STRATEGIC RELOCATION

North American Guide to Safe Places

3rd Edition

By Joel M. Skousen
and
Andrew L. Skousen

Strategic Relocation

Maps and illustrations by Andrew L. Skousen

Cover and typesetting by Elizabeth S. Lindsay

Third Edition

Copyright 2016 by Joel M. Skousen

(Original 1st Ed. Copyright 1997; 2nd Ed. 2001; 3rd Ed. 1st printing 2010)

The information is accurate to the best of our knowledge. All recommendations are made without guarantee on the part of the authors or publisher. Due to the nature of crises, disasters and threats to life or property, the authors cannot foresee every possibility and disclaim any liability in connection with the use of this information. For additional information please contact Joel Skousen, 290 West 580 South, Orem, UT 84058.

Printed in the United States.

ISBN 978-1-56861-262-1

CONTENTS

Section Two: North American Analysis 59

Chapter 7: US and Canada Geography and Climate 61

Chapter 8: Freedom and Politics 73

Chapter 9: Crime, Health and Quality of Life 84

Chapter 10: War, Invasion and Terrorism 98

Chapter 11: Government Intrusion on Liberty and Individual Lives 106

Section Three: Strategies 111

Chapter 12: Customize a Plan for Your Own Situation ... 113

Chapter 13: Choose a Safe Place 119

PREFACE

This third edition is a complete re-work of the previous editions of this book and not only has entirely revised content and layout, it also has updated information as of 2016. The most significant changes in this edition include a new world-wide analysis of countries, state and province-specific reviews of the US and Canada and dozens of new maps and tables to make information more accessible. We hope these changes will be helpful as you consider relocation opportunities around the world and particularly in North America.

The Value of Strategic Thinking

What you are about to read in this book is a reflection of our world view—a view that sees multiple threats to our well-being and liberty. Indeed, some threats loom so large they cannot be avoided, only mitigated by moving to a strategically safe place. Although you may not agree with all our views, our purpose is to inform you of the principle threats that we see, including those not generally considered by the average population and evaded by mainstream commentators.

In our experience the process of analyzing threats will require some unpleasant considerations and some tough thinking to really prepare for these threats and the strategic decisions necessary to survive the difficult times ahead. This "tough thinking" deserves some explanation. After years of experience consulting with families about high security residents and retreats, Joel feels strongly that soft people won't do well in a severe crisis, and neither will children from homes where their parents don't require mental and physical toughness. In the first edition Joel wrote:

"I don't trust the commonly held, rosy-eyed view of life held by most people. While not a pessimist, I believe in seeing what is real in life, not what we wish it to be. I firmly believe that excessive optimism or positivism can lead to a partial blinding of our ability to see the future, especially relative to security issues. Today we live in a world awash in illusions of peace, prosperity and security and if you build your life around these illusions, they can leave you woefully unprepared when things get really bad.

"From my observations of history and people I have come to the inescapable conclusion that it is the tendency of all societies to slowly degenerate into chronic bad judgment, insensitivity to higher moral values and dullness of conscience. This is happening in all Western societies today, without exception. The end result is the eventual destruction of liberty, most often through war, tyranny and economic depression

"Even though most people are at least partially aware of the societal problems around them (debt, profligate spending, war and moral decline), they almost always fail to be sufficiently concerned to raise the alarm and change direction before society passes the point of no return. Sadly, I feel that our Western culture has passed that point of no return. It isn't that it can't be turned around, only that it won't. One must understand the innate tendencies of most men in order to understand why this true.

"Consider why most people fail to come up to a significant level of enlightenment and proper action even when they know better. Although the world still has millions of good people, they almost all suffer from soft thinking habits. When surrounded by such people, especially in high density urban areas, your personal security is at risk because you live within an area prone to group thinking and bad judgment, manipulated by the media and the long-term effects of soft and mistaken social ideas promulgated in public education."

This "soft thinking" problem is essentially the innate resistance of some people to the tough truths that would lead to enlightenment. Most people constantly seek comfort, look for the easy way out, or the least painful solution to problems and ignore more permanent and honest solutions that are tougher or more costly emotionally. Often in dealing with other people's problems, individuals evade confronting the core issues to avoid conflict. This often postpones or exacerbates problems. The same happens when people fail to confront their own weaknesses with honesty and a willingness to change.

Evading hard mental effort leads to soft thinking, which we see in popular ideas like "everybody is special", and "I'm OK and you're OK." The world's problems simply don't go away by making ourselves blind to the differences between us. Differences have to be confronted, often with patience, but confronted nonetheless.

Soft thinking philosophies promote, for example, the illusion that out-of-control criminal minds will reform if given enough "understanding" and that "self-esteem therapy" is a good substitute for real competence. These philosophies promote the idea that rebellious children will "come around" if given enough "unconditional love" and acceptance. Sometimes they do (because they have an innately good spirit), but mostly they go into adulthood with chronic bad judgment and weaknesses. Soft thinking also promotes the false notion that communist dictators really can be reformed by giving them enough aid and military concessions. The list of human judgment errors is seemingly endless and, sadly, fatal in the long-term, when done on a national level.

In our opinion the future probabilities for peace and prosperity are not good in a society which is over-confident in its soft thinking, and its mainstream eduction sources of information. Character-wise, people are only attracted to what they want to hear and thus are generally lacking in real wisdom. That said, we do have hope for the relatively small group of people we have seen scattered throughout every community, who seem to sense that something is wrong with the world. This book is written for this group to hopefully give them a strategic ability to analyze the long term trends that will affect their safety and security so they can prepare.

The Role of an Active Conscience

You cannot develop good strategic judgment without a very detailed and accurate view of what is going on around you. Some of it involves getting access to the right sources of news and analysis but the most important source is good judgment as directed by an active conscience.

You can actually improve your ability to be sensitive to the feelings of conscience by listening to them more carefully and following through when prompted and by heeding nervous feelings which come to warn you of error or danger. We have two small rules which can help you and your children develop increased sensitivity to the small signals of conscience and will help you develop an increased ability to follow through:

> *Never do anything you feel nervous about, as to the correctness.*
> *Always force yourself to do what you know you should do, especially when you don't feel like it.*

These principles have served our family well for decades. We hope this book will encourage you in your quest to make some beneficial changes in your lives and those of your children. Otherwise, strategic relocation is just a change of scenery without improved security.

INTRODUCTION

What do we mean by "strategic relocation?" In our modern culture it is not uncommon for individuals or families to relocate multiple times during their life. Change in employment is probably the number one reason people move, but other factors usually include proximity to family, educational opportunities and desirable climate. A less-common and often overlooked reason is that of finding an area with better long-term security from natural or man-made disasters. Unlike most relocation books, this guide will not teach you where to buy a house in the best school districts or where to find the best golf courses.

Strategic Relocation was written to help our readers make assessments about the strategic safety of places in the long-term. Planning this move requires careful forethought for the future to assess and deal with the threats that are most likely to impact you.

Foreseeing future strategic threats can be very hard to do. In this book, we work to give you information about obvious threats, such as natural disasters and crime but also provide information about less obvious threats like nuclear war, tyranny and social unrest. We believe these latter threats to be more dangerous than any other danger in the long term and yet they are largely ignored by the media and, hence, the general population.

Joel has spent decades analyzing current events and has found consistent patterns of a larger agenda. In the US, for instance, government leaders in both major political parties consistently only produce results that advance the same globalist agenda, actively promoted by advisors from the Council on Foreign Relations and other internationalist organizations. The goal to "unify" everyone under one system may seem laudable for "easier commerce", "world peace", and "freedom" for all, but the true result is just centralized control over all people in a worldwide hegemony with more beauracratic red tape, increasing wars and more restrictions on personal liberties.

Even controlled legislators cannot make everything on the globalist agenda legal fast enough, so most Western governments resort to illegal means. In recent years we have caught glimpses of warrantless spying, torture, indefinite detention without due process — denial of constitutionally protected rights, the rule of law suspended in critical court cases and all levels of government agencies that have acted contrary to their legal obligations and sometimes even their normal roles. All of this is done in secrecy, of course, until glimpses come to light and then blame is placed on a few low-level rogue agents, but it is almost always systemic.

There is evidence that secretive, powerful groups have accumulated enough influence within US and other governments that they can manipulate a wide range of economic, judicial and political forces to their ends. The proof is the controlled legislators that move to legalize the illegal acts of government that come to light. There are many excuses for these "necessary evils" such as the fight against the never ending bogeyman of terrorism.

One of the most important steps for finding your best strategic retreat is to learn what the real threats are—threats to the liberties and freedoms that allow for our way of life and happiness, not the trumped up fears touted by the news to deprive us of liberty in exchange for false promises of "safety." Terrorist attacks, social unrest, racial tensions and war are all used to create excuses for undermining personal liberty and national sovereignty. As a result, world problems only get worse each year despite trillions spent on police and military intervention.

Because these secretive groups also control the surveillance machinery of the State, and have the power to hide illegal activities behind the veil of state secrets, tracking these people and obtaining evidence to stop them or prosecute them is almost impossible. Despite all the rhetoric and words by our leaders, actions speak louder than words and they are currently leading Americans and free people everywhere toward a disastrous outcome.

We will examine the real strategic threats in this book. Because of the specifics involved in assessing the dangers to each area, we present our analysis in successive layers of detail. This book is written in four sections that describe the threats and best options beginning at the international level and then narrowing down to specific cities in the US and Canada.

Section One: Selecting a Safe Country

Thinking about getting out of the US and living abroad? This section introduces the strategic threats facing the world and then reviews specific countries in light of these criteria—including popular tax-haven countries and cheaper Central and South American getaways. Even if you are not planning on becoming an expatriate, we recommend reading this section since we introduce all significant threats here. This section will educate the reader on things to consider about climate and scenery, politics and taxes, crime and standard of living. These chapters also present the prospects for war, invasion and terrorism around the world. The last chapter reviews the most popularly considered countries around the world.

Section Two: North American Analysis

We still consider the US and Canada as the most reliable nations for safety in the future. This section describes the threats that are specific to these countries. We cover the differences among states and provinces for factors like geography and weather, freedoms and taxes, natural medicine, homeschooling, crime and, finally, safer areas from war, tyranny and social unrest.

Section Three: Strategies

Once you know what threats we face and have some idea of the location you are considering, these chapters present the most important aspects to consider as you attempt to narrow down your choices. This section covers selecting property, building security into your homestead or vacation retreat and finding a balance between current life and future security. We also discuss factors such as social networking, employment options, contingency plans and exit strategies for living in less secure areas.

Section Four: Regional and State Ratings

Want more specific recommendations? This is a largely expanded version of our popular list from previous editions highlighting the areas that we consider more secure for the long term. In this new edition, we not only analyze the relative strengths and weaknesses of the larger regions in the US, but we also present three regions of Canada and an entirely new state-by-state analysis which includes summarized data, ratings and details about living near the largest cities. We have also coordinated this data with detailed color maps of each state.

Whether you are looking for a secure retreat, building your dream home, preparing to retire or planning to purchase a vacation home, we hope this book will teach you how to weigh your options and give you the tools and information necessary for finding your own safe place.

SECTION ONE: SELECTING A SAFE COUNTRY

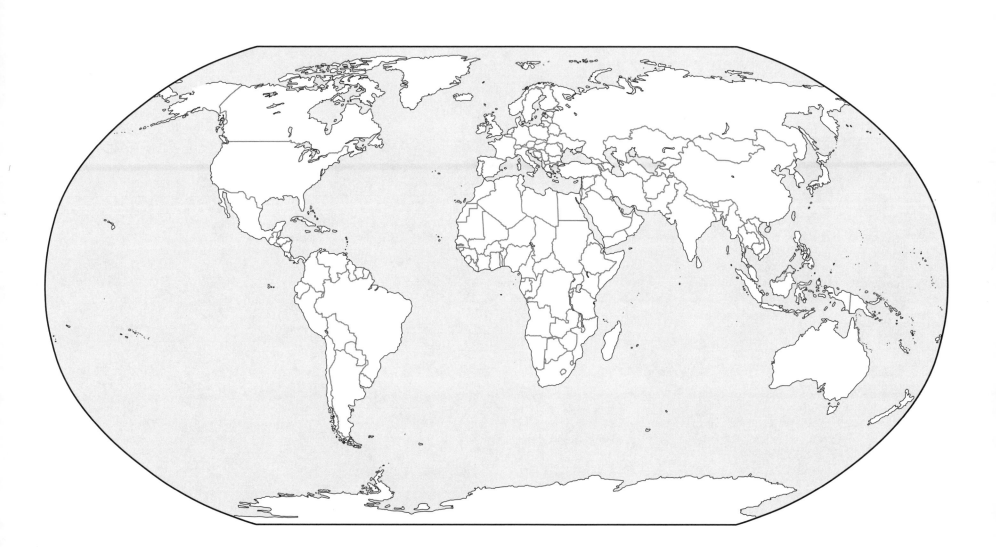

Chapter 1

ESSENTIAL CRITERIA

Choosing a place to live can be a daunting task with all the factors and benefits advertised by developers and real estate agents, city committees and even countries inviting you to invest your money in their areas. Oceanfront properties, tax havens, upscale condo towers, golf courses, and many other amenities attract people into settling near comforts and conveniences. But living life is not always about the conveniences. Many conveniences are near long-term threats. Earthquakes in California, hurricanes in Florida and hurricanes in Texas. People also like conveniences so these areas have high population densities, expensive land, scarce natural resources, and restrictive local laws.

There are two categories of criteria that determine how people assess where to live: The positive aspects which make life convenient and comfortable, and the negative threats that have to be weighed against the positives, and which can negate them in an instant.

The positives are what we look to fulfill and enjoy in the short and medium term. The positives are nice to have, but the lack of them isn't necessarily fatal. However, if we disregard the strategic or local threats, we could eventually suffer irreversible, harmful consequences. These two criteria combine to provide the motivation to relocate in search of a balance between an improved quality of life and enhanced long-term security. Realistically, however, almost no place provides both high security and a fulfillment of all our positive wants.

As you prioritize things keep in mind the following: negative criteria are far more important in the long-term than most positive wishes since failure to take them into consideration is much more damaging to your way of life. For example, taking up residence in a communist nation like China because of a good business opportunity would be a poor choice strategically. The limited civil rights and ultimate threat of losing your business and your freedom overwhelms any short-term business advantage. Many people still enter into these types of deals, despite the risks, because they don't see or don't want to see the threat. Potential profit can often lead to blindness about danger. They don't want to see the historical track record of the Chinese Communists that reveals how they are experts in strategic deception and at putting on a benevolent front to draw in foreign investment.

This illustrates one of man's most prominent weaknesses: we readily accept the risk of devastating, but uncommon failure just to get a smaller immediate benefit. We run red lights to save a minute and build houses near unstable cliffs for the view ignoring the probabilities that will someday catch up with us. Some people sense danger a long way off but get

distracted by the illusions of our current peace and relative prosperity. In this chapter we will try to awaken our readers to the most critical threats. You can't make a decision about threats if you don't see them, and some of the biggest threats are deliberately downplayed by our own leaders and the establishment media.

How Much Do You See?

In order to begin thinking strategically, we must establish a habit of looking at the big picture first, so as to cultivate the correct perspective and a realistic strategy for future safety. Part of this big picture is recognizing that conflict and strife will always be with us. The liberal view that world peace is just a matter of mutual understanding misses the crucial point that systematic evil exists in the world, and that no amount of understanding will ever deter that evil—only force. There is a tendency among soft, good people to see good in everything, and to deny the existence of real evil—which often hides behind the facade of diplomacy and worldly success. Facing up to the existence of systematic evil in the world is perhaps the most important single step you can take toward protecting yourself from being blindsided by foolish optimism and naiveté.

Ignorance about what is really going on in the world is surprisingly prevalent today, but it is not always people's fault. A wise history professor once said, "Anyone who claims to know the history of the world, and yet knows nothing about the secret acts of conspiring men, does not know history." So even if you read a newspaper every day, you will never really know what is going on in the world, behind the scenes. It is nearly impossible for good men to know certain crucial facts, because there is a broad-based conspiracy among those in positions of power to cover up each other's illegal acts. Governments, for instance, hide illegal acts behind the veil of "national security." Only occasionally do the perpetrators make mistakes big enough for a conspiracy to show its ugly head—and even then, conspiracy is downplayed and covered up quickly by the establishment media whose top editors and owners are part of the conspiracy and work to protect those in power above them.

How Do You Process the News?

Part of the reason for people's inability to see a threat has to do with the number of superficial issues that divert us from focusing on more important ones. Most people suffer from both information overload and the failure to differentiate between crucial issues and superficial facts. Partial blame can be attributed, as we said, to the purposeful omissions of controversial truths and facts by both the establishment media and by government spokespersons. The establishment media loves to bury issues which they deem harmful to their unsaid "support whatever government does" agenda.

Liberals in the media also have their own anti-free market agenda which is dangerous to your health and pocketbook. Everyday establishment journalists are busy promoting the latest EPA scare stories about "carbon pollution" and the phony "man-made global warming" scenarios.

These are false threats promoted by dishonest academics, yes-man journalists, and government-funded foundations and environmental groups anxious to undermine individual and property rights. After years of only limited success in changing American law, they are increasingly turning to international environmental law to gain effective control over national sovereignty, energy and private land.

Our purpose is to help you see the real threats amid the media clutter of bogus threats meant only to generate reasons for more government control. Not all of our readers may see things exactly as we do, but hopefully you will learn from considering our point of view. Even the things you disagree with will be helpful since it may cause you to reassess what the media puts out as fact.

What Threats Do You See?

It's helpful to consider the following specific aspects of threats to remind yourself how to be aware of them and more realistically weigh them.

Visibility: What threats exist out there? Are they obvious? What are the types of threats that people fail to perceive? How do we learn to see these?

Timing: When is a threat going to strike? Can it be foreseen or will you always have to be ready? Will you be able to see trigger events ahead of time like provocations to war?

Degree: How bad or dangerous is a threat? How much damage will it cause when it comes?

Location: Where are these threats most likely going to strike? Can they strike anywhere?

Personal Probability: How likely is it that you are going to be personally affected by this threat even in a high threat location? Often you can find specific areas that provide partial safety even in a threat zone.

Causes: Are the causes of natural disasters random and natural, or does God sometimes intervene to cause these events—and if so, why? Will we be spared because we try to always do what is right? Are man-made disasters (economic, political, intrigue, war) the result of circumstantial and natural conflicts inherent to man or are they caused or influenced by conspiring men as part of a larger control agenda?

Prevention and Mitigation: What can we do to prepare against, lessen or mitigate the threat? Can we postpone the time of relocation by careful disaster preparedness?

Each of the aspects above is very important but some threats may apply to you more than others depending upon the category of potential danger. We will attempt to amplify some of these aspects as we discuss both moderate and serious threats facing us in the future. To analyze each of these threats strategically, we have to look beyond the obvious, present-day threats to perceive what we believe are serious, hidden threats. If you relocate to avoid the most deadly threats and correctly prepare against the lesser threats, then you have a high probability of coming through the upcoming periods of danger with your life and property intact. That is our goal.

Some threats should be avoided and some mitigated. For example, avoid living near volcanoes and military target areas even if the threat seems unlikely. In contrast, some threats lend themselves to mitigation and preparation. Many people can live in moderate threat areas such as those subject to hurricanes, tornados and earthquakes by taking steps to lessen the risks and preparing to survive in place. We all have to accept some amount of risk, but we can minimize the chances of death or major destruction of property if we know what the risks are and how to avoid them. If you must stay in an area of significant risks, do some minor relocation to lessen the threat. For example, if you are right on the beach in a state prone to hurricanes, move further inland or at least to a sheltered bay that is not subject to direct storm surge. If your home is situated on a piece of sandy soil with a high water table in an earthquake area (liquefaction potential), move to higher, more stable ground.

How We View the World

With this information as background, it is helpful at the outset of this book to briefly review for you how we see the present world. This will help us set the stage as to what we view as strategic threats in the future and their origins. We will begin our assessment by analyzing some key factors of economy, culture and politics and their impact on the safety and stability of the world.

Long Term Economic Threats

The United States has been the driving economic force in the world during the 20th century for two reasons. First, America's relative free market allowed for the fastest rate of high tech innovation and development ever known in the world and, second, the dominance of the formerly gold-backed dollar as a world currency gave the US financial advantages not available to other nations. The US has lost ground dramatically by increasingly restricting free markets and by reneging on the dollar's redeemability in gold, but it is still using the residual strength of the US economy to bail out much of the world with paper dollars.

Inflation and debt are the prime negative factors in the declining health of nations in the world. All are playing the inflationary money game to hide deficit spending. Many smaller countries are at risk of default due to debt excesses of the past two decades. Powerful nations get away with it for longer periods, but eventually they too will fail. This is the only reason that the US dollar is maintaining any strength at all—because all other currencies are inflating their money supply as well. However, other countries don't have the huge volume of currency outstanding as does the dollar, so even moderate inflation shows up quicker as higher prices in Europe or England than it does when the US Federal Reserve inflates.

We expect general inflation to continue worldwide in the 5%-15% range, and eventually even higher. Don't rely on government numbers to judge the real rate of inflation. Every nation is taking a cue from the US and falsifying its inflation rates. This can't go on forever. The ticking time bomb is the interest on that growing debt. Many countries, including the US will reach the point of technical bankruptcy within a decade or two when income from taxes is no longer sufficient to pay the interest on the national debt, let alone the trillions in social welfare benefits demanded by the public.

As we write this in 2016, the US maintains a dominant influence on the world economy but it is still growing slowly after the deep recession of 2008. The US influence is largely due to the Federal Reserve control over the rate of inflation of the dollar, and short term dollar loans keep the EU banks afloat. Many are predicting either collapse or hyperinflation, but we think neither is realistic in the short term. Hyperinflation cannot happen unless government establishes an automatic mechanism to index people's wages to inflation—without it you get stagflation as people can't keep up with rapidly rising prices and stop buying.

The FED can continue to create money and feed it selectively to the insider banks to stave off any collapse, and if they keep the real rate of inflation below 10% most people can adjust—they've been doing so for 20 years. Most of the money they create and inject goes to insider banks and Wall Street brokerages and thus stays within the speculative economy. Only about 20% of that leaks out into the real economy. That is why certain speculative futures markets in currency, bonds and stocks balloon while the normal economy is relatively stagnant.

We expect the financial powers that be (PTB) that control the US will continue to keep the US and world economy afloat by moderately inflating the money supply. They can keep doing this as long as they keep the real rate of inflation below 10%, and if existing tax revenues are sufficient to pay the interest on the debt. At the present rate, a default wouldn't happen until sometime in the latter part of the decade 2020-2030. They are, we believe, preparing a way out so they don't get the blame. When facing default, the major players on the world stage will create a crisis sufficiently large to justify walking away from the debt—most likely another major world war.

Europe was the strongest economic power in the 19th century, but lost it in the 20th century due to the decreased incentives of socialist business control, high priced unionized labor and the rise of social welfare systems. Europe and other developed nations like the US have seen a decline in job growth that has begun to cause tension among various groups that vie for government unemployment benefits. Outright austerity measures by governments like Greece, Iceland and Ireland have threatened the civil order itself. The percentage of people on government payrolls in these nations is simply too high to survive major cutbacks in government spending—so all they can do is create money and postpone the day of reckoning.

Current and former third world countries achieved high rates of growth in the past two decades as labor-intensive industries in the West sought out the lower regulatory and labor costs of Mexico, India, China and other Far East "Asian Tigers." After the worldwide recession that started in 2007 and 2008, many of these nations began to stagnate as debt-driven growth and foreign investment leveled off. Although the working class got a taste of free markets and fast growth, corrupt or tyrannical governments failed to complete the transition to a modern society as did Japan and Taiwan. There is a certain amount of pent-up frustration among workers that persists in these third world nations.

Asian Tigers had less structural restraints to change in their socialist laws and regulations, compared to Europe, and began to free up access to their markets, at least temporarily, for economic advantage. Foreign capital flowed in dramatically, first to Japan, then to Taiwan and now to China, Singapore, and Hong Kong. The Far East is the sector of the world economy that has been the fastest growing sector for almost two decades and still has the greatest growth potential. The oriental labor force is hard working and has the massive numbers to keep labor prices low.

Japan led the way in the latter part of the 20th century with its low cost, highly educated and industrial labor pool, but has stagnated for over a decade due to skyrocketing price inflation of assets and the economic contraction that always accompanies too much social spending and growth restrictions. Eventually Japan lost its cheap labor advantage to Taiwan and Taiwanese labor is now losing its price advantage to China. This process is inevitable as long as manufacturers are able to jump ship to another country and there exist new pools of cheap, competent labor.

Despite many internal problems (social unrest, human rights violations, inflation, growth, pollution, and energy shortages), China is the world's second largest economy after the USA. But even China is not in good economic health. Its credit and banking structures are in a huge bubble due to artificial expansion and an easy money policy from the Chinese central bank. China only tolerates a partial and temporary free market atmosphere in order to entice foreign investment, steal technology, and use those funds to further their aggressive military intentions.

In China, communist control still abounds in every sector (though often kept hidden from foreign view) and the effects are starting to be felt as the boom times of unlimited foreign investment have slowed. China is woefully overextended in real estate—partly because of many bad loans that were directed to poorly run state companies. With the slowdown of the world economy, China's voracious appetite for natural resources has slackened, causing a dramatic fall in commodity prices and containerized shipping, but China's secret military expansion continues unabated.

China is notoriously non-transparent in its financial dealings. Analysts fear that China's banking sector is on thin ice with hundreds of multi-billion dollar loans going bust if Western consumption of Chinese products stops growing at its previous pace. China has bought so much of the debt of other countries that it is vulnerable in a different way—to debt devaluation. As the US and Europe inflate their way out of this huge debt (which is inevitable and ongoing), China can and will be left holding billions in bonds of declining value. That is why China has historically spent so much on commodities—trying to convert dollar and Euro holdings into foreign property and other real goods. Individuals should also be doing the same, over time.

Threats of Cultural Conflict

Cultural differences will always be with us. They only become a serious threat to national stability when they combine within a single social welfare state that pits various ethnic groups against one another in the pursuit of "their share" of the productive pie. Even the US has moved into that dangerous position. When cultural differences are too pronounced, integration becomes almost impossible. That is why it is better for many cultures to stay relatively separate and homogenous. Studies have shown that a base culture can absorb up to about 10% of another diverging culture without too much conflict, but when the invading culture begins to compete for dominance and majority rule, conflict is certain and often violent. Look at Palestine, the Balkans and now Europe.

The Middle East has suffered years of globalist intervention from an agenda to not only control vast supplies of the world's oil, but also to foment small wars and displace millions of muslims to bring tremendous social instability and conflict wherever they flee, including all the way to Europe and other Western countries.

Certain areas of the world and their culture are more susceptible to manipulation and deception than others. It is politically incorrect to talk about differences in cultural groups, but we cannot avoid them if our readers are to have a clear understanding of the manipulated nature of a threat. Societies that have a large majority of simple people with only basic intelligence and education are much more susceptible to mass hysteria and propaganda than cultures with a larger percentage of savvy, well educated people. No society has a majority of smart people, but some have much larger percentages than others. Survival in a conflicting world requires that we develop a keen eye for cultures that are stable and inherently capable of good critical thinking. In particular, look for cultures that can evaluate themselves and their own culture honestly, according to sound principles.

No country has a perfect (or even entirely acceptable) cultural base, strategically speaking. We can only recommend playing the odds by staying within your own culture but away from severely unstable areas in Africa, the Middle East and many countries in Latin America and Asia. Even for the West, with its highly developed thinking culture, mandatory education is overrated and does not guarantee wisdom or good judgment among the population as a whole.

Religiosity and goodness are valuable indicators but not enough when superficially practiced. Lacking the spiritual sensitivity to see through deception, good people—even smart people—can be convinced to go along with many things that contain evil, hidden agendas. Look at what happened to the highly educated and religious people of Germany in WWII. It is therefore important to look at the history of a culture. Only those cultures that have a history of being free will have sufficient will to fight for it in the coming conflicts.

Political Threats from Conspiracies of Power

The most stable political systems allow for an orderly resolution of conflict and a voting method that allows the highest percentage of citizens to participate in the governing process. However, that process must be limited by strict constitutional provisions that prohibit even majorities from using law to impose their will upon minorities when it is a violation of fundamental rights—most often used to redistribute wealth by force.

It is essential to develop a universal understanding in law of the fundamental rights of individuals and the family unit. Free markets (where the rights of all are equally defended from predation and crime) are the least conflicting of political and economic systems. Socialism in its varying degrees of using government force to redistribute wealth is the most conflicting, always pitting competing groups against each other—like the poor against the productive class. The only restrictions in a free market should be against predatory practices and coercion, but individuals must always be free to make discriminatory judgments as to worth and competency in employment and other voluntary dealings.

Aside from those crucial ideals, the greatest safeguard to citizen control of government is to watch for and stop secret combinations of power that strive to gain control of major corporations, governments and judgeships. Conspiring men are always working to manipulate and control governments from behind the scenes, and have been from the beginning of civilization. While most third world countries are ruled by strongmen and their coterie of thugs, first world countries are controlled by one of the following three predatory combinations of power that transcend national boundaries.

The most powerful is what we call the "Anglo-American establishment." This powerful coterie of wealthy men in America and England began by creating a system to control money and international banking and have since gained manipulation or outright control of most governments in the Western world and their major media outlets. It is most useful now to refer to these big players in the world of political control as globalists since they actively conspire to diminish national sovereignty in favor of a globalist New World Order under their exclusive control.

The second group we refer to by the banner, *Socialist International*, a combination of leftist political control created by the Soviets in Moscow during the cold war. It still operates today under Russia's hidden hand and is semi-secret so that its smaller, above-ground namesake doesn't really represent its true influence. Yes, we are saying that Russia still is a world power with hegemonic goals of world conquest.

The smallest, in terms of numbers of nations controlled, is the power block controlled by China. China is just emerging as a world player in politics like the first two and its true hegemonic intentions won't be visible until another world war rearranges international boundaries and sorts out the winners and losers. China is playing hardball in business, buying up energy sources, ports and shipping companies on every continent in the world in anticipation of future control. China doesn't make any deals unless their front companies hold a 51% controlling interest. The Chinese are making the strongest inroads into economic control in Australia, New Zealand, Latin America and Africa.

It is primarily the British and American globalists that threaten our liberties directly, so we will mainly address their movements toward world hegemony. They do not have absolute power, but they do exercise effective control over most aspects of government, finance and the media in the West. It really doesn't matter who "they" are since they uniformly control the surveillance machinery in each nation and possess immunity from prosecution by controlling the highest judges in each country. Even without knowing their names, their pattern of control and operation is fairly clear to those willing to take a hard look.

They have been patient and have taken decades to work their own people into key positions of authority in government so that they can effectively determine who gets hired. Mediums of communication are bought up in each country so that public opinion can be influenced.

They have also concentrated on controlling teacher education, public school text books and curricula.

Politically, these Anglo-American globalists have been able to control both major political parties in America, and the largest political parties in Japan, the UK, France, Germany, Spain and Italy. Third parties in America and the smaller parties of Parliamentary systems in Europe (whether left or right) are uniformly anti-establishment, and sense correctly that the political system is rigged against them. They all realize that the enemy of liberty hides within establishment power structures.

It is a different story however, in Russia and the former Soviet states of Eastern Europe. One has to be very astute to ferret out the smaller "democratic" parties that have been created by the Communist Party. The Communist Party still exists, both above and below ground. Today in Moscow, you still hear leaders talk about "the Party" and how its dictates must be followed—and they aren't talking about Putin's *United Russia Party*—one of many fronts for the Communist Party. Any party, on the right or left, that is allowed to have any degree of power in Russia, or the other post-Soviet states, is not a legitimate opposition party, only a controlled one.

Threats of Nations in Conflict

India and Pakistan are currently not at war but are prone to escalating ethnic conflicts both within and outside their borders. Both have been allowed by the East and West to become nuclear powers in order to counterbalance each other. India has traditionally been a client state of Russia and an enemy of China, and the tension with China still exists today. Pakistan used to be a Chinese client state and is now returning to China's embrace now that the US has worn out its relationship through years of intervention and drone strikes. Both Russia and China are now reestablishing their military client relationships with India and Pakistan respectively.

The Middle East is going to remain a region of continual conflict. We predict with confidence that there will never be peace between Israel and the Arabs. We feel strongly that continued US intervention in the Middle East and in central Asia will exacerbate conflict and increase terrorism against the West. These insurgency wars against US and NATO occupation are completely unwinnable, despite the false appearances of victory in Iraq where conflict is still ongoing and will only increase.

Sadly, the US has lost much good will around the world, especially in the Balkans and in Muslim and Arab countries through its ruthless interventions in the name of spreading democracy—which never was the real reason. This intervention has caused many countries to become hostile to Americans and that hostility is now very much deeply ingrained.

The targeting of Iran, though temporarily on hold, has long been a globalist goal since Iran is the only Muslim country trying to become independent of both East and West in their military armaments. Although Israel is willing to lead the attack on Iran (knowing the US military will take over), they don't want Iran's ally, Syria, to retaliate right on their border. Taking down Syria has proven very problematic despite arming multiple rebels and creating ISIS; the attack on Assad has been set back (perhaps irreversibly) by Russian intervention, but the globalists have not given up. The US seems intent to bring more force into the game using Saudi Arabia and Turkey as the primary surrogates to arm, train and possibly even join ranks with the radical Islamists fighting Assad. Eventually, we will see another major war in the Middle East after Israel finally attacks Iran and the US is drawn into the conflict (as planned). As a result, the rest of the world will suffer from dramatically higher oil prices, and the US and NATO will become even more hated by the Muslim world.

Note the contrast between the way Iran and Syria are threatened incessantly with military destruction while North Korea is excused or allowed to continue being the nuclear pariah and conventional weapons proliferation champion of the world. Yes, the rhetoric is harsh but there is never any teeth to those threats. China ensures that NK survives any sanctions. We think this is because North Korea is being preserved as the trigger event for WWIII.

Iran, however, is scheduled for a more immediate military takedown. The West will never tolerate a Muslim country achieving weapons independence from the major powers. But, this future war with Iran will not, in our opinion, lead directly to the next world war, but rather to a regional war in which Israel will become the dominant power in the region—and hated even more for it.

Latin American countries are slowly returning to the far Leftist roots that have prevailed there for many years. The US lost a lot of favor in Latin America during the globalist interventions that began during the George W. Bush administration. A majority of nations in Latin America are now being governed by communists—some virulently anti-American as in Cuba and Venezuela, and others playing a more moderate role for now, taking advantage of favorable trade relations with the US, but waiting for and planning on the coming revolution when Russia and China give the signal. The major Latin American nations with Far Left governments are Brazil, Venezuela, Cuba, Boliva, Nicaragua, El Salvador, Ecuador, Uruguay, and Chile. The latter may surprise those that keep thinking Chile is the free-market champion of South America—but Chile's current woman president, Michelle Bachelet, is a "former" communist, trained in East Germany and is awaiting the return of Chile to the Left. The only allies the US has presently are Mexico, Costa Rica, Guatemala, Peru, Panama and Colombia and all of these have tremendous problems with corruption and violent crime. Panama also has deep ties with China.

In summary, you can see there are many aspects of the world that are not easily visible but which will affect your future. All the factors mentioned above affect the long-term stability of every country. Choosing the best strategic retreat for your situation will hinge on a thorough understanding of these factors and their affects.

Customizing Your Strategy

Each individual must make their own evaluation of the specific circumstances and threats around them. In the following chapters we will introduce specific threats in more detail and endeavor to give you the tools to plan out your best move. Everyone's life and timing is different, but do not to put off implementing your strategies until it is too late. Decide for yourself which threats you need to avoid and which you will have to mitigate (because you can't avoid them) and then work out a timeline for implementing these strategies. It might be helpful to work up two timelines—an ideal and a worst-case timeframe before which you'll get each step of your preparation plan finished. We hope the following information and maps will be instrumental in your efforts.

Above all, remember that there is no perfectly safe place—safety is only relative, and there are a lot of trade-offs and compromises to consider. Do not be deceived by the current illusions of safety in various countries. You have to project how these nations will change during the coming wars and upheaval to correctly evaluate them for the future.

Chapter 2

GEOGRAPHY AND CLIMATE

It's nice to still have the relative freedom to choose a different climate or geography as we consider relocation. There are real differences here that some people are unaware of, having lived in one place or climate all their lives. We have found that a non-flat geography offers a more enjoyable and aesthetic surrounding. In fact, a hilly or mountainous geography has strategic advantages too. Mountains are natural barriers to many threats and if they're tall enough to be seen in your neighborhood they provide a constant visual cue to your orientation when traveling around locally. Lakes and rivers provide aesthetic appeal, diversion and important water storage, and sometimes are barriers to travel. Living in areas with fertile farms or orchards provides a comforting quality of life and good access to local produce and self-reliant neighbors. Even the deserts have certain advantages that can be enjoyed including clean, crisp air, scenic vistas and generally less people and pollution.

Having said this, everyone has different preferences for their environment. Often these tastes are influenced by previous location experience or what one considers comfortable. When considering a new location for security, however, we have to consider the strategic factors. Sometimes these dictate that the most comfortable areas are not the most secure. We will look at geographic factors first and then aspects of climate as they relate to long term safety and retreat potential.

Geography

Geographic features that lend themselves to security do not have to be at the expense of beauty. Although it may take time to adjust to an area that has some rigorous aspects, we recommend locating in areas that have a variety of geographical features, while avoiding the extremes of desert, high altitude, swamps, coasts and flatlands. Here are our summaries of the basic geographical considerations.

Altitude

Higher altitude geographic areas are usually more secure than lowlands. In the mountains, look for areas with some variety. Forests and lakes are not hard to find at extreme upper elevations, but suitable farm land is. For some people, it takes time to adjust to high mountain climates because of less-humid, thinner air and colder, snowier winters. Finding a building site in mountainous areas isn't always easy. Much of the best property is owned by the federal or state government. But keep in mind that even in non-mountainous areas you can often find forested terrain with rolling hills.

Young people of good health have little trouble adapting to altitudes up to 10,000 feet. Some older people with health problems can have trouble breathing at even 6,000 feet. Above 6,000 the growing season is shortened sufficiently to make it difficult to grow anything but cold weather crops (root vegetables and hay). The best growing conditions are found below 4,500 feet.

Forestation

Isolated deserts can sometimes serve as good retreat areas, but the isolation is tough to endure during normal times—and costly if you have to drive to town a lot. Some isolated desert areas of the Intermountain West are especially beautiful with dramatic, red sandstone cliffs, wind carved shapes and delicate arches.

Areas with some forested land are important if you ever have to retreat and need some cover and concealment. Even in flat, farming areas, there are usually pockets of trees and forests. In desert climates, trees can indicate where more prevalent water sources are located—although sometimes that is merely an indication of winter snow accumulation.

Consistently damp areas can produce dense undergrowth and forests such as in tropical lowlands, rain forests and jungles. These forests are not recommended for security. Insects, disease and a less-industrious population are more common here, creating an unhealthy atmosphere in many respects.

Coastlines

Many people wish they could live in coastal areas. Despite being very therapeutic (fresh air, sea breezes and access to the ocean), coastal areas have more disadvantages strategically than advantages. Strategically speaking, coastlines are transition areas (water to land masses) with a formidable barrier on one side. It can be too easy to find yourself with no place to go in an emergency. Coasts are often entry points for external threats, both natural and military. Only with very careful contingency planning can you find long-term safety on a coast, and even then, never right on the beach where so many are tempted to live. That doesn't mean you can't have a beach house, but it shouldn't be your primary residence.

Defensive Geography

It is important for the ideal nation to have some imposing terrain features within their borders that allow for good strategic defenses in case of war. Mountains, hard winters, large rivers and bodies of water are excellent defensive barriers. For example, in WWII it was mostly the rigors of the Russian winter combined with extended supply lines that doomed the German offensive into Russia.

Ask yourself these questions when choosing a country of residence: Does the surrounding terrain lend itself to good long-term security with natural barriers to invasion? Is the national military structure of the nation sufficient to provide protection against international threats? The country must be large enough to have sufficient natural resources and have enough people to provide defense while allowing for continued industrial production—without depending on imports.

Nations such as Japan, Israel and New Zealand have learned to get around the limitations of size and lack of natural resources by using a vigorous policy of international trade. While such strategies work during times of peace, nations that live or die on imports and exports are extremely vulnerable to war, natural catastrophes, labor strikes or international boycotts.

Effects of Geography on Climate

Coastal areas with onshore wind flows always provide a moderating affect on temperature. Salt air can be very corrosive if you live closer than a couple of miles from the beach. Mountain ranges close to the coast will always be very wet as they soak up the first waves of clouds and precipitation moving inland.

The largest and most dramatic effects of geography on weather come with the size and shape of the continent. You can see this in the weather pattern contrast between North and South America. North America has the bulk of its size in the north, whereas South America ends in a narrow strip of mountainous land at the southern tip of Argentina and Chile. Both have the same moderation of temperatures from the coastal areas on the west, but incoming moist air masses change into different forms because of the different size of the land mass they traverse from west to east.

In North America, storms generated in the Gulf of Alaska travel from west to east, dropping most of their moisture in the western coastal or Rocky Mountains and then proceed to become large masses of dry air as they travel across the wide, cool expanses of Canada. These drier, cooler air masses only cause severe weather as they descend over the mainland portions of the central plains in the USA and mix with hot humid air coming up from circulation originating in Mexico and the Gulf of Mexico.

This same phenomenon doesn't happen at the corresponding latitudes in South America because the continent is too narrow down south for the air masses to dry out extensively. Thunderstorms primarily occur further north where drier air from Argentina meets the tropical air masses in Brazil and Paraguay. This same phenomenon also affects southern Africa even though it is not as long and narrow as South America.

Climate

People feel partial to many factors related to climate. Sun, heat, humidity, precipitation and wind all factor heavily into our perception of ideal locations to live. Here is our assessment of these basic factors and a few more to consider in regard to secure climate areas.

Solar Exposure

The Human body needs exposure to sunlight to produce Vitamin D and maintain good emotional health. This factor does not necessarily correlate with a region's annual level of precipitation. Some places get a lot of rain all at once, with otherwise sunny days. Other places get the same amount of rain spread out over nine or ten months, and are plagued by constant cloudiness. The former will be more pleasant relative to sunshine exposure.

Temperature and Humidity

The human body is comfortable within a very narrow range of about 70-80 degrees Fahrenheit. Except for a few rare places, most of us have to deal with keeping warm or cooling off during the changing seasons of the year. Humidity is a big factor in how much the temperature affects us. Hot, dry climates are much easier to tolerate, in our opinion, than hot, humid climates. Any area that has a lot of locally generated summer thunderstorms is going to be hot and humid. Paraguay and Brazil have a lot of heat and tropical vegetation that generate moist air locally. In the summer, they often have daily thunderstorms at about 2 p.m. Other areas, like the Intermountain West in the USA, which is normally dry, only get thunderstorms when humid air masses come up from Mexico. Some areas have large bodies of water that generate humid columns of air that turn into local thunderstorms. Even large, irrigated farm lands can act as sources of rising humidity when the sun evaporates the moisture.

The humid Midwest area of the USA only gets relief from the heat and humidity when fall weather comes and cool, dry Canadian air descends into the US pushing the warm, muggy air southward. This same phenomenon occurs a bit later in the fall in the humid southern states, where days will alternate between humid gulf air and cool Canadian air.

The trade off between humid climates and dry climates are pronounced. The dry, high desert climates as in the Intermountain West are generally more comfortable in the summer and winter because of lack of humidity. The price is lack of greenery. And the price of greenery is rain and humidity, which is abundant in the Pacific Northwest, the Midwest, the South and the East Coast of the USA. There is also a price for greenery beyond rain. The wooded areas in rainy or humid areas are generally overgrown and full of noxious weeds like poison ivy. In contrast, the drier pine and fir forests of the West are much less overgrown and easier to enjoy when hiking and camping.

Precipitation

Moisture is essential to life, but it makes a difference depending on the form it takes—either rain, sleet, hail or snow. It's also important to know when and how the year's total precipitation comes. It is generally not helpful if it all comes during one season. If it is spread out during nine months of the year, the cloud cover can get rather dreary. Tropical areas of the world in equatorial regions are subject to monsoon type rains which are very heavy and unpleasant. Extreme northern coastal areas like parts of Norway and Alaska experience such frequent cloud cover that they may have only a couple of weeks of sun total and usually no more than a day at a time. The Pacific Northwest of the USA has nine months of cloudy weather. The Nebraska plains area of the US gets most of its summer rains from thunderstorms. Rain and snow storms are fairly fast moving in the Intermountain West region, so they don't linger for long, leaving lots of sunny, cold weather during the winter months. We prefer living where it is drier: 20 to 40 inches of moisture a year. This is not enough to grow crops without irrigation, but it provides for a pleasant, sunny climate. Your tastes, of course, may differ. People with dry skin, for example, like humid climates more than dry ones.

On the other hand, insufficient rain can lead to severe water shortages, especially where cities rely on underground water. The Rocky Mountain areas which stockpile water in mountain reservoirs are mostly desert. Now that the reservoir infrastructure is in place, they have the advantage of gravity fed water supplies, as opposed to flat land cities that have to pump water into above ground towers. Twenty to thirty inches of rain and snow per year is sufficient in the arid west to provide sufficient water to the reservoirs– unless they outgrow the water supply as they have in Las Vegas, Nevada and Southern California.

Wind

Wind is generally not a pleasant factor except when light breezes are needed for cooling, as in tropical areas. Those looking for wind in order to generate power must realize that power from windmills grows exponentially with wind speed—meaning that good wind power areas will be quite uncomfortable to live in. Even staying indoors, one is subject to the noise of wind whistling around the house. Mountainous areas often have steady winds in the morning or afternoon, especially if you live near a canyon in the path of winds flowing to higher and lower elevations.

Strategically Balanced Climate

Ideally, a balance is desired between a climate that can sustain life in an energy crisis and yet not be so comfortable as to attract the soft, comfort-seeking elements of society. A climate that is too severe, especially in cold temperatures, requires heavy expenditures of energy to sustain the population during the winter. While this is somewhat beneficial in terms of attracting only the hardiest of immigrants, it is a distinct liability in a crisis, where one has to expend increasing amounts of valuable energy and funds just to preserve the quality of a warm or cool existence. On the benefit side, cold, dry climates have fewer insects and diseases.

Climate extremes don't serve as isolators from certain types of people like they used to. With the almost universal use of heating and air conditioning, people are shielded from the oppressive heat and humidity of hot tropics or deserts as much as they are shielded from the severe cold near the poles. We predict that in a long-term energy crisis there would be a massive migration of people back to the climates that better match what they can tolerate. In hard times, the hardier climates will always tend to attract and keep those who are more rigorous in their endurance of cold or desert conditions and better capable of handling climate stress.

Natural Disaster Threats

Natural disasters are the most unpredictable of the threat groups. Scientists are getting pretty good at forecasting certain types of storms after they form and begin to get threatening, but the key elements of what causes them originally (such as El Niño weather patterns) or exactly when and where a tornado will strike, still eludes them. It will probably always be out of reach of human science, and perhaps it is meant to be that way. It is even possible that the increasing frequency of natural disasters we experience each year is a type of a subtle divine warning meant to nudge sensitive people to think more about preparedness.

People are amazingly immune to the voices of warning. It seems that almost everyone keeps trying to see a silver lining in everything; trying to look for a positive future. In weather, for example, you can analyze storm tracks and details for years without getting a feeling for an ominous pattern that we think is developing of bigger and more destructive storms each decade, pressing in on certain locations. Until now, you may have survived several hurricanes on the south Florida coast or several earthquakes in California. A lot of people now think they can withstand anything nature can deliver or rebuild afterward with the aid of government handouts. This is false confidence. In our opinion there are huge catastrophes coming in the future that will forever alter the way we think about certain locations.

Rather than let our recent experiences lull us into complacency, let's keep an eye on these new trends. If we feel they are getting worse, let's not wait around for the "big one." Instead, we should providentially decide to relocate when times are still good—otherwise we'll simply be caught in the panic of a mass exodus with all the rest who waited too long, and then there won't be any property value left to salvage or sell. Move before the big one and you stand a good chance of keeping your life and accumulated assets intact.

Severe Storms

As part of your strategic planning, look at the locations and geographic patterns where you find the highest probability of damage from severe storms: coastal areas, large lake shore areas, mountain passes, and flat plains. What do these have in common? They are exposed to high flows of either air or water because of lack of obstruction or even channeling of those elements. The secret to a safe location from storms is to find a place with shielding elements. Forests and hills are good examples of this. Mountains are even better as long as you stay off of the steep parts of the mountain itself and out of the passes or approaches to the passes. Always look for sufficient elevation to avoid flood waters. Horizontal distance from prevalent storm tracks can also be helpful.

Severe Storm Recommendations

To enhance your probabilities of storm avoidance consider the following location guidelines:

- In coastal areas, locate at least behind the first set of hills inland and away from coastal mountain rivers subject to flooding in torrential rains. Locating near a small river is desirable for other reasons, but make sure you have sufficient elevation and distance away from the stream to avoid flooding.

- Inland, in cold or cool climates, avoid the lowest parts of the valley where cold air seeks to settle or flow. Seek locations on sheltered bench areas (slightly elevated areas where valleys transition to hills or mountains) but away from direct avalanche or rock fall areas so as to avoid cold winter airflows from mountain passes that follow open, low-lying stream beds.

- In the plains areas, try to find some slightly higher ground away from flooding rivers or lowlands, and pick a site in the lee of any small forested area for protection against high wind. Keep trees sufficiently away from the house to avoid damage from fire or falling branches and tree trunks. During the winter blizzard season, don't let your car gas tank get below the 1/3 level, and always carry emergency equipment in your trunk including blankets, energy bars and hand warmers to help you ride out a blizzard if stranded in your car.

- In all areas, stockpile extra plywood sheets, tarps, rolls of plastic, duct tape and a few varieties of roofing nails in your garage (especially plastic top nails for fastening plastic sheeting) to make emergency repairs to the roof or cover and seal broken windows. In the event of winter storm damage this is the only way you'll be able to keep life-saving heat inside the home. Within hours of a damaging storm, there will be a run on these types of repair items at all hardware stores, so stock up beforehand.

Hurricanes

Much of what was just discussed is applicable to hurricanes. Hurricanes are only generally predictable despite lots of money spent on tracking them. Weather forecasters can determine where they are with great precision, but they never really know where they will go next—especially as they approach landfall. As hurricanes interact with other air masses over land, it often causes them to turn in unpredictable directions. On the Atlantic seaboard, they can make very abrupt turns and reversals without much warning. Because hurricanes lose power in direct proportion to how far inland they go, there are two basic ways to protect against them. If you wish to live in a coastal area subject to hurricanes, you must build on ground which is always a little higher than the surrounding terrain, but still shielded from on-shore winds (this tends to eliminate good view spots). You should build with reinforced masonry construction, such as the modern ICF concrete insulated forms. If you can't afford high-security construction, you should locate at least 50 miles inland (preferably 75 to 100 miles).

Hurricanes have historically caused as many or more deaths from flooding than wind damage. If you must locate in a high risk hurricane zone, implement strong construction measures. In the future we expect more big storms to hit coastline communities so we recommend overbuilding a little for security and protection. Pick the more sheltered locations rather than the more risky view points. Homes in moderate risk areas further inland (which are only occasionally impacted) need only a secure room retreat.

Hurricane Recommendations

- Avoid the exposed high ground, as well as the low lying land which may flood during high rains.

- Locate your home in wind sheltered locations such as forested areas that absorb a lot of wind energy.

- Keep trees in your own yard at a safe distance, or tether them together with wire cables.

- Integrate a reinforced masonry storm room into your home.

- Invest in unbreakable, acrylic plastic storm windows (Plexiglass is one brand name).

- Add hurricane ties to your roof and walls to secure the roof framing to the top of the wall and the wall to the foundation.

- Pay particular attention to large eaves or overhangs on your house that are susceptible to wind uplift.

- Select siding materials that are rigid and well fastened (brick veneer or stucco are best).

Tornadoes

Thunderstorms themselves are very powerful micro-storms and deserve a healthy amount of respect. Under specific conditions thunderstorms can produce tornadoes, bringing the wind power right to the ground. Fortunately, it takes a certain mix of air masses to produce the necessary conditions for tornadoes and these conditions are not common throughout the world. The highest tornado potential develops as warm, humid air masses clash with dry, cold air. This geographic situation requires a continental shape and size like North America, as described previously. The most pronounced area is in the southern Central Plains of the United States, which is known as "Tornado Alley" because this is where the vast majority of twisters occur. Tornadoes have occurred in other areas with significant thunderstorm activity, such as the F4 tornado in South Wales, Australia in 1970. But occurrences outside the US are so rare we will leave this discussion until Section Two when we discuss natural disasters in the US.

Tornado Recommendations

Build a below-ground or basement safe room, preferably accessible from an adjacent basement space in the house. Our book *The High Security Shelter - How to Implement a Multi-Purpose Safe Room in the in the Home* has plans and details to help you build a solid shelter not only for tornados but also the full range of physical threats to your security.

Floods

There are three or four types of floods that you need to prepare against, depending upon your location: tidal waves, river flooding, lowland flooding and flash floods.

Tidal Waves

If you are located directly on the coast or on nearby sea level land, you need to prepare against tidal waves. Tidal waves differ from storm waves in that they are caused by distant earthquakes under the ocean which generate wave pulses capable of creating ocean swells as high as 30 feet. When they make landfall, they can rise to even 90 feet. Even non-seismic coastlines are susceptible to this danger since they can be generated by earthquakes thousands of miles away. These waves roll outward from the epicenter like a giant ripple, hitting coastlines in a 360 degree arc. When unobstructed, these waves have rolled inland over half a mile and there is precious little you can do to stop them. Even worse, they always hit in a series of waves and the rip tides going back out to sea can be just as deadly as the incoming force.

For example, on August 16, 1976 in the Philippines, an 18 foot tidal wave struck and swamped the islands of Mindanao, Sulu, Basilan and Tawi Tawi causing 8,000 deaths. An even larger wave struck Sumatra on December 26 in 2004 causing 225,000 deaths with millions losing their homes. Don't underestimate these monsters if you live on the coast. If you must build near a shoreline with a view, pick a small bluff to build on which gives you height above this kind of massive wave action. But make sure the cliffs are very stable. Soft sandstone bluffs and cliffs in California are slowly eroding away in some areas and threaten both homes and highways.

Tidal waves are only a real danger on sea level beaches. On the west coast of Canada, only the lower shallow beaches around Vancouver are susceptible. In America, the Hawaiian Islands have many vulnerable beaches, as does the Pacific Coast area of California. Many cliffs on the Pacific Coast, particularly in Oregon and Washington are safe from tidal waves because of height above the sea. The northern Atlantic Coast areas from New England to Nova Scotia in Canada are susceptible to tidal waves produced from off-shore earthquakes, although the "ring of fire" fault lines mostly encircle the Pacific Ocean. A tidal wave in 1929 hit Newfoundland and killed 27 people—the Atlantic Seaboard's worst tidal wave death toll.

River Flooding

The most common flood danger is along large, wide, meandering rivers like the Amazon or Mississippi. The flat plains surrounding the river immediately begin to flood when the river level rises. In America, billions have been spent to build levies along the Mississippi so that farmers can cultivate the flat lands next to the river. This strategy delays the onset of flooding beyond the levies but exacerbates the flooding and destruction when the levies are breached. Many flood planners now realize that it would have been better to never have built levies so that the river could spread out early and evenly. Levies tend to channel big rivers into rushing torrents. Without levies, homes and even small towns could have been built on artificially elevated ground, for less total cost than levies. Obviously, flood plains are not good locations for any permanent structures. But, if you have no choice, build them on artificial, elevated mounds, and make sure you have an inflatable boat in the garage or barn.

Lowland Flooding

The third form of flooding is that which happens on flat land. During severe rain storms, especially in Monsoonal areas, huge amounts of rain can descend in a matter of hours. If you are located in an area even a foot or two below the surrounding plain, and a severe storm dumps 12 inches of water on the area in a couple of hours, you could find yourself in a few feet of flood water (or worse if the terrain funnels more water your way). Look at the precise elevations of land whenever you build or buy a home on what appears to be flat land. Always pick the higher ground. It is also wise to make sure the high ground is shaped like a peninsula giving you a high ground escape route away from floods, rather than forming an island which can trap you.

Flash Floods

The fourth form of flood to watch out for is flash floods. These affect people who locate in relatively narrow canyons or valleys that descend from nearby mountains. A large summer thunderstorm can generate tons of water and funnel it down a canyon—forming walls of water and debris 20 to 50 feet high, depending upon the geography of the canyon. Even if you are outside the canyon itself, but in a valley along its path, you can be exposed to its destructive force. The solution is, again, higher ground and increased distance from the threat. If you have already purchased a home in one of these danger channels, build diversion barriers so that your house will only be subject to the rising water, not the initial wall of mud and debris.

Flooding Recommendations

In summary, here is your flood protection checklist for those not able to avoid locating in a flood hazard area:

• Stay out of the direct flow area (which is destructive as well as wet).

• Select sites with favorable elevation. Build berms and artificial hills if you need more height.

• Build diversion walls of boulders and logs tied together with cable and wire fencing and then backed by earth to divert flash floods or tidal waves. Remember to build diversion walls for the return flow in tidal wave zones (on the back side of the house).

• Always have a boat and a cellular telephone.

• If you have a basement, get a gas powered suction pump (to do salvage work in basement areas).

• Make sure you are tied into a local warning network—especially for sudden floods like tidal waves and flash floods.

Earthquakes

Earthquakes are most common where tectonic plates in the earth are slowly migrating north or south or riding up on an opposing plate boundary. These plate fault lines often conform to coastlines and mountain uplift areas. This can be seen in seismic maps of the world. There are notable exceptions, however, such as the New Madrid fault in the central USA. It extends 120 miles from the area of Charleston, Missouri and Cairo, Illinois south through New Madrid and Caruthersville and down to Marked Tree, Arkansas. It crosses the Mississippi and Ohio Rivers various times. The New Madrid fault is somewhat less active than other faults in the US but when it does give way, the tremors are felt for many more miles around because of the flat terrain and underlying water table—causing wave action.

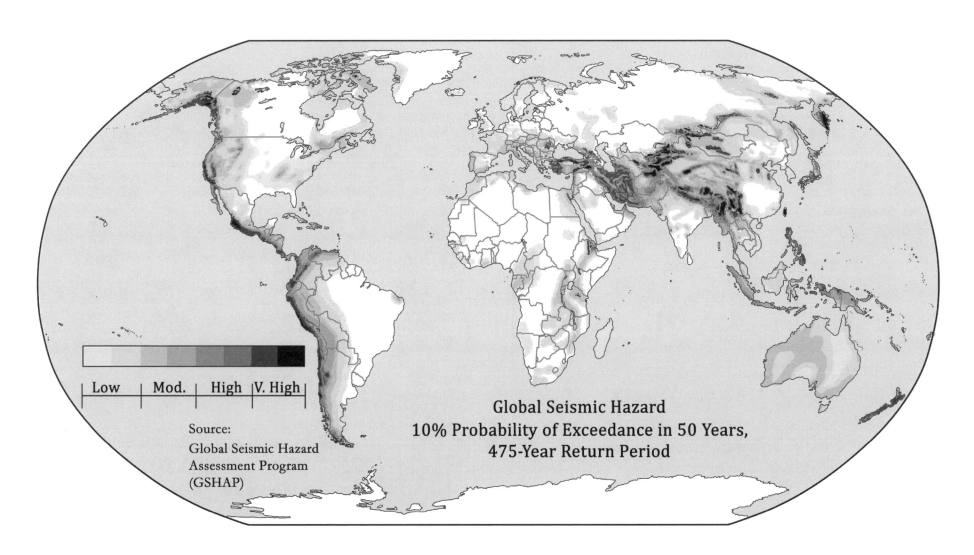

| Low | Mod. | High | V. High |

Source:
Global Seismic Hazard
Assessment Program
(GSHAP)

Global Seismic Hazard
10% Probability of Exceedance in 50 Years,
475-Year Return Period

World's Most Devastating Quakes

Compared to the rest of the world's earthquake record, North American seismic events have been comparatively mild. The following is a list of the world's deadliest earthquakes. Note how the death toll is usually more dependant on the construction methods of stone and unenforced masonry than on the magnitude of the quake itself. Remember that the magnitude is based on the Richter scale which is logarithmic—each higher number is 10 times stronger. As a general gauge any magnitude less than 3.0 is imperceptible, 3-5 are mild to moderate quakes, 5-6 are strong quakes and 7-9 magnitude tremors can cause real devastation. This list is in reverse chronological order—most recent first.

World's Most Devastating Earthquakes Since 1900				
Date	Location	Magnitude	Fatalities	Notes
January 12, 2010	Port-au-Prince Haiti	M 7.0	230,000	
May 12, 2008	Eastern Sichuan, China	M 7.9	87,587	
October 8, 2005	Pakistan	M 7.6	80,361	
December 26, 2004	Sumatra and Andaman Islands	M 9.1	227,898	Triggered a tsunami that hit 14 countries including South Africa.
January 17, 1995	Kobe, Japan	M 7.2	6,425	Great Hansin Earthquake. Major destruction to city of Kobe.
September 30, 1993	Latur, India	M 6.4	22,000	Five separate Magnitude 6-7 quakes. People were killed in 36 villages.
June 20, 1990	Caspian region Iran	M 7.7	50,000	100,000 injured; 100,000 homeless.
December 7, 1988	NW Armenia and Russia	M 7.0	Over 25,000	18,000 injured.
October 10, 1986	San Salvador	M 7.5	1,500	20,000 people injured, 300,000 homeless, many buildings collapsed in the city of San Salvador.
September 19, 1985	Mexico City, Mexico	M 8.1	10 to 12,000	40,000 injured.
November 23, 1980	Irpino, Italy	M 7.2	2,735	Near Naples. Over 7,500 injured, many missing.
September 16, 1978	Tabas, Iran	M 7.9	26,000	Town of Abas was completely flattened.
July 27, 1976	Tangshan, China	M 7.8	655,237	Approximately 779,000 injured, millions homeless.
February 4, 1976	Guatemala City, Guatemala	M 7.5	23,000	Quakes and mudslides. 80,000 people were injured and 1.5 million people were made homeless.
December 23, 1972	Managua, Nicaragua	M 6.5	7,000	600,000 homeless.
May 31, 1970	Yungay, Huaraz and Chimbote, Peru	M 7.9	70,000	600,000 homeless.
May 23, 1960	Santiago and Concepcion, Chile	M 9.5	Over 10,000	Most powerful earthquake recorded. After-effects included tidal waves and volcanic eruptions.
August 1, 1949	Ambato, Ecuador	M 6.7	6,000	100,000 homeless.
Source: USGS and Wikipedia				

World's Most Devastating Earthquakes Since 1900				
Date	**Location**	**Magnitude**	**Fatalaties**	**Notes**
October 25, 1948	Ashgabat, Turkmenistan, USSR	M 7.3	110,000	
January 24, 1939	Concepcion, Chile	M 8.3	25 to 30,000	95 per cent of buildings were damaged or destroyed.
May 22, 1927	Xining, Tsinghai China	M 7.9	200,000	
September 1, 1923	Tokyo and Yokahama, Japan	M 7.9	140,000	2.5 million people homeless.
December 16, 1920	Jiangsu province, China	M 7.8	180,000	
January 13, 1915	Avezzano, Italy	M 6.9	30,000	In Avezzano only one multi-story building remained. 96 percent of population died.
December 28, 1908	Messina, Italy	M 7.2	82,000	A tidal wave followed, causing more devastation, also to the town of Reggio across the straits.
April 4, 1905	Kangra, India	M 8.6	19,000	
Source: USGS and Wikipedia				

Mitigating the Danger

In our opinion, it is worth preparing houses in even moderate seismic areas for some earthquake forces. Horizontal steel straps can help connect major structural members together, shear walls will brace upper floors and anchor bolts are critical to secure the base of walls to the foundation during horizontal movements.

Within high earthquake danger areas, you can minimize the destruction of local quakes on your own home by selecting the building site. The key is to build a flexible structure (wood or steel stud) on solid soils—preferably rock or rocky soils. Stay away from locations with clay, silt, sand or loose gravel such as at the bottom of valleys or near coastlines. Poorly compacted fill or river deposits allow bigger quake wave movement because of their loose consistency. Even worse is when loose soils are over a relatively high water table. These are very likely to liquefy during an earthquake and allow heavy parts of a building to settle and lean or fall over.

The soils and water tables underlying major portions of Mexico City are typical of this worst case scenario. Major portions of this city are built over an old lake bed of sandy soil on top of deep clay which retains ground water. When a quake hit Mexico City in 1985, the loose soils easily moved and rippled causing severe shaking and soil liquefaction all over the old lake bed. Parts of buildings settled during the shaking causing splitting, cracking or toppling. A few portions of the lake bed are underlain by old volcanic rock and these

areas stayed stable and the buildings suffered much less damage. You can find information on soil types for your potential area at the local building authority or local library (in a developed country) or directly from the geological survey in the US.

Building in the mountains will usually expose you to some earthquake risk, but it can still be advantageous. It's much easier to find good soil with rock layers below the surface providing a potentially safe spot even if relatively close to a minor fault. In an earthquake the mountain area may receive one or two jolts directly from the quake movement down in the fault, but without the ripple wave action through the soil, it may not be as destructive. Be careful of building right next to a steep mountainside, where rocks and boulders come crashing down. Also beware of building on the scenic edges of sandy foothills where the land wants to continue sloughing downward. These foothills can become unstable in an earthquake, taking your house and foundation with it.

Volcanoes

Volcanoes are almost like a nuclear attack—only potentially bigger and without the radiation fallout. When Mount St. Helens erupted in 1980, she blew a third of the mountain top off and converted it almost instantly into ash, gravel and dust that was sent into the troposphere and carried clear across the United States. The majority of the ash fell in eastern Washington, Idaho and Montana. Joel describes his experience at the time:

"I was living only 50 miles from it when it blew. In fact my office had a large picture window pointed in that direction. Due to west-southwest winds, almost all the ash bypassed my location, except on one or two days. And on those days you can't imagine how bad that gritty, grinding dust was. It gets into everything and destroys or damages many moving parts in a vehicle. One must avoid driving through an ash storm or even when significant quantities cover the ground. Almost everyone had to wear a face dust mask outdoors, which was not pleasant."

The following map from the US Geological Survey (USGS) shows the most active volcanoes around the world.

shifting magma. The volcano threat will affect you if you are seeking a secure location in and around the beautiful, forested Sierra Nevada or Cascade Mountains in the West. These volcanic threats are noted on the corresponding state maps in the last section of the book.

Volcano Guidelines

- Stay an absolute 10 miles away from these volcanoes in any direction to avoid blast damage.

- Do not locate closer than a mile from any river or stream that comes down from these mountains to avoid mudslides and flash flooding.

- Stay at least 50 miles away from any location 30 degrees either side of the prevailing wind to avoid the heaviest ash fall.

- Always carry a supply of high quality dust masks in your car, plus an extra car air filter in case you get trapped and have to drive out of an ash fall. You must be prepared to leave the area during an eruption cycle where you are exposed to a lot of ash on the ground—to avoid having to drive in it regularly and breathe the dust. The ash is not toxic, and is actually pretty good fertilizer—but not good to breathe. If you don't have an extra auto filter and your car air filter gets clogged, remember that you can open up the filter housing, take the filter out and pound it against your tire or the road and make most of the dust fall out. Put it back in and keep driving till it clogs again, and repeat as necessary. Buy these things in advance, to avoid the run on these items within hours of an eruption.

Prominent Volcanoes of the World

Source: USGS

"End of the World" Scenarios

The largest volcanic eruptions seem to be triggered in relation to the solar and lunar forces that cause ocean tides. Although 7 out of the 8 smaller eruptions of Mt. Saint Helens occurred between strong tidal periods, the big blast eruption that took off the top of the mountain was triggered by a big earthquake under the mountain during the time of maximum solar and lunar pull. In other words, there is a correlation to high tidal periods and pressure on tectonic plates just prior to an eruption, which coincides with an earthquake. An eruption of magma pressures tends to happen between these high stress periods—almost like the molten core of the earth is adjusting to the stress periods by

This is controversial subject is popular for fictional summer movies but some theories are being seriously discussed in halls of government. The two principle sources of "the-sky-is-falling" type ideas are pseudo prophecies of a spiritualistic and New Age origin and from bad scientists and sociologists promoting false environmental catastrophes. Both base their theories on forces or aspects of nature that we don't fully understand.

The first group's theories are usually cosmic in origin such as planets aligning to disrupt the moon's orbit, the earth's axis/magnetic field, etc. all of which are proclaimed to have dire consequences. Sometimes there are rigid time-dates surrounding all this speculation but virtually all of the previous earth-change predictions for a specific date have come and gone without effect.

We are skeptical of any prediction from New Age or spiritualistic sources especially when the idea involves an "end of the earth" scenario. We rely on the fact that God has his own divine purposes for preserving the earth as a testing ground for mankind, and isn't going to allow cosmic forces to destroy it.

As an example of this, we find it highly improbable that mere chance has preserved the earth from a major asteroid collision for so long. Every other planet in our solar system shows extensive damage from large asteroids. The moon is completely pock-marked. We have only had a couple of minor asteroid hits during recorded history—all in unpopulated areas and with no significant effect. We suggest it is best to simply trust in God in things that are too big for man to control. Consequently, we feel that spending billions on an anti-asteroid missile system, etc. is neither feasible nor necessary.

The second group of doomsayers is more difficult to dismiss. Using bits of data and science they predict the downfall of the world through global warming, overpopulation, pollution, etc. Fortunately, cooler heads in the scientific community can be found who help sort out the falsehoods. Temperature fluctuations in our climate can be almost totally attributed to sun cycles. Economic development gradually brings cleaner energies and methods with it. The difficulty is that these environmentalists and their scientific smoke screens divert large resources to inefficient pet causes, and tie up the world's limited attention span on utterly false solutions. Worse yet, the dangerous legislative edicts that come out of these international treaties on climate control will present a constant and pernicious threat to your pocketbook and liberty.

As with the previous threat, we don't believe that God will allow man to destroy the earth entirely. However, he does allow men to torment each other through false ideas and theories. The governmental response to these fake threats becomes the true danger to our way of living. We will discuss the threat of bad government in the next chapter.

Chapter 3

FREEDOMS AND POLITICS

Nothing is more important to your overall security than the structure and form of government in the country which you live. Tyranny can happen even in democracies, especially when the tyrannical steps are made in relative secrecy or hidden behind false premises such as national security.

This chapter will describe some of the most important factors to consider about governments. There are certain ideal principles of freedom and protection of rights that are vital for sustaining liberty in a government. Some aspects of government aren't as clear cut, such as taxes, but can be almost as detrimental. Certain countries are inherently strategically safer because of natural resources. To our knowledge no country on earth fully matches all these criteria perfectly, but some are much better than others. Your liberty and freedom will be proportional to these factors.

As you evaluate potential countries and their current freedoms, pay attention to the historical legacy of the country's background. Historical precedents can predict if people within a nation have a tendency to resist the onset of tyranny within, or become pawns of government power, especially during war when governments get away with many crimes. People who are accustomed to being dictated to by government are much more likely to start taking orders, without question, during war than those with a history of liberty and resistance to tyranny. Look for governments that are stable. Countries with a history of coups and uprisings can never be trusted to provide security. Neither can countries like Russia or China whose people have acquiesced to decades of surveillance and control.

If the country you live in becomes tyrannical, you may be able to mitigate the risk temporarily by keeping a low profile and not making waves. But unless you can look and fit in like a native you are bound to be noticed eventually. If you are the type who can't stand by and see people being abused (a good thing), then you will have difficulty keeping silent in the face of oppression. Be prepared to get out of the way or go partially underground before it gets to the point that resistors are being rounded up. Learn the lessons of East Germany. One day they woke up and the border was sealed by troops. The next day, barbed wire was in place. The next week the cement wall was begun. Thousands made it to freedom on the first day by acting immediately. Those who waited had a much more difficult time getting out. It will happen again—count on it.

Government Threats to Fundamental Rights

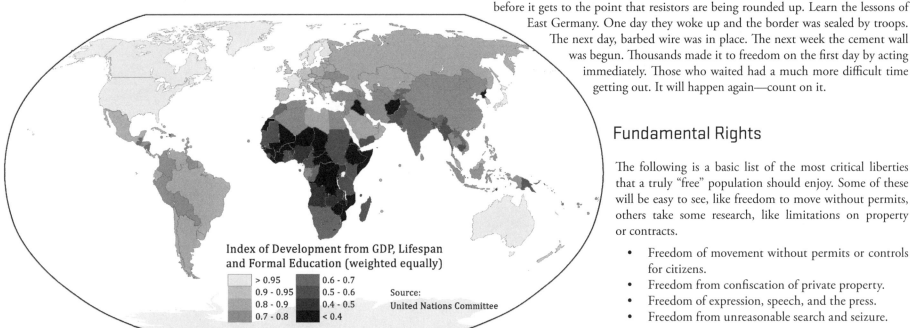

Index of Development from GDP, Lifespan and Formal Education (weighted equally)

> 0.95	0.6 - 0.7
0.9 - 0.95	0.5 - 0.6
0.8 - 0.9	0.4 - 0.5
0.7 - 0.8	< 0.4

Source: United Nations Committee

Fundamental Rights

The following is a basic list of the most critical liberties that a truly "free" population should enjoy. Some of these will be easy to see, like freedom to move without permits, others take some research, like limitations on property or contracts.

- Freedom of movement without permits or controls for citizens.
- Freedom from confiscation of private property.
- Freedom of expression, speech, and the press.
- Freedom from unreasonable search and seizure.

- Freedom from arbitrary arrest, delays of justice and judgment without a trial by jury.

- Freedom to defend oneself by force of arms.

- Freedom to discriminate between people you wish to associate or do business with.

- Freedom to engage in any activity not violating the fundamental rights of others.

- Freedom of ownership and control of private property.

- Freedom from redistribution of income by government via confiscatory taxation.

- Freedom to contract freely with other willing parties without government regulation or licensing.

- Freedom to choose how to medically care for yourself and your family.

Some of the freedoms listed above are ideals, like no redistribution of wealth for welfare, government housing, etc. which all countries participate in. The extent of encroachment on this liberty, however, does vary. Look for a maximum of these partial freedoms and avoid countries with a history of corruption, which is common with redistribution of property.

Patterns of Government

The fundamental rights listed above should be established within the framework of government. Many countries respect these rights through legal precedent, like Canada and England, but without a tightly worded constitution. In our opinion it is better if these rights are spelled out formally in a constitution that is binding upon the government. Even the US constitution, as good as it is, has too much general language and loopholes that have been exploited by activist judges to erode many of the principles and rights outlined above.

Beyond a rigid framework of defending rights, a secure nation must have two essential political frameworks:

First, a secure country must be governed by a representative system of government with universal suffrage for citizens. But the power citizens can exert through representatives must be restricted by narrow constitutional limits. These powers, whether at the national or state/province level, should be strictly limited to the defense of fundamental rights and should not allow the majority to vote themselves personal or group benefits.

Second, a secure nation must also possess a national legal system that actually defends fundamental rights. A list of rights in the constitutions is only helpful if the courts defend those rights. These courts should also establish criteria for criminal prosecution and punishment which effectively deters crime, prosecutes fraud and enforces contracts.

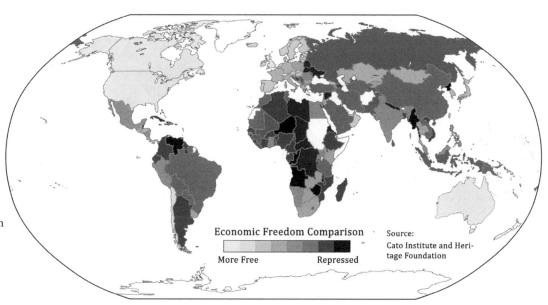

Economic Freedom Comparison

More Free — Repressed

Source: Cato Institute and Heritage Foundation

Freedom and Corruption

On pages 20-22 are three map-style comparisons of countries around the world: economic freedom, world development and corruption. Unfortunately, no one country is perfect in any of these respects. The maps comparing economic freedom and world development generally represent the freedom to transact business and retain profits from taxation. However, they do not represent all freedoms since some critical rights such as bearing arms and freedom from search and seizure are not represented by these graphics. The corruption map represents ratings obtained from surveys of businesses about the perception of corruption in their country. Transparency International, the author of the study that generated the information, maintains that this method is more reliable than measuring the number of corruption charges or cases since often the police and courts are also corrupt and do not prosecute.

Usually found among the top 10 countries for freedom are Hong Kong, Singapore, Switzerland, New Zealand, the USA, Chile, Ireland, Canada and Australia.

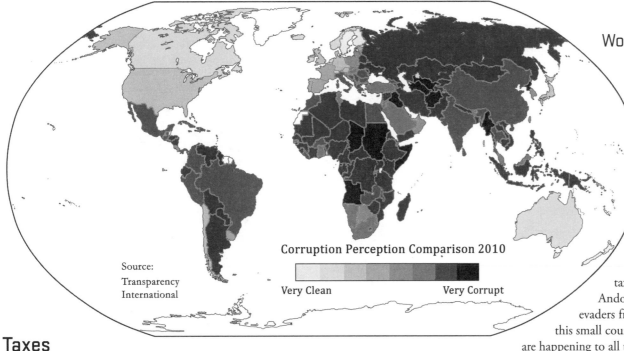

World Tax Rates

The table on the next page shows some of the tax rates in countries usually considered for relocation, minus the countries that we consider untenable for long-term security. As with all tax strategies, it's important to research how each location will impact your specific income situation.

Andorra, Europe's smallest country, has been a traditional tax haven in Europe, as you can see from the following table. Recently, the country has fallen on hard times with the decline in tourism, duty free trade and restrictions on bank secrecy and is starting to follow the rest of Europe by implementing the VAT tax. The EU, Spain and France have threatened to deny Andorra's principality status if it doesn't crack down on tax evaders from France and Spain that have stashed their earnings in this small country in the Pyrenees Mountains. These kinds of pressures are happening to all the world's small tax havens.

Corruption Perception Comparison 2010

Source:
Transparency
International

Very Clean   Very Corrupt

Taxes

"In this world nothing is certain but death and taxes" (Benjamin Franklin) is applicable no matter which country you live in. Even tax haven countries like the Virgin Islands raise limited revenue through license fees and import taxes which are passed along to people living there.

When evaluating the tax burden in other countries look for these and other hidden taxes. A common hidden tax is the value added tax (VAT). Unlike the sales taxes in the US which are added at the register and made obvious to the consumer, VAT taxes are hidden in the sticker prices since they are collected along each step of the manufacturing process. People don't feel this tax as much. In the US the sales tax can only rise to around 10% before people start fighting or avoiding the tax. VAT taxes have been sustained at up to 17% and even 21%. They drag down even historically strong economies like that of Germany. In France, the majority of tax revenue comes from VAT taxes.

The most onerous tax in the United States is easily the income tax. The US is usually the leader in developing tax code in this area and every year it gets more complex. We haven't found much respite from this in other countries, however, since their governments are constantly learning from the American IRS.

Despite these outward pressures, we are convinced that some world leaders and other corrupt people in league with governments are given immunity from discovery. For example, when the giant Union Bank of Switzerland was forced to reveal thousands of secret bank account holders to the US government, the secret accounts of well-connected government officials and other insiders were exempted from discovery.

In the UK, the Isle of Man and the small Channel Islands have served as traditional tax havens for the wealthy from both Europe and America. In the western hemisphere, certain islands of the Caribbean have served as tax havens including: British Virgin Islands, the Caymans, Antigua and others. Much has changed in the past decade as the United States has put extreme pressures on these islands to break down bank secrecy. A good current listing of tax havens can be found on Wikipedia.

Don't be tempted to relocate based solely on avoiding taxes. Almost all of the tax havens are tiny countries or islands that are vulnerable to invasion and external threat. They have no appreciable defenses and are protected by other powers that use the banks to secretly stash their own or their leader's ill-gotten gains. These havens are allowed to survive as long as they serve the Powers That Be.

World Tax Rates			
Country/Region	Individual	Payroll Tax	VAT / GST / Sales
Andorra	0-10%	N/A	4.5% or 1%
Argentina	9%	44%	21%
Australia	0-49%	4.75-6.85%	10%
Austria	0-50%	N/A	20%
Belgium	0-50%	37.84%	21% (6% food)
Bolivia	0-25%	13%	13%
Brazil	0-27.5%	31%	17-25%
Canada	0-29% (federal) 0-21% (provincial)	9.9%	5% 0-10%
Chile	0-40%	10-20%	19%
Colombia	0-33%		16%
Costa Rica	0-25%	9%	13%
Denmark	29.68-51.95%	8%	25%
Dominican Rep.	0-25%	20%	18%
El Salvador	0-30%		13%
Finland	7.71-62%	20.64%	24%/14%/10%
France	5.5%-45%	66%	19.6% (5.5% food)
Germany	14-45%	15% Nat'l Ins. + 26% social security	19% (7% food)
Guatemala	5-7%	17.5%	12%
Iceland	37.3-46%	6%	24-12%
India	0-30%	2-12.5%	5.5-14.5%
Ireland	20-40%	0-11%	23% (Goods)
Italy	23-43%	39	22% (4% food)
Jamaica	0-25%	6.75-31.75%	Up to 20%
Japan	5-50%	25.63%	8%
Liechtenstein	1.2-17.82%	11.6%	3.6-7.6%
Source: Wikipedia			

World Tax Rates			
Country/Region	Individual	Payroll Tax	VAT / GST / Sales
Luxembourg	6-52.45%		17%
Mexico	1.3-35%	35	16%
Monaco	0	38-54%	19.60%
Netherlands	36-56%		21%
New Zealand	10.5-33%		15%
Norway	0-46.9%	0-14%	25% 15% (food)
Panama	0-27%		7%
Peru	0-30%	17.33%	18%
Portugal	14.5-48%	34.75	15-23%
South Africa	0-40%	18-40%	14%
Spain	20-49%	36.25	21% / 10% / 4%
Sweden	31-59.7%	31.42%	25%
Switzerland	0-13.2%		8%
United Kingdom	0-45%	25.8% Nat'l Insurance	20%
United States	0-39.6% (federal) 0-13.3% (state)	15.3-19.1%	0-11.725%
Uruguay	0-30%		22%
Virgin Islands	0	10-14%	N/A
Source: Wikipedia			

Regional Self-Sufficiency

The nation or region most likely to survive a serious economic depression must have the majority of resources needed to survive within its own borders. Look for a nation that is completely self-sufficient as to the essentials of food, water, electric power generation, fossil fuels and manufacturing of raw materials. Strategic minerals are very important to a high technology nation like the USA, which must stockpile in advance of a crisis (which it is not presently doing). Ultimately, though, food is the most critical. It is disturbing how many nations are not self-sufficient in food supplies anymore and depend on significant quantities of imports.

On a smaller scale, avoid living in heavily industrialized or geographically isolated areas that must be supported by a continuous stream of food and supplies. These areas are likely to suffer more in an emergency when supply lines become reduced or held-up.

The US is the clear winner here. Brazil and Argentina also have a full range of industrial capability, though not as high tech. The USA is completely diversified and self-sufficient except for some strategic minerals. Canada is also diversified and self-sufficient for food. However, it has developed a high reliance upon US imports, rather than develop its own complete industrial base. It's not that it did not want to do so, but it was not as efficient to build domestically compared to buying what was already made in the USA.

This same lure of efficiency and lower prices is weakening US self-sufficiency in the long-term. By shipping jobs and factories overseas to China and Mexico, the US industrial base has been weakened significantly, even though lower prices have increased the standard of living of its citizens dramatically. During the next war, it will take several years to rebuild this capacity when trade is cut off. Fortunately, the US has all the technology to do so rapidly.

Chapter 4

CRIME AND STANDARD OF LIVING

Many positive factors on your wish-list will combine to create a beneficial standard of living and low-crime should be at the top of the list. Several demographic statistics can point to neighborhoods with good qualities and away from areas with crime. We find that quality of life is also greatly dependant on health affects, such as pollution and access to medical help and by schooling opportunities. We examine each of these aspects in general in this chapter.

Crime and Demographics

The people surrounding us can have a significant impact on our quality of life and on our ultimate security. This section covers important qualities to look for in the surroundings you are considering for relocation.

Moral, Industrious Culture and People

National stability is never any stronger than individual religious and moral stability, as manifested through the family unit. Certain cultures really are less prone to corruption and violence as a whole. While every nation has both good and bad people, certain political and cultural climates induce a higher or lower degree of morality and work ethic in the local populace. While it is not politically correct to point out cultural or character deficiencies or differences in ethnic groups, they do exist.

The role of religion in Western countries as a determinant of moral norms has declined severely, especially with the youth in Europe and America. Most are worldly and indifferent to religion. We completely disregard statistics on the percentage of populations that claim to be associated with various religions—especially nations that have a state sanctioned church such as Italy, or Russia or Germany. In fact, the easiest way to destroy or corrupt religion is to subsidize it with government money. Religious fervor is significantly weakened in nations where everyone is a member by birth in a state sanctioned religion.

Religious Diversity

The most secure locations have religious diversity. By that we don't mean the diversity of two warring factions between major religions vying for state recognition and control. The real test of religious diversity is the freedom to start smaller religions without having to gain permission from the state or other major churches. You don't have to adhere to any one religion to take advantage of the generally elevated stability that surrounds most mixed religious communities. There will always be fringe elements involved in a religion, but as long as they are not harming others, they should be tolerated. Beware of communities that are prone to becoming agitated against smaller minorities—you could be one of those targeted someday.

Population Density
(People per km²)

0   350   700

Source:
NASA

Common-sense communities tend to be more stable and tolerant—especially when they have personal knowledge of the minority groups around them. Problems most often arise during a crisis when minority groups are persecuted and forced to flee as a group to new areas. Residents of these areas absorbing the new immigrants get fearful that somehow they are going to lose control over their community. We don't know of any way of foretelling how a community would react to such a situation, except that the more diverse the religious makeup of the population, the more tolerant they become (of peaceable religions).

Population Density

People tend to group together in cities and communities because they can focus their abilities and still make a living because there exists a larger base of potential buyers or clients. For long term peace and security, however, we recommend that high density population areas be avoided.

High population density almost always correlates with high instability in a crisis for the following reasons:

- Excessive specialization. Not enough people have the general abilities to take care of their own basic needs in a crisis, or maintain employment—desperation results.

- Few sources of local food. The ratio of farm land to people is very low, or non-existent, so supplies must be shipped in on a nearly uninterrupted basis.

- Financial dependence upon regular paychecks. Employee work forces are susceptible to strikes and work stoppages even if only a portion is directly involved with organized labor. Everyone's finances are more vulnerable to bank runs.

- General psychological feelings of insecurity in a sea of humanity. This leads to a defensive propensity characterized by the "survival of the fittest" e.g. power plays, gangs, and mob tactics. Power group segmentation occurs in a crisis due to lack of moral or ethical cohesiveness.

- Potential for mass epidemics. Disease can spread rapidly in close quarters.

- Friction of movement. Traffic increases irritations, but in a panic, normal vehicular movement is paralyzed.

- Politics are dominated by liberal and leftist politicians who maintain power by promising and delivering welfare and education benefits. These costs inevitably outrun the supply of tax funds.

As the previous list of density problems illustrates, the tighter the mass of people living in any given area, the more specialized and interdependent the economic and social fabric. In a crisis, almost all of these dependencies and interconnections will fail. Food won't be delivered and people have little space to grow any substitutes. Water and gas may be cut off and people have little access to wood or other alternative fuels to cook or heat with.

Gasoline will run short and transportation will potentially grind to a halt. Even without fuel shortages, any crisis that requires a mass movement of vehicles or people will result in rapid paralysis of the transportation system.

Work Ethic and Class Conflict

Look for areas with a good mix of middle class, hard working people with a lot of self-employed owners, farmers, etc. The self-employed population is usually more self-reliant and stable in tough times. Self-employed people (compared to employees of larger corporations) also seem to understand the effects of excessive government regulation better and are more willing to fight for liberty and just causes. Areas with many employees are not bad, necessarily, but we do recommend against communities that are built around industries controlled by organized labor unions. The bigger unions are always corrupt.

In the USA, the power of the unions has been partially broken and persists mainly in holdover industries such as automobiles, manufacturing and government. But other countries like Europe are still deeply entrenched in a labor union-dominated job structure. Their entire transportation system can and is regularly held hostage by striking workers.

Organized labor is dangerous because of the excess tyrannical powers granted to them by government—not because it is wrong for workers to band together to protest bad employer practices. In our opinion, a worker's true rights in the free market are to enforce existing working contracts or seek employment elsewhere. Boycotts or mass exits by groups of workers are an appropriate way to send a really strong message—when performed voluntarily by the workers. Sure it is tough to quit and find another job, but that is part of the price of freedom.

Unions, however, have been given special legal status that forces the employer to negotiate with them, and keeps employers from hiring replacements. Unions are really anti-other-workers (the ones who would be willing to do their job for less money) as well as anti-employers. The hatred they show toward potential strike breakers proves this underlying hostility to competition. "Worker Solidarity" is just a sham and a propaganda stunt for those who hold the existing jobs.

Why this criticism of unions? Because unions are inherently corrupting and divisive in society. Every union has access to forced contributions from workers who may not agree with union leadership (closed shops). Because of these huge sums of union funds, organized criminal elements and powerful leftist political elements have always gravitated to union activity and power. Consequently, every community that has large blocks of union workers is divisive and subject to the poisonous class-conscious doctrine that leftist union leaders preach. Unions are often hostile to workers even within their ranks who work "too hard" and who make the others look bad. This kind of corruption infiltrates the work ethic of any region with large industrial concentrations. Avoid these areas.

You also need to avoid areas with high concentrations of wealthy, sophisticated people. Although usually associated with lower internal crime rates, concentrations of wealth and expensive homes tend to elevate land and housing prices and also attract envy and resentment that is not good for long term security.

Crime and Social Unrest

The old sociological excuse about people turning to crime because of pure environmental causes like hunger and poverty is not really true. At least it doesn't have to happen that way. Stealing for the sake of real hunger is certainly the exception—and is far different from the true criminal act. When it happens, the perpetrators are rarely violent, nor do they contribute appreciably to crime rates. In contrast, real criminals are greedy, self-gratifying, uncaring, insensitive and aggressive (even though they may well exhibit more humble qualities after being arrested or when they are before a jury). Some of this is innate; other parts are learned by a long history of bad habits.

Factors Affecting Crime

Serious crime is not simply a manifestation of the fatigue and irritation that comes with high density areas as people grate against people. Big populations do, however, create natural conflict as density adds to the difficulty of coping with life and increased neighbor and domestic disputes. The crime we will concentrate on is the predator crimes—crimes that are a conscious decision on the part of some to willfully steal from or attack other innocent people for personal gain. It is a manifestation of chronic character problems that develop not out of poverty per se—but from a history of violating the signals and promptings of conscience.

Crime is primarily a degradation of the human soul due to chronic bad desires and a history of bad judgment (sometimes in combination with innate, rebellious tendencies which manifest themselves in their youth). The primary personal weakness that affects the propensity for criminal activity is the unwillingness to forego instant gratification—which comes from a combination of being spoiled by permissive parents or teachers and not being required to develop and use self-control themselves. Parents don't have to be well off to spoil children. Any time parents continually let kids get away with things they shouldn't be doing, they are being spoiled—which we define as getting addicted to having one's own way when it isn't right. Not all spoiled kids turn criminal because of this. The key difference is the innate rebellious drive that may be inside a person. It is the quality of the basic soul inside each person that really makes us all different.

Society itself can encourage crime. Large cities attract poor people because of welfare benefits—initially in the private sector but later (and less discriminately) by government. In either case, organized welfare is only effective at gathering money, not in distributing it according to the worthy. In fact, using rigid rules, sometimes the worthy go hungry and the indolent, once in the system, become perpetual takers. We don't believe in the idea that "everyone who is poor" is worthy of assistance. We believe that people who are prone to chronic bad judgment, and who consistently reject good counsel, need to experience their own consequences (even if severe) in order to break them of bad habits and weak judgment. Welfare, even private welfare, that is "non judgmental" is ultimately detrimental to improving character. Careful judgment doesn't have to be harsh, necessarily, but it often must hold to a tough standard lest it become permissive of slovenly behavior. Human beings do respond to strong deterrents. We need more deterrents and more consequences for bad judgment early on, so that the criminal system doesn't have to apply so much severity later on (which it isn't doing anyway).

High crime areas are directly proportional to high concentrations of low class people. Note that we didn't say "poor" people. There are some poor people who are hard working but limited in their skills and will never achieve any wealth in life. But they can achieve a fair standard of living. These are not necessarily low class. We define low class as people who have chronic bad judgment, insensitivity to conscience, and who lack the ability to sacrifice short-term cravings for long-term advantages. This form of personal corruption afflicts all economic levels though it shows up more in the poverty levels simply because chronic bad judgment almost always takes a person toward poverty. A few problem people are able to evade the consequences of vices or bad personal judgments for a while, but it eventually catches up with them.

The worst criminals usually have evil innate tendencies, but among those who do not, a certain percentage can be led down the path to corruption by bad environmental influences—the earlier in life the worse. It may start in the home with a set of permissive or neglectful parents, and then is solidified by contagious contact with other dominant, cocky, corrupt kids—usually in the public school system. We single out the public schools for primary blame because they have institutionalized permissiveness in education. They no longer have the will to discipline or correct bad behavior, let alone bad attitudes, except perhaps in the most egregious cases, which they cannot avoid. Even the good teachers can't discipline effectively because parents won't support it and bad law threatens them with losing their job if they do.

We take the time to explain these root causes so that you will be able to make determinations about how to avoid the future growth of crime in a locality. Otherwise, you may well sink your fortune into your dream home, only to find you are forced to move 10 years later due to excessive criminal pressures.

Interestingly, crime is not always directly related to population density in and of itself. There are certain cultures that have a higher than average number of innately good children born to parents that possess a natural inclination for good discipline. Later when we look at specific statistics on crime in the US, we will discover that there is a general correlation between population density and crime, but also that there are a few high density areas that have relatively low crime rates. When you look into the makeup of the community and culture, you will see a discernible lack of low-class families in that culture. These cultures are eroding, but not as fast as western culture in general. Does this mean we recommend these high-density, low crime areas? No, not for the long term. We believe strongly that even good cultural traditions (of the passive variety) will not survive the contagious aspects of corruption in a high density society. Yes, you can gain some time living in and around such cultural oases in the short and medium term, but long term safety is really only found in less dense communities where good parents have more influence and more maneuvering room—but that can only occur with careful monitoring of or shielding from public school influences.

Crime Areas of the World

Mexico is a prime example of a high crime nation that is the result of cultural, political and socioeconomic components. There is a culture of petty theft and housebreaking in Mexico and all of Latin America generally. Wealthy homes are surrounded by high masonry walls topped with broken shards of glass to deter burglars. Many employ guards, and all windows have iron bars on them. The political component has a long history of payoffs, bribes and vote-buying in Mexico. Corruption is rampant from the bottom up, also typical of most countries in Central and South America. Then there are the narco-syndicate gangs in Mexico that are in full warfare against the Federales and competing drug lords. The civilians are caught in between and American tourists are targets of kidnapping for ransom.

Other continents have the same pattern, and sometimes worse. African nations have a long history of corrupt strongman governments that prey on everyone except their own cronies. Worse, tribal hatred and warfare is epidemic in areas that have a long history of civil war.

In drug trafficking countries like Colombia, we can count on narco-revolutionaries to add significantly to the statistics on violent crime. When leftist governments hinder the hands of police and military, right wing death squads emerge to invoke sometimes much needed vigilante justice.

In short, stay out of countries that are in their own little war zones. For institutionalized crime, we'd also recommend staying out of the former Soviet Eastern European states. Criminal gangs tied to the money flows of the Russian mafia abound in these transitional states. While tourists are left alone, generally, so as not to kill the golden goose of tourism, immigrant residents and newcomers are often targeted.

Crime in the UK and Europe is on the rise. A large portion is due to the rise in drug related crime in combination with the fact that unarmed citizens are seen as easy targets.

Pollution

Staying healthy is a core aspect of self-sufficiency and any strategic plan for relocating and surviving in a disaster. Long-term pollution can slowly degrade your immune system and overall health—especially in combination with overeating and poor quality food, which taxes the glands and overloads the system. Many people don't realize the damaging effects of their surroundings until later in life because the human body is so resilient to gradual effects when it is young.

Many long-term health problems arise from air and water pollution. Almost all these threats are man-made hazards and all are directly related to high population, industrial and vehicular density. The solutions we will give greatest emphasis to are first, avoidance, by staying out of such high density areas if you can, second, corrective natural health therapies and third, a return to proper nutrition. Unfortunately, in this last area, both the establishment medical community and government have become the two biggest obstacles in achieving a restoration of long-term health, and are threatening to become even more intrusive and controlling. Here are the details on the various health threats and the strategies necessary to mitigate the risks.

Air Pollution

We consume tremendous quantities of water and air over our lifetimes. Our bodies end up acting like huge filters in their attempt to remove suspended particles and chemicals. The primary air filters are the mucous membranes in the respiratory tract (nose, throat and lungs) which absorb these particles and expel them in phlegm or mucus. It's a slow and inefficient process, but otherwise sufficient except when the quantity is overwhelming. The key to avoiding long term air pollution damage is to make sure your exposure to medium and high concentrations is brief or infrequent.

Air pollution risk is normally separated into six monitored forms:

1. Nitrogen dioxide from burning coal, fuel and industrial processes. Very dangerous to the lungs and a part of smog.

2. Sulfur dioxide from coal, oil, fuel and industrial processes; contributes to smog.

3. Ozone from auto exhaust, industrial processes, paints and solvents; contributes to smog.

4. Lead from leaded fuel, industrial processes, coal.

Air Pollution by City

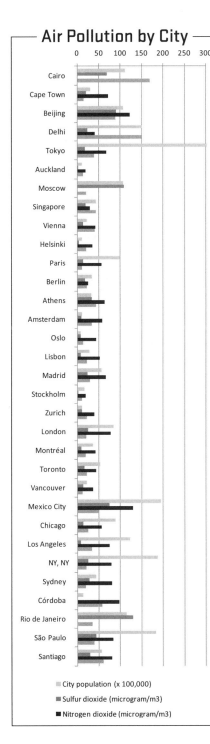

■ City population (x 100,000)

■ Sulfur dioxide (microgram/m3)

■ Nitrogen dioxide (microgram/m3)

5. PM-10 (particulate matter 10 microns and smaller) from smoke or man-made dust particles.

6. Carbon Monoxide from smog, fuel burning; toxic to humans in significant quantities.

The chart on this page shows the pollution levels in various cities around the world (source: worldbank.org). Europe, the United States and Canada have made the most progress against air pollution. Third world countries like Mexico and China are at the top of the list of dangerous levels of pollution. The air in Beijing and Mexico City is some of the worst in the world and caused by both vehicular traffic and industrial waste being pumped into the air. Other third world cities are just as bad in total pollution but have the advantage of coastal breezes which move the pollution further inland. Both Mexico City and Beijing sit in somewhat of a geographic bowl which traps the pollution in one place. Only occasional storm systems will scavenge out the air in these places. Cairo has very high levels of particulate matter—this is partly a result of being near a desert but it is also significantly related to man-made factors.

Water Pollution

Water pollution in today's world takes three forms: first, the lack of purification in rural areas of third world countries; second, the inflows of farm fertilizers and industrial chemicals into both surface and ground water, which eventually gets into the public water supply; third, the excessive use of modern chemicals including chlorine and fluoride to treat the water in modern cities. Dysentery, cholera, parasites and other intestinal tract diseases are the common plagues of untreated water. Sometimes locals develop a sort of immunity to some of the pathogens in local water, but newcomers can be severely affected.

Europe has made the most progress in switching from chlorine as a water purifier to oxygen and ultraviolet light purification systems. The USA is particularly bad about denying the dangers of long-term exposure to chlorine and fluoride on public health. The heavy use of chemical fertilizers, as well as hormones and antibiotics in huge feedlots in America also pollutes the ground water—more so than other countries which still rely on animal waste fertilizer.

Nuclear Power Pollution

The issue of nuclear waste is overdone, in our opinion. The quantity produced by power plants is very small. Twenty-five years of waste from one plant fits under a coffee table. It is safe to bury deep in the earth, but we are in favor of keeping it at power plants where it presently resides—which is much safer than shipping it across the country. Europe has a much higher percentage of nuclear power than the US, but is also plagued by increasing environmental demands against nuclear material use.

We are in favor of nuclear power as the second most efficient and cleanest way to produce electricity after hydro-power dams. The safety record of nuclear power in the West is very good with the exception of old style plants and those at risk in earthquake or tidal wave zones—like Fukushima. Even in Fukushima there have been very few fatalities (despite the hype).

The risk of a Chernobyl-style meltdown is a near impossibility with well-designed plants. Chernobyl was a disaster because of bad Russian engineering and construction. When considered in the light of the growing threat of nuclear war, as we will discuss later, the risk of nuclear power pollution in the West is minuscule compared to the benefits.

Nuclear power plants are still at risk of small, localized catastrophes in very rare, worst-case scenarios. Nuclear reactors do not explode like atom bombs they just melt down from overheating if by some rare chance the core parts cannot be separated in a disaster. This situation is almost impossible in today's modern designs.

Nuclear power plants could be targets in war where a big enough bomb could broadcast the radioactive material and create more fallout, but power plants are not in key strike areas and would only result in a few more civilian casualties. Primary targets are strategic military bases so we show nuclear power plants as secondary targets only. Your retreat or home still should not be within 25 miles of one or 100 miles downwind.

On the following page is a map of the current nuclear power plants in operation around the world. Nuclear power plant locations in the US and Canada can be found on the individual state and provincial maps provided in the state specific reviews in the last section of this book.

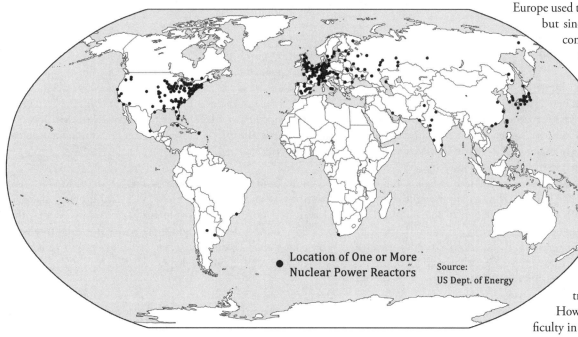

Europe used to be the haven for alternative therapies among developed nations, but since the noose of the ever-tightening European Union has taken control, medical panels continue to push for more controls and restrictions on alternative health. The European Union's Food Supplement Directive places direct restrictions on food and health supplements including outlawing some forms and restricting or regulating all others. This directive has been adopted by the World Trade Organization in their *Codex Alimentarius* and there are efforts to adopt similar regulations in the US. Fortunately, there is a high degree of resistance to accepting these European dictated controls. The pervasive control of the establishment medical system on hospitals, medical schools, and state licensing laws has driven millions in America to seek alternative medical care including resorting to getting treatment in Mexico, which is more tolerant of choice and cheaper too.

The Far East has a much longer history in the use of Oriental traditional medicine and these methods are still very much in use. However, due to the language barrier, English speakers will have difficulty in wading through the myriad of choices.

● **Location of One or More Nuclear Power Reactors**

Source: US Dept. of Energy

Health and Medicine

We consider the freedom to choose how to care for yourself medically to be one of the fundamental freedoms and a critical factor when considering relocating to another country. In our experience, Western establishment medicine creates many problems as it dogmatically affirms the almost exclusive use of drugs for medical care despite their long list of side-effects and often detrimental outcomes. One of the greatest dangers to this very important aspect of personal liberty is the tendency of Western nations to legally restrict or prohibit people's access to and use of natural health remedies—even when found to be effective in practice. The medical monopoly clearly intends to eventually restrict free public access to vitamins and herbs. Incredibly, while drugs are widely approved, advertised and pushed upon the world by doctors despite their long lists of deadly side effects, the establishment medical control system wants the use of herbs banned or regulated if there is only one minor side affect.

Proofs of effectiveness of alternative remedies are hard to come by because governments and medical boards only accept random control, double-blind studies which are very costly and often subject to skewed results by professional bias. Because none of the drug companies have any incentive to prove the efficacy of alternative therapies, the world's body of knowledge comes mostly from anecdotal evidence, coupled with a lot of trial and error on the part of the user.

Schools and Education

Some nations have much better technical and scientific education systems than the US. Europe is generally far superior at the primary, secondary and even college levels at state supported schools. However, the US is viewed as superior or on par with other European nations at the upper-college and post-graduate level.

Persons looking to relocate in foreign countries should keep the following in mind: there are American style schools in almost all foreign countries that cater to the children of business people and diplomats working overseas. We do not recommend them except when living in a country where foreigners must keep their children secluded for safety reasons. The uniformly bad education philosophy of American schools (especially in the social sciences) pervades these foreign schools with their mostly American or Americanized teachers.

Our experience living overseas has demonstrated that children will get a much better education experience going to local schools where they are forced to learn the local language. We never recommend that a parent leave all education to the schools anyway. All schools teach a lot of junk science and bad social theory—most of it oriented toward leftist Democratic Socialism and politically correct jargon. The "best" schools are usually

First World Education Levels		
	15 year-olds at or below PISA reading literacy level 1	
	Percent of non-native and first-generation children in school	Non-native and first-generation children (%)	Other (native) children (%)
JAPAN	0.1	14.4	9.1
ICELAND	0.8	35.7	13.8
ITALY	0.9	33.3	17.8
CZECH REPUBLIC	1	24.2	13.2
FINLAND	1.2	28.6	6.1
HUNGARY	1.7	23	22.2
SPAIN	2	30.6	15.3
IRELAND	2.3	6.5	10.4
PORTUGAL	3.1	31.6	25.2
NORWAY	4.6	31.4	16
GREECE	4.8	48.5	22.7
DENMARK	6.1	43.5	14.9
UK	9.3	20.9	10.8
AUSTRIA	9.7	40	11.1
SWEDEN	10.5	28.5	10.1
FRANCE	12	26.5	12.5
BELGIUM	12	48.6	13.8
USA	13.6	27.7	15.4
GERMANY	15.2	44.3	14.2
NEW ZEALAND	19.6	19.7	10.5
SWITZERLAND	20.5	44.2	13.1
CANADA	20.5	12.2	8
AUSTRALIA	22.5	14.5	11.5

Source: UNICEF http://www.unicef-irc.org/publications/pdf/repcard4e.pdf

the worst when it comes to pushing bad ideas upon your children. Aside from the language experience of having your children in local schools, teach the important subjects of life to them yourself.

Home schooling is an exploding phenomenon in the USA, where it is legal in all 50 states, but not so in Europe. It is banned in most foreign countries. However, as a foreign resident, you can almost always get away with home schooling.

The table on this page compares fundamental reading levels within first-world rated countries. Of particular note is the percentage of immigrant and first generation children of immigrants in the school systems. Although this is not necessarily an indication of immigration percentages in that country, it is a very good measure of how much the country allows immigrants into the social and welfare structure, and the corresponding burden on citizens and taxpayers.

Chapter 5

PROSPECTS FOR WAR, INVASION AND TERRORISM

Through a series of carefully crafted deceptions, the Western World has been led to believe that Communism is now dead or has somehow become benign through the attraction to free markets. We are told that the biggest future threats are terror and regional conflicts from the Middle East. Sadly, this isn't true. A third major war will someday descend upon the world, and it will come without much warning—especially with leaders in the West lulling their own citizens to sleep about the nature of the real threats.

It is true that the world is still beset with numerous regional wars, particularly in the Middle East, but we believe these will eventually grow in intensity until another major world war erupts. The onset of war won't necessarily be a gradual process related directly to those smaller conflicts. Most likely, one regional war of intervention after another will exacerbate the growing hatred toward the US and NATO by the Muslim and Slavic nations until Russia and China finally feel confident and justified enough to initiate their long-planned nuclear attack on the West.

Terrorism is touted incessantly, but that is mostly a diversion to keep citizens ignorant of the growing threat of world war, and to justify US intervention in smaller nations that will eventually bring the larger war to the forefront. Despite all the media propaganda to the contrary, Russia and China together are the only axis of evil that will truly threaten the West. Muslim nations have always been pawns of Eastern or Western powers, and will continue to be used as cannon fodder in coming conflicts.

In this chapter we will examine the hidden motives and military power of these two communist nations, as well as the motives of our own globalist leaders in covering for Russian resurgence and downplaying the Chinese military buildup.

Both Russia and China are actively building weapons of mass destruction and taking severe measures to conceal those preparations. Despite Russia's reputation for weakness since the so-called fall of the Soviet Union, it is using a large portion of its oil and gas wealth to arm for a future World War.

Ultimately, we believe China is the greater danger. Not only will it join with Russia to attack the West, but it will remain as a threat even after Russia is defeated. With its huge population it is capable of creating an army larger than anything in the West. The Chinese communists are presently milking the West of every bit of technology they can buy or steal and are aggressively building the full range of modern conventional, nuclear and biological weapons.

Terrorism

Real terror does exist in the world, but there is a hidden side to terrorism that few people in the world realize. A large percentage of terrorist acts are provoked and fomented by covert or "black" government operations, both in the East and the West. US black operations that provoke or foment terror are kept secret from the European and American people. The War on Terror has given the US government an almost unlimited excuse to intervene whenever and wherever it wants to in the world—which will eventually create sufficient backlash that it will foment a great war against the West. Note: this is a much condensed summary of years of past analysis found in the *World Affairs Brief*, Joel's weekly analysis of all the most critical current events and forecasts (*www.worldaffairsbrief.com*).

Islamic terrorism does exist, but what few in the Western World realize is that most of this hatred toward the West and Israel has been cultivated by years of CIA intervention, US military occupation, and black operations funding terrorist leaders like Yasser Arafat and dictators like Saddam Hussein and the Ayatollah Khomeini. For example, few people know that Yasser Arafat's secret Swiss bank accounts, where he squirreled away over $300 million dollars in aid money intended for the Palestinian people, was set up for him by Israel with help from US-linked criminal billionaire Marc Rich (pardoned by Bill Clinton). Islamic terror is now a much greater problem than it would have been naturally if not for these purposeful provocations, covert assistance and training.

The ethnic wars in the Balkans were fomented and exacerbated by CIA operatives in Bosnia and Kosovo. Few Americans realize that US operatives funded and trained the Marxist Kosovarian revolutionaries in Albania, and falsified certain massacres on the border with Serbia and Kosovo to cast blame upon the Serbs. It was, in fact, the Kosovarian revolutionaries that marched into Kosovo and gave the orders to tribal leaders, demanding the mass exodus of Kosovo's Muslims—which the US government blamed on the Serbs. That isn't to say there wasn't wrongdoing on the part of Serbs, but it never would have escalated to war without covert US intervention. In the US air bombing campaign against Serbia they purposely hit civilian targets to create hatred against the West. One Air Force pilot was even ordered to shoot at a civilian convoy of refugees after he radioed back that there were no enemy combatants to be seen. It is no wonder that goodwill toward America evaporated among the Slavic people, even in Russia, after this trumped up "War of Liberation."

The September 11 attack on the World Trade Centers unleashed the formal "War on Terror" by the United States. This false flag attack was planned as a "New Pearl Harbor" to provoke the American people into going to war, and it was just as effective as Roosevelt's eight point plan to provoke the Japanese attack on Pearl Harbor as outlined in Robert Stinnett's excellent work: *Pearl Harbor, Day of Deceit*. Despite the atmosphere of incredulism surrounding "conspiracy theories" about 9/11, our research indicates that this was, in fact, a carefully crafted US operation using terrorists trained under the false flag of al Qaeda—itself a creation of US and Saudi black operations. This provided the Powers That Be in the US the rationale to justify not only an invasion of Afghanistan and Iraq (which had nothing to do with the attack), but the curtailment of US civil liberties (under the mislabeled US PATRIOT Act).

The evidence of US instigation and direction of the entire event is too voluminous for this book but can be found in summary detail on Joel's website *www.worldaffairsbrief.com* under the "9-11 Update" link. The website *www.911truth.org* is another credible site. For those of you who want credentialed testimony see Architects and Engineers for 9/11 Truth. Their website (*www.ae911truth.org*) contains volumes of witness testimony and evidence that explosives were used to bring down the three World Trade Center buildings that day.

While the American public is always fed the line that our government is assisting other governments in their fight for democracy, it simply isn't true—it's a cover story. Pakistan and Saudi Arabia are good examples. The US uses a variety of threats to keep corrupt regimes in power in both these nations. Both are used in different circumstances to create and maintain private terrorist groups that provide a constant flow of terrorism in Iraq and Afghanistan for conflict creation purposes. In Pakistan, the CIA uses the Pakistani intelligence service (ISI) to direct and control elements of the Taliban and al Qaeda in order to keep the war on terror going—all while claiming publicly to be fighting the Taliban and al Qaeda. US secret agencies do a lot of bribing, arm-twisting and blackmailing to make sure that leaders of other allied countries don't oppose this secret globalist agenda. Nations that don't go along with US pressure, like Iran, are eventually targeted for attack as nations "harboring terror" or illegal "nuclear ambitions."

Biological and Chemical War

Most people think that biological and chemical war agents died with the fall of the Soviet Union, or that now they are the exclusive domain of terrorists. But, in fact, the fears should be reversed. There is a lot of disinformation floating around about "loose nukes" and "stolen vials of deadly viruses," but we have not found any of these threats to be credible. Suitcase nukes are the crown jewels of nuclear technology and neither the Russians nor the US have lost any such weapons. Even if they had, the nuclear triggers go bad quickly and have to be renewed regularly. The only occasion of loose nuclear material actually making it to terrorists occurred in 1994 when the German Foreign Intelligence Service arrested

several terrorists who were carrying weapons grade plutonium, and even that turned out to be a situation created and funded by German intelligence so they could put fear into the public about the "dangers of nuclear proliferation."

As for chemical weapons, the US has, in fact, destroyed most of their stockpiles, but the Russians still have secret stockpiles in bunkers never inspected by the US. Nobody really knows what the Chinese have, but they are engaged in developing the full range of weapons of mass destruction, so we assume they have biological and chemical weapons as well. All our research indicates that only the West has engaged in disarmament and destruction of these materials.

Biological weapons are real as well. Several Russian defectors claim that the post-Soviet Russian government under President/PM Putin has created new state-of-the-art biological and chemical weapons factories underground in the new bunker system at Yamantau Mountain in the Ural Range.

In past disarmament proposals by the Obama administration, former Secretary of State Hillary Clinton assured Americans that the US has been verifying Russian compliance and will continue to do so. This is an outright lie. The Russians have never allowed US inspectors into all of their facilities including new sites like Yamantau Mountain, they are only allowed into the older, outdated ones.

Nuclear War

Nothing should take precedence over your concerns for this potential threat. Just because it never happened during the Cold War is no guarantee that it is not going to happen. If the media and the leaders aren't concerned, Americans think there is nothing to worry about. Top military leaders are concerned, but those that protest against the government's hidden policy of "speak no evil" about Russia or China, are not promoted.

Here is some of the evidence we believe shows that Russia is intent on launching a nuclear/biological or chemical war against the US in the future:

- Russian scientist and recent defector, Vil Mirzayanov, revealed that Russia is continuing to develop and build new chemical and biological weapons in violation of the chemical weapons treaty ban.

- Russia continues to sell nuclear technology to at least five different countries—all who are sworn enemies of the USA.

- Russia continues to build new intermediate and Intercontinental Ballistic Missiles in violation of the INF and START treaties.

- In 1996 it was revealed by anonymous US intelligence agents and declassified satellite photos that Russia is continuing to build a huge underground military complex in the Ural Mountains, with a total subterranean land area the size of the Washington DC metro area. This facility at Yamantau Mountain includes underground bunkers, biological and chemical weapons production and nuclear missile factories on a huge scale.

- In violation of the 1972 ABM treaty, they have installed a system of mobile interceptors that are moved each week.

- In 2010 the Russians announced 5,000 more nuclear shelters would be built in and around Moscow.

- Russia claims to have stopped targeting US cities, but this is meaningless since the Russians don't intend to strike cities in a first strike,

- Russia has increased industrial and military spying by nearly two-fold according to FBI sources. The recent arrest (and repatriation to Moscow) of nine suburban spies is telling. They were given medals by Putin in 2010—so much for Russia being an ally.

- Russian subs continue to stalk and practice attack maneuvers on the US Navy at sea. China does so as well.

- The Russians are constantly demanding limitations to a joint US/European ballistic missile defense system, including restricting the missile speeds to below 3,000 feet per second—the speed needed to catch Russian ICBM's in the first stage.

- The US paid millions to Russia for the disarming of all Ukraine's obsolete nuclear missiles, and then allowed Russia to take possession of all the warheads, which are being stockpiled and potentially reused.

- The Russians have a long history of lying, deceiving and delaying US treaty compliance inspectors until they give up.

The actions above are not defensive in nature since there is no clear threat of attack that would justify Russia acquiring this level of armament, which already exceeds the US arsenal by several times. How do we reconcile all these actions when the Soviet Union supposedly has collapsed and reformed?

The Phony Collapse of the Soviet Union

Depending on one's ability to sense truth amid falsehoods, you may or may not be surprised to know that there is powerful evidence to indicate that Communism is not dead and its powers within Russia have purposefully gone underground in a feint of weakness to trap the US at some future time when the West lets down its guard. Here is some of the evidence. Nobody knows the full story, as is always the case with carefully guarded military secrets, but what we do know is enough to convince most people.

Creating the Illusion of Collapse

The collapse of the Soviet Union was orchestrated with great expertise, and with the knowledge or partial knowledge of western media sources who would have to have been blind not to see the contradictions. History has shown time and again that tyrants never relinquish power voluntarily. Yet that is essentially what we are to believe in this case. Here is an abbreviation of the official version of events compiled from Wikipedia sources:

1985—Mikhail Gorbachev becomes the youngest General Secretary of the Communist Party after only five years of membership, defying long-standing tradition. He makes several key position changes among the party, replacing many old-line party members.

1985 to 1989—Gorbachev implements new policies of perestroika (political and economic restructuring) and glasnost (partial increased free speech and access to information), which slightly diminished specific portions of political oppression. Despite his reference to economic changes as "free market," key aspects of economic power were not released such as price controls, prohibition of private property ownership and government monopolies over key sectors of the economy.

An outward policy of non-intervention in Soviet States was publicly adopted toward local governments of Warsaw Pact countries, and allowed for the appearance of open elections for even non-communists. Secret orders were given to not crack down on demonstrations demanding independence to give the appearance of freedom. All of the new governments formed in post Soviet States as a result of the "Velvet Revolutions", were still socialist, and still controlled by closet Communists within their governments. Chinese anti-communists thought they perhaps could get away with similar protests, but they were cut down in Tiananmen Square.

1990 to 1991—Economic weakness in Russia continued to feed public discontent and resulted in demonstrations. An outward restructuring of government took place allowing Party Chairman Gorbachev to assume the Presidency until Boris Yeltsin was elected to the office in June of 1991 (Gorbachev retaining the position of General Secretary over the Communist Party).

August 1991—The definitive turning point in the transition of power from the Communist Party to the Russian Federation was a remarkably small attempt by eight of the most powerful men in Russia. This "Gang of Eight" included Vladimir Kryuchkov, the chief of the KGB; Dmitry Yazov, the highest ranking military leader; Valentin Pavlov, the prime minister and Gennady Yahayev, the vice-president. But all these men were newcomers to power and had only recently been promoted to their positions by Gorbachev.

During the coup, the KGB is said to have arrested several powerful people including Gorbachev, who was placed under house arrest without communication. Yeltsin, incredibly, was not detained. Tanks, military vehicles, paratroopers and Special Forces are said to have entered Moscow and surrounded the Russian Parliament building. Yeltsin arrived at Parliament and made a speech decrying the military action as "unconstitutional." He gave another speech on one of the tanks (while the press took photos) and was then allowed to leave. The military surrounding Parliament is then reported to have disobeyed a direct order from the Grand Marshall (Yazov) and backed down. Gorbachev was released the next day. That was the sum total of resistance by "hard-line apparatchiks." The KGB never arrived in their black cars to arrest the troublemakers. Only three protesters died.

Western media reported that the leaders of the "August Coup" had "fled", but who were they fleeing from? These were the leaders of the police and military. Two were found dead, one with his wife, and their deaths were declared suicides. Others were arrested but soon pardoned and lived inconspicuously in Russia afterwards. In the next few months the Soviet Union was officially dissolved. Several countries moved toward independence including Ukraine, Estonia, Latvia and Lithuania during "The Singing Revolution."

1992 and beyond—Anatoly Chubais heads the restructuring and privatization of the Soviet Union's considerable state-owned businesses and very lucrative natural resources and utility companies to "private parties" who all turned out to be "former" top communist leaders who helped put Gorbachev and the Gang of Eight in power. With loans from Russia's Central Bank they "bought" Gazprom, the electric power system, the state oil company and other industrial factories. These men became the new "Oligarchs."

The Oligarchs lived mostly in western Europe and wielded significant unseen power for a decade or so commensurate with their control of key industries. Boris Berezovsky was the chief Oligarch and began his public role after the "Fall" as Secretary General of the newly formed Commonwealth of Independent States. After Berezovsky made himself rich and "fled" the country, Vladimir Putin declared him public enemy number one, but Spanish Intelligence reported that they met five times in Berezovsky's villa in southern Spain the year before Putin became President. Infighting comes to even secret leaders in tyrannical systems, however, and in 2013 Berezovsky was forced out of the oil group Sibneft and died in London under suspicious circumstances just seven years after his associate, Alexander Litvinenko, was killed by polonium poisoning.

Contradictions to the Official Story

The biggest contradiction in the official story is the way the power change occurred: credible Sovietologists know that changes to the power structure in Communist systems always happens secretly, whether by assassination or arrests in the middle of the night. There is never any open struggle with big displays of tanks and soldiers. The new leaders are simply announced the next day. As the deceptions became more complex it is even hard to tell whether the new public figureheads are the real leaders or puppets for a power

behind the scenes. Consider these contradictions in the unprecedentedly rapid collapse of the Soviet Empire compared to the normal pattern Soviets operations:

- The eight leaders who composed the junta were only mid-level communist leaders a year before they were appointed by Gorbachev to their new (highest level) government posts. None of them were powerful military or KGB leaders before they took charge. People don't rise to the top in Communism by being chosen—they rise by eliminating their opponents ruthlessly. These were advanced to be the fall guys in the phony coup.

- Gorbachev himself was only a mid-level arms control official when he was suddenly vaulted into the Premiership—evidence that others behind the scenes were really running the show.

- Yeltsin and other so-called pro-democracy leaders were not arrested in the night prior to the coup, but were allowed to rally the people without hindrance. Television and telephone lines (controlled by the Communist Party) were not cut off during his televised speeches, allowing Yeltsin a platform for his message.

- The military made only a token show of force with a few armored personnel carriers bashing buses in front of Parliament—which made for good camera footage for the eager Western media. Is the Soviet military really as inept and unsure of itself as we were led to believe? Was such a claimed mass defection and refusal to take orders really possible in the ruthless Soviet military? Where is the historical evidence of elite Soviet units failing to act in total unity with a Soviet superior's command? There is none.

Yeltsin and his group of reformers are also former communists who have never come clean with a full confession of their evil acts, and who most probably are playing the role of "team B" (Gorbachev was "team A") to pacify the freedom movements within Russia so that legitimate anti-communist leaders do not emerge. When one team falls from favor, the leaders can switch support to team "B" and avert a popular uprising. We believe that only in the Baltic States, in Belarus, and in Georgia was there originally a legitimate anti-communist leadership which was not part of the tyranny of the past. But the reforms in Belarus and Georgia were eventually overthrown by "reformed communists" under suspicious and non-democratic circumstances. Only the Baltic States truly broke with Russia.

The Western television media said all the right things, almost as if they were reading a script. Journalists can be terribly blind sometimes when they are told by their bosses how to view the "facts." Not once did the media ever question the veracity of their communist sources of information about the anomalies and contradictions that surrounded this botched coup. "The back of the Soviet military has been broken" and the "KGB is no longer a significant power" were trumpeted about, setting the stage for another propaganda coup—that we in the West can now safely disarm.

The phony nature of this coup, coupled with what appears to be western media complicity, makes us also question the demise of Communism in the Eastern European countries. Eric

Honeker, former East German communist chancellor, revealed before he died in exile in Chile that he was ordered to step down by Moscow and to allow the student demonstrations to go forth in Leipzig that led to the "fall of the Berlin Wall."

That the people in Eastern Europe have legitimate longings for liberty is not in question. But what is truly in question is whether the so-called "former" Communists who now have been "elected" are really playing a false role as well. The elections were all hastily arranged and gave little time for organizing a truly effective opposition.

The so-called reformed governments of Romania and Yugoslavia are the clearest examples of old tyrants in new clothes. East Germany made a near-total reform by unification with the West, with the West Germans picking up the tab.

Now over 20 years after the phony "fall of Communism" defectors have come forth to reveal that Lech Walesa of Polish Solidarity fame was a Communist agent all during the years he was the supposed champion of union solidarity and freedom. Defectors in Czechoslovakia also produced evidence that Vaclav Havel of the Velvet Revolution was also secretly an agent. So was Ion Iliescu of Romania, the supposed "former" communist who took over after dictator Nicolae Ceausescu was executed on orders from Moscow when he refused to step down.

We are convinced the communist leaders are still in control of all the real levers of power in Russia and most of the former Soviet States. The other less strategic states have been let go in Eastern Europe (with a mere semblance of independence) simply because the Russians know they can be retaken by stealthy means as is happening in Ukraine. Under the terms of the 1992 "Mutual Security Treaty" signed (mostly under duress) by the former Soviet Republics, Russian troops are stationed at their host's expense in Georgia, Belarus and all others except the Baltic States and Azerbaijan. The Russians moved millions of ethnic Russians into Ukraine, Georgia, Belorussia, and the Baltic states specifically to cause ethnic conflict that could someday be used to retake these former Soviet states.

Possible Russian Motives for Feigning Collapse

What is the reason behind all this deception? First, the Russians reap the benefits of having the West take over the financial support and subsistence of their former Eastern European satellite states, which was causing a tremendous drain on Russian resources.

Second, they are now in a position to milk aid and technology from naive or duplicitous Western governments. Western oil companies did most of the modernization of the Russian oil and gas fields that now provide billions monthly for Russia in new revenue. This aid allows them to channel more internal funds to their secret military projects and to continue to build up foreign client states that will join in the attack on the West (like North Korea, Iran, Syria, and others). The former communist hierarchy is being enriched

by their temporary switch into organized crime and positions as Oligarchs, which now support the same elite lifestyle they used to enjoy as the "Nomenclatura" in Soviet life.

Russian Motives for Waging a Nuclear War

Russia's ultimate intent is to launch a nuclear pre-emptive strike on American military forces in order to blackmail the rest of the Western world into submission. They want to conquer Europe without a destructive fight, so as to harness this huge economic engine on behalf of Communism (which cannot sustain itself without external economic support). We believe that North Korea is being preserved as the trigger event for this nuclear strike on the West.

We do not think they intend to invade or occupy the USA, mainly because of the deterrence of so many private arms in the hands of citizens, and the distances involved in maintaining such an occupation thousands of miles from their bases. It would be a Vietnam for the Russians in terms of long supply lines. They figure that a nuclear surprise attack would cripple the US ability to retaliate and induce Europe to capitulate without a fight.

The Russians don't have to worry any longer about their people longing for "free markets." The powers that be in Russia and their Russian Mafia allies have given free markets a very bad name by abusing their government control of money and insider status to enrich themselves at the expense of ordinary citizens. The Russian's limited experience with "liberty" was sabotaged early on by not allowing sufficient freedom to make it work.

Putin never misses an opportunity to champion the return of Russia to its position of world hegemony and the Russian people love it. In our opinion most Russians aren't really keen on liberty and long for the prideful days when Soviet power was respected and feared. Threats against the West are becoming a weekly occurrence.

Western Disarmament Continues

Presidents Bush and Obama have made the United States increasingly vulnerable to a first strike nuclear attack by proceeding with suicidal unilateral disarmament. We say unilateral, because the Russians have never lived up to their part of the agreements, and we have not ever required any disarmament from China at all.

The US has already decommissioned all 50 Peacekeeper MX missiles—the only land based missiles capable of penetrating Russian hardened targets, even though the Russians reneged on their portion of the Strategy Reduction of Forces Treaty (START). The US has agreed to stop keeping nuclear armed B-52s on alert. We have removed the nuclear capabilities of the B-l bomber and most of our Naval Fleet. We have agreed to not build any more Trident submarine bases except those in Bangor, Washington and Kings Bay, Georgia, and to keep half our submarines in port at any given time. This makes it easy for the Russians to target them. The US has removed all the multiple warhead from our remaining 450 Minuteman III missiles, reducing our nuclear deployed warheads by two-thirds.

But here are some even more troubling questions for the leaders of the US, who appear to be covering for Russian hostile intentions:

- Why has every US administration, both Democrat and Republican refused to prosecute any past treaty violation or even report them to the American people? Why have they classified these violations as top secret and prohibited all intelligence agencies from revealing them?

- Why does the US continue to disarm when they know the Russians are not reciprocating or worse yet, allowing Russian and Chinese military people to have special briefings and nearly open access to all our top secret facilities, both military and private?

- Why did the US government ship, via special air courier from Kennedy International Airport each week during the 1990s, millions in US currency to Russia—all in crisp, new $100 bills? We think you will find an interesting correlation between these bills and the ones Europeans complain are flooding their countries at the hands of hundreds of big spending Russian Mafia chiefs—all "former" communist leaders.

The Start of War—How We Think it Will Play Out

It appears as if the Russians are attempting to gain the maximum disarmament they can get from the West before initiating conflict. They are also using the time to maximize their industrial espionage of US military systems to bring their equipment up to, or as close to, US technology as possible. Russia also needs to allow for China's military rearmament as China is expected to attack and control the Pacific Rim nations to protect Russia's rear.

Possible Timing and Signs of War

While it is impossible to know when war will start, we don't think Russia and China will be ready before the beginning of the next decade—when their newest weapons systems are scheduled to begin deployment. As of this writing, Russia is already beginning to retake Ukraine, and China is becoming extremely aggressive in the East and South China sea area. It is using military naval forces to bully all its neighbors, Japan, the Philippines and Vietnam. China has also bought up most of the mineral rights in Australia.

Watch for the following signs that war is coming:

1. Russian-instigated provocations in the former Soviet States of Ukraine, Poland, and the Baltics so Russia can move in to "protect" the Russians living there. These

Russians were moved into these countries specifically to provide a trigger for future conflict. It has already started in Ukraine.

2. Russian challenges and threats to NATO, including the cutoff of natural gas supplies to western Europe, which has become increasingly and unwisely dependent on their eastern neighbor. This squeeze for gas has already started due to the Ukraine crisis.

3. Trigger events like a North Korean invasion of South Korea that could lead to a larger nuclear war very quickly. North Korea has such overwhelming conventional forces opposing South Korea (and the thousands of US troops there) that it is likely the US would have to use tactical nuclear weapons to stop the North Koreans from overrunning US troops. That could easily hand Russia or China an excuse to launch their long-awaited pre-emptive nuclear strike on America.

History Revisited

The nuclear attack on America and the UK is intended to remove the US and British military and their ability to stop a Russian advance. We do not believe that this plan will ultimately succeed. We along with other military experts believe the US has developed significant secret weapon systems, perhaps even space based anti-missile systems. They will still allow a first strike to take out the US military so Americans will be forced to give up our sovereignty and regroup in a militarized New World Order. Then they will bring out the secret weapons to rally and beat the Russians. The Russians cannot sustain a long war, especially if the West can induce China sometime during the war to turn against Russia and attack it from the rear similar to Russia turning against Germany in WWII. This projection on our part is quite probable given China's intent to achieve world hegemony someday. China knows that eventually Russia will have to be eliminated before it can achieve world domination. We are confident they will take that opportunity when Russia is fully at war with the West during the next big conflict.

As for our own leaders in the West, they will come out of their bunkers and proclaim that "The Russians deceived us. We didn't know this was coming." It will be a lie, but in America's damaged and desperate state, the public will only cry out for government to save them. It will be easy for our globalist leaders to convince Americans to join in a New World Order to prosecute the war—a world order that will transform itself into a full-scale world government with military power as the war progresses.

The reason we believe the US will absorb the nuclear first strike is because in 1997 during the Clinton administration, the US completely revamped its nuclear strategy and ordered American missile forces in Presidential Decision Directive 60 (PDD-60) "not to rely on launch on warning" but to be prepared to absorb a nuclear first strike and retaliate afterward—prompting one of the top Marine Corps generals to say, "Retaliate with what!?"

He was right. Launch on warning is a key military tactic that allows the one who launches second to gain the advantage. Russian and Chinese missiles take about 20 minutes to arrive on target. If the US launches its silo based missiles before enemy missiles arrive, the Russian and Chinese attack hits empty silos and are wasted.

While our missile forces still practice launch on warning, they cannot launch if the codes are not received from the White House. PDD-60 was a warning not to expect those codes to arrive. The entire purpose of allowing the first strike to hit us completely is so that globalist leaders can justify driving Americans, and the entire West, into accepting a militarized global government, since the US military will be effectively decapitated in a first strike. Sadly, American sovereignty will never be returned, even if the war is won.

Summary

We recognize the terrible news this chapter must be for some people. Most of our readers likely have some inkling that the world is not right but few recognize something of this magnitude is in the works: The groundwork is being laid for the most serious war humankind has ever faced, and it will happen in the near future. The evidence for it is not yet so clear that you can run to your friends with the proof, but there are warning signs and they will get bigger as it draws closer. By the time the threat is obvious, it will be too late to stop (just like in previous wars when Japanese and German war buildup was downplayed until it was too late). War usually comes as a dreaded surprise for the laypeople. Only a few conspiring leaders really want war and they are prepared to sacrifice part of their country and military to ignite the event, but only if it looks like a surprise. Don't be fooled by the way they ignore the larger danger even as it looms on the horizon.

Ultimately everyone must follow their own feelings, but don't dismiss these warnings out of hand. Like many others, we sense that something is very wrong, and that the dark side of the US government knows what is coming. We are dealing here with several masterfully kept secrets. There is tremendous internal political pressure being put upon Western intelligence agencies not to say anything critical about Russian rearmament, and China's efforts to gain advanced weaponry on a large scale. Why else are our leaders building huge bunker systems deep underground? Certainly, these are not out of fear of some minor terrorist attack. But they are not warning people in the West to prepare as they are, we have to have develop that foresight for ourselves.

The rest of this book will provide you with recommendations for improving your strategic safety based on the foregoing threats. Repositioning your life to weather these events will take considerable time and money and require a serious commitment, but take the time to review the facts and think through your best options. There is time to consider our warning and take careful action. Confidence will replace fear if you know what lies ahead and prepare for it.

Chapter 6

REGIONAL SCORECARD

Selecting a Country

After reviewing the preceding principles for an ideal nation and the most important threats we face, we will now look at the countries available today for relocation potential. No nation in the world qualifies as ideal under all the criteria of liberty. We will not comment on every country specifically, since many are not suitable for relocation, but we will spend extra space on those nations with good possibilities.

We have used the categories outlined in the previous chapters in our deliberations, but they are not weighted equally. The highest weighted threat is the potential for future war—not simply whether or not there will be war, but chances of surviving it when living in a particular nation. The destruction that comes with war, invasion and occupation can make all of your retreat preparations for safety null and void in a moment. So can a systematic roundup of foreigners or the confiscation of their property in nations that end up taking sides against America. All these things must be considered.

The next most important criterion is safety from violent crime. Petty theft and burglary are not nearly as dangerous as violent crime, especially kidnapping of foreigners for ransom—usually in connection with leftist guerrillas and drug lords who come after foreign residents as a source of income.

Analyzing each country for these threats and the principles described above can be daunting, but we have tried to include the most important points about countries outside the US that are most often considered for relocation. We hope the following descriptions prove helpful.

Western Europe

Europe has always been the geographical and aesthetic crown jewel of the earth, but it has been fought over and contested many times because of its sometimes strident cultural differences thrust together in a small geographical area. Diversity is nice, but too much cultural diversity in close quarters leads to near constant conflict, as illustrated by European history from the dark ages on up through both world wars. Europe has developed a tarnished track

record for stability and safety. Today's conflicts are and will be the result of the large influx of Muslim immigrants from African and Eastern countries.

There are no economic advantages for Americans retreating to the UK or Western Europe. It is uniformly more expensive than the States (especially London), and while the value of Europe's two primary currencies (the Euro and the Pound) went down during the initial crisis of 2010, all Western currencies will probably continue down the path of inflation because all the central banks have no other avenue left but inflation of the money supply. In addition, taxes in Europe are very high.

If money is no object, Europe is a wonderful place to live. The old world culture, including the healthy and fresh cuisine, is a delight. Natural medicine is far more advanced in Europe than America although it is becoming restricted by EU legislation. Europeans have long resisted the over-commercialization of food products, so finding wonderful, natural food is the rule rather than the exception. Sadly, that is also starting to change as even Europeans are beginning to succumb to the lure of cheaper prices from mass production techniques like feed lots for cattle.

On the down side, European economies will always be in the grip of socialism. The ever-tightening control by the EU legal structure will guarantee that Soviet-style controls return to haunt Europe, even before the next war. As an American resident you can avoid most of these controls and taxes, except the heavy VAT taxes on everything you buy.

National governments in Europe sway back and forth between the grip of leftist parties still under the influence of the Socialist International and the center-right parties aligned with the Anglo-American globalists. Either way, Europe is on a losing track. During the next war, Europe may not be attacked with nuclear weapons (Russia wants to preserve Europe's economy for itself and will aim its pre-emptive first strike at the US and perhaps the nuclear arms of the UK), but parts may become occupied.

Western Europe has a deep-seated conflict brewing. Almost sixty million Muslims from Africa and the Middle East now live in Europe. Muslim immigrants have a much higher birthrate than Western Europeans and are overwhelming the socialized medicine and public school systems. One university calculated that almost 25 percent of the population in Europe will be Muslim by 2025. Permissive immigration laws in Western countries have encouraged cheap labor from former colonies, but the social unrest is coming back to haunt them. Muslim religion and culture are so deeply intertwined, the assimilation of Muslims is much worse than the assimilation of Mexicans within the US economy. This clash of cultures is exacerbated by the socialist mentality whereby one's share of productive profits is linked to the political power of your ethnic minority—a recipe for constant divisiveness and conflict. Radicals have no trouble inciting social unrest with constant harangues about being disadvantaged, poor and not getting "our fair share." These multicultural conflicts flourish in the major metropolitan areas, but even small communities are affected as they are forced by EU nations to accept thousands of refugees.

Switzerland

If Europe is your destination, Switzerland is the premier nation for safety, beauty and political stability—but bring a fat wallet. Benefits of Swiss residency are:

1) A fair tax system, 2) a central location in Europe with ease of travel to neighboring states, 3) a nice four season climate; beautiful mountains and valley geography, 4) a superb train system that runs on time, 5) excellent hospital care and numerous natural health clinics, 6) good personal privacy in banking—as long as you are not a target of the American IRS, 7) solid political stability and 8) a history of evading war. There has been no war or invasion of Switzerland since 1515. Switzerland evaded Hitler's demands by agreeing to hold Germany's gold. However, we do not believe Switzerland will go unscathed in WWIII. All of Europe will be occupied for a period. Nevertheless, no other country in Europe is better prepared to actually defend itself against invasion than the Swiss. Most homes have personal fallout shelters, and the army has numerous enclaves in mountain bunkers to wage a long costly war of attrition with any occupier.

Gaining residency is tougher for Americans than Europeans who now can live and work in any EU nation without permits. For people under 55 and not EU citizens, it is difficult to live in Switzerland, because permits are tied to employment with a company working within Switzerland. However, you can retire in Switzerland and obtain a Class B residency permit if you are 55 years or older even if you are not an EU-15 citizen. After 55 years of age, you won't have to work within Switzerland. Your wife, even if she is not 55, can of course join you as well as your children below 18 years of age. You will be expected to actually live in Switzerland most of the year, but there are exceptions possible if done in good faith. You also need to show some ties to Switzerland such as owning property, Swiss friends, relatives living in Switzerland or other ties.

A retreat in Switzerland should include plans for a concealed fallout-protected safe room underground. If you plan on riding out a future war in Switzerland, pick a mountain location and prepare places to hide and disappear. If you are planning to leave war-torn Europe before occupation sets in, choose a location in the French speaking sector which is closer to France and Spain—your best places to find a way out of Europe if invasion comes.

Spain

Spain used to be our top pick in Europe because of relatively cheap living, warm climate, and distance from traditional wartime invasion routes far to the East—but no longer can we recommend the Iberian Peninsula. Due to Spain's dire financial condition, they have been targeting the rich and the foreigners with arbitrary taxes and fees both on the national and local level. Expats from Britain are leaving in droves.

One angry foreigner wrote on an expat website: "The Spanish government, provinces and town halls have benefited from & milked ex-pats for many years with the draconian and sometimes illegal demands for more money from dubious taxes. Now the ex-pat community are voting with their feet and saying enough is enough. Throw in the land grab laws, corrupt town halls and property buyers uncertainty over whether their property is legal when control of the town hall changes political parties, is it any wonder many are leaving for a more just, transparent and law abiding country[?]"

Another expat site (*www.bidstrup.com/expat-country.htm*) warned about Spain's land grabbing laws several years ago, "Many local governments, in an attempt to attract developers, have created property laws that make it easy for developers, working through local governments, to seize your property—with no compensation to you! The Spanish federal government has been indifferent to what has been going on. It's called "land-grabbing," and the result is that the hordes of British retirees that moved here years ago are now selling, if they can."

The law in question has been used to reclassify rural land as urban without the owners' permission—effectively giving developers compulsory purchase rights on foreign-owned homes at a fraction of the market value. Clear back in 2006, acting upon the complaints of hundreds of foreign victims in Spain, the EU Commission demanded that Spain change the law, but Spain only made token adjustments and the problem remains.

Then there's the 2013 foreign assets reporting law: According to Spain's new reporting requirements all residents have to declare assets abroad worth €50,000 or more (per category) before the end of April. While this law was aimed at the Spanish rich taking their money abroad to evade taxes (same thing is happening in France) it ends up affecting expats living in Spain who have no vote. Fines start at €10,000 for failure to report foreign assets.

The bottom line is: Even if expats are given an exemption, Spain is too greedy and desperate now to be trusted so stay away. For those who want to risk it, we offer the following:

Obtaining Spanish residency is not hard if you don't plan to work (a "non-lucrative" permit). You need to show sufficient savings in a Spanish bank ($75,000 dollars in the bank and $15,000 for each family member). It takes several months to complete the process. Bring lots of copies of birth and marriage certificates. If an American plans to work in any EU country, including Spain, the process is fairly involved. A company has to sponsor you and submit paperwork that they have posted the job in Europe and not found a qualified EU citizen to fill the position. Many expatriate websites recommend hiring a European lawyer if you are serious about it.

Portugal

Portugal is now better than Spain, but it is also in dire economic straits and is raising taxes and changing laws on land that affect expats, though in far less radical ways than Spain. Expats in Portugal are being urged to check their property rights under new rules that could see them lose coastal or riverside homes or face a hefty land tax. The law only affects people with holiday homes within a short distance of the coast or rivers and built after 1951. Waterside homeowners must prove that their home was built on private land and gives government the power to take back any land which was originally owned by the state.

Expat residents in Portugal are required to pay tax on their worldwide income, and the government is trying to raise tax revenue by a whopping 30% due to its national austerity program, mandated by the EU. Portugal's tax burden is now higher than the UK, France, Spain, Germany and Italy.

Portugal is like Spain with a slight inferiority complex. It is also a socialist country and there is a certain amount of anti-capitalist and anti-American spirit among the university crowd. But the average person doesn't feel that way. Crime is probably the lowest in Europe so Portugal is very safe—if you discount the dangers of driving in a nation that has traditionally not obeyed traffic rules. It is clamping down on driving rules so that may change.

More Portuguese speak English than do Spaniards. Spanish is such a predominant world language that many Spaniards are used to foreigners knowing enough to communicate. In contrast, Portugal is a poor country with high debt and low tourism. They realize that their native tongue is more difficult to hear and understand than Spanish, so more Portuguese make the effort to learn English or other languages.

With less tourism you might expect the Portuguese in restaurants and shops to be more inviting to foreigners, but they are stand-offish and reserved. The lay people, however, are very hospitable, especially if you know the language. Few non-business people speak English.

We recommend Northern Portugal which gets more rain and is very agricultural. Land and homes are cheaper there too. Southern Portugal is sunnier and attracts most of the tourists, but this makes it more expensive. Do learn the language if you intend to stay.

Residency is fairly easy to obtain. You must apply to your nearest town hall in Portugal or to the Portuguese Immigration Service for a Registration Certificate during the 30 days following the 3-month period since you entered the country. This certificate will be valid for 5 years from the date of issue. You need to have a passport and evidence of one of the following:

1. Working or self-employed.
2. Self-sufficient financially with enough to support yourself and your family.
3. Enrolled in a course of study plus sufficient funds to support yourself and your family.

Italy

Italy is another economic basketcase in Europe so beware of their income tax (23-43%) and high social security requirements compared to other countries in the EU. Italy also has a high VAT tax. It is much more expensive than Spain and less secure geographically, unless you have an exit plan by boat. As a long narrow peninsula, it has many of the strategic disadvantages of an island. My favorite parts of Italy are all in the north along the border with Switzerland and France. These are the Alpine regions and offer some of the advantages of

Switzerland without the high Swiss prices. If you have to leave in a hurry by land, it's best to be in this northern region where you have quick access to Switzerland and France. The people are generally more industrious and ambitious in the North compared to the South. There has long been a secessionist movement in the North since it produces most of Italy's income while the South absorbs most of the government welfare spending.

The rest of the countries in Europe should only be considered if you have relatives, close personal friends or long-term business relationships that help mitigate the strong strategic disadvantages. In general, all the northern and central European countries are in the path of a future invasion from Russia, which will cause massive social unrest just as in WWII.

Germany

Germany, in particular, is a threat to any enemy due to its well-deserved reputation for military prowess and an industrious people. Germany is at the strategic center of Europe with few major mountain obstacles, except in Bavaria to the South. If it weren't for this lack of strategic obstacles to invasion, Germany would be a great place to live. Most people speak English, German and at least one other language. The living standard is equal to the US. However, population densities, as in all of central Europe are unacceptably high. Large, open spaces and extensive farmland like we enjoy in the USA are very limited. Germany also has some of the most intrusive laws relative to free speech, liberty, and home schooling. People who disagree with the official version of the holocaust, even in one or two small details are put in prison if they speak out or write about it. The Germans are very much in the New World Order (NWO) camp and collude with the NSA in spying on its own people, including foreigners.

If you pick Germany as a destination, look for property in the rural, mountainous areas of Bavaria or the northern farm country near Denmark. Both offer the fastest escape routes out of Germany if there is an invasion from the East.

Austria

Austria is similar to Germany but has fewer problems. Due to its fairly robust minority of anti-EU political parties, it is not as big a proponent of the NWO. Countries whose citizens can see the danger of expanding EU powers and diminished national sovereignty are better places of safety. However, as in the case of Austria, they also become targeted for elimination and isolation by these powerful globalist forces, just as the international community ganged up on Austria when its anti-EU Freedom Party was allowed into the ruling coalition. In short, if you want to live in a Germanic speaking country, Austria is better than Germany itself. Its mountainous terrain also offers greater safety.

France

France has much more open farm land than Germany and is one of Europe's big agricultural centers. That's a plus for finding some safety in southern France, coupled with partial self-sufficiency. The French "provence" (rural areas) are quite distinct from the large urban centers like Paris, which are not safe for dozens of reasons. For retreats we recommend the mountain meadow/alpine areas in southern France near the Italian border, or near the southern mountains next to the Spanish border.

France is a wonderful place to live and visit during peacetime, although it can be very expensive. The French are not particularly friendly to foreigners. French pride gets in the way unless they get to know you better. Few speak English well, and the French people are fairly intolerant of foreigners who try to speak French, especially if they don't have perfect pronunciation—which really grates on their ears. But even more troubling is the fact that France has the highest level of ethnic unrest in Europe with its significant number of Muslim immigrants from North Africa. Powerful unions also hold the nation hostage to strikes and demands that can paralyze the transportation system in a matter of hours.

Retreating to a foreign country depends in large measure on your ability to blend in. In France, that is nearly impossible for non-French speakers. France is also very much involved in the New World Order plot to undermine national sovereignty. Like Germany, the government cannot be trusted to uphold French sovereignty in the face of constant attempts by the EU to create a monolithic and all-powerful European government. France is also in tough economic straits and will continue to deteriorate toward "soak the rich" taxes due to a staunch refusal to accept any austerity measures.

The Netherlands

The Netherlands is a mix of many contradictions, positive and negative. Its language has Germanic roots, but they resent the Germans dearly for the ruthless Nazi occupation during WWII. The Dutch-speaking sector is very distinct from the French-speaking Belgium sector which is more like France (though the French won't agree). The divisions are like two different countries. One advantage is that almost everyone speaks English because English is taught in school and everyone receives English TV broadcasts from across the Channel. However, the country is rife with ethnic competition and excessive population density. The big disadvantage is that land is at a premium and a large portion of the coastal areas have been reclaimed from the sea by huge sea walls and dykes—which make the whole nation vulnerable to an attack on those sea walls. As everywhere in Europe, the transportation and communications net is modern and efficient, but telephone and internet utilities are more expensive than in the US. The Dutch are more tolerant of drug use and loose moral conduct than the world in general.

Belgium

Crime is on the rise there and Brussels Belgium is one of the most dangerous cities in Europe. The French influence here has led to a pleasant softness that is fine except when it leads to permissiveness in standards and criminal prosecutions—which is fast making this country a no-go destination. It also has a very high population density.

Scandinavia

Norway and Sweden are now our top picks for safety in Europe, but not Denmark. Although the Russians will have to occupy the southern portions of both countries (and all of Denmark) in a future war scenario to secure safe passage for their Baltic fleet, the northern areas of both Norway and Sweden will provide many forested and mountainous places of refuge—as long as you have implemented a concealed basement safe room. Be prepared for long cold winters.

The Scandinavian countries are somewhat like the Netherlands in culture. They have become quite secular, liberal and tolerant of drugs and immoral behavior. They used to be a hardy and even hard-nosed people, which the climate demands. But with the arrival of modern conveniences, central heating, and cradle-to-grave socialist care, the people have lost some of their historical strength—but there are notable exceptions in rural areas.

English is widely spoken in all three countries, which is an advantage. But of the three Scandinavian languages (which are similar in written text), Danish is the most difficult to understand due to its closed and imprecise pronunciation. We found the people very friendly and helpful in all of Scandinavia.

Finland and the Baltic States

Finland has the same retreat advantages as Sweden and the same cold-weather disadvantages. However, the Finish language is one of the most difficult in the world, particularly for foreigners who want to learn and speak it well. English is spoken by the young generations, but not by the older people. The Finns were one of the few countries to give the Russians a real contest when Russia tried to snuff out Finish freedom in WWII. There still remains a fair amount of hostility toward Russia in Finland and the Baltic States.

We prefer Estonia to Lithuania and Latvia. The Estonian language is similar to Finnish so it is difficult to learn—a disadvantage, but almost all the youth speak English and everyone likes people from the West, except perhaps for some in the Russian minority. All three Baltic States have significant Russian minorities that were brought in during the Soviet years to give Russia future claim on retaking these nations. Estonia has the highest level of

hostility to Russia, and Lithuania has the least. Latvia is in between. None of those are recommended due to the future Russian threat. If you have to pick a country for temporary safety, pick Estonia and then try to get to Finland on your way to Sweden or Norway.

Eastern Europe

Russia and its Former States

These countries include Belarus, Ukraine, Georgia, East Germany, Poland, Czechoslovakia, Hungary, Bulgaria and Romania.

Except for former East Germany, you can forget about the previously Russian-ruled countries in Eastern Europe for safety. Even though life is cheaper there, and old cities like Prague are culturally attractive, communists still lurk in their governments and are set to take back control of these nations during the next world war. The so-called "reformed" governments are often headed by persons only feigning to be anti-communist. In fact many, such as Lech Walesa of Polish Solidarity fame, were later discovered to be Soviet agents pretending to be in opposition to Soviet Rule. Legitimate anti-communists have come to power, but they are usually ousted within a short time by forces still loyal to Russia. Americans won't want to be caught behind the new iron curtain.

Middle East

Israel, Jordan, Kuwait, Lebanon, Oman, Qatar, Saudi Arabia, Syria, Turkey, Iran, Afghanistan, UAE, Yemen

Currently this is the most unstable and war-prone area of the world and is unsafe for Westerners generally. Israel is an exception to this hostility toward Westerners, but is itself vulnerable to attack. War between Israel and the Arab nations that surround her (especially Lebanon and Syria) is an ever-present threat. Globalist leaders in the US and NATO are determined to destroy Iran's military might and have tasked Israel to start the attack against Iran's nuclear enrichment program. The US will join the war against Iran as will Israel's enemies, causing a broader Middle East war. This is why the US wants to defeat Assad and Syria's significant weapons—to lessen the retaliation against Israel. But she will still be attacked by her Arab antagonists in Lebanon and the various Muslim extremists that will be allowed to take over Syria. But she will still be attacked by her Arab antagonists in Lebanon and the various Muslim extremists that will be allowed to take over Syria.

Because of the world's increased hatred toward Israel and the US, Westerners will never again be safe in these nations. Many American Jews have moved to Israel during the past 40 years, but many are leaving and returning to the states due to the high levels of regulation, cost of living, poor job markets and lack of security. The climate is moderate only in the areas bordering the Mediterranean Sea.

Pro-western Arab nations such as Jordan and Saudi Arabia have been bought off by Western aid and military ties. There are also secret protection treaties wherein the US government keeps these corrupt Arab leaders safe from being overthrown by factions within their own countries. While this appears to add to stability in the region for now, the built-up hatred against US interference in these nations will eventually create greater instability.

Southern Asia

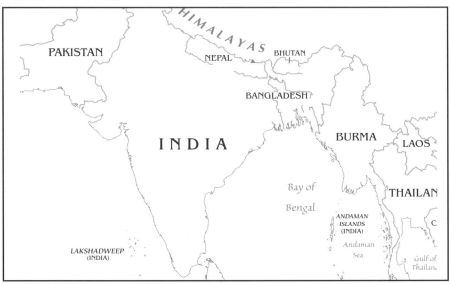

India, Pakistan, Bangladesh, Sri Lanka, Burma (Myanmar)

This area is also not recommended. It is in the monsoon climate belt making it vulnerable to heavy rains, flooding and a humid climate. Pakistan will probably never recover from the intervention of the West which has caused extreme tension between fundamentalist Muslims and secular groups, and corrupted the political process. Pakistan has chronic poverty throughout most of the nation due to pernicious levels of socialism and government control. China is now moving back into Pakistan for military influence.

Burma and Sri Lanka are mired in communist-backed insurgencies. India is the only nation that is growing toward modern integration with the West, but that modernization only touches the well-educated minority in a few major cities. The rest of India is still wallowing in poverty, religious infighting and heavy-handed provincial governments that enforce a rigid form of socialism on all aspects of business. Countries with huge population densities such as India, coupled with systematic socialist corruption, will never be stable.

Both India and Pakistan are nuclear nations armed by other competing world powers. They have a long-standing hatred for each other and engage in military clashes on a regular basis. China was the major historical benefactor in Pakistan while Russia backed India. Although the West has dominated Pakistan for two decades it is losing influence and is making a major move on India. The West views India as a counterweight to Chinese dominance in the region. It is the only nation in the world that has a population base comparable to China. The subcontinent area will be a very dangerous place in the next world war, so avoid it.

East Asia

Asia is generally overcrowded in the extreme—except in some of the vast areas of China, but limited freedoms there make it a bad destination for Asian immigrants. True, there are small oases of economic semi-liberty in Singapore, Taiwan and the formerly free Hong Kong. However, all of these have no long-term future. The Chinese dragon, in my opinion, is destined to make war on both the East and the West in some future decade after it is allowed to grow strong on Western trade and technology.

Asia also has a troubling philosophical dichotomy which is noteworthy. While its eastern religious base tends to be viewed as liberating and open minded to the "higher essences" of life, such philosophical pronouncements don't tend to carry over into the minds of the governing class—who historically have shown a callous disregard for human life in war, population control and genocidal measures. Even the Russian leaders with their frigid and heartless disregard for humanity haven't been quite as ruthless as the Oriental tyrants.

China

China is the dominant player here, even over Japan—despite the latter's mature economic strength. China's overwhelming population numbers, coupled with a growing military and industrial prowess, guarantee that China will continue to threaten Asia with total hegemony. Taiwan and South Korea are growing competitors to Japan's industrial export economy, but not a threat to China's growth.

The major threats of natural disasters are earthquakes and flooding from heavy rains except in the Siberian north. Pollution is a major problem in China, where old industrial processes are still operational. The air in Beijing is simply not fit to breath. Water pollution is epidemic in all of China due to unsanitary disposal methods near rivers and streams.

China is unsuitable for everyone not born there, and even for freedom-loving Chinese. Despite the façade of openness, China is still a communist run state with a deceptive and predator mentality. No other positive factor can hope to compensate for this major threat to personal and family liberty. North Korea is its vassal puppet and most likely will be used as a trigger event for some future war against the West.

South Korea

South Korea is a bustling Asian tiger and is a growing competitor with Japan for industrial dominance in the free portion of the Far East. However, it is unsuitable for permanent residence for Westerners because of its extreme vulnerability to attack from North Korea—an event which surely must come. South Korea also does a lot of stupid things in law because of the extreme influence of the US military and its American doctors—like mandating circumcision for all male babies. Nobody in the world does this as a mandate anymore, except South Korea.

Japan

Japan is the most westernized and modern of all the East Asian states, but it is still difficult for Westerners to find a permanent home there and even more difficult to fit in. Before considering Japan, read this interesting list of frequently asked questions about cultural differences: *www.thejapanfaq.com*.

Politics in Japan are very much under the control of competing combinations of power that operate in secret—by the same forces as in Western industrialized nations. The largest parties are tied to the Anglo-American Trilateral Commission, a globalist power center that is dangerous to liberty. The cost of living is very high (except in rural areas), real estate prices are astronomic and business is a fairly closed game among Japanese power brokers with insider ties to government. Also keep in mind that the biggest threat to being a Western expatriate in Japan is that China has a grudge match to settle there (Japan invaded China prior to WWII and committed many atrocities there). When China finally strikes out at the West, expect Japan to be over-run and fully occupied. Don't be there when that happens.

Southeastern Asia

Brunei, Burma, Cambodia, East Timor, Indonesia, Laos, Malaysia, Philippines, Singapore, Thailand, Vietnam

None of these nations are recommended for safety or liberty. Cambodia, Laos, Indonesia, Vietnam and East Timor are still dominated by the Far Left and outright communists. Businessmen who are lured in for the temporary advantage of open trade will rue the day when their foreign investments get confiscated.

Thailand and the Philippines are the only two nations that have some attraction to Westerners. The cost of living is low, but both countries restrict foreign ownership of property and have high crime rates in urban areas. They are also both deteriorating into long-term conflict—especially Thailand, which is very unstable politically. Communist-backed insurgencies are prominent in most countries of this region, including the Philippines. Kidnapping of Westerners is a common tactic, so don't put yourself at risk. One of the big negatives that Western tourism and trade has brought to Thailand is a huge demand for sex slaves, drugs and prostitutes, feeding black market corruption.

The Philippines will always harbor resentment towards America owing to our less-than-savory reputation during the colonial days. There is a minority that still longs for the return

of US influence. Since the US left, instability and corruption have reigned in this nation. Communist and Muslim insurgencies still abound there and play upon the idea that the West is planning on returning to take back their former colony. These nations also have the monsoon climate that is never pleasant for comfort or long-term health. Bacteria, viruses and mold are real problems in such humid environments. However, the most important negative for long term security in this region is the potential for occupation during the next world war. We expect China to occupy all of the countries in this region in the next war.

South Pacific Islands

Samoa, Tahiti, Polynesia, etc.

Many have longed for an idyllic island retreat in the warm climates of the South Pacific, but the realities are often otherwise. Many of the governments in the South Pacific are socialist, but they are fairly benign to tourists owing to their need for tourist dollars. Ultimately, the fact that an island is an island provides a set of vulnerabilities that are dangerous. The climate is warm and humid, but Islands are only a paradise as long as there is a steady flow of imports—food, fuel, raw materials and manufactured goods—and those always cost a premium due to shipping and limited supplies. None of the islands are self-sufficient except at a Robinson Crusoe level of existence.

Islands are also security traps, surrounded by water. In an invasion scenario or during social unrest that accompanies a cut-off of supplies, you have only three options: stay put and try to compete for supplies, fly out on one of the few commercial flights leaving or find a boat. For those who have lived among the native populations for years and have lots of friendly contacts, staying put may be a possibility. Speaking the local language helps a lot in that regard. Otherwise, one should provide for a retreat potential either by private aircraft or by ocean-worthy boat. Both provide advantages over staying but also involve formidable obstacles—not the least of which is distance over water needed to get to a safer haven. Few small general aviation aircraft have the range to reach a mainland destination without refueling, and that leaves you vulnerable to the possibility that no other island along your route may be safe to refuel.

Leaving by a slow sail boat or motor launch will get you a lot farther over the water to safety but at the slow pace of 3 to 8 knots. Be prepared with a variety of small arms to defend yourself against pirates and marauders which will roam the sea lanes, and whom you won't be able to outrun. There are however, some high-speed, long range, ocean going speedboats (the kind the drug runners use) that will outrun most predators, but they take a fair amount of skill to operate when the water gets rough. In short, if you are immigrating to an island primarily for the climate and tourist lifestyle, it won't be enough to overcome the disadvantages long-term. Always prepare a backup plan to your home country (if safer) and don't burn your bridges back to a much larger land mass.

Australia and New Zealand

Australia used to be the great last frontier in the world, but it too is rapidly succumbing to the same socialist ravages and gun control mania as Europe. Both Australia and New Zealand suffer from ideological vestiges of their colonial English roots—which are somewhat hostile to the American type of laissez-faire liberty.

Australia

Australia is a continent-size island and has many of the advantages of the West in the US—lots of dry arid land and few people. But it takes a hardy lot to make it in the wilds of the outback in Australia. Australia is also a socialist country that, like all redistributive democracies, is having severe budget problems due to government overspending. The globalist government movement also has its tentacles deep into Australia, controlling high politicians in both major political parties, right and left. Worst of all, the Australian government has gotten deep into bed with Red China—which has been sold rights to the development of a lot of Australian resources. We fear that Red China fully intends to make Australia a colony or at least occupy it someday during the next world war, when China will take possession of all the Far East.

Australia also makes it difficult to establish retirement residency, and they want big dollars. *ShelterOffshore.com* says that the "Investor Retirement Visa is a temporary 4 year visa renewable for further periods of 4 years at a time. This visa category will not lead to permanent residency in Australia or to Australian citizenship and it is for those aged 55 or over (although an accompanying spouse can be under this qualifying age), who have no dependents and are able to fully financially support themselves in Australia. In terms of the amount of money an applicant will need, it is quite substantial. A second visa application charge of AUD 8,000 per person is made, then an individual or couple have to prove they have assets available for transfer to Australia to the net value of AUD 500,000 if settling in a regional area, or AUD 750,000 if settling in a non-regional area."

Perhaps most troubling is the fact that Australia is wont to become the world's guinea pig for every new experimental control mechanism the New World Order wants to try out on its hapless people—like the latest round of draconian gun control measures.

New Zealand

New Zealand has experienced a strong turnabout from an almost fatal dose of Socialism (which brought it to the brink of bankruptcy) in the 1980s. Since 1984 the country has rebuilt itself around free trade principles and its exports increased substantially. But only time will tell if it is only a respite or a permanent lesson learned. Historical precedents warn that once the masses get accustomed to being "on the take" (government benefits), they will only forego reduced benefits for a short time—until the productive class gets on its feet again. Then the benefit-corrupted majority will come back with a vengeance demanding "their fair share" of the (other people's) wealth.

With the recession of 2008 still in full swing, New Zealand is now going deeper into debt due to residual social spending and a diminishing tax base. NZ also runs a trade deficit instead of surplus, despite being export oriented.

There has been a net outflow of population from NZ, mostly to Australia where jobs were better. During the boom years, housing prices in major cities like Auckland went through the roof, as they did in California. Just as in the states, many sold out in the big cities and started cashing in on rural real estate which was much cheaper. If you move there, you should plan on rural living as well. One expatriate said, "Many retirees move to the Waikato, a region to the south of Auckland, or Tauranga in the Bay of Plenty. Southland is a rural area with no large cities and it has suffered from depopulation."

You might expect NZ to be anxious to invite people into the country, especially retiring Americans, but they only want you if you have lots of money. NZ does not even recognize the permanent retirement immigration category. That said, there is a two year visitor visa which is renewable for those over 66. According to *news.emigratenz.org* The main requirement is money—a whopping "NZ $2,600 application fee, and then you must invest NZ $0.75 million in New Zealand for two years, and have ownership of NZ $0.5 million of maintenance funds and an annual income of NZ $60,000 at the time you apply. The Investor Category is even higher: approximately $1.5 million for five years, and be under the age of 55. Other work visas are available but the forms are long and complex."

In short, while there are delightful places to live in New Zealand and Australia, the long-term outlook on government policy is not good—especially in Australia. New Zealand has also experienced increasing earthquake damage in recent years, so stay clear of the most vulnerable areas.

Africa

Africa is home to a billion people and is quickly sinking into the dark hole of tyranny and corruption. It is not called the "dark continent" for no reason. This is one of those cultures that has huge, overwhelming majorities of simple and uneducated people that sometimes can be whipped up into mindless hatred and violence against their perceived "oppressors." This isn't politically correct to say, but, even with the history of colonial exploitation, most middle class Africans now realize that there was never a time of greater relative peace than during colonial days. They may have lacked democracy but at least they had predictable law and order that was relatively fair to all.

Africa's downfall began when the various colonial powers in Portugal, France, Germany, Britain and Italy (all Socialists) bent over backwards to make sure their colonies were turned over to outright Marxist revolutionaries who have destroyed what the colonies left intact. When you hand over a mix of productive lands and millions of dispossessed minorities to raw democracy, it becomes a free-for-all of taking and socialist redistribution. That is primarily why Africa is still in poverty and political turmoil today despite huge resources and billions in foreign aid. Instead of being exploited by colonial nations, these nations are now exploited by corrupt strongmen and tribal leaders. Naturally, the predatory powers of Western Globalists still have their fingers in the pie, providing arms to various strongmen and buying off the corrupt leaders with billions in aid, much of which is diverted to personal use.

Northern Africa is composed mostly of Arab regimes with only the façade of representative government. They range from corrupt monarchies to outright tribal death squads and anarchy. Piracy and pillage are rampant wherever these "strongmen" rule. The black African regimes in the rest of Africa are rich in oil, diamonds and other natural resources but corrupt to the core. It is one eternal struggle: one strongman toppling another and promising change which never comes. Each has the secret backing of various competing Western or Eastern powers and illicit arms dealers under their employ. There isn't a single nation in the whole continent we can recommend for safety—not even South Africa.

South Africa: This former jewel of Africa only survives on the residual vestiges of law, order and wealth that came during the days when the Dutch, Germans and English had some control over their own property rights. But, with raw majoritarian government now in the hands of the ANC and its black Marxist cadres, it is only a matter of time before SA goes the way of Zimbabwe. Crime, kidnapping, car-jackings, murder and rape are widespread in many parts of the country, and land redistribution and confiscation is happening slowly as well.

Westerners may still view a vacation in Kenya or South Africa with nostalgia, but it's only a façade that hides the official corruption underneath. It won't last. Joel remembers talking to various white farmers in Rhodesia as the British government was undermining this nation and handing it over to Robert Mugabe's Communists. They were incredibly resistant to believe in his warnings of future danger. They were all too confident that they'd "never have to leave." Now they can't leave (with their money) and all their major land holdings have been confiscated by the government. Many are dead. Currency controls also kept South African whites from voting with their feet when the communist ANC took power. And, even though things have not deteriorated as quickly as Zimbabwe, they are heading in that same direction. We recommend no country in Africa—None!

South America

For comparison purposes, we like to divide South America into three different groups of countries: first, the Andean Mountain nations of Colombia, Peru, Bolivia and Ecuador (all of which, except Bolivia, have coastal, mountainous and jungle areas); second, the fully tropical jungle nations of Venezuela, the Guyanas, Paraguay and Brazil; third, the southern nations of Uruguay, Argentina and Chile. Chile and Argentina both have towering Andean mountains, but are so distinct from the other Andean nations that they must be considered separately.

Even though Latin America is now free of its colonial taskmasters, it is burdened with a large poor sector that is highly susceptible to the egalitarian call of Marxism and Democratic Socialism, which has kept these nations in the economic basement for far too long.

Fortunately, the realities of world economic competition have forced these traditional socialist strongholds to take a more free market oriented approach in previous decades. We must not forget, however, that they haven't lost their Marxist passion but are only playing semi-capitalist, for now, to gain in economic strength and military power. That partial pro-free market trend made a significant reversal after the economic bust of 2008 when free market policies got blamed for the collapse (when in fact it was corporate corruption and collusion with government that was the real culprit).

The electoral gains by Marxist leaders in Venezuela, Bolivia, Peru, Ecuador, Brazil, Argentina and Uruguay during the start of the new century do not bode well for the future of Latin America where the Far Left is coming back with a vengeance. Therefore, despite the future potential of another World War, the present liberties available in North America outweigh the liabilities and make it a better choice for strategic relocation for Americans and Canadians.

Like Central America, Virtually all nations in South America are socialist and therefore inherently unstable and subject to heavy public debt and periodic social unrest. Some, like Venezuela, Bolivia and the Guyanas are led by outright Marxists whose leaders are openly hostile toward free markets and America. Even Brazil's outgoing president, Lulu de Silva is a Communist, but he is playing as if he is a moderate for economic advantage in world trade. De Silva holds an annual conference in Sao Paolo for communist revolutionaries in South America to plan for an eventual takeover of all South America. His replacement, Dilma Rousseff, is also a Communist. Even Chile was ruled by a closet Communist, Michelle Bachelet. She got elected by promising to continue Chile's free market business policies while increasing socialist benefits. Slowly, all around South America, this return to more socialist demands is sapping the strength out of the freer markets allowed during the 80s and 90s.

Argentina

In general, the three southern nations of Chile, Argentina and Uruguay offer the most favorable climate for American and European expatriates who want to live in a semi-European atmosphere for half or a third of the cost. Of the three, Argentina has the biggest economy, filled with plentiful resources. It is most like the USA with its variety of regions and climates. You can find tropical areas up north, high desert and mountains in the center-west of the country and fertile plains in the center all the way south. Argentina is an agricultural paradise. Almost every type of crop is grown indigenously within the country. Naturally, it's a major exporter of food around the world. It has tried to diversify into manufacturing, but can't seem to compete with Brazil, the industrial powerhouse to the north.

Argentina would be my natural pick as a wonderful retirement and retreat area for Americans if it were not for the total and chronic level of corruption in government, labor unions and business that have plagued this nation historically. Bad as it has been in the past, it has reached its pinnacle under the corruptive dealings of the Kirchners, a husband and wife political team who have both served as Presidents of the country. Cristina Kirchner has finally left office and is replaced by Mauricio Macri, a pro-business leader more on the right. How long this favorable turn for their economy will last is unknown.

Kickbacks and payoffs run everything in Argentina, including elections. You cannot run a business there without huge payouts. Still, business prospers in Argentina's wildly fluctuating cycles, due to high profits when the government occasionally frees things up. Increasingly, however, the corruption of the Kirchner years will continue to demand higher taxes, and export duties, putting the nation's export profits at risk.

Argentina, like Mexico, also has a history of confiscating people's bank accounts, stealing the dollars they have hoarded as protection against rampant inflation, and giving them worthless government bonds in return. While all nations have been forced by world markets to be less predatory in the past decade or so, the mentality for "stealing from the rich" is still latent in all Latin American countries.

American expatriates mostly congregate in and around the capital of Buenos Aires (BA)—a cosmopolitan city that reminds me of everything in Europe, with wide boulevards, street side cafes and pedestrian streets downtown lined with fancy shops. Most of Argentina's Indian peoples are in the tropical regions up north, so everywhere else you find descendents of Spanish, Italians and Germans. Banking services are modern, living is relatively cheap and people are friendly—especially if you take the time to learn the unique form of "Rio De La Plata" Spanish they speak there. Many people speak some English.

Although Buenos Aires is fun to visit, we prefer the country towns and cities. It is not difficult to become self-sufficient agriculturally there with the fertile land and climate of central Argentina. The "campo" of Mendoza is very much like the US. The central-south Pampas are the vast fertile plains of Argentina where the best grass-fed beef in the world originates. Bahia Blanca is the major agricultural port in the south-central region, but the real gems for living are the small towns in between Bahia Blanca and Buenos Aires. You can even find mountain communities very much like the Swiss Alps near the Bariloche and the Chilean border—but a lot of Europeans flock there and the prices are high. The public transportation system is very good (except the trains), so you can even do without a car. Long range coach style buses take you everywhere in Argentina. It's too bad the trains have gone into disrepair. High speed trains would be a natural there where distances rival those in the USA.

With all of Argentina's great resources, the government is not friendly to foreigners. You can wait months trying to get through the bureaucratic red tape of getting a residence visa. As International Living points out, "It is difficult to get permanent residency here unless you buy property. If you buy property through a corporation and make yourself the director of the corporation, you can basically write yourself a letter offering yourself a job [opening the way for a 'Business Work Visa']. If you don't want to buy a property, you could rent, but you would be able to spend only six months in the country (enter on a three-month tourist visa and then extend it at the immigration office for another three months). Renting may be the way to go for people who just want to spend three to six months in Argentina, especially right now, as rents are pretty low. Also, remember that Argentina enjoys opposite seasons to the U.S. If you time your six-month stint appropriately, you could live with year-round spring and summer temperatures."

"The country is very bureaucratic and requires official documents for everything—which means standing in lines for hours to get through the process—and there are always delays so you have to come back time and again. Whether entering with a visa or a tourist card, it is important to carry a passport at all times. Police can, and occasionally do, demand identification. A passport is usually required to check into a hotel, cash traveler's checks, and conduct other routine business."

While Doug Casey and other financial gurus have developed communities in Argentina and tout it as a great expat location, I think it's too corrupt and unstable to depend upon for the long-term. The Argentine government will someday turn on expats.

Uruguay

Tiny Uruguay just across the river from Buenos Aires is much friendlier (bureaucratically) to foreigners and the preferred destination for many savvy expatriates. Uruguay has gone out of its way to be open to foreign investment, and it shows. The populated areas, from the capital Montevideo to the community of Punta Del Este (the major resort destination up the Atlantic coast), are modern and first world rated. For that reason it is also more expensive than Argentina in these areas, but still less expensive than America and Europe. In fact, a lot of things are priced in dollars. The local business people got tired of being burned in previous inflationary periods and got used to dealing in dollars.

However, the interior of the country is still third world and very cheap. We prefer it, but you really have to learn Spanish to take advantage of the easy living in this part of Uruguay. You also won't have the same infrastructure as in the capital—rated quite high because of clean water, efficient telephone connections (within 48 hours) and quick setup for internet. Not so in the interior. You can still get fairly good services, but the wait is longer and more frustrating.

Uruguay has wide pampas (grassy plains) like Argentina so its cattle and sheep industry is every bit as developed as Argentina's. However, Uruguay doesn't have the range of climate that Argentina has, and so must import some of its food from Argentina and Brazil. The

end result is that all the good food found in Argentina is available in Uruguay, but not all of the industrial goods. And if it isn't, it's a quick trip to either Buenos Aires or Brazil to get it.

Here are some specific recommendations:

To be close to Montevideo, but still find cheap farm property, try Santa Lucia or Canelones.

To beat the extremely high prices of beach towns like Punta Del Este and Maldonado, try Rocha farther up the Atlantic coast. It is more inland, but not far to get to the beach.

All of the interior towns in Uruguay are regional agricultural centers—all suitable for relocation but a long way from any major commercial centers. I much more prefer the border towns, where you have access to international products at reasonable prices:

Rivera and Artigas: Both towns are right on the border with Brazil, where you get easy access to all the Brazilian food and imports.

Fray Bentos, Concepcion, Paysandu and Salto: On the Argentine border, separated by the Uruguay River, you have bustling border towns that cater to Argentine tourists and provide access to all the products of Argentina. And when you travel between Buenos Aires and Uruguay, you'll probably use one of the high speed ferry boats which cross the wide Rio De La Plata and docks in Colonia—which is surrounded by good farm land. It's a good rural location if you want frequent access to Buenos Aires in Argentina, and is a little over an hour to Montevideo.

Uruguay is our top pick for relocation in South America, despite being dominated by the Frente Amplia (wide front of Leftist parties). They are too smart to mistreat foreigners who provide so much income to the country—unlike Argentina. Recent Marxist President José (Pepe) Mujica left the country in better economic shape through pragmatic decisions and a humble lifestyle void of corruption. He was someone hard not to like who didn't bash people with Marxist rhetoric, lived in near poverty (unlike almost all the other communist leaders in the world), and gave most of his salary to the poor. Something the current president, Tabaré Vázquez, will have a hard time following.

According to International Living you should apply for a residency visa through the immigration office in your country of residence. In general terms, the requirements are: "owning a property in the country and/or a bank account with adequate funds, having a clean police record in the country of residency and having proof of income in Uruguay or a work permit. All documents will have to be authenticated by a public notary—but it is more involved and more expensive than typical US notaries. All Latin American nations require this and it is a real hassle. Any person visiting Uruguay for business purposes can go to the consulate or embassy of their respective country."

Chile

Chile had a serious bout of communist rule under Salvador Allende until he was overthrown by Gen. Augusto Pinochet, guided by the CIA. Pinochet was thus universally reviled by the leftist press around the world, not only for overthrowing a democratically elected Communist but because he brought serious free market reforms to Chile that allowed Chile to prosper well above the Latin American norm. Of the three nations in the southern group, Chile has the most laissez-faire free market, but also the highest percentage of native Indians, which always provides the base group of campesinos that Leftists play upon to portray as victims of Capitalism and demand more socialism. The minority of Chileans is of European descent, and this group provides the vast majority of business entrepreneurs.

Chile has a lower level of corruption than most Latin American countries, but it is still there. It has an excellent system of roads due to its relatively long but narrow geography, requiring fewer roads. The overall living standard is good by Latin American standards because of its strong export income, and it has first-world quality telephone and internet services.

Healthcare facilities are excellent and most senior doctors have training either in the US or Europe. Prices are comparable with America before Obamacare. Medical insurance is affordable by Western standards.

Chile has income tax on foreign retirement benefits, pensions, and social security payments and it has "no double taxation" agreements with the US, so it's either/or not both. Foreign sourced income is free from income taxes in Chile for the first three years of an expat's residency.

Santiago is the capital and largest commercial center and Vina del Mar is the swanky coastal town that caters to the wealthy. As in all South American capitals, these cities are cosmopolitan, efficient and filled with cultural amenities. There are also the bad areas which foreigners need to avoid—but far fewer in number than other large cities. Santiago is a very modern city due to its powerful export-driven economy, and home to 7 million people with world class festivals, museums, parks and shopping experiences.

But Chile is not the cheapest country in the region and Santiago has a higher cost of living than similar cities in either Argentina or Uruguay. It is an hour from the coast and close to skiing in the nearby Andes mountains. The main coastal town is Valparaiso, with its fishing wharfs and commercial district. This town is cheaper than the resort community of Vina del Mar just to the north.

Still on the high end, La Serena is one of Chile's oldest cities, at the end of the Elqui Valley, with some of Chile's most popular beaches—miles of white sandy shores, restaurants and apartments. The numerous towns around Concepcion, further to the south have more economical beach properties, but beware that the water is very cold due to the Humbolt current coming up from Antarctica.

Iquique: If you are thinking of retiring in the northern half of Chile, consider Iquique which has a mild climate and many natural and archaeological sites.

The Lake District of Chile in the south is colder, but wedged in between dramatic mountains and lots of lakes. Retirement communities like Pucón near Lake Villarrica, has the look and feel of Lake Tahoe before it got crowded, with great views of the mountains and lakes.

However, as in all of Latin America, the cost of living goes way down when you live in rural small towns and live and eat as the locals do. The farther south you go on the central highway the cheaper life becomes generally, and the more rural the countryside.

Charles Spencer explains the best way to get residency in Chile on his website *www.allsouthernchile.com*. "The investor visa is easy to obtain, and very difficult to keep. Immigration will audit your business in the second year to determine if it is a viable business and will examine in detail your business plan. An investor visa is also typically thousands of dollars more expensive in terms of procedures that must be completed." But then he explains the more friendly, "Chilean Retirement and Income Visa."

"The key requirement is a basic recurring income that will support you in the future. Among just a few of the sources that Chilean Immigration will accept are pensions, social security, rent from real estate, long-term contracts, interest income or Annuities. Any source that will periodically recur in the future. Your other resources are also considered. It is not only a recurring source of income. Immigration would, for example, consider a small social security check you receive every month, in addition to a large savings account, stock portfolio, or property you own in Chile as proof that you have sufficient assets. Some of the secondary assets that Chilean immigration will consider are savings, stocks, property in Chile or other countries, investment in a business in Chile, and so on."

"Chilean immigration for the most part will not tell us or anyone else exactly what the magic number is in terms of monthly income or other assets that is required to qualify. All they will say is that it must be sufficient to live on in the area you are intending to reside. So, for example it is much more expensive to live in Las Condes in Santiago than a small town in Southern Chile. A good rule of thumb across Chile is that you should be able to show $1,000 US per person including yourself and any people you claim as dependents on your application. This is sufficient to live a middle class lifestyle in almost every part of Chile." As in Argentina, there are several American funded expat retreat and retirement communities in Chile, but be careful not to invest or buy into planned developments "on paper only" that don't have existing infrastructure.

Venezuela, Bolivia and the Guyanas

We do not recommend the three Guyanas (Guyana, French Guyana and Surinam), nor Venezuela or Bolivia. All are directly controlled by the Far Left or outright Communists like the late Hugo Chavez, and radical successor Nicolas Maduro. Venezuela now has shortages of everything, plus currency and price controls, and inflation above 100% per year.

Ecuador

Ecuador has a large contingent of expatriates and is highly rated by the editors and writers for International Living. Living is cheap and the climate in the highlands is ideal, which is about all they consider important, as long as the law allows foreigners to live there. However, they completely overlook the fact that Ecuador is ruled by Rafael Correa, a far left socialist president and ally of the late Hugo Chavez and his Bolivarian movement—advocating a Marxist revolutionary approach in Latin America to counter US influence. If this far left control in Ecuador continues, we think there is a high probability that Americans' property will someday be confiscated.

Ecuador, like most of Latin America, has a history of bad socialist economics. As the Heritage Foundation wrote, "Ecuador's financial sector has been bankrupted by corruption and inflation, obliging the government to bail out institutions and freeze accounts. Foreign investment and new business traditionally has been discouraged by regulations and practices favoring existing monopolies. And despite small steps such as creating transparency commissions and signing international conventions, efforts to curb corruption have not taken root. Furthermore, price controls and subsidies to make food and medicine affordable have warped markets and sustained government spending in the face of impossible debt."

Things are more stable for now, so Ecuador has become one of the cheapest places for expats in all of Latin America. There are three distinct climate types in Ecuador, coastal, highland, and jungle. The highlands (La Sierra) have a much cooler climate that varies with altitude. Quito, the capital has an average summer temperature of about 61 degrees F. Avoid the hot steamy jungle areas in the east (El Oriente) where guerrilla activity and dangers are the highest.

Foreigners can't own property within 50 km of the borders or coastlines, and banks won't lend long-term—usually only from 1-7 years. So, even though the property is cheap, unless you plan on flipping it within a few years, I suggest you rent rather than buy. Rent is relatively cheap too.

The two major cities in Ecuador are Guayaquil (coastal) and Quito (highlands). Both have all the advantages of big cities as well as the disadvantages of crime, dirt, and traffic. Here is one expats pros and cons about Guayaquil:

Pros: Good medical care available throughout the city; lots of cultural activities to do like museums, concerts, parks and the Malecon; government offices are readily available as is the US and many other consulates; reliable and affordable public transportation; cheap housing prices; cheap prices for most food; and friendly people.

Cons: High crime rate, including auto theft; hot and humid six months of the year; some parts of the city are dirty; long waits at government offices; people are not punctual; high prices for electronic items and everything that is imported.

That list applies for most cities in Latin America. Quito stands out, however, for its very mild climate. Cuenca is a highly rated retirement haven because it is relatively cheap, is the cultural capital of Ecuador, has great views of the Cajas Mountains and also has mild weather. But that mild weather is more of the Seattle variety (rainy) than So. California—and it is 8300 feet high, so people with breathing problems shouldn't go there. The city is also plagued with diesel fumes from all the buses and trucks.

Many others prefer the sunny climates of Vilcabamba south of Loja which is still in the mountains. Tena is about the only tropical town that still has a mild climate. San Clemente is a small beach town where the prices are still low. There are many other unspoiled places in Ecuador, so there is lots to choose from. If it weren't for its bad government, Ecuador would indeed be a paradise.

Colombia and Peru

Colombia and Peru are more favorable towards Americans, but both are socialist nations at in the past have had significant dangers from communist guerrillas (FARC) and the drug cartels, which are often in league with each other. The guerrilla problem is somewhat now under control and the drug trade stabilized (meaning the CIA-backed drug cartels have finally conquered most of the competition), so things are better now than in the past decade. While the insurgency with the guerrillas ebbs and flows, Americans will always be looked upon as intruders by the Far Left, so you still have to be careful. Colombia has a long history of being under the influence of US black operations in Latin America—one of the principle forces causing resentment against the US. Colombia has discontinued permanent residency status and so expats now have to renew their residency every 5 years, which is a bit of a hassle and costs about $500.

There are 3 major cities in Colombia: Bogotá has a moderate climate, Cali is much hotter, and Medellin has a spring-like climate year-round. In each of these Colombian cities, foreigners will only find certain areas suitable and safe for expat living—unless you are fluent in Spanish with a Colombian accent and have the looks to fit in like a native. The majority of the other areas of the cities are working class areas or lower class ghettos, which are completely unsuitable. There are not a lot of Americans in Colombia because of the former dangers during the drug wars and guerrilla conflicts.

In Peru, there are two major cities to consider: Lima, the capital, is on the coast and has about 9 million inhabitants, and Arequipa which is 8,000 feet high in the mountains and has close to a million people. These are also the two largest commercial centers. Unless you need to be in and around the capital, with its high level of commerce and some crime, we prefer Arequipa for a better climate and lifestyle.

Paraguay

Paraguay is rampant with crime and police corruption. It used to be fairly stable under the dictatorship of General Alfredo Stroessner, but that was at the price of liberty. Under his watch Paraguay became a smuggler's route for Brazilian products into the rest of South America. Smuggling and its black market was driven by outrageously priced protective tariffs that drove people to break the law. When Stroessner was ousted, the closed corruption system he tolerated became open corruption and it has been bad ever since—although there have been token crackdowns from time to time. Often police are known to shake down foreigners and locals alike when they drive out into the countryside. The cost of living is very cheap but the climate is very hot and humid. Not recommended.

Brazil

You can find almost everything in Brazil, good and bad. Brazil is the biggest country in South America and the most advanced and prosperous—although you might not know it if you dare to travel through some of the many ghettos (Favelas) in major cities. Few people realize that half of South Americans speak Brazilian Portuguese, not Spanish. The culture is both eclectic and captivating—especially the music. The country is a mix of dozens of races and cultures, but the black Mestizo culture predominates. Government corruption is big in Brazil too, where the Rousseff government is plagued with allegations of corruption and favoritism. Crime is a big problem in Brazil especially in and around the Favelas of Rio de Janeiro and Sao Paulo. The standard of living ranges from luxury in first world parts of major cities to abject poverty.

There is a lot of wealth in Brazil, but it is sad to report that most of the big business concerns gave up the fight for liberty in Brazil when Marxist Lula Da Silva got elected. They succumbed to his party's not-so-subtle threats if they opposed his increased socialist demands. Da Silva was a radical Communist who led the thinly-veiled revolutionary movement from his annual leadership Forum (Foro de Sao Paulo). But he and his hand-picked successor, Dilma Rousseff, have been smart enough to play the same role as Red China—giving businesses a certain amount of liberty in order to build up the Brazilian economy, so that, in turn, he can build his armed forces. Brazil is doing just that. It has major aircraft manufacturing factories (both military and civilian) and manufactures a full range of weaponry. It is even working on nuclear weapons, the first in Latin America.

The Zika virus is a new problem for Brazil, although it is spreading to other countries. Adults may not have symptoms or just experience a rash, but unborn infants can have microcephaly (deformed heads). Some scientists note that the microcephaly could be the result of the larvacide pyriproxyfen (commonly sprayed in those areas) in drinking water.

We don't generally recommend relocating to Brazil unless you intend to become fluent in Portuguese. It is large enough that you can get out of the big cities and into safer territory, but you must speak the language well. Fortunately, there are enough fair-haired Brazilians of German descent that Portuguese-speaking Americans can blend into certain areas where Germans settled.

One of the safer places in Brazil is Santana Do Livramento on the border with Uruguay—giving you an escape route to the south if needed. But that is a long way to Sao Paolo for major commerce. The entire Rio Grande do Sul has the same gaucho (cowboy) feel as Uruguay with a lot of cattle ranches and a moderate more temperate climate. The closest major city is Porto Alegre, which is safer than Sao Paolo.

Both Sao Paolo and Rio De Janeiro are dangerous cities—even outside the slums—and traffic is horrendous. Lots of foreigners have been robbed at gunpoint and even killed. That said, you can find nice areas of town in both major metro areas but crime can hit even there—so never let your guard down.

Brazil is a big country with hundreds of large towns, so you can find almost anything you want, including some excellent beach locations—but it can be fairly primitive in rural Brazil, so it's better to stay within an hour of a moderately sized city.

If you don't want to take up a paying job in Brazil, it is fairly easy to gain resident status, either as an investor or retiree. Wikipedia says this about the visa policy of Brazil:

"Resident investor status may be granted to foreign nationals wishing to invest a minimum of US $50,000 in a Brazilian business or productive activity. There is a requirement to demonstrate a good knowledge of Portuguese. Investment funds must be submitted through the Central Bank of Brazil. Investor visas are issued for an initial 5 years, renewable on approval of a satisfactory investment plan and on confirmation that the investor has created jobs for at least 10 Brazilian nationals. Resident investors can apply for Brazilian citizenship after 4 years; prior to this they have many of the rights of citizens, except for voting rights."

For retirees, "Foreign nationals aged over 50 can apply for a permanent visa if they will be transferring the equivalent of at least US $2,000 to Brazil every month. Visas are also issued to up to two dependents, but there is a requirement to transfer an additional US $1,000 per dependent per month. Documentary proof of income and a bank declaration authorizing the monthly transfer are required."

Central America and Mexico

There is perhaps no other area of the world that has attracted so many American expatriates as Central America and Mexico. This area is relatively close to the USA, has a mild (though humid) climate, and has many friendly people eager for the economic boost that American dollars bring. On the negative side, crime is increasing dramatically and there is an entrenched Latin American bureaucracy that is hard for Americans to handle. A lot of money has to be thrown at local attorneys and the results are not always satisfactory or legitimate. In some countries, legal roadblocks are thrown up arbitrarily and bribery is necessary to pay your way out of trouble.

Americans are increasingly having trouble finding banks that will allow them to transfer a lot of monetary assets from the states without enormous fees and red tape. Now that the new Foreign Account Tax Compliance Act (FATCA) has gone into affect, the cost of compliance and the risk of being sanctioned by the US financial authorities is driving many banks to the point of refusing to deal with American accounts. The US government is putting a lot of pressure on these banks to track American attempts to take their money offshore. Increasingly, local governments are looking at ways to tax or limit large financial transactions at ATMs to force Americans to transfer their money in country. But that too is dangerous given the propensity of certain countries to confiscate dollar accounts and replace your money with local currency at unfavorable exchange rates (or worse yet, government bonds) as has happened in Mexico and Argentina.

There is also an ever-present minority of government bureaucrats and officials that are on the far left and hate Americans. The many Marxist state universities in Latin America are notorious for their anti-American sentiment and they produce thousands of trained radicals each year. This increasing hatred of America, which took a major leap forward during the Bush years of American intervention around the world, will someday tempt these governments to confiscate the property of foreigners.

In Nicaragua and El Salvador communist guerrilla leaders have been able to take over the nation politically by offering socialist promises and ideological attacks on the wealthy. This trend does not bode well for foreign expats looking for a haven from government tyranny.

Our advice is: don't take all your money or assets off-shore and don't burn all your bridges back to the states. If you discount the increasing corruption and crime factors (which you shouldn't), you can live quite cheaply in Mexico or Central America. Limit your risk by withdrawing only small transfers at a time through ATMs and living in rented facilities. That way, there is nothing to confiscate.

Many choose Latin American waters as a good place to retreat to using a live-in sailing vessel. They travel up and down the coast to find the best weather and change locations at will depending on the changing economic and political climate. But this is not a good long-term solution due to the increased numbers of pirates operating in the Caribbean, especially off the coast of Venezuela. Most countries don't allow you to have firearms on boats but you would be foolish not to have some weapons hidden away anyway. When attacked, you won't be able to depend on local authorities for help even if they could get to you in a timely manner—which they can't. As for safety, this will vary from country to country. Guatemala is currently the least safe place for foreigners, followed by Mexico.

Mexico

We have lived in Mexico at various times and it was delightful, but now things have changed dramatically. Mexico is a cauldron of corruption and drug violence that threatens the stability of the whole country. Americans are particularly at risk due to the increasing attention given to illegal immigration and the border conflict with Mexican drug lords. There is a violent turf war being waged by the established cartels and the constant competition that is always emerging from breakaway drug dealers who want to establish their own cartels and take a larger share of the loot. What the American public doesn't realize is that certain cartels (ie: Sinaloa) are an extension of the official Mexican government which, in turn, is in league with our own government's black operations which has its own drug pipeline through Mexico. That's why our border patrol often has to deal with the Mexican military crossing the border in support of drug haulers. With this kind of official collusion, drug violence will never end. Worse, it leads to a culture of corruption on both sides of the border as high officials increasingly have to step in to cover up what's really going on.

We believe that American tourists are increasingly going to be targets for the kind of kidnapping for ransom that plagued Central America in the 1980s. For this reason, American expatriates are tending to concentrate in gated American communities in Mexico, such as those in and around the seashore town of Ensenada and in the southern highlands. However, what good does it do to retire in Mexico if it is no longer safe to travel on the roads outside your community? How fun is it to live in a luxury ghetto for the affluent? Of course, things aren't that bad yet. Americans still do travel fairly freely in Mexico but it is with increasing risk. The trends for safety are not good in the long-term—especially when you can't depend on getting any justice in the corrupt Mexican system.

For now we have stopped driving our own vehicles into Mexico. There is too much danger of being stopped for minor traffic violations (or for no reason at all) by crooked police and forced to pay a bribe or fine. There are also a few dangerous bands of criminals that block the roads in rural areas and rob people or worse.

Costa Rica

Expatriates have also been particularly attracted to Costa Rica because of its political stability, relative low cost of living and low property prices, but now with over 50K Americans in the country, all that has changed. Prices are much higher and real estate is no longer cheap. Still there are advantages and Americans keep coming. The national health care system is modern and low in cost with affordable health insures for around $200-$300/mo. Expatriates are exempt from tax on overseas income, and there are lower property taxes than in the U.S. and no capital gains taxes. Costa Rica also offers generally drinkable tap water, "high-speed" Internet (that actually isn't very fast) and good phone service. Taxis and buses are abundant and not too expensive, but some Taxi drivers overcharge gullible foreigners.

On the downside, Costa Rica is very humid in the lower altitudes which always produces a lot insects and bugs. The better places to live are at the higher elevations. While there are no taxes on foreign retirement income, gasoline in this country is expensive at over $5 per gallon. Petty crime is high including home break-ins and property theft, but violent crime and murder rates are low. There is, as in all Latin America, a good deal of corruption in both government, police and business. Unemployment and poverty are high among the less educated. Wages are low, so hired help is cheap.

You can expect to pay $4,000 a month or more to live on the beaches of the Pacific unless you get away from the favorite American hangouts for more reasonable housing. A persistent problem all over Costa Rica is "Gringo Pricing" (especially high prices for Americans) and, unless you are fluent in Spanish and know what the real local prices should be, you'll be taken advantage of on a regular basis.

A lot of Americans complain about everyday "Ticos" (what Costa Ricans call themselves) being liars or untrustworthy in their dealings. Part of the problem is something endemic to much of Central America—their lack of precision about everything, including verbal responses to questions. It's almost impossible to pin anyone down about a price, procedure, time commitment or directions to somewhere. It is very frustrating to get five different answers to a precise question or get a different answer the next day. It's not necessarily pernicious, as much as sloppy mental thinking, a lack of commitment, and not taking the effort to be precise and correct. The higher classes however are a lot better at accurate communication and keeping commitments.

Most expats live on the coast or in more rural areas of the Central Valley. Here are a couple of specific locations that are recommended:

San Jose, the capital of Costa Rica, has about a million people in the metro area. It is rich in culture and commerce including the best shopping and dining possibilities in this nation the size of West Virginia. The city starts at 3,000 feet of altitude and has even higher hills surrounding the city, so despite its tropical latitude, it has a very temperate climate—rarely hot and never cold. Buying good housing in San Jose is expensive but renting is cheaper. Security is pretty good in peaceful times in the suburbs and middle class areas of San Jose, but there are a lot of poor areas (as in any Latin American city) that you shouldn't venture into at night. But don't expect this security to remain during a major crisis or world war where masses of people will be out of work and tourism dries up. It would be best to be very rural when that happens.

Atenas: This quaint town of about 5K people in central Costa Rica has very moderate temperatures due to the higher elevation—about 60 and 80 degrees F. year-round. Many expats live up in the rolling hills near town with beautiful vistas. Atenas is some 45 minutes from the beaches on the Pacific and a half-hour from San Jose. San Jose is where all the shopping malls, theater, museums, and major hospitals are, but most expats prefer the cheaper and slower lifestyle in the smaller towns.

Nosara: This is a beach town on the Pacific with about 5K people, but away from the big tourist destinations. As with all beach towns it is more expensive than its rural neighboring towns, but much less expensive than most coastal towns in the US. The average coastal property rents for about $2,000 a month. The downside is the distance to San Jose and any major hospitals—a five-hour drive, but you have to get that far away to get decent housing prices near the beach. The nearest international airport is a two-hour drive.

San Ramon: This city of about 15K is a cultural center about an hour away from the hustle of San Jose. This is home to the University of Costa Rica—the top university in the country—and a couple of museums. It's a regional center for the area so you have the full range of commercial facilities as well as cultural opportunities including a symphony.

There are two basic types of residency in Costa Rica:

Residency for Pensioners or Retirees (Pensionados or Rentistas). If you earn $600 per month from your pension or $1000 a month from your investments you can qualify.

Residency for investors (Inversionistas). If you invest at least $50,000 US dollars in local businesses as approved by the Center for the Promotion of Exports and Investments (PROCOMER). The current priority investment areas of business are ornamental plants, leather articles, spices, fruits and vegetables, processed foods, wood products and tourism. If you prefer an area of investment not listed by PROCOMER, you must invest $200,000 US dollars in that business.

Costa Rica is still one of the safest countries in Latin America, especially compared to Guatemala and Mexico where crime and kidnapping is a real problem for foreigners. But don't ever make your decisions about going south of the border based on current expat experiences as extolled in all the many expat web sites. These conditions won't last. Every country in Latin America has a lot of Marxists and people who hate Americans—and many of them are in academia, the press and the bureaucracies. Someday when tough times hit, and locals look for people to blame, and the government looks to "tax the rich" the foreign expats will be a prime target.

From a long-term safety perspective, our biggest concern with Costa Rica is that its economy is mostly based upon foreign tourism and the money brought in by expats and tourists. In a world war, most of that is going to be cut off and foreigners will be left without access to their money and more than half of Ticos will lose their source of income, creating severe economic and social disruption.

Panama

Because of the Panama Canal and a major US Air Force base, there has been a lot of American influence in this country, both good and bad. But after the invasion of Panama by US forces people here either love Americans or hate them. But time tends to heal bad relations and Americans are still choosing Panama as an expat location.

Panama has two distinct weather seasons—the wet season April to December and the dry season from mid December to March. Generally, it is rainier on the Caribbean side and drier on the Pacific Side. Typical of Central America, it is hot and humid in low elevations and drier and cooler at higher elevations.

The top income tax rate in Panama for individuals is 27%, but you also have to pay a national sales tax (VAT) on everything. Healthcare is generally modern but less expensive compared to the states. Medical health insurance is much cheaper as well, around $1,000

per person, per year. In a misguided bid to control inflation, Panama just implemented price controls this year—which always causes shortages in time.

Panama attracts a lot of foreign expatriates because its banking system is fairly friendly as far as Latin American countries go, and that is still true, but in the long-term Panamanian banks will fare no better than most in a worldwide banking crisis, and unless you are an insider, don't expect the system to protect your funds. Before you invest or open an account in any foreign bank check the current status of banks and corruption on some of the websites that cater to expatriates, like *www.Internationalliving.com*. Don't take their recommendations blindly. They are commercially skewed and full of promotional hype. But do read realistic comments by bloggers and contributors to the site.

Despite Panama's reputation as an international banking center guaranteeing privacy, most of those advantages are now gone due to bureaucracy and corruption. Many suspect that some of Panama's top banking officials are already on CIA and DEA payrolls in order to protect US drug pipeline profits. Many expats have had problems with Panamanian ATMs. If they are out of cash (which you don't know until you've entered your bank card), some Panamanian banks debit your account even when they don't give you the cash—and then depend on you prove the error. It's very difficult to get those funds back, especially if you don't have an account where the ATM is connected.

Probably the root of the problem is that the ATMs in Panama are older types and they are getting hacked. Banks are too cheap to buy new machines and claim they are not responsible so the card holder gets shorted. Without ATM protection, you've lost one of your main sources of getting funds in a foreign country if you choose to not open a local account. In most foreign countries I recommend using the ATM exclusively and keeping your money in the US. In Panama because of ATM problems, you will have to open a local account and get a VISA debit card to pay for things—but only transfer as much money each month into the bank as you need. Panamanian banks are mostly complying with FATCA and are willing to deal with Americans—but don't count on privacy anymore.

As in most expat situations, I recommend renting rather than buying. There have been many instances where expats have been defrauded by sellers and corrupt lawyers. You don't want to have to deal with the corrupt legal system in a contractual dispute.

Panama has a well deserved reputation for corruption and drug dealing, having long been in collusion with the CIA ever since the time of Manual Noriega, who was running the CIA drug pipeline for our government. He was taken down by the CIA for taking too big a cut. Now that the US has abandoned the canal, the Chinese have established a commercial shipping foothold and are well aware of the strategic position of the Panama Canal. All over the world the Chinese are trying to control shipping lanes and Panama is the key country in Central America. This doesn't bode well for Panama in the next world war, or for the Americans living there, so beware. Hospitality towards Americans could change rapidly in bad times.

The biggest city is Panama City, which is modern in most respects and has all the commercial conveniences plus a major international airport. It is also hot and humid year-round, and traffic is very heavy day and night. During boom times there is the constant noise and dust from construction. It also is no longer very cheap—expect to put out $2000-2500/month in living expenses.

The Interior highland is cooler and less expensive. Centered around Distrito David in the mountainous area in Western Panama. This is the regional commercial center. Higher and cooler, this area is used for crops that need cool weather such as strawberries or coffee. Boquete, just to the north of David is the best known and most developed highland city for retirees and it is more affordable than the capital. Housing costs have fallen somewhat since that past boom time.

Almost all the beach resorts on the Pacific side near Panama City are expensive and crowded. You have to go farther west to the Azuero Peninsula to find rural, inexpensive beach living—like Las Tablas.

Panama goes out of its way to attract pensioners, and, being a dollar based economy, it is easy on Americans with dollars. The Panamanian balboa has been tied to the dollar (which is legal tender in Panama) at an exchange rate of 1:1 since its introduction and has always circulated alongside dollars. Inflation in Panama has been running higher than the US, hence the unwise drive for price controls. All things imported are more expensive in Panama than in the states.

One of the best things about Panama is its visa for foreign retirees, called the Pensionados. According to International Living as of August 2008 the "pensionado" requirements are: "Applicants must draw a minimum pension of $750 and invest at least $100,000 in property in Panama or you must have a pension of at least $1,000 per month (no real estate requirement). You can pool your pension with your spouse's to meet the minimum pension requirements. The benefits are big: 15 - 50% off everything from medical and energy bills to entertainment and public transportation.

Belize

A former British colony, Belize is a favorite of many who are looking to live in a foreign country. English is the official language but the locals mix it with Creole (with a British accent). There are a variety of immigrants in Belize besides US expats, such as European Mennonites, a lot of Asians (industrious owners of shops and grocery stores) and various Latinos from the Americas. The Mennonites are quiet and unassuming. The Asians keep

to their business side, but the Creole blacks are loud, jovial and sometimes aggressive when corrupt. You'll see a lot of wretched human beings in Belize City—half starved and depraved. You get accosted a lot by beggars and drug peddlers.

Belize is often recommended for the typical tourist reasons: ocean beaches, clear water, isolated retreats, Mayan ruins and rainforests. However, the climate is hot and humid most of the year, with a monsoon-type period May to November. There are snakes and the bugs are very bad, especially the sand flies. Beaches are often only so-so (ugly near Belize City).

Parts of Belize City have a growing gang problem including gang warfare and drug problems, but they are limited to no-go areas of Belize City which locals know to avoid. The rest of Belize, especially the Cayo District (higher altitude, cooler, less bugs) or Corozal or on Ambergris Caye (near Mexican border), is quite safe.

Other problems are petty crime in the big city (as in all of Latin America), unreliable electricity, and bad roads.

Belize's Tourism Board administers a program for "qualified retired persons" (QRP), much like Panama's Pensionados above. According to International Living, the QRP "offers significant tax incentives to those who become permanent residents of Belize. Foreign residents under the program are exempted from all taxes on income from sources outside Belize. They can own and operate international businesses based in Belize, again exempt from all local taxes. They can also import personal effects without paying import duties."

However, most expatriates never learned that Britain turned the government over to a Marxist political party when they granted independence and that influence is still under the surface. If the world turns against Americans, they won't want to be in Belize.

Nicaragua

We don't recommend Nicaragua because it has never been the same after the Sandanista revolution when communist rebels came to power, thanks to efforts by the US State Department to undermine pro-Western president Anastazio Samoza. The Sandinistas lost power after many years, but strongman Ortega is now back in power courtesy of raw democracy and the draw of socialism.

Guatemala and El Salvador

Guatemala and El Salvador also had similar bouts with communist guerrillas but came to a forced negotiated solution (by the US). The Far Left has been kept at bay during subsequent elections, but they have now gained electoral control of the country through the ballot box. Both El Salvador and Guatemala have a small but growing group of libertarians—owing almost exclusively to a free market university (San Marroquin University) in Guatemala City. Guatemala is currently not recommended because it has a very high rate of violent crime. Police are almost completely ineffective and corrupt. Foreigners who want to buy or rent are at the mercy of a corrupt legal system that makes you pay Guatemalan lawyers unnecessary fees for every contract. El Salvador, however, is one of our favorites because of the number of principled and sharp businessmen that successfully fought against the US favored Marxist insurgency. The US State Department is full of leftists and globalists that work to undermine free markets in Latin America. But, sadly, the Salvadoran business sector has been labeled as "Oligarchs" and no longer can stem the tide of social democracy as championed by the far Left.

Honduras

Honduras is similarly not recommended due to the strong leftist influence in political life and current instability. Manuel Zelaya was elected as a conservative and then took Honduras into the Far Leftist ALBA association and joined forces with communists Chavez and Castro. He was later overthrown by the military. Currently, a more Western-friendly government is installed but the Left will ultimately return to power. Crime and corruption in Honduras is widespread as well as poverty for most.

The Caribbean

Certain islands of the Caribbean are viewed as safe havens for your money: Barbados, Cayman Islands, British Virgin Islands and the Turks & Caicos, all of which have ties to the UK and have their banks audited by the Bank of England. The Bahamas have also been popular in the past, although banking privacy laws have recently been somewhat compromised. Ultimately, the rules can change anywhere suddenly, so don't count on anything staying the same. I no longer expect banking privacy anywhere in the world as the Foreign Assets Reporting Law (FATCA) is put into force. But that is probably just as well, because I've always felt that when war comes few Americans (and only those with insider connections) are going to be able to get access to foreign accounts and get it transferred to America.

Climate-wise, Caribbean weather is wonderful most of the time with mild tropical sea breezes. However, the islands are very vulnerable to tropical storms and hurricanes. Many of the top ten storms of the last decade occurred in this region. While storm numbers and levels of destruction vary from year to year, the overall trend seems to be more numerous and more powerful storms each decade. In general, we do not recommend retreats on small islands because you have no place to go if and when that island is occupied and your situation becomes compromised.

US and Canada

The North American continent (excluding Mexico) offers arguably the best long-term future security for Americans and Canadians despite the fact that the US and Canada will be the target of a pre-emptive nuclear strike sometime in the future. As we describe in the section on US nuclear war, this will affect the whole country, but not equally. If you take our advice and relocate for security before that really big threat comes, you can survive it and the following social unrest. We get a lot of calls from Americans thinking about re-locating outside the USA specifically to avoid this future strike. That seems logical if you only consider the initial aspects of war and not living through the aftermath. Consider the following:

1. Nuclear war is very survivable if you are not living in a target area or immediately downwind—and if you prepare some form of safe room that shelters you against fallout. Unlike nuclear reactor meltdowns, which have significant quantities of radioactive fuel, fallout from nuclear weapons dissipates within a few weeks depending on factors such as the distance from the blast zone.

2. Social unrest in the aftermath of a nuclear war can also be mitigated by relocating or having a retreat in rural areas with a contingency plan to get there quickly.

3. In the longer-term aftermath, nations will take sides, or be coerced into joining one side of the conflict or other. If in a nation that has a population that is hostile to America or the West, you could become a hunted person. Americans and foreigners will likely have property and bank accounts confiscated or nationalized as times get worse.

4. There are significant advantages to living in your home country during world turmoil. Few people can blend into a foreign culture and language sufficiently to build a network of resources to sustain them when times get hard and foreigners become unpopular.

5. Canada and the United States have total self-sufficiency in food and water, and the residual technological know-how to recover rapidly.

6. Most importantly, there is no other country on earth other than America that has so many millions of Conservatives schooled in the values of liberty and constitutionally limited democracy who are capable of banding together to form a resistance to the expected tyranny of the New World Order as it forms in the aftermath of war.

For these and other reasons, we have concentrated the rest of our relocation advice to this area. The remainder of this book provides more detail about the areas presented in the previous chapters as they impact the residents of the US and Canada.

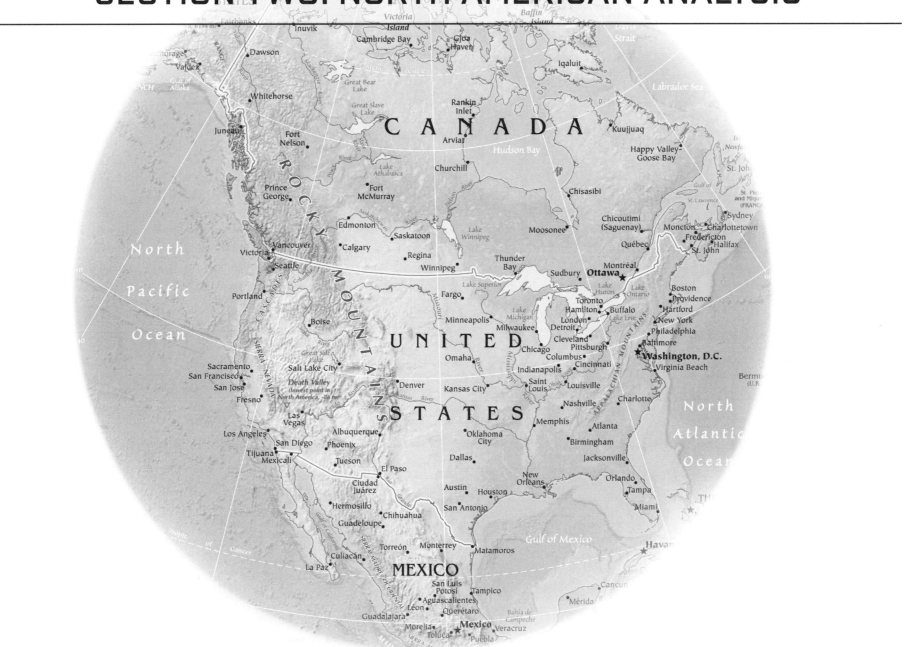

Chapter 7

US AND CANADA GEOGRAPHY AND CLIMATE

As we begin our focus on the valuable locations within North America, we present here climate factors for the US and Canada. Keep in mind that the criteria should not just be for comfort but to sustain life in a crisis.

Specific Environmental Factors

The United States has the largest number of preferred areas which meet the sustainability criteria. Most of Canada's southern regions, close to the US border are also adequate for basic gardening. Far northern Canada lies within an extreme climate zone that is sufficiently cold in the winter that it does not qualify for self-sufficiency except for the most hardy and adaptable families. In the US only regions with very high altitudes or without sufficient water are untenable.

Growing Season

The maps on this page and the next show the average US and Canadian growing season. That is, the length of time between significant frost periods. We recommend a minimum of 90 days and preferably 150 days or more. As you can see, outside of the upper mountain areas, most of the US and some of southern Canada is sufficient for crops.

These maps do not tell the whole story about good growing potential, however. Plants need sunlight and water in the right ratio, and good soil. Some plants, like tomatoes, need a period of sufficient heat to "set" so some areas up north may have a reasonable growing period but lack the right high temperatures during the summer. Farmers here should consider a greenhouse. Also note that the darkest

areas are not necessarily better, such as the dry deserts of Arizona or the damp Everglades in the south of Florida where only certain plant species grow well.

Cloud cover and moisture over the Seattle and Vancouver, BC areas can make it hard for some crops like wheat. The angle of the sun in northern latitudes is lower in the sky, even during summer, so position your garden in these areas appropriately to catch enough rays.

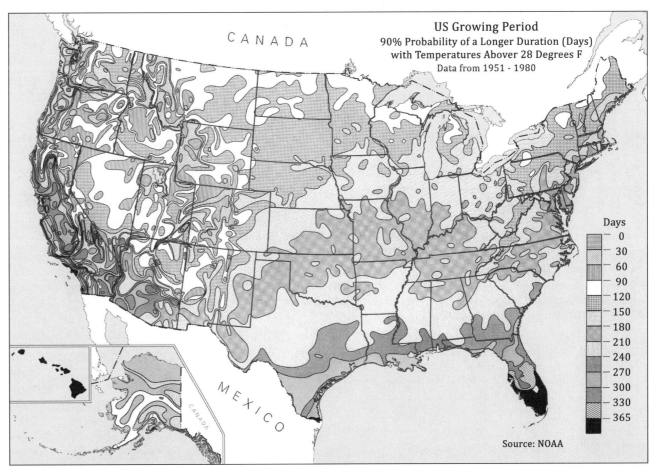

US Growing Period
90% Probability of a Longer Duration (Days)
with Temperatures Abover 28 Degrees F
Data from 1951 - 1980

Days
- 0
- 30
- 60
- 90
- 120
- 150
- 180
- 210
- 240
- 270
- 300
- 330
- 365

Source: NOAA

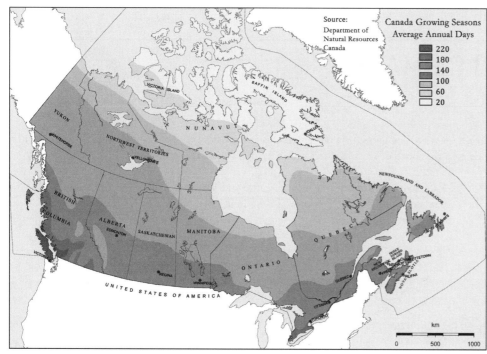

Sunshine and Cloud Cover

Sunshine is critical for physical wellbeing. It produces Vitamin D, an essential vitamin for overall immune system function. The risk of skin cancer from regular, moderate doses of sunlight is overblown. Skin cancer is more related to how many times you get sunburned, not how much general exposure to sun you receive. But even if you live in a sunny area, those who work indoors all of their lives rarely get the benefits of sunshine, unless they make the effort to eat lunch outdoors or exercise after work while it is still sunny.

The abundant sunshine of the American West is one of the reasons it continues to grow and attract people away from other climates with long cloudy seasons or even sunny but highly humid climates that are exposed to thunderstorms and hurricanes. Sunny weather is also good for your mental health. Depression is more frequent and harder for people to overcome in areas with little sunshine like Alaska or Seattle. Take a look at the US annual days of cloud cover map on p. 63 near the descriptions of Pacific maritime climates.

Inland southern California and Arizona are the true sunshine states, despite Florida's nickname. The Florida sun is more intense when it is shining, being closer to the

Precipitation and Humidity

The precipitation map on this page shows increasing darkness for larger amounts of precipitation (rain and snow). Thus the small shaded areas in the western deserts are mostly for snow in the mountains.

Cold penetrates or feels colder in humid climates because humidity lessens the insulation value of air. In like manner, warm weather accompanied by humidity higher than 80% is much more difficult to cope with than that same temperature in a dry area like the mountains or high deserts where the humidity is often below 50%. We show US humidity maps for January and July on p. 64 with the descriptions of climate areas in the Central Plains and Gulf Coast.

Constantly humid climates are breeding grounds for mold, bacteria and disease, not to mention insects and pests. Humid climates, however, usually have an abundance of water for growing crops and many people like the moisture in the air. We recommend dry climates for health and comfort as long as your skin can tolerate the dryness and you have enough water for living and crop irrigation. Vegetable crops need at least 6" of water per week in summer months and 4" per week in cooler months.

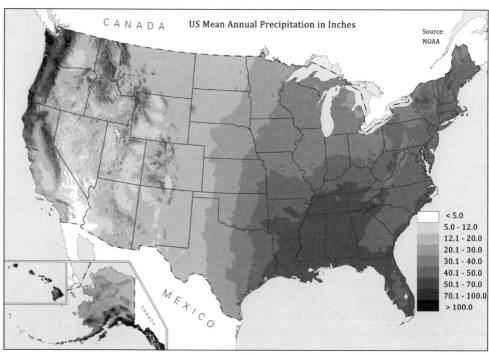

equator, but it also generates a lot of cumulous clouds due to the humid weather. The dry desert Southwest has many more cloudless days. In addition, it rarely gets humid, except when air flows up from Mexico. The climate is very hot and dry in the low altitude areas of Phoenix and Yuma. Southern California is still very sunny but milder in temperature because of the moderating effect of the cooling westerly flows of maritime air.

One of the main reasons for seeking more sunshine is to outfit your home with solar energy. While solar energy is still not nearly as cheap as public power, it is essential for partial self-sufficiency in a crisis. All areas of the country are vulnerable to power outages because of the way in which the national electric grid is tied together. Having some independent solar power with a battery storage bank is a wise option.

Temperature

As you study the temperature maps in this section, keep in mind that in a crisis you will likely not have access to central air conditioning and could be without central heating unless you have a wood stove or other alternate source of heat. If you have a choice, it is better to choose a cooler climate than a warmer one since it is easier to make heat in a crisis than to cool down with no electricity.

These maps show the average daily temperature during the hottest and coldest months. We recommend the areas that average above 0.0 degrees and below 100.0 degrees Fahrenheit.

Forestation

If you love forests and mature trees, you're in luck. Forestation is an important strategic factor in our analysis. Beyond aesthetic appeal, trees are valuable for many reasons. Trees can shield you from the elements, shade your property or conceal yourself and your retreat. Wood is an excellent building material, and a very valuable fuel. The downside of heavy forestation is the fire danger—especially now that arson is a factor that will increase over time. Building in the forest requires creating a cleared distance of 100 feet (minimum) from the forest as well as clearing out undergrowth beneath the trees. We recommend a fireproof exterior, metal roof, and ample water with large capacity pumps.

The Pacific Northwest has the most conifer forests at low altitude. The Northeast has mostly deciduous trees, and the South has a mix of pines and deciduous trees. The plains states do have trees, but mostly in patches, left by farmers to provide variety and shade for animals. The deep topsoil is just too tempting for farming cash crops like corn and soybeans to leave many trees.

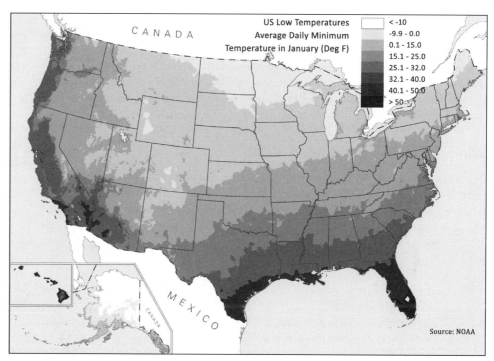

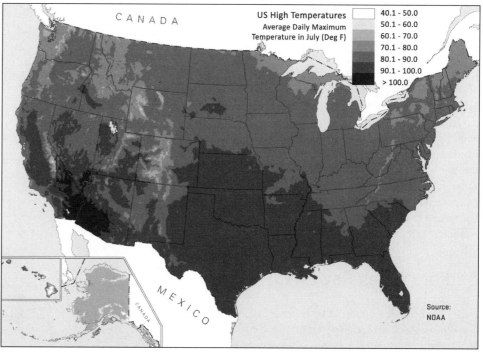

There is a general correlation between rain and forested areas. However, in the high desert states of the West, slow snowmelt provides the moisture to grow aspens and firs at altitude. Thus, in the high desert areas forests are rarely found below 6,000 feet except along river banks in the valleys or where planted by man and watered by irrigation systems. General forested areas can be seen visually on our national and regional maps in the colored maps of chapter 16.

Wind

The most consistently windy areas are found along coastal areas and where large lakes create temperature differences between the air over land and water. The great lakes, for example, often have steady winds along the shorelines. High storm winds and on-shore or off-shore flows give coastal and lake areas their windy reputations. Alaska has high winds along its southern coasts and especially in the Aleutian Islands. Hawaii has regular trade winds in the 12-25 mph range from May through November.

The central plains states get the most consistent wind in the continental US. They are in a transition zone between the cool, dry air from Canada and the hot, humid air from the Gulf of Mexico. The jet stream over the US and Canada flows in an undulating way from west to east carrying an alternating pulse of low pressure systems from the west and intermingling the north-south opposing air masses with dynamic effects. This combination generates steady north-south winds and violent thunderstorms and tornadoes.

In the Intermountain West, different air masses get caught on one side of the mountains and the pressure difference pushes air through some valleys making them very windy. Wyoming, for example, sits astride a relative low spot in the continental divide, and gets a steady flow of wind right along the I-80 corridor. This west-to-east flow has a sort of wind-tunnel effect, causing the wind speed to increase as it is forced through the restricted mountain passes. Nowadays, one can often gauge high wind areas just by the presence of wind farms. We don't recommend these areas for living, however, since winds have to be high and steady to be profitable for wind generators and, therefore, are not comfortable for full-time living.

Climate Areas Reviewed

Below is a brief description of each climate type so that you can make an informed choice between the range of environments that exists. Remember not to discount the extremes simply because we have

modern heating and air conditioning systems. These comforts may not be available during a crisis. Some discomfort is important, however, to keep you isolated during times of social unrest.

Arctic

Alaska, Yukon and the Northwest Territories make up this region that is famous for its extremes—and it's more than just cold weather extremes. Because of the wide variation in solar input from summer to winter, the arctic and sub-arctic regions have warm, humid summers with long days of extended sunlight. Alaska and Northern Canada have plagues of bugs and flying insects in the summertime. The winter days, conversely, are dark, cold and wet on the coastal regions and snowy and dry in the continental interiors.

Northwest Coastal Maritime

This region extends northward from the California coast above San Francisco up to parts of Alaska. It includes the land between the ocean and first set of mountains - the Coast Range in CA and the Cascade range in OR, WA and British Columbia. In southern BC,

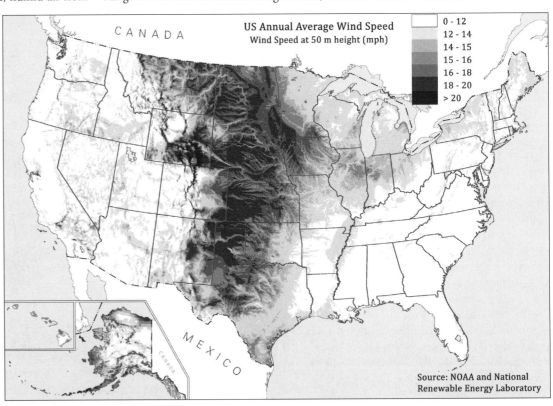

US Annual Average Wind Speed
Wind Speed at 50 m height (mph)

☐	0 - 12
	12 - 14
	14 - 15
	15 - 16
	16 - 18
	18 - 20
■	> 20

Source: NOAA and National Renewable Energy Laboratory

the Cascade Range joins up with the Rockies and stops its coastward encroachment. This area is very wet and experiences cloud cover most of the year. The Olympic Peninsula, particularly, is a rain forest, except near Sequim, Washington. The valleys east of the coastal mountains are drier and can be more pleasant.

This climate is usually mild in temperature, due to moist ocean air masses brought inland by the prevailing westerly winds. The moisture grows lots of beautiful, lush forests—almost too lush and overgrown. In winter, the ocean air masses come swirling down out of the Gulf of Alaska in low pressure storm systems bringing residual cold air behind them. This creates a pattern of rain, followed by freezing rain, and then snow. But the snow never stays for long due to the intermixing and alternating of these warmer ocean air masses and the subsequent Alaskan air masses. Ocean water at the beach is cold year-round due to the descending Alaskan current.

California Coastal Maritime

This area extends south from the San Francisco Bay area to San Diego and from the coast to the Sierra Nevada mountain range. When not foggy, many think this is the best climate in the entire continent. Along the coastal areas there are almost always perfect temperatures for human comfort. California's Central Valley, however, gets somewhat overheated in the summer and foggy in winter and spring. The humidity is also fairly comfortable in this region—staying in a moderate range of 60-70% on average. The Sierras themselves are not really part of this climate zone but add spectacular contrast to the sometimes barren California deserts.

This climate zone is considered Mediterranean and is fairly dry, getting only between 10 and 20 inches of rain a year. Thus, vegetation is not nearly as green and lush as the Northwest. The coastal beaches are beset by morning banks of fog which tend to keep the beaches obscured until at least mid-day. By afternoon in summer, it has burned off.

Intermountain West and Great Basin Region

This area is composed, climatologically speaking, of a medium altitude desert basin which lies between (and includes) the Sierra Nevadas and the western slope of the Rocky Mountains. Geographically, this refers to eastern Oregon and Washington, southern Idaho, parts of Utah and Nevada, northern Arizona, western Colorado and Wyoming. The entire area experiences dry, medium altitude desert air and is shielded from the heavy coastal rains and the extreme cold continental air masses from central Canada. Utah and southern Idaho usually stay about 10-15 degrees warmer than parts of Wyoming that are on the eastern side of the continental divide. Even this may still seem too cold for those who dislike anything approaching freezing but the mountains also keep out humid air which helps moderate the cold. The dry air allows clothes to insulate the body much more effectively.

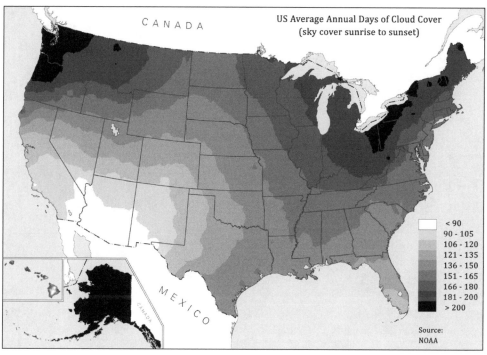

US Average Annual Days of Cloud Cover (sky cover sunrise to sunset)

< 90
90 - 105
106 - 120
121 - 135
136 - 150
151 - 165
166 - 180
181 - 200
> 200

Source: NOAA

Temperatures in the summer often exceed 100° F in elevations lower than 3500 ft, such as Las Vegas. The temperatures are more moderate at altitude (above 4500 feet). Salt Lake City is the hub of the region. Its weather pattern is a balance between cold and hot: 134 freezing days a year, 60 days in the 90+ range, 125 clear days and 139 cloudy or partly cloudy days (most of which is due to localized thunderstorms generated over the Great Salt Lake). Note that out of those 130+ partly cloudy days, there are only 40 days of rain in the year. Only during an average of 3 days in the winter do temperatures dip below 0°F. The growing season in the Intermountain West is moderately long in the valleys and marginal in the higher elevations—which are restricted to cattle and feed crops.

Desert Southwest

This area encompasses the southern deserts of California, Nevada, Arizona and New Mexico below 3000 feet in elevation. This area is similar to the Great Basin zone in many ways, except that it is a lot hotter. The heat in the summer can be fatal in Death Valley, southern Nevada, southern Arizona and New Mexico. There is hardly any rainfall (less than 10 inches per year) so it is a true desert. This region is very dry and sunny almost all year round.

Temperatures are in the 100-120 degree range almost all summer long. Cloudy days number fewer than 70 and winter temperatures only drop near freezing 10 days a year. But without

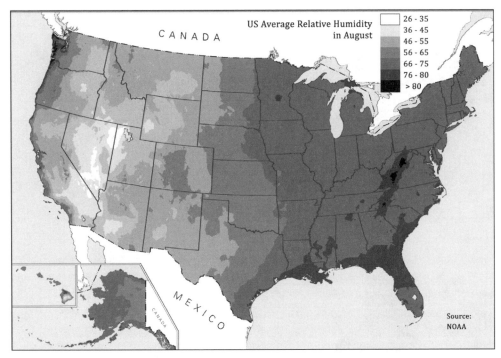

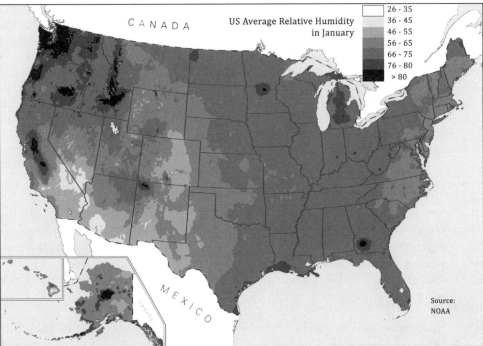

massive amounts of air-conditioning, the area is barely livable in the summer. Winds are fairly mild, except for the occasional hard blows that come from the southwest storms of Baja California (Mexico) penetrating into El Centro, California and Yuma, Arizona.

Crops can grow abundantly here but only with copious amounts of irrigation water from the mountains (which is quite limited). The growing season is the longest in the country.

Central Plains

This area is generally defined by the eastern front range of the Rocky Mountains on the west to the Mississippi valley on the east. It can be divided into two subgroups—the northern plains states of N. and S. Dakota, eastern Colorado, Nebraska, Kansas, Iowa, Illinois and Indiana; and the southern plains states of Texas, Oklahoma and Missouri. Both Missouri and Oklahoma transition into the Ozark mountain country of Arkansas.

This climatic zone is a vast playground for violent weather forces generated by two great air masses—the warm, moist tropical flows from Mexico and the Caribbean and the cold, dry northern Canadian masses. They react together in striking and sometimes dangerous ways. Winds generally travel from west to east at jet stream altitudes. Lower winds often have different flows.

In winter, the cold, dry Canadian air masses which settle down to ground level often descend deep into the plains, bringing cold air and horrendous blizzards with high winds. In the summer, the tropical southern air masses from both the west coast of Mexico and the Gulf Coast invade the region. All this tropical moisture turns these plains into a relatively hot, muggy, insect-buzzing farmland. Summers are spent dodging thunderstorms and occasional tornadoes. The climate in the plains is very pleasant in late spring and early fall as cool Canadian air masses keep the humid gulf air masses to the south. The growing season is long here and therefore optimal in areas where there is sufficient rainfall. Refer to the humidity maps on this page for relative percentages in summer and winter.

Gulf Coast and Deep South

This area of the US below the southern boundary of Tennessee and Virginia is a fairly uniform climate zone. It is noted for warm, humid, semi-tropical weather patterns. The major air masses that affect this region come from the Atlantic Ocean farther east and travel into the gulf where they are forced to turn northward as they collide with westerly air masses coming across Mexico and the southwestern US.

This northward turning movement can occur as early as Florida or be delayed until making landfall in Texas.

As these warm, water-laden air masses converge against the westerly flows (which are usually drier and colder) they generate new storm systems, including many thunderstorms. These southern storms are rarely cold, lending to the south's mild climate reputation.

Although rare, cold northern air masses occasionally penetrate this far south. When they do, it can be catastrophic to winter fruit crops in Florida and to home plumbing systems that are not protected from freezing temperatures. The rest of the time winters rarely produce hard frosts. This is part of the reason insect infestations are more vigorous here since this climate provides year-round breeding for pests—especially cockroaches and termites. High humidity climates also grow lots of mold and mildew. People who are sensitive to these health hazards should be mindful of this.

The Deep South has a higher-than-average number of hazardous insects, snakes and animals which you should be aware of—alligators in Florida and Cottonmouth and Water Moccasin snakes throughout the South.

Northeastern Continental Mix

This area takes in the states and provinces from the Great Lakes on the east to the Atlantic Ocean, and as far south as the southern Tennessee-Virginia borders. There is a wide mix of weather in this zone. It is not nearly as uniform as the others, and gets air mass flows from a variety of different areas depending upon the season. This area is hot and humid in the summers, being awash in strong, humid air masses that come up from the south. But during the other three seasons, there is an alternating pattern of ebb and flow where the humid, southern moisture retreats in front of dry continental air from Canada. For example in the Washington, DC metro area, you can have hot, muggy spring and early summer weather and then get a cool northern wind the next day, making it seem like a whole different climate. These changes happen most often in fall and winter.

The Atlantic northern coast gets an occasional "nor'easter" when a storm brings moisture from the Atlantic eastward over the northern states, usually causing severe weather (wind and snow) or rain. Lake effect is a constant factor in the states downwind of the Great Lakes. Insects—particularly gnats—are bad around northern Virginia and southern New York. It's no wonder screened porches and bug zappers are the rage. On the other hand, what can compare to the evening lights of the fireflies that abound in these moist summer climates? The soils are clayish in the east due to all the leaf fall from deciduous trees—a real mess to work in if the moisture content is excessive. But the growing seasons are very adequate.

Canada

Canada's most habitable areas are mostly within the southern climate zones. The province of British Columbia is mostly a northwest coastal maritime climate. Alberta is much like the Intermountain West because of the Canadian Rocky Mountains. Saskatchewan and Manitoba are similar to the US northern plains states. Ontario is mostly influenced by the large cold and dry continental air masses, but it also sometimes experiences hot muggy summers in the south where it joins the Great Lakes. Quebec, in the heavily populated South is similar to northern New York State. The Atlantic maritime provinces of Newfoundland, New Brunswick and Nova Scotia have northeastern Atlantic maritime climates, only much colder and more severe than New England.

Still, Canada diverges from the US in some of its interesting weather extremes. For example, it has the lowest tides in North America (0.1 meter in the Arctic) as well as the highest tides (16 meters in the Bay of Fundy, Nova Scotia). Twenty-seven percent of Canada's land mass is north of the tree line—very barren. While it has many fewer tornadoes and hail storms than the US, when they do occur, they can be very destructive.

Probably the most pleasant climate in Canada is in the large southern Okanagan Valley of British Columbia. This area is a true "banana belt" where warm air comes up from the Intermountain West. It is an ideal fruit growing area, with the longest growing season in Canada, and has many beautiful lakes. Kelowna, the largest city in the area, also has the least winds in all of Canada. Summers are mild and warm and have made this a favorite vacation spot for Canadians and Americans. Nearby Kamloops has the warmest summer periods. However, the highest number of clear days is found in southern Saskatchewan—a large, grain growing area. Prince Rupert Island, just south of Alaska, is the rainiest area of Canada and the cloudiest. Windsor (near Detroit) is the most humid and nearby London, Ontario, has the most thunderstorms. Medicine Hat on the eastern side of the Canadian Rockies (near the southern Alberta border), is the driest part of Canada. St. John's, Newfoundland is the foggiest place in Canada, as well as the windiest, and has the most days of freezing rain in winter.

Natural Disasters

Within the climactic areas mentioned above, there are big regions that we recommend avoiding because of excessive exposure to natural disasters. In general, natural disasters can be easily survived with proper preparations. However, you should still locate away from property exposed to the most severe or most frequent occurrences. Here is information about the most significant natural threats for the United States.

Storms

There are four major areas of the US and Canada that are subject to strong storm systems.

Pacific Coast from British Columbia to California: These areas (predominantly from San Francisco northward) take the brunt of all the pacific storms generated out of the Gulf of Alaska. While southern California gets fewer storms, when they do come they tend to do a lot of damage as they precipitate mud slides or flash floods. Pacific storms occasionally reach typhoon strength and are capable of very strong winds accompanied by heavy rains or snow.

Southern California experiences hot Santa Ana wind storms flowing out of the high deserts. When combined with wild fires, these winds create fire storms that have consumed millions of acres of brush and the houses that get in the way. Many of these fires are caused by arson, making them a constant danger in the future.

Central Plains receive big thunderstorms constantly in the summer. In the winter months, pacific storm masses dry out over the western mountain chains and then reform over the plains as warm, southern air masses collide with cold Canadian air. These storms generate the life-threatening blizzards that the Midwest is so famous for. **Northeastern coasts** of the US and Canada experience fierce winds and lots of rain or snow from strong storms generated by north and south air mixing along the Atlantic coastline. This batters the coastal areas from Connecticut northward.

Great Lakes Storms: The US has to contend with additional storm strength when cold Canadian storm systems pick up strength and moisture over the Great Lakes. These are known as "lake effect" storms and can dump significant amounts of extra precipitation where they make landfall such as in Michigan, New York and even northern Pennsylvania.

South Atlantic and Gulf Coast: These areas, from the Mexico-Texas gulf coast to North Carolina are the prime targets of all the Atlantic tropical depressions. These tropical storms and hurricanes come out of the southeast Atlantic Ocean primarily in summer and fall.

The least stormy areas, in general, are in the western inland valleys of the Intermountain West. These are largely protected from the west by the Cascade and Sierra Nevada mountain ranges and to the east by the Rocky Mountain line. The south-central Appalachian area of Kentucky and Tennessee are also mild weather areas. These areas do have storms, of course, but most have lost their ferocity by the time they get this far inland.

Hurricanes

The following is a list of the deadliest hurricanes to strike the US. It is interesting to note that many times hurricane deaths were the result of flooding rather than the hurricane force winds. Storm surge, strong rains, and dikes breaking have all been significant causes of deaths during these massive storms. This list was compiled from information from *www.farmersalmanac.com* and *www.wikipedia.com*.

- Hurricane Camille hit the east coast in 1969. This was a category 5 storm with winds of over 200 mph and caused 256 deaths. Half of casualties were due to flooding in the Appalachian mountains after drenching rains.

- Great New England Hurricane of 1938 was a category 3 hurricane with winds of 186 mph. 250 people reportedly died, tying with Hurricane Camille in US casualties. This storm made landfall further north than most tropical storms, catching residents and weather forecasters by surprise.

- New Orleans and Texas hurricanes of 1915. There were two category 4 storms that hit close to each other. The strongest had 135+ mph winds. These caused a total of 275 casualties and serious damage.

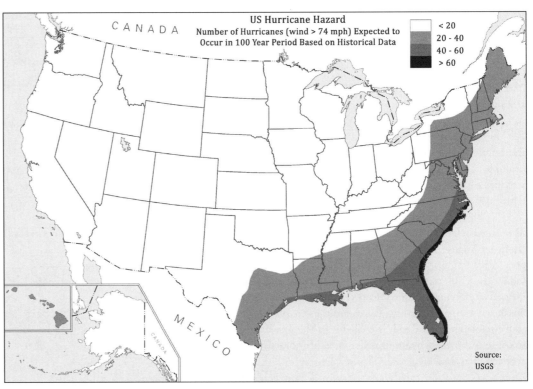

- Florida Keys and Texas storms of 1919. With winds close to 150 mph, this storm sank many ships resulting in 287 casualties.Grand Isle, LA hurricane of 1909. Wind speeds only reached 80 mph but storm surge caused significant flooding of lowland areas and resulted in approximately 350 deaths.

- Widespread storm hit Miami, Pensacola, Missouri and Alabama in 1926. 150 mph winds caused 372 deaths. Most of the damage occurred in Miami where residents came outside when the eye crossed over them and they thought the storm had passed.

- Florida Keys storm of 1935, category 5. 185 mph winds and 408 casualties. Many deaths were road workers stranded on the Florida keys as the storm hit, wiping out their only escape routes.

- Hurricane Audrey, that hit Texas and Louisiana in 1957. This category 4 storm had 135 mph winds causing 419 casualties mostly in the low lands. Water from storm surge flooded as far as 25 miles.

- Hurricane Katrina of 2005. Rated as a category 3 storm when it actually hit landfall. This storm had winds of 175 mph. Of the approximately 1800 people who died, most actually survived the storm but died in subsequent flooding.

- Lake Okeechobee, Florida storm in 1928. This category 4 storm had 160 mph winds and caused dikes to collapse creating a wall of water that swept houses and residents away. Around 4,000 people were killed as the water swept some of them all the way to the Everglades.

- Galveston, Texas storm of 1900. This category 4 storm had 150 mph winds. It is the deadliest natural disaster to strike the US. Storm surge swept over Galveston Island flattening the town and washing many houses away. The situation was made worse because the access bridges to the town were also swept away so help was slow coming. 8,000 people were killed, many of them died in rubble waiting to be rescued.

Pacific hurricanes, called typhoons, rarely make significant landfall in North America. The track is usually from the southwest, hitting the Mexican Baja coast and sometimes causing stormy weather up into Arizona and as far east as southern Texas. Occasionally, you get a major typhoon as far north as Oregon and Washington, such as the famous Columbus Day storm in 1962. Storms such as these seem to have greater impact and cause more damage in areas that rarely experience them.

Many people choose not to spend the money on reinforced construction or damage control when the need only arises every 100 years or so. But it only takes one big disaster to change your life. We recommend avoiding the darkest areas of this map completely, and if you build in the lighter areas, do make it more secure by building with sturdy materials like masonry or brick veneer. Otherwise consider hurricane ties and shear walls. It's not worth the risks to live in a weak house, whatever the storm probabilities. Also avoid low lands and property in runoff areas even in the lighter shaded areas as these can be subject to flooding from all the rain these storms carry.

Tornadoes

As we pointed out in the climate section, tornados are a fairly rare occurrence in the world. Only a few land masses have the right elements to spawn them. The south central US is prime territory for all these elements and has become known as "tornado alley." The highest tornado potential develops as warm moist air masses clash with dry, cold air masses. The tornadoes that emanate from these squall lines are very powerful and often fatal to life and property.

Tornadoes occur as far north as the central plains of Canada when southern air makes it this far north. We don't consider this threat significant to Canada. The south-central region of the US is the most dangerous place for tornadoes. Every home in this six state area should have a concrete shelter capable of withstanding the destructive winds. Below ground shelters are best, but concrete shelters can also be built at ground level. In Chapter 10 we explain how you can order Joel's book for building a multi-purpose shelter into an existing home (also look for it under bibliography and resources in the Appendix).

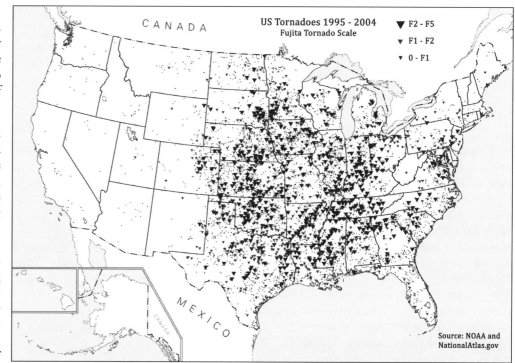

US Tornadoes 1995 - 2004
Fujita Tornado Scale

▼ F2 - F5
▼ F1 - F2
▾ 0 - F1

Source: NOAA and NationalAtlas.gov

The following map shows locations and concentrations of tornadoes between the years 1995 to 2004. You will see the higher danger areas quite clearly. The more symbols in close proximity represent a higher probability of tornadoes in the future.

If you have to live in any area with tornado potential or that has regular, heavy summer thunderstorms you should take some precautions. We recommend that in addition to the tornado shelter or safe room, you do the following:

- Install acrylic storm windows if you are in the tornado belt proper. They don't break like glass under impact.

- Train your family in tornado emergency procedures, especially for occasions when family members are not at home.

- Tune into weather radio during large thunderstorm activity.

- Acquire a cell telephone or portable two-way radio (family band type) for emergency communication when not at home and make sure all family members know how to use them.

Earthquakes

The following is a list of the most powerful earthquakes that have occurred in the US since 1800. Note that almost half were in unpopulated areas of Alaska, accountng for a low fatality rate. These are in chronological order so note the inreasing frequency of both magnitude and damages. All of the quakes listed are big earthquakes so although the epicenters were in relatively rural locations there was often still considerable damage.

The US and Canadian seismic maps on the following page show the locations where the earthquake risk is the highest. The darker gray scale areas are the most active and potentially dangerous. The biggest seismic risk areas are in proximity to the "ring of fire." This is

US Biggest Earthquakes			
Date	Area	Magnitude	Summary
1811 Dec. 16	New Madrid, MO	8.1	A series of 3 massive quakes about one month apart. Little loss of life. Shocks were felt through Eastern Cities and toppled chimneys in Boston. A similar quake with today's population would be devastating.
1857 Jan. 09	Fort Tejon, CA	7.9	Major damage to existing buildings.
1872 Mar. 26	Owens Valley, CA	7.8	Located south of the Sierra Nevada Mountains.
1868 Apr. 03	Big Island, HI	7.9	Relatively unpopulated area. Destroyed primitive buildings.
1892 Feb. 24	Imperial Valley, CA	7.8	Earth displaced horizontally some 15 feet for 40 miles along the fault. Few deaths, major damage.
1899 Sep. 04	Cape Yakataga, AK	8.2	Relatively unpopulated area. Destroyed primitive buildings.
1899 Sep. 07	Yakutat Bay, Alaska	8.2	Close proximity to the Yakataga earthquake.
1900 Oct. 09	Kodiak Island, Alaska	7.9	Knocked over chimneys, cracked windows.
1906 Apr. 18	San Francisco, CA	7.8	Most of city destroyed by fires after earthquake, over 300 died.
1915 Oct. 03	Pleasant Valley, NV	7.7	Quake formed an escarpment 22 miles long where the earth separated vertically up to 15 feet.
1927 Nov. 04	Lompoc, CA	7.3	Poorly built masonry walls toppled. Cornices and chimneys fell.
1938 Nov. 10	Shumagin Island, AK	8.3	Underwater earthquake. Tremors felt in Anchorage.
1964 Mar. 27	Ankorage AK	9.2	Quake took place at sea in Prince William Sound. Large land areas sunk up to 12-25 feet, damage to roads, buildings.
1965 Feb. 04	Rat Island, AK	8.7	Located in the far Aleutians.
1983 Oct. 28	Borah Peak, ID	7.3	Dramatic faulting, artesian water formed fountains. Significant damage to unreinforced masonry and block buildings.
1986 May. 07	Adreanof Island, AK	8	Near Adak, Aleutians.
1987 Nov. 30	Gulf of Alaska	7.9	At sea, produced significant tidal waves.
1989 Oct. 17	Loma Prieta, CA	7.1	South of SF. Called the World Series Quake. Extensive damage throughout San Francisco Area; freeway bridges collapsed.
1994 Jan. 17	Northridge California	6.7	Most costly US earthquake. Toppled elevated freeways and overpasses, and many "earthquake resistant" structures. A similar quake in the same area occurred in 1971 (M 6.6) in Sylmar, Ca.
2007 Dec. 19	Andreanof Islands, AK	7.2	Located in Aleutian Islands.
Source: USGS			

a line of volcanoes and seismic activity corresponding to the convergence of continental plates in the ocean off the western US coast and continuing northward near Alaska and under the Aleutian islands and eventually forming a great circle in the Pacific Ocean. The earthquakes that form offshore along this line can also produce tidal waves such as the damaging wave that hit the Alaskan coast and islands in 1964 following the "Great Alaskan Earthquake" on March 27th. Alaska is a very active earthquake zone.

From the map we see that the West Coast has the highest risk areas. Large quakes can also happen in the Mississippi Valley, although it does not have the dangerous fault lines like in western mountain ranges.

Seismic events in the East tend to follow the Appalachian Mountains but hazards are also spread out along the St. Lawrence Seaway into Canada. The Hawaii chain lies on a fairly active rift on the ocean floor, accounting for its volcanic and earthquake activity.

The maps show potential seismic ground acceleration (movement). The ratings compare the horizontal accelerations to the acceleration of gravity or "g". Thus on the US maps an area with 1.0 g could produce as much horizontal force as gravity itself, or to think of it another way, it's as if the foundation were tilted up to vertical. We recommend avoiding

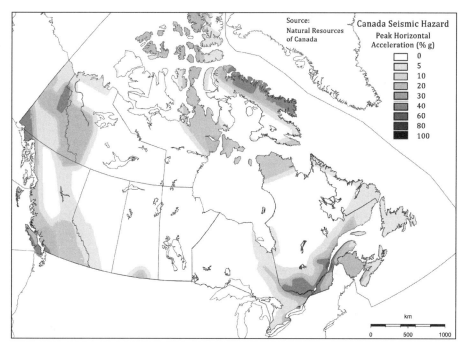

the very high seismic risk areas with horizontal accelerations of 80% "g" or higher. For a color version of the US map refer to the front of the color maps at the end of Section Four.

Many of our recommended areas are in moderate seismic areas but you can mitigate your risk to this threat if you:

1. Don't live or work in buildings or houses not specifically designed to sustain a strong quake.

2. Try to avoid living or working deep inside urban centers where it is difficult to get out after an earthquake.

3. Select a home with the most geologically safe soil as described in the earthquake primer in Section One.

4. Plan alternate routes if you commute on elevated roadways, bridges or overpasses that might become compromised or even collapse in an earthquake, so that you can still get home. Long, arching, spaghetti-bowl type freeway exchanges are the most vulnerable, followed by elevated highways crossing large bodies of water.

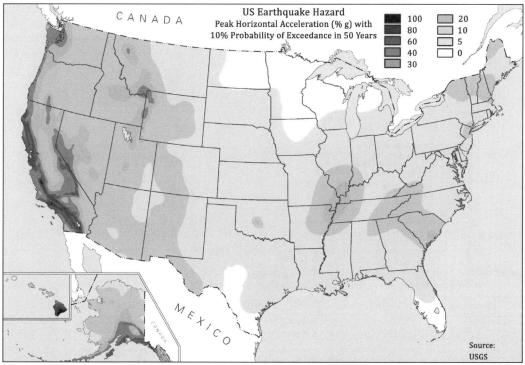

Volcanoes

North American volcanoes are mostly found along the west coast of the continental US, Canada and Alaska. Almost all the volcanoes in the Cascade Range of California, Oregon, and Washington are still potentially active, though dormant now. The most dangerous include: Lassen Peak (east of Redding, CA), Mount Jefferson, Mount Bachelor, Mount Hood, Mount St. Helens, Mount Baker, Mount Rainer and Mount Washington. Geologists have noted that the entire Sierra Nevada chain in California is occasionally alive with thousands of little tremors—called swarming. Lassen Peak is sure to blow its top someday. Mount Hood is always steaming. Mount St. Helens, the most recent erupting US volcano, is re-growing its dome and could erupt again. If Mount Rainier near Seattle

blows, it will be very devastating—not only because of ash fall, but because of the huge glaciers on its slopes. During an eruption these glaciers melt and send catastrophic flash floods down the slopes, devastating wide areas below—even in areas that would normally be protected from ash fall due to westerly winds.

Outside of the Cascades the most significant volcano threats are from the Long Valley Caldera near Mammoth Mountain in California and the caldera at the basin of Yellowstone National Park. Both of these geological depressions were formed from massive volcanic activity that caused mountains to form around the sides as the center collapsed into a sunken valley. Geological hot spots still exist under these areas as evidenced by geothermal heating, geysers, hot springs and earthquakes. The USGS monitors the seismic activity of these areas to watch for signs of further volcanic danger. We recommend staying at least 50 miles from these possible "super volcanoes" but the area of potential hazard could extend 100 miles away.

The following is a map of the most significant volcanoes for the US and Canada. As you can see, most volcanoes are along the western coast. Neither the US nor Canada has volcanic activity on the eastern side.

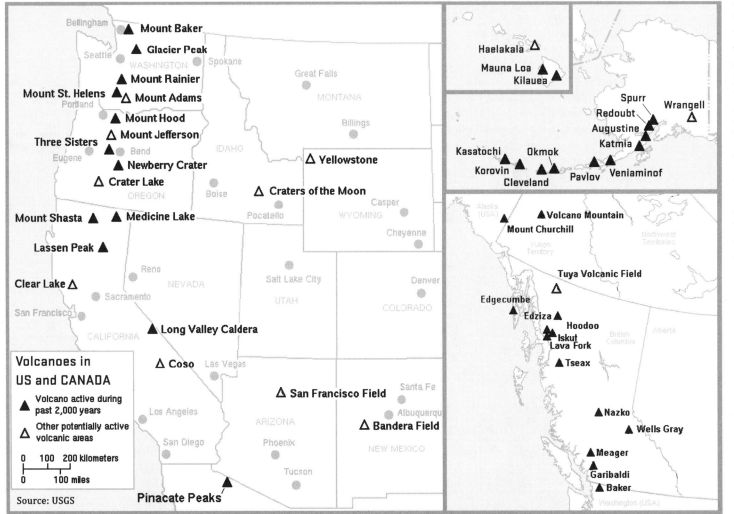

Chapter 8

FREEDOM AND POLITICS

The United States and Canada have historically provided some of the most personal freedoms for its citizens. Canada inherited a legal system that respects individual rights from Great Britain. The US had a unique governing system that established a representative government restricted by a constitution that specified limited powers to government and delegated the majority of power to the states while safeguarding individual rights by listing the most critical in the first 10 amendments.

In the rest of this chapter we will examine the differences in freedoms and characteristics of the states and provinces (where applicable). The powers vested in the states have been a dual-edged sword for freedom. Because the states have some autonomy in writing state law, one can compare between states and find those that offer the most freedom and the least onerous laws and taxes. We will compare factors like tax rates, property use restrictions and firearm ownership laws as a comparison with the rest of the country. Note that many of these factors are compiled for each individual state in the state summaries in Section Four. We will show you how these and other significant differences can help you relocate for greater freedom and security.

Liberty in the US

The restricting provisions of the US Constitution were not written in tight legal language and over time, the "elastic provisions" have been exploited to write or interpret laws in a way that undermines the original document. The most egregious recent instance is the idea that the "regulate interstate commerce" provision can justify national healthcare legislation.

Congress now violates many critical rights by taking away property and redistributing wealth, creating new government agencies that perform unwarranted searches and seizures and writing laws that undermine self-defense rights. The executive branch is engaging in foreign wars without a declaration of war and directing secret activities, torture and surveillance against foreign and US citizens alike. The legislative branch has repeatedly turned a blind eye to the constitution or has ruled against the original intent using creative interpretations. The legislative branch is the key to protecting the constitution by overruling bad laws and reigning in the executive.

Many encroachments on fundamental liberties are justified in the name of defending against terror. Since the attacks of September 11, 2001, several noteworthy cases involving citizens who the government claims are "terror suspects" or of assisting terror have

completely diminished our confidence in the US legal system. Most notably, the right of Habeas Corpus (show just cause for holding a prisoner), the right to a speedy trial and the right to be tried by an impartial jury have been denied. These cases show that the last bulwarks to personal freedom in the US can be overturned.

These actions have progressed so far in the US that we are sorry to conclude that the constitution is essentially dead. It can be discarded at will any time the government or judges determine it's necessary—or a matter of "national security." In our experience this excuse is often used to stop investigations into illegal activity by government agencies. Most of the limitations on government power by the constitution have been weakened or eliminated, although officials and judges keep paying lip service to it to maintain the illusion that it is still in force. For more information about this topic look at the "Philosophy on Law and Government" link at Joel's website (*www.joelskousen.com*).

Canadian Liberties

Sadly, Canada displays an equal disregard for citizen rights under the mantle of battling terror. Border crossing between the two countries is now an intrusive and delay-filled experience. In both countries, if one objects to questioning or abusive procedures, law enforcement immediately uses excessive force and treats a person as a criminal. Officials have overstated or even blatantly lied about people's conduct and demeanor in order to justify their abusive behavior. Airport searches are excessive, as in the US.

These losses of liberties are a serious threat to the traditional friendliness of Canada and the United States toward freedom. Sadly, there are no other countries that are not following the same path toward secrecy and tyranny.

Demographics

The freedoms and politics of a democratic nation are largely dependent on the makeup of the people in that country. Alexis de Tocqueville famously recognized the most important of these—that the greatness of America was dependent on the goodness and morality of the American people. We have found a steady downward trend in this area, but some regions are significantly better than others. Percentages of immigrants and political ideology can change the atmosphere of an area significantly. Let's look at these factors across the nation.

Moral, Religious Culture and People

Moral and cultural values are closely related to the influence of religion and a classical education focusing on libertarian thought and morality. Not all religions are equal, however, in promulgating their values and expecting their members to live them.

In both the US and Canada, the single largest factor keeping American religion vibrant is the rise of Christian Fundamentalism. Evangelical sects, although based upon the same general doctrines of the Protestant mainline churches, are much more concerned with spiritual action (not only to say, but to do according to the Word). These churches have often broken off from the hierarchical control of larger Protestant conferences. Their youth can better articulate values and address issues of controversy and doctrine. Missionary work and service are both actively supported by youth groups. Fundamentalist congregations tend to be smaller and less popular compared to the mainline congregations, and much less well funded than the televangelists and mega-churches (which people often attend for social status).

The rise of less accepted Christian sects (Mormons, Jehovah Witnesses and Seventh-Day Adventists) have also had an important impact on the nation's religiosity. Of these we see strategic value in locating near groups with good values. Mormons, in particular (now the fourth largest religion in America) are conservative politically, tend to hold their youth to high moral standards and believe in preparedness for hard times.

These values tend to provide a bulwark of safety in areas of the Intermountain West where they predominate. Most of these rural mountain valleys, including Utah (where Mormons are in the majority), are areas where conservative Evangelical Christians also thrive and this corresponds with good long-term safety. Having a base community of hardworking, religious people cannot be underestimated, even if you may not subscribe to any particular religion.

The Amish areas in the East are also desirable for reasons of self-sufficiency and healthy back-to-the-land attitudes. Unfortunately, the Amish communities are mostly found in or around the high population density areas of the eastern US and are not as safe in the long-term, despite the Amish presence.

Immigration Demographics

North America would also lose much of its wide open spaces if it had to find room for and maintain order for all the peoples of the world. This is one of the dangers in being a magnet for freedom and jobs. When coupled with a government that is intent upon allowing illegal immigration to flood its border areas, America is on the road to the same kind of social conflict found in Europe.

No nation can sustain rapid, uncontrolled growth, especially with masses of illegal immigrants of a different culture, and still maintain stability. Both Europe and America seem to be suffering under the same agenda of open borders promulgated by their respective governments.

Americans are rightly concerned about the penchant of both major political parties to entice millions of illegal immigrants to America by allowing them numerous job and welfare benefits. Regular offers of amnesty keep drawing them here as each tries to get inside before the next deadline.

Despite the supposed ever-present threat of terror (more provoked than real), and the current flood of illegal immigration, past and current administrations have refused to seal off America's porous southern border. It is almost as if the federal government keeps delaying and stalling any effective corrective means until mass cultural dilution of America is a "fait accompli."

There seems to be a perverse and hidden agenda to force multiculturalism down American's throats, just as in Europe. It is an evil goal that pits one culture against another in a race to get "their share" of government benefits. It also forms part of a dangerous globalist agenda—to justify forming a regional government such as a North American Union and create economic controls such as the euphemistically-named Free Trade Agreement of the Americas (FTAA).

Humanity doesn't deal well with large or rapid changes, or mixing of dissimilar cultures. Such circumstances all too often are so threatening that even normally free, liberty-loving people acquiesce to tyrannical government controls in the quest to sustain order. Unfortunately, these controls are difficult to dismantle after the crisis, especially when government wants those controls kept in place.

The top rating for a peaceful, pleasant people in North America must go to Canada, although it too has a growing problem with unwise immigration policies. The cities are generally cleaner than the US, and most people don't try to get ahead as fast. This lack of aggressiveness tends to make people more mellow and enjoyable. Canada is probably always going to be a little higher on the moral scale than the US for that reason.

Forced cultural diversity, however, could change much of Canada's advantage, especially in urban areas like Toronto and Vancouver where immigrants are pouring in. Unlike America, Canada has opened its doors to nations all over the world and thus has more potential problems with excessive diversity. Extreme diversity tends to produce a wide variety of cultural sinkholes or ghettos within a nation, which lead to gang membership and crime. Still, Canada, with the exception of the Quebec separatist extremists, has a more pleasant feel to it in most places.

US Voter Distribution

The states with the worst reputation for regulation and controls are those with large Democratic Party majorities. Although it's worth noting that some southern states where Democrats dominate are still fairly conservative in their support of family values. Interestingly enough, almost every state in the union is conservative in its rural districts and heavily liberal in its urban areas, where benefit-corrupted majorities dominate. In those states where the better part of the state's population resides in one metro area, rural voters get outvoted consistently. Oregon and Washington are prime examples of this constant 51%-49% split, making these states act extremely liberal when, in fact, liberals have only a narrow majority. But it's still enough to win almost every election.

The following maps show some of this graphically. The first map represents the percentage distribution of republican versus democratic voters in the 2008 presidential election by county. The second map shows the voter switch during the 2010 mid-term election when disapproval of democrats was high. Note the areas of strong, democratic voters, even in 2010 and the areas that can switch by comparing the maps. Note that this does not accurately show the numbers of voters. Urban areas and cities have many more voters in their small areas. Rural conservative areas have much fewer voters spread out over large areas.

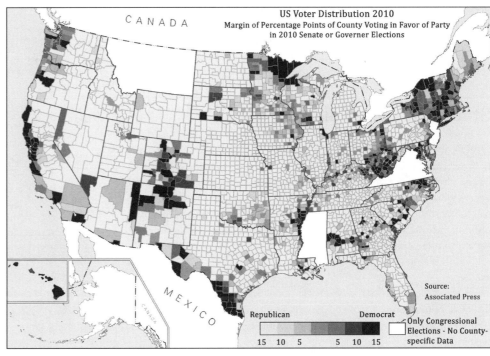

A prime factor that affects voter distribution is the presence of a large, liberal newspaper that dominates every urban area, and therefore affects a good share of public opinion. Here are some examples of liberal and highly regulatory states together with large-circulation liberal newspapers:

- Boston, MA / Boston Globe
- New York City, NY / New York Times
- District of Columbia / Washington Post
- Chicago, IL / Chicago Herald-Tribune
- Denver, CO / Denver Post
- Dallas, TX / Dallas Morning News
- Portland, OR / Oregonian
- Seattle, WA / Seattle Post-Intelligencer
- San Francisco, CA / SF Chronicle
- Los Angeles, CA / LA Times
- San Diego, CA / San Diego Union-Tribune

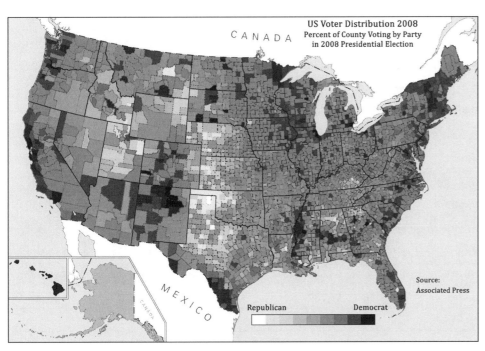

If you have to live in these states and metro areas, be prepared to endure a constant barrage of left-liberal misinformation that will influence local opinion and reflect in state politics. The same thing occurs in Canada — all the major cities of Vancouver, Toronto, Ottawa, Montreal and Quebec are controlled by liberal newspapers.

State Taxes and Spending

Overall, we've found the tax burden in the US is high but still significantly lower than in Canada and Europe. The federal government takes the largest chunk of personal income ranging from 10 to 35 percent. Social Security tax takes another 15% and the state's tax burden adds another 7 to 10.5 percent. Each state raises money differently and thus, depending on your income type and amount, may provide a significantly different tax amount depending on where you live.

State Tax Rates

The Tax Foundation, a policy research group, developed the information we display in the average tax burden table for individuals from each state in 2011.

This table takes the total state revenue and divides it by the total resident's income. However, unlike many such tables it accounts for state income from taxes on natural resources and taxes paid by out-of-state visitors. The "Taxes Paid to Other States" column accounts for taxes collected out of state, such as Alaska and Wyoming taxes on oil and gas that is paid by consumers around the country. Another example is tourist taxes such as hotel taxes or car rental taxes.

Note that these are still average numbers and could be different for you depending on your sources of income. County and local tax rates can also dramatically affect your tax burden. For example, according to a report by the city government of Washington DC (*cfo.dc.gov*) local taxes on a family of three earning $50,000 annually vary from 4.4% in Cheyenne, WY to over 20% in Bridgeport, CT.

Alaska rates as a low-tax state on this list since it has neither an income tax nor a sales tax. Most of its revenue comes from oil and gas taxes, but Alaskan citizens do experience high property taxes and local government licensing fees. Property values in Fairbanks and Anchorage have increased to around 250k on average, making property taxes quite a shock to low-tax

State	Rate	Rank (1 is highest burden)	Per Capita Taxes Paid to Home State	Per Capita Taxes Paid to Other States	Total State and Local Per Capita Taxes Paid	Per Capita Income
U.S.	9.80%		$3,064	$1,152	$4,217	$42,473
Ala.	8.30%	41	$1,926	$961	$2,886	$34,763
Alaska	7.00%	49	$2,109	$1,210	$3,319	$47,354
Ariz.	8.5%	41	$2,170	$1,074	$3,244	$38,174
Ark.	10.30%	12	$2,484	$921	$3,405	$33,182
Calif.	11.40%	4	$4,075	$1,061	$5,136	$45,254
Colo.	9.00%	32	$2,916	$1,303	$4,220	$46,767
Conn.	11.90%	3	$4,885	$2,264	$7,150	$60,287
Del.	10.10%	15	$2,467	$1,741	$4,209	$41,521
Fla.	9.20%	31	$2,471	$1,228	$3,699	$40,296
Ga.	8.80%	35	$2,251	$985	$3,237	$36,611
Hawaii	9.60%	20	$3,160	$1,100	$4,259	$44,255
Idaho	9.50%	24	$2,157	$1,032	$3,189	$33,741
Ill.	10.20%	13	$3,458	$1,200	$4,658	$45,664
Ind.	9.50%	22	$2,430	$955	$3,385	$35,592
Iowa	9.30%	29	$2,639	$1,101	$3,740	$40,147
Kans.	9.40%	26	$2,566	$1,283	$3,849	$40,913
Ky.	9.50%	23	$2,291	$877	$3,169	$33,435
La.	7.60%	46	$1,883	$989	$2,872	$37,889
Maine	10.20%	14	$2,801	$1,035	$3,836	$37,701
Md.	10.60%	7	$4,077	$1,520	$5,598	$52,805
Mass.	10.30%	11	$4,002	$1,584	$5,586	$54,321
Mich.	9.60%	21	$2,616	$890	$3,505	$36,641
Minn.	10.70%	6	$3,687	$1,171	$4,858	$45,552
Miss.	8.40%	40	$1,782	$838	$2,620	$31,067

Source: www.taxfoundation.org

State	Rate	Rank (1 is highest burden)	Per Capita Taxes Paid to Home State	Per Capita Taxes Paid to Other States	Total State and Local Per Capita Taxes Paid	Per Capita Income
Mo.	9.00%	33	$2,298	$1,081	$3,380	$37,651
Mont.	8.60%	38	$1,994	$1,143	$3,137	$36,407
Nebr.	9.40%	25	$2,775	$1,216	$3,991	$42,281
Nev.	8.10%	43	$1,957	$1,263	$3,221	$39,947
N.H.	8.00%	44	$2,093	$1,677	$3,769	$47,349
N.J.	12.30%	2	$4,659	$2,017	$6,675	$54,422
N.M.	8.60%	37	$2,089	$955	$3,044	$35,328
N.Y.	12.60%	1	$5,258	$1,364	$6,622	$52,417
N.C.	9.80%	17	$2,621	$943	$3,564	$36,195
N.D.	8.80%	36	$2,688	$1,369	$4,057	$46,218
Ohio	9.70%	18	$2,777	$911	$3,687	$38,073
Okla.	8.50%	39	$2,143	$1,044	$3,187	$37,617
Ore.	10.10%	16	$2,838	$1,023	$3,861	$38,219
Pa.	10.30%	10	$3,224	$1,150	$4,374	$42,268
R.I.	10.50%	8	$3,223	$1,452	$4,676	$44,367
S.C.	8.30%	42	$1,868	$916	$2,784	$33,603
S.D.	7.10%	48	$1,700	$1,352	$3,052	$43,212
Tenn.	7.60%	45	$1,835	$942	$2,777	$36,525
Tex.	7.50%	47	$2,109	$979	$3,088	$41,269
Utah	9.40%	28	$2,287	$1,017	$3,304	$35,224
Vt.	10.50%	9	$3,028	$1,323	$4,351	$41,634
Va.	9.20%	30	$3,112	$1,357	$4,469	$48,498
Wash.	9.40%	27	$3,116	$1,250	$4,366	$46,456
W.Va.	9.70%	19	$2,297	$863	$3,160	$32,708
Wis.	11.00%	5	$3,387	$1,089	$4,477	$40,741
Wyo.	6.90%	50	$1,638	$1,862	$3,500	$50,805
D.C.	9.7%	(20)	$4,394	$2,247	$6,641	$68,795

Source: www.taxfoundation.org

seekers. Only if you live in rural Alaska and away from local government restrictions, can you get truly low state taxes.

Wyoming consistently ranks among the lowest states in individual tax burdens because most of its revenue comes from natural resources.

Useful Tax Strategies

Income tax: The best way to find lower taxes is to pick places where the types of taxes they collect are primarily in areas that don't correlate to your income or spending patterns. Don't move to a no-income tax state until you see where the state does collect its taxes, and compare that with your assets and spending patterns. If you have a high income independent of your location, by all means pick a no income tax state like Washington, Wyoming, South Dakota, Nevada, Texas, New Hampshire or Tennessee. All of these have some good relocation sites. Florida also has no income tax but is not a recommended state for relocation. New Hampshire and Tennessee only tax income derived from dividends and interest.

Sales tax: If you have a low income you may not mind living in a state with an income tax. Take a tax break by picking a state with no sales tax like Oregon, Montana and New Hampshire. Delaware and Alaska don't have state sales taxes either but are not recommended due to the high cost of living. Sometimes buying on the internet can get around sales taxes, but shipping costs often negate this benefit.

Investment taxes: If you have a large investment portfolio, avoid states like Florida that tax "intangible personal property" (Stocks and bonds). Tennessee and New Hampshire extract taxes on interest and dividends. Many states don't tax interest on state-issued bonds.

Property taxes: If you live in a state that levies a high tax on houses, buy a modest home—it's good for keeping a low profile. Put your money into good self-sufficiency equipment and pleasing interior décor. These items are very rarely taxed. Check property tax rates in surrounding counties or nearby states to your ideal location. Sometimes it is worth a little travel as a compromise. Be aware of different appraisal methods. Some counties automatically adjust the appraised amount upward every year. This might affect the bottom line more than a percentage comparison between states.

Playing the Border Advantage

The secret to avoiding sales and income taxes is to live in a no income tax state that borders a state with no sales tax. This occurs in MT/WY/SD, and WA/OR/ID. Many people choose to live in Washington, a no-income-tax state, near the Oregon border. They drive into Oregon to do most of their shopping without sales taxes and still live in a no-income tax state. This advantage only works for those working and living in Washington. Oregon law collects income taxes on anyone employed in Oregon, even if they live in Washington.

Likewise, there is no sales tax in Montana, and no income tax in Wyoming and South Dakota. New Hampshire has no income tax and no sales tax so you get both living there, but property taxes are almost double the national average. So, if you are self-employed in the Boston market, consider commuting to New Hampshire, you'll have a relative tax haven.

Canadian Taxes

Canada's burgeoning welfare state is taking a big bite out of Canadians' incomes. Canada's tax rates are even worse than those of the US. Canada's federal tax has four major tax brackets: 15% up to $45K, 20.5% on $45K-$91K, 26% on $91K-140K and 29% on $140K-200K, 33% on everything else. There is a universal sales tax called a "Goods and Service Tax" (GST) which is 5% everywhere. Add to this 15% to 30% for province and local sales taxes and you have a hefty tax burden to shoulder. Only four provinces have no provincial sales tax. Nova Scotia, New Brunswick, Newfoundland and Labrador have merged the GST with their sales taxes.

The following table shows tax variations across Canada. Note that these numbers do not reflect other forms of taxation such as property taxes or federal income tax.

Canada Province and Territory Tax Rates 2016

Provinces / Territories	Income Tax Rate(s) (Canadian Dollars)	GST + Prov. Sales Tax	Approx. Tax on $100K
Newfoundland and Labrador	Five tax brackets from 7.7% on first $335K to 15.3% on the amount over $175K	13%	33%
Prince Edward Island	Three tax brackets from 9.8% on first $32K to 16.7% on the amount over $64K	14%	35.4%
Nova Scotia	five tax brackets from 8.79% on the first $30K to 21% on the amount over $150K	15%	35.7%

Canada Province and Territory Tax Rates 2016

Provinces / Territories	Income Tax Rate(s)	GST + Prov. Sales Tax	Approx.: Tax on $100K
New Brunswick	Six tax brackets from 9.68% on first $40K to 25.75% on the amount over $250K	13%	34.7%
Quebec	Four tax brackets from 16% on first $42.4K up to 25.75% on the amount over $103K	14.975%	36.3%
Ontario	Five tax brackets from 5.05% on the first $41.5K to13.6% on over $220K	13%	31.1%
Manitoba	10.8% on the first $31K, + 12.75% on the next $36K, + 17.4% on the amount over $67K	13%	35%
Saskatchewan	11% on the first $44.6K, + 13% on the next $82.8K, + 15% on the amount over $127.4K	10%	33%
Alberta	Five tax brackets from 10% on first $125K to 15% on amount over $300K	5%	31%
British Columbia	Five tax brackets from 5.06% on the first $38.2K to 14.7% on the amount over $106.5K	12%	30%
Yukon	Five tax brackets from 6.4% on the first $45.3 to 15% on the amount over $500K	5%	29.8%
Northwest Territories	Four tax brackets from 5.9% on the first $41K to 14.05% on the amount over $133K	5%	30%
Nunavut	4% on the first $43.2K, + 7% on the next $43.2K, + 9% on the next $54K, + 11.5% on the amount over $140.4K	5%	28%

Source: http://www.cra-arc.gc.ca/tx/ndvdls/fq/txrts-eng.html, Wikipedia

State Spending

The more revenue governments collect, the more they spend. States that have low populations and few resources are forced to economize on expenditures, as do states with a high percentage of low-income residents. The poorer the state, the less the legislature can extract from the people in taxes. States like Alaska and Wyoming with large revenue sources from energy taxes can spend more without taxing.

Canada's provinces have some of the same imbalances in income as do the states. For example, Alberta's spending is 40 percent higher than Ontario, 30 percent higher than British Columbia and 15 percent higher than the average in the other nine provinces, but its revenue from oil is much higher as well.

Welfare Spending

State welfare spending is important because it represents how much grip the benefit-corrupted welfare society has on a state legislature. We recommend avoiding states that rank high on welfare expenditures. It is not a sign of compassion but of willingness to corrupt society by taking from the productive class by force. Ultimately welfare states will have to cut benefits or go broke since "needs" always exceed what productive people can be taxed.

Canada is a social welfare state much like Europe. However, as a confederation of provinces, the welfare burden falls upon each province and there is considerable disparity between the ability of each province to provide funding for the federally mandated programs. The Canadian government has numerous avenues for subsidizing welfare and equalizing benefit payments where poorer provinces are deficient but this is constant source of contention in the country.

Property Rights

The ultimate right to control your own property is one of the most significant areas in law where Americans have lost ground in the past 100 years. Due to the advent of zoning laws and building codes, and now through the intrusion of eminent domain takings by government, property owners find themselves increasingly restricted on what they can do with "their" property, or whether their property is at risk for confiscation to benefit someone else's private development scheme. We expect many of our readers who are relocating will want to build a new home or relocate a business. We recommend looking into the regulatory atmosphere at the local level of the city or county where you want to reside. Our state-summaries section has some building code information for each state, but we cannot cover this level of detail for every county. Here are the general categories to consider:

State Spending 2013

State	Spending Per Capita	Rank	State	Spending Per Capita	Rank
U.S.	$4,795	–	Montana	$5,621	15
Alabama	$4,498	34	Nebraska	$4,125	41
Alaska	$13,808	1	Nevada	$3,247	49
Arizona	$3,583	47	New Hampshire	$4,627	33
Arkansas	$4,930	26	New Jersey	$6,316	11
California	$4,907	27	New Mexico	$6,086	12
Colorado	$4,260	39	New York	$6,491	10
Connecticut	$6,781	7	North Carolina	$4,109	42
Delaware	$7,972	3	North Dakota	$6,603	9
Florida	$3,196	50	Ohio	$5,165	21
Georgia	$3,515	48	Oklahoma	$4,855	29
Hawaii	$7,991	2	Oregon	$5,437	18
Idaho	$4,060	44	Pennsylvania	$5,374	19
Illinois	$4,638	32	Rhode Island	$6,666	8
Indiana	$4,186	40	South Carolina	$4,780	30
Iowa	$5,096	23	South Dakota	$4,421	36
Kansas	$4,277	38	Tennessee	$3,619	46
Kentucky	$5,476	17	Texas	$3,674	45
Louisiana	$5,575	16	Utah	$4,737	31
Maine	$5,804	14	Vermont	$7,202	4
Maryland	$5,208	20	Virginia	$4,398	37
Massachusetts	$7,061	6	Washington	$5,155	2
Michigan	$4,433	35	West Virginia	$5,809	13
Minnesota	$4,975	25	Wisconsin	$4,855	28
Mississippi	$5,031	24	Wyoming	$7,123	5
Missouri	$4,084	43			

Source: usgovernmentspending.com.

State and Local Welfare Spending 2013

Rank	State	Public welfare spending per capita	Rank	State	Public welfare spending per capita
1	Alaska	$1,543	26	Montana	$637
2	California	$1,199	27	North Dakota	$634
3	New York	$1,193	28	South Dakota	$570
4	Massachusetts	$1,156	29	Virginia	$565
5	Connecticut	$1,054	30	Wyoming	$557
6	New Jersey	$1,051	31	Kentucky	$551
7	Rhode Island	$977	32	Louisiana	$542
8	Pennsylvania	$928	33	Indiana	$532
9	Maryland	$889	34	Utah	$521
10	Vermont	$882	35	Tennessee	$514
11	Minnesota	$848	36	West Virginia	$508
12	Oregon	$845	37	Oklahoma	$497
13	Ohio	$830	38	Iowa	$493
14	Maine	$808	39	Arkansas	$493
15	Illinois	$807	40	New Mexico	$448
16	Delaware	$768	41	Florida	$446
17	Wisconsin	$762	42	Idaho	$442
18	Washington	$747	43	Georgia	$442
19	Nebraska	$707	44	Arizona	$423
20	Hawaii	$703	45	Mississippi	$419
21	New Hampshire	$692	46	Kansas	$408
22	Nevada	$677	47	Missouri	$405
23	Michigan	$672	48	Texas	$382
24	Colorado	$640	49	South Carolina	$348
25	North Carolina	$638	50	Alabama	$325
State Average $740					

Source: www.usgovernmentspending.com

Zoning and Planning Commissions

Avoid states that mandate zoning criteria at the state level. This is indicative of a state's propensity to control its citizen's free use of property. In Oregon, which started this process, state mandates create a great deal of hardship and controversy for rural cities and counties, which used to have the ability to modify zoning for local needs. Fighting zoning battles at the state level is too costly for the lay person. Once state zoning powers get started there is no stopping them. In today's atmosphere of worshipping everything "green" it is almost impossible to repeal bad environmental protection once enacted. The new watchword for comprehensive, state-mandated zoning is "smart growth." Don't fall for its euphemistic appeal.

Avoid communities that are changing the zoning statutes. Suppose you buy a piece of commercial property and before you can develop it or sell it, they reclassify it as a residential zone. Now, you can't use it for what you purchased it for, and you may not be able to recoup the premium price you paid because it is worth less now.

Talk to developers and contractors to see if there is a general atmosphere of reasonableness in city planning officials. Avoid cities that are in the habit of writing intrusive and arbitrary "architectural standards" into zoning laws that dictate the "look" of new construction. Even if you agree with the architectural standards, it's dangerous to build in a city that usurps the authority over the aesthetic appearance of private property. The only proper role of governments is to protect neighbors from true harm or legal nuisances (smoke, traffic, noise, hazards) caused by other developments or uses. Once planning bodies start dictating colors and styles, you don't have any real property rights anymore. Look elsewhere.

Building Codes

Most states dictate some or all of the building code requirements for new construction and then local jurisdictions usually add restrictions on top of these. Building permits are hardest to obtain in or around big cities. Local jurisdictions, particularly in New York and California, can be very onerous and will even require a permit for building a shed or changing kitchen appliances. There are still counties out there with few restrictions. Everyone requires a new construction permit, but sometimes this only entails permitting the septic system. We have found *www.cityapplications.com* has general summaries of state building permit requirements, but a call to a local jurisdiction can also be very informative. They are usually very willing to explain their requirements.

Eminent Domain Laws

Eminent domain laws are also a threat to your property rights ever since the US Supreme Court (*Kelo v. New London*) improperly held that local governments could take other people's property and sell it to private developers as long as there was a "general public purpose." It used to be that it took a very specific government purpose like military bases or roads to justify an involuntary taking.

Some states have recently passed laws prohibiting the implementation of the Kelo decision. Some of these laws protect property rights better than others. An important aspect that needs to be carefully defined surrounds the state taking property because of "blight" or aesthetic reasons. Often this loophole allows states to force the sale of land to a private party. The Institute for Justice, a libertarian institution dedicated to championing rights and fighting bad law, published the grading system of the eminent domain laws of each state shown in the table below.

Environmental Protection Laws

It is the proper role of government to keep others from producing pollutants that would be significantly harmful to others who have not agreed to be subject to those health risks. But the science of determining how much is harmful, in what dosages and over what period of time is not precise. There must be a balance between low levels of harm and the costs involved in eradicating the problem. The world is presently heading in the direction of excessive environmental regulation. Laws involving minor endangered species, ozone depletion and global warming are, for the most part, based upon bogus science and a political agenda to control property and energy production in the name of preserving the environment. In our analysis, most environmentalists are not part of this agenda, but a cadre of top environmental leaders is part of this scheme as are the political and corporate leaders who fund them.

Environmental regulation is an area where virtually all nations are being steamrolled into submission by several scenarios of environmental catastrophe, such as global warming. Both the US and Canada burden their own people with massive regulations requiring very costly engineering changes in all types of consumer and industrial equipment for energy production. The debatable ban on Freon in air-conditioning systems was absorbed without too much economic damage, but "cap and trade" schemes to restrict a naturally-occurring emission such as carbon dioxide will be a costly disaster.

US Eminent Domain Comparison			
Grades of States that Passed		**Grades of States that Failed**	
Florida	A	Idaho	D+
North Dakota	A	Illinois	D+
South Dakota	A	Kentucky	D+
Virginia	A	Maine	D+
New Mexico	A-	Nebraska	D+
Michigan	A-	Alaska	D
Arizona	B+	Connecticut	D
Delaware	B+	Maryland	D
Georgia	B+	Missouri	D
Nevada	B+	Montana	D
New Hampshire	B+	Ohio	D
Oregon	B+	California	D/F
South Carolina	B+	Rhode Island	D-
Alabama	B+	Tennessee	D-
Mississippi	B+	Vermont	D-

US Eminent Domain Comparison			
Grades of States that Passed		**Grades of States that Failed**	
Kansas	B	Arkansas	F
Louisiana	B	Hawaii	F
Utah	B	Massachusetts	F
Wyoming	B	Mississippi	F
Minnesota	B	New Jersey	F
Indiana	B	New York	F
Pennsylvania	B	Oklahoma	F
Iowa	B-		
Texas	B-		
Wisconsin	C+		
North Carolina	C-		
Colorado	C-		
Washington	C-		
West Virginia	C-		
States received an "F" for failing to pass any degree of eminent domain reform.			
Source: www.castlecoalition.org			

All countries are on this bandwagon, so there seems to be no way to relocate around it. But some states are worse than others. The worst state for environmental regulations in the US is California. Every radical, excessive, and industry-killing environmental initiative seems to start in this state. For example, restrictions on diesel fuel emissions became so tight that the whole US vehicle industry was forced to make changes to their exhaust systems (rather than make California-specific models). European standards would have been sufficient, and could have allowed car manufactures to import more "clean diesel" vehicles to the US. As it is, few are willing to take the risk of bringing new diesels to America because of these requirements.

Firearm Rights

When all competent citizens have the right to possess and use personal arms for self-defense, it provides the most effective defense against a criminal aggressor when police are not readily available—which is almost always the case. Simply put, a criminal's greatest advantage is when no one is available to deter his aggression with force and this is eliminated by the armed homeowner or businessman with an effective weapon. Indeed, criminals go out of their way to target subjects who they view are least likely to be armed and in areas with long police response times. Allowing citizens to conceal their weapons is important so thugs don't know who is and who isn't carrying a defensive weapon. The threat of prosecution after the fact is hardly a deterrent to hardened criminals, but the fear of meeting an armed citizen truly is.

Only an armed citizenry can provide the deterrence necessary to truly reduce violent crime. In fact, it is interesting to track the rapid decline of violent crime in virtually every jurisdiction that has encouraged and implemented the right to carry concealed weapons for personal defense.

The second reason for private arms is not often considered but it is critical for long term security. The founders of the US Constitution recognized that only citizens bearing arms can deter government tyranny and aggression. There is not a single tyrannical government that has come to power without first disarming the civilian populace. This was also the primary reason, beyond the helping hand of God, that Americans won the revolutionary war against Britain: they didn't have to rely on a formal army. The Americans could muster a volunteer militia on their own, using local citizens and private weapons.

Ultimately, you can't avoid all crime and we recommend obtaining and learning to use a firearm for self-defense. Owning a firearm isn't practical unless you have it when you need it, so get a concealed weapons permit. We cover each state's gun laws in Section Four. A state's allowance for or restriction of private concealed weapons is a key element

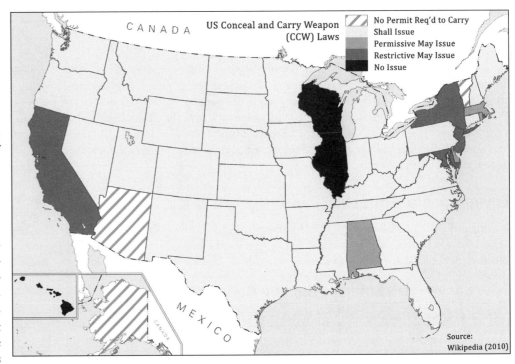

in choosing a safe state. We recommend relocating only to a state that allows conceal and carry weapon (CCW) permits and where states "shall-issue" the permit if you meet the qualifications. "May Issue" states can arbitrarily deny your right even if qualified. The few states that still don't allow concealed carry by permit also restrict firearms in other ways that affect your safety. The allowance in a state for concealed carry permits is a big deterrent to crime. Florida crime rates dropped significantly when they started issuing permits to carry a concealed weapon.

Low Regulation States

These are becoming harder and harder to find. The worst thing that happened to individuality in state governments was the national and regional conferences for governors and state bureaucrats. They get together regularly and share ideas about the latest regulatory scheme that is working for them and other states rapidly follow the latest fad.

New York has long been the leader in intrusive regulations, but California now leads in many ways. California, however, has often had to back down because of backlash from frustrated residents. California has pushed people so far toward the extremes of people control and high taxation to pay for it, that people are lashing back at the state. Who would have thought that high-taxing California would eventually approve the strongest

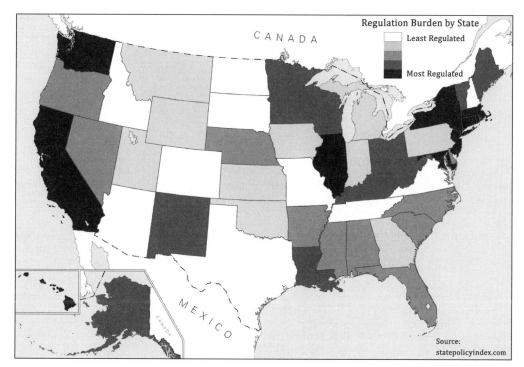

Regulation Burden by State
Least Regulated
Most Regulated

CANADA

MEXICO

CANADA

Source: statepolicyindex.com

Other states that have no safety inspection requirements or state-wide emissions requirements are:

- Alabama (only upon sale or transfer)
- Arkansas
- Florida
- Iowa
- Kansas
- Kentucky
- Maryland (only upon sale or transfer)
- Michigan
- Minnesota
- Montana
- Nebraska (only safety inspection when bringing car from out of state)
- North Dakota
- Oklahoma
- South Carolina
- South Dakota
- Wyoming

of all property tax limitations? Who would have thought that their radical affirmative action injustices would finally set the stage for a partial rebellion? Sadly, the bureaucrats are learning to get around tax limitations, and the courts are undoing voter-approved legislation against state regulatory tyranny, so it is eroding fast. But it does demonstrate that even with the highest levels of power politics in the world, government controllers still have to fear popular backlash.

There is another side to the conformity among state trends. Certain states have steadily exhibited a stubbornness to change and conform to what other states do. Incredibly, Oregon continues to outlaw pumping your own gas, under the mistaken notion that they are saving jobs. They need an economics lesson on how a forced diversion of consumer funds to one area always inhibits their beneficial use in another. On the positive side, Oregon still doesn't have a mandatory vehicle safety inspection, with no higher accident rate based on mechanical failures. Oregonians also refuse to implement a sales tax—although their leaders keep pushing them toward this alternate means of additional taxation. Many Oregonians still remember getting pushed into the income tax trap under the siren call of "support education with a small tax" that grew into a monster tax (like the national income tax).

The rest of the states require either an annual or biannual safety inspection. Some allow for new cars to be exempt for the first few years. Emission tests are usually limited to counties with large urban cities.

A website dedicated to representing the various ways states enact limitations is at *www.statepolicyindex.com* where each state policy (taxes, spending, property rights, gun rights, etc.) is given a weight and tallied up for combined comparison with other states. The map below shows a visual comparison of this index. The lighter shades are less regulated states.

Your local standard of living is dependent on thousands of factors related to your surroundings, your own lifestyle and preferences and those of the people around you. Many people see these as the most significant factors for relocation, but they pale in light of the bigger threats we see in the long-term. Fortunately the most critical factors for quality of life can be found in safer areas. Here are the most important criteria from our point of view.

Chapter 9

CRIME, HEALTH AND QUALITY OF LIFE

Crime

Crime is like a localized natural disaster affecting the victims. It is always worst in high density urban areas. Crime in sparsely populated areas is usually limited to more moderate property crimes, although the recent inroads of meth labs into rural areas is changing that somewhat. In our analysis, crime is locally bred. Here are some of the factors we see affecting crime.

Trends and Patterns Affecting Crime

In our research, we have noticed four general factors that affect an area's crime potential: population density, household income, minority composition and political leaning. One factor alone is usually not enough to indicate high crime, but two or more are sufficient.

The following table shows the ten highest and ten lowest crime cities in the US, rated according to crimes committed per person. We also show demographic factors for each city to look for general trends that affect crime.

Let's look at why these factors might affect crime.

10 Low Crime Cities in US					
(Population Over 50,000)	Population / pop. Density	Income	% Black	% Hisp.	% Vote Rep in '08
Clay, NY	59K/1225	$62.5K	3.4	1.4	39
Greenwich, CT	62K/1304	$128.4K	1.6	6.3	41
Rancho Santa Margarita, CA	50K/4030	$100.2K	1.5	14.9	51
Laguna Niguel, CA	65K/4411	$103.0K	1.4	10.7	51
Ramapo, NY	113K/1892	$75.8K	16.5	8.2	47
Flower Mound, TX	66K/1717	$116.0K	3.1	10.8	62
Mission Viejo, CA	95K/5073	$93.3K	1.5	16.7	51
Orland Park, IL	56K/2886	$80.3K	0.5	8	23
Naperville, IL	143K/4061	$101.9K	3.7	14.6	44
Yorba Linda, CA	65K/3414	$126.0K	2.3	11	51
Average	**77K/3001**	**$98.7K**	**4**	**10**	**46**
Sources: City-data.com (top 101 cities list) and Census Bureau					

10 High Crime Cities in US					
(Population Over 5,000)	Population / pop. Density	Income	% Black	% Hisp	% Vote Rep in '08
East St. Louis, IL	29K/2046	$26.1K	97.7	0.7	38
Hammond, LA	19K/1553	$33.9K	45.2	1.6	65
South Tucson, AZ	6K/5966	$18.5K	2.3	81.2	47
Florida City, FL	9K/3086	$18.3K	56.7	32.1	42
St. Louis, MO	347K/5723	$22.9K	51.2	2	50
Anniston, AL	24K/521	$34.5K	48.7	1.7	66
Tukwila, WA	17K/1917	$53.8K	12.8	13.6	28
Hartsville, SC	7K/1499	$32.4K	42.5	0.8	50
Morrow, GA	5K/1880	$50.6K	36.1	6	17
Riviera Beach, FL	36K/4371	$37.6K	67.8	4.5	38
Average	**50K/2856**	**$32.9K**	**46**	**14**	**44**
Sources: City-data.com (top 101 cities list) and Census Bureau					

Population density: Cities with smaller populations distributed over wide areas are almost universally low in crime. Small towns don't invite professional criminals without the presence of modern upscale subdivisions or resorts. Smaller populations also make it harder for outside criminals to blend in where people know who their neighbors are. As population density increases, crime also increases. This relationship is not always proportional. To see some of the other factors, we chose low-crime cities with relatively large populations (50,000 and above) for our table. These are also the cities that are better for strategic relocation. For the 10 high crime cities in our table we limited it to population areas of 5,000 people or more so that we could zoom in on the data and factors for crime. For example, the larger Palm Beach area in Florida has generally higher crime, but Riviera Beach, specifically, has the highest crime within that area, so we focused on the factors there.

Estimated Average Household income: This factor alone does not lead to high crime, as many small town and farm communities have very low incomes, but its effect is significant when combined with high population density or any of the factors below.

Minority composition: While it is not politically correct to discuss racial demographics in general, most people recognize this as a significant factor for crime. From our list this factor was more common than any other in the high crime cities, whereas only one of the low crime cities have Black or Hispanic percentages over 10% of the population. We show here visual representations of these factors nationwide. Most maps show the variation by county so remember that the percentage is usually concentrated in the city not throughout the county area shown.

Political leaning: This factor is not as directly correlated as those above, but we believe it is a factor. Welfare policies in large urban areas tend to attract dysfunctional families, which produce the majority of problem children. Union oriented labor areas are usually centered around big cities and draw people that believe government owes them benefits or at least ought to intervene to make sure they get "their share" of the productive pie. Deserved or not, the Democratic Party has the reputation of delivering more benefits than Republicans. This factor has become somewhat less reliable now that most Republicans also vote and campaign for benefits.

Neighborhood factors: State or national crime statistics are only relevant to the general area. All crime is local as far as it directly affects your safety. Except for violent crime that targets you specifically (someone trying to murder you), crime is a matter of opportunity and location--such as being in the wrong part of town. Virtually all major cities have high crime areas and safe areas. Find out where the bad areas are and avoid them. If you want to move to Nashville, for example, the overall crime rate doesn't do you much good. You want to know where the specific areas are that have high crime. There are websites that show crime specific to area within a city or zip code (e.g. *http://www.neighborhoodscout.com*).

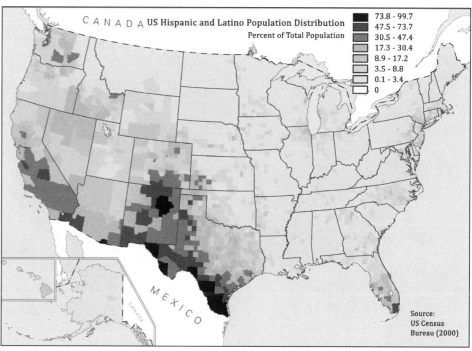

There is much euphoria in the media about the downturn in crime statistics across the United States. But this seems surprising. First and foremost, none of the following fundamentals of human action that breed crime have changed:

- Permissiveness in the home
- Bad influences and little discipline at public schools
- Exposure to increasingly corrupt morals in television and movies
- Judges and leaders who refuse to apply effective deterrents throughout the judicial system
- Use of drugs and alcohol that lead to criminal behavior to pay for these vices
- Gangs that prey on people as a matter of challenge and habit

So how do we explain the lower numbers? Criminal statistics have always been unreliable since it is generally left up to individual reporting units to decide what and how crimes are reported. For years, there was a great discrepancy between police units that were reporting honestly and those who were fudging things in order to make someone at the top look good. The result, sadly, was that honest police chiefs in problem areas were increasingly made to look bad, while corrupt cities were looking better, statistically. Anywhere a governor or mayor makes a big issue out of crime and spends a lot of taxpayer funds to control it there is a lot of pressure to make it appear successful. To a large degree, it seems

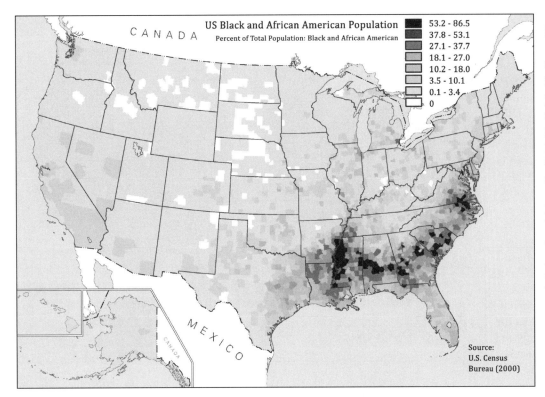

US Black and African American Population
Percent of Total Population: Black and African American

■	53.2 - 86.5
■	37.8 - 53.1
■	27.1 - 37.7
■	18.1 - 27.0
■	10.2 - 18.0
■	3.5 - 10.1
■	0.1 - 3.4
□	0

Source:
U.S. Census
Bureau (2000)

Crime in Canada

Canada has a lower crime rate compared to the US across the board. But it still has the same problem of crimes being concentrated in large metropolitan areas, especially where immigrant gangs predominate. As a group, native-born Canadians are less prone to violence than most Americans, partly because corrupted elements of society don't like harsher climates. As personal corruption and foreign immigration increases in Canada, however, its citizens will have no personal arms to deter criminals and protect themselves as Americans do. Ultimately they may be worse off from crime.

Remember as well, that Americans can't take their personal arms across the borders into either Canada or Mexico, so they are more vulnerable there. Do carry pepper spray or, if you are going camping, you might consider a small plastic flare gun (that boaters use). It isn't a firearm, but it is very effective against both criminals and the big bears you may meet in the Canadian wilds.

Pollution

Some areas of North America are definitely more dangerous to your health than others. In the US and Canada pollution in the air, water and ground is usually related to densely populated cities or areas with industrial plants (past or present). Rural farm areas are also increasingly polluted because of large-scale agricultural practices where chemical pesticides and fertilizers are used. A great many of us live in one of these areas and it can require great care and cost to filter or avoid these pollutants. We will try to help you sort out which communities are the worst, and recommend that your long-term location be outside of these areas.

Air Pollution

Air pollution is concentrated where a source of pollution is located in a geographic depression or encircled by mountains that capture the pollution. The worst case of this is in Los Angeles where the on-shore air flow is slowed or stopped by the coastal mountains. This traps the significant pollution from both industry and population-density resulting in LA's infamous haze and smog. Salt Lake City has less pollution but the nearby mountains can trap the pollutants during winter periods when air is stagnant and temperature inversions are common. The only relief there is when a storm system blows through and scavenges out the bad air.

everyone has climbed on the concealment bandwagon in order to survive politically. More and more police chiefs are chosen for political reasons rather than honesty and competency.

Some deterrence has increased, which explains part of the reduction. A lot more money has been thrown at enforcement. SWAT teams are part of even small-town police forces and huge amounts of manpower and resources are applied to criminal take-downs—often to the detriment of civil liberties. This, combined with the growing number of concealed weapons permit holders, is having some deterrent effect. More mandatory sentences are being handed out for violent crimes and more prison space has been built (though a system with real deterrence would not need more prison space, with its related expense).

There has been an improvement in crime havens like New York City, where subway gangs have been vigorously rooted out with a much higher police presence, but the federal money paying for much of the increased police jobs will run out in a few years. In the long term most of these temporary deterrents will lose some of their edge. Criminals will adapt and get smarter and find other targets. Eventually hardened criminals will learn to adapt to the new pressures and become more selective in their targets. They may even take crime to more rural areas where the police are few in numbers and where the victims can be isolated.

There are six major air pollutants measured by the US Environmental Protection Agency (EPA): nitrogen dioxide, sulfur dioxide, ozone, lead, particulate matter (PM-10 and PM-2.5) and carbon monoxide.

Of the six major pollutants lead is the most toxic, but not a major problem now that leaded fuel is not burned in cars. People who have lived near busy streets often experienced high residual levels of lead contamination in their body. This pollutant can severely damage the immune system and leads to susceptibility to chronic fatigue syndrome and a host of other weaknesses of the nerves and brain.

Particulate matter 10 microns (PM-10) and smaller (PM-2.5) is presently the most controversial form of regulated pollution. Dust from roads, construction, wind-whipped dirt,

Worst US Cities for Air Pollution (2010)

	Ozone Pollution	Year-round Particle Pollution	Short Term Particle Pollution
1	Los Angeles-Long Beach-Riverside, CA	Phoenix-Mesa-Scottsdale, AZ	Bakersfield, CA
2	Bakersfield, CA	Bakersfield, CA	Fresno-Madera, CA
3	Visalia-Porterville, CA	Los Angeles-Long Beach-Riverside, CA	Pittsburgh-New Castle, PA
4	Fresno-Madera, CA	Visalia-Porterville, CA	Los Angeles-Long Beach-Riverside, CA
5	Sacramento-Arden-Arcade-Yuba City, CA-NV	Pittsburgh-New Castle, PA	Birmingham-Hoover-Cullman, AL
6	Hanford-Corcoran, CA	Fresno-Madera, CA	Sacramento-Arden-Arcade-Yuba City, CA-NV
7	Houston-Baytown-Huntsville, TX	Birmingham-Hoover-Cullman, AL	Salt Lake City-Ogden-Clearfield, UT
8	San Diego-Carlsbad-San Marcos, CA	Hanford-Corcoran, CA	Visalia-Porterville, CA
9	San Luis Obispo-Paso Robles, CA	Cincinnati-Middletown-Wilmington, OH-KY-IN	Modesto, CA
10	Charlotte-Gastonia-Salisbury, NC-SC	St. Louis-St. Charles-Farmington, MO-IL	Hanford-Corcoran, CA
11	Phoenix-Mesa-Scottsdale, AZ	Charleston, WV	Merced, CA
12	Merced, CA	Detroit-Warren-Flint, MI	Philadelphia-Camden-Vineland, PA-NJ-DE-MD
13	Dallas-Fort Worth, TX	Weirton-Steubenville, WV-OH	Provo-Orem, UT

Source: http://www.stateoftheair.org/2010/city-rankings/most-polluted-cities.html

Cleanest US Cities (2010)

	Ozone Pollution		Year-round Particle Pollution		
1	Bismarck, ND	1	Cheyenne, WY	13	Duluth, MN-WI
2	Brownsville-Harlingen-Raymondville, TX	2	Santa Fe-Espanola, NM	14	Pueblo, CO
3	Coeur d'Alene, ID	3	Honolulu, HI	15	Cape Coral-Fort Myers, FL
4	Duluth, MN-WI	4	Anchorage, AK	16	Palm Bay-Melbourne-Titusville, FL
5	Fargo-Wahpeton, ND-MN	5	Great Falls, MT	17	Sarasota-Bradenton-Punta Gorda, FL
6	Fayetteville-Springdale-Rogers, AR-MO	6	Tucson, AZ	18	Billings, MT
7	Honolulu, HI	7	Amarillo, TX	19	Fargo-Wahpeton, ND-MN
8	Laredo, TX	8	Albuquerque, NM	20	Port St. Lucie-Sebastian-Vero Beach, FL
9	Lincoln, NE	9	Flagstaff, AZ	21	Lincoln, NE
10	Port St. Lucie-Sebastian-Vero Beach, FL	10	Bismarck, ND	22	San Luis Obispo-Paso Robles, CA
11	Rochester, MN	11	Salinas, CA	23	Bangor, ME
12	Sioux Falls, SD	12	Fort Collins-Loveland, CO	24	Burlington-South Burlington, VT
				25	Midland-Odessa, TX

Source: http://www.stateoftheair.org/2010/city-rankings/most-polluted-cities.html

diesel and vehicle exhaust, industrial smoke and wood or coal burning stoves are all sources of these tiny particles that become suspended in air. Some rural areas are regularly out of compliance due to blowing dust, which we don't consider as harmful as pollution dust from traffic and industry which is more likely to be measured from PM-2.5 levels.

Ozone is three oxygen atoms combined, or O_3. It is thought to be formed when vehicle exhaust combines with volatile organic carbons (VOCs) from industry or common chemicals evaporating. This combination in sunlight and heat forms ozone which significantly contributes to smog and is considered hazardous to inhale. There is some debate about benefits from this molecule including its use as a disinfectant. Notwithstanding this debate, we consider this a good indicator of population and industry pollution together.

Carbon dioxide is an example of a purely politicized danger. This ubiquitous compound is not a pollutant in any manner, so we will not cover it as such. We do not consider global warming a serious, scientifically justified threat.

The following table lists the worst US cities for air pollution considering ozone and particulate matter. Note that many of these locations are located in geographical basins which exacerbate the effects of pollution during certain environmental conditions like inversions.

Water Pollution

Water pollution differs from air pollution in that there is almost always a treatment facility between the source and what we ingest. In 1974 the federal government passed the Safe Drinking Water Act that established federal guidelines for maximum levels of various pollutants and pathogens. These restrictions caused water treatment plants to not only purify the water but also to inject disinfectants such as chlorine into the drinking water to kill bacteria in the pipelines. This latter process has chemical side effects that essentially produce a second form of pollution. Let's look at pollutants in water sources and supply systems each in turn.

Water source pollution includes sediment, microorganisms, organic compounds and inorganic chemicals. All of these are reduced as water is processed in treatment plants, but only the contaminants mandated by law are measured and cleaned out—to their required levels. Many water sources have pollutants and heavy metals that are not regulated and even the minimum regulated amounts of some, like lead, we consider still unhealthy over time.

Try to avoid communities that take their water from large, polluted rivers or lakes (like Lake Michigan). These sources have heavy metals that do not get eliminated during processing. Moreover, the chlorine levels in these waters are usually at or near maximum levels to combat the additional pathogens in these waters. Many of the largest cities' water supplies are undesirable for cooking or bathing, let alone drinking. You can search for information

Drinking Water Disinfectant Contaminants

Disinfectants		
Contaminant	Potential Health Effects from Long-Term Exposure Above the MCL (unless specified as short-term)	Sources of Contaminant in Drinking Water
Chloramines (as Cl2)	Eye/nose irritation; stomach discomfort, anemia	Water additive used to control microbes
Chlorine (as Cl2)	Eye/nose irritation; stomach discomfort	Water additive used to control microbes
Chlorine dioxide (as ClO2)	Anemia; infants & young children: nervous system effects	Water additive used to control microbes
Disinfection Byproducts		
Contaminant	Potential Health Effects from Long-Term Exposure Above the MCL (unless specified as short-term)	Sources of Contaminant in Drinking Water
Bromate	Increased risk of cancer	Byproduct of drinking water disinfection
Chlorite	Anemia; infants & young children: nervous system effects	Byproduct of chlorination
Haloacetic acids (HAA5)	Increased risk of cancer	Byproduct of chlorination
Total Trihalomethanes (TTHMs)	Liver, kidney or central nervous system problems; increased risk of cancer	Byproduct of chlorination

Source: EPA

about specific water quality by zip code at *http://www.ewg.org/tap-water/whatsinyourwater/* including a history of when it exceeded healthy and legal levels.

Water treatment chemicals injected at the end of the purification process are a significant source of daily chemical consumption for most people. Chlorine, for example, doesn't kill everything and leaves behind cancer causing residuals (e.g. Trihalomethane-THMs) that are dangerous. The above list shows the most common disinfectant chemicals and their byproducts. The EPA maintains that their maximum levels are set to produce "no known or expected risk to health." We think otherwise, as do many alternative health sources. We recommend chemical filters to remove chlorine in your drinking water and preferably in your showers also.

Fluoride is a controversial chemical that is added to many water sources. Our research concludes that it is a dangerous chemical whose benefits do not outweigh its dangers. Most chemical fluoride added to water comes as a byproduct of aluminum production and is highly poisonous. Fluoride has been advocated by the dental community because it changes the natural chemical process during re-mineralization of teeth. Minerals in saliva are always rebuilding teeth surfaces. When fluoride is present during this process it is more reactive than some of the minerals creating a very thin layer that is thought to be more acid-resistant. Excess fluoride, however, impedes the natural process creating fluorosis which results in mottled, pitted or discolored teeth and brittle bones. Fluoridated water supplies have been found to reduce IQ in developing children (*http://www.fluoridation.com/brain.htm*). Even small doses of fluoride are being found to affect the body in subtle ways, though we still don't know the complete effects. It has been observed, for example, that fluoride competes with iodine, a critical element for health and thyroid function. In our opinion it should be strongly avoided. For improving dental health we recommend increasing your nutrition from mineral-rich sources like bone broths and reducing the intake of sugar and refined flour and foods.

The Center for Disease Control allows a search of fluoridated water sources at *http://apps.nccd.cdc.gov/MWF/* and we list the percent of fluoridated water in each state in our state-specific reviews in Section Four.

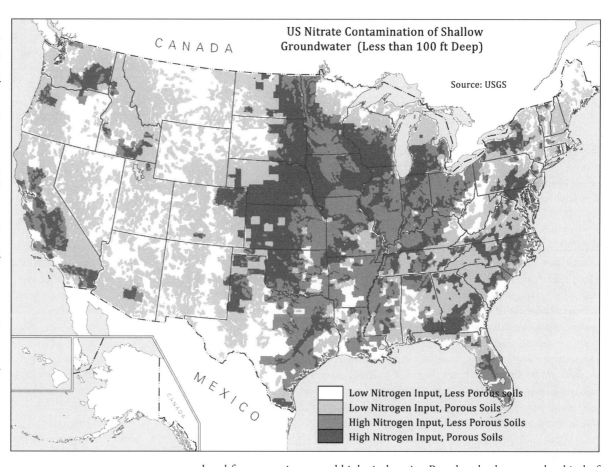

US Nitrate Contamination of Shallow Groundwater (Less than 100 ft Deep)

Source: USGS

Low Nitrogen Input, Less Porous Soils
Low Nitrogen Input, Porous Soils
High Nitrogen Input, Less Porous Soils
High Nitrogen Input, Porous Soils

Smaller water systems that use wells are usually better than treated river or lake water since ground water is naturally filtered as it seeps through soil and porous rock, but some agricultural fertilizers and chemicals are polluting these sources too in areas with heavy concentrations applied over porous soil. The above map shows the worst areas for this contamination in shallow soils. A more detailed colored map is available at the front of the color maps at the end of Section Four.

Another factor to consider is the presence of bad smelling natural chemicals in underground aquifers. Water is the universal solvent and tends to leach out naturally occurring chemicals in the ground as it percolates downward. Many areas of Ohio have a strong sulfur smell in the water. When you take a shower there, it smells unpleasant, though not harmful, necessarily. Some areas of southwestern Colorado have a foul mixture of oil and gas residues in the ground water, which adversely affect private wells that are drilled for drinking water. Whenever you purchase a rural home with a well, make sure you have the

water analyzed for contaminants and biological purity. But also check to see what kind of filtration equipment is in the home. If it has a complex system, then you may well suspect they have a problem with water quality. Have one of the filters pulled out and inspect it for residues. Taste the water and smell it. Try to find water that tastes almost neutral and that has virtually no smell.

Toxic Sites

Thousands of sites throughout the US have been tagged by the EPA for cleanup of hazardous substances. These sites were dubbed "superfund" sites after congress voted to allocate billions toward their cleanup in 1980. A list of these sites, called the National Priorities List (NPL), is maintained on the EPA's website (*www.epa.gov/superfund*) together with location maps, current cleanup status and information about the hazards. Although some sites with hazards are not listed here and sites listed may already be sufficiently contained, we still recommend using their "Where you live" tool to look up your potential relocation areas to ensure you are not near these clearly hazardous sites.

Medical Help and Regulations

It used to be that rural areas with poor sanitation and unsafe water were considered unhealthy and more prone to disease than urban living. Today, it is the rural areas that are usually healthier. Higher population density areas yield greater contact with more varieties of disease and a greater exposure to pollutants.

We have found that in matters of nutrition, medical treatment of ailments, childbirth and disease prevention, it is wise to return to time-honored practices and rediscover the benefits of the old ways of living. We explain a few of these methods here as they pertain to states that have regulations affecting their practice.

Access to Healthy Foods

Most readers will probably not be able to make the ultimate lifestyle change for good health by moving to a rural farm. However, modern methods do allow us access to many of the same benefits for a little extra cost and time. In our opinion, the most important foods are fruits and vegetables that are in-season and organic together with meat, eggs and dairy from animals on pastures, not feed lots or crowded "cage-free" hen houses. Fortunately, the trend toward buying these products from local farmers is growing in many areas. Farmers markets are proliferating. Look for small-scale operations where you can see for yourself how your food is prepared. Get to know your farmer and make sure that your food is not tainted by pesticides or strong disinfectants and that trace minerals are replenished in the soil from mulch and manure not commercial fertilizer.

The most significant threat to small-scale operations is often over-regulation by national or state governments. Legislation requiring documentation and inspection can often be a burden that small farmers and ranchers can't afford. Federal legislation has been proposed to track all food from seed or birth to consumer. State restrictions on raw milk are perhaps the most obvious case of banning a valuable food source. Raw milk is quite safe to drink provided the cow is raised naturally on grass and free from overcrowded, disease-prone feed lots and large-scale dairies. Many people with lactose intolerance have been able to consume this whole food. Nonetheless, most states have some restrictions and some ban its sale outright. Some exceptions are made if the consumer owns part of the cow, so cowshare programs are popular in some states. The website www.realmilk.com lists the restrictions of each state. Currently Canada outlaws the sale of raw milk.

So far, it is still possible to get pasture-fed animal meat and local organic vegetables. We recommend that everyone learn to find sources for these in their area. We have become convinced that good sources of grass-fed animal fat are vital to a healthy diet. Native populations isolated from refined foods historically had healthy bones, perfect teeth and virtually no degenerative diseases. Their diet had considerable amounts of natural animal fats and cholesterol. We recommend reading about the invaluable studies of these populations by Dr. Weston Price. For more information go to *www.westonaprice.org* or refer to our bibliography and resources.

Ultimately, there is no better way to get vegetables than to grow them yourself. A key part of your long-term strategy should be learning to grow and preserve your own food with a garden. Start small and build on your knowledge. It can be surprising how much food can be grown in small areas or even on balconies. There are many valuable sources out there and we've listed a few in our bibliography.

Establishment vs. Alternative Medical Treatment

Twenty years ago, it was commonly held that medical science had solved or was in the final stages of solving all the world's big health problems. Today the medical establishment is experiencing numerous backlashes from their practices of using drugs and vaccines. Many so-called cured infectious diseases are now starting to make a comeback with new, mutant, drug-resistant strains. All synthetic drugs developed in the past have bad side effects and many are found to have long-term damage or eventual ineffectiveness.

Medical science does have great expertise in surgery, but they know almost nothing about prevention or helping the body improve itself holistically with nutrition. They treat and diminish symptoms, but, in most cases, don't cure. Most cures come from the body's immune system, in spite of the drugs. Some of what they do is certainly good, but most procedures are laced with damaging side effects. True cures only happen to people who make real changes in their lifestyle. Improving nutrition, using natural herbs and remedies, exercise and improving your environment are the only changes substantial enough to bring about strong change.

You may not be immediately convinced of trusting alternative health methods over establishment practices, but if you start studying from alternative health sources, you will begin to realize that there is a lot of competent information available. Don't delay. Don't wait till you get cancer to start finding out what your alternatives are. You'll be under the gun from relatives and doctors pushing you to make decisions that may not be in your best interest. It takes many years to learn enough to take care of yourself.

We have included a list of recommended books in our bibliography about establishment and alternative medicine. Every good health food store will also have some recommendations for you. It's worth noting that the alternative field is just that —everything else out there. There is a fair amount of spiritualistic, new-age philosophy, which should be avoided or overlooked. The truth is in-between.

In the preparedness and survival community, many are worried about finding drugs to fill their prescriptions or doctors and hospitals. We strongly believe that people need to learn about natural nutritional solutions over drugs for both prevention and cure. Consider instead, storing and saving herbs and basic vitamin supplements. This will also reduce your dependence on establishment medicine which will largely be unavailable after a catastrophe. Moreover, if you become connected with ways of healing yourself naturally you can limit expensive medical insurance to more minimum levels. Perhaps just to cover catastrophic accidents and thus save thousands.

Vaccines and Drugs

As for vaccines, we recommend extreme caution. We do not subscribe to the establishment medical enthusiasm for vaccines. Vaccines have a history of creating damage to the human immune system. Young children have weak and untrained immune systems. Babies, in particular, are susceptible to the contaminants and preservatives in vaccines.

There are many heartbreaking stories of parents whose children experienced immediate, prolonged fits of pain and screaming after receiving vaccinations. In rare cases the child has even died. When this happens, medical authorities almost uniformly talk the parents out of their obvious conclusion that the problem was caused by the vaccination and attempt to label it under the vague "sudden infant death syndrome."

There are many things to weigh when considering vaccinations so we recommend reading up on some of the balanced discussions about this controversy. We recommend books by Aviva Jill Romm, *Vaccinations: A Thoughtful Parent's Guide* and Stephanie Cave, MD, *What Your Doctor may Not Tell You About Children's Vaccinations.*

Access to Alternative Medical Practitioners

Restrictions to the freedom to choose alternative medical care will increasingly be important to your strategic situation. It is not inappropriate for states to have some form of voluntary licensing, if it honestly acts as a "certification" of state competency and does not prohibit others from practicing medicine except in cases of true fraud or misrepresentation.

We expect the establishment medical system is destined to be completely controlled by the government someday, and will be one of the prime ways in which the government controls people. The passage of Obamacare was a significant step in this direction. If you stay out of this system now you will have more freedom later on when everyone else is trapped and ignorant of the alternatives.

It is important to locate appropriate health practitioners who are competent in alternative herbs and honest nutrition. The natural healing methods are not precise and take a great deal of experience to know what works for you. Start now to find the right way to eat and start listening to the body's warning signals when things aren't right. There are a lot of mystical, unsound theories out there that attach themselves to alternative medicine. Study and search out the best sources and forge some good links with people that you can trust. You can search for a naturopathic doctor via their website (*http://www.naturopathic.org*).

US and Canada Naturopathy Laws				
	State Regulation or License	**Prescribe Drugs**	**Perform Minor Surgery**	**Prohibited by Law**
United States				
Alaska	√			
Arizona	√	√	√	
California	√	√		
DC	√	√	√	
Florida	√			
Hawaii	√	√		
Idaho	√	√	√	
Kansas	√	√	√	
Maine	√	√	√	
Minnesota	√			
Montana	√	√		
New Hampshire	√	√		
Oregon	√	√	√	
South Carolina				√
Tennessee				√
Utah	√	√	√	
Vermont	√	√	√	
Virginia	√			
Washington	√	√	√	
Canada				
British Columbia	√	√	√	
Manitoba	√			
Nova Scotia	√			
Ontario	√			
Saskatchewan	√			
Source: Wikipedia				

Restrictions on Practicing Midwives

The practice of midwifery is one of the oldest professions in the world and significant percentages of births are still cared for by these women around the globe. We consider this an important aspect of your freedoms and a reasonable gauge of how restrictive a state is.

There are several types of midwives with varying levels of training and credentials, depending on the laws of each state. Nurse Midwives are licensed by the medical establishment and work in hospitals or birth centers. They are trained in non-medicated pain relief techniques and largely operate under hospital protocols including drugs and medical intervention techniques in childbirth which have their own problems and side effects. In contrast, Certified Professional Midwives (CPM) are taught through alternative, accredited schools and in some states they may be licensed to carry life-saving drugs. Lay Midwives are taught through assisting experienced midwives.

We consider the right to bear offspring outside the establishment medical hospital system an important aspect of long-term security. The health care system is gradually becoming the only approved entrance point into society and could become a control point for mandatory restrictions such as inoculations or the licensing of parental "competency" (which someday could exclude parents who believe in Christian "indoctrination" and physical discipline). We provide short descriptions of the restrictions on midwifery in our state-specific reviews in Section Four.

Schools

Unlike other books on relocation, we will not cover the neighborhoods with the "best" public schools. Instead, we recommend relocating to states that favor the alternatives: private schools, religious schools and home schooling. Here's why.

Public Schools

We can't recommend public schools on principle. This institution is a monopoly because of their access to tax money, which requires everyone using alternate schools to pay twice for education. Moreover, all education has values associated with it, and values should never be enforced or taught by government controlled processes or even by majority rule. All values should be free to compete for adherents, and the only way to do that is to allow everyone to put his education dollars where they wish—without government tax compulsion.

There are several problems inherent in the public schools including bad textbooks, large classes, lack of discipline, bad teaching (with some exceptions), unionized employees, bloated administration costs and expensive facilities. Crime, abusive attitudes and heavy social pressures abound. While some very good kids are partially immune, most are not and parents are constantly waging a losing battle to counter the attitudes their children pick up at school. The curriculum is written in favor of government intervention, political correctness, skewed history lessons and incomplete economic lessons about social welfare. This kind of thinking predisposes them to resist many of the warnings about critical threats and trains up a non-thinking population dependant on government and the establishment media.

Private Schooling

Private schools produce a better quality education for less than half the operating cost of public schools. That said, it is important to be selective. The expensive elite private schools are always better than the public schools in academics, but the lofty social attitudes there aren't necessarily any better for your children than the undisciplined public schools. But, at least they aren't violent, and there is considerably more discipline. No real education takes place without disciplining the mind and the body. We object to public and private schools that subscribe to the false philosophy that education should always be fun. It can be, but mostly good education is hard mental work.

The most economical schools are church-related private schools, where religious congregations help subsidize tuition voluntarily, which is laudable. However, price isn't everything. If you don't subscribe to the religious views taught, you can either counter-indoctrinate at home, or pick schools which don't mix religious doctrine with the curriculum. You may have difficulty in some religious backed schools if you have contrary beliefs.

Home School Laws

The ultimate right to control your children's education is an essential liberty and will become more important as public schools get worse or as more conditions are required to enter them, such as vaccinations. Every state in the US now allows for home schooling, even though seven states are hostile to home schooling and put up significant bureaucratic barriers to parents. These are ND, NH, VT, NY, PA, RI and MA.

Oregon was one of the first states to go so far as to attempt to shut down all private schooling and force them to fall under the control of the state public school system. This attempt was overturned in the famous Supreme Court ruling, Oregon vs. Society of Sisters. Oregon has had the most unregulated private education laws ever since—because of backlash—not because of any wisdom on the part of Oregon's education establishment.

It took a major legal battle against the State of Nebraska (which had even imprisoned some pastors for defending religious schools and homeschoolers) and the shooting of a home schooling father in Utah to cause enough backlash and embarrassment for many state legislatures to start making exceptions for home schooling.

Twenty years ago, every state had uniform compulsory attendance laws for schooling that severely restricted a parent's liberty to take their children out of school. At best, some states allowed for licensed and regulated private schools, but no state recognized that the parents had any right, let alone the ultimate right to take charge of their children's own education. Now all states have some type of law allowing home schooling.

The most uniform type of law carved out by the legislators was that parents had no "right" to determine the education of their children, but that the state could, under strict controls, grant them approval to do so. The following map is a visual representation of states' home-schooling requirements. It is broken down into four levels of state requirements for parents who want to home school:

1. No notification.

2. Low regulation, state requires notification by the parent.

3. Moderate regulation, parents must send notification, test scores and/or professional evaluation of student progress.

4. High regulation, all the moderate requirements and more, such as curriculum approval, parents having teaching qualifications or home visits by state officials.

Most states with high regulation require that if a student fails to perform to certain standards, then they must return to the public schools. None allow the parent to demand the same right if the student fails to perform in the public schools. This is proof that the issue is not one of quality of education, but of who will have the ultimate sovereignty over the child's education—and the state clearly thinks it has the ultimate authority. This is always the danger with the "compelling interest" doctrine established by the Supreme Court. In reality, it doesn't matter who claims to have a "compelling interest". The only critical issue is who has the "ultimate interest" or the "ultimate authority." Compelling interest is merely a euphemism for the underlying assumptions of state sovereignty over parent rights.

We provide specific information about homeschooling requirements in the state-specific reviews in Section

Four. The best website for more information on specific state requirements is the *Home School Legal Defense Fund* (*http://www.hslda.org*).

Colleges

No matter where you get your education, college degrees are becoming the most important factor for getting into the workforce. We recommend looking at the colleges in areas you consider. Our family left the small-town life specifically because we needed better opportunities for the growing children to go to college, and couldn't afford to pay room and board away from home. We chose a town with a good junior college. We don't recommend living specifically in college towns because they often harbor strong liberal influences. Many colleges have historically been biased against homeschoolers entering easily. But homeschooling has gained sufficient mass now that it's usually not an issue to test into most schools.

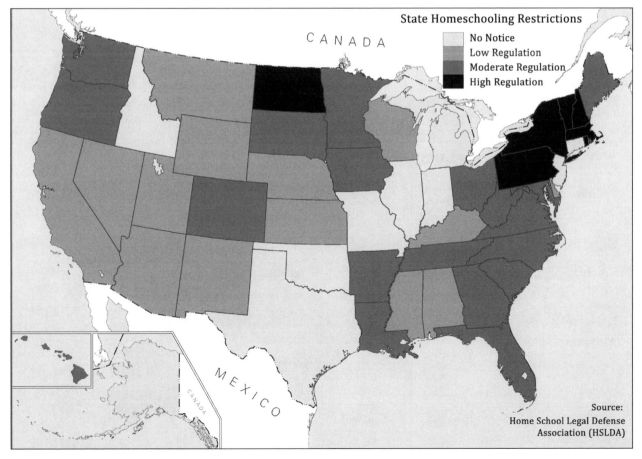

State Homeschooling Restrictions

- No Notice
- Low Regulation
- Moderate Regulation
- High Regulation

Source:
Home School Legal Defense
Association (HSLDA)

Cost of Living

As we described in Section One, we predict all governments will continue to inflate their currencies to pay for government programs. Thus, a significant factor for strategic relocation is to find a state or city that still has a reasonable cost of living and moderate housing prices. Investing in solid commodities is also an important tactic to mitigate the effects of inflation on your savings. Housing is one of those commodities, so don't buy in states where prices are highly inflated.

Low housing prices are reflective overall of the general cost of living. Look for houses in slow, steadily growing communities, but beware of "good deals" in depressed areas. There may be a reason the area is being vacated—crime, minority influx, flood plain, or a dying city like Detroit.

Home Price Comparison

The following table has data from Coldwell Banker's 2015 Home Price Comparison Index. It represents the cost of a 2,200 sq. ft. single-family home with 4 bedrooms, 2 1/2 baths, family room (or equivalent) and 2-car garage. The neighborhood is estimated "typical for corporate middle-management transferees." To see what your current house would cost in another city, divide the 2015 market value of your home by the index number of your current city and then multiply that value by the index number of the destination city.

Home Price Comparison Index (2015)

Market	Average Price	Housing Index	Market	Average Price	Housing Index
Alabama			**Arizona**		
Huntsville	$176,104	49	Flagstaff	$391,129	108
Mobile	$173,264	48	Mesa	$206,967	57
Alaska			Phoenix	$199,111	55
Anchorage	$374,731	104	Scottsdale	$505,391	140
Fairbanks	$238,074	66	Tucson	$284,821	79
Arkansas			**California**		
Fayetteville	$266,351	73	Bakersfield	$310,268	86
Pine Bluff	$136,233	37	Carlsbad	$716,180	198
Little Rock	$172,332	47	Davis	$634,710	175

Home Price Comparison Index (2015)

Market	Average Price	Housing Index	Market	Average Price	Housing Index
Encinitas	$874,667	241	San Mateo	$1,463,455	404
Fremont	$884,316	244	San Rafael	$1,042,405	287
Fresno	$257,395	71	Santa Barbara	$1,328,700	366
Grass Valley	$413,309	114	Santa Clara	$869,647	240
Irvine	$989,860	274	Santa Maria	$341,352	94
La Mesa	$497,953	138	Santa Monica	$1,460,912	402
Lancaster	$203,234	56	Santa Rosa	$584,419	161
Long Beach	$739,455	204	Sonora	$337,631	93
Mission Viejo	$725,737	201	Thousand Oaks	$723,076	199
Modesto	$279,172	77			
Napa	$777,569	215	Victorville	$196,360	54
Newport Beach	$2,291,764	635	**Colorado**		
Oakland	$698,583	219	Boulder	$1,044,656	288
Palo Alto	$2,066,600	573	Colorado Springs	$252,157	69
Pasadena	$1,317,808	365	Denver	$542,575	149
Placentia	$653,032	181	Fort Collins	$459,014	126
Pleasanton	$978,586	271	Durango	$412,000	113
Ramona	485,300	134	Montrose	275,370	75
Riverside	$412,136	114	**Connecticut**		
Sacramento	$318,253	88	Danbury	$411,935	113
San Bernardino	$273,861	75	Fairfield	$713,425	196
San Diego	$584,913	161	Greenwich	$1,290,921	356
San Francisco	$1,360,189	376	Milford	$538,700	148
			Ridgefield	$685,668	189
San Jose	$871,158	240	West Hartford	$384,034	106

Home Price Comparison Index (2015)

Market	Average Price	Housing Index	Market	Average Price	Housing Index	Market	Average Price	Housing Index	Market	Average Price	Housing Index
Washington D.C.	$784,038	216	Dalton	$188,604	51	Bloomington	$207,159	58	**Louisiana**		
Delaware			Macon	$237,779	65	Joliet	$181,778	51	Baton Rouge	$244,126	68
Wilmington	$281,311	77	Savannah	$245,491	67	Peoria	$182,890	51	Lafayette	$267,633	74
Florida			**Hawaii**			Springfield	$166,222	46	Monroe	$211,234	59
Boca Raton	$427,446	117	Honolulu	$1,133,400	196	**Indiana**			New Orleans	$225,994	63
Clearwater	$234,922	64	Kapolei	$568,519	149	Fort Wayne	$166,029	46	Shreveport	$213,236	59
Fort Myers	$231,072	63	**Iowa**			Indianapolis	$215,312	60	**Massachussets**		
Gainesville	$254,014	70	Des Moines	$171,363	48	Lafayette	$235,602	66	Arlington	$692,825	193
Jacksonville	$191,370	52	Burlington	$183,300	51	Muncie	$144,996	40	Boston	$609,704	170
Lynn Haven	$259,360	71	Cedar Rapids	$175,723	49	Schererville	$315,526	88	Cambridge	$1,106,991	308
Miami	$353,667	97	Sioux City	$130,798	36	South Bend	$170,064	47	Canton	$676,433	188
Naples	$394,303	108	**Idaho**			Valpariso	$291,928	81	Framingham	$473,353	132
Orlando	$237,610	65	Boise	$215,432	59	**Kansas**			Lexington	$983,388	274
Palmetto Bay	$525,019	145	Bonner's Ferry	$237,909	66	Kansas City	$118,904	33	Maynard	$422,720	118
Panama City	$330,493	91	Caldwell	$166,841	46	Leavenworth	$176,186	49	Springfield	$169,322	47
Pensacola	$177,661	48	Coeur d' Alene	$283,394	79	Overland Park	$240,331	67	Wilmington	$595,985	166
Port Charlotte	$206,862	56	Idaho Falls	$146,037	41	Topeka	$143,686	40	Winchester	$1,049,739	292
Sarasota	$358,165	98	Lewiston	$272,185	76	Wichita	$171,453	48	**Maryland**		
Tallahassee	$207,346	57	Payette	$121,480	34	**Kentucky**			Annapolis	$587,252	163
Tampa	$276,055	76	Pocatello	$144,790	40	Bowling Green	$209,954	58	Baltimore	$221,812	62
West Palm Beach	$283,377	78	Rexburg	$191,011	53	Lexington	$221,722	62	Bethesda	$782,300	218
Georgia			**Illinois**			Louisville	$221,221	62	Columbia	$395,919	110
Athens	$197,869	54	Chicago	$257,159	72				Frederick	$318,307	89
Atlanta	$207,491	57	Highland Park	$556,872	155				Joppa	$302,704	84
Columbus	$159,588	43	Lake Forest	$774,649	216				Ocean City	$570,372	159
									Salisbury	$232,918	65

Home Price Comparison Index (2015)

Market	Average Price	Housing Index
Maine		
Augusta	$139,552	39
Bangor	$183,441	51
Brunswick	$266,391	74
Portland	$396,591	110
Michigan		
Ann Arbor	$148,000	41
Commerce	$326,735	91
Detroit	$81,616	23
Dewitt	$272,700	76
Flint	$95,482	27
Grand vRapids	$204,720	57
Hillsdale	$137,775	38
Lansing	$143,124	40
Monroe	$170,891	48
Newport	$215,867	60
Traverse City	$329,103	92
Minnesota		
Bloomington	$396,563	110
Lake Minnetonka	$668,786	186
Minneapolis	$693,388	193
Roseville	$375,215	104
St. Cloud	$264,140	73
St. Paul	$425,886	119

Market	Average Price	Housing Index
Missouri		
Kansas City	$229,696	64
Poplar Bluff	$188,710	53
Springfield	$210,323	59
St. Louis	$248,585	69
Mississippi		
Biloxi	$201,825	56
Clinton	$169,306	47
Gulfport	$170,891	48
Jackson	$118,406	33
Madison	$250,794	70
Tupelo	$167,691	47
Montana		
Billings	$239,039	67
Bozeman	$394,184	110
Great Falls	$181,135	50
Helena	$244,278	68
Livingston	$242,775	68
Missoula	$333,030	93
Kalispell	$199,625	55
North Carolina		
Chapel Hill	$406,313	113
Charlotte	$242,371	67
Fayetteville	$197,089	55
Greensboro	$204,628	57
Raleigh	$284,791	79

Market	Average Price	Housing Index
Wake Forest	$262,031	73
Winston-Salem	$207,175	58
North Dakota		
Bismarck	$248,069	69
Fargo	$231,914	65
Minot	$273,361	76
Nebraska		
Columbus	$197,577	55
Norfolk	$125,064	35
North Platte	$125,826	35
New Hampshire		
Amherst	$441,317	123
Manchester	$252,417	70
Salem	$363,994	101
New Jersey		
Atlantic City	$205,774	57
Bridgewater	$538,564	150
Edison	$507,476	141
Hillsborough	$539,308	150
Jersey City	$348,859	97
Monroe	$535,929	149
New Brunswick	$257,568	72
Newark	$159,448	44
Woodland Park	$385,033	107

Market	Average Price	Housing Index
New Mexico		
Alamogordo	$222,559	62
Albuquerque	$274,045	76
Carlsbad	$265,165	74
Farmington	$276,802	77
Las Cruces	$182,503	51
Santa Fe	$440,714	123
Nevada		
Carson City	$314,663	88
Elko	$289,078	80
Las Vegas	$252,409	70
Reno	$313,436	87
Sparks	$273,650	76
New York		
Albany	$178,222	50
Buffalo	$110,429	31
Chester	$407,665	113
Queens	$793,500	219
Rochester	$120,018	33
Rome	$141,288	39
Staten Island	$555,562	153
Syracuse	$131,746	37
Ohio		
Akron	$136,839	38
Cincinnati	$210,590	59

Home Price Comparison Index (2015)

Market	Average Price	Housing Index
Cleveland	$74,502	21
Columbus	$205,467	57
Dayton	$137,390	38
Eaton	$203,658	57
Fairborn	$167,413	47
Lancaster	$209,198	58
Oklahoma		
Norman	$233,690	65
Oklahoma City	$190,164	53
Tulsa	$198,281	55
Oregon		
Bend	$411,119	114
Grants Pass	$260,301	72
Klamath Falls	$237,781	66
Medford	$295,704	82
Portland	$400,319	111
Salem	$286,225	80
Pennsylvania		
Erie	$156,491	44
Hanover	$239,058	67
Lewisburg	$348,479	97
Newtown	$568,069	158
Philadelphia	$252,102	70
Pittsburgh	$171,506	48
Reading	$208,923	58
Waynesboro	$294,632	82

Market	Average Price	Housing Index
Rhode Island		
Providence	$188,013	52
South Carolina		
Charleston	$336,138	94
Columbia	$197,297	55
Greenville	$239,973	67
Myrtle Beach	$256,756	71
Tennessee		
Chattanooga	$149,197	42
Knoxville	$242,198	67
Memphis	$152,271	42
Nashville	$284,395	79
Texas		
Abilene	$213,352	59
Amarillo	$221,627	62
Austin	$362,030	101
Corpus Christi	$240,138	67
Dallas	$216,160	60
El Paso	$191,079	53
Houston	$237,204	66
Laredo	$201,703	56
Midland	$297,050	83
Plano	$233,865	65
San Antonio	$215,233	60

Market	Average Price	Housing Index
Utah		
Cedar City	$199,570	56
Ogden	$210,790	59
Orem	$240,162	67
Provo	$231,000	64
Salt Lake City	$374,063	104
St. George	$294,109	82
Vernal	$231,719	64
Virginia		
Alexandria	$577,500	159
Charlottesville	$345,013	96
Chesterfield	$236,940	66
Fredericksburg	$324,943	90
Norfolk	$207,100	58
Richmond	$233,209	65
Virginia Beach	$302,853	84
Vienna	$641,783	179
Virginia Beach	$302,853	84
Vermont		
Burlington	$431,283	120
Milton	$308,600	86
Rutland	$168,683	47
Washington		
Everett	$369,410	103

Market	Average Price	Housing Index
Olympia	$329,835	92
Seattle	$674,309	188
Spokane	$200,918	56
Tacoma	$346,409	96
Tri-Cities	$283,058	79
Walla Walla	$257,134	72
Wisconsin		
Ashland	$131,438	37
Eagle River	$239,700	67
Green Bay	$159,451	44
Madison	$243,886	68
Milwaukee	$162,514	45
West Virginia		
Bunker Hill	$208,183	58
Huntington	$153,232	43
Martinsburg	$223,346	62
Wyoming		
Casper	$232,580	65
Cheyenne	$214,835	60
Evanston	$203,965	57

Source: http://hlr.coldwellbanker.com

Chapter 10

WAR, INVASION AND TERRORISM

The threats in this chapter may be difficult and unpleasant to consider and analyze for many readers but we believe many of them to be the most important considerations for your ultimate security. As we laid out the background to these threats in Section One, we described our analysis of the global terrorist threat and why we conclude that most terrorist events are manipulated to create conflict and justify intervention and the restriction of liberties. We explained why we expect a Third World War where Russia and China attack America with nuclear, biological and chemical weapons.

We believe all these events are part of greater plan—a plan of crisis and war that will manipulate people into accepting a consolidation of world power. In its basic terms, this is how we see this plan: 1) A terrorist threat is created and manipulated by Western leaders to justify military intervention in other nations. 2) This continual intervention and meddling around the world creates hatred against the US and eventually justifies the long-planned nuclear attack on the West by Russia and China. 3) Anglo-American globalist leaders will emerge from their bunkers (having had foreknowledge of the war) and convince Western nations to yield essential sovereignty in favor of a militarized global government with conscription and taxation power sufficient to prosecute the war. 3) This new World Government will eventually beat the Russians and use the residual threat of Chinese hegemony as an excuse to retain this world army and supra-national authority. 4) There will be the usual persecution of dissidents and critics, commensurate with a systematic loss of individual and national rights.

Here we examine these significant threats in more detail as they affect the US and Canada.

Terrorism in America

We see the war on terror as an essential part of this plan for world power. It is the favorite conflict creation vehicle that leaders throughout history have used to justify radical changes, expand military power and reduce civil liberties while ostensibly working to combat this shadowy threat.

The idea that terrorists hate the US for its freedoms is just plain propaganda. There is hatred toward the US but it is a result of CIA and State Department manipulation of other country's leaders that create bad feelings. If that weren't enough there is military intervention and occupation. blackmail, political arm-twisting, financial enticements with IMF funds, weapon deals and the creation of destabilizing opposition groups. In almost all cases this manipulation favors the wrong side of the conflict—it consistently undermines democracy and works to put socialist and communist dictators into power. This manipulation goes back decades and is the real cause of deeply seeded tensions and distrust even among our allies.

These manipulations have been especially active in the Middle East where tribal and ethnic conflict is ever present and easy to inflame. True terrorists do exist there, but they are too small and juvenile to carry out the really high-profile attacks that occurred on September 11th. In our estimation, a majority of terror attacks in Western countries today show strong evidence of government infiltration and guidance by agent provocateurs for the purpose of creating the appearance of a deadly threat that will drive people into acceptance of increased government control and power.

This manipulation and creation of conflict is often referred to as the Hegelian Dialectic: Create wars and attacks to justify a diminution of civil rights and constitutional protections. For instance, as we write this, Americans are being subjected to significant new search procedures at airports that are unjustifiably intrusive. The shoe bomber and underwear bomber were not real terrorists. No trained terrorist would have been ignorant of the fact that you can't set off plastic explosive with a match. You need blasting caps. We think these two patsies were set up just to give the government the excuse to control travel.

Evidence of Government-Sponsored Terror

There are many examples in history of governments fomenting attacks against their own people and then blaming another group to justify greater wars or crackdowns. Here are some examples:

- The arson attack on the Reichstag in 1933 was blamed on a Dutch bricklayer who was portrayed as a Communist, creating a fervor that solidified the Nazi party and allowed a bill that rescinded critical civil liberties in Germany. Historians agree that this event was pivotal for the Nazi party and Hitler's rise to dictatorship.

- The attack on the Gleiwitz German radio station in 1939 was one of several attacks against German nationals living in Poland that Germany used to "justify" their invasion into that country and formally begin WWII. Details from the Nuremburg trials revealed that it was Gestapo agents dressed up as Polish soldiers who attacked their own countrymen in a false-flag operation called "Operation Himmler."

- The second highest man in IRA security force, Keven McGuire, was a British agent. Unlike a typical spy, however, he worked actively to create IRA violence. He personally authorized the killing of honest British agents that had infiltrated the IRA at lower ranks.

- During the war in Iraq, British agents were caught dressed in Arab garb in southern Iraq trying to plant explosive charges within the city under coalition control. The British government refused to explain what they were doing, even as it demanded their release.

- Al Qaeda is not what you think. It turns out to be a false flag terror organization, financed out of Saudi Arabia and run at the top by persons like Osama bin Laden who was a reported CIA covert asset.

- According to whistleblowers, the CIA leased a C-130 Hercules cargo plane to deliver shoulder fired anti-tank and anti-aircraft missiles to the IRA.

- All of the 2010 terrorist convictions of young Muslims in the US were done by FBI agent provocateurs who incited disgruntled young immigrants and provided them with the knowhow and fake explosives to justify their prosecution. It is clear that none of these ignorant Muslims would have been able to engage in terror without government provocation and guidance.

Here's a more recent example: The Belfast Telegraph revealed in November 2010 that when

"addressing his peers in the House of Lords, Lord James of Blackheath revealed that he had been involved in the laundering of billions of pounds of terrorist money, specifically that of the IRA and various North African terrorists at the behest of the Bank of England."

"James' comments reveal even more secretive activity when he begins to discuss the shadowy organization, Foundation X as he calls it that contacted him with the proposal to aid England in the payment of its debt. Undoubtedly, the stature of Foundation X ranks higher than any organization we are currently aware of. As Lord James attempted to connect Foundation X with the appropriate individuals within the House of Lords and the Bank of England he says, 'I found myself between a rock and a hard place that were totally paranoid about each other, because the foundation X people have an amazing obsession with their own security. They expect to be contacted only by someone equal to head of state status or someone with an international security rating equal to the top six people in the world.'"

What about Nuclear Terrorism?

Both the US and Russia have built nuclear suitcase bombs—powerful enough to destroy a one mile area of an American city. But the claim that as many as 10 of these have been "lost" or allowed to pass into the hands of Middle Eastern terrorist organizations is unlikely (or just meant to put blame on Iran or foment more fear). These weapons are some of the most closely guarded assets ever. In planting this story, government propagandists are taking advantage of the public's naïve belief in the fall of the Soviet Union and a decrepit security structure around their nuclear weapons. Nonsense. We have found no credible information that this is true. The only known loss of nuclear material was done on purpose by German intelligence in a supposed sting operation against terrorists. In fact, the terrorists were trumped up too, so it was just a publicity stunt to encourage more aid to the Russians to "secure their nuclear stockpile." Even if a suitcase nuke were lost, a few years ago as claimed, it wouldn't work now. The nuclear tritium triggers in these devices have to be renewed very often, rendering them useless to a terrorist if not used soon after they get them.

Summary

Although we still consider every event as it occurs, we have found that most terrorist attacks against the US are phony or not indicative of a threat at this time. We see very few small-scale terrorist events in the US that are more common around the world. Our borders are essentially open, and there are limitless opportunities for these strikes.

If you are concerned about being hit by the next 9/11 type of terrorist attack, consider that false-flag events are most likely to occur around high profile areas and city centers. This is yet another reason to move to suburbs and rural areas. We have also noticed that some airports, like JFK in New York City, seem to have a disproportionate number of airline disasters. We attempt to fly out of other airports, where possible.

Nuclear War

As we describe in Section One, we conclude that an overwhelming nuclear attack against the West is imminent. Here is what Americans need to know.

The Coming "Surprise" Attack

It will be a surprise to America but not to our leaders. There are ominous signs that the US leadership knows something is coming, but they are unwilling to warn their own citizens. On December 10, 1997 National Public Radio announced that President Bill Clinton had signed a presidential decision directive, PDD-60, addressed to the military that changes US nuclear doctrine: that the US would no longer plan to win a nuclear war, only deter it, and that the US military will no longer plan to launch on warning. Supposedly we would prepare plans to react after absorbing a nuclear first strike. "Retaliate with what?" we ask.

Any military strategist can see that this is a suicide pact not a strategy. The only effective strategy to deter a nuclear war is to let the enemy know you plan to launch on warning. This ensures that our side is able to launch the majority of our nuclear weapons before they are destroyed in their silos by the incoming attack.

Although hailed as a peaceful move in the event of a "nuclear accident," PDD-60 can only give the Russians confidence that their first strike will be the most effective. If the US is going to absorb the first strike, then the Russians should make it a massive one with thousands of warheads, knowing that they may only get one chance to obliterate all possible US targets and lessen the possible retaliation.

US missile commanders have not, in fact, been told directly or unambiguously that they will not be allowed to launch on warning. Clinton only changed the nuclear doctrine about depending on launch on warning. The military still plans on it—but they don't have control of the process. No missiles can be launched without White House approval. After observing the actions of our political leaders, we think our military commanders will be watching the Russian and Chinese first strike in progress and waiting in vain for White House approval to launch.

After that first strike, our only ability to retaliate will be by nuclear submarines still intact after the first strike. Keep in mind that even that potential has been downgraded by our government. Pres. Clinton unilaterally agreed to keep half our ballistic missile subs in port at any given time—supposedly to assure the Russians of our peaceful intentions, but it just makes them more vulnerable to a first strike. Even the submarines at sea, however, will not be able to launch if the Russians can take out all our communication systems. That is why they and the Chinese have developed anti-satellite missiles.

US Strategic Nuclear Forces

In order to understand where the US will be hit, here is a brief overview of US nuclear and strategic forces and their support systems that we consider likely primary or secondary targets in a nuclear war. All this information is available publicly through a variety of sources. Most of our information came from the US military's website (*www.globalsecurity.org*) and the *Bulletin of Atomic Scientists* (*www.thebulletin.org*).

Intercontinental Ballistic Missiles (ICBM): These are the core of our nuclear deterrence strategy but the US continues to disarm, while the Russians only pretend. The US has deactivated the 50 Peacekeeper missiles (the most powerful and versatile US land based missile) and the components are stored near Hill AFB in Utah, making that base and the nearby Dugway Proving Ground a prime nuclear target. The US is now relying solely on the Minuteman III missile whose warheads have been reduced

from 3 down to 1 and those warheads lack the power to penetrate many of the Russian hardened silos.

Each US missile silo is also hardened and requires a direct hit by a nuclear weapon to be compromised. Therefore the missile fields of Malmstrom Air Force Base (AFB) in Montana, Minot AFB in North Dakota and Warren AFB on the southeast corner of Wyoming with 150 missiles apiece could be hit for each silo. That is why these areas show such a mass of targets.

Inactivated US silos are being destroyed by explosive demolition as required by the disarmament treaty, START I—eliminating any possibility of reversing current disarmament. The US is now considering converting some portion of these expensive missiles to conventional warheads to be used against terrorist threats needing immediate action (missiles can get to any part of the world in the fastest time).

Submarines: The *Ohio*-class SSBNs (Sub Surface, Ballistic, Nuclear powered) are the only ballistic missile submarines still in the US arsenal. All subs belonging to older classes have been decommissioned or converted to other uses. The US has built 18 *Ohio*-class submarines: 14 are nuclear-powered SSBN, with 24 Trident II missiles each, and 4 are nuclear-powered Ohio class boats that have been converted to SSGNs (cruise missile submarines), each capable of carrying 154 Tomahawk cruise missiles with conventional warheads. SSBN submarine bases with Trident missile storage are located at Bangor, WA and King's Bay, GA. Attack submarines are also located at the large West Coast Naval Facilities in San Diego, CA.

Bombers: The B-1B has been converted to a conventional bombing role. The B-52H force has been scaled back to a total fleet of 71 planes, although only 44 are on active duty at any one time. Despite its age (the last was delivered in Oct. 1962) the B-52H airframe is estimated to be good for service until at least 2030 (this is 83 years after the B-52 program's inception). Plans for retrofits and upgrades (including reengineering) of the B-52H are underway. The B-52H force will be split between Minot AFB, North Dakota and Barksdale AFB, Louisiana. The Northrop Grumman B-2 is operational and fully nuclear capable. The B-2 squadrons are based at Whiteman AFB, Missouri, and at our island base in the Indian Ocean, Diego Garcia.

Nuclear Weapon Manufacturing: All manufacture of nuclear materials for weapons has been halted. There is now a stockpile surplus of weapons-grade Uranium (U-235), Plutonium (Pu-239) and lithium deuteride. But one of the problems with nuclear weapons is that the tritium trigger mechanisms decay over time. With production of tritium cut off, tritium taken from weapons being retired will be used to replace the triggers in stockpile weapons so that no new tritium production will be needed until 2011 (allowing a 5 year reserve). Preliminary planning is underway to develop a new tritium production capability at Savannah River, South Carolina, by this date.

Weapon Storage: As of mid-1995 the US had nuclear weapons stored at 20 sites in 17 states, and at 13 sites in 7 foreign countries (not counting ballistic missile submarines on patrol in the open ocean). The US has an estimated 500 nuclear bombs in Europe, mostly B61 gravity bombs stored at eight bases: Belgium (Kleine Brogel), Germany (Norvenich, Buchel, Ramstein), Italy (Ghedi Torre and Aviano), Netherlands (Vokel), Turkey (Akinci, Balikesir, Incirlik), and the UK (Lakenheath).

Strategic Communications HQ: We speculate that there are significant bunker structures in place that are truly secret, but we only expect these to protect the conspiring leaders that are fomenting this war. Most published locations, like the Mount Weather Complex near Washington DC in Maryland, are officially deactivated but may still be hit in a war.

NORAD (North American Aerospace Defense) has their central command located inside Cheyenne Mountain near Colorado Springs. This complex controls all satellite and space communication and defense and has recently been upgraded to withstand EMP effects. During the upgrade many NORAD systems were moved to or are controlled from Peterson AFB in Colorado Springs, putting that city at risk. Offutt AFB has all the backup command and controls for our military nuclear forces.

There are several space satellite tracking and communications stations as well as more dated low frequency submarine communication systems scattered around the US. These systems are setup to communicate with nuclear submarines and transfer the launch codes for the Trident missiles.

Refueling and Transport Bases: The Air Force and Air Force Reserve bases with refueling and transport aircraft are a critical component of our strategic conventional forces. These are listed in our state-specific summaries in Section Four and shown on the state maps.

Nuclear Research and Development: Our nuclear weapons are maintained, developed and updated by a network of laboratories that we think will be primary and secondary targets in a nuclear war. These facilities would likely be targeted and include the National Laboratories like Los Alamos, Sandia, Idaho National and Lawrence Livermore facilities. Processing and enrichment equipment would likely be targeted as well, including old infrastructure that is currently mothballed but not dismantled. Descriptions and locations of these facilities are included in their respective state-specific summaries in Section Four.

During our research into military and strategic targets throughout the United States, we have compiled 146 primary targets (not including every one of the 450 Minuteman III silos targeted individually), and our estimation of over 150 secondary targets considered from public information sites. The following map shows the primary targets nationwide.

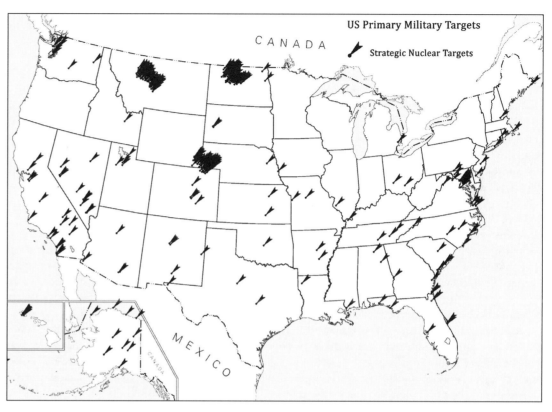

US Primary Military Targets

Strategic Nuclear Targets

Canadian Nuclear Forces

Canada has a very limited tactical offensive capability. It has no strategic weapons—no missiles and no long range bombers, and therefore no nuclear weapons delivery capability. Its forces have been traditionally linked with the US military in defending the North American Northern sector. The "Dew Line" is still in place along Canada's far northern boundary. It has 11 minimally manned long range radars for detecting incoming aircraft and missiles, 36 unmanned gap-filler radars, and 4 minimally manned coastal radar sites (1 on the Pacific and 3 on the Atlantic).

Canada's main mission for its military has changed significantly during the past 10 years. It is now commissioned to serve a defensive role at home and an international support role to the UN when overseas. It has several well-trained and capable F-18 Hornet squadrons as its primary defensive arm. Most of these units are in Cold Lake on the Alberta/Saskatchewan border. Major deployment bases for defense are further north, presumably to counter incoming aircraft from Russia over the poles. It has several C-130 Hercules transport and air refueling squadrons and 3 anti-submarine warfare (ASW) squadrons on the coasts (1 in BC and 2 in Nova Scotia). In light of this, her only primary nuclear targets of interest to the Russians would be radar sites. Secondary targets would be the main fighter bases, especially the 4th Wing at Cold Lake, and the ASW bases at Comox, BC and Greenwood, NS.

Fallout

We have eliminated a fallout map in this edition because there is no accurate way to show predictable fallout directions. This is because fallout will be affected partially by surface winds and partially by high-altitude jet stream winds. Surface winds change often. High altitude winds at the jet stream level undulate over the US and Canada in a wave form, generally from west to east due to the rotation of the earth. After a nuclear event, the top portion of the mushroom cloud will reach jet stream heights and scatter radioactive material in a broadening plume to the east, northeast or southeast.

Some of the most radioactive particles will settle close to the impact area or where carried by surface winds. Lower altitude winds vary considerably from the jet stream depending on low and high pressure systems, geographic aspects and the season. While most areas have a prevailing wind direction, we don't recommend relying on this as the wind could be different on the day you need to evade fallout.

If you live within 100 miles of a target, do pay attention to the directions in which wind may come in order to have some idea of how much fallout may be heading your way. Learn the various wind directions and study weather patterns so you can predict which way they will turn after a storm front passes. If you are near a geographic boundary like a canyon, mountain pass or off the ocean coast, you may get daily reversals of wind directions due to air masses shifting and flowing up or down the canyon or on and off shore.

When a storm passes, winds usually change directions according to the passing mass of air or "front." The storm front pushes the air ahead of it aside creating winds parallel to the broad face of the front. When the front passes, the wind changes since you now feel the wind that is driving the front forward. Generally expect a 90 degree wind change after storm fronts pass.

Watch the evening news weather so you can get familiar with what local weather fronts look like and how the wind changes. You want to be able to make basic wind direction predictions even when you don't have access to forecasts.

You can easily determine prevailing wind directions by viewing local airport runways on satellite images (all the popular online map viewers show these or have satellite images of them). The runways will be pointing in the directions of the area's prevailing winds. There will be more than one runway for areas that have varying winds but the largest will be aligned with the prevailing direction.

Because of the reduced number of nuclear targets in Canada, it's likely that the fallout danger in many parts will be lower than in the US. Depending on wind flows, however, fallout could easily drift North, particularly over the populated areas in the eastern half of the country. We expect a fair amount of dispersed radioactivity to blanket all of North America and recommend making some preparations for it wherever you live.

EMP (Electro-Magnetic Pulse)

During testing of nuclear weapons after World War II, it was discovered that upper atmosphere nuclear explosions interacted with the earth's magnetic field creating an electronic storm of electromagnetic waves that can cover the entire nation depending on the altitude and size of the explosion.

Russian and Chinese nuclear attack doctrines call for an early use of high altitude nuclear explosions to cause large electromagnetic pulses to radiate down onto the earth's surface. These pulses cause extremely high voltages to be generated in every form of electrical wiring, especially long power lines. This attack would knock out radar sites and communication equipment. Since the nation at large would be targeted, an EMP may give you several minutes warning about a nuclear attack if you are watching for it.

The resultant power surges occur faster than lightning strikes and could blow out transformers and power plant lightning protectors. Everything connected to the grid or a long piece of metal will conduct some of this electrical wave. Light bulbs, computers, and almost everything that is plugged in at your home or business could be burned out. It is even possible to damage equipment that is not turned on or plugged in if there is sufficient wire within the equipment that can flow through computer circuits.

A total cessation of electricity, radio and television may alert you to this impending disaster. If that happens you can assume a nuclear blast is imminent in the target areas outlined above within 10-30 minutes.

An EMP attack from a single warhead launched by a terrorist group or rogue nation is unlikely to be devastating. It would take six or more EMP bursts distributed over the US for the full effect and only Russia and China have that capability. They won't strike until they can also stop our EMP-hardened military from retaliating.

Fundamentals for Surviving a Nuclear Blast

Outside the five mile destructive radius of a nuclear weapon, you can survive the shock waves and the flying debris by getting into a basement space and crouching down near the walls closest to the target area. For example, if you are in San Diego, get up against a basement wall which is closest to the Naval Bases and facilities. Blast waves will break your windows, but the house will likely stand if more than 5 to 10 miles away.

Getting out of town alive with massive amounts of fallout raining down will be another problem—if not impossible. Remember, only particles caught up in the mushroom cloud of a blast become radioactive. The radioactivity of those particles doesn't make anything else radioactive—they just radiate their energy until it naturally dissipates. Most radioactivity will decay in a week or two. This isn't like a meltdown of a nuclear reactor which can spew heavy isotope radiation for months and have deadly effects for years.

If you are not living in a blast zone, but are potentially downwind of one, make a quick calculation of the present wind and how long before the fallout arrives. Make every attempt to travel away from the blast and get to a fallout shelter or at least a basement space at home, or perhaps even at your office, if you have that capability and foresight. You need to have enough shelter and supplies to last you at least two weeks, and perhaps a few months, if there are numerous strikes thereafter.

Forewarning

Advanced warning can make all the difference. Joel puts out a weekly newsletter entitled *The World Affairs Brief*, which not only covers his analysis of world news each week, but will provide advance warning of dangerous future events. It is very inexpensive and comes to your email box every week. Go to *www.worldaffairsbrief.com* for more information.

Shelter Considerations

If you absolutely have to live in a blast zone, you must build an underground blast shelter with very expensive components such as blast doors, high-tech ventilation system and blast valves. Even after all this expense, the chances are slim you will have sufficient warning to be able to take shelter there when the strike comes. If you must live in a high threat blast area, you should at least locate your residence so there is a substantial hill between you and the target area, so that your home will be somewhat shielded from the pressure wave. Remember, however, that many of the explosions will be in the air, not ground bursts.

If you take our advice (after all, that's what this book is for) and relocate away from blast areas, then all that has to be dealt with is fallout. It takes much less money to prepare against fallout and because this threat is likely to spread out and cover most of North America, we recommend this precaution for everyone.

A good fallout shelter needs to stop radiation by placing dense material all around you. Four inches of lead will work, but 10 to 12 inches of solid concrete, 2-3 feet of dense earth or 3 feet of water will also stop or reduce radiation down to a tolerable level. We recommend constructing the shelter underground or in basement areas under your residence so you get the benefit of dirt around you without having to go outside to get there.

The shelter should have a source of filtered air, a secure metal door, food and water supplies, sanitation facilities and solar/battery powered electricity. There can be no windows in a shelter, so you need to have plenty of light available. There are many other things to think about, including secondary escape paths that we can't detail here but shelters are explained in Joel's books as referenced in Chapter 15 and in the "Sources" at the back of this book.

Summary of Recommendations

- Relocate away from direct target areas, or at least locate where you are blast shielded.
- Plan on preparing a shelter against fallout wherever you relocate.
- Establish a network of people who are knowledgeable of the threats, which can give you additional signals, or advance notice that something is imminent.
- Prepare an emergency 72 hour kit and keep it in your trunk for taking temporary shelter in the basement of some home or office. Even if you have no food it is better to stay put in a basement than venture out during heavy fallout.
- Train your children about what to do if they are away from home when a nuclear attack strikes. Teach them how to meet up with you and to leave notes on the inside of windows that tell where they are going if they have to move on. That really helps if a parent goes searching their last known location.
- Prepare your home for self-sufficiency with equipment for multiple alternate energy options so you can live if public utilities and other services are cut off.

Chemical and Biological War

Despite the claims that everyone has eliminated chemical and biological weapons, we don't trust the Russian self-reports about their disarmament. Moreover the Chinese have never even made any promises to disarm. Prudence would dictate that we should be prepared for widespread use of biological and chemical weapons.

Russia has the most extensive arsenal in the world. We expect that Russia will rely on its nuclear arsenal in the beginning, but will use chemical and biological weapons extensively if any Western armies try to combat Russia in the conventional field of battle. Chemical and biological weapons are some of the easiest weapons to manufacture and deliver compared to the devastation they wreak. Even small nations like Iran and North Korea are working to increase stockpiles so as to even the playing field with the US. None of these countries have any regard for the potential retaliation on their own people. In fact, it is highly probably that the sensitivities of Western countries would not allow them to use such weapons even if our own soldiers were attacked with them. Morally, we support this position of not attacking armies with weapons of mass destruction, but we do support attacking the leaders of aggressive foreign nations. Why spend time killing the rather innocent foot soldiers when it is the leaders who are the ones responsible for sending them into battle?

Unfortunately, there is little protection from biological agents. Relocation to rural areas is the greatest safeguard. Chemical is much easier to protect against. Keep personal gas masks in your car trunk or at least a commercial grade paint respirator (much cheaper and quite effective). Don't rely on loose medical face masks, although they are better than nothing.

We can't emphasize enough how important it will be for you to be able to get far away from civilization when plagues and diseases strike. If the disease doesn't get you, the government's inevitable draconian quarantine measures will probably ensure that you are trapped in areas where you are exposed to the disease. Get out of populated areas before quarantines are imposed. In rural areas, concentrations of these pathogens will be so minute or non-existent that you may have a real chance of survival, especially if you eat right and have a healthy immune system.

As outlined in Joel's book, *The Secure Home*, there are whole-shelter Nuclear Biological, Chemical (NBC) filters made to military specs that you can install to give you standard levels of protection from chemical and biological warfare agents. Unfortunately, they are expensive and difficult to acquire. If you can't afford them, you can use regular HEPA filtration systems (costing a few hundred dollars) and then supplement with stored gas masks inside a shelter when a danger is imminent.

Invasion

It is our considered opinion that the Russians or Chinese will not try and occupy America after the strike since that would involve millions of troops and extended supply lines that could not be maintained. Moreover, the millions of gun owners in America would quickly form into a formidable guerrilla force. Even unorganized, millions of armed citizens can play havoc with an occupation. We believe the Russians simply want us out of the picture so they can blackmail the rest of the world into submission.

However, it is entirely probably that there will be a massive invasion of humanity from Mexico after the radiation danger has passed. Law enforcement will be too preoccupied with their own survival and that of their families to worry about waves of illegal immigrants. We don't recommend living near the southern US border.

Social Unrest

Much of the threat of social unrest in other countries is related to labor disputes, racial tensions, student demonstrations, riots and uprisings. The population in the US is less affected by the same factors such as socialist laws, labor unions and welfare groups, although these factors are growing in the US. Currently, mob actions in the US have only occurred in large metro areas with concentrations of low class minorities and whites that can be induced into mob violence when some injustice (real or perceived) triggers an excuse.

We have noticed a criminal aspect to riots in large US cities when police do not stop looting. The unorganized criminal world learned a dangerous lesson from the first of the LA riots. They learned that police were intimidated and would not stop them from looting as long as the pillaging was done in sufficient numbers. The masses of people who join riots when it involves looting, as opposed to peaceful demonstrations, prove there is an undercurrent of personal corruption within American Society. It shows that some people harbor wantonly resentful and greedy habits that allow them to overcome their conscience and steal if they can hide in a crowd. We believe this is reinforced and justified in their minds when they receive government-mandated social benefits because of their "needs." During the looting in the LA riots the police were unwilling to take assertive or physical crowd-control actions to protect private property which would likely have kept the demonstrations shorter.

These isolated instances of social unrest, however, are not the key threat we think you should plan around. They are very small compared to the nationwide social upheaval following an EMP strike and nuclear attack.

After the Bombs

It is hard to imagine the world after a nuclear attack, but we are certain it won't be the end of the world. We think that most Americans will survive the initial blasts. We cannot tell how many waves of nuclear weapons will fall over the US, but we expect a massive first strike followed by secondary strikes in the next few days. Most nuclear weapons will be expended by then and the war will become conventional.

Despite the massive devastation, people outside of the major target cities will not immediately die. However, surviving for the long term amid starvation and without commerce will be much more difficult. After an EMP strike, many components will have to be replaced all along the electrical grid. We expect most of America will be without electricity for over a year, possibly much longer in some areas. America's infrastructure will be almost completely disabled without electricity. Even after some power plants begin to come back online, there will be huge holes in the electrical grid until new parts can be installed or manufactured. Governments will be under pressure to institute rationing of power for short periods of time in different locations.

During this time there will be little communication and news. Most land-line telephones and all cell phones and internet communication will be lost for an indefinite period. Without power there can be no credit card transactions and no bank processing. People will resort to cash (make sure you store small bills for exact change) and even start bartering for basic goods. Gold and silver coins will come out of hiding when the cash is gone. Gold coins will be at a disadvantage because no one will have change for such a high-value coin. Silver dollars will be a better barter coin to use.

Other utilities will also stop or be unusable. With power out, the water pumps and processing plants will be stopped or impaired. If you live in an area without gravity fed water sources, the tap water could even cease. Natural gas and city-supplied fuel sources must be compressed by pressure stations that operate on electricity, so this source could also stop working.

Gas stations will be unable to pump gas. It's unclear whether many cars will be running after the EMP strike, but we suspect that some will be, depending on how strong the EMP pulse is in your area. Keep some reserve fuel on hand. Trucks and trains, however, will largely cease operation for an extended period of time. Most interstate commerce will stop or be limited. Isolated cities like Honolulu and Las Vegas will be cut off from the steady supply stream they are used to. Rural communities will be isolated as well, but that will probably be an advantage since we expect social unrest to begin in large urban areas and spread out from there.

Without a constant stream of supplies from trucking, stores will run out of food within hours or days. Looting and pillaging will erupt in most business districts. Millions of refugees will flee the areas near the blast not knowing what is happening or hoping to escape the fallout. This will clog every freeway and major roadway within an hour of an attack. Many will not have a destination but will just try to get away. Thousands will spread out on every alternate route and side road making these also impassable for a time.

Desperate crowds will likely start searching houses systematically for food supplies or barter items. At first they will search the empty houses but eventually the houses that look like they have food stores will be targeted. In time hungry crowds will spread out from the cities into the suburbs. Refugees stranded on highways will scavenge everything within a few miles of the roadways and even further where signs of civilization are apparent. Once the major roads become passable, a steady stream of desperate people will spread from every populous city looking for food, security or shelter. This is a real issue and all ultimate retreats must be prepared. In Section Three we outline some strategies to mitigate the dangers from this threat on your home or retreat.

Lessons from History

We get some idea of the dangers from social unrest by examining cases in history where large portions of the population have been affected by major catastrophes. Before and after major hurricanes or storms principle roads, highways and freeways have been clobbered with traffic from people trying to leave big cities. Cars have run out of gas sitting in endless lines going nowhere. In most urban freeways there are barriers on either side of the road that keep cars from getting off except at exits. In an emergency, don't get on a freeway unless it doesn't have side barriers—even if traffic seems to be moving.

In the days after hurricane Katrina there was widespread looting and social unrest. Police and National Guard personnel had to be pulled away from rescue efforts to contain violence, shootings and arson, but largely allowed looting to continue. Mob looting and social unrest is a big potential problem anywhere there are high density populations containing ghetto type areas. When times get hard, however, the number of people participating seems to increase with the scale of the emergency. During the aftermath of hurricane Katrina even some of the locals who were part of the police force and in uniform were found looting.

During World War II systematic looting of houses took place as soldiers and refugees looked for food or valuables. Desperate for food, gardens were picked clean, houses emptied of goods and every kind of animal was killed and eaten. At times whole cities would evacuate to escape approaching armies. In these cases refugees choked roads, bridges and mountain passes making them virtually impassable unless people had alternate means available to them.

Avoiding Social Unrest

By its nature, the threat of social unrest is directly proportional to the density of the population around you. Relatively uninhabited zones around big cities are also at risk. In Section Three, we discuss how to locate a retreat in a safe area away from these high density threats. But even after choosing a good retreat site and building up your supplies, it is likely this threat will still reach you in some significant way. We will also talk about keeping a low profile with all your preparations including hiding goods and provisions. We don't recommend making your home look like a fortress; in fact, we recommend you protect your goods first by concealment, and as a last resort with arms.

One of the hardest things you must think through beforehand is what you will do when confronted with masses of people needing help. Wide-spread social unrest will always accompany war, just as it did at the end of WWII. Particularly after nuclear war there will be so many sick and dying that it is almost futile to try to be a Good Samaritan for those badly irradiated. Everyone will have to make some really tough decisions. Prepare backup plans for yourself along every step of your planned emergency escape route. If you don't use all your preparations, you can refer others to them (e.g. your basement stores in your suburb residence) and share. Above all, remember that you don't do yourself any good by giving everything away trying to help people who haven't prepared. It only takes a few minutes of unlimited giving before you are all starving. Every person has got to be trained to fend for themselves and seek shelter on their own. Make sure your family members know how to get to the shelter you have prepared.

In the entire course of human history, there are few circumstances or events of any major significance (war, assassinations, major changes in the control of people's destiny) that have not been accomplished through the combined efforts of conspiring men. As one historian

Chapter 11

GOVERNMENT INTRUSION ON LIBERTY AND INDIVIDUAL LIVES

put it, "no one knows history unless they know the history of conspiracy." Although many conspiracies are small in scale and isolated we see a single or broad conspiracy with a common thread weaving down through the centuries.

Evil men have always conspired to control the world for their own gain. Most people have no trouble seeing this idea operate in organized criminal networks but they have a hard time seeing how it could grow to control a complex democratic government and countries where there are many changes in leadership and seemingly opposing parties.

It is true that in an organization where the public has regular input, it is difficult for a conspiracy to have absolute control. However global power doesn't require absolute control or influence over everyone, only on the ones that control key positions. Since these positions often come about through seniority or political spoils, conspiring powers have considerable time to influence and control those who are allowed to rise within the system to fill these vacancies.

Conspiracy to Control Government

People all over the world are having to deal with a slow, methodical loss of liberty. This is not the work of some individual tyrant for selfish reasons, nor is it the product of mere general socialist trends (though that does play a role). Instead we see it as a small group of people working within our own government toward the slow, systematic erosion of national sovereignty and eventual loss of individual liberty. This threat will possibly have the longest and most far-reaching affect on your strategic efforts to find safety in the future. In this chapter we will discuss generally the hidden conspiracy of power that we believe is behind the effective control of governments and that fully intends to bring the majority of nations into a One World System of global control. Conspiracy is a great subject of derision in the popular press; nevertheless, we are sure of its reality after scrutinizing the evidence for years.

When we speak of conspiracy, we do not mean to say that everything is controlled or planned, or that everyone involved knows the whole agenda. Those that conspire have a definite direction in which they are headed—in this case, a New World Order of nations under statist control. In this system, the march toward greater government control continues unabated even when leaders change through manipulated democratic elections.

This conspiracy seems established enough to accommodate even large events beyond their control—not only natural disasters, but glimpses of their power that could awaken a portion of the people.

The key to understanding how the present system works is found in the principle of using predictable men (who have a limited knowledge of what is going on) wherever possible to carry out the general direction of the agenda. In this way only a very few men at the top echelons of power need to fully conspire, as long as there is a large pool of people they can hire whose behavior is so predictable that they never have to reveal the conspiracy to them, and yet can accomplish all they need them to do. This is, in fact, how the present conspiracy works, but there are a few basic principles a conspiracy must follow to make it operate smoothly in a democracy.

First, they must have a regular way of influencing the thinking of a majority of people. Since a conspiracy very rarely has absolute military or police power, they must always keep the people from finding out the truth. This is a complex issue that has taken more than a century to refine and perfect. It involves careful manipulation not of everyone, but only of the majority, with attention to the following:

- Mandatory public schooling and control over the ideology and content of education.

- Control of the establishment press by controlling funds or flow of information to higher level editors and owners.

- Cultivation of believable and likable political leaders who can be manipulated, even if they are not part of the conspiracy itself. Each leader must be an effective and believable liar in order to put out numerous brush fires of controversy. A conspiracy always makes mistakes which have to be covered up.

- Control of all major political parties so that they can switch to team "A", "B" or "C" and give the appearance of reform, while sabotaging that reform with something false or ineffective.

Second, a conspiracy must control the courts, especially the appellate and high courts so that non-cooperating lower judges can be overturned. Because a democracy can sometimes fail to produce enough unprincipled men in Congress to manipulate all legislation, it is necessary to use the courts to change law or make good law ineffective. These back-up avenues of control are important to avoid suspicion that might arise from too much direct control in Congress.

Third, they must control the military and police forces. This is almost always accomplished in a democracy by making sure that military and police leaders are totally committed to civilian control, and that their allegiance to defend the Constitution is made ineffective by emphasis on mandatory obedience to hierarchy first, without question. To be safe, all non-compliant, powerful, and independent personalities are regularly purged from the ranks as they demonstrate strong differences of opinion. We do not believe there will ever be another Douglas MacArthur or George Patton allowed up through the ranks to high positions in the US military.

A Theoretical Organization Table

In order to accomplish these principles of control, our analysis has come up with four hypothetical levels of participants in this over-arching conspiracy in order to maintain the power they seem to exert. No one outside of this conspiracy has full knowledge of the system and lives to tell about it.

The top level is the relatively small ring of conspirators themselves. Frankly, we don't really know for sure who is in this group. We have some suspicions, but only a member of this group would know for sure. No one invites themselves into this group. It is by invitation only after one has gone through a long, careful selection process (coming up through the ranks, so to speak). They must show that they are completely committed to the cause of control by power, and that they are absolutely without principles or scruples. They must have demonstrated that they are entirely callused against the promptings of divine conscience.

People in this group hardly ever take a top level position in government. Though they may assume mid-to-upper level bureaucratic positions, to gain experience, and to watch over and drop messages to those in more visible positions of leadership and government.

The second level is made up of those who have reached the pinnacle of power in government: advisers and handlers of puppet presidents—the ones who call the shots. After a while on the job, everyone in the White House knows who the real bosses are and not to cross them. Almost all of these leaders have somewhat of an elitist attitude, no matter what they profess in political speeches. They believe that people in a democracy have to be managed and fooled into doing what is good for the whole of society. These second level people are always very well educated, very ambitious, and excited to work for the real Powers That Be (PTB).

These might be called "directors"—people like Henry Kissinger and his associates who rotate in and out of government and exercise control even when out of office. Founders and leaders of the Trilateral Commission and other globalist organizations are also at this level. The advisors in this group are quite visible—and, in our opinion, include such notables

as Sandy Burger, Strobe Talbot, Brent Scowcroft, and Zbigniew Brzezinski. A recent true story demonstrates how powerful these second level controllers are.

Barack Obama's National Security Advisor **James Jones** made an incautious remark at the Munich Security Conference in February, 2009: "As the most recent National Security Advisor of the United States, I take my daily orders from Dr. Kissinger, filtered down through General Brent Scowcroft and Sandy Berger, who is also here. We have a chain of command in the National Security Council that exists today." This is a tangible admission of conspiracy: NSA Jones has no legal authority to be allowing Kissinger and others to dictate "daily marching orders" to him or the Obama administration, but it happens in every administration. As of this writing, this quote was still available on the website of the nation's foremost globalist leadership group, the Council on Foreign Relations (CFR): *http://www.cfr.org/publication/18515/*

The third level is made up of yes-men at all levels of government who do their jobs and take orders in exchange for worldly benefits, positions and, eventually, just to "survive" in their career. These are the predictable hirelings we talked about. Most know there is a control system underlying the "democratic system" but they rationalize it away as benevolent or a necessary evil. By their obedience training, and partial weakness of character, they end up doing the legwork for these globalist causes that have other hidden purposes.

They will keep any secret no matter how horrible simply to preserve their career and keep the considerable benefits and future pension coming. These include most heads of government, a good portion of the non-leaders in the Council on Foreign Relations, the Federal Judiciary, most Senators, most Congressmen, many governors and a good portion of heads of government at all levels. As much as possible, bright people with predictable philosophies and compromised morals are selected to staff the higher positions in government so that they can be easily manipulated and influenced without being told too much.

For example, in 1996 Spain's neophyte puppet president Jose Marie Aznar told one interviewer (renowned Spanish commentator Inaki Gabilondo) that his very first official visitor after being elected was Henry Kissinger, who doesn't speak Spanish and is not an expert on Spain. Aznar said that "he was explaining to me how the world worked."

There are also hundreds of powerful men in the private sector who are part of this level. These include major heads of international corporations, chief owners and editors of major media sources and heads of most of the powerful tax-exempt foundations that fund so many bad causes.

These men all get to where they are because they very badly want to be in a position of power, and are willing to compromise certain moral principles to get there and to stay there. However, since some of these people (though politically and socially liberal) have strong, independent egos, they are never allowed to go any farther than this level. Lee Iacocca, former Chairman of Chrysler Corp. was a good example. He was a high-level player with plenty of power potential—but he couldn't and wouldn't allow others to control him. His ego was too big. A conspiracy doesn't like people with independent, big egos that cannot be controlled by others.

The fourth level is made up of low-level enforcers. These are unprincipled police and former military yes-men who are willing to use force without scruples. They carry out "black operations" in sectors of various government agencies, and have connections with the organized criminal world. These are "dirty tricks gangs" that form cells in every federal police force—especially CIA, FBI, Secret Service, DEA and ATF. These are necessary to carry out threats, "suicides" and assassinations (as necessary) to keep other government yes-men from defecting or letting their conscience get the best of them.

Each of the federal services (FBI, CIA, ATF, INS, Secret Service, etc.) has many good and patriotic people working for them. The good guys are the regular, naive, patriotic types who are assigned the legitimate tasks of government enforcement. Virtually every agency head knows about the black side of his organization. No one is allowed to run these agencies unless he can be trusted to execute the special orders that come down via discrete private channels. Upper level managers who are part of the conspiracy are always watching and judging the above ground side of personnel, testing for lack of character to see who can be drawn in and trusted to do corrupt work. That is also one of the main purposes for the government hiring so many hundreds of thousands of private military contractors. They are sifting through the ranks of former military to help recruit personnel for dark side government operations.

The public got a glimpse of this "Good ol' Boy" network after one particularly egregious social gathering in 1990 (entitled: The Good ol' Boys Roundup) which was videotaped by one of the newcomers (thinking it was funny) and the tape found its way into the media's hands in 1995. Nothing would have come of it except that there were a lot of racial gags and insults that caused an outrage in the media, but only over this aspect. Obviously, the smell of secret gatherings of cross agency thugs didn't bother them. The subsequent investigation revealed that this inter-agency party is an annual secret convention—a kind of inter-service party where certain enforcers get together to exchange war stories and revel in their own powerful connections. Members even have a special ring which they wear occasionally when together. Their leaders always deny such activities when confronted directly.

Cover-ups and Evidence of Conspiracy

In a cover-up, government agents, policemen, military officers, medical personnel and a host of other people have to get involved to silence the truth. These cover-ups always occur whenever the government has to do some criminal act in public, or at least when the suspicions of foul play reach the public. Witnesses who observe government criminal activity have to be threatened, silenced, bought off, or convinced that they didn't see what they saw. Innocent government personnel recording events in their normal line of duty have to be sworn to secrecy. The fact that the government often has legitimate reasons to keep things secret is often used by these innocent government workers to suppress their normal misgivings. They are, in fact, taught never to question why something is ruled secret.

We will not go into any of these cover-ups in any depth, but here is a list of some of the bigger ones:

- The Assassination of President John F. Kennedy, which involved multiple professional hit men directly connected to CIA, the mafia and elements of the Secret Service. The official Warren Commission investigation falsified and omitted evidence in order to promote the lone gunman theory. The president's body was altered during a pre-autopsy in order to cover for multiple hits from different directions.

- The Martin Luther King assassination that led to the passing of multiple Civil Rights legislation. There was also the subsequent sealing of the FBI files on Rev. King's blatant immoral lifestyle with prostitutes and alliances with Communists.

- The Robert F. Kennedy Assassination, where police recovered 9 bullets supposedly coming from the six shot revolver of Sirhan Sirhan.

- The POW/MIA cover-up from World War II, Korea and Vietnam where thousands of captured soldiers were abandoned. Some of these were subjected to medical experiments, and others were found to have died in Russian, Korean, Chinese and Vietnamese gulags, all after the supposed release of all prisoners. All this was done with the full knowledge of our government.

- The missile downing of TWA flight 800 out of New York and the subsequent buying off of witnesses who would not recant that they saw a missile in flight. Significant falsification had to be done on the salvage aircraft mockup.

- The Vince Foster Murder and the false evidence and reporting about his claimed suicide filed by "Independent Counsel" Kenneth Starr.

- The death of Commerce Secretary Ron Brown in an airplane "accident" in Bosnia. A later autopsy was covered-up with X-rays showing that Brown had a bullet hole in the head, and that one of the Bosnian tower operators was told to shut down the navigation beacon before Brown's plane arrived.

- The government involvement in the Oklahoma City Bombing, with its multiple explosions and multiple accomplices protected by the FBI.

- The attacks of September 11, where considerable evidence and witnesses attest to explosions inside the buildings, including building 7, which was not hit by hijacked aircraft.

Joel continually reviews and analyzes these events as they develop in his World Affairs Brief. You can read much of this analysis from previous years at his website (*www.worldaffairsbrief.com*).

The Ultimate Threat

Government itself will only be a serious threat to a minority of its citizens—those who really suspect what is going on behind the scenes and who are prepared to object or resist in some meaningful way. This is because the conspiracy fully intends to make sure it always has believable, normal looking people at the heads of all governments. This is very important toward their continual efforts to keep the public as well as the media (which they directly control, for the most part) in the dark about a conspiracy big enough to control government.

The majority of people don't have the ability or inclination to see through a complex conspiracy such as what we are dealing with in the West. Sadly, this is true of most Americans who do not see what is going on with their country. This is partly because of their lack of critical thinking about what they see and what the media feeds them. This starts with the highly edited version of history they learn in public schools and their dependence on the establishment media for news coverage of current events.

Strategies for Protection

Considering the many cases in history of government oppression and instances when opponents to government were targeted, incarcerated and eliminated systematically, you might be wondering if there is really any place to relocate to for absolute safety. There probably is not such a place, or at least not a permanent place. Preparations must involve both strategy and location. Every principled person will have to find their own path through this threat. We can only give general hints. You will have to work out the details according to your individual inclinations and circumstances.

In general, one has to stay within society as long as possible. Blend in among the majority, as long as it does not require you to compromise your principles. As government works to crack down on liberties and citizens in opposition to its aims, the majority will become more and more fearful of doing anything that would get them targeted by the establishment. Stay active in only the most important causes. Avoid traps like the tax protest

movement, which we think is being purposely allowed to attract independent people who still think they can get justice in the courts on the tax issue.

Keeping a low profile does mean being very careful who you express objections to, and only revealing your strongest feelings and objections to injustice when you are dealing with someone you can really trust. People of strong ideological feelings have a difficult time doing this. It also means holding back some of what you know, depending on the preparation of the person. Only try to give additional information to people who sense something is wrong on their own.

Pick an area to live that has like-minded people. This is best done in suburban or semi-rural settings where there are others who match your living style. All active resistance to tyranny (if that becomes necessary) must be done privately, and all public resistance should be done in the most orderly, generic and proper forms possible.

Do not live in a survivalist community. Every one of these places will eventually be targeted for infiltration, provocation and disruption by hostile government agents or will be fractured by strong contentions and infighting. The leaders of these communities are almost always people with very strong personalities who sometimes lack wisdom and restraint on key issues. It only takes one or two issues that appear "extreme" to turn the surrounding community into suspicious or hostile observers—even when the group's basic plan and motives are sincere.

Develop contingency plans and resources. Keep your published address, phone number etc. in an urban or suburban location, but consider establishing one or more layers of retreat locations that fewer and fewer people know about. Never live full time in a true retreat—it leaves too many tracks. Retreat structures should be designed with multiple levels of self-sufficiency to avoid the need to commute into town often. One of the most interesting contingency retreat options is to get in a motor home and "disappear" on the road for awhile. But that can't be done during really hard times when there is no fuel and when you need land to grow food.

Secondary retreats can be vacation spots. Make friends with the neighbors, but avoid the ones who are overly nosy or curious. Avoid being secretive, since nothing attracts more attention than someone trying to keep a secret. Ultimate retreats should ideally be in forested, hilly terrain to avoid being too visible. Stay away from associations or owning a condo, unless the association is friendly and non-intrusive. Your retreat should have a safe room with a concealed entrance and an alternate, concealed exit. Never plan on defending your retreat against a siege standoff with large numbers of intruders. Always leave discreetly via your private access before you become trapped.

Only a few of the most visible resistors will need the ultimate type of retreat to safeguard against being rounded up as a threat to tyranny. There are only two possible strategies and they involve some form of disappearing act—either by blending in with society or physically hiding. Each of these two can be accomplished in either a rural or an urban setting.

Summary Thoughts

If the subject of conspiracy in government and the potential for war is new to you, this section on US threats has likely been somewhat disturbing. It used to be more difficult to convince good people that all of this was happening during a Republican administration when President George W. Bush was pretending to be both a conservative and a devout Christian. Christian conservatives are too trusting of those who claim to be one of them even when their actions betray their words. Now it is easier to believe. Under the Obama administration, it has become all too obvious that government control and tyranny is accelerating faster than ever; but remember, all of it was started (or was continuing) under George W. Bush.

The threat of nuclear war may seem to loom larger since it will threaten every American physically but we think the threats of social unrest and then tyranny will ultimately become more dangerous as our own government starts eliminating our liberties and cracking down on people like no invader could. In this next section, we will discuss more strategies for the threats described here and help you decide how to mitigate their affects through your own relocation, preparedness and contingency plans, including for those that have to stay within unsafe urban environments.

SECTION THREE: STRATEGIES

Chapter 12

CUSTOMIZE A PLAN FOR YOUR OWN SITUATION

Your personal strategy for safety will depend on many, often competing factors. As we consult with people we often find spouses who disagree about their priorities or who struggle to make changes around children. It is rare to find a place that will satisfy everyone completely. The trick is to weigh the factors and find the right compromise. In this chapter we hope to help you distinguish the important issues from the superficial considerations that too often impair these critical decisions.

Assess the Threats

In Chapter One we discussed the process for evaluating threats. This is a very important part of your analysis. We divided the threats we face into two major groups, threats to avoid and threats to mitigate. Now that we have discussed each threat in more detail, here is a summary of where these threats fall:

Threats to Avoid

Remember that these are serious threats that will sweep through large sectors of society but in relatively localized places. These will offer little mercy and almost no warning. They will be worst where people are concentrated in high risk areas. Avoiding these risks is not simply a preferred strategy—it is a must do strategy. We have worked to document or map out each of these threats in previous chapters. Although none of these risks seems looming at present (which is why millions of people choose to live in the shadow of these threats), their effects won't be seen until it's too late. If you don't get out of these high danger zones before that happens, you will be trapped. Nothing less than getting out will give you any real chance of long term safety. Here is a summary of these threat areas:

- **Big natural disasters:** These are areas where the threat of death or injury from nature is high. This includes potentially active volcanoes, serious earthquake zones, coastal hurricane or tsunami areas and housing developments in dry forest areas subject to wild fires.

- **High pollution areas:** Although this isn't a quick, devastating threat, it is localized and very dangerous in the long-term. Like the other threats, once the effects hit and your health is suffering, you've waited too long to leave. Avoid cities with year-round exposure to air or water pollution and localized, even rural areas near dangerous polluters, past or present.

- **High crime zones:** Obviously these are worst in already high crime cities. Avoid even driving through the bad parts of these cities.

- **Military target areas:** Move away from these potential blast areas in a nuclear war. The blast radius is 5 to 10 miles from ground zero. We show a 10 mile radius ring around the targets in our color maps.

- **High density urban areas:** These areas are extremely susceptible to panic, social unrest or martial law during a crisis.

Threats to Mitigate

These are threats you can't avoid completely because of their widespread effects, but you can mitigate your exposure by at least modest relocation and advance preparations. Often the need for big preparations is inversely proportional to the distance of your relocation. Here is a short summary of these threats, how to mitigate them and ways to prepare for their effects:

- **Moderate natural disasters:** Mitigate by staying far enough away that you have time to move or seek protection. Prepare with basic reinforcement to your buildings or surroundings.

- **Plagues and health threats:** Mitigate this threat through isolation and distance from big populations. Prepare by learning to stay healthy and practicing natural remedies.

- **Widespread social unrest:** Mitigate with distance from big populations. Prepare with concealed, defendable stockpiles.

- **Economic problems:** Mitigate and prepare by developing alternate skills and building up savings in money and certain material goods.

- **Effects of war:** Mitigate by staying away from military targets. Prepare by maintaining and developing communications alternatives for news and information.

- **Government persecution:** Those who resist tyranny must prepare to fight the erosion of liberties and mitigate their risk by keeping a low profile.

Specific Strategies

Earthquakes: Those who live in California really need to take the earthquake hazard seriously. The big quakes are survivable if you live in a single story reinforced wood frame building on decent soil. Avoid older masonry buildings. Try not to commute on elevated bridges or freeways and plan routes around these after an emergency. Check out local county soil and seismic maps that show which areas are less susceptible to liquefaction and multiple reverberations. You can also reinforce a portion of your home to provide a safe area to retreat to during the quake. Make sure that you have at least a 1 month supply of food, water and household supplies in your home, even if you have a retreat (in case you can't get there).

Hurricanes: Don't live in hurricane country, if at all possible. It's really much wiser to enjoy the Gulf Coast and its climate during a vacation than to live there full time. What measures the government can take in a major hurricane are somewhat futile, and may quickly turn into harsh control tactics as we saw in Hurricane Katrina.

The Federal Emergency Management Agency (FEMA) has plans to relocate refugees in natural disasters to public buildings where they are not free to leave. In the future, they may even place people in private homes, without the consent of the owners and with little or no government support. If the refugees are low class and hostile, they may even take over and not allow you to keep order in your home or make the rules of conduct and without any legal right to evict them. You will be the host and the hostage at the same time.

If you cannot avoid localized storm threats such as tornadoes and hurricanes, you should implement a high security safe room in your house. Don't forget to make advance preparations at work, where possible. Preplan your routes of escape. If you live in a hurricane area, harden the exterior of your home or buy materials to board-up windows. Stockpile supplies and make contingency plans for moving further inland or to higher ground.

Pandemics: To avoid the increasing risk of contagious diseases, move to rural suburbia. High density regions are the cauldron of plagues and contagions. Keep your kids out of public schools when there is a high probability of picking up contagious diseases. In a major public health outbreak, even if you are a dedicated natural health person, your immune system can only stand so much bombardment of chemicals or pathogens. You are at risk if your children get sick from contact with others in school and bring it home to you. You can keep other sick people away, but not your own children. Only by living in rural areas, in greater isolation from other sick people, will you have the best chance of avoiding the worst outbreaks.

Economic problems: If you are between jobs, it may be a good time to relocate. Keep your relocation strategy in mind as you search for new employment. Don't be afraid of branching out into new areas of your profession or even other professions that provide practical work experience. A broad range of skills may help you in the future and knowledge and tools to fix problems at home or on your car can also save you considerable money. Live within your means and go without instead of going into debt. People who are overextended are

going to lose most of their assets someday. If you are thinking of changing jobs or think your job is unstable, prepare for a loss of income by slowly buying a little extra food each month and storing it. A minimum 2 or 3 month's supply of savings and supplies can sustain you while in transition.

War and its aftermath: You must avoid blast zones by relocation. Prepare to mitigate fallout. Only count on short travel periods to get to a shelter. This can best be done by building a safe room within your basement. After the initial threat of radiation has passed, the threat of famine will face those who have survived the first strike. Conceal your stockpiles to avoid physical confrontation with looters.

Crime and home invasion: People stuck in urban areas should take extra precautions against social unrest and crime. Crime is an ever-present problem in all metro areas, so make a few extra security precautions. Have impact resistance doors and jambs (preferably metal), pick-proof locks, acrylic storm windows (which also inhibit intrusions), a solid door with a strong jam and locking knob on each bedroom (very important to keep you and the children safe at night from surprise intrusion) and a defensive firearm close to your bed. Get in the habit of always locking your bedroom door so that any intruder will have to get through the door before he gets to you. This will also give you time to wake up and react.

Determine Your Financial Options

One of the first steps in realizing your relocation goal is to make sure you can sustain your family financially in the new location. Most people will have to make compromises between total security and personal desires regarding their income stream. Jobs with a certain company or self-employed business plans can rarely be transferred to rural safe locations. Often you will have to make the most of your business within local metropolitan areas while times are good and make plans to retreat to a more rural safe area later. As you become more financially independent you may even be able to retire early in a more secure location.

Balancing Income and Relocation

If you are young and just starting out, it may be wise to relocate sooner so that you don't have to uproot your business or profession in the middle of your career. In these troubled times it is often better to set up shop in a smaller town in a safer area than take the big paying job in New York or Los Angeles. If you can't do that, then structure your career to be as flexible as possible. For example, you may consider joining a company that has branches in safe areas to which you can transfer someday.

The potential of deep financial problems in the US and world economies is large enough that location becomes partially irrelevant for avoiding a bad economy—it will affect you wherever you are. However, depending upon your specific job and abilities, some locations can give you more room to maneuver than others.

Some areas of the economy are less robust against recessions because of demographic factors. For example, areas with high concentrations of retirees, who are completely dependent upon invested income and pensions, are the most vulnerable. Florida is one of the highest in this category. Areas that have experienced rapid gains are the most susceptible to collapse. The boom of high tech companies (e.g. Silicon Valley) has fallen. Rapid housing growth has fallen and created greater economic struggles (e.g. Las Vegas, Florida). The best areas will be those with moderately-sized metro areas that have had steady but moderate growth, are well balanced and diversified and are surrounded by an agricultural base.

Don't be in a job or business transition when these economic problems strike, if you can help it. Due to the severity of the financial bubbles created during 2000-2008, we are already in serious trouble in 2010, although it is still only affecting the market selectively. About 20% of Americans are hurting, but the rest are still doing well. Those still in good shape need to protect yourselves while you can. If you are starting a business, build slowly to avoid debt wherever possible. There were dozens of very profitable businesses that went under from 2008-2010 simply because they were too far extended into debt.

If you decide to move, carefully weigh the practical needs of finances with your feelings about when to make a move. Here are some basic questions to ask yourself:

- How long will it take to be firmly reestablished in a new and safer location before things get worse? Ideally you want to have your business contacts, business ties and backup strategies already established before the market gets thinner or a crisis hits.

- Do I have a fallback position, in terms of job, talents, skills, funds, reserves, etc. in the new location? If not, how long will it take me to create and establish them?

- Will there exist a need for my fallback talents in the area I am presently living, or do I have to move to find an area with more potential clients in a crisis? For example, electrical engineers and computer programmers may be able to fall back to computer or electronic repair and maintenance, but not in San Jose, California where there would be an oversupply of competition.

- Does my location allow for total self sufficiency, if I have to revert back that far? Is there land to grow a garden? Will I have space for a garage or shop and tools? Will I have secure storage room or space for a secure room at home? Only move if you have the ability to stockpile supplies, grow food and maneuver.

- What will my network be after the move? How long will it take to build it up? If you don't have a significant network of like minded friends and relatives to help you give and take in a crisis, you are more vulnerable and without recourse.

Economic Survival

The biggest single factor you have to consider when relocating during relatively peaceful times is maintaining your financial resources and income stream after a disaster. As much as we see the value in relocation for safety, you must keep your priorities straight. Don't let your relocation goals get ahead of your financial ability to make it happen. We have consulted with many well meaning people who make the move too soon to rural living before they are prepared to sustain themselves financially. Self-sufficiency and security aren't cheap. Too many also get panicky thinking that they are "out of time." There are no shortage of "the sky is falling" stories on the internet to make one feel that collapse is imminent. Someday it will be imminent, but you must get a good handle on your ability to discern between what is real and what is just scaremongering. Bad things tend to take longer to fully mature than people think. That's no reason to relax, but you must keep your security plans within your means to pay for them.

Work on developing financial stability or independence by reducing or eliminating unnecessary expenditures. Grow a garden and buy unprocessed foods (it's cheaper and healthier over time). Budget time and some funds for immediate emergencies and then keep your contingency plans up to date so that you can "get out of town" quickly if needed. The minimum is a good 72 hour kit and storing some spare fuel. During this developing period you may have to make plans with friends or relatives who live in safer places. Stay as independent as possible since they will fall back on their security means in hard times too, but sometimes you can make your own precautions in parallel with like-minded family or close friends. It's best if you have your own safety net but don't be too proud to ignore dependency plans with others when you have no alternative. Ultimately, you will always have to deal with the delicate balance of how much of a network to build and rely on versus going it alone. Something in-between is usually best.

Don't take this advice lightly. This is the most common error that people make in reacting to their valid assessment that the world is headed for trouble someday—they move too far, too fast, rather than in stages with built-in contingencies. Joel had dozens of families come to him for consultation during the Y2K (Year 2000) scare, having put themselves into the predicament of selling everything and moving to an area where they couldn't sustain themselves financially. Now, they were stuck and he had to advise them to move back into a more sustainable location (better than before, but still less rural). So, as a basic ground rule let's establish the following three principles:

First, consider the degree to which you are independently self-sufficient. After a calamity, can you do all the work to keep yourself alive and do you have the tools to do it? If you do, then you are one of the few who can retreat to the safest rural areas. We encourage people to work toward this kind of self-sufficiency, where possible. For all other services we will have to work together with some degree of interdependent commercial society which will take time to develop.

Second, recognize what kind of person you are and cross-train yourself in as many areas as necessary to ensure your value in a world that will someday only value competency in practical areas. You will always do better in a future world of uncertainties by maximizing your usefulness within your given talent pool. Better still; try to increase the breadth of your talents—as long as you are realistic about your limits. Even though everyone someday will need more food, not everyone has the kind of stamina and practical savvy about growing things that a farmer has. Farming doesn't take a lot of brain power, but it sure does take a lot of practical experience, practical knowledge about fixing things, and a good internal spiritual warning system about what to plant and what the weather threats are going to be. Everyone at least ought to know how to grow a garden, but even in a crisis thinkers and creators can better leverage their talents by creating solutions and fixing problems, than by trying to grow food for barter.

Unfortunately, some current professional and artistic jobs have virtually no monetary value in a crisis economy. If you have a profession that has no usefulness in a collapsing social and economic world, train for another in your spare time. Swallow your pride and get some other useful skills that will serve you well. For example, if you are a financial guru, what will you do when financial instruments collapse? Certain high tech engineering and computer jobs are only good as long as well-financed corporations can produce the products they design. Technical types should be prepared to retrench back to maintenance and repair and become experts in helping people make do with existing hardware and software and modifying them to fit new, essential needs. Doctors with exotic specialties should be retraining in alternative medicine and more practical, well-rounded family practice services. Business types ought to broaden their product lines so as to withstand shifts in the markets. Investment gurus should learn how black markets and barter markets operate.

Third, bolster your resources by stockpiling what you can't produce yourself. In a world of overabundance, the cheapest and easiest way to prepare against the future is to stockpile. It's cheaper than buying a farm and equipment. It's safer than saving tons of money where there is a high risk of eventual loss. It's also the smartest thing you can do to ensure that your business remains viable longer than the competition in a crisis. Stockpile as much of your business essentials as possible but be careful how you do it to avoid a tax drubbing. One of the greatest economic risks we face today is the excess reliance on "just in time" inventory practices. When the highly sophisticated distribution systems fail, America's entire business structure will come to a screeching halt. Don't be caught without inventory and you may still be in business when products start reappearing.

Investment Survival

If you are financially self-sufficient or if you have significant resources, you are still at risk—sometimes even more than the person with less money. Large bodies of assets have to be invested because they exceed your reasonable consumption needs or exceed your present time resources to put them into productive, tangible holdings. What can you do? Right now you've probably put your excess money and capital into paper investments. Whenever you have lots of money invested in intangible markets you run the risk of losing all or most of it from inflation or a financial melt-down. Even if you have invested in gold and silver as a hedge against inflation, you probably haven't taken physical possession of it, or can't without a secure room in which to store it.

If you have excess wealth beyond your preparedness needs, we recommend that you invest in one of two areas of the market that can survive even a war or partial economic collapse. Nothing is foolproof but these two have the best chances of success depending on your income needs.

For passive income, invest in commercial or industrial buildings that are leased to government, utilities, or medical professionals. We think that those three types of tenants will always have first access to continuing funds, even in war. Make sure you pick a location that is not subject to destruction during war. Pay for these outright and keep them debt free.

For active income, create a service business focusing on something that will be essential in hard times, or set up a small manufacturing outfit that can be operated without a lot of manual labor. All service businesses will require some stockpiling of materials you can't produce locally—the same with small manufacturing, unless you are into recycling.

Examples of service businesses are: computer or appliance repair, small engine repair or a machine shop. The best jack-of-all-trade handymen could do well setting up a total recycling center/junk yard in combination with a full spectrum welding, machining and repair shop and then concentrate on scavenging parts and creating working cars and appliances out of the most repairable equipment that comes in. Salvaging and rebuilding computers will someday be an essential service. Small manufacturing might include ammunition reloading, or refining methane, bio-diesel or ethanol fuels on a small scale. Downsized or small-unit equipment is available now, but won't be in a crisis.

A number of warehousing businesses can be created by stockpiling essential equipment in anticipation of a future shortage. The tough part of this business is watching out for obsolescence and waste through dated materials. The best way to protect against that is to be supplying the current tradesmen with a rotating and constantly updating inventory at a profit.

Relocate and build strategic, practical reserves (physical commodities for use or barter) with some of your investment income. In other words, take a sufficient portion of your reserves and convert them from at-risk-investments to very low risk assets that you will use for personal protection and security in a crisis. In a nutshell, this means preparing to eliminate your future need for money by stockpiling homes, cars, equipment, food, water, tools, parts, and supplies.

Naturally, to do this, you have to be sure you have selected the optimal long-term location to ride out the future crises. If you make the wrong choice, you risk having to leave behind not only your investments, but your fixed strategic reserves as well. The compromise, of course, is that often the best locations are so remote that one loses most ties with the world in order to live there. This is rarely wise either, except in the most extreme crises. Better to select a compromise that has a little more risk, but which ensures you don't starve or run out of ways to make a living before the need for high security arises.

Consider Your Network - Family and Friends

No man is an island unto himself. Despite the growing deterioration of society in general, hard times will always bring out the best in a smaller portion of society. At some point, even the hardened isolationist will need the help and cooperation of others to survive the most difficult threats ahead. Bartering basic items or combining labor to complete large projects will become vital to survival and rebuilding. Start to take note of who makes up your support group and maintain contact with the people you trust.

This support group is what makes up your "network"—the people that you trust and who you can rely on for support or favors when you really need it. The kind of people you would call in an emergency or trust for favors like picking up your child from school or holding a spare key to your house. This network is very important to your relocation. People naturally recognize this and often avoid moving away from friends or family because of it. We caution you to make a balanced decision in this regard. There are friends to be made wherever you move. Don't move to the middle of Boston just to be near family, or fail to move because you don't want to separate your kids from their friends. If you find yourself in a tough crisis surrounded by ill-prepared, good friends your network has only served to keep you from getting to safety.

Take the time to share some aspects of your view of the world to help you find out who is like-minded or not. You never know what kinds of friends you really have until you broach difficult topics and current problems. Go slow at first and test their reaction. A knowledge of which friends are similar-minded is important for your long-term support group. If liberties become suppressed, this network will become vital for maintaining basic freedoms such as communication, travel and exchange of goods. In the past, many members of oppressed societies had to learn who was trustworthy and who was not.

Your network will mostly be made up of family, close friends and support groups like church congregations. You will also know many local acquaintances such as coworkers, neighbors or casual friends from social groups or sports who are not part of your trusted network, but who may become so after a time.

Family

For most people, family members will be the most important part of your network. Most families already combine to share resources, knowledge and efforts to help each other. Family members are used to working together for mutual benefits without contracts or agreements. Be careful not to abuse this understanding and keep a balanced relationship of help flowing both ways. Even parents get tired of giving unending support to a capable child.

It's easier to develop a standard of trust and reliability with family members or, conversely, if someone is not fully trustworthy it is usually known to family. Be careful not to overlook failings and weaknesses in siblings, spouses and children. This is a common mistake among families so try to see people as they really are. Usually you already know more about these people, their opinions and abilities than any others in your network.

Family connections, unlike friends, are not based on similar tastes, values or opinions, necessarily. It is important to test the waters of extended family members by sharing parts of ideas and seeing where their interests are. Where there is clearly hostility toward ideas of preparedness we have found it is often better to keep your ideas to yourself. Be careful not to constantly discuss your preparations with others who aren't making any similar efforts lest they assume they can just "come to your house when things get bad."

This is a real thing to consider. It is hard enough to make sufficient preparations for yourself, let alone for others too. It will be very hard to turn people down if they come knocking at your door in a crisis. Depending on your circumstances, you may want to prepare an extra stage of security that you can give to others if you don't use them in an emergency. We recommend having multiple such stages of security: a basic stage of 72 hour kits, a second stage at work with more food, water and supplies, a third stage at home (if you don't have your shelter there) with a few month's worth of food, water and essentials and, finally, your ultimate retreat with the real solid resources to live things out. Hopefully you will make quick progress to your retreat and you can leave arrangements for the unused portions to be found by those who haven't prepared but are worth helping.

One of the biggest hurdles to effective preparation and relocation is when a wife or husband is not convinced that hard times are coming and doesn't want to move or make the changes necessary to weather future threats. In the end you have to do your utmost to save yourself and your family from impending destruction. Teaching and sharing the reasons for concern are all important to communicate. All of these preparations take time and after a while many spouses will become accustomed to your "hobby" of becoming more prepared. Sometimes compromises can be made to convert a personal room such as an office or garage space into a secure room. Establish an understanding of respect in this regard so your careful plans are not spilled by the other's flippant remarks someday.

Friends

The friends we make throughout our lives are the second most important part of our network. For those who cannot locate near family or who don't have any support from extended family, this may be your primary network. Fortunately, one can often find and develop friends wherever they move, so this part of your network is inherently more flexible.

There are different levels of friendship and trust, however. Few friendships are strong enough to really help each other out in the same way family would. These life-long friends are almost harder to keep around you than family but even long-distance friendships can be good parts of an extended network.

Keep your extended network in mind throughout this process. It should be made up of people who you can trust in hard times. Whether you stay where you are or relocate, try to keep those essential contacts in other parts of the region and world intact. You never know when your lives will meet up again and provide opportunities to help each other. When you travel, always keep a current list of these contacts on hand so if you are stranded in some faraway place when trouble hits, you know who to seek out. Also, don't just see the sites when you travel; try and get to know interesting people wherever you go.

Church and Communal Groups

Your church congregation can also be a valuable part of your network. Some congregations are close-knit and can provide a lot of support. Others are more of a social gathering place. Regardless of this both can be good places to meet potential friends who have similar morals and ideals. Some church groups are like small towns—helpful in a pinch but often nosy.

Although we encourage banding together and networking, we do not recommend joining any communal living efforts or formal survival groups intent on building a shared community. It may be fine for friends to move close together or in the same general location, but too much interdependency breeds unnecessary friction. The best long term relationships have just enough distance so that independence is fostered and personal friction over minor differences is minimized. Yet, in a crisis, they are close enough to be of assistance—in other words, establish loosely organized preparedness communities providing full autonomy for each family.

Prepare Immediate Essentials

While you are preparing to relocate or are working on building up your safe place, be sure to make some preparations for your current situation, wherever you are. The first step of making 72 hour kits can be started in one evening just by gathering things from around the house. After that, make steady, incremental increases over time until you have some basic security.

72-hour kits of emergency supplies can be easily put together and stored in your trunk or where you can get to it in a hurry. Pack such things as energy bars for emergency food, pre-packaged opaque plastic containers or pouches of water, a first aid kit, flash lights, small Dacron blankets, Mylar plastic survival wraps (space blankets), incidental fix up things (e.g. nails, screws, tape, glue, screwdriver, pliers) and a whistle to alert rescuers to your location. Pack extra engine oil, anti-freeze and spare parts like fan belts in your trunks with a modest tool kit to do minor repairs.

It is also a good idea to purchase high quality, industrial dust or chemical respirators for emergencies where smoke, dust or ash is present. These are cheaper and less obtrusive than a gas mask, but are much better protection than regular dust masks. Store one in the car along with a few regular masks for unprepared friends. A real gas or smoke mask may be more helpful in an emergency where you have to quickly rescue someone. This is not a fool-proof or totally risk free solution to smoke inhalation, but it may save someone's life. We also recommended having masks at home in parent's and children's bedrooms to ensure they can get out of a smoke-filled house in a fire.

For nuclear fallout situations, we recommend carrying one of the small radiation stickers that show accumulated radiation exposure. They only cost a few dollars (*www.ki4u.com*) and can be stored in 72 hour kits or in a wallet. There are also key-chain detectors for around $150 that chirp depending on the level of radiation in the area (*www.nukalert.com*). All these can help you decide if it is safe to try and travel to a more secure location, or when to leave a temporary shelter for a better one.

People who commute in large cities and risk getting caught in massive traffic jams should pack a small, portable, lightweight bicycle in their trunk. If you have to ditch your car, these folding or take-apart bikes can get you home much faster than walking.

Be sure that you have adequate stockpiles of food, water and other essentials in your everyday home so that you could live there for at least a month without going to the store. Two months is better. Build these up slowly by buying a little extra when things are on sale or in bulk. These should be foods you eat on a regular basis, so you can rotate through them.

The last essential step for true preparation is some minimum alternative energy resources in the home, such as a battery powered light system with a few solar panels for charging, a small generator and some fuel barrels to keep you out of the gas station lines until things get back to normal. Although most people have gotten used to not having power outages, in previous years our family often used our minimum 12 volt lighting system run off of a small battery bank during power outages when others were lighting candles.

Chapter 13

CHOOSE A SAFE PLACE

Joel has worked with many people considering relocation for safety and he has found that most people are not able to make a clean break from city or town life and live in rural retreat areas full time. Constraints of work and income or schooling combined with social ties like family and church gatherings all keep people tied to urban life. Many of our clients can only find a reasonable compromise between all their criteria by having two properties. Urban obligations are often met by keeping a moderate house in the suburbs or small cities and (since strategically secure land is often out-of-the-way and cheap enough) they also buy a little retreat property in a rural area and use it for vacations. The retreat should allow you to live safely away from the much longer and more serious problems within society. We discuss these contingency options in detail after we help you consider your present situation.

What is the Best Retreat Option for You?

Although we cannot explain a strategy for every person here, it is helpful to consider the general places in which most people find themselves. We'll divide these into four areas: rural, small town, suburb/small city and big city. Each of these represents a successive level of higher population density, and we have found that most people can't jump from one extreme to the other. People used to living in city centers may not be comfortable moving right to a farm lifestyle, but they are comfortable in a suburb. This isn't to say it's impossible, just that the changes can be abrupt. Often people can handle moving in stages. Here are our general concept strategies for each group.

Rural Areas

Many farmers and ranchers are in this group and many already live in strategically safe areas. However, most people who live off the land must live in more fertile lowland and flatlands which are lacking some safety features. Just being rural isn't good enough—we still recommend mountain valleys or forests for safety, particularly if they have good growing potential. These rural areas were previously populated only by back-country folk but increasingly there are communities of independently wealthy, retired and self-employed people who are moving back to the land or have found a way to commute to nearby cities.

In the past, people in rural areas were familiar with gardening and possessed multiple skills for fixing things and being self-sufficient. This is changing as big discount stores make it into smaller population areas and provide cheap, modern conveniences and division of labor. On the flip side, modern conveniences and especially internet communication options are gradually making their way into rural areas allowing more self-employed people to move to these safe locations and still make income from a variety of internet related businesses.

As a whole, people in rural areas are still more prepared for difficult times and will be better neighbors in a crisis, although most are still unprepared for the biggest threats of fallout and social unrest. You will still need a shelter and the full range of concealed food, water and supply stockpiles. The rest of the people around you will likely still survive the coming threats but not without some sickness and significant discomfort. Consider and study the recommended area maps and state descriptions in Section Four for more recommendations for these kinds of areas.

Small Town

Some small towns and cities with less than 100,000 people offer the next level of security. People in these areas are usually middle-class income earners. Crime is usually low and people often watch out for each other. Many people in this group are practically in the rural category and are just as self-sufficient, though they earn their living in town instead of off the land. Land is usually much cheaper and most areas have access to fast Internet connections. Often houses in town can safely be outfitted with shelters to provide reasonable long-term security if proper concealment is made. Every town is different, however. Avoid or relocate away from the towns near nuclear targets and within 100 miles of big cities that have grown up next to major traffic corridors and interstate freeways.

Possibly the ideal relocation setup is a moderate farm or ranch house in a small town, or a secure piece of land in nearby hills or mountains for a very strategic retreat. The principle residence in town should be on at least a quarter acre for a garden and fruit trees.

Suburb and Small City

Most readers will probably fall into this group of people that live in suburbs or cities with between 100,000 and 200,000 inhabitants. This group also has the widest variety of situations and factors. Depending on how well prepared the surrounding population is, you may find some security at the periphery of these towns, if your area is far away from principle corridors and big cities. A rule of thumb for distance to big cities is 100 miles for every one million inhabitants for safety from social unrest. Some people will be able to make the move from here to small towns or rural areas, for the rest of you, consider buying land for a vacation retreat and make the extra preparations required for a dual strategy. We cover several specific strategies for individual cities in our state-specific area descriptions in Section Four.

Big City

As we have repeatedly warned, we see inherent dangers in all large population centers and recommend people move away from these areas if at all possible. We realize, however, that some people are tied to these areas and cannot easily extract themselves. We encourage people in this situation to make significant contingency preparations, including alternate properties and retreats. This is more costly and takes more careful preparation to map out an exit plan for a crisis, but it can be done. We have details on this in the next chapter.

Farm or Mountain?

One of the unfortunate dichotomies we have found is that the best retreat locations are not usually good for farming, and the best locations for growing are not usually private enough for retreats. One can, in fact, find locations that serve both purposes if you know how to watch for areas with extra sunshine and water. Those who want that property for a vacation retreat have the added problem that farmable acreage usually cannot be left unattended in the same way a cabin can. Usually you need to work out arrangements with nearby farmers to rent the land, and watch over the machinery sheds or barns. If one has the capability of maintaining a small rural farm as a retreat, they will truly have the capability of becoming self-sufficient almost indefinitely—depending upon the security of the area. We highly recommend this, though even we cannot find the time to maintain such a retreat.

We recommend forested, mountain or hill country areas for retreats and lower elevation land for full time living where food can be grown more easily. Forested hill country or mountains offer much more seclusion, privacy and interesting views than open flat land. The terrain also keeps people from seeing you from a distance. Some of the best retreat land will back up to state or federal forest land which insures that the adjacent land and water supply will always be protected and free from development. It also gives unlimited access for recreation. The one caveat you need to be careful about is backing up to high profile National Parks like Yellowstone. We expect governments will someday declare a several mile wide "buffer zone" around parks as they collaborate with the UN in establishing "World Heritage Sites." We expect they won't take away property at first, but they will likely prohibit most development in these zones.

Access to a Moderately-Sized Metropolis

One of the great disadvantages of rural living, far from the centers of modern commerce, is the amount of time and expense required to travel back and forth on errands for basic goods. A small percentage of the population is capable of living a sufficiently restricted lifestyle as to avoid these commutes—mainly by learning to be self-sufficient, stockpiling supplies in advance, or doing without many of the nice-to-have (but relatively non-essential) conveniences many of us are used to. Often one's lifestyle can be much healthier away from the convenience of fast food and grocery stores full of processed or prepackaged foods.

However, most of us cannot live this way and still engage in our specialty professions. Even those who can are often unwilling to live this way when there are still other choices available. We find that it is worth the extra effort to prepare multiple contingencies in order to have the best of both worlds. You should attempt to stay within society as long as you can—while having reasonable access to safer retreats or farm areas. Even people who have become self-sufficient financially often don't have the total freedom to "get away" from it all. For example, many people still have children living with them who need access to education.

In short, the best of both worlds is to find a good retreat area that has at least one medium-sized metro area (not in a high density region) within reasonable range for commercial shopping. Fortunately, with today's rapid communication and transportation links, even small cities are becoming quite complete in their access to high-tech supplies. But for those who need access to high-powered technicians and expert employees, one must live near an active metro area.

We prefer areas that are upgrading or intending to upgrade their communications infrastructure to take full advantage of telephone, cell phone and fiber optic technologies. These are vital to access the burgeoning information base in the world without having to live in a major metro area. If your area does not have local Internet providers you might consider satellite receivers so you can access this cyber-information library without slow, long-distance phone lines. If you haven't become computer literate including communicating by email and using the Internet for searching out information, we highly recommend you do so. This will likely be the last source of uncompromised information.

Rural and Suburban Housing

For a variety of reasons, the locations that provide the highest quality of life with reasonable security for most people are in rural suburbia. This is because most people have to work in or near a city. Rural suburban areas encompass the suburbs at the farthest edge of a major city. This is important in order to avoid being trapped by traffic in the central areas during a crisis. If at all possible, you want to avoid having to commute deep into downtown areas on a daily basis. If this cannot be avoided, prepare a contingency plan for getting out of catastrophic traffic jams in a crisis.

We recommend avoiding areas with rapid growth. Everyone seems to move to high growth areas—mostly in search of jobs. But high rates of growth are always disruptive and bad for society in the long term. Local governments tend to make bad decisions in the heat of public "demands" to solve new growth problems. Remember, it is an illusion that enticing new companies to move into an area (through tax breaks and condemnations of private property) will build an increased tax base. On balance, the increased costs of additional infrastructure (schools, sewers, water systems and roads) always exceed the growth of the tax base—not to mention the injustice to the economic rights of those whose business and trade is threatened by those who can start up new companies on subsidized property or with unfair tax breaks.

For those who only need weekly or occasional access to the city, we highly recommend going completely rural. With today's land planning intrusions, you almost always have to buy larger tracts of land in order to build in rural areas. But if you buy an existing place, you can sometimes get reasonably small acreages. For most people, we recommend around an acre for self-sufficiency. You can grow all you need to live on in an acre without having to buy any larger machinery than a big garden tiller. For more than an acre, better machinery is needed and the land begins to eat up all of your time. With all that said, if you have the inclination and time to work a larger tract of land and are willing to acquire all the machinery and other equipment and outbuildings, go for it. But if you are the professional type who only wants to dabble in gardening and not dedicate the majority of your time to self-sufficient, back-to-the-land labor, don't get a lot of land (unless you want to use it as an uncultivated buffer around your property). A forested buffer gives you privacy and does not tie you down with much maintenance.

Vacation Retreats

For a vacation retreat, try to find something you can travel to on one tank of gas from your primary residence and, ideally, at least 100 miles away from most metro areas. I only recommend a 200 or 300 mile radius from the big monster areas like New York, Newark, Philadelphia, Chicago and Los Angeles. Most other metro areas have some retreat areas within driving distance.

Vacation retreats have some distinct advantages over retreats on your full-time property. It is preferable if all your societal connections do not know where you will be in hard times but if you live any kind of normal life, you make too many tracks to your everyday home to try and keep it very private. Secrecy only invites more curiosity.

Vacation retreat properties should still be used with some regularity so you are familiar with the surrounding area and people. Pick an area that is safe, not too high profile, and that offers some vacation opportunities. You'll probably want to invite select friends there but don't brag about the concealed storage and shelters for you and your family. The external hardening is for many purposes including security from thieves and vandals. Secure storage rooms should be concealed with secret entrances. It is essential to have a normal pantry with the basic food stuffs separate from the main storage room for use while on vacation with guests.

When you are looking for a retreat site, look for something that is relatively secure, either by its remoteness or by its being part of a protective development. The more secure the location, the less time and money is needed on hardening the exterior against intrusion—at least this is true of suburban locations and primary residences. In reality, when picking a remote retreat site, harden it anyway because of the potential of someone happening upon your property and doing damage to it. The temptation is too great for intrusion into homes that are unoccupied and isolated in remote areas. The higher insurance rates on a second home are proof of this. If your location is extremely rural, with no visible neighbors, it may be necessary to make the retreat nearly impregnable to entrance and wired with an alarm system. Sometimes our clients have chosen to have the alarm system make a lot of noise and dial them directly rather than call the local authorities since false alarms can become a high profile nuisance. A caretaker or trusted neighbor may be very helpful if you need someone to go and check on the property.

If someone already has a high profile in society, they definitely need a retreat that few others know about. If one has the funds, a third property that is even more remote is sometimes advised. As a matter of long-term planning, we always recommend thinking about "where do I go from here if this situation becomes compromised?" Obviously, there is only so much that you can plan for and it doesn't pay to overdo it. We find that intuitive feelings can be counted on to know what level of preparation is right for you.

Local Requirements

Once you have chosen a likely spot for a retreat, it is helpful to do additional research to find out how hard it will be to make the changes and prepare the property for your long-term goals. Consider the following criteria for the area around a good retreat:

Surrounding Society That Can Take Care of Itself

Part of the strategy we recommend as you seek to make long-term strategic decisions is to seek out regions that have the ability to revert to a non-specialized society. This is very important. The more self-sufficient an area is in its supply of all the basic necessities, the easier it is for a certain percentage of the high tech experts to stay during a crisis. Some people can't easily expand their narrow talents to become self-sufficient. But it only takes about a third of the people in any given area to be generalists, for the other two thirds to remain mostly specialized and hire out their basic needs. Even when national economies contract out substantially, certain regions (which have a broad range of goods and services) can remain fairly healthy by relying upon intra-area work.

Moral Society with a Mix of Conservative Leadership

Don't be squeamish about making judgments here. Areas do differ in people makeup. Optimally, you want a good mix between working class people and managerial and professional types. High powered metro areas with lots of highly educated people are inherently lopsided and unstable—morality and friendliness almost always decline. On the other hand, predominantly rural, agricultural areas have plenty of nice people, but very little in the way of intellectual stimulation or good thinkers. We don't wish to insult these people, only to say that in today's sophisticated world of bad environmental law, excessive regulation and excessive urban planning, the communities that often get rolled over by these over-educated and liberty-destroying city planners are the rural communities. To their credit, rural people can often sense when something is wrong, but the levels of discussion, over time, get so sophisticated and muddled by the opinions of city attorneys telling people what they "must" do, that rural communities almost always lose the battle against the regulators. Worse yet, when rural people decide to "become modern" and jump on the regulation bandwagon, acting as members of city councils or school boards, they can do some very stupid things that unknowingly destroy others' liberty.

In short, it is very frustrating dealing with people who are relatively incapable of understanding difficult arguments and who haven't the inclination to expand their thinking abilities to learn. There are many people who become frustrated with small town living. We still consider rural life valuable for retreats, but not for daily living, so, look for a balance. We've found that balance most often in the medium sized towns that are within an hour's drive of a medium-density metro area. You should research local news articles about events and local changes to get some idea of where the community is moving.

Non-Intrusive, Local Government and Associations

One of the most disappointing things we have seen in various rural communities is that every community, no matter how small, has a ruling power group that is hard to deal with. Dominant people tend to rise to the top, whether in public schools or the business world. Large metro areas have the worst power group politics to contend with and they are almost always corrupt, statist or leftist in their orientation. The only counter-advantage one has in dealing with metro politics is a larger base of people available to gather a following on a given issue, so that you at least have the appearance of a counter base of influence.

Unfortunately, in small towns with a much higher percentage of non-professionals, it is hard to change opinions and initiate action over issues that involve difficult arguments and complexity. There is only a narrow range of populist issues that rural people get excited about, and rarely do these issues allow changes in the fundamental nature of the local government—especially in gaining some relief from the increasingly pervasive intrusion of state and federal regulatory mandates in land use, building codes and environmental restrictions.

Try to stay out of an area that requires emission inspections on vehicles. EPA emissions compliance zones almost always center around high traffic metro areas. Unfortunately, these often also include everything in the entire county (even if it is mostly rural). If you have multiple vehicles, the hassle of dealing with yearly safety and emission inspections just adds to your burden and expense in life. You will surely have to rely on older vehicles someday and tight emission requirements will become a costly compliance issue.

In selecting a town or rural area, talk to locals about the following:

- How are the building department restrictions? Is it easy to improve your property as you see fit? Try to talk to someone who has built a home or significantly renovated recently.

- For private developments or areas with homeowners associations ask about local regulations.

- Look into water rights and restrictions as well as water quality. Stay away from fluoridated water supplies or ones that reek of too much chlorine.

- Try to get a feel for the people in the area. They determine the character of the area.

- See if the development or city allows small domestic animals such as chickens or goats.

When looking for property in a development, try to avoid being part of an association. This isn't always possible nowadays, so if you can't, make sure the rules are reasonable and don't give too many arbitrary powers to a committee such as "architectural review." Any time you put your property under an association, you have lost many of your rights to that property. There is always friction between groups vying for advantage or attempting to enforce upon you their aesthetic point of view. When you get outvoted, you still have to pay dues on what you didn't want. The ideal situation is your own moderate sized suburban or rural plot of land, with clean non-treated water, clean air and good soil, adjacent to some public or private forest land, no debt and no group associations. This is harder to find—but keep looking, it is out there.

Chapter 14

MAKE CONTINGENCY PLANS: IF YOU MUST LIVE AND WORK NEAR A BIG CITY

We have many clients who have to live in or near one of the US or Canadian metro areas with over 200,000 people. For these we recommend a two or three stage contingency plan:

1. Choose a full time residential location as far to the periphery of the metro area as possible, consistent with your commuting limitations.

2. Prepare a secondary farm residence or vacation retreat within the range of a tank of fuel so that you can escape from high density social unrest when necessary.

3. Prepare a second retreat in one of the high security rural locations that we will outline later. This option, however, is only necessary for a few who must remain deep in population dense areas and will have to travel far to escape the masses spreading out behind them, and some outspoken liberty fighters who may become persecuted by government someday.

In general, your primary residence should be within normal society. It doesn't have to be within a subdivision, but that is where most people find it convenient, especially if they do not have the time to develop all their own self-sufficient utilities and resources in a rural location. Rural suburban land from a quarter acre up to two acres is ideal—unless you know how to take care of more land. Even an acre can be a lot to take care of for one small family.

Preparations for an Urban Residence

The primary residence doesn't need to be a fortress, but normal security precautions are important. You will need to beef up most security aspects because you may have to face some initial threats here. Doors, jambs and locks should all be upgraded, but we recommend stopping short of bullet proofing the exterior of the house. This is expensive so only do this for a secure room or closet. Hopefully you'll get out to your contingency options before real serious looting starts.

The main residence, if located near a high density population, needs the following basic preparations:

1. Multiple types of transportation, kept in secure garages, for retreating out of an area. Besides normal commuting cars, we suggest a 4WD van or pickup with a long fuel range and capable of hauling a load. Used Sport Utility Vehicles (SUV) are excellent all terrain vehicles, but look for one with interior cargo space. Trucks can work for this if they will fit everyone. There are also minivans with AWD capability but they usually have limited clearance—make your retreat plans before you buy to determine what you need.

2. Mountain bikes and bike racks to mount on your retreat vehicle are vital in case of a break-down or serious street impediment for the car. If you are seriously considering the bicycle option it wouldn't hurt to have a small trailer for carrying things behind your bike. Your 72 hour kits should be in backpacks to easily grab and wear on a bike. Bicycles are still a lot better than walking. Ideally, if your retreat is fully stocked (including clothing and food) there won't be much of anything to haul from your permanent residence in an emergency.

3. Boats or planes. A limited number of people, who are pilots, have developed transportation contingencies using their airplanes to reach a retreat, when out of vehicular range. Some people can use a sailboat (with an engine in case of no wind) but only if you can access it near your home and your destination. We recommend carrying a small portable bike in the boat or plane to send one person to pick up a vehicle parked at their retreat—since most retreats will not lend themselves to having an airstrip or dock within walking distance.

4. Motorcycles or ATVs. These are even better under certain circumstances, especially if the distance is beyond a couple of day's bicycle range. Stockpile enough fuel in portable containers to be able to fuel vehicles before departure in order to make it to the next safe retreat.

5. Cellular telephones and portable radio communication. In a crisis, the potential of jammed communication lines is very high. It is important to be able to locate family quickly and get them rounded up. Cell phones are fairly inexpensive now, and so are ham or public band radios. Learn to use them and allow older children to carry them as well, especially during periods when the risk of danger seems high. Develop contingency plans for the family so that if they cannot get home or in touch, you know which predetermined friends or relatives they are to try and contact or reach. Make sure they keep a list of names, addresses and telephone numbers with them.

6. Some minimal vault room or "hardened" closet to safeguard valuables and allow temporary safety from social unrest or intrusion. It is also nice if this security chamber has at least one private exit to the outdoors and/or garage, so that transportation can be reached without confronting an intruder.

7. A minimum of one month's supply of food, water, parts and tools. Having a second retreat lessens the amount of stockpiling you have to do for the long-term in your primary residence. The purpose of this minimal stockpiling is to make sure you can wait out a short term crisis, or at least pick your best time to leave for the contingency retreat.

8. An alternate source of heat with reserve fuel for 3 months.

9. An alternate source of electricity (generator setup or small solar/battery/inverter) for one month.

10. Reserve fuel for your vehicles—at least enough to fill each tank.

11. A security system and personal firearm protection.

Make an Emergency Family Plan

As you plan out your exit strategies it is important to consider the worst case scenarios. For example, how will you round up the family in a timely manner? What will you need if you have to stay put until after the initial crush of panic rather than take to the road in the midst of it? When you take the risk of staying, even for the first week, will you be prepared to avoid confrontation with localized threats? People won't be starving yet, but they probably will start looting stores. Considering what happened after hurricane Katrina, house looting should be limited to isolated instances at first.

With or without warning, it is essential to prepare the whole family well in advance and train them for what to do in a crisis so they can react quickly and predictably. That way you have a good chance of making it out of town faster than others. Almost everyone else will simply try to get home and gather everyone but many people won't know where their family members are or how to round them up for safe keeping.

Unfortunately, even with the convenience of cell phones, in a large crisis the circuits will be jammed with callers. It is very important that you develop a plan for all family members to meet at one or two locations in a crisis. It is also a great idea to have everyone carry a pad of sticky notes with them and something reliable to write with. If they leave their current spot or where the family expects them to be, they can write where they are going on the sticky side of the note and place it inside a window close to the exit door. That way it won't blow away and if you try to find them you can have some indication of where they have gone. Work on this kind of coordination. One person missing can delay the entire family's expeditious retreat.

Emergency Facilities at Work

Part of your contingency preparations should center on your workplace and your commute. Exiting from downtown in a crisis will be a very difficult hurdle. Hopefully you'll have some advanced warning but think about worst-case options. Some people may actually be able to establish an emergency temporary shelter in the midst of the danger zone in which they work. Let's suppose you take our advice and establish a suburban primary residence in a safe, but not excessively high profile area. You also establish a secondary vacation retreat. But, as one of those 18 hour-a-day executives, you may suspect that the chances of your getting stuck "downtown" in the midst of turmoil are pretty high—too high to have any assurance of reaching home during situations of panic within the city. There are a few possible strategies in this case.

Prepare alternate ways out. Store a fold up bike in your trunk. If you need to cross a water way, store an inflatable dinghy in a locker or closet for small rivers. Work out arrangements for a bigger boat for wider water crossings. Put away some food and water stockpiles so that if traffic or social unrest catches you downtown by surprise, you have some reserves until you can get out.

It may be a wise contingency to prepare some means for sleeping and cooking within your office complex for emergencies. There are many clean, small camping stoves. Make sure you have some independent communication available to contact your home, so you can discuss the alternatives with your family. Consider discussing emergency preparedness with your business associates to develop a stockpiling plan for essential supplies necessary to keep your business running in a transportation strike or other threat that causes shortages. Certainly the 1997 UPS strike made a lot of businesses wish they had prepared in advance.

Mapping out an Exit Plan

Your contingency plans hinge on being able to get out ahead of the first wave of people. This will require very careful planning and preparation. You have to live on the outskirts of the city you are tied to. Only the outer suburbs have a chance of getting out before traffic stagnates on most roads. Prepare your travel vehicles in advance and have the items you need ready to easily throw in or strap on to make all possible speed. This includes any standby vehicles—a motorcycle on a trailer or bikes prepared on racks. The sooner you get on your prepared route, the better your chance of making good time. Prepare fuel for more than just the minimum.

When you plan out your retreat route, remember these guidelines:

Locate all significant obstacles

1. Assume the following will be impassable: all tunnels, most freeway bridges, all freeways, principle highways and all heavily traveled arterial roads. Color these red. Some roads with a slight chance of being open can be made orange.

2. Look for two lane roads that are less known and traveled, not just frontage roads. Consider residential roads where possible. Choose the best, widest of these and color them green even if not on your expected route.

3. Plan around geographic and infrastructure obstacles such as rivers, lakes, mountains and freeways. These are barriers that block your path and funnel traffic into narrow corridors for passage—what we will call choke points. Mark the choke points you are avoiding in red or orange and other lesser-known options in yellow or green. Don't buy a main residence in urban or suburban areas that can only be accessed through a few choke points.

4. Look for crossing points of freeways and highways that do not involve on and off ramps that could be backed-up. Look for dedicated over and under passes.

5. Try to talk to locals familiar with less-traveled bridges that can be driven over. Ask about the traffic levels and sturdiness of the bridge.

Locate possible crisis points and disaster areas.

6. Consider the natural disasters in your area and locate weather-related obstacles such as low spots prone to flooding, roads that are impassable in winter, infrastructure that could collapse in an earthquake, roads affected by landslides, etc.

7. Locate on your maps nuclear targets and a 10 mile radius to avoid the most significant destruction. Refer to the colored maps of each state for our perception of these threats. at the end of Section Four.

Plan your route carefully

8. Avoid areas with dense concentrations of people. Once you make your way to rural areas keep out of towns with over 50,000 people, where possible. As you travel out of town avoid shopping districts and town centers that could be prone to looting and mobs.

9. Plan multiple routes. Highlight your expected routes in different colors for primary and alternate routes.

10. Make separate maps for alternate travel such as 4WD on unpaved roads or motorcycle, bike or foot travel. Look for trails that may be unmarked on city maps.

11. Travel your routes and become familiar with them and local geography in general. Verify you have not planned routes through gated communities, toll roads, fenced areas, etc.

Sample Exit Plan

To illustrate how to develop an emergency exit plan, we have selected one of the most difficult areas in the United States—the NYC/Newark, NJ area, one of the largest and most densely populated areas in the country. It may be even more difficult to escape than the Los Angeles area because there are numerous rivers and small creeks that must be crossed by bridges (choke points). Even if you don't live in this area, you can learn a lot about your own exit planning by following along with this example.

We've chosen the suburban community of Livingston, NJ as a starting point. This suburban location represents a suitable compromise location for a busy professional that must commute into Newark or NYC, yet still allow for a head start out of town in a crisis. There are two major Beltways around Newark and the Livingston suburb is outside of the first but inside the second (I-287). Obviously, it is better to live outside both beltways, but we assumed there were tradeoffs to consider.

To map out an exit plan you must first know where you are headed. It is not enough to simply get a few miles out into the rural countryside and think you are safe. In a widespread crisis of social unrest it would only be a matter of hours or a day before the near country-side around major cities is flooded with refugees trying to escape the chaos and panic. You must pick a retreat destination that is both lightly populated and distant enough from the population centers that refugees can't get to you easily.

For the NJ/NYC area, the closest retreat areas are in rural Pennsylvania or upstate New York and Vermont. Why did we choose not to go south to Virginia, Tennessee and Kentucky? Because it would be unwise to try to get around the huge population centers of Philadelphia and Washington DC. By the time you got there, all the roads would be jammed and impassable.

You have to go west from Newark before you can go north to upstate NY or Vermont. If you were to take off from Livingston directly north, you would be competing with too many others for space on the smaller roads. Freeways will clog first, then secondary roads and then residential streets. You can see why it's better to not try for the "faster roads" if you haven't gotten out of town first. In fact, you'll have to be careful about driving on residential roads that are too close to feeder roads. Access intersections may back up for blocks and you may not be able to cross.

As we have said previously, never plan on leaving by way of the freeways unless you can see that it is flowing freely and it isn't headed into a major city where the way will surely be blocked with traffic jams. Once on a freeway, it is nearly impossible to get off when traffic is backed up. Most freeways have side barriers, ditches or fences to impede getting on or off except at an exit. So, if you aren't on a freeway, freeways now become trap zones.

because you can't get passed them except at an overpass, underpass or exit. Never try to cross a freeway at an exit. Chances are good that it will be clogged with people trying to get on or off the freeway.

If GPS satellites are working (possible in natural disasters but doubtful in war) the automated traffic warning information might be invaluable. But, don't rely on GPS exclusively. Have paper maps with routes marked and have them in your vehicles.

To create your maps, we encourage you to get on a computer and use web pages that show street maps and satellite views (e.g. *www.maps.google.com*), alternating between the map view and the satellite view to find passage over or under a freeway that doesn't pertain to an off ramp. You can usually zoom in with sufficient resolution to see options or obstacles such as if there are exits or underpasses at freeway crossings. In the end you have to drive your routes to make certain.

The map on this page (see color version on p. 209) can't show all the detail that you can see on satellite images, but it should illustrate the process. In our example we have first chosen to go SW in order to find rural roads that don't go through the dense subdivisions. Then we turn northwest after going under a freeway where there are no exit ramps and head for a non-exit crossing below I-287. Once on rural roads, try to pick a path that doesn't go through towns where traffic jams can occur, even if it means going out of your way. In our sample, we had to make choices between taking a more rural route over more bridges and choke points to stay out of towns or take the chance of going through more populous rural sections. We take you only as far as Newton but one could continue in the same manner. We have some route planning tips out of major cities in the state analyses in Section Four.

Notice that we have mapped out at least one alternate route. In reality you should map out as many as possible. The most direct routes will usually take you through

other subdivisions, which you want to avoid if possible. Be prepared to take however many side detours necessary to avoid congestion that may be visible ahead. Turn off onto alternate roads well before you get up to the traffic jams to ensure you don't get stuck in traffic yourself.

The real key to getting out of a crisis of panic and social unrest is timing. We encourage everyone to have access to alternate news sources that may assist you in anticipating when major crises are imminent. Your first line of defense has to be having advance warning. Consider getting Joel's weekly newsletter *The World Affairs Brief,* as one of these sources. He not only covers his analysis of world news each week, but will point out any advance warnings we can see of dangerous future events. It's very inexpensive and comes to your email box every week (see *www.worldaffairsbrief.com*).

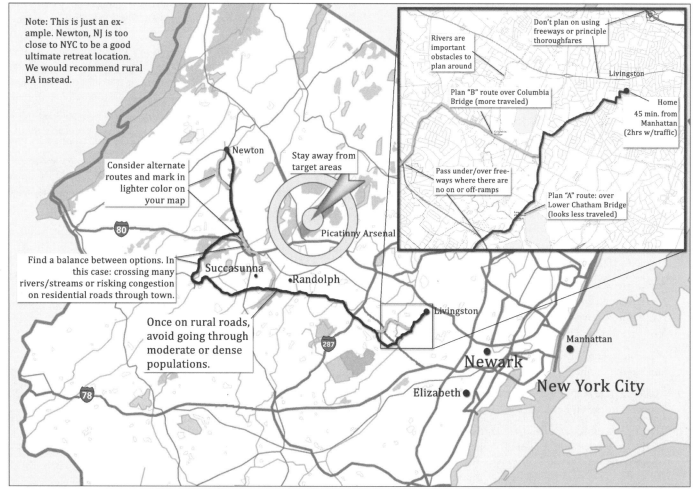

Chapter 15

PREPARE FOR THE WORST

We encourage you to take our advice and relocate away from high density inner cities, war zones and blast areas, so that you will only have to mitigate the effects of social unrest, lack of food, lack of water/electricity and (in a nuclear war) radioactive fallout. A retreat property with essential living arrangements and a multi-purpose safe room is the only way to protect against home invasion, crime, fire and radiation and serve as a reliable secret storage of valuables and supplies.

Ideal Aspects of a Long-Term Retreat

Some people planning a retreat want to make it the ultimate safe spot and extremely secure. We recommend against planning anything that would get them into a "last stand" situation. We think history shows it is always better to work toward concealment, alternate back doors and further retreats. The freedom to maneuver is always a better strategy than to put all your eggs in one fortified basket. A retreat's main purpose is to provide comfortable and self-sufficient living away from the threats of the metropolitan areas you stay close to in order to work and live a normal life.

One also needs to take into consideration how many people they are going to prepare to assist in a crisis. No one has unlimited resources to help everyone, so it is important to plan ahead—especially in limiting the number of people who know about your secondary or tertiary retreat system. The more people who you invite to visit your facilities, the greater the possibility you will have "uninvited" guests showing up at your door in a crisis. So be selective. There are many preparations to be made just for yourself and your family. Here's a list of the essential aspects of a good retreat:

Concealed storage: Whether a vacation retreat or a farm, provide for large, underground, concealed storage with enough supplies for a minimum of one year, preferably two.

Good source of water. A reliable, non-public water supply with internal storage tanks of at least 200 gallons. The best systems are renewable by a mountain spring or a rain water cistern.

Reinforced exterior: A durable construction form for outside walls should provide fire resistance, vandal resistance, intrusion resistance and even some bullet protection. Provide ample eaves for water protection and use a metal roof for fireproofing.

Conventional appearance: Buildings should not be high profile or flamboyant in style. Also avoid allowing it to become rundown as this could invite tramps.

Concealed entrance and exit: These allow you to get in or out unobserved if vandals are occupying your place when you get there.

Enclosed garage: A secure, enclosed garage will protect your investment in vehicles. Utility vehicles such as tractors, ATVs, mountain bikes and motorcycles can be important parts of a complete stockpile.

Partial energy self-sufficiency: Provide for some alternate energy system. A minimum system to provide electricity, space heating, cooking and water heating will allow a basic level of subsistence. Usually solar panels and wood stoves are the primary option if the area has sufficient sunlight.

Basic repair facilities: Store these with some spare parts for essential equipment. A minimum of tools ought to be kept in the secure storage and shelter area. During a radiation period, you need to be able to repair items in the shelter without having to leave its protection.

Fuel storage: Enough gas or diesel to fill every vehicle. Kerosene, propane and wood as required.

Preparing a Shelter and Safe Room

Here's a brief primer on what it takes to design a moderate safe room with radiation resistance. We think everyone should plan on preparing against some degree of fallout unless you are on the extreme west coast where there are almost no possible targets upwind. This is probably limited to southern Oregon and northern California. Any other place could receive substantial amounts of fallout, depending upon the winds.

A good fallout shelter needs to stop radiation with dense material all around you. Four inches of lead will do it, but that is too expensive in most cases. Fortunately 10 to 12 inches of solid concrete or 2-3 feet of dense earth will also stop or reduce radiation down to a tolerable level. We recommend constructing the shelter underground or in basement areas so you get the benefit of dirt around the outside of the vertical walls. In addition this gives you direct access from your home to the shelter without having to go outside. You will also need a source of filtered air, a secure metal door, food supplies, water supplies, sanitation facilities and solar charged batteries providing minimum electricity. There are no windows in a shelter, so you need to have some source of generating light. This is a basic setup and there are many other things to think about implementing to make it more secure, such as secondary escape paths.

A shelter doesn't have to be wasted space. If you add the security door it can easily be a multi-purpose safe room that can serve many useful purposes even if the big disasters don't come. Above all, having a fire-proof, earthquake proof, storm proof, intrusion proof and radiation proof vault room gives you a great deal of peace of mind, and that is worth a lot in today's uncertain world.

If you already have a basement, it could take as little as $3,000 to $20,000 to make basic preparations against fallout. This should be well within the potential of most middle class wage earners. You can nearly eliminate the potential consequences of the nuclear attack threat. Fallout travels relatively slowly, so there will be few scenarios in which you could not get to your shelter if fairly close.

Tips on Constructing Retreat Houses

There are several ways to add security to a retreat home but be careful not to overspend on one aspect while ignoring another that could be a weak link. For instance, it can be wise to install steel doors and jambs but not without protecting the windows. If metal roll down shutters are installed, intruders may take a chainsaw to the walls. That isn't to say you shouldn't harden a home but that you have to do so with balance. Try to give fairly equal treatment to all the weak links.

The difficulty with constructing a vacation retreat is to secure it during the long months when it sits unattended. In one rural situation, Joel designed an A-frame cabin with all the doors and windows on the ends, with a deck that matched the roof line. When the owners left the cabin unattended, they simply used a 12 volt winch to lift up the deck that was hinged to the foundation on one end and mated to the roof when raised so that all access to windows and doors was denied. This was a fairly inexpensive, but effective solution to their needs.

In other styles of homes, we recommend some form of durable, low maintenance exterior such as brick or stone outer walls or a stone base wall with stucco or log siding above. We recommend unbreakable acrylic plastic storm windows, heavy duty steel doors and steel jambs (wood jambs are an often overlooked weak link) and high-strength, pick-resistant locks and deadbolts. Where masonry (brick, concrete or stone) is too expensive, we use a special form of double wall construction. The outer wall is filled with gravel of a

certain size to deter forced entry. This is also the cheapest way to make a wood wall highly resistant to a chainsaw or even stray bullets. We recommend metal shutters on the ground floor windows.

Other more expensive ways to build secure homes involve the use of poured cement in interior or exterior walls. Log homes can also be made pretty difficult to get through if metal reinforcing rods are laid between the logs during construction—it dulls a chainsaw blade in a few seconds. This is not to infer that anyone should ever defend his retreat as an armed fortress. There are other strategies that don't involve a western style shoot out.

Always make sure that the secure structures and features don't look conspicuous. Joel discouraged one notable group from installing a large, underground complex with a cellar type door leading down out of a parking lot. He reasoned that it would invite a lot of curiosity seekers wondering what all these cars were doing parked out in the middle of nowhere, around a big trap door. We prefer designs that don't draw undo attention to themselves, and which have a conventional structure over a shelter so that no one thinks twice when you go inside.

For this reason, as well as for cost, we discourage total underground construction or reinforced dome construction. The notoriety among the builders, workmen, neighbors, building officials and anyone else who hears about it is too great for safety. A design should look fairly conventional. If you want an underground house for energy conservation or security, build a believable portion of it above ground so that there is at least the semblance of normalcy. Anyway, with today's super-insulation design techniques one can get underground energy efficiency above ground—without the waterproofing problems that plague underground homes. There still may be reasons for going below ground level, but not for energy conservation alone. All below ground security rooms should have normal access (even if concealed) from inside a home or from an outbuilding that avoids public views.

While we design a lot of solar features in homes and retreats, we try to avoid using large glass walls for solar heat. Not only is there the security problem of protecting so much glass, but also the problem of having a high profile look that attracts too much attention.

How to Get Plans

For a complete guide to converting space in an existing house into a secure room and shelter consider our recently updated book, *The High Security Shelter - How to Implement a Multi-Purpose Safe Room in the Home* available from Joel's website (*www.joelskousen.com*). This short book includes a complete set of plans and details for a do-it-yourself multi-purpose high security shelter with a concrete block shell for radiation protection and secure living and survival facilities. These shelters can be built at ground level but preferably should be below ground for concealment and added protection. They will provide secure, hidden storage if you implement some of the concealment features presented.

Those of you considering a more significant remodel or plan to build a preparedness home from scratch should take the opportunity to implement security features during the construction process. This will allow you to implement many valuable aspects such as radio antennas and alternate energy systems. There is a lot of information to consider in this process. Joel's significant architectural design book, *The Secure Home*, provides details for most of these systems in over 700 pages of material. It covers everything from high security construction to total self-sufficiency using solar, wood and multi-fuel heating and cooking sources. The appendix has hundreds of listings of hard-to-find sources of the best equipment and supplies. For more information see Joel's website.

These two books also explain how to read your radiation meter and deal with radiation sickness. Having a meter is essential so you know when to come out of the shelter, and when to go back in. Otherwise you are just guessing, since it will likely take a long time before TV and radio stations start broadcasting again.

Stockpiling Supplies

Once you have a secure room, you will need to stock it with essentials. If this is a temporary secure room in your urban residence, we recommend preparing a one to two month supply of food, water and basics. If you are stocking your ultimate retreat you should keep a full year's supply of long-term food storage.

You should also prepare some or all of these packages of items:

- Barter items and small, easily identifiable goods that most people need. Ammunition, soap, toiletries, fuel, stoves, laundry detergents and canned goods.

- Cash in a variety of bills. Gold coins are not as practical in an emergency since most people can't tell their value and they are hard to subdivide. Bulk silver is probably better (look for US dimes and quarters minted before 1964), but some gold coins could buy your way out of a bad situation.

- Tools, batteries, spare parts, gas welders, electric welders, generators and basic repair items.

- Communications equipment. Citizen's band (CB) radio, short wave radio, hand-held units.

- Equipment and plans for a business after a severe crisis. Candle-making equipment, metal working tools, etc.

- Firearms and reloading equipment.

- Water filtering equipment if you don't have a good source on your property.

- Medical equipment and natural methods for treating yourself when hospital help is not available.

These are just a few of the many items you might find helpful after an emergency. For more in-depth ideas and lists of supplies and equipment refer to Joel's booklet, *10 Packs for Survival* (see *www.joelskousen.com*).

For long term food storage consider a combination of dehydrated foods (for variety) and large bulk supplies of whole grains, beans and white rice for main subsistence. Note that brown rice is nutritionally better than white rice, but it has a shelf life of only 6 months without refrigeration or freezing whereas white rice will store for 18 months to 2 years on the shelf. Coconut oil is the only oil that won't go rancid after 2 years and is very healthy.

Supplement these stores with canned goods that you like to use. This can take more effort if the retreat cabin is used only once or twice a year, since you'll have to move the stock of canned fruits and vegetables that need to be rotated. Below-ground storerooms should keep them cool enough to last up to 2 or 3 years without noticeable loss of taste. Canned goods can even go longer if kept at 50 degrees or below. While the taste of canned food deteriorates over long periods, as long as no swelling occurs in the cans, it may be possible to eat it after the printed expiration date in an emergency. Dehydrated foods also have a problem with deterioration of taste when stored for long periods. Only whole grains and some beans do not deteriorate if kept cool and dry. Beans do get very hard after a few years of storage and will be somewhat crunchy when cooked, unless you add 1/4 tsp of baking soda per pound of beans to the cooking water. It is important to integrate bulk foods like beans and grains into your diet beforehand so that they are well tolerated by the body and there is no food aversion. It is good preparation to learn to live without junk food now.

Stockpiles of supplies often need to be concealed. Nosy people, hungry neighbors and even government may criticize people who store food, labeling them as "hoarders." This could lead to efforts to confiscate your hard earned preparations or limit your ration coupons, penalizing you for having the foresight to store food in advance. Don't let this happen through blind neglect—prepare to keep the bulk of storage hidden. You may want to share voluntarily, but not at the barrel of a gun. And if you do share, don't show all that you have. Keep your main stocks private and secure so you can decide when you need to stop sharing without inviting jealousy.

Maintaining all these security features around children can be difficult. Your kids may become interested in all your preparations particularly if it includes "secrets" and "hideouts." They may unwisely reveal security preparations to their friends which can make it the object of widespread conversation among family or friends and compromise your retreat. We recommend keeping them uninvolved and only introduce it as necessary. Help them see it as a "grown-up" project at first and later explain that it is "just for our family" rather than it being a "secret" which is always hard for kids to keep. Treat them as grown-ups and explain it as clearly as possible when it is inevitable that they know.

We mention stockpiling medical supplies in the list above and this deserves an added note. We don't expect hospitals to be able to handle the overwhelming numbers of unprepared people who will begin to get sick when fallout comes. Very few doctors and nurses have protection and therefore, they will be as sick as the rest or even dying. We strongly recommend being prepared to treat your own illnesses, but this takes significant preparation beforehand by learning alternative therapies in natural medicine with herbs. Get as much knowledge as you can—it will be helpful no matter what happens. Don't forget to put reference manuals in your stockpile.

Preparing to Live After a Nuclear Attack

With all the dire events impending upon the world, it is hard to imagine putting life back together afterwards. Although we don't pretend to know how things will ultimately stand, people will need to be prepared to grow much of their own food and use cash or barter for the rest. Plan on having enough stored food to last through the first harvest. It is essential that you prepare as a family (or jointly with others) a few acres where you can grow a garden including some root vegetables that can be stored for the next winter. Don't expect food commerce to knit back together in anything less than a year or two, and it may be longer depending on how much infrastructure is destroyed.

You can find archives on the Internet of a 1958 farmer's bulletin No. 2107 that has some practical considerations for civil defense in this regard (*http://www.scribd.com/doc/37878078/Farmer-s-Bulletin-No-2107*). It's a little generic and outdated, but many of the principles still apply.

There aren't any failsafe ways of testing for trace radioactive particles on food or in the soil, so plan on using time to ensure things have decayed to safe levels. If you take potassium iodide (KI) tablets, your body should be able to survive the low-level lingering doses. Historical documents show that people in eastern and northern Europe significantly reduced their chances of thyroid cancer after the Chernobyl disaster by taking KI tablets even with the longer-lasting radioactive isotopes inherent from a reactor meltdown (as opposed to the shorter decay time of most nuclear weapons).

Growing Food

Plan to have enough food storage to last until the first crops can be grown. The ground should be clear enough of contaminants to safely grow crops after a year. We expect nuclear attacks to come in winter and, if so, most high radiation fallout in the air should have subsided by spring, but there will still be some long-term radioactive particles in the ground, particularly near areas that experienced significant fallout. Particles such as Strontium 89 and 90 take 6 months or more to decompose, but you can't be certain that all dangerous dust in the soil will have decomposed until after 12 to 18 months. Depending on what the fallout concentrations were in your area, you can plant some long-term crops like potatoes or grains as early as a few months after the attack (in the spring). Even if the crop is contaminated, as long as the plants don't die off before the harvest, you can store this food until they are safe. Potatoes are probably fine if they are washed and peeled.

Depending on the exposure in your area, trees and plants will survive but the fruit may be tainted by the fallout. Stick to your food stockpiles. If you can gather food outside when it is safe to come out, consider drying it or preserving it for a few months to ensure any radioactivity has declined. The radioactivity may actually prolong the shelf life of food since it kills living organisms like bacteria.

It is especially important to practice growing a garden before disaster strikes, so that you know how to get the soil in good shape, establish watering systems and have the tools and seeds at hand. Be sure and stockpile heritage seeds, not hybrid seeds. With heritage seeds, you can save part of the crop for seed and use them again next year. Hybrid seeds have been genetically modified and may not reproduce the same plant the next year. Seeds are susceptible to radiation and should be stored in your shelter.

Protecting Animals and Livestock

If you raise chickens, pigs, goats, cows or other animals it is a good idea to plan a way to keep these alive for future food sources. Ideally animals need the same protection as humans, but anything is better than nothing.

Keep the animals in a covered structure to keep fallout dust off them and their food. You should store at least a 6 month's supply of hay or feed in a covered area, preferably in a barn or enclosed area. In a worst case scenario it's better to keep the animals alive on some compromised feed and water than to let them starve. Use water from a covered water source or flowing stream.

Milk is more susceptible to radioactive contamination so extra precautions must be made before consuming this from compromised sources. Milk from cows exposed to radioactivity may be all right if the feed is clean. In a dire state, preserve the milk or make it into cheese and wait for a few weeks before consuming it to allow any radioactivity to decline.

Summary

There are many more aspects of preparation, stockpiles, supplies, food preservation, gardening, concealment, survival, etc. than we can present here. But we hope this gives you enough information that you can make a decision about how to relocate. We will focus the rest of the book on more specific details about locations in the US and Canada to which you can apply the tools above and choose a strategic safe place.

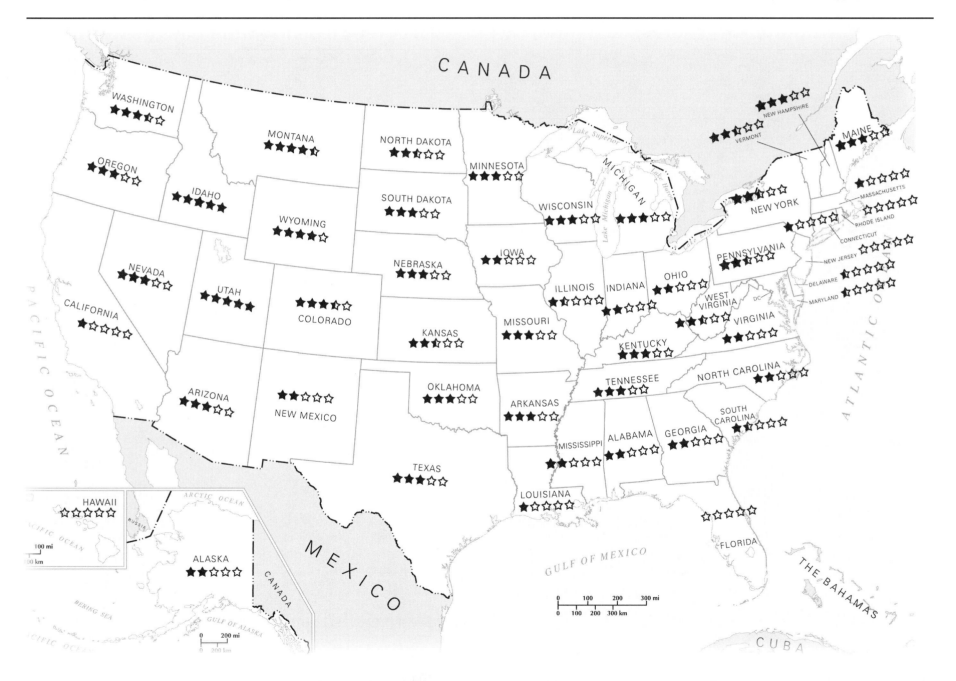

Chapter 16

REGIONAL ANALYSIS

In the previous sections we have presented our criteria for safe places, shown you how the US and Canada compare overall and explained our ideas for preparing strategies and retreats. Now let's examine the US and Canada in more detail by looking for general regions of safety or danger and discussing how to select one for a retreat. Many of these areas overlap state boundaries so we've broken up the US and Canada into larger "regions."

As we have said before, there is no place on earth that is absolutely safe from all threats, but some regions are much safer than others, and these will be our focus. If you are one of the fortunate people that has the financial freedom to relocate at will, then this section will help you narrow down your study to the specific states or provinces that make up the best regions. If you can't relocate, you may want to consider a retreat in the safest region nearby and make contingency plans to get there before a full crisis breaks out.

If you don't have the ability to move to one of these safe regional areas, then you will have to make the best choice you can within your surroundings or in an area that you can move to, even though it may not be one that has the highest rating. Because so many readers fall into this latter category and don't have the full range of choices, we have tried to point out even less-than ideal options in all regions. In the next chapter we do a full analysis of all states and their major cities, even though a few have almost no hope for long-term safety.

The Color Maps

At the end of this chapter we provide color maps of each of the regions in the US and Canada that we will discuss (pp. 147 to 156). Color allows us to highlight details like forestation, mountains and lakes. As you read our discussion on each region, keep a finger in the map section so you can refer back and forth as needed.

The maps have red dots that correspond to population density. Cities with more people have concentrations of red dots in proportion to their density and extents. This gives you a dramatic visual cue about where the danger of social unrest lies. Similarly, we have depicted the main freeways in red because, even if officially closed by authorities, they will still become the main thoroughfares of exiting people—even if they are on foot. Almost all major towns are linked by freeways or have sprung up around these transportation corridors and people will first head for other cities where they hope to find food and lodging. It is only when they discover that almost all other towns are suffering from the same calamity of panic that they will start fanning out into the countryside looking for

shelter and food from individual farms and houses. Historically, this is what happened in WWII when whole cities emptied out and took to the roads to flee a massacring army such as the Germans fleeing from the Russians at the end.

Naturally, volcanoes and nuclear targets are also shown on the maps. Pay attention to prevailing wind directions but recognize that winds can always change. To ensure safety from fallout or volcanic ash, have a safe room with fallout protection overhead no matter which way the wind blows.

The best potential retreat areas are circled in yellow on the regional maps. Some areas include national or state parks within their borders—but property is often available in and around these parks. We have kept these areas general but in your individual analysis you could find good areas outside them. We give more specific recommendations in our state-by-state analysis in the following chapter. Our purpose in pointing this out is to give you an easy graphical representation in which directions you could plan your exit strategy.

A Note about Canada

Unlike the US which is surrounded by either water or another country on every border, Canada has a wide open northern area, almost entirely free from threats because of the severe cold and relative lack of humanity. If one can tolerate the cold, and the lack of resupply, virtually the entire northern areas of the populous regions of Canada are suitable for retreats. Because the area is so vast, we will have to forego specific comments and we focus our analysis to southern areas where most Canadians live and work. The relatively open border between the US and Canada is lightly fenced in the middle of a clear cut of trees, and is a kind of temporary safe haven for citizens of both countries. Anyone who might run afoul of some over-zealous government edict on either side can cross easily.

We encourage Canadians to acquire a residency permit for living in the US. Many in the US can do the same in Canada. Having dual citizenship or residency can come in handy someday. Canada has made a change in the law recently which allows children of any Canadian born person to become a Canadian citizen with just a bit of paperwork. There were many Americans who went to Canada during periods of hardship and who had children there. These children were Canadian citizens and any child born to them, even after coming back to the USA, can now qualify as Canadian Citizens—but only the first generation.

Hawaii and Alaska

We don't cover Alaska and Hawaii in the regional analysis but they are covered in the state analyses. We repeat a warning about islands like Hawaii, Puerto Rico or Guam. The fact remains that you are trapped by the surrounding waters when resupply is cut off. In addition, on most islands the food growing potential is limited by the available land and the high density of population. Hardly any islands are self-sufficient. Prices for imported supplies are high, and can be cut off quickly by a shipping or labor strike. Alaska is, in many ways, similar to an island in its isolation and difficulty of resupply in a crisis.

Regional Ratings and Population Density

As we look at these areas, keep in mind the biggest threats we are working to relocate around. The most catastrophic threat one would encounter in North America would be a surprise nuclear attack on the American and Canadian military and satellite early warning and communications stations. After this threat we foresee incomparable social unrest and instability for upwards of a year.

Some of the threats we have described earlier in the book may not apply to you personally, but the much broader danger of social unrest will affect everyone to some degree. When electricity, water and gas utilities stop and the crisis is widespread enough that no level of government can come to the rescue, it will endanger many people. The ultra high densities of some American cities make it virtually impossible to survive without panic and pillaging if food supplies cease to arrive and government services go down for anything longer than a few weeks. This can happen in a major natural disaster and certainly during a war where the US is attacked.

Part of the reason for social unrest is that many key people who help react to emergencies such as doctors, government people, police and emergency workers will likely die or become sick as they initially do their jobs but are unprotected. Depending on the fallout levels in each area, serious sickness could occur in a matter of days. Everyone will become desperate. Beyond people's own stores there will be no official supply line, almost no public utilities, no water and no news to let you know what it's like elsewhere. The few ham radio operators who have radios in their basements are going to be the only ones with any news during the crisis and during the initial recovery.

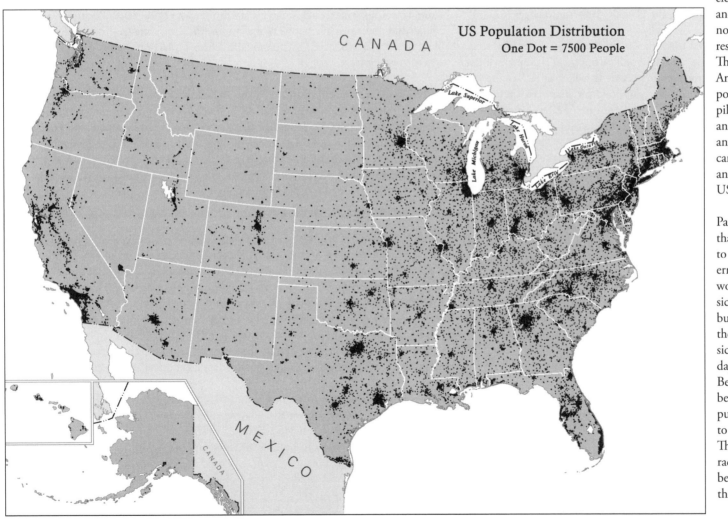

US Population Distribution
One Dot = 7500 People

To be honest, some people will survive even in cities that are direct nuclear targets, just like some did in Hiroshima and Nagasaki as long as they were outside the blast zones. But survivors exposed to some fallout will have sickness, and some will die later on. Consider that well when you tell yourself, "I just can't leave" an unsafe city. Do you think it will be any easier after disaster strikes, when you have no choice? It won't be, so if you live in one or more of the high density urban areas that are likely targets of a major threat someday, don't try to play the odds and be on the last train out. Your chances of doing that are very slim—especially if what we now see coming in the future becomes obvious to most, and you find yourself competing with hundreds of thousands at a time trying to leave. It will be like Hurricane Katrina bearing down on New Orleans all over again.

Most will not be smart enough to leave the area initially, and few will be prepared to do so quickly enough to avoid the rush and will get stranded in endless traffic. They will stick around hoping for government to take action. But it will take only a week or two for a panic of food shortages to develop. By then it will be obvious that government isn't coming to the rescue and isn't able to stop the lawlessness that is developing. It will be "everyone for himself" and that's when the scavenging for survival starts. When the stores become emptied, people will really start to panic—even good people. They are desperate to get food for themselves and their families and emergencies turn even good people into desperate survivalists. But good people won't be able to compete with the ruthless, low class people and gangs that will pillage with that "grab all you can get" mentality, probably accompanied by armed violence. Good people will have to flee the cities.

The eastern US is the most vulnerable to danger in a nuclear war. Not only are there multiple local targets in the East, but fallout from targets to the west will likely drift east on the jet stream, eventually. The effects of fallout will be gradual but near constant for quite some time up to a hundred miles downwind of blast zones. We predict that in war where the US is attacked, urbanites will start a mass migration westward, trying to escape the mass competition for food in the big cities. There will be long columns of people on foot, just as in former world wars, heading for any smaller city or development that appears to be faring better than the ones they just left. Rumors about safety here or food there will abound and people will stream in those directions for survival. When those sources are picked clean they will fan out into the countryside. This is what you need to relocate around.

The Top Rated Area

The top rated area in the US and Canada is an area surrounding and including the Intermountain West. We see this area as extending from the Okanagan Valley of Alberta and British Columbia in Canada, south through all of Idaho and Utah (excluding the major cities) and including western Wyoming, western Montana, eastern Washington, eastern Oregon, northern Nevada, northern Arizona and western Colorado. This area is the gold standard.

The Intermountain West is centered around Salt Lake City, Utah. Though that particular city is not considered safe, this location serves as a focal point to illustrate the strategic advantages of the area. Its greatest virtue is its low population density, wide open spaces and vast distances that provide a buffer zone to major metropolitan areas in all directions.

To the west are hundreds of miles of barren Nevada and Oregon deserts that will be difficult to traverse if fuel is not available. It will keep much of the huge populations of central California from reaching this area. To the south are several hundred miles of the Mojave Desert that would keep the masses in southern California from migrating very far north. They might make it to Las Vegas, but we expect this will be a terrible trap zone, due to its isolation in the desert and nuclear targets near the principle interstates. To the east are more deserts plus the main formation of the Rocky Mountains that provide 500 miles of hardship between Salt Lake City and Denver, the next biggest problem city in that direction. To the north is sparsely populated high desert valleys and forested mountains with no major cities at all.

Most of the "best areas" for retreats are in and around mountainous, forested land which the government has often appropriated for national or state forests and parks. Generally you will find this to be an advantage if you can find land that backs up to these forested areas. It is like having a big backyard for free. There is a fair amount of private land in and around these state and national forests.

Be careful, however, of the "inholder" trap: land that is completely inside federal forests. The federal government has been trying to coerce the inholders (as they are called) into selling their land. Most have refused but the government could someday use eminent domain proceedings against all the inholder parcels except those that are fairly close to highways running through the forests. That is why we do not recommend purchasing these holdings, attractive as they are. An inholder property would be acceptable only if it was part of many other homes where you might join together in concerted action to defend your legal rights.

Some of the best private land is found along roads that bisect or cross national forests. Pioneer homesteads almost always were allowed to remain along the roadways even after the surrounding land was taken by the feds for national forests. These are probably safe from confiscation since the roadway keeps them from being ruled as "wilderness" or other environmentally sensitive designations. In short, don't be discouraged with the state map, where most of the land that we have circled is not private. The government has claimed almost all the beautiful forested land everywhere—especially out west where the greatest safety lies. Look for the niches of private property surrounding and going through federal lands.

Other Areas with Value

There are other areas of the country that have the virtues of cheaper land and forested mountains at lower altitude than the Intermountain West—like the Appalachian mountains in the east from Maine down into North Georgia, including the Alleghenies, the Cumberland Plateau and the Ozarks. Food is easier to grow here and there's more water. So why aren't these areas rated more highly?

We do recognize the virtues of these areas which are of particular interest to our readers on the East Coast, but all of these have one big disadvantage—they are too close to the huge population densities in the East, like the core cities around the Washington DC-New York City corridor, and major metros in the Carolinas, Georgia and Florida.

Right now all of these excellent eastern retreat areas, which we will cover in detail in the individual state analysis, appear to be very rural and not very accessible to outsiders. But when that sea of humanity floods out from the East Coast, there is a much higher probability that retreats even two or three states away will eventually face more desperate people as compared to the Intermountain West. Still, a retreat in the eastern mountains will definitely buy you some extra time before the threat arrives, and it will be much diminished when it arrives. People will always pick one area clean before moving on to another, and that could allow you to increase your level of preparedness and concealment or move on before the threat arrives.

Some have postulated that the plains states will do alright because they can grow food better than anywhere else. There is some validity in that, but the influx of refugees from the east may well compromise many farms in the central plains since the terrain is open and largely indefensible. The best counties in the central US are those that have a lot of hilly terrain mixed with farmland. All of the plains states have some hills within their boundaries so look there first. Land is cheaper here than out west. This area also has its own high-density population areas around Chicago and the Great Lakes that will fan out into the rural areas for food and relief.

Imagine growing a garden for your own family's survival with tens of hungry travelers around waiting for the crops to ripen. It makes for a very difficult situation when your land is visible and accessible to all. Real distance from civilization is crucial for any retreat, but especially in flat land farm country where you don't have mountains to deter people or provide some invisibility. Coverage behind lots of trees is helpful.

We don't want to sound fatalistic about these retreat areas in the East. Many will be able to survive there, and if that's the best choice for you given your particular restraints, you can make it work for you. In fact, we are convinced that some people, who find the right piece of property with good privacy and who have implemented sufficient concealed storage/living areas in basement spaces will be able to survive even multiple visits of marauders if they can stay concealed sufficiently. Disappear and let people search through the empty above-ground portion of the house. The strategy of hiding out and evading refugees rather than confronting them takes careful pre-preparation to do effectively. You can even prepare a house with electronic activation of pepper spray to make it unlivable for intruders.

As we now go into our regional analysis, we hope that everyone can find something that improves their situation. Don't be consumed with finding perfection—go for the best that works for you and your situation. We will begin our analysis with six regions in the United States and three regions of Canada, proceeding from west to east. The state–by–state analysis follows in the next chapter.

US Northwest Region ★★★★☆

This region encompasses most of our favorite places including the northern half of the Intermountain West. The hills and forests around the big cities in Washington and Oregon are some of the closest safe areas to populous cities that we know of (though still not ideal). Both the Seattle and Portland areas detract from their respective state's survival ratings because the majority of residents are Democrats and liberals who have bought into most environmental control schemes that undermine private property rights.

Washington and Oregon Areas

Western Washington has several of the biggest strategic nuclear targets in the naval and air bases around Seattle, including the Trident Submarine base near Bangor. Because of the prevailing west winds, there is a high probability that nuclear fallout from targets in the Puget Sound will not only blanket Seattle but also drift over the Cascade Mountains to eastern Washington and even Idaho. The Puget Sound area also faces a major earthquake threat. There are also volcanoes along the Cascade Mountain range that separates the populated valleys from the most secure areas in eastern Oregon and Washington. The volcanic ash will generally affect areas to the east.

After a nuclear attack, the probability of massive panic in these high density corridors along I-5 from Eugene to Seattle and points north is extremely high. On the map, these dangers correspond to the red populations and highway corridors which highlight the major outflows of people from the cities. Don't locate in any of the retreat areas that are close to the concentrations of dots or near the freeway corridors leading from them as these areas will be overrun by scavengers or worse problems.

There are areas along the Washington, Oregon and northern California coast that will be fallout free, except perhaps from a little residual radiation coming from Japan if it is hit. Those are the areas on the map starting at the Olympic Peninsula and following the coast mountain range south almost to Santa Rosa, CA. The Oregon and California coasts are more populated than the Washington coastal area, which could serve as a retreat area for people who must live in the Seattle area. All the coastal areas are rainy, so you won't need much irrigation to grow crops, but the weather is fairly mild. Retreats here do not have the buffer distance from major population centers but we suspect that it will not be a direction many refugees will go. On the other hand, this area is home to not a few roughneck types that could provide serious security problems. Stay away from the beach itself which puts you up against the sea without a good retreat. Land is also much cheaper if you stay east of Highway 101.

There is a small area on the NW tip of Washington from Port Angeles to Port Townsend that centers on a little town called Sequim (pronounced by the locals as "Squim") that is unique because of its optimal climate. Unlike the rest of the area in and around Seattle, this area is relatively dry. The Olympic Mountains soak up so much of the rain from the west, that there is little left over for this little pocket on the lee side of the mountains. It's a fair drive from here to Seattle, however, since you have to drive south around the very large Puget Sound. This area is ideal for Canadians who live on Vancouver Island and who want to keep a foot in the US which is just a 30 minute ferry ride across the channel.

The Cascade Mountains provide close retreat property for the agricultural valleys where most of the people in Oregon and Washington live. The western slopes are the most accessible for those who want to live full time in a retreat setting and still commute to work in the cities, but depending on the quantity of people around and from California, these areas may have to deal with refugees after the suburbs and valley farms have absorbed most of them. We therefore recommend the eastern slopes of the cascades where there is less rain and where pine forests start to compete with the firs. Don't locate downwind of one of the volcanoes, however. Check out the ash fallout patterns that came from Mt. Saint Helens near Vancouver, WA when it blew its top during the 80s. There were also major mud flows down all the rivers leading away from the mountain, so avoid those areas too.

As the Cascade Range goes farther south toward the California border, it nearly merges with the coast range in southern Oregon. This forms the highly rated area around Medford and Grants Pass. This was the original retreat capitol of the survivalist movement popularized by Mel Tappan and others. It's still a good area, though it has become somewhat liberal with the influx of people from California. The Cascades separate again after descending into California and they become wholly pine forests around Mt. Shasta (another volcano hazard). It's a beautiful area, and would be more recommended if it weren't in such a heavily Democratic state.

There are excellent rural areas around the city of Yakima, a major fruit capital of Washington, but stay west of the city to avoid fallout from the NSA listening post which we think is a strategic target. You must also be prepared for major damage from ash if any of the three local volcanoes erupt.

Northeast of Seattle there are some good retreat areas on the eastern slope of the Cascades, especially around Wenatchee and along Highway 2. Mt Baker, near the Canadian border, is a volcanic threat so avoid locations up to 50 miles east and along prevailing wind directions to avoid the worst ash plume. Primary residences with small farm acreages are abundant on the western sides of this area, but as in Oregon, they will have to contend with some refugees.

Even better retreats abound in the far northeast part of this zone, in and around the Coleville National Forest in northern central WA. The area is dry, with pine and scrub forests. For those who do not like the wet weather of the Pacific Northwest, always locate east of the Cascades where the rainfall drops off rapidly. There is also a lot of beautiful forested land north of Spokane. Fairchild AFB is a major base for aerial refueling and therefore a nuclear target, but this area is far enough north to be free from most fallout unless winds blow contrary to normal wind patterns (from the south). This is a prime pine forested retreat area for the Spokane area, and also serves as a US retreat for Canadians.

Central Oregon as two major farming and mountain areas that make for good retreats, if you like small town living. These are the best long-term retreat sites in Oregon, and a far distance from any major metro. One is around the Blue Mountains. The climate is dry, the forests are mostly pine and the farmland to the east around La Grande and Baker is excellent. The only drawback here is that you have to fit into a rural farm lifestyle and job market to make a living here—unless you are financially self-sufficient.

An even more remote ranching area than Baker and La Grande encompasses the gorgeous Wallowa Mountains with the Eagle Cap Wilderness area. Ranching is about the only business in this area, so it is a solidly conservative area and bucks the normal Oregon liberal trends. You can find good forested land at low altitudes anywhere in the area. Elgin is also a very nice town.

Idaho Areas

Idaho is a top-rated state for strategic safety. It has a conservative populace with an agricultural base. It also has a large forested portion of the Rockies in its central and northern sectors, offering excellent farm, ranches and retreats. The Boise area also has a lot of high tech companies moving in, providing a more diversified economic base. This growth largely stopped during the recent recession, but we see this as a good thing because it will help stabilize growth.

The area labeled "Northern Rocky Mts." on the corresponding map is in the heart of Idaho. This is one of the prime areas for retreats for people who live and work in any of the farm communities of the Snake River Valley or the Boise area. Prime locations are found along Highways 75, 93 and 28 on the east side of this range, and Highways 56 and 95 on the west including the Bitterroot Valley of Hamilton Montana. Each highway goes through a mountain valley with abundant private lands that back up to the national forests. This is one of those areas that has a very good chance of evading almost all the strategic dangers.

The northern extension of this area leads to the Coeur d'Alene area. The terrain and the people are different here so it merits its own category. The area has grown out of a rough and tumble mining and logging community and is Idaho's pocket of liberal voters. It has some spectacular retreat areas, both for farm and vacation, but does not have the same conservative base as the southern Idaho farming areas. Coeur d'Alene is the crown jewel of beauty in Idaho, and although it has the trappings of a resort town, we still like it. The better areas are to the north in Sandpoint and Boundary County, which have few building code requirements. The old neo-Nazi compound, Aryan Nations, has been shut down, so it no longer attracts the hoard of federal agents and infiltrators that plagued the area in past decades.

Farther to the south is the Lewiston and Clarkston area on the Washington border which has a milder climate than most of the state with a long growing season at a comparatively low altitude. Nearby Orofino is nice as well.

Montana Areas

Toward the east of the panhandle of Idaho is the highly rated area of Kalispell Montana. This area has nearly the same forestation as northern Idaho, but is somewhat colder, being on the eastern side of the Rockies and exposed to the cold Canadian air masses that come down out of the north during the winter. The Flathead Lake Valley has mountains on both the east and west and has an excellent base of mostly conservative Christian people, although a lot of liberals from California have moved in as well, creating tension.

Montana has a very high rating for strategic purposes, because of its mountains in the west. One of its detractions is that it has a mining background, with the corruption that accompanies that industry. There is something about the early mining mentality that leaves its mark on the future inhabitants and their attitudes about religion and morals that still plagues the liberal element of the state. As you can see from the map, there is a major missile field spread out in central Montana, and much of the eastern portion contains some fairly barren plains, so only Western Montana rates highly.

Moving southeast on the map, there is a pocket of mountains east of Helena—the "Little Belt and Big Belt Mountains". This is fairly dry and not as fully forested as the western Rockies, but is suitable for austere retreats. This area is at partial risk from fallout from the Malmstrom AFB base missile silos to the north, if the winds come from there.

The Gallatin Forest area would be a top rated area except for its proximity to Yellowstone. Much of this area has the potential of being declared a "buffer zone" around the park— the environmental lobby's way of getting more private land for non-development without having to pay for it. Stay at least 10 miles from the park boundaries and your property should be safe from this designation. There is a lot of cabin land in the area. The Yellowstone area is off limits to private cabins, but the volcanic caldera underlying the park makes it totally unsafe for retreats anyway.

Farther to the east are the Bighorn Mountains. Custer's last stand took place just south of the Crow Indian Reservation. It ties into the Bighorn National Forest coming out of Wyoming. It has a lot of retreat potential though it is fairly isolated from any big city.

Wyoming Areas

Wyoming is another top-rated state, with one of the lowest population densities, low regulations, and low taxes. Its two major drawbacks are the lack of water and the windy, cold climate. In the flat areas of Wyoming, the wind seems to always be blowing in the winter. The Wyoming plains are a low spot in the continental divide through the Rockies, thus forming a wind channel. To avoid these winds, you must seek out protected locations in the mountains to the north or to the south around Evanston or Laramie.

The Grand Teton area, excluding Yellowstone National Park, is the crown jewel of Wyoming retreat country. Land is expensive on the Wyoming side of the Grand Tetons because so many of the rich and famous have bought second homes there. The mountain views are spectacular. The climate is very cold and rigorous in the winter and averages about 3 feet of snow all winter, so it's not for the faint hearted. The best areas for retreats are in the southern part in either Star Valley or Swan Valley on the Idaho side. All of these give you close access to the Tetons without the high price.

Wyoming does have a portion of the Black Hills, but most development parallels the commercial activity which is oriented toward Rapid City, SD—the only significant city for miles around. The Black Hills area is the only retreat land available in South Dakota, which otherwise is composed almost entirely of vast level plains.

There is also some nice cabin land in the Laramie Mountains, south of Casper. The main mass of the Colorado Rockies extends a little into southern Wyoming offering limited private land. These are an extension of the Colorado Medicine Bow Mountains. Typical for Wyoming, they are cold and windy, but excellent retreat sites for the inhabitants of Laramie and Cheyenne. Cheyenne is surrounded on the east by the missile fields of Warren AFB, home of some Minuteman III missiles and other secret things, so it should be avoided.

The visible portions of Utah, Nevada and Colorado in this region will be covered in the SW region.

US Southwest Region ★ ★ ★ ☆ ☆

This corner of the US has a few more areas to avoid, but some excellent safe areas as well. As in Oregon and Washington, none of the areas in California will be highly rated because of this state's reputation for intrusive regulation—not to mention the inevitable bankruptcy that comes from providing too many welfare and education benefits. California's codes and regulations are monstrous compared with any other state. This is a shame because some of the most restricted areas, particularly in northern California, could be some of the safest areas around. Bureaucrats behind the scenes are still fanatical in this state, especially when it comes to enforcing environmental or conservation laws. Sometimes the only way you can buy into any existing restricted area is to buy something already built because new construction is either totally prohibited or prohibitively expensive after complying with all the costs of regulations (including hiring high-priced professionals to lead you through the complex red tape). California also contains three major metro centers that are sources of social unrest (Los Angeles, San Francisco, and San Diego), as well as several primary nuclear targets and many secondary targets.

California Areas

The northern California forested area outlined on the corresponding map is probably the best in all of the state. Northern California in many ways should be a different state from the central and southern areas where most of the problems are. The coastal side of this retreat area begins at the Russian River above Santa Rosa and includes all the coast north, wraps around above Redding and includes the Sierras down to within 10 miles of I-80. Redwood trees abound in the coastal region because there is a lot of rain. The eastern side has a drier climate that allows mostly pine forests to grow. These areas provide retreats for those in the San Francisco and Sacramento area. Excellent farming retreats can be found near the foothills as the central valley begins to rise to the Sierras. Retreats in this area, however, will experience a lot of refugees when the San Francisco and Sacramento urban areas seek food elsewhere.

The Sierra Nevada area (south of I-80) includes the spectacular Lake Tahoe area, which offers expensive vacation retreat potential but is riddled with building permit hurdles and restrictions. It is best to live on the Nevada side of the line. This area will certainly be overrun by people coming over the Sierras on I-80, so any cabin must be well off the beaten path.

In the southern Sierra Nevada Range, the forests extend beyond Yosemite on the west to below Bishop on the east and then turn into high desert near Bakersfield. There is a large, semi-active volcano area around Mammoth Lakes and Mono Lake that is going to be dangerous in the future. Many small swarms of tremors are being monitored by the USGS and we think the entire zone is unstable. The Bishop area on the eastern slope is a very fine retreat area, but one must beware of the potential of earthquakes and volcanic ash fall.

The central California coastal area (Santa Lucia Mts.) represents a marginally safe coastal area of California from Monterey down to Santa Barbara. It is primarily not a true retreat area, but excellent for main residences if you must live in California. The coast offers the best air quality and the scenery is spectacular, but prices are elevated. Some retreat sites are available in the mountain areas, but they really are not of the same caliber as those in the Sierras since the coastal zone will be overrun by people fleeing northward from the LA basin.

There are two mountain cabin areas around the LA basin that may tempt you as a retreat—the Santa Maria and San Bernardino Mountains. The Santa Maria zone is fairly dry and unattractive, but this offers a positive barrier to development. There are very few private holdings in the zone until you get up on the high desert side where Lancaster is located. The air quality is better out of the basin, but if you plan to commute to LA it will be very difficult to access this area if you don't get home before the crisis begins. In a major exodus from LA, the few passes through the mountains (like the Grapevine or the El Cajon Pass) will be clobbered with traffic. Your best bet is to pre-plan exit routes through some of the mountain roads or even jeep trails (consider a 4WD SUV). We expect a lot of refugees to flood the high desert someday.

The San Bernardino Mts. area includes the beautiful Lake Arrowhead resort area. While expensive, it does have some fair retreat areas that get you out of the smog and into some beautiful pine country. Some people actually commute from here to San Bernardino or Riverside each day. These mountains even get snow in the winter and have skiing. They will be mostly overrun, however, as people flee the valleys.

The mountains south of the LA basin down to Escondido have a lot of steep rocky hills that can offer temporary respite from refugees that will mostly stay in the valleys. However, we can't assure you of any long-term safety in a major crisis of social unrest. There are simply too many millions at risk after government services and food deliveries fail.

For those in and around San Diego, the southern Cleveland Forest area has some possible retreats and residences but be aware that this area is too close to the Mexican border for comfort. We expect there could be a major influx from that direction in the aftermath of major social unrest. Stay some distance away from I-8 leading to El Centro—a major exit point from the San Diego area.

Nevada Areas

Nevada has certain strategic advantages due to its mostly barren landscape. Few will venture out into those deserts on foot. Even pioneers had trouble transiting this state due to lack of water. There are, however, several oases of high desert mountains with snow capped peaks and pine forests, such as the Santa Rosa Mountains north of Winnemucca, the Humboldt National Forest north of Elko, and the Ruby Valley and Mountains south of Elko.

The majority of the southern part is dominated by the Nevada Nuclear Test Site and Area 51, the top secret test base for experimental aircraft and other unknown projects. This is certainly a nuclear target just because the Russians don't trust anything the US military does in public and will hit all top secret bases, just in case, after having taken out all the primary targets.

The farm and ranch valleys around Carson City near the Sierras are probably in the best retreat area in Nevada. Reno to the north will absorb a huge amount of refugees coming over the I-80 corridor.

Utah Areas

The Utah area contains some of the top rated retreat areas for long term security. The state is in the center of the intermountain area and has a major international airport at Salt Lake City with direct flights and good connections everywhere. This is one of the few states where excellent long-term retreat sites are within an hour of a major airport hub (Delta). Almost any place but the Salt Lake Valley itself is an excellent location. Despite being medium altitude desert, there is sufficient water stored in the mountain reservoirs for farm and cabin type retreats. Most of Utah, southern Idaho and northern Arizona were founded originally by Mormon pioneers and Mormons are still represented in these areas in large numbers. This is an advantage in our mind as Mormons are largely preparedness oriented, conservative and are familiar with government tyranny in their past. All this makes for a good population base for security. Despite the common grumbling to the contrary, we have found Mormons are very friendly and tolerant of other faiths in their midst.

The front of the Wasatch Mountains is visible to the east as you drive along I-15, the north-south freeway which connects all the cities in the area. The mountains look dry from the highway because of the west sun which melts the snow too fast to grow trees, but the back sides of the mountains are heavily forested, especially around all the best ski resorts and mountain valley retreat sites. These back mountain valleys provide maximum security and still have relatively quick access to a moderate-to-low crime metro area. Salt Lake City has less crime than most urban cities, and only has a problem in areas where non-religious and low class people live. This supports our correlation between crime and lack of religious feeling. The valleys directly to the north and south of Salt Lake are low crime, highly cultured and moral. These communities are the best compromise locations near significant civilization.

More austere retreat areas are available farther to the east in the Uinta Mountain Range—the highest peaks in the intermountain area. Land for retreat sites and ranches are limited and found only along the periphery of this area, but look in Wyoming as well as Utah. The area is a long way from civilization and will fare well in hard times, if you can survive there financially in the meantime.

We rate the central Utah Wasatch Mountains as one of the highest rated areas in the entire continent for long-term security. It is far enough south from the populated Salt Lake areas that it will always be free from high density people problems. There are many private plots of land available in all the small farming communities. Sanpete County gets our highest rating. The people are down-to-earth, pioneer-type people, favorable to self-sufficiency and very friendly. However, as in all the best retreat areas, it is not a good area for finding employment.

The Mormon Range of mountains in the Dixie National Forest around St. George, UT provide good but high altitude retreat sites for those moving to southern Utah. St. George is a banana belt, sunny resort area that offers year round vacation potential. It experienced fast growth after Las Vegas got too expensive. This is Utah's red rock country and it is gorgeous. St. George itself is not the best area, so we like the rural towns to the west in Green Valley and to the north such as Hurricane, La Verkin or Toquerville. Water is limited in this area, so make sure any rural land comes with water rights. Cedar City to the north is a growing educational and cultural center. It is high desert and colder than St. George, but not as hot in the summer.

Utah's red rock country extends over into eastern Utah around the red rock mountains near Moab and Monticello. Moab is a mountain bike resort destination, noted for its miles of bike trails that travel all over the beautiful red rock country. The area has a dry, sunny climate where water comes from mountain snowmelt.

Arizona Areas

Fifteen years ago, Arizona was more highly rated than it is today. As the Phoenix mega metro has grown larger, so have the liberal tendencies of its government. It still has many conservative roots, but they are more and more in danger of becoming a permanent minority.

Arizona still has some top rated retreat areas in the mountains, however. Generally, they are very dry in terms of rainfall, but the earth has a special area of impervious clay and rock that holds water and creates artesian wells where water springs out of the ground in a few totally dry areas. The locals will know how to find these areas. Arizona also has an interactive website where you can see the details on every water well drilled in the state, its location, depth and flow rate---invaluable for checking on your chances of finding good water in any area: https://gisweb.azwater.gov/WellRegistry/

There are large pine forests north of Phoenix around Flagstaff and farther east. They exclude a large dry area known as the Natanes Plateau and the Gila Mountains where the San Carlos Indian Reservation is found. Many of the rural landowners around flagstaff have to haul water because the water table is too deep for drilling domestic wells. These National Forest areas are full of pockets of private land—but check for water availability. The best sites are around the cities of Payson, Heber, and Snowflake—and north of Clifton by the New Mexico border.

Colorado Areas

Colorado has all the makings of a top-rated state in terms of geography and distance from major problem areas. The only problem is the obvious city center of Denver which taints the whole state in our minds. This highly intrusive, Democratic controlled center of the Rocky Mountains is a regional base for US government black operations and illicit activities. Several major nuclear target areas are also in Colorado such as Cheyenne Mt. near Colorado Springs, Buckley CIA base in Denver and the missile silos from Warren AFB in WY that extend into the north corner of the state. Stay clear of Colorado Springs and Denver altogether.

Central Colorado is home to the backbone of the Rocky Mountains and they are formidable indeed. We don't recommend retreats at the ski resorts unless that's the only way your spouse will agree to have a home in the Rockies. There are many more rural retreats available away from the resorts but still close enough for easy access to the ski areas. The top rated area for rural farm retreats is around Montrose where they have many orchards as well as nearby mountain locations. The climate is more mild here than in the higher altitudes.

The best area for forested mountain retreats in western Colorado is between Durango and Pagosa Springs, in the southwest corner, and areas east and west of Montrose. However, because of oil and gas wells in the area, you must work hard to find good well water that isn't contaminated with some of these natural substances. Another excellent area, away from the high ski resort prices, is the valley north of Salida on either side of Highway 24. There are other sites in this large area which are too numerous to mention.

There is also a northern section of the Colorado Rockies above the I-70 corridor. These are the best areas in which to find retreat sites if you live in Denver, Boulder or Fort Collins.

New Mexico Areas

New Mexico has very few retreat areas due to the heavy influx of illegal aliens from Mexico, which have almost reached a majority status in the state. There are also several significant strategic nuclear targets in the state such as Los Alamos and Sandia nuclear research laboratories, White Sands missile test range at Holloman AFB and the Trinity Site north of White Sands. The last site has multiple primary targets such as satellite and missile tracking stations as well as nuclear stockpiles. NM also has a large new-age population around Santa Fe. While New Agers are not aggressive or threatening in any way, their spiritualistic roots may not lend long-term stability or good judgment to the area.

A portion of Colorado's Rocky Mountains does reach into northern NM, which makes for the best retreat areas in the state. The mountainous areas shown in southern NM are not highly rated due to their proximity to Mexico and Fort Huachuca.

US North Central Region ★★★☆☆

This map is dramatic for its lack of retreat areas. You will also notice on the corresponding map that there are several areas of high population density around the lower Great Lakes: Chicago, Detroit, Cleveland and Cincinnati. These were all great cities born and raised up during the American industrial heyday—and are now dying. These areas are high concentrations of blue collar and union workers and will be just as much a refugee threat to the Midwest as the East Coast is to the Appalachian mountain retreat areas. When the government-provided infrastructure in these major industrial cities collapses, people will take to the highways leading westward into the central plains states to look for food in the "breadbasket of America" (which sadly only grows GMO corn and soybeans of late).

Ozark Areas

The Missouri Ozarks to the south and the northern Minnesota and Wisconsin Lake country will be the prime areas of safety for those wanting to get out of the refugee flow.

The Ozarks of Arkansas, Oklahoma, and Missouri constitute one of the best retreat areas in the nation, except what is within reach of the future refugees that will pour out of the East Coast and Florida. It has beautiful hardwood forests, abundant game animals, clear rivers and a good mix of people who like their privacy. Its only drawback besides accessibility to others is that its fine reputation for privacy and beauty has attracted a few survivalist groups which have established small communal compounds. None of these people would present a problem except their presence attracts government agents who are constantly attempting to provoke survivalists into some rash act for which they can be taken down and prosecuted. For this reason, we never recommend joining formal survival groups in establishing common living territory. If you are good friends with people there, then stay connected but separate. You can always band together when the time for action arrives.

Minnesota and Wisconsin Areas

The Minnesota lake country is far enough north that few from the cities will seek out this area in their search for shelter and food. This area, with its vast maze of forests and lakes is an outdoorsman's paradise—except for the insects. Because of the hot, humid summer climate the insects breed abundantly and are a real drawback. The locals seem to know how to deal with them, perhaps by stocking up on repellant. Winters are rugged here with lots of cold Canadian air and snow.

In like manner, the northern Wisconsin woods and land around the Ottawa National Forest are good retreat areas. This forested lake country is very similar to that in Minnesota, but it has a weather pattern heavily influenced by the great lakes which nearly surround it to give it more breezes, more humidity and more snow in the winter. This also applies to the only safe place in Michigan—the Upper Peninsula. Its greatest disadvantage is the potential to be isolated by peninsular geography. With the potential of serious social unrest from Chicago down south or Minneapolis/St. Paul to the southwest, this area could conceivably have few exits in a long-term crisis. Cold weather could be your ally here.

US South Central Region ★ ★ ☆ ☆ ☆

The southern sector of the US is at greatest risk for the continuing influx of illegal immigrants from Mexico. They are already reaching majority status in many areas of the SW and Texas. This will impact ratings in south Texas especially. Notice the red areas on the map. That's a pretty good depiction of where the population flows will travel seeking relief. When they don't find it, they will branch off sideways toward small towns, homes and farms looking for food. The recommended areas shown in yellow are the least likely areas (or at least the last areas) to take on unwanted visitors.

Texas Areas

On the corresponding map, the "South Texas Hill Country" north of San Antonio centers around the town of New Braunfels. The landscape is hilly and wooded with Oak, Juniper and some Pine. It doesn't have a high population density, but there are already plenty of rural subdivisions where the wealthy from Austin and San Antonio have built second homes. These are more upscale developments that will absorb most of the refugees passing through, so if you build a retreat in a hilly, private area with few people you may have a

chance of evading some of the danger. The downside of this area is that there is a lot of solid rock subsoil so underground rooms require blasting or jack hammering throughout the excavation.

The "South Texas Pine Forest" area offers good retreats for people in the Dallas area. This area is between I-10 to the south and I-20 along the top and extends from I-45 on the west to the Louisiana border on the east. This follows our general rule that retreats be at least 10 miles away from major freeways, and always out of direct visual sight of all highways.

You will also find some modest Texas hill country up north by the Oklahoma border. The Red Plains area of north central Texas isn't particularly spectacular, but it covers a vast area for farm retreats that has good odds of rarely meeting any outsiders. The Panhandle area of Texas also has a lot of undeveloped territory. It isn't mountainous but it does have a lot of distance between it and other major population centers. Few refugees will venture into the far reaches of this area.

Oklahoma and Arkansas Areas

Oklahoma has some nice mountain retreat areas in the eastern part. The Arkansas and Missouri Ozarks intrude into Oklahoma, as do the Ouachita Mountains to the south, which are better on the OK side than in AR.

The Ouachita forests are similar in terrain and landscape to the Ozarks to the north, and have a variety of pine and deciduous forests. One caution about this area—stay clear of the Mena, Arkansas federal airstrip. This is where the CIA operated its 10,000 foot runway for "special operations" like illegitimate covert operations that ran drugs.

US Southeast Region ★ ⯪ ☆ ☆ ☆

The map clearly shows the high density population areas of the South. There are two major threats within this region: first, the massive number of people concentrated in the Atlanta area and second, the high density, high crime areas of southern Florida. Florida is particularly problematic because it will become almost unlivable without food, air conditioning and transportation. Millions will have only one way to get out of the area someday, and that is north.

The small towns of southern Georgia, Alabama, Mississippi and Louisiana will be particularly hard hit with refugees, not only from their own urban areas on the coast, but also from the rest of Florida. It is doubtful that many people will flow towards Atlanta since any thoughts of safety there would be quickly dispelled by the streams of people leaving the Atlanta metro area.

Southeastern Mountains and Plateaus

As the corresponding map indicates, the best four retreat areas are the Blue Ridge Mountains, the Cumberland Plateau and the Ozark and Ouachita Mts. of Arkansas and Missouri, covered previously.

The Blue Ridge Mountains are the least secure of the four because they will have to absorb the first wave of refugees from Atlanta and the Carolinas. It's not a lost cause however, because most of the refugees will stay in the lowland valleys heading up into the Carolinas or on toward Knoxville in Tennessee.

The Cumberland Plateau gets our highest rating in the east because it will receive far fewer refugees than the Blue Ridge Mts. The Plateau has a formidable look to it when approached. It is fairly steep so we believe that most people flowing out of Atlanta to Chattanooga or Knoxville will stay in the valley. There is a wide valley cutting through the Plateau NW of Chattanooga, and most people will keep on heading toward Nashville and the wealthy horse farm country to the west rather than attempt to climb up on the Plateau. Those steep approaches are also very defensible. That's what makes this a good area for safety.

Southeastern Forests

That said, there is some hill country areas in the northern parts of Alabama and Mississippi that you should consider as well, but they are a little too close to major cities to give long-term safety.

The Holly Springs Forest area southeast of Memphis and north of Oxford and Tupelo, Mississippi are suitable for some retreats. The Bienville Forest area between Jackson and Meridian, MS is a similar area, but fairly close to these two cities.

In Alabama there is an area surrounding Bankhead National Forest that includes all the rural counties south of Decatur and northwest of Birmingham. There is also the area surrounding the Talladega forest between the Tombigbee and Alabama rivers and the Talladega Mountains east of Birmingham toward the Georgia border.

There is also a bit of rural hill country situated in Louisiana, east of Alexandria, south of I-20 and east to I-55 in Mississippi. It encompasses the Homochitto National Forest and extends south nearly to the eastern "boot" of Louisiana. There are numerous deciduous forests in this area, as well as pine and open land for farm retreats.

US Northeast Region ★☆☆☆☆

In general, the eastern half of the US has fewer secure retreat sites, not because of lack of beautiful forested hill country, but because of shear population density. As you can clearly see on the population density map at the beginning of this chapter, the northeastern United States is by far the most dangerous region in the country in terms of high density urban areas. For more precise figures on state average density, see the summary analysis pertaining to each state in the following chapter.

In our analysis the high threat in this region will be from social unrest and masses of refugees. Keep in mind that it is almost one long, continuous city from Washington DC to Boston. As populations in these areas contemplate fleeing they will try to flee away from other big cities. The south portion around DC will mostly try to flee south and west. From Boston people will run to the north or west. People in the Newark-New York corridor are really stuck. They are surrounded by water to the east, and masses of other suburbs to the north and west. That's where the most turmoil will be. Those already in the eastern suburbs will flow west. Most roads lead toward Philadelphia or Syracuse and Albany in rural NY.

The best retreat areas are outlined in yellow on the corresponding map. These are mostly mountainous areas with light population densities. The rule of flow with refugees is that they will head for medium-sized cities before taking to the open countryside. Large masses will only head into the mountains as a last resort. We predict that most masses will flow around and between these yellow recommended areas. Even though pillaging and marauding will eventually reach the mountains, it will be lighter than the pillaging of the cities and towns, where the pickings are easier and seem better to people.

You can also see the high density urban areas to the west on the northeast regional map, including Chicago and Detroit, as well as the other industrial towns ringing the Great Lakes. These cities present a big problem for people fleeing the east, since those that make it into the valley and mountains toward eastern PA will see other crowds of people from the Midwest converging against them as they also seek shelter farther into the mountains. People caught in these combined refugee flows will be mostly in close Midwestern cities such as those in Ohio, West Virginia and western Pennsylvania. Most of the larger Midwestern cities will flow west, and secondarily north and south.

The foregoing is why the Alleghenies and Central Appalachians will get very crowded. Our recommendations therefore are to go farther north or south for retreat sites. You'll have competition everywhere in the east but your chances are best the farther away you get. Consider VT, NH, or Maine to the north or the Appalachian and Cumberland plateaus to the west. Even better, consider one set of mountains past the Appalachians themselves.

Appalachian Areas

North-Central Pennsylvania is the least populated hill country of the east. The best areas here are north of I-80, which is also the least travelled of the freeways in the area. The Pennsylvania Appalachian area extends from Scranton to Johnstown, PA and includes the Allegheny Mountains near Erie, PA. There are so many rugged ridges of hills and mountains in this area, everyone has their own private mountain to name. While population densities in Pennsylvania are high, crime rates are lower (percentage wise) due to the long history of Pennsylvania-Dutch and Amish cultures. These areas have the lowest population densities as is common with land that is tough to work.

The Appalachian Plateau of West Virginia runs into the hill country of eastern Ohio and is part of the coal region. It's a poverty stricken area and not that friendly to newcomers, but it's the best of the Midwest alternatives.

The Daniel Boone Forests of Kentucky and the northern Appalachian chain of mountains are an extension of the Cumberland Plateau which is the highest rated area in the east. The farther south into TN you can get on the plateau the better.

Northeastern Mountain Areas

The Catskill Mountains are the playground of the New York elite. There are still a few affordable areas, if you search for them. The mountains were originally a high level plateau that was eroded away into deep valleys, thus explaining the abundance of elevated, flat forested areas unlike the rest of the Appalachian chain to the southwest.

The Adirondack Mountains encompass a huge area of upstate New York to the west of Lake Champlain. This area offers more remoteness than the Catskills and cheaper land

The Green Mountains of Vermont are good for retreats because the climate is a little rigorous for some, keeping the general masses down toward the southern areas (which will always be more susceptible to refugee flows than the north).

The White Mountains of New Hampshire are some of the best in New England, but only those in the northern half of the state will be far enough away from the mobs fleeing Boston someday.

The Northern Appalachians of Maine are the most remote and farthest away from the population centers. The insects in the summer and the cold winters will make city folk in New England think twice before venturing up there. These mountain areas of VT, NY and ME have the slight disadvantage of not allowing you much maneuvering room if you

decide to go further west in the midst of turmoil. The routes will be blocked once long term unrest begins, so you'll need to stay put or go farther north into Canada.

Southwest Canada ★★★★⯪

The area outlined in the corresponding southwest Canada map (British Columbia and Alberta) has features in the south resembling the terrain, vegetation and climate of the US Intermountain West and eastern Washington State. It's like a composite of the terrain from Washington State to the plains of Colorado all compressed into a much smaller area. It's a wonderful area for living and has our highest rating for Canada. In fact it would rate a full 5 stars if it weren't for Canada's draconian gun prohibitions. The southern part of this area borders the retreat areas of WA. It is free from direct nuclear targets, although it is possible to receive fallout from the Seattle area under certain wind conditions. There is no shortage of dormant volcanoes in the coastal mountains, as can be seen on the map.

British Columbia

The area known as the Okanagan valley is our favorite area in Canada—by far. It has a good climate, a normal growing season, lots of fertile land, and there are lakes and forests on the east and west for prime forest or farm retreats. The towns are small and friendly and the people are very nice. We like Osoyoos, right across the border from Oroville, WA or Penticton at the south end of Okanagan Lake. Kelowna is the biggest town in the valley, also on the Lake.

Anything north of Kamloops is too rural for most people to make a living, and the north country of BC is also a land of thousands of lakes and rivers, making it hard to travel.

Vancouver is the main city in BC and is a sprawling, modern metropolis with a growing crime rate—mostly due to the influx of Chinese and Muslim immigrants. Canada's open immigration policy has really hurt the country as a safe haven for Canadians. 52% of the residents speak a foreign language as their native tongue. Vancouver has an international boating harbor that is the gateway to a world of sailing around the surrounding waters. The rural areas between Vancouver and the US border are too crowded for good retreats. We recommend you either locate north of the Fraser River or around Abbotsford which puts you on the eastern edge of the Metro area—and closest to the best retreats in the Okanagan Valley.

Except for one Canadian Air Force base, most of coastal British Columbia north of Squamish is suitable for retreats, farms and mountain homes. Once you get 75 miles north of Vancouver the entire province is very lightly populated and is largely composed of trackless forested wilderness areas. But you can find any number of retreats within a reasonable commuting distance to Vancouver. The big drawback of the western-most area is the heavy rain, but it's the price you pay for all that greenery.

Vancouver Island is a partial exception to our philosophy against island retreats. It is so large that you can establish private retreats there with agricultural self-sufficiency and still have a lot of privacy. It is also very lightly populated, so there isn't much danger of hundreds of thousands of people pouring out of cities in search of food. Victoria is the main city on the island and it is so focused on ferry traffic back to the mainland that most people would probably hold out for evacuation to the mainland rather than take to the relatively empty forests in search of food. The other benefit of Vancouver Island is its proximity to the mainland. It doesn't take an expensive boat to transit the region if you need to. You must take great care to watch the currents however. They can be quite swift and overwhelm small motors.

Alberta

There are also a lot of possible mountain retreats in the Canadian Rockies of Alberta, although there is less private land available compared to the Rockies in the States. Almost everything away from the centers of the big cities and a few miles from the major highways could be considered retreat property here. This includes the areas surrounding the Canadian Rockies, with its gorgeous vacation resorts like Banff and Lake Louise. Of course the best areas for retreats are further away from these expensive tourist spots, but virtually all of the major cities in these two provinces have access to a significant number of good retreat areas.

Calgary is the largest city in Alberta and is Canada's "cow town" because it plays host to the famous Calgary Stampede and is surrounded by extensive ranching assets. The city itself is at the edge of the Great Plains of Canada and within 10 miles of the mountains. You can find numerous farm retreat sites along the foothills, and Hwy 8 and 22 lead to forested sites fairly close to town.

Edmonton (also an energy city) and Red Deer are farther north and out in the plains, but are still acceptable for safe farmland because the population densities of Canada are low. Note the nuclear target north of Edmonton and one farther east at Cold Lake, as indicated on the map, which must be avoided.

Edmonton is Alberta's capital city, and is the most northerly major city in the country. Edmonton is the energy capitol of Canada and near the largest oil fields and most of western Canada's oil refineries. Almost 75% of the province's population lives in the Calgary-Edmonton corridor.

Once into Canada's plains, you will find the dry continental climate that is typical of central Canada with warm summers and cold winters—often extremely cold in winter where temperatures can change rapidly. Arctic air masses in the winter produce extreme minimum temperatures varying from minus 65 °F in northern Alberta to minus 51 °F in southern Alberta. Summers are mild and warm.

South Central Canada ★ ★ ★ ☆ ☆

Saskatchewan and Manitoba

Geographically, these provinces differ mainly in water resources. Manitoba is a land of huge lakes which both moderates the temperature and generates thunderstorms and lake effect rain and snow. Saskatchewan is devoid of any large bodies of water and thus doesn't generate its own weather. It is subject to the extremes of temperatures from the north and the humid summer air coming up from the south. The hottest temperature ever recorded in Canada happened in Saskatchewan: 113 °F in Midale and Yellow Grass. Of course, one winter Prince Albert (north of Saskatoon) also registered a record of minus 60 °F.

Regina is the capitol city and where most of the people of Saskatchewan live. 45% of the grain in Canada is grown in Saskatchewan, but it also is second to Alberta in gas and oil. There are only a million people in the province so it has very low population densities. The geography is flat, but there are forested sections that make for good retreats. Both Saskatchewan and Manitoba overcome much of the weaknesses of a plains-region that most US farm retreats have by virtue of the fact that there just aren't enough people for hundreds of miles to bother you. Very few refugees are going that far north into what appears fairly bleak country. The downside, of course, is that it's hard to make a living as a lone family retreating to the plains.

Manitoba is likewise an agricultural state. But extensive agriculture is found mostly in the southern half of the province. Cattle ranching in this province exceeds grain farming. Its capitol and largest city is Winnipeg where 60% of the population of the province lives. The province has over 110,000 lakes, which channels traffic into corridors, making it more difficult to maneuver in a crisis.

Southern parts of both provinces experience tornados, being at the far north end of the plains that make up Tornado Alley in the USA. An average of 12 to 15 tornados occur each year and a few have even developed into F5 twisters. The strongest officially recorded tornado in Canada was an F5 storm that devastated parts of Elie.

Temperatures exceed 86 °F during the summers and feel hot and humid. Carman, Manitoba holds the record for the highest percent of humidity in Canada.

We recommend only living in the outskirts of the two major cities in the region just to make sure you are not surrounded by people in a panic. Generally, anywhere north or south of the transcontinental Hwy 1 is fine for farm retreats. If you can find forests, so much the better for privacy and protection—not to mention a winter supply of firewood during Canada's cold winters.

Southeast Canada ★★☆☆☆

Southern Ontario

This peninsula has a humid continental climate. Summers are hot and humid with numerous thunderstorms and occasional tornados as big as F4. Annual rainfall is 37 inches, and the growing season is pretty good because of the moderating affect of the great lakes on both sides. Winters are generally cold with occasional mild periods. Windsor is not located in the lake effect snow belts that affect the US states to the south and east of the lakes.

The high density population regions (shown with clusters of red dots) of Windsor-London-Toronto and Ottawa-Montreal are the two primary danger zones in eastern Canada. To be fair, they have not grown together into two massive metro areas yet as we find in the New York City-Newark metro areas. There is a fair amount of rural farmland between each town, but it is mostly flat and offers little cover.

Even these moderating effects are counterbalanced by some serious threats from nuclear power plants, close proximity to Detroit and increased crime and cultural unrest similar to Europe where large minority groups from Muslim countries were encouraged to immigrate to Canada. There are organized crime groups connected to Chinese immigrant communities and gang activity from various minority sectors is on the rise.

The following analysis from a Wikipedia article on "Muslims in Canada" offers some surprising facts. According to a census in 2001, the majority of Canadian Muslims live in the province of Ontario and the largest groups are in or around the Greater Toronto Area. British Columbia also has a large Muslim population, mostly from the Middle East and Iran. "Canada's national capital Ottawa hosts many Lebanese and Somali Muslims, where the Muslim community numbered approximately 40,000 in 2001. Greater Montreal's Muslim community neared 100,000 in 2001. It is home to large numbers of Canadians of Moroccan, Algerian and Lebanese descent, as well as smaller Pakistani, Syrian, Iranian, Bangladeshi, and Turkish communities." The numbers of Muslims there have almost doubled since 2001.

Only a relatively small percentage of Muslims are a problem currently, but it is the minority that has historically been taken advantage of by agent provocateurs working as informants

for government. Because the Muslim religion and culture does not mesh well with Western historical traditions, it is easily provoked when youthful dissatisfaction is fomented and taken advantage of during hard economic times.

There are numerous traps zones involved in planning a retreat strategy in this area. The Great Lakes nearly surround the high density Southern Ontario peninsula and the St. Lawrence River and Seaway forms a barrier to the south of this population corridor. In addition there are numerous lakes and small rivers laced throughout the area between Toronto and Ottawa, as well as in the more rural areas to the north that create additional trap zones and force most travel onto established roads.

We recommend that most Canadians who live in the southern Ontario peninsula (1.5 stars) have retreats outside this area, except those that are very rural and that have basement potential to build a concealed safe room. It is safer to the north because of the lower population density and distance from Detroit. The best areas that still give you reasonable access to civilization are north of Hwy 7. It is difficult to find property where concealed basement space can be created because of the numerous lakes in the area and corresponding high water table. We don't recommend creating a retreat anywhere near populated areas where conditions don't allow hidden underground safe rooms. Encountering pillaging or marauding people someday is inevitable and you must have a place to hide and evade conflict. Interestingly, the southern Ontario Peninsula does have more elevation and less water table problems for basements than the less populated areas to the north, somewhat offsetting the disadvantage of closeness to big cities. So, if you can leave the area, do so. If you can't, get some below ground secure space built.

North of Hwy 17, where the population density is even thinner, you have the same problem with lands of thousands of lakes and high water tables. But some basements are possible on higher ground. Sometimes you can find areas where partial basements can be built and covered with bermed landscaping. This is one of the reasons why Alberta and eastern British Columbia are so much more highly rated. Basements are much easier to build in these drier areas.

Toronto is the largest city in the area and requires special attention to avoid getting trapped in a crisis. If you must live close to Toronto, we recommend picking one of the several small cities that lie outside Hwy 407 to the NW. By commuting into town but not living in town you have a much better probability of avoiding traffic traps in a crisis. Living as far away as Newmarket on Hwy 9 is even better, but a longer commute. If you are trying to get north to a retreat, watch out for the bottleneck created by the single main road (Hwy 400) leading north between the Georgian Bay and Lake Simco. Hwy 12 is a possible alternate on the east side of Lake Simco, but if it is clogged there are almost no other alternatives.

Once you get north of Cornwall on Hwy 401, the US boundary line ceases to follow the river and goes directly east for a number of miles. This area of Quebec south of the river is rated 2.5 stars. This forms a portion of Canada that is sandwiched between the US border and the St. Lawrence Seaway. It is actually a better retreat area than most of the land to the north of the Montreal-Quebec line of cities. The land to the north of Montreal is not very high and is filled with a thousand lakes. Water tables are high in most parts, making it difficult to put in basement space.

To the south, there is a lot of good farm land and far less population density, but you may get driven across the US border by refugees from Montreal or Quebec. Don't attempt to flee northward. The Seaway is a formidable barrier with very few bridges and those mostly lead to major metro areas that will block entrance from the south. Sherbrooke and Drummondville are the major towns in the area which provide for suitable commerce.

Eastern Maritimes

New Brunswick shares the same advantages of good farmland, higher ground and close proximity to the USA, as the area just mentioned and is probably the best retreat site in eastern Canada. The population density is low and there are no major threats except the cold and dampness in the winter and the bugs and humidity in the summer.

Nova Scotia, **Newfoundland** and the other islands are safer than other islands we have discussed because they are quite large and lightly inhabited. Temperatures are moderated by the Gulf Stream in this region of Canada so it is not as cold as in the western and central provinces. Cape Breton is a little rocky and hilly, but the "mainland" part of Nova Scotia has very fertile sections. Halifax is a world class city with many cultural attractions, two universities, and an international airport with flights to Europe.

Housing prices never collapsed in Canada when the US housing declined, but housing prices in the Maritime provinces (NB, NS, NF, PEI), are still very reasonable. Prince Edward Island (PEI) is similar to NS except that the conservative Fraser Institute has called it the least free state or province in North America economically.

It is also unlikely that the Maritimes would be targets of hostile occupation or takeover in a war. Their only military value is for transiting the Atlantic between Europe and the USA. They do have access to the fishing grounds of the Atlantic and might be coveted for that. If or when occupation does become a threat, make sure you have a means of getting off the islands.

Montreal and Quebec metro areas desire special attention in developing a retreat plan out of these cities. As in all large cities, you want to pick a location on the outskirts so that in a crisis of social unrest you can have a fair chance of exiting the city without clogged roadways.

Montreal: The first decision to make is whether you want to retreat to the south or the north. If south, locate on the south side of the seaway. If north, you have to be NW of both river channels that divide the land Montreal and Laval are built around. It is best if you are outside the 640 Beltway. Inside the beltway, you have to plan routes that get outside the beltway where there are no access ramps that will become clogged. Any of the towns over 20 miles away to the NW should provide sufficient distance from the metro area to avoid most refugees.

Quebec: Within a 10 mile radius of Quebec to the NW, there are dozens of small towns in the mountains and hills that provide good retreats. Try to keep at least 10 miles away so that any refugees will be absorbed by the smaller cities nearby. If you live on the safer southern shore of the seaway, stay south of Hwy 20 so that it does not restrict your exit strategy.

Trois-Rivières presents much fewer problems but stay north of the V formed by Hwy 40 and 55/155.

Northern Quebec and **Labrador** are mostly uninhabited lake country without much strategic value except as a major buffer zone to the north. Most of the inhabitants live in the south of Quebec or on the eastern seacoast of Labrador. Even most Canadians wouldn't accept a retreat in these remote and isolated areas. It is somewhat like Alaska—great retreats for those that can stand the cold and the isolation—but it gets low marks for convenience and livability except in the worst of world situations.

In summary, Canada offers a significant amount of retreat territory for Canadians and a secondary retreat for Americans. The down side is the dependency of so many on universal care from the government which will surely fail someday. When social unrest erupts, Canadians will be ill-equipped to resist the tyranny of the New World Order with a decided lack of weapons. Otherwise, in good times it's a wonderful country to live in with lots of scenic beauty where almost everyone is friendly.

US Primary Threats

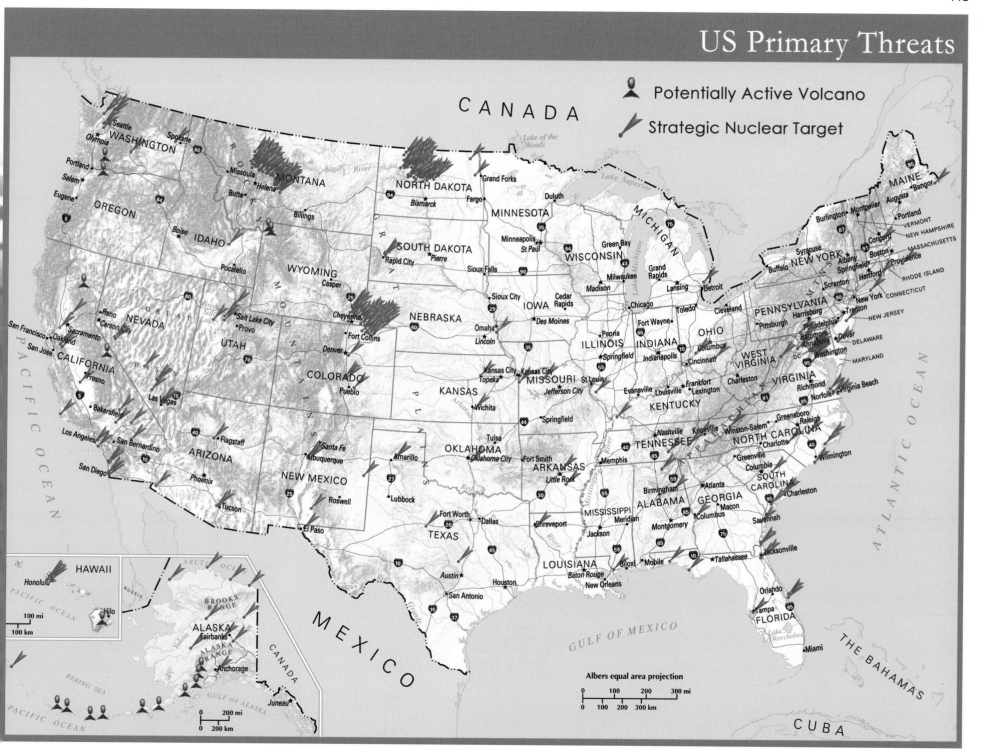

Potentially Active Volcano

Strategic Nuclear Target

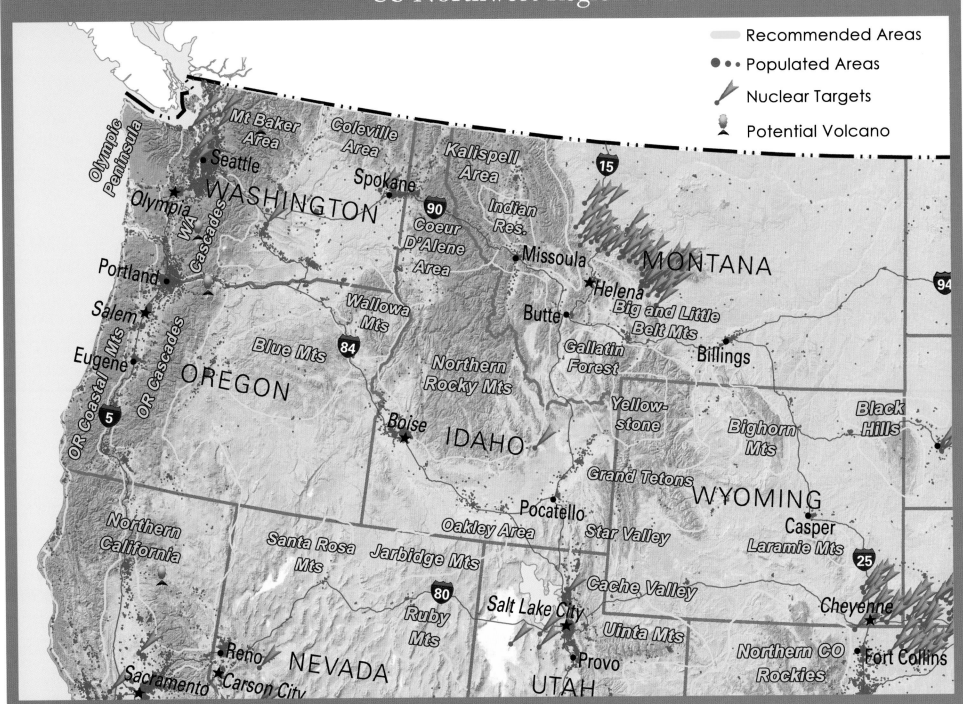

US Northwest Region and Recommended Areas

Recommended Areas
Populated Areas
Nuclear Targets
Potential Volcano

Olympic Peninsula
Mt Baker Area
Coleville Area
Kalispell Area
Seattle
Spokane
Olympia
WASHINGTON
WA Cascades
Indian Res.
Coeur D'Alene Area
Portland
Missoula
MONTANA
Helena
Big and Little Belt Mts
Salem
OR Cascades
Wallowa Mts
Butte
Gallatin Forest
Eugene
OR Coastal Mts
Blue Mts
Billings
OREGON
Northern Rocky Mts
Yellow-stone
Black Hills
Boise
IDAHO
Bighorn Mts
Grand Tetons
WYOMING
Northern California
Pocatello
Oakley Area
Star Valley
Casper
Laramie Mts
Santa Rosa Mts
Jarbidge Mts
Cache Valley
Ruby Mts
Salt Lake City
Uinta Mts
Cheyenne
Reno
NEVADA
Northern CO Rockies
Fort Collins
Sacramento
Carson City
UTAH
Provo

US Southwest Region and Recommended Areas

Recommended Areas

●●● Populated Areas

⚔ Nuclear Targets

⚱ Potential Volcano

US North Central Region and Recommended Areas

Recommended Areas

Populated Areas • • •

Nuclear Targets

NORTH DAKOTA

Grand Forks

MN Lake Country

Duluth

Upper Peninsula

MICHIGAN

94

Bismarck

Fargo

MINNESOTA

Northern WI

35

75

Minneapolis

St Paul

Green Bay

94

WISCONSIN

Black Hills

SOUTH DAKOTA

Pierre

90

Sioux Falls

Madison

Milwaukee

43

Grand Rapids

Lansing

Detroit

Lake Erie

Rapid City

Chicago

Cleveland

Sioux City

Cedar Rapids

IOWA

Toledo

NEBRASKA

29

Des Moines

Peoria

Fort Wayne

INDIANA

OHIO

80

Omaha

ILLINOIS

65

Columbus

Lincoln

35

Indianapolis

70

Cincinnati

Springfield

Charleston

55

Kansas City

Kansas City

St Louis

Frankfort

Topeka

MISSOURI

Evansville

Louisville

Lexington

KANSAS

Jefferson City

KENTUCKY

Cumberland Plateau

Wichita

44

Springfield

Ozarks

Nashville

Knoxville

TENNESSEE

US South Central Region and Recommended Areas

★ Santa Fe

Texas Pan-handle

OKLAHOMA

Ozarks

Tulsa

40

Memphis

Amarillo

★ Oklahoma City

Fort Smith

ARKANSAS

27

Red Plains Area

Ouachita Mts

★ Little Rock

55

EXICO

North TX Hill Country

30

Roswell

Lubbock

MISSISSIPPI

Meridian

Fort Worth

Dallas

Shreveport

Jackson

20

TEXAS

10

South TX Hill Country

45

South TX Pine Forests

59

LOUISIANA

Biloxi

Austin

Houston

Baton Rouge

New Orleans

35

San Antonio

37

Recommended Areas

●●● Populated Areas

Nuclear Targets

US Northeast Region and Recommended Areas

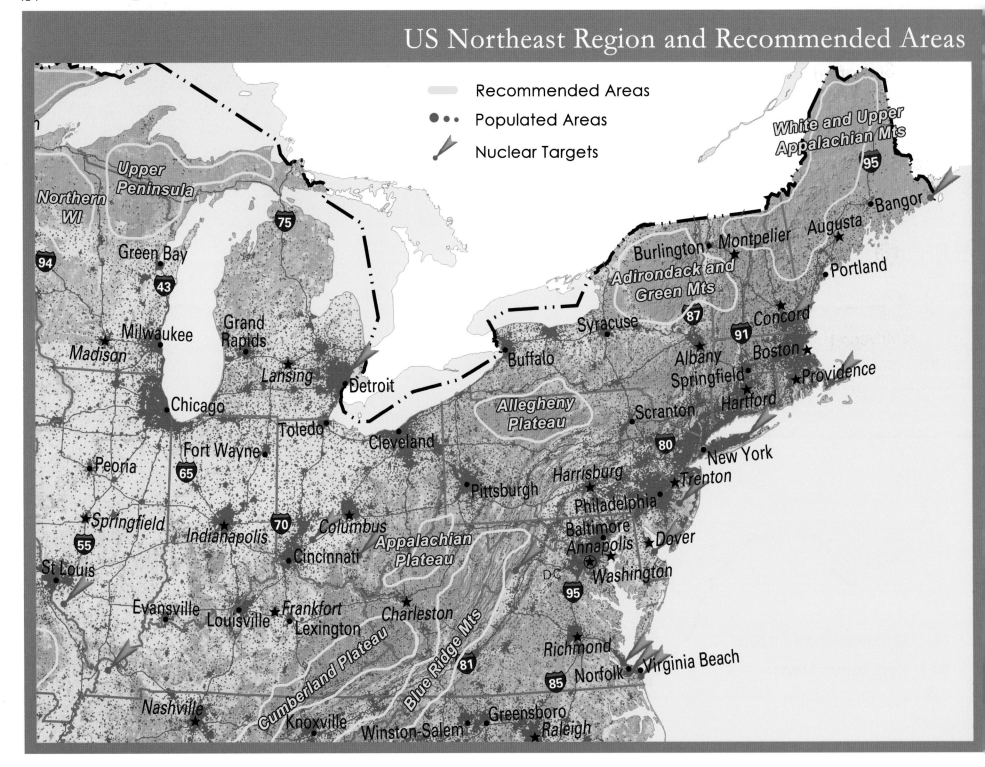

Recommended Areas

Populated Areas

Nuclear Targets

Upper Peninsula

Northern WI

White and Upper Appalachian Mts

Green Bay

Bangor

Burlington

Montpelier

Augusta

Portland

Milwaukee

Grand Rapids

Adirondack and Green Mts

Madison

Lansing

Syracuse

Concord

Albany

Boston

Chicago

Buffalo

Springfield

Providence

Toledo

Detroit

Hartford

Cleveland

Allegheny Plateau

Scranton

Fort Wayne

New York

Peoria

Harrisburg

Trenton

Pittsburgh

Springfield

Columbus

Philadelphia

St Louis

Indianapolis

Appalachian Plateau

Baltimore

Annapolis

Dover

Cincinnati

DC

Washington

Evansville

Frankfort

Charleston

Louisville

Lexington

Richmond

Nashville

Cumberland Plateau

Blue Ridge Mts

Norfolk

Virginia Beach

Knoxville

Winston-Salem

Greensboro

Raleigh

US Southeast Region and Recommended Areas

Springfield

Fort Smith

ARKANSAS

Little Rock

30

TENNESSEE

40

Memphis

Holly
Springs
Forest

Nashville   Knoxville

Cumberland Plateau

Blue Ridge Mts

65

Bankhead
N.F.

59

Birmingham

Atlanta

Talladega N.F.

MISSISSIPPI

55

Meridian   Montgomery   **85**

Jackson   Bienville
N.F.

Homochitto
N.F.

ALABAMA

65

LOUISIANA

59

Baton Rouge

New Orleans

Biloxi   Mobile

10

GEORGIA

75

Columbus

Macon

Savannah

Tallahassee   Jacksonville

Greensboro

Winston-Salem   Raleigh

NORTH CAROLINA

Charlotte

85

Greenville

40

Wilmington

Columbia

SOUTH
CAROLINA

95

Charleston

Shreveport

Orlando

Tampa   **95**

FLORIDA

Miami

Recommended Areas

Populated Areas

Nuclear Targets

Southwest Canada

VOLCANO

- Potentially Active
- Active in last 2000 yrs

NUCLEAR WAR TARGETS

- Primary Target
- Secondary Target

ALTITUDE IN METERS

5 000
4 000
3 000
2 000
1 500
1 000
700
500
300
200
100
0 Sea level

FEDERAL LANDS

- National and Provincial Parks
- Populated Areas

Source: Natural Resources Canada

CFB = Canadian Forces Base

Atlin
Tuya Volcano Fields
Dease Lake
Mt. Edziza
Iskut-Unuk Volcano Field
Stewart
Tseax Cone
Terrace
Masset
Queen Charlotte Islands
Prince Rupert
Kitimat
Smithers
Burns Lake
BRITISH
Fort St James
Vanderhoof
COLUMBIA
Bella Bella
Prince George
Quesnel
Bella Coola
Williams Lake
Port Hardy
100 Mile House
Mt. Meager
Campbell River
Mt. Garibaldi
Lillooet
Kamloops
CFB Comox
Whistler
Courtenay
Vancouver
Nanaimo
Squamish
Vancouver
Tofino
Abbotsford
Island
VICTORIA
Penticton
CFB Esquimalt

Fort Smith
Fort Nelson
High Level
Fort Chipewyan
La Crête
Fox Lake
Fort McMurray
Fort St John
Spirit River
Peace River
Dawson Creek
Slave Lake
Lac La Biche
Grande Prairie
ALBERTA
Cold Lake
CFB Edmonton
CFB Cold Lake
EDMONTON
Hinton
Leduc
Lloydminster
Jasper
Red Deer
Stettler
Golden
Banff
Calgary
Revelstoke
Brooks
Salmon Arm
High River
Kelowna
Cranbrook
Medicine Hat
Trail
Lethbridge

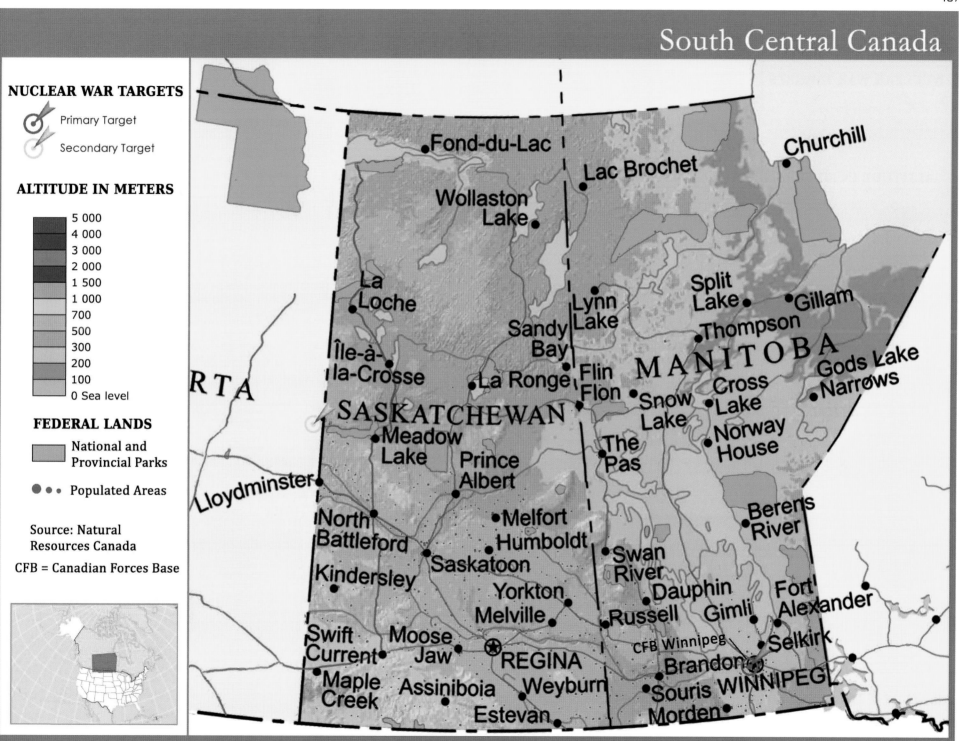

South Central Canada

NUCLEAR WAR TARGETS

Primary Target

Secondary Target

ALTITUDE IN METERS

5 000
4 000
3 000
2 000
1 500
1 000
700
500
300
200
100
0 Sea level

FEDERAL LANDS

National and Provincial Parks

••• Populated Areas

Source: Natural Resources Canada

CFB = Canadian Forces Base

Fond-du-Lac

Lac Brochet

Churchill

Wollaston Lake

La Loche

Split Lake

Gillam

Lynn Lake

Thompson

Sandy Bay

MANITOBA

Île-à-la-Crosse

La Ronge

Flin Flon

Gods Lake Narrows

Cross Lake

Snow Lake

Norway House

SASKATCHEWAN

Meadow Lake

The Pas

Prince Albert

RTA

Lloydminster

Berens River

North Battleford

Melfort

Humboldt

Dauphin

Fort Alexander

Kindersley

Saskatoon

Swan River

Yorkton

Russell

Gimli

Melville

Selkirk

Swift Current

Moose Jaw

CFB Winnipeg

REGINA

Brandon

Maple Creek

Assiniboia

Weyburn

Souris

WINNIPEG

Estevan

Morden

158

NUCLEAR WAR TARGETS

 Primary Target

Secondary Target

ALTITUDE IN METERS

5 000
4 000
3 000
2 000
1 500
1 000
700
500
300
200
100
0 Sea level

FEDERAL LANDS

National and Provincial Parks

••• Populated Areas

Source: Natural Resources Canada

CFB = Canadian Forces Base

CFS = Canadian Forces Station

Chapter 17

STATE BY STATE REVIEW

This chapter contains specific pros and cons about each state to help you find the best one for your situation. If you can't leave a particular state but you still want to find the safest locations nearby, these state reviews will give specific information about the biggest cities, their dangers and how to retreat from them. We also list where retreat properties might be found within that state—although some states are very marginal. We realize that most of our readers don't have the option of just choosing any state they want, and we still want to help everyone prepare a specific strategy within their constraints.

We have tried to give every state a semblance of equal treatment as to seeing its best potential. Unlike some other survival analysts, we don't write off 60% of the states as totally unsuitable. Not everyone can leave, and each person needs to know how to make the best of their current situation if they can't relocate.

That said, we have not given every state the same amount of space or analysis, for a couple of reasons: First, we spend more time on states that have either a lot of good security potential or those that have serious problems so residents understand how to plan for contingencies and get to a safer area. Second, some states have more complexity in geography, climate and obstacles. Flat plains states like Kansas or North Dakota are pretty uniform and require less analysis. Where there are states with miles and miles of rural farm land, we don't need to analyze every part of it. The reader must use the specific criteria of finding land with some partial forestation and privacy in order to select the right degree of seclusion.

Color Maps

At the end of this chapter we have provided full-color maps for each state detailing the cities, principle corridors, largest towns and primary threats. We recommend referring to the corresponding color map together with the state description to see, for example, where the military targets and state parks are located relative to cities.

Additionally we show a few color maps of national threats. These maps occur before the state maps and include a US national seismic map, US groundwater danger from agricultural nitrates and the retreat route example from Section Three. Each map contains additional information or more details in color.

How Each State is Rated

We show a table at the beginning of each state with a summary of facts, ratings and our overall star approval for the state. Below this summary we have notes and information on specific cities.

Summary Facts and Ratings

We start off with a summary of facts and ratings on climate, population density, crime, etc. that bring together in synoptic form much of the information presented nationwide in Section Two. This way you have summaries of all the state information at your fingertips so that you don't have to go back to tables and general maps. Here are the categories we analyze and some sources of our information, where appropriate.

Overall Rating: Each state is given an overall star rating next to the state name—from 0 to 5 stars. Only two states have a 5 star rating and only three are rated at 0. One shouldn't assume that everyone needs to get to the highest rated states. Part of Montana deserves a 5 star rating but the state gets 4.5 stars because it has a large target (missile field) in the center. Many people will have to settle for a state rated at 3 stars because of their ties to work or family. The chances for having an easier time are proportional to a better rating. For example, as we explained in the regional analysis, the entire East Coast is high risk because of high population densities from Boston down through Florida. Obviously everyone can't leave the East, so even though the states that contain the Appalachian Mountains (or the even higher rated Cumberland Plateau) are the safest places in the east, they are only rated 2-3 stars due to their proximity to these high population threat centers. Not all states on the East Coast are rated at 0. Some are rated as 2 or 2.5 because they have rural mountainous areas in a portion of the state where people can have retreats. They aren't as safe as being way out west where retreats are protected by miles of open country, but it's the best many people can do in the East.

Climate: Here we describe the general climate type and significant weather information. For states that have tornados we provide the average number per year according to *http://www.noaa.gov*. The tornado threat is very real in states with over 25 tornadoes per year. If you are not sure how it feels to be in a certain climate type, we suggest you take a trip to that area and find out if you can tolerate it, in summer and winter, before you move.

Population Density: We list the people per square mile and the percentages of significant minority groups. These are very important criteria. Safety in a crisis of social unrest is inversely proportional to the population density. We used Wikipedia's article "list of U.S. states by population density." Minority concentration is also important as an index of potential problems that often surface with immigrants. This is usually only a problem when there are sufficient numbers of them so that they don't integrate well in society or if they are prone to criminal acts. These factors are much more dangerous when minorities concentrate in ghettos. That's when gangs become prevalent. Specific information about these demographics can be found on *www.citydata.com* and from US census data (presented in map form at http://demographics.coopercenter.org/DotMap/index.html).

Cost of Living: This is not a dollar amount but rather an index constructed using costs added together and compared to other states. We tell you whether the state is above or below a standard index, whose average is 100 according to Missouri State's compilation of data from several sources (*http://www.missourieconomy.org/indicators/cost_of_living/index.stm* as of 2015). This is an important factor for many people who want the most value for their money.

Private Land Availability: We report the percentage of the state that is owned by government. This relates to how much is available to the public to buy as well as the price of land. Sadly, the top rated states in the west have had to cede over half their land to the feds just to become a state. Note that just because the percentage of private land is low doesn't disqualify a state, it just makes things more expensive. Information from *http://www.nrcm.org/documents/publiclandownership.pdf*.

Building Permits: We list some of the state requirements for building permits. Most states require permits for all new home construction but there are often differences for remodeling requirements or for small structures depending on how much authority is allowed to the local jurisdictions. While we wouldn't make or break our decision about a state over this issue, more freedom to build what you want is better, and usually a lot cheaper. We gather most of our information from *http://www.cityapplications.com/* and you can find additional in-depth information on most county websites.

In this space we also list the possibilities of building a basement in the state. Basements are essential to a good, secure home as they are the ideal locations for a safe room and concealed, cool storage. In general, basements are more commonly installed where there is freezing weather, since most foundations have to be dug below the frost line. Usually it's worth it to put a little more material in and create a basement. Warmer areas often don't have them unless people specifically want them. If your property has rock, hardpan soils (e.g. caliche) or high water tables it can make basements prohibitively expensive.

Land and Urban Planning: We list where the governing authority lies with regard to the land-use rules in the state. Some states are starting to dictate these requirements from the state level making it increasingly difficult to appeal or work with the process.

Food Production: We list the length of the growing season and the annual rainfall since these are the most important aspects for a retreat where you intend to grow food to restock stored supplies. Everyone eventually will have to do this. Where rainfall is insufficient, you need to provide for irrigation or well water. We talk only generally of soil types. There are extension services in each state that can help you determine more specific soil types where you move to. Most soils need some improvement, but if the soil is infertile, too alkaline, acidic, contains too much clay, is rocky or sandy the costs may be prohibitive.

Health Environment: Unhealthy environments are mostly a site-specific problem and we can't get into that much detail. But we do list the general level of air and water pollution in the state. We also list the percent of the population with fluoridated water (*www.nidcr.nih.gov*), which we always recommend avoiding. Even in states with fluoridated water flowing into over 70% of the population's drinking supply one can still find small towns or well water that does not use this harmful chemical.

Traffic: This is not a direct issue for retreats, but is important for your standard of living and is an indication of how hard it will be to "get out of Dodge" when things suddenly fall apart. The worst traffic cities have the most population to road infrastructure ratio. Therefore, they are also the most difficult to plan an exit from. We compiled this information from many sources including "*America's 75 Worst Commutes*" from *www.thedailybeast.com* For interest, we also list those states that authorize the use of red light and speed cameras. That doesn't mean they are used everywhere in the state; they mostly occur in the largest cities (information from *http://www.iihs.org/laws/cameramap.aspx*).

Politics: Here we present a summary of the political makeup of the state. We have found that conservative states are generally safer and more economical in the long run. Democrats almost always have control in states with high density populations. This is often because of the base of union workers, liberal newspapers, poverty, crime and the many minority groups that can deliver votes in return for welfare benefits. All of this is a recipe for social unrest someday when the benefits stop flowing. That said, even democratic states have a lot of good conservative families who live in rural areas where they can find greater safety. If you can join them, you will still suffer from bad, restrictive laws popular with urbanites that are enforced upon the whole state. Conservatives can pass bad laws too, but they don't usually break the budget. Almost every liberal democratic state is now having severe budget shortfalls, and many will probably demand a bailout by the federal government rather make the cuts necessary to balance the budget. The breakdown of registered voters is available from the US Census Bureau.

Taxes: The state and local tax burden is a combination of all the taxes an individual pays, on average, to their local and state government in each state as compiled by the Tax Foundation for the year 2011 (*www.taxfoundation.org*). We may also list information for income taxes, sales tax and property tax. Low taxing states have almost always been among the most efficiently run. This should be an important factor on your priority list.

Corruption: This is an important factor for our star rating of each state. But it is also a difficult category to assess because the most corrupt states have the means to hide or otherwise provide immunity for those high up in government. Corruption always involves prosecutors, law enforcement and judges. Often there is an inverse relationship between the number of corruption cases and real political corruption. Sometimes, the most corrupt states have few convictions relative to their population size. But it isn't always true. Sometimes major corruption comes to light and the local powers that be have to prosecute just to keep up the appearance of justice. The corruption continues underground and they become more careful. We try to give some examples of the corruption that exists in each state. Almost all states are deeply corrupt, but a dozen or so are much more corrupt than the average. These are the states that are run by political machines operating through controlled elections since the 1800s.

There isn't a lot you can do about corruption, except to elect leaders who aren't part of the establishment. Though Democrats have the worst reputation for running corrupt big city political machines, both Democrat and Republican administrations can be and are corrupt. Don't trust any reformer who comes from establishment circles—even if he or she promises to clean up City Hall. If there are establishment roots, they are probably just fronting for more powerful people behind the scenes, or will bend to their pressure. Once in a while, a true reformer is elected, but the corruption system stays alive below the surface and awaits the return of "one of their own." Once corruption gets deep inside a state it is very rarely rooted out—they just get better at hiding and covering for their illegal acts. We don't have the space to detail all the corruption in a state, but we give a general rating and list the specifics in the notes with some prominent examples.

Corrupt states are usually high taxing states, but the biggest reason you want to avoid them is that the powers that be at the federal level keep track of individual corruption so they can use it for leverage in getting leaders to go along with the dark side agenda of government. Don't expect any protection of civil rights from a corrupt state when the federal government gets more tyrannical. Many states are passing 10th Amendment resolutions meant to placate conservatives who then think the state will stand up to unconstitutional federal mandates, but these are mostly for show—they have no intention of really fighting federal intervention.

Crime: The two most important statistics are the number of violent crimes (murder, rape, assault, etc.) per hundred thousand and the number of property crimes (burglary, theft, break-ins, etc.) per hundred thousand (data per FBI *www.fbi.gov/about-us/cjis/ucr/crime-in-the-u.s*). The crime index from *http://www.neighborhoodscout.com* represents the percent of cities with higher crime (100 is safest). High state crime rates are always tied to the largest major metros in the state, so crime rates can often be discounted if you don't live in the city. Sadly, meth labs are seeking out the small rural towns and raising the crime rates even there. Fortunately, these crimes aren't as violent, overall, as in the urban areas. High crime rates in a city mean that those same criminals and gangs that prey on city dwellers will pour out of the cities into the surrounding towns once they have run out of plunder. These armed thugs will constitute the really serious point threats that can challenge the best of rural residences nearby that normally never see crime. Do pick states with low crime rates. It improves your chances immensely of evading roving bands of terror.

Personal Liberty: This is a state ranking by *Mercatus.org* which we have found to be pretty accurate. This rating weighs fiscal, regulatory and personal restrictions. Fiscal freedom encompasses the many restrictions on business and finances, regulatory examines the courts and legal restrictions, and personal freedom reviews factors such as education alternatives, medical liberty, gun rights, and personal moral liberty. Some states with high personal freedoms like Alaska still rank low because of economic restrictions or limitations. A rating of 20 out of 50 or below is acceptable.

Gun Liberty: This deserves a separate rating even though it is connected to personal liberty because it is so crucial to your survival and self-defense in a crisis. When law enforcement isn't readily available (and it almost never is), you must be able to defend yourself and your family. Don't live in a city or state that is hostile to personal gun ownership. Most states that allow concealed weapons are "shall issue" states—that is, their laws are written so that permits must be issued if an applicant meets the legal requirements. "May issue" states leave the decision up to arbitrary local authorities even if an individual meets the requirements of the law and are usually very restrictive in issuing permits. We found the information at *handgunlaw.us* helpful for this topic.

Alternative Medicine: This is another essential element in liberty. The establishment medical boards have tried to control people's liberty to choose treatment for decades. Almost every state has a law that defines what constitutes "the practice of medicine." They are uniformly tyrannical in arrogating to certified doctors the exclusive right to even diagnose any illness or symptom. That's tantamount to saying that no private individual can give any advice whatsoever without illegally engaging in "the practice of medicine." The states rarely prosecute individuals but they regularly go after alternative practitioners on that basis. Avoid states with this medical mentality.

We note the states that have a licensing board and legal pathway for naturopaths, but you can check whether naturopaths are listed as practicing in your area at *www.naturopathic.org*. We consider the liberty to have children with a midwife or alternative caretaker outside of a hospital as another one of our most important health freedoms. We report on the licensing possibilities for Direct Entry Midwives (DEM) as opposed to nurse midwives who must finish the nursing program first and operate under hospital requirements. Some states only allow Nurse Midwives. We found the Midwives Alliance of North America (*http://mana.org*) helpful in our research.

Vaccination laws are a key aspect of your medical freedom. Most laws restrict access to public schools unless vaccinated. This is but one reason to get out of public schools. Don't let medical professionals push shots on your kids if you are uncomfortable with the risks. All states allow a religious exemption exept Mississippi and West Virginia. 18 states have philosophical or "personal belief" exemptions—see each state's ratings.

Home Schooling: This is another essential freedom for parents to have alternative options and ultimate control over the education, training and discipline of their own children. The ability to opt out of the public system will become increasingly important as the public schools get worse in crime, fostering bad attitudes and false education philosophies. We found state requirements from the Home School Legal Defense Advocates website (*www.hslda.org*) to be very helpful.

Military targets: We list the most important military targets, their general location and their likelihood of being hit in a nuclear war. Every state has them, so the best you can do is know where the threats are and make sure you are outside the 5 mile estimated circle of destruction. If you have to live nearby, locate in a sector of town opposite the threat and sufficiently outside the high density developments so you can get a head start leaving if an attack occurs. The target level rating is based on our own analysis. Primary strategic targets are the most likely to be struck in a nuclear first strike. Secondary targets we expect to be hit in subsequent strikes, if at all. Tertiary targets are not shown on our map; they represent possible targets but are low enough on the strategic list we don't consider them significant enough to influence your relocation sites. We use the following acronyms: NG is National Guard, ANG is Air National Guard, USMC is US Marine Corps, USN is US Navy, USAF is US Air Force.

Nuclear Power Plants: It's important to know where these are because if they are attacked the fallout from these is much more deadly than an atomic bomb, and the effects last for years rather than weeks. Don't be in any downwind direction of these plants (and know how the winds usually shift). We show these on the state maps as secondary targets so people will stay away, but we recognize these plants are very safe in normal operation and are probably only a danger from an attack during war or from terrorists rather than because we expect any one of them to meltdown.

Notes

Here we include additional comments and information about the state that we compiled during our research. This is where we list the in-depth cases of corruption and provide

more lengthy descriptions about specific issues or benefits of each state in any of the categories mentioned above.

Strategies for Populated Living Areas

This could be one of the most important sections for those that have to live in or around a dangerous high density metro area. We give you suggestions as to where the best retreat sites are relative to this city, but only within the state under discussion. Keep in mind that your best option may be to head for a retreat outside the state—refer to our regional analyses and maps above. We also direct your attention to potential trap zones (water courses, freeways and other obstacles) that will restrict your ability to maneuver when exiting the city. Obstacles force traffic into a few roads that go around them, or worse, over bridges. These you must avoid because the funneling affect of these obstacles makes it likely that you will be hopelessly stuck in traffic when you can least afford it. You want to be outside these trap zones so that you can easily exit the area before others clog the roads and before authorities shut down freeways.

Retreat Areas

We cover the best areas to find retreat property in each state, denoted by the closest city or town. Just because we mention possible retreat areas in each state doesn't mean these are just as safe as areas in higher rated states. They probably aren't. But everyone needs to know what the possibilities are within the state they reside—even if they choose to retreat to other areas. We want people to have the full range of choices because not everyone can relocate to optimal areas. We sometimes have a listing of **Rural Farm Areas** in lieu of retreat areas. This is because many states, particularly in the Midwest, have no forested or mountainous geography for an ideal retreat. But they do have a lot of rural farm land that is suitable for a retreat as long as it is remote enough from cities and major roads. These farm areas usually have an advantage over mountain retreats in that food growing is easier and more productive. However, they don't always have the advantages of privacy from view nor safety if you have to flee from an area out in the open. For this reason, we state that your best defense in a flat farm area is to have a concealed and hardened basement safe room where no one can find you. Hiding out is better than open warfare when you are outnumbered.

Here then, are the state specific reviews in alphabetical order. We did not consider Washington DC separately as it is not a safe area, in any way. You can find it included with Virginia since it shares many aspects with Arlington, VA. We hope you will find these reviews useful.

ALABAMA ★★☆☆☆

Summary Facts and Ratings

Climate:	Humid subtropical climate with long summers and short, mild winters.
Population Demographics:	Low average density: 93 ppl./sq. mi. (27th in the nation). Black 26%, Hispanic 3.2%, mixed 1.1%, Asian 1%.
Cost of Living Index:	Low. 91 (average is 100) and ranked 6th least expensive.
Private Land Availability:	Good. 3.85% of the land is government owned (state and federal).
Building Permits:	Required for new construction, renovations of existing buildings and demolition. Basement construction is feasible, though not common in most places as the high water table is an issue in some parts.
Land and Urban Planning:	Mostly local control. Cities and municipalities may create comprehensive plans but the plans must be "substantially consistent" with state enabling acts.
Food Production:	Very good with a growing season of 240-270 days. Rainfall averages about 58 inches per year. Rich soil, good gardening, sometimes too wet.
Health Environment:	Water pollution is about average, but ground water away from big commercial farms is OK. 78.4% of the people have fluoridated water (major cities). 64% of adults are obese or overweight.
Traffic:	Moderate traffic problems in Birmingham, rated only 37th of 75 bad traffic cities. Red light cameras are used but not speed cameras.
Politics:	Dem 55%, Rep 40%, Ind/3rd party 5%.
Taxes:	Low: 9th lowest tax burden at avg. of 8.7% of income. 4% state sales tax and some high local taxes. Mobile city taxes add 10%.
Corruption:	High. See notes below.
Crime:	High. Violent crime is 431/100K, property crime is 3351/100K. Crime Index Birmingham 1 (only 1% of cities have higher crime, 100 is safest), Huntsville 4, Mobile 6 and Montgomery 6. Meth labs abound in the ghettos of Birmingham and have made inroads into the rural areas.
Personal Liberty:	18th out of 50.
Gun Liberty:	No permit required to purchase firearms. "May-issue" state but friendly to open carry.
Alternative Medicine:	Natural health practitioners are free to practice, but licensure is unavailable to lay midwives effectively prohibiting the practice. School vaccine exemptions: religious and medical.
Home Schooling:	Low regulation, the state requires parental notification only.
Military Targets:	**Fort McClellan** east of Anniston. Army Reserve NG training site; not a target. **Anniston Army Depot**. Chemical weapons stockpile; primary target. **Redstone Arsenal** near Huntsville. Marshall Space center, rocket engine development and army aviation and missile command; primary target. **Fort Rucker** west of Enterprise. Army aircraft training and testing; not a target. **Birmingham airport**. ANG station; not a target. **Maxwell AFB**, Gunter annex. War college and airlift as partial tenant; secondary target. **Barin Field** east of Mobile. Practice field for Navy & Marines aviation; not a target.

Notes

Alabama has a lot of lovely rural areas with a mix of southern pine and deciduous trees providing significant cover and privacy for plots around good farmland. It lacks mountain retreats, however, except in the north. Alabamans are mostly friendly, gentle and gracious. White residents are mostly conservative and religious. Blacks are religious and mostly liberal. Democrats outnumber Republicans but they are conservative Democrats because of the religious roots. Income taxes are moderate and property taxes are the lowest in the nation thanks to a state constitution requirement that requires a voter referendum to raise them.

The coastal area is significantly warmer in wintertime than the central and northern parts of the state. On average there are only 20 tornados per year, but an F5 tornado in 1974 nearly wiped the town of Guin off the map. Its path through the Bankhead National Forest could be seen on satellite pictures for months.

We rate this state low because of major corruption in state and local affairs. Former Birmingham mayor, Larry Langford, was found guilty of 60 counts of various types of corruption. Federal authorities rounded up 11 people guilty of using gambling in casinos to corrupt the legislative process. Charges were filed against four state senators and two casino operators. Corruption is easy to find, even among judges and local police.

There are also significant dangers here during war or social unrest. This state has quite a few danger spots such as military bases and nuclear power plants. The potential for social unrest is high because of its high welfare population and long-standing dependency upon federal dollars. Like Mississippi, it is also in the path of major escape flows from other areas: I-20 and I-85 from Georgia, I-10 from points east, including all of Florida and Georgia (impacting Mobile). The biggest cities and towns in AL are along major freeways, so readers will want to position themselves away from those refugee flow areas. If your plan is to retreat to a western state, you could run into problems getting out. The big problems in getting through MS to the west is getting across the Mississippi river itself. It has very few bridges that aren't freeways and susceptible to being jammed with traffic.

Strategies for Populated Living Areas

Mobile: Not a recommended city due to numerous trap zones and the presence of I-10. To avoid the trap zones of water and freeways, stay north of I-10 and west of I-65 coming down from Montgomery.

Dothan: This is a nice area in the south except it is sandwiched between two danger spots: Rucker Field to the northwest and the nuclear power plant to the east. We recommend staying west of the city beyond the beltway.

Montgomery: Most of the city is south of the Alabama river as is the military target at Maxwell AFB, so we recommend locating north of the river in Prattville on the west side of I-65 (leading to Birmingham). The intent is not to prepare to retreat north to the problem capitol city, but west to Selma on secondary roads and then on to Meridian or northwest to Greensboro or Eutaw where you can cross rivers away from freeways.

Birmingham: Birmingham is the worst city in this state due to crime, urban sprawl and various trap zones making it difficult to exit the area in a crisis. The safest retreat areas are to the north in southern Tennessee, the Cumberland Plateau in eastern Tennessee or to the west via Mississippi. We do not recommend heading NW toward Memphis, a major problem area. The northern exit routes are bounded by the 3 fingers (west to east) of I-22, I-65 and I-59. There are water courses blocking each fan-shaped exit direction. To get to central/southern TN, locate between I-22 and I-65 to avoid crossing freeways. Head west to Jasper and then north to Moulton, which allows you to cross the lake without going through Florence. If heading toward the Cumberland Plateau, you want to locate between I-65 and I-59 but make a plan for getting around the Huntsville threats and Guntersville Lake. Hwy 79 to Guntersville and Scottsboro allows you to thread the needle.

Retreat Areas

Rural farm retreats are your best option for surviving a crisis in Alabama itself. There are a lot of southern pines and other deciduous trees that give privacy and cover, but the state is also laced with many rivers and creeks that make it difficult to get to rural areas away from the cities. There are several state and national forests in Alabama which allow you to back up to government land. The important thing about choosing a rural farm retreat is not to be very visible from any main or secondary roads and to be far away from the general path of refugees, who will be stopping to look for food and shelter.

ALASKA ★★☆☆☆

Summary Facts and Ratings

Climate:	Alaska has a severe, arctic cold climate in the interior and northern parts of the state and a cool, coastal climate in the south and on the panhandle.
Population Demographics:	Extremely low: 1.2 ppl/sq mile. Eskimo15.5%, Hispanic 6.4%, Asian 5%, Black 4.2%.
Cost of Living Index:	High. 133 (average is 100), 6th highest in the nation.
Private Land Availability:	Relatively low. 90% of the land is government owned but it is a big state.
Building Permits:	Required in urban areas for new construction and significant remodeling. Elsewhere they are limited to land use permits over environmental concerns. Basements are possible but the foundation has to be below the deep frost level.
Land and Urban Planning:	Controlled at the local level, except in regard to state environmental regulations.
Food Production:	Poor. Greenhouses are advised. Growing season is 0 to 120 days.
Health Environment:	Very good outside of industrial areas of Anchorage. Water quality is perhaps the best in the USA. 53% of the population has fluoridated water including Anchorage.
Traffic:	Low. Lots of campers and trailers in the summer. No red light or speed cameras.
Politics:	Generally conservative/libertarian (60-40 right/left split). Dem: 15%, Rep: 25%, Ind/3rd party 60%.
Taxes:	Good, for now. Lowest rated tax burden at 6.5%. No income tax and no state sales tax. 62 municipalities impose local sales taxes that range up to 7%.
Corruption:	Very high, especially among elected officials.
Crime:	Very high. Violent crime is 640/100K, property crime is 2,885/100K. Crime Index: Anchorage 8 (100 is safest), Juneau 18.
Personal Liberty:	13th out of 50. Mercatus ranks personal freedom as very good but taxes and regulations are moderate.
Gun Liberty:	Excellent. No gun registry. "Shall issue" state for concealed weapons and open carry is permitted, including cars.
Alternative Medicine:	Good. Naturopaths can practice with a license. Direct entry midwives are licensed using the reasonable NARM exam process. School vaccine exemptions: religious and medical.
Home Schooling:	No regulation.
Military Targets:	**Fort Greely**, 70 miles SW of Fairbanks. Anti-Ballistic Missile defense station with 25 to 30 missiles; primary target. **Fort Wainwright**, Fairbanks: Light infantry base and army training site; less than secondary target. **Fort Richardson**, Anchorage. NG training site; not a target. **Clear Air Station** between Fairbanks and Anchorage. Home to 13th Space Warning Squadron (SWS) and comprises the Ballistic Missile Early Warning System. Primary target. **Advanced Radar Sites (ARS)**. There are currently 15 remote ARS sites throughout Alaska including 12 of the original MAR (Multifunction Array Radar) sites: Cape Lisburne, Cape Newenham, Cape Romanzof, Kotzebue, Tin City, King Salmon, Fort Yukon, Indian Mountain, Murphy Dome, Tatalina, Sparrevohn, and Cold Bay on the Aleutian Chain. There are three sites from the original DEW (Defense Early Warning) line sites: Point Barrow, Oliktok and Barter Island, and three locations at Elmendorf; all primary or secondary targets. **Eielson AFB**, Fairbanks. F-16 training and KC-130 refueling; secondary target. **Elmendorf AFB**. F-22, C-17, E-3 AWACS air superiority base; primary target. **Eareckson Air Station**, tip of the Aleutians. COBRA DANE radar warning system; primary target. **Kulis ANG base** at Stevens Airport, Anchorage. Not a target.

Notes

Alaska is generally remote, isolated, cold and wet in the habitable areas. Fairbanks is an exception with its dry climate and only 10 inches of average rainfall. Summer temps here are in the mid-60s which is 10 degrees higher than Juneau and Fairbanks. Western Alaska is a subarctic oceanic climate, with over 100 inches of rain in the coastal mountains. Anchorage and southern central Alaska have a cool, coastal climate with more sun and less rain (16 inches) compared to Juneau. The southeast and panhandle is fairly mild but cloudy for all but two weeks in the whole year. Rain varies from 50-275 inches per year and rarely freezes due to the proximity to the ocean.

Alaska is excellent as a retreat site but only for the hardy individualist who has adapted his income or work to this specialized economy and climate. Because the state is not self-sustaining except on a bare survival level, almost everything must be shipped in, so living costs are high. Even gasoline is imported because there is insufficient refinery capacity to meet Alaska's domestic needs. Many Alaskans don't realize that the Alaska Pipeline is vulnerable if the power grid goes down. If this happens, pumping will cease as will the thousands of refrigeration elements that keep the permafrost ground frozen around the pipeline supports which could thaw and sag creating a rupture. Food and supplies are so dependent on shipping that Alaska is almost like an island.

For living or doing business in Alaska, business regulations are strict on mining and other environmental issues where there are a dozen or so agencies to deal with. However, for the small businessman, regulations are not that burdensome. Wages are high for those in government or energy work, but normal people's salaries have not kept pace with wage/price inflation.

Alternative medicine has a strong following in Alaska. As in most states, state medical boards are hostile, but doctors are given a lot of leeway especially in the rural areas. There are many alternative health practitioners, and the workers compensation statutes allow a fair amount of alternative therapy.

Corruption is a significant problem at higher levels of government, such as the recent scandal with former Senator Ted Stevens. Major corruption came to the Klondike with the billion dollar oil service contracts. Kickbacks and special deals with lawmakers were common, such as in the Veco Services company scandal. Corruption seems to be lower at the local levels where police complaints are low. Crime is a problem, though, particularly in the cities. It is exacerbated by the transient nature of people coming here to get rich quick.

Taxation is moderate but state government is heavily subsidized from oil revenue which is declining. While there is no state sales tax, Alaskan deficits are climbing into the billions of dollars since they are not cutting spending fast enough. Some predict a huge budget collapse. They have been tapping into their savings and are running out. There are lots of creeping taxes (alcohol, cigarettes, excise, etc.) that the state is using to cope with declining energy revenue. Only 25 municipalities in Alaska (cities or boroughs) levy a property tax but these are high and occur where the majority of people live. Local sales taxes can be high. Juneau, for instance, is 5%. Anchorage, Fairbanks. Kodiak and Wrangell are the highest at 7%.

As for threats, strategically there are significant military installations in Alaska (as indicated on our maps) which should be avoided, including the downwind areas of the installations that are considered primary nuclear targets. Earthquakes and volcanoes are a constant threat in Alaska, since it is sitting on the "Ring of Fire." Tidal waves have been significant on the coastal areas, along with oil spills. Regarding local threats, while it is relatively easy to get away from civilization in Alaska, predatory wildlife is a threat to those not skilled in dealing with big animals like grizzlies and wolves.

The threat of pillage and social unrest is mostly due to the fragile shipping lifeline that could be cut off in war or natural disasters. That said, the hardy nature of those in the wilds will probably not have to confront social unrest since pillagers will not dare get out too far from their source of stolen food. Neither will the social unrest last long in winter. The scavengers will probably die quickly as soon as there is nothing easy left.

Local Perspective: One Alaskan reported, "In a long-term collapse, the residents of Alaska's densely populated coastal cities will likely starve and/or freeze to death. Meanwhile, those in inland towns, albeit better fed, will be geographically isolated so that commerce with the coast will be difficult if not impossible. Bush pilots will eventually be grounded due to lack of fuel, lubricants and spare parts. The only people I foresee surviving are a few seasoned Sourdoughs and native tribe members that still have well-honed outdoor survival skills and are still capable of reverting to a self-sufficient mode. The best set up for this would be a small settlement on a clear water (non-glacial) stream with an active salmon run and a couple of productive 'fish wheel' salmon traps."

Strategies for Populated Living Areas

Fairbanks: Stay northwest of the city to avoid the military target areas.

Anchorage: Stay to the northwest in the valley where Wasilla is located or southwest in the Kenaii peninsula.

Juneau: There is no road to Juneau. It takes a ferry or an airplane to get in or out which is not good in a crisis. But if you want to live in the major city of the panhandle, this is it. It has mild, rainy and very wet weather making it cloudy most of the year.

Retreat Areas

One of the biggest problems with living in Alaska is the extreme lack of roads. There are only a few dozen paved roads in Alaska and you often have to drive into Canada to get back to the US mainland. There are simply thousands of square miles of trackless wilderness in Alaska. Road maintenance is average but asphalt roads don't hold up where subsoil base is soft. The distances between fuel stops are very long. It would be easy to get stranded during a crisis because of lack of fuel. Many island cities in the Alaskan panhandle are accessible only by air or ferryboat. This is great if you are prepared to stay put, but not if you have to maneuver. Anyone trying to survive in this area should have a plane or a long range, ocean-capable boat, unless absolutely prepared to survive without resupply.

Growing potential in even southern Alaska is marginal. Without greenhouses, only cold weather crops grow well here due to overcast conditions, cool nights and the short frost-free growing season. Carrots, beets, potatoes and salad greens grow fine. Most Alaskans are not capable of food self-sufficiency.

ARIZONA ★★★☆☆

Summary Facts and Ratings

Climate:	Dry, hot, desert climate. More moderate high-desert climate in the north (more typical of Intermountain West). Four tornadoes per year.
Population Demographics:	Moderately dense: 56 ppl/sq.mi. (33rd in the nation). Hispanic 31%, Native American 5%, Black 4.5%, Asian 2.6%, mixed 2.5%.
Cost of Living Index:	Average. 98.8 (average is 100).
Private Land Availability:	Poor. 80% is state and federally owned, including almost all of the best forests and mountain land.
Building Permits:	Required everywhere for new construction, significant remodel. Basements are not very common but can be built in areas without caliché hardpan soil.
Land and Urban Planning:	AZ does have a smart growth initiative, but so far no statewide mandates.
Food Production:	Good—but only with irrigation. 22 in/yr rain in the north and 8 in/yr in the south. Sandy soil. Growing season is long at 280 days.
Health Environment:	Water quality is only fair. 58% of people have fluoridated water. Air Pollution is low except in the polluted metro area around Phoenix.
Traffic:	Phoenix area ranks 29 out of 75 worst traffic cities. Tuscon is #60 Traffic is light elsewhere. Red light and speed cameras are used in Phoenix area.
Politics:	Conservatives predominate except in Latino or native Americans areas like Tuscon and Apache county. Pheonix is barely red with establishment conservatives while eastern suburbs like Mesa, Gilbert and the northern counties have more Tea Party voters. Dem 34.6%, Rep 40%, Ind/3rd party 25.5%.
Taxes:	Relatively low: Ranked 34th best with an effective tax burden of 8.8% of income. Ranked 39th in property taxes.
Corruption:	High in state government and metro police, but low in rural areas.
Crime:	Medium high: Violent crime 417/100K, property crime 3400/100K. Crime index: Phoenix 10 (100 is safest), Mesa 18, Chandler 30.
Personal Liberty:	Very good, 11th best out of 50.
Gun Liberty:	Good. No permit to purchase firearms. "Shall issue" state and recognizes permits from some states. Open carry allowed, including cars.
Alternative Medicine:	Very good for full range of natural health practitioners. Direct entry midwives are licensed and about 20 have practices for home birth. School vaccine exemptions: philosophical, religious and medical.
Home Schooling:	Low regulation. State requires parents to send notification only.
Military Targets:	**Fort Huachuca and Libby Army Airfield**, Tucson. Army Intelligence Center, Helicopters, prison camp; secondary target. **Yuma Proving Grounds and Laguna Army airfield**. Munitions, vehicles, armor, etc. testing ground; secondary target. **Navajo Army Depot**. Storage of conventional munitions and decommissioned Trident C4 missile motors; primary target. **MC Air Station Yuma**. Harrier and F-35 base and training center; primary target. **Davis-Monthan AFB**, Tucson. A-10, C-130 and aircraft graveyard; primary target. **Luke AFB**. F-16 training; secondary target. **Air Force Plant No. 44**, SW of Tucson. Air-to-air missile production plant by Raytheon; primary target.
Nuclear Power Plants:	**Palo Verde** Nuclear Generating Station, 30 mi. east of Phoenix.

Notes

Arizona may be a desert but there are aquifers in northern Arizona where impermeable rock layers capture water, creating year-round springs and streams. In the few places where you can find good water supplies, combined with Arizona's abundant solar potential, you have the makings of a good retreat. Northern Arizona has advantages of cooler temps, forestation, mountains and distance from the Phoenix area. The limited access to good agricultural survival and water supplies, however, is a problem almost everywhere. Most agriculture is hay and cattle in northern Arizona near the mountains. The southern part has a very long growing season where large, irrigated farms grow melons, etc. well.

Arizona's lowland deserts have been a relocation target for Californians intent on cashing in on their real estate value. In the Phoenix-Scottsdale metro area, this has been a factor that drove up real estate prices and population density (3373 ppl/sq.mi.). The growth then moved south and east through Gilbert and Mesa, bringing with it increased traffic and crime. The Phoenix area has significant and problematic minority populations that are linked to gangs and crime. The violent Latino gangs are the most numerous and dangerous.

Arizona's biggest threat is illegal immigration and the future potential of being "reclaimed" by Latino militants. Its southern border counties are already becoming war zones where the border fence is not complete. Armed human traffickers and even more heavily armed drug runners, known as "Coyotes," invade the US border areas sometimes accompanied by the Mexican military.

Arizona is also home to black operations of the CIA and the DEA which facilitate and protect their own drug runners. This adds to the corruption of many law enforcement personnel, but particularly those at higher levels which have to be compromised and paid to look the other way. Local police and judges in the Phoenix area are corrupt to keep this information in the dark. In our analysis, an additional aspect of corruption among upper law enforcement and judges is an effort by the PTB at the state level to create a network to suppress the considerable numbers of conservative citizens in the state.

The long-term social unrest from a major war or economic collapse will mostly impact the Phoenix area and cause a major exodus to the north and the east. Like Nevada, the network of roads is fairly limited due to major geological features like mountains, deserts and the Grand Canyon. All these make it difficult to flee the area in a crisis.

Strategies for Populated Living Areas

Phoenix area: If you must live in the Phoenix area, we recommend staying in the northern suburbs, outside the 101/202 beltway. This gives you first access to highway routes going north. I-17 to Flagstaff will be clogged within 30 minutes to an hour of a crisis. Highways 87 and 88 are better alternatives leading out of the Mesa/Apache Junction area. Don't live in the southern sector of the metro area, since you won't be able to retreat north. Pima, Maricopa, and Yavapai counties have the highest property taxes in the state, but are still lower than the national average.

Tucson: While we don't recommend Tucson at all due to its military installations and proximity to the border, if you have no other choice, pick areas in the northern part of the city (Oro Valley or Catalina).

Flagstaff: This is a beautiful area but it is a major exit route from Phoenix, and will also collect everyone coming from California trying to avoid the Las Vegas bottleneck. In order to bypass the impassible Colorado River Gorge (which blocks the path from Hoover dam

on the west to the Grand Canyon on the east), travelers have to go through Flagstaff. You want to be above I-40 and on the north side of Hwy 89 past Flagstaff proper. However, be aware that the water table in most of the rural lands surrounding Flagstaff is too deep to economically drill a well, so many rural landowners haul their water.

For information on water wells in Arizona go to https://gisweb.azwater.gov/WellRegistry/ for a catalog of every water well in the state. Zoom into the area you are interested in, and then click on the individual red dots in that area and it will give you the depth of the well and the flow rate—just the information you need to have some idea of what kind of water resources exist, and how costly it will be to drill.

Sedona: We used to recommend Sedona, but it has become very expensive now and puts you in the path of everyone coming from the south on Hwy 89. A good compromise outside Sedona proper is the farmland and homes along Oak Creek between Cottonwood and Sedona. It does flood once a year, so make sure the land is out of the flood plain.

Retreat Areas

While Sedona and Flagstaff do have mountainous areas in the vicinity which offer potential retreat sites, the best areas are farther away from the future refugee flows that will come out of Phoenix. Most of the good farm/ranch retreat areas were former Mormon colonies in Arizona. The pioneers always picked areas with good water supplies for irrigation. You will find **Cottonwood** near the Verde River between Prescott and Sedona. North of town there are lots of irrigated farms that make fairly good retreat sites, but watch out for flooding.

Payson is a fine ranching and farming community at the base of Arizona's northern mountains, but it too is the first major town refugees traveling up highway 87 will meet. Look for retreat property in the **Star Valley** area or farther north up into the mountains. Off of highway 288 you find the small town of **Young** which is in a small valley surrounded by rugged mountains.

The towns north of these mountain ranges offer the best survival potential because they are shielded from the arrival of most refugees. **Heber and Show Low** are the favorites—deep in the mountains and the closest to pine forests, but the altitude may be too high for warm weather crops. **Snowflake** is a farming community at lower elevation near the mountains but is fairly barren of trees. As in most places in the high desert, you must get above 6 or 7 thousand feet in order to get enough moisture from snowfall to grow forests. **Springerville** farther east is also a farming town and closer to the mountains.

We recommend nothing in Southern Arizona even though there are some well-watered canyons and year-round springs coming out of the Chiracahua and Huachuca mountain ranges.

ARKANSAS ★★★☆☆

Summary Facts and Ratings

Climate:	Humid, subtropical climate with hot, humid summers and cool, drier winters. Twenty-one tornadoes per year (moderate high risk).
Population Density:	Average. 55 ppl/sq.mi. (34th in the nation). Black 15.8%, Hispanic 6%, mixed 1.5%, Asian 1.2% .
Cost of Living Index:	Low. 91.4 (average is 100), ranked 10th least expensive.
Private Land Availability:	Good. 12% is state or federal government owned.
Building Permits:	Required for all construction and issued at the city level. Basement potential is limited and expensive in the mountains because of rock foundations. The valleys are better except where the water table is high.
Land and Urban Planning:	Primarily at the city and county level. The state encourages multi-county planning primarily to enhance economic development and coordinate government services.
Food Production:	Very good. Growing season of 180-240 days. 45 in/yr of rain. Rich soil, except in the Ozarks where it is rocky.
Health Environment:	Ground water pollution is way below average and some rural streams pristine. The Mississippi river is not. 70.6% of the population is obese or "overweight" only just behind Mississippi's 70.7%. 67% of the population's water is fluoridated, including the major cities.
Traffic:	Heavy traffic is a problem in Little Rock (ranked #59 of 75 bad traffic cities). No red light and speed cameras.
Politics:	Dem 70%, Rep 25%, Ind/3rd party 5%. Even though Democratic registrations far outnumber Republicans, many vote Republican at the national level.
Taxes:	High. Ranked 14th highest with an effective rate of 10.1% of income. It has high income taxes, but low property taxes (43rd in nation), plus a 6.5% sales tax.
Corruption:	High, see notes in text.
Crime:	High. Violent crime is 460/100K, property crime is 3603/100K. Crime index for Little Rock is 1 (less than 1% of other cities are safer; 100 is safest).
Personal Freedom:	Moderate. Rated 32 out of 50 (lower is better)
Gun Liberty:	Fair. No permit to purchase firearms. "Shall issue" state and recognizes some permits from other states. Open carry is prohibited.
Alternative Medicine:	There is no licensing available for naturopaths, but it is not prohibited. Direct entry midwives are licensed. Mothers using midwives must also see a physician or health clinic for two visits and must file a back-up plan with the Health Department. School vaccine exemptions: philosophical, religious and medical.
Home Schooling:	Moderate regulation. State requires parents to send notification, test scores, and/or professional evaluation of student progress.
Military Targets:	**Pine Bluff Arsenal**. Chemical weapons storage; primary target. **Little Rock AFB**. Largest base of C-130 airlift aircraft; primary target. **Fort Smith Airport**, near Ebing. A-10 ANG base; below secondary target.
Nuclear Power Plant:	**Arkansas** Nuclear Power Plant, 6 miles NW of Russellville. 2 reactors, both operational in 1978.

Notes

Arkansas is a southern state with a mix of many different European immigrant groups, but the European cultures have been almost totally absorbed by the southern culture. Blacks and Hispanics are the largest minorities. The mountain people of the Ozarks are part of a self-reliant culture which is pro gun and pro private property. The native population in the mountains is typical of most mountain folk in the US—they keep to themselves and don't trust strangers from the East Coast. Once they get to know you they are solid, faithful friends. Of course, there are a certain percentage of Rednecks with low-class lifestyles and attitudes. Meth labs have also made their way into the rural areas and Ozark Mountains.

Arkansas has not recovered from the corruption days of Bill Clinton, where he fronted for many dark side government activities, including federal drug running through the Mena airport in Scott County. The police in even the rural areas became deeply corrupted. A local of that county found out the Sheriff himself was growing marijuana and reported it to the DEA. Instead of investigating the DEA gave the Sheriff a recording of the meeting and the citizen became threatened and intimidated. When the Sheriff died in an accident the Quorum Court appointed the late sheriff's wife in his stead—a cafeteria worker with no experience in law enforcement. This is cronyism at its worst.

We downgraded our rating principally because of this major corruption between state and federal government. Once a state is corrupted by illicit federal government actions involving police, judges and state officials, it almost never recovers. There were 26 public corruption convictions last year, but most of the high level corruption is never discovered or prosecuted. Since the days of the Clintons, the state offices and legislature are still dominated by Democrats, but Arkansans voted Republican in the last two presidential elections and elected a Republican Senator in 2010.

Military targets are the Pine Bluff Arsenal and Little Rock AFB, home to C130 military airlift units. Arkansas would be more highly rated if it were not for the history of federal and state corruption combined with it being in the path of refugee flows coming out of Memphis—a social meltdown waiting to happen.

Strategies for Populated Living Areas

Little Rock: This single major city in Arkansas has several trap zones, not unlike St. Louis, Mo. It is bisected by the Arkansas River and has an AFB target across the river to the north. If you have an exit strategy to the north, we would normally recommend you locate in Sherwood which is north of the river barrier, but that puts you a bit too close to Little Rock AFB and Camp Robinson. A better strategy, although with a longer commute, would be to select Conway, taking care to note the only way to cross I-40 outside of an exit: Hwy 64 to Hwy 25. If your retreat is in the western Ozarks, you want to be south of the Arkansas River, west of the 430 beltway and north of Hwy 67.

Retreat Areas

Rural farmland: Eastern and southern Arkansas are relatively flat river bottom areas, which lie in low and gentle contrast to the rugged, forested Ozark Mountains. There is a fair amount of deciduous trees in these farm areas, so they make OK farm retreats and good water wells. The best farm areas are south of Pine Bluff. The land is too wet and swampy further north. The best rolling hill farm area is north around Jonesboro.

The Ozarks: these are the only significant mountains between the Appalachians and the Rockies, and thus cannot be overlooked as a great retreat sight for the Midwest. The Ozarks are particularly suited for retreats with plenty of wild game, fish and an endless supply of firewood. The water is excellent from both springs and wells. Interstate 30 bisects the state from SW to NE and the Ozarks lie to the NW of this. However, due to the illicit federal activities at Mena airport south of Fort Smith, the best areas are in northern Arkansas above I-40 and west of I-30 as it extends past Little Rock towards Jonesboro. Keep a 50 mile distance from Little Rock itself and keep some distance from the major roads leading out of Little Rock to the west and north.

The Arkansas River parallels I-40 from Little Rock up to Fort Smith. This presents only a few crossings, which could be a problem in a crisis. What this significant barrier means is that you should pick either the northern area or the southern area of the Ozarks and make sure your travel plans to either place don't cross any major barriers.

CALIFORNIA ★☆☆☆☆

Summary Facts and Ratings

Climate:	There is almost every climate type in California. Oceanic climate in the north with temperate weather and heavier moisture on the coast. South of San Francisco is a Mediterranean climate that is dry and arid but with fog and moist breezes on the coast. Warm, humid conditions in the inland valleys. Further east it becomes more arid and dry in high deserts and low lakebeds, like Death Valley. There are high, cold mountains and dense forests. CA has an avg. of 5 tornadoes per year.
Population Density:	Moderately high: 244 ppl/sq. mi. (12th most dense in the nation). Hispanic 37%, Asian 13%, Black 7%, mixed 2.5%.
Cost of Living Index:	Very High: 134 (average is 100).
Private Land Availability:	Fair. 42% state and federal ownership, including most of the best forests.
Building Codes:	Widespread and restrictive on almost all construction and land use permits (partly the result of coercive Smart Growth initiatives). Basements can be built in most areas, but southern CA and the high desert often have hardpan soil.
Food Production:	Long growing season of 280 days. Avg. rainfall is 33 in/yr in the north, 13 in/yr in the south. You will need water in the arid regions, but water bills are high now. Good soil in the Central Valley but stay away from depleted soils on the big farms.
Health Environment:	Water quality is fair to poor in the largest cities and wells in the Central Valley. Water is good along the Sierras with access to mountain runoff. 63.7% of municipal water systems add fluoride. Air Pollution is high in or downwind of cities, but is worst in the LA basin. Pollution is moderate in the Bay Area due to sea breezes and very low in Northern California.
Traffic:	Very heavy in all major metros. LA is rated the worst and the Bay Area 5th worst in the nation. Red light cameras are used but not speed cameras.
Politics:	Very liberal in the Bay Area and LA basin, overwhelms the historically conservative population of Orange County. Conservatives now dominate only in rural parts of the state. Decades of illegal immigration has affected the political makeup. Dem 43%, Rep 35%, Ind/3rd parties 22.3%.
Taxes:	High. Ranked 6th highest with an effective tax burden of 10.9% of income. Sales taxes vary from 7.5 to 8.75%. Very high property taxes unless you've owned your property for many years, thanks to Proposition 13. The state is in serious financial difficulty and debt, which means higher taxes in the future.
Corruption:	Very high in state government and in metro cities. Low in rural areas. Police are corrupt in all major metros, but the Highway Patrol is less corrupted. Judges: Very high levels of corruption and collusion with the PTB at all levels. Bankruptcy court corruption here was the worst in the nation during the 1980s and 1990s.
Crime:	High. Violent crime is 402/100K, property crime is 2658/100K. Crime Index: LA is 25, SF 3, Fresno 8, San Diego 30, Sacramento 11 (100 is safest).
Personal Liberty:	Very poor. Rated 49th.
Gun Liberty:	Terrible. Guns are allowed but strictly regulated. Some counties like LA have extra laws. Assault weapons are broadly defined and restricted. Military rifles (like AR15 and M4) require modifications like a "bullet button" or tool to release the magazine. New magazines are restricted to 10 rounds, but some larger magazines are okay if you had them before 2000. Almost all weapon purchases (even from private party or family) must be transferred through a licensed firearm dealer resulting in de-facto registration on these guns. "May issue" state, effectively "no issue" in cities and "shall issue" in some rural counties. No recognition of other state permits.
Alternative Medicine:	Good. Naturopaths are licensed and exist in many varieties, but are highly regulated. Direct entry midwifery is licensed and legal in California. Schools require vaccine unless medical exemption is signed by doctor. Some CA colleges also require vaccinations.
Home Schooling:	Low regulation. State requires parents to send notification only.

Military Targets:	**Fort Irwin**. Army mechanized armor training range; tertiary target.
	Sierra Army Depot. Storage and destruction of conventional munitions; secondary target at best.
	Tracy Army Depot. Supply depot; tertiary target.
	Sharpe Army Depot. Supply depot; tertiary target.
	Camp Pendleton. 1st Marine Expeditionary Force; primary target.
	China Lake Naval Weapons Center. USN development and testing range; secondary target.
	Lemoore Naval Air Station. Home base for 4 carrier fighter wings; primary target.
	Twenty-nine Palms, USMC training base and firing range; secondary target.
	North Island NAS, San Diego. Navy fighter and helicopter base; primary target.
	Miramar, north of San Diego. Marine Corps fighter base; primary target.
	Port Hueneme, Oxnard. Seabees and Navy supply base; primary target.
	Port Mugu Pacific Missile Test Center, Oxnard. Primary target.
	MC Logistics Base, Barstow. Supply depot and repair facility; tertiary target.
	Concord Naval Weapons Station. Large ship munitions loading site; secondary target.
	Moffett Federal Airfield. Joint Civilian, military and ANG airfield; secondary target.
	Stockton Naval Communications System. Low frequency transmitter for navy communication; primary target.
Naval Weapons Station: .	**Seal Beach**. USN weapons and munitions storage, loading and maintenance; primary target
	Beale AFB. U2 and Global Hawk reconnaissance and ballistic missile warning radar; primary target.
	Edwards AFB. USAF flight test center and NASA Dryden research; secondary target.
	Travis AFB, Sacramento. 60th Air Mobility Wing for global airlift; primary target.
	Vandenberg AFB. Satellite launch facility, spaceport, missile testing center; primary target.
	Los Angeles AFB. Space Command and Space and Missile Systems Center; primary target.
	March AFB. Largest USAF reserve site; secondary target.
	Over the Horizon Radar, Lost Hills. Research radar transmitting site; primary target.
	Over the Horizon Radar, Los Banos. Research radar receiving site; primary target.
Nuclear Plants:	**Diablo Canyon Plant**. 10 mi. west of San Luis Obispo.
	San Onofre Plant. Between Dana Point and Oceanside.

Notes

California has been a magnet for people seeking beautiful weather, landscape, farmland, riches or just plain jobs for decades and has resulted in overcrowded cities and a left-leaning population such that it is no longer a safe haven. That is a shame because California has some of the most spectacular and varied landscapes in the nation, from breathtaking coastlines to the majesty of the Sierra Nevada forests and lakes. The Central Valley is the most productive area per acre in the nation providing Californians and much of the nation with the best organic and non-organic produce.

All the beauty and wealth of the Golden State, however, comes with a price in the form of significant and choking regulations, taxes and restrictions. California has a regulatory agency for everything, including the California Coastal Commission, California Department of State Architect, California Energy Commission, California Commission on Aging, California Environmental Protection Agency, and California Environmental Resources Evaluation System, to name a very few. All of these agencies combine to form a web of restrictions that can be a costly nightmare to navigate for businesses and individuals—usually requiring the help of lawyers and engineers. It is no wonder that businesses are fleeing the state in record numbers.

There is a lot of potential crime and racial or social unrest. Although large black populations in Los Angeles are slowly being displaced by Latinos, the potential of a Watts-like riot is still there. Increasingly, it is the militant Latinos that are pushing the envelope of law enforcement tolerance. Population densities exacerbate crime and the Bay Area metro is fairly dense with 1,100 ppl/sq. mi., but it pales in comparison to the 7,068 ppl/sq. mi. in the LA basin, which is the most densely populated metro area in the US. Personal safety is compromised from both sides as crime increases and the ever expanding list of banned weapons threatens your ability to defend yourself. The cost of living is high and housing costs are still too high even after declining one third their boom time values.

The state is a prime destination for illegal aliens escaping the Arizona crackdown. The word is out that this is a sanctuary state ever since the California Supreme Court overturned the citizen initiative to cut off welfare, medical benefits and public education access to illegals. Mexican illegal immigrants have not only created the largest gangs here, but have also formed radical political organizations such as Aztlan, La Raza, and Mecha intent on fomenting revolution and "retaking" California. They are also driving many blacks out of the inner cities so they can take over.

As for threats, California has them in abundance. There is the ever-present threat of earthquakes and horrific wildfires caused by lightning and arson. As the state color map indicates, there are dozens of nuclear targets, ranging from San Diego's concentration of naval assets to Lawrence Livermore's nuclear labs near the Bay Area. Unless you are living within a five mile circle of these targets, however, your biggest threat will be the massive social unrest and pillaging that comes from having so many people living in one confined area, such as the LA basins. This basin is surrounded by mountains which not only traps the bad air, but also concentrates all roads leading outside the valley to a few passes that are easily clogged with traffic, even in normal times. The populated southern half of the state is largely isolated by the vast distances of the deserts in Nevada, Arizona and Mexico. The corridors east and north are relatively few.

City-Specific Strategies

If you must live near one of California's mega-metros, consider locating on periphery areas such as those described below so you have a head start leaving when things melt down. We can't name all the potential areas, but these samples will give you an idea.

Bay Area: The biggest obstacles in the Bay Area are the people and the water courses, including not just the bay itself but the spider-like network of tributaries of the Sacramento River basin. This is a huge triangular area from I-580/205 to I-5, north to Stockton and Sacramento and back south again on I-80. To get to the safety of the Sierras or north to the rural areas above the Napa valley, you have to get around these huge areas of water and marsh. Try not to work where you have to cross a major bridge to get home or to your retreat.

The San Francisco Peninsula is the most confined area with the longest escape route. To leave SF without attempting the dangerous bridge bottlenecks you have to get to the beach side of the mountains and go south far enough to get around the huge population center of San Jose. Go down to Santa Cruz and then take the 152 to Los Banos to get past I-15 and Hwy 99 to the mountains. You may also want to consider having a boat in a slip if you need an alternative to a bridge. Either take this boat all the way to a retreat or to a spare car somewhere.

If your escape route is north, try to live and work north of the Golden Gate Bridge, perhaps in San Rafael, for example. If Highway 101 is clogged (guaranteed), there are several small mountain routes between Highway 101 and 1 that can get you to Petaluma, then on over to Highway 29 above Napa and on to the Clear Lake Area. Avoid the Santa Rosa area, unless you work there; it is the last big clogged traffic area going north.

Oakland: This side of the bay is less confined but you still have to get around the delta area and there are very few roads to choose from besides I-580 going east. If you are trying to go north above Sacramento, consider Hwy 160 which cuts through the delta. Skirt the west side of Sacramento until you get around it. About the only way east from the Oakland area without using freeways is to take Hwy 84 out of Freemont to Livermore and then Mines Road down to 130 and on east to Patterson. Plan alternate routes and know where the rural roads are.

Central California Coast: The only area we can partially recommend (for medium term security), is the south-central coastal area around San Luis Obispo and north to Paso Robles. It is far enough away from Vandenberg Air Force Base and has good agricultural potential. Santa Cruz has some hill country areas that offer respite from the crowds. Monterrey is beautiful, but too high priced for most.

San Diego: If your exit direction is toward Arizona, try to live east in El Cajon and Santee and a few miles north or south of I-8. If you prefer to live north of San Diego, plan to avoid the military targets and fallout by staying north of Miramar and east of I-15. Don't get sandwiched in the growth area between I-5 and I-15 where there are hardly any ways to escape these two N-S freeways that could act like barriers. Any overpasses that coincide with an exit will be clogged during a panic and impassable. To exit the area from the east of I-15, use Hwy 78 going further east to Blythe and then north on 95.

Los Angeles Basin: This is a real problem area. There are only five main exit paths out of the entire valley for 20 million people and these passes are all occupied by freeways which will surely be blocked within an hour of a major crisis, if not shut down by federal orders: The coast highways (101 and 1) to Santa Barbara, I-5 to the San Joaquin valley via the "Grapevine," Hwy 14 to Lancaster/Palmdale (high desert), I-15 to Victorville (high desert), and I-10 to Palm Springs and Arizona.

Aside from a handful of jeep trails, there are two lane roads near towns that are sufficiently outside the main urban valley. Consider these places and get on these roads before they are clogged: from Ojai plan an exit north on Hwy 33 to the San Fernando valley; from Santa Paula go north on Hwy 150 or east on the 125 where you will find one non-exit crossing of I-5; from Santa Clarita use multiple mountain roads to the high desert if Hwy 14 is clogged; from Azuza take the 39 north to the high desert; from San Bernardino take Hwy 18 to the mountains, then the 138 or 173 to the high desert; from Highland take the 330 to Hwy 18 until Big Bear; from Redlands take 38 east into the mountains; South of

I-10 head for the Salton Sea and then east on Hwy 78 to Blythe. With 20 million people competing for exit routes, you will have to be the first to these roads.

High Desert: This area has now become the overflow area from the LA basin. This population exodus includes a lot of minorities which are negatively impacting the demographics and crime statistics of the area. Still, it is within commuting range of the basin and allows one to be outside the trap zone of living in the basin itself. It does suffer from diluted air pollution that drifts up from the valleys below.

Retreat Potential

Northern California offers by far the best retreat areas compared to the south. The population density is much lower, but so are the jobs (they are reciprocal). Between the coast and I-5 beginning with the Clear Lake area and heading north you have hundreds of good retreat sites available (good except that you are still in the tyrannical state of California). The beach areas can be too foggy for comfort, but staying inland a bit brings more sun. The best coastal retreat areas are around Crescent City and the Smith River area to the north is spectacular.

The northern counties of Humboldt and Trinity have good potential. They feel more like southern Oregon except one still has to deal with the liberals down south that write the laws. Police are noticeably reluctant to enforce the laws with the same vigor as in populous areas, but the bottom line is they are always hanging over your head. As one local put it, "if they want ya, they got ya." There are also remnants of the hippy movement in Humboldt County and Arcata who are generally good people, just different.

There are excellent ranches on both the east and west sides of the mountains that back up to the Trinity National Forest along highways 299 and 36. There is lots of nice farmland from Ukiah on north if you stay to the east of Hwy 101 in this area to avoid Fort Bragg.

On the drier east side of the Coast Mountains, we like the Scotts Valley area around the town of Etna. On the east side of I-5 in the north is the Mt. Shasta area. You should avoid locating any retreat in the plume shadow of this volcanic mountain, so stay north and west. The mountains to the east of Montague are a relatively safe distance from I-5 as is the town of Mt. Hebron on the other side of the mountains. In the northern Sierras, above I-80, you have to watch out for Mt. Lassen. Susanville is downwind. You have to get as far south as Quincy to get some safety—a great survival area, as is everything east of Oroville and Paradise.

In the Sierras south of I-80, we also find some volcanic activity around Mono and Mammoth lakes, so stay clear of that area. The forests around Lake Tahoe are gorgeous, but too expensive for most. If you pick a retreat site there, make sure it is isolated from the normal tourist areas and not too visible. I prefer the Nevada side for a more builder-friendly regulatory climate.

On the western side of the Sierras, there are nice retreat sites east of Placerville near Pollock Pines (Hwy 50). Check out Hwy 88 out of West Point, and Hwy 108 out of East Sonora. All these access roads into the mountains have cabin sites left over from pioneer claims. Avoid Hwy 120 and 140 leading to Yosemite because they have too much traffic and casual observers. In the middle of the Sierras range, we particularly like the foothills and cabin areas east of Clovis on Hwy 168. Outside of Visalia and Three Rivers, check out Hwy 198 into the mountains.

COLORADO ★★★⯪☆

Summary Facts and Ratings

Climate:	High desert in the west, Mountain Continental climate in the Rockies, and Continental Plains climate east of Denver where it is hot and humid in summer and cold and dry in winter. Eastern CO has some 24 tornados a year.
Population Density:	Below average: 48.9 ppl/sq.mi. (37th ranking in the nation). Hispanic 21%, Black 4.4%, Asian 2.7%, mixed 2%, American Indian 1.2%. Denver is less than 50% Caucasian now.
Cost of Living Index:	102 (average is 100).
Private Land Availability:	Fair. 40% is state and federally owned, including most of the best forests and mountain land.
Building Permits:	Permits and regulations are required statewide. Small town areas have less inspection requirements. Basements are common in most parts of the state.
Land and Urban Planning:	Local jurisdictions have planning control but are required to coordinate with the state. The Colorado Land Use Act requires local governments to identify areas that should be classified as areas of state interest. Once identified, these areas are protected from development by procedural requirements.
Food Production:	Growing season of only 90-180 days and 16 in/year of rain in the west. The eastern part gets 180-200 days and a little more rain.
Health Environment:	Water quality is excellent where fed by mountain springs. Quality is only fair from wells in the valleys. 72% of Colorado's water supplies are fluoridated. Air pollution is not a problem except in Denver. Good solar potential.
Traffic:	No major traffic problems except in Denver and Colorado Springs where it is moderately heavy. Red light and speed cameras are used.
Politics:	Colorado pits Democrats in the big metro areas with Republicans in the rural areas. Dem 30%, Rep 37%, Ind/3rd party 34% (this group makes the difference).
Taxes:	Below avg: Ranked 34th, effective rate is 8.9% of income. Sales tax is a low 3%, and CO has below avg. property taxes (ranked 38th in the nation).
Corruption:	Moderate. High corruption in Denver but low corruption in small towns.
Crime:	Low. Violent crime 308/100K, property crime 2658/100K. Crime index: Denver 12, Colorado Springs 11 (100 is safest)
Personal Liberty:	Good. 19th best.
Gun Liberty:	Fair except in Denver. No state purchase permit but a background check is required on all private sales. Dealers must record handgun sales. "Shall issue" state that recognizes permits from many other states. Denver bans assault weapons and requires a permit to carry openly (permitted elsewhere in the state). As of 2013 magazines are limited to 15 rounds (8 shotgun shells) unless owned before July 2013.
Alternative Medicine:	Very good with full range of natural health practitioners. Colorado law permits Direct Entry midwives to attend homebirths and to provide prenatal care to those women who meet risk assessment criteria. School vaccine exemptions: philosophical, religious and medical.
Home Schooling:	Regulated. State requires parents to send notification, test scores, and/or professional evaluation of student progress.
Military Targets:	**Fort Carson**, south of Colorado Springs. 1st-4th Brigades and 10th Special Forces Group; secondary target. **Pueblo Chemical Depot**. Chemical weapons storage. Destruction to begin in 2015; primary target until complete. **Buckley AFB**, Denver. Secret CIA base, 460th space wing, tracking and missile warning and satellite control; primary target. **Schriever AFB**, east of Colorado Springs. Military space systems control center; primary target. **Peterson AFB**, Colorado Springs. NORAD and Air Force Space Command who assume duties from Cheyenne Mountain which is now on "warm status;" Primary target. **Cheyenne Mt. NORAD** command center plus other secrets; primary target.

Notes

Colorado is a magnificent mountain state with impressive altitudes and many secure retreat sites. Dry land farming is good in the eastern state extension of the Great Plains, with altitudes ranging from 3500 to 5500 ft. This area is not nearly as productive as the central plains states, however, due to limited irrigation water from wells and streams. Ranching, irrigated farming and dry land farms predominate in the high altitude western half.

Colorado would be very highly rated except that Denver is the central hub of dark side government activities in the West and the big population centers of Denver and Colorado Springs are becoming increasingly liberal—or, worse, home to dumbed-down Americans who easily go along with "progressive" ideas while thinking they are conservative. The push for gun control legislation during 2013 is served as a good litmus test for the makeup of each state legislature, and Colorado's politicians rate poorly as they succumbed to outside pressures (the gun control lobby pushed hard for a win) and internal pressures (the increasingly liberal trend in the big population centers) to pass new gun restrictions. Although this bill had to be watered down due to the tough fight every gun bill goes through, conservatives ultimately lost—and that is a bad sign. We expect many other less-visible forms of liberty-restricting bills to become law in CO and this prompts us to downgrade the rating of this state as of 2013 despite the many excellent retreat locations in the western half of the state.

Various whistleblowers have told about the dark side of the federal government controlling Denver judges, police, insurance companies and financial firms. The extensive cover-up of facts surrounding the Columbine school shooting and Aurora movie theater shooting is telling of collusion between federal and local entities and the suppression of an honest investigation. There were 44 public corruption convictions last year, but that masks the tremendous amount of unprosecuted corruption in the Denver area in the judicial system and among the police where there are complaints and evidence of police brutality.

Many insider government corporations, insurance companies and military contractors locate here because of this control and collusion. There is no greater manifestation of this than the top-secret intervention of the federal government in the construction of the Denver International Airport. Huge underground levels were added for secret government purposes and then hidden from public scrutiny in what was billed as "gross cost overruns." The brazen use of numerous Masonic and occult symbols, sculptures and murals in the interior décor of the main terminal are also indicative of the dark side of government and its involvement in the Denver area.

In addition, in our work as high security designers we have come across various builders who have personal knowledge of numerous high government and CIA retired officials who have built underground bunker-type safe rooms into their retirement homes in various ski resorts in Colorado. While we certainly applaud the use of secure living areas in homes, the fact that these former government officials seem to know about dangerous future events is both telling and ominous, especially since they have refused to warn the American people about what they know is so life threatening.

There are secret military units, stationed at Buckley AFB near Denver, which is also the new home of a major domestic intelligence division of the CIA and to the Aerospace Data Facility which is the major U.S.-based satellite downlink for intelligence operated by the National Security Agency and the National Reconnaissance Office (NRO). Both the proverbial "black helicopters" and the "silent helicopters" have been observed at Buckley field at various times.

Even more dangerous threats to the local residents are found 70 miles farther south in Colorado Springs. The U.S. Northern Command and 21st Space Wing are based at Peterson Air Force Base in Colorado Springs. Nearby Schriever AFB is home to the 50th Space Wing of the Air Force Space Command which provides command and control for most of the government's navigation and communications satellites. Both of these are important first strike nuclear targets, putting everyone at Colorado Springs at risk of severe harm. The military put civilians at even greater risk by moving day to day operations of the NORAD command out of the bunker system at Cheyenne Mountain and into non-hardened buildings at Peterson. The official reason was that "they are no longer concerned about a threat to their operations from an intercontinental nuclear attack." Really? Then why is the federal government building so many new bunkers for officials and why are they keeping Cheyenne Mountain in "warm standby, fully operational and staffed with support personnel should the need arise?" Obviously, the military doesn't believe its own propaganda which is meant to keep ordinary Americans unaware and unprepared.

If the weird Masonic and occult connections of the Denver Airport weren't telling enough, you will find that the small city of Crestone in SW Colorado (two mountain ranges west of Pueblo) has become a Mecca for new age religions. This area of Colorado is competing with Santa Fe as the new age capitol of the US. New World Order and globalist financier Maurice Strong created a "world spiritual center" there with numerous iconic images and statutes. He bought up a controlling interest in a dying development and sold or donated parcels of land to various Eastern spiritual religions. There you will find Hindu, Zen and Carmelite monasteries and temples. Maurice Strong is an integral part of the New World Order conspiracy so we do not recommend you locate anywhere where he has a strong presence.

The eastern part of the state has all the negative aspects of the plains states (cold, wind-driven winters and hot, humid summers) but without the compensating ample water and deep soil. That isn't to say that you can't find pockets of good, small farm plots, but you still have the liability of being in the wide open spaces with little shelter and cover.

Fortunately, western Colorado beyond the front range of mountains is more conservative and resistant to the liberal influences of the Denver front range of cities. We exclude the luxury ski resorts in our recommendations for obvious reasons. The western Colorado ranch and mountain country is the only area of Colorado that we can highly recommend. It is also free from nuclear targets but will likely be exposed to fallout from targets farther west.

City-Specific Strategies

Denver: If you must be near Denver, you definitely need to establish a retreat in the nearby mountains. Avoid the center of this huge metro area and the suburbs to the east and south, which put you on the far side of where you'll need to go to safety. Locate on the western arc of the following suburban cities closest to the mountains: Littleton, Lakewood, Golden and Arvada. Select those subdivisions that give you close access to Hwy 285, 74, 40, 6 and 93 (but avoid I-70) into the mountains, depending on which leads to your retreat. If you are south of I-70 and you intend to go north, ascertain where you can cross under or over the freeway without contending with the congestion of an exit. Broomfield is a good location for those who intend to use a local airport to get out of town. It's close to either Rocky Mountain Metro Airport or Erie Municipal.

Traffic is very heavy going north into the more distant bedroom cities of Boulder and Longmont, but both these cities will be better for getting to the mountains via Hwy 119, 7, and 66. Loveland and Fort Collins are even safer since they give you an exit into the mountains through Hwy 34 to Estes Park.

Colorado Springs: If you are unfortunate enough to be located in Colorado Springs, you should be at least 5 miles away from Peterson AFB, which is co-located with the Colorado Springs airport. Fortunately, Schriever AFB (formerly Falcon AFB) is out in the plains to the east and less of a direct threat to the city itself. We recommend you also avoid Fort Carson to the southwest since it is closer to Cheyenne Mountain. The most secure location is west of I-25 and near Hwy 24 leading to Manitou Springs and Cascade, the best route out of the area in a crisis.

Retreat Areas

Montrose Area: This is our top-rated area in western Colorado for safe town living and for retreats closer to the mountains. Whenever you find a really safe town, you can often do without a separate retreat. Montrose is particularly nice because it has a major regional airport, good access to irrigated farmland and orchards, but is still surrounded by mountains in the distance. Other towns in the area such as Cimarron, Olathe, Delta, Cedaredge, Paonia and Crawford also provide retreat areas, although they are more remote than Montrose. The Ridgeway area along Hwy 550 is the area for beautiful cabin sites close to the mountains. This is the same highway that leads over the mountains to Durango.

Durango Area: The best area for forested mountain retreats is between Durango and Pagosa Springs, in the southwest corner of the state. Beware of water problems in the Durango area because nearby oil and gas wells often contaminate the water coming from wells. There are a lot of good farm or cabin retreat sites up along Falls Creek Road and on Route 501 going north from Bayfield to Vallecito Reservoir. Bayfield is east of Durango on Hwy 160. Pagosa Springs is further on this same road and is superior to Durango in safety but more isolated. It has abundant rural farm and mountain cabin sites.

Grand Junction to Glenwood Springs: Neither of these towns are suitable due to the I-70 corridor running through them but there are numerous farm and cabin sites to the south up against the rising mesas and plateaus that are distant enough to be safe, if not visible from the freeway.

Past the last ranges of mountains (almost to Utah) are a few very small towns such as Dolores near Hwy 160 and Nucla, Norwood and Naturita on Hwy 145 that are very safe for rural farms or ranches by virtue of their relative isolation.

CONNECTICUT ★☆☆☆☆

Summary Facts and Ratings

Climate:	Humid continental climate except along the southern shoreline which has a humid subtropical climate with temperatures moderated by the Long Island sound.
Population Density:	Very high: 726 ppl/sq mi. (4th highest in nation). Black 10.4%, Hispanic 12.3%, Asian 3.6%, mixed 1.5%.
Cost of Living Index:	132 (average is 100) making this the 6th most expensive state.
Land Ownership:	6% is state and federally owned.
Building Permits:	Required for new buildings and most renovations involving building structure. Many homes have basements.
Land and Urban Planning:	The state encourages and assists municipalities with planning and zoning. Most state agency projects regarding economic growth, preservation and conservation are not backed by any comprehensive state smart growth initiatives.
Food Production:	Adequate in lower elevations. Most soil is rocky and acidic but there are pockets of clay where forests have dropped leaves for decades. Growing season of 150-200 days. 50 inches of rain is spread out evenly through the year.
Health Environment:	Bad surface water quality. EPA rates it one of the most polluted in the nation. Aquifer water is good in rural farms. 90% of the population's drinking water is fluoridated. Air quality is a problem around Providence but only on no-wind days.
Traffic:	Traffic is heavy in Hartford (ranked #33 worst). No red light or speed cameras in the state.
Politics:	Connecticut used to be a hardnose Yankee state, but has grown soft and liberal over the decades. Dem 34%, Rep 23%, Ind/3rd party 43%.
Taxes:	Very high. Ranks 2nd in the nation (only NY is higher) with an effective tax burden of 12.6%. There is a 6% state sales tax and property taxes are among the highest in the nation.
Corruption:	High. Political corruption has been widespread at all levels.
Crime:	High. Violent crime 263/100K, property crime 1974/100K. Crime index: Hartford 5, Bridgeport 13 (100 is safest)
Personal Liberty:	Low. Ranked 40th.
Gun Liberty:	Very bad. After the Sandy Hook shooting state legislators enacted the most restrictive gun laws in the US. Permits with broad background checks (criminal and mental health) are required to purchase a handgun, rifle, shotgun or even ammunition. De facto gun registry due to paperwork sent to state on all sales/transfers. 10 round gun magazine limit. Grandfathered larger magazines must be registered. "Shall issue" state but local authorities can legally deny, revoke or delay permits resulting in "may issue" state. Broad assault weapons ban.
Alternative Medicine:	Naturopaths are licensed by the state and there is even a private school for Naturopathic Doctors (ND). Direct Entry midwives are not legally recognized nor prohibited by the state. School vaccine exemptions: religious and medical.
Home Schooling:	Low regulation. No state requirement for parents to initiate any contact.
Military Targets:	**New London Naval Submarine Base**. Only East Coast base for attack submarines; primary target.
Nuclear Power Plants:	**Millstone Plant**, on the coast near Waterford; 2 reactors.

Notes

Connecticut is by many measures the state of most concentrated wealth in the nation, although it has been steadily losing ground with the demise of the typical Northeastern industry and many military facilities. That wealth has led to a loss of the Yankee spirit of toughness and self-sufficiency. Even though Independents predominate, the state is now a reliable Democratic State with high taxes and high regulation. New Haven, Hartford and Bridgeport have been plagued by crime and have lost manufacturing jobs and people. The state is hostile to small business and very much controlled by big insurance companies. Small business growth is hampered by high taxes, heavy regulation and health insurance requirements that demand coverage for everything under the sun.

Although the living areas are fair in the northern part of the state, they are still way to close to NYC and the high density urban corridor to be safe for even the medium term. Southwestern Connecticut is part of the New York metropolitan area, including three of Connecticut's eight counties and most of the state's population. Connecticut's rural areas and small towns in the northeast and northwest corners of the state contrast sharply with its industrial cities, located along the coastal highways from the New York border to New Haven. Northeastern coastal forests of oak, hickory and maple cover much of the state. Horse property abounds in the state and it is said to have 47,000 horses—one for every 72 people, making it the highest ratio in the country even compared to Kentucky.

Corruption has been high in this state. There were 23 public corruption convictions just in 2009. The mayors of Bridgeport, Waterbury and other towns have been convicted on corruption charges, and Governor John Rowland had to resign to avoid similar charges in 2004.

Population density is very high in this state but this is mostly concentrated along the entire coastal area north of NYC. It is only moderately dense in the northern half of the state where rural towns and estates along the NY border are home to NYC commuters.

Despite its beauty Connecticut is often rated as one of the worst states for retirees due to its high cost of living and tax burden. Specifically, high property taxes and high personal income taxes hit retired couples hard in the Nutmeg State.

City-Specific Strategies

Bridgewater-Hartford corridor: We will cover the entire corridor because it constitutes a high density dividing line through the state from SW to NE. While it isn't one continuous line of cities, the individual cities are sufficiently populous that there are no safe rural areas in between. We highly recommend that you locate to the NW of this line of cities. While there is an equal amount of rural farm land to the east, all of those locations are sandwiched between this line of cities and the line following I-95 to Providence RI. Your chances of finding privacy and escape from social unrest are much better to the NW where you have relatively unimpeded access to the more rural escape routes either north to upstate NY and Vermont or farther west into north-central PA. Give Hartford a wide berth because of the crime factor and higher population density. The outskirts of West Hartford would be best if you must live nearby.

New London: Avoid this area. It is lovely, but it is also the only primary nuclear target in the state. Stay at least 5 miles north to avoid the blast affects.

New Haven-Port Chester corridor: This is the commuter corridor to NYC and should also be avoided. It is better than the NYC-White Plains corridor, but only if you locate north of this corridor in the countryside.

Retreat Areas

Danbury: The area north of Danbury (New Milford, etc.) is the only area offering any real safety. Danbury itself and further south are the commuter suburban areas that offer less safety. There are lots of rock outcroppings in the area mixed with sometimes gravelly or clayish soil, so shop for land carefully to make sure you can sink a basement under the house for a safe room. You'll need it in this area. You will also have to watch out for eventual influxes of refugees, so select locations far away from secondary roads.

Windom: This is the central town in the eastern half of CT. It has a lot of rural land with only moderate population density but as we pointed out earlier, it is less desirable because you would eventually be overrun with refugees from cities farther east flowing westward. That isn't to say it is inevitable, but your safety would be highly dependent upon being able to disappear into concealed quarters. The line of high-density cities from Bridgeport to Springfield, MA would make it difficult to maneuver under such conditions.

DELAWARE ★☆☆☆☆

Summary Facts and Ratings

Climate:	Delaware is in a transition zone between a humid, subtropical climate and a continental climate. The southern part is warmer than the north despite its small size.
Population Density:	High: 453 ppl/sq mi. (6th highest in nation). Black 21%, Hispanic 7.2%, Asian 3%, mixed 1.5%.
Cost of Living Index:	103 (average is 100) making this the 18th most expensive state.
Land Ownership:	7% of the land is state and federally owned.
Building Permits:	Required for new buildings and most renovations involving the structure. Many houses have basements except in the southern part where ground has a high water table.
Land and Urban Planning:	The Delaware Office of State Planning Coordination is the state planning agency and the state's Land Use Planning Act requires state agencies and local governments to coordinate land use decisions of more than local concern.
Food Production:	Adequate productivity everywhere. Soil varies from sandy to clayish and wet in the south. Growing season is 150-200 days. 45 inches of rain is distributed regularly throughout the year. The southern portion of the state has a somewhat milder climate and a longer growing season than the northern part of the state.
Health Environment:	Bad surface water quality—EPA rates it one of the most polluted in the nation. Aquifer water quality is good in rural farms. 86% of the population's drinking water is fluoridated. Air quality is not a problem except in Dover's industrial area on days with little wind. There are 14 superfund sites in DE, half due to industry pollution and half from improper landfill use.
Traffic:	No major traffic snarls in Delaware. It does use red light cameras in Dover.
Politics:	The state used to be a bellwether state but now Democrats consistently hold a majority of registrations in Delaware. Dem 50%, Rep 33%, Ind/3rd party 23%.
Taxes:	Fairly high. Ranked 17th highest with a tax burden of 10.2% of income (slightly below the national average of 9.5%). The income tax tops out at 6%, and property taxes are below average.
Corruption:	Medium high. Delaware was number one in the personal crimes category because of forgery and embezzlement.
Crime:	Very high. Violent crime 491/100K, property crime 3065/100K. These figures are mostly a reflection of the concentrated population in Wilmington which has a crime index of 1 (less than 1% of other cities have higher crime;100 is safest). Rural Delaware is somewhat safer.
Personal Liberty:	Slightly better than average. Ranks 17th.
Gun Liberty:	Good. No permit to purchase firearms. "Shall issue" state, but applicants for a concealed handgun permit must post their names in the newspaper. Open carry friendly state.
Alternative Medicine:	Alternative medicine is discouraged by Medical Practice laws. Direct Entry Midwives are legal by licensure. No Medicaid reimbursement for homebirths. School vaccine exemptions: religious and medical.
Home Schooling:	Low regulation. Parental notification to the state is required.
Military Targets:	**Dover AFB**. Largest airlift base operating C-5s; primary target.

Notes

Delaware is the second smallest state in the Union and located in the northeastern part of the Delmarva Peninsula. The western peninsula is shared with Maryland. Delaware is on a fairly level plain, with the lowest mean elevation of any state in the nation. Some rolling hills occur in the north among part of the Appalachian Piedmont. The main part of the state, deep into the peninsula, is part of the Atlantic Coastal Plain with flat, sandy soil and sometimes swampy ground.

Delaware has taken advantage of state's rights to create laws that make it advantageous to visit and do business there. Leaders pioneered liberal laws of incorporation and now more than half of the nation's corporations are incorporated in Delaware. The state also hosts the 10 biggest credit card companies. These credit card banks are one of the largest employers after the military. Delaware's policies have paid big tax dividends as out-of-state visitors pay a large share of Delaware's taxes through tolls, corporate fees, franchise taxes and gambling at the race tracks. Out of state revenue has allowed Delaware to levy no sales tax and reduce income taxes several times.

These trends toward propriety and responsibility have not kept personal corruption from the political leaders. According to Ron Williams in The News Journal, when Senator Chris Coons served as the President of the County Council, he diverted untold millions of taxpayer dollars as payoffs to his political buddies and top staff. Coons did this by exploiting a loophole in the county's pension program. Delaware Governor Ruth Ann Minner in 2006 was accused of special favoritism for her friend, a liquor distributor.

Delaware isn't all that bad to live in during normal times, but it is just not safe in a major crisis because the whole peninsula is boxed in by Wilmington and Philadelphia, which will be major sources of social unrest. Most of the rivers run E-W toward the ocean and thus require many bridges to travel N-S through the state, creating lots of bottleneck areas. The lack of escape routes is the biggest danger for this small state in a crisis. Those who already live there should have access to a sturdy boat.

City-Specific Strategies

Wilmington: Fortunately, the main traffic corridor of I-95 goes through the middle of the city leaving the NW section of the city wide open for retreat routes into southern PA. These routes are far enough southwest of Philadelphia to beat the crowds that will flow outward during a crisis. In fact, the rural suburbs of NW Wilmington and Newark are the only places in the state where you are not living in a trap zone.

Dover: In order to stay out of the 5 mile blast radius around Dover AFB (a primary nuclear target), don't live in Dover proper. Stay in the outskirts to the north and west of town.

Retreat Areas

As stated in the Wilmington section, the only exit out of Delaware is to the NW through southern PA. If you can't live in NW Wilmington where you have quick access out of the area, you need to have a very private rural retreat where few people can find you. Considering Delaware's coastline, it would be a good idea to have a boat stashed somewhere to give you one more option. We don't recommend a house right on the coast, since some marauders will likely use boats and shorelines for scouting out new scavenging sites.

FLORIDA ☆☆☆☆☆

Summary Facts and Ratings

Climate:	Subtropical in the northern and central regions with a true tropical climate in the south. FL averages 45 tornadoes a year.
Population Density:	High. 344 ppl/sq mi (8th highest in nation). Black 16%, Hispanic 22%, Asian 2.4%, mixed 1.5%.
Cost of Living Index:	Average. 100.5 (average is 100)
Land Ownership:	26% of the land is state or federally owned but most of this is the Everglades Park.
Building Permits:	There are many kinds of permits. Several apply to new construction and remodeling. Remodel permits are more stringent to satisfy hurricane codes and sometimes require additional electrical and plumbing inspections. Basements are not common because of the high water table.
Land and Urban Planning:	The State Comprehensive Plan sets long-range policy for twenty-six areas. Local governments are required, through the Local Government Comprehensive Planning and Land Development Regulation Act, to prepare and adopt plans that are consistent with the goals and policies of the state plan.
Food Production:	Good, but only for certain crops like citrus and ranching. The growing season is in excess of 240-280 days. Average rainfall is 54 in/year, and it rains more in the northern panhandle than in Miami. Soil is sandy and lacks nutrients.
Health Environment:	Water is polluted above the national average. The air quality throughout the state is not good generally, and there are EPA red zones along the coastal cities Miami, Tampa, Orlando, Pensacola and Tallahassee. Aquifer water quality is poor from agricultural pollution and porous soils. 78% of the population's drinking water is fluoridated—all the big cities.
Traffic:	Miami is the 10th worst traffic metro in the nation. Tampa is the 23rd and Orlando is 46th (out of 75). Red light cameras are used.
Politics:	Fairly even split between major parties. Dem 40%, Rep 40%, Ind/3rd party 20%.
Taxes:	Moderate. An effective tax burden of 8.9% of income, just above the national average of 8.5%. FL has no income tax. Its state sales tax rate is 6% and property taxes are average.
Corruption:	Very high at all levels.
Crime:	Very high. Violent crime 470/100K, property crime 3105/100K. The worst crime is in and around Miami whose crime index is 4 (100 is safest)
Personal Liberty:	Average. Ranked 23rd best.
Gun Liberty:	Moderate. No permit to purchase firearms. "Shall issue" state for concealed firearm licenses. No open carry allowed.
Alternative Medicine:	Alternative medicine is discouraged by medical practice laws but largely unprosecuted. The practice of midwifery by direct-entry midwives is regulated by licensing. Practicing without a license is a felony. 80 midwives are licensed and practice primarily in out-of-hospital settings. School vaccine exemptions: religious and medical.
Home Schooling:	Moderate regulation. State requires parents to send notification, test scores, and/or professional evaluation of student progress.
Military Targets:	**Jacksonville Airport**. F-15 Air National Guard—not a target. **Jacksonville Naval Air Station**. MCSF Blount Island, Mayport Naval Station. Major naval base with loading facilities, airport, P-3C patrol aircraft, helicopters and home to 4th fleet; primary target, possibly multiple hits. **Key West Naval Air Station**. Navy Fighters, electronic surveillance aircraft, water special forces; secondary target. **Panama City Naval Support Activity**. Naval research and development lab; secondary target. **Pensacola Naval Air Station**. Navy training station; not a target.

Military Targets continued:	**Cape Canaveral AFS, Patrick AFB**, west of Orlando. Satellite tracking and launch facilities; primary target.
	Eglin AFB, Hurlburt AFB, E of Pensacola. Satellite tracking, fighters; primary target.
	Homestead Air Reserve Base, south tip of FL. F-16 global fighter base; secondary target.
	MacDill AFB and Avon Park Range. Joint reserve base. Marine Corps F-18 and Air National Guard, KC-135 Aerial refueling; primary target.
	Tyndall AFB, Panama City. F-22, F-15 Fighters and training; primary target.
Nuclear Power Plants:	**Crystal River Plant**, 75 mi N of Tampa. 1 reactor.
	St Lucie Plant, S of Ft Pierce. 2 reactors.
	Turkey Point Plant, S of Miami. 2 reactors.

Notes

Hawaii and Florida are the only two states that rate a zero rating. They are wonderful vacation spots, but they are very vulnerable to almost every threat. Florida is almost totally unsafe, even in the short-term. It is subject to tornadoes, thunderstorms and hurricanes. Corruption is strong, crime is very high and there is a high-density population that is totally unprepared for any significant crisis.

As we analyze this state, we find it is one big trap zone. Even the panhandle is so covered with military targets that it will be unsafe someday. Like an island, the best exit routes involve a large, fast boat. Food production is not easy, and most cities are dependent upon imports. Even if you wanted to build a safe room and disappear during turmoil, there are few places high enough to get out of the shallow water table. Almost every crisis scenario would hit this state hard. When electricity is gone, the heat and bugs of this climate will be very uncomfortable to live in. If you have a vacation home here, enjoy it, but live and have a retreat in a safer zone.

There isn't much terrain cover here either, which will make it difficult to grow food in a crisis with thousands of people just waiting for your crops to ripen. There are 4 growing zones in FL. The panhandle area does freeze in the winter and trees lose their leaves. Frost can get down into central FL on rare occasions. Some of the coastal areas are swampy. The heat and humidity is relatively high during most of the year, so only certain types of plants grow in FL. Watering is required during the dry season.

Politically, Florida has some interesting anomalies. In sixty years Florida went from a small southern state, overwhelmingly Democratic, to the 4th largest state with Republicans and Democrats fairly evenly split. Democratic strongholds continue with black communities and where liberals have migrated from the urban centers of the NE states. The latter are often concentrated in Broward and Palm Beach Counties on the Gold Coast. Unlike California, a large percentage of Latinos here vote Republican rather than Democratic—mostly because of the Cuban hatred of heavy-handed government.

We don't hold out hope that politics will turn Florida around, however. Corruption in Florida is a principle reason for the low rating. There were only 12 public corruption convictions last year; so many more are being covered up. Former Governor Charlie Crist secretly betrayed his get "tough-on-crime" campaign promise when it came to his Republican supporter, Louis J. Pearlman. Lou Pearlman's model scouting scam was run by convicted fraudsters. After two years of investigation, the Attorney General's Office virtually whitewashed the whole affair. To get there he had to fire the assistant attorney general in charge of the case. Upscale Palm Beach County had two major sex scandals, first by Rep. Mark Foley and then his successor, Tim Mahoney. U.S. Attorney R. Alexander Acosta just announced corruption charges against 18-year Palm Beach county commissioner Mary McCarty.

City-Specific Strategies

Miami Beach to Palm Beach: This is the high density coastal community in southern Florida. It is utterly unsafe to live here. Every city except Palm Beach at the northern end is sandwiched in between the Everglades and the ocean. That means there are no rural roads leading to safety when the main roads are clogged. We cannot emphasize enough that if you live south of West Palm Beach, you will need a boat to escape massive social unrest.

Central Coast Beach Cities: These cities are much safer because they are not boxed in on the west. There are rural roads that can get you out in a pinch. Beware, however, of the significant swampy areas and small lakes out in central Florida that can cut off your retreat or create bottlenecks. Carefully map out and pre-drive various routes. Going north, you have to get to the west of the Orlando metro area before you can go north. Ideally, you want to cross I-75 and take the secondary roads that are to the west of this N-S freeway. Most of the others will be on the east side where the population centers are.

Orlando: This is a major urban center with many water traps surrounding it, especially to the west where safety lies. Fortunately, there are numerous rural roads threading their way through the lake country. Locate on the outskirts of Orlando (as in Mt Plymouth). That gives you secondary routes both east and north for retreat. If you live in the west, such as Winter Garden, keep heading west during an exit. Try to get past I-75 to Brooksville and then go north.

Tampa/Clearwater: We would only recommend living north of Tampa so that you are the first to exit out. If you live on the coast, you'll have to be farther north still (Hudson area) to be out of the highest density coast communities. Don't get trapped down in the St. Petersburg peninsula unless you have a boat.

Jacksonville: This is one of the most dangerous cities in Florida, not only because of the multiple military targets but because of the minority composition and crime potential of the area. The only safe strategy is to locate outside the 295 Beltway to the west, preferably north of I-10. Sadly, there aren't very many rural roads leading north to Georgia. Don't even think about taking I-10 very far. The further west you go, the more problem cities you will find blocking your route. Try to get to one of the two highways that go around the Okefenokee Wildlife Refuge which is also blocking your path (either Hwy 2/94 to the west or 23/1 to the east).

Retreat Areas

General advice: There is farm and ranch country in central Florida and in the panhandle, but even these do not offer much privacy unless surrounded by dense, tall overgrowth. Britton Hill, in the Florida Panhandle, is the highest point in Florida at 345 feet above sea level. It is located in Walton County, about 1/2 mile south of the Alabama border and about 68 miles northeast of Pensacola. Other relatively high spots are Clearwater (where it rises 50 to 100 feet in some places), some spots north of Ocala where elevations are at least 8 feet above water tables and some rolling hills in North Florida, if at least 25 miles away from the coastline with elevations ranging from 100 to 250 feet. The highest point in southern FL is Sugarloaf Mountain (312 ft) in Lake County.

If you are close to the coast and at risk for hurricanes, you need to build with reinforced concrete and have protective rolling shutters on your home. Acrylic storm windows are also very effective and much less costly than shutters.

GEORGIA ★★☆☆☆

Summary Facts and Ratings

Climate:	Largely humid subtropical climate. Summers are hot and humid, except at the higher elevations in the NW. GA averages 20 tornadoes a year.
Population Density:	170 ppl/sq mi. (18th highest in nation). Black 30.2%, Hispanic 8.3%, Asian 3%, mixed 1.3%.
Cost of Living Index:	Below Average. 92 (average is 100), making this the 12th least expensive state.
Land Ownership:	5% of the land is state and federally owned.
Building Permits:	Varies by city, but generally you will need to obtain a building permit for most new construction work or significant remodel affecting an existing structure. Counties in the north Georgian mountains do not require more than a septic permit and state electrical inspection. Basements are possible in most areas but are not common.
Land and Urban Planning:	There is no current statewide plan. Local governmental entities are encouraged to plan and the state's Planning Act requires a statewide plan to be assembled after local and regional entities have planned.
Food Production:	Good except in the northern mountains, which have thin, stony clay soils and the coastal areas which are swampy. The growing season is 180-240 days. Heavy rainfall with 45 inches on the plains to 75-80 inches in the mountains.
Health Environment:	Georgia's waters are rated average for pollution, which is better than most southern states. The air quality throughout the state is not good with Atlanta leading the way. All medium-sized cities have some pollution. Most of the EPA superfund sites are located in the industrial corridor or are landfills. Agriculture has polluted aquifer water to varying extents even in rural areas. 96.3% of the population's drinking water is fluoridated—very bad.
Traffic:	Atlanta is the 22nd worst traffic metro in the nation. Red light cameras are used.
Politics:	Dem 42%, Rep 48%, Ind/3rd party 10%.
Taxes:	Moderate. Ranked 16th highest with an effective tax burden of 9.9% of income. The progressive income tax rate tops out at 6%. State sales tax rate is 4% and property taxes are average.
Corruption:	Very high, particularly in Atlanta city politics.
Crime:	High. Violent crime 379/100K, property crime 3,411/100K. Most of the crime is in and around the Atlanta metro area.
Personal Liberty:	4 out of 5 rating.
Gun Liberty:	Poor. No permit to purchase firearms. "Shall issue" state for permits that are required for both open and concealed carry.
Alternative Medicine:	Alternative medicine is discouraged by medical practice laws, but practitioners are largely unprosecuted. Practice by Direct-Entry Midwives is effectively unlawful because certification by the Department of Human Resources, as required by law, is unavailable. A few midwives still practice in the open and are not prosecuted. School vaccine exemptions: religious and medical.
Home Schooling:	Moderate regulation. State requires parents to send notification, test scores, and/or professional evaluation of student progress.
Military Targets:	**Fort Benning,** Lawson Field, SE of Columbus. Principle airlift launching point for army. Home of 3rd mechanized infantry division, ranger school; primary target. **Fort Gordon**, W of Augusta. Officer school and houses NSA and intelligence agencies from many branches of the military; secondary target. **Fort Stewart**, Hunter Army Airfield, W of Savannah. Home of 3rd infantry and armored unit; primary target. **Marine Corps Logistics Base Atlantic**, Albany. Supply depot, repair facility; tertiary target. **Kings Bay Submarine Base**. Atlantic base for submarines carrying nuclear trident ballistic missiles; primary target, multiple hits.

Military Targets cont:inued	**Dobbins ARB**, Marietta. Lockheed Martin production plant including F-22s. USAF Reserve base for C-130 airlift; secondary target. **Moody AFB**, NE of Valdosta. A-10 and global search and rescue; secondary target.
Nuclear Power Plants:	**Hatch Nuclear Plant**, Donalsonville. 2 reactors. **Vogtle Nuclear Power Plant**, E of Waynesboro. 2 reactors and 2 more possibly built by 2015.

Notes

Georgia has been, since 1990, one of the fastest growing states in the nation. Most of the growth is in the Atlanta metro area, although not in the core city which has little room to grow and is not too far away from the ghettos of old Atlanta. Most of the growth has been to the north of Atlanta where tens of smaller towns have been absorbed into the metro area that now measures almost 100 miles north to south. Hardly any of the roads are straight, so traffic is a tangled mess clear out into the suburbs. Atlanta is both the greatest draw of Georgia and its greatest danger zone during tough times.

Georgia used to have a near majority of black citizens and, thus, very powerful roots in the Democratic Party. However, most of the newcomers during the boom years from the 90s to the present have been white with strong conservative attitudes. This growth reduced the state's black percentage to 30% in 2000 and it is still slowly dropping. Republicans now strongly dominate the state. The growth effects have been good for conservative politics and a robust economy but bad since they create a lot of high-density suburban areas with traffic problems. Atlanta has become the de facto economic center of the south and attracts a variety of products, services and jobs. Kasim Reed, Atlanta's mayor, however, is a staunch Democrat and was even voiced about as a vice president possibility for Hillary in 2016.

This growth has also fueled corruption in the Peach State and Atlanta is the corruption leader. Atlanta's former mayor, Bill Campbell, was convicted of tax evasion and has fought to maintain Atlanta's racial set-aside programs. Lately, city and county minority officials are resigning and pleading guilty to a variety of corruption charges revolving around racial set-aside programs—aimed at Campbell's friends and favored contractors. Fulton County has a similar history of abuse of racial-preference programs and set asides. There were only 38 public corruption convictions last year, so many are being covered up.

City-Specific Strategies

Atlanta: Your only hope of getting out of this major metro is to be fairly far out from the central areas bounded by the 285 Beltway. But even that isn't far enough if you want to get rural. Along I-85 leading NE, it's crowded clear out to Suwanee and Lawrenceville. The only safe GA retreats are in the northern mountains, so we recommend locating north of 285 and within the sector formed by Hwy 19 to Alpharetta on the east to I-75 on the west. That would not include the busy and populated corridor of I-75 which leads to

Marietta and passes by Dobbins Air Reserve Base, but rather the more lightly populated areas in between. There are some very nice subdivisions in all directions around Atlanta, but we prefer the ones to the north since you don't have to go a hundred miles around the metro area to exit to safety. Wherever you choose to live, you must carefully map out alternate rural routes that do not include the major freeways or secondary roads. These are clogged during normal traffic, let alone during a crisis. This is one city where you must have advance warning to make it out during a time of social meltdown.

Other Cities: None of the other cities of GA even compare to Atlanta in terms of high density population threats. Just follow our general council about locating on the outskirts and map out retreat routes north by predetermining freeway crossings where there is no on or off ramp. Take note of the list of military targets above and locate outside the 5 mile radius blast zones associated with them.

Retreat Areas

There are lots of potential rural farm retreats all over but they aren't safe in the long term due to potential confrontations with refugees coming up from Florida to seek food in the countryside. There are some big nuclear military targets on the coast, such as King's Bay above Jacksonville, which will drive thousands towards the center of the state. Refugees always flow toward cities because that's where all the roads and signs lead—but when they get there they will find it is futile. It is only when they can't go on that they start fanning out into the countryside—that is your major threat in a non-mountainous rural area. If you try retreating from most of the rural parts of the state toward the north, you'll have a major problem getting past Atlanta.

The Atlanta region is rolling hills where you find a good mix of forest and fields which give you some privacy for permanent residences. It's beautiful but very high density. The mountains of north GA around Clayton and Blairsville are mostly national forest, but there is still enough private land along the roads and rivers for retreats. Ultimately, the GA Mountains will be affected by refugees who will be driven there after easier pickings in the valleys are consumed. This is inevitable due to the massive number of people in the Atlanta area who have to go somewhere. That's what makes the mountains better, and why these first mountain areas as not as safe as the Cumberland Plateau in Tennessee, which is more distant and more difficult to reach.

Blairsville and Morganton: This area in the heart of the Blue Ridge Mountains has the most private land around it and much of it is forested hills, not just farmland. There is also a nice lake in the area for water.

Clayton: There are only farm retreats along the roads and rivers here (where the pioneers settled) but the seclusion and forestation is spectacular. The county has minimal requirements for building permits and inspections which is good for privacy. There are a dozen small towns scattered throughout the area, including Hawasee to the west that has a beautiful lake.

HAWAII ☆☆☆☆☆

Summary Facts and Ratings

Climate:	Hawaii's climate is tropical with humid air and temperatures ranging between 70 and 90 degrees. The trade winds are fairly constant making the windward side of the islands less hot than the leeward side.
Population Density:	High on Oahu (1,650), low on other islands. 201/sq mile statewide. Asian (mostly Japanese) 38%, White 30%, Pacific Islanders 9.2%, mixed 18%.
Cost of Living Index:	Very high. 168 (average is 100), making this the highest in the nation by far.
Private Land Availability:	Poor. Only 13% of the land is state or federally owned, but almost all the private land is owned by 39 owners, all large land trusts. Most homes are built on leased land.
Building Permits:	Very strict on Oahu, but not as much on the islands populated by native Hawaiians. Almost no basements are built on the island due to the coral base, but they can be done.
Land and Urban Planning:	The State has responsibility for education, zoning and planning. No local control.
Food Production:	Marginal. Poor soil, insects and diseases prohibit all but native crops like papaya, mango, taro root and sweet potatoes. Rain is 130 in/yr on the windward sides of the islands but the leeward sides only get about 18 in/yr. Fishing is an excellent source of food.
Health Environment:	Abundant fresh air, but the warm, humid climate breeds lots of insects and some mold. Good water quality, low in chlorine and only one city adds fluoride.
Traffic:	Honolulu is very high, ranked #2 after LA. Rural areas have moderate traffic mostly because there are few roads. No red light or speed cameras.
Politics:	Heavily democratic state—almost 4:1.
Taxes:	Ranked 13th highest in the nation with an average tax burden of 10.2% of income. Property taxes are high. The income tax brackets go up to 11% and there is a 4% state sales tax.
Corruption:	Very high. All levels of government and in the police. Racial prejudices occur.
Crime:	Average violent crime: 252/100K (mostly in Honolulu), but above average property crime in Honolulu and Hilo of 3054/100K. Crime index for Honolulu is 7, Hilo is 6 (100 is safest). Crime is moderate in other cities.
Personal Liberty:	Terrible, ranked 47th in the nation.
Gun Liberty:	Very bad. Permit required to purchase. Gun registry. "May issue" state but authorities say they will "never issue" concealed/open carry permits.
Alternative Medicine:	Allowed and encouraged in deference to native Hawaiians. Direct Entry Midwives (DEMs) are legal by statute, but licensure is unavailable. School vaccine exemptions: religious and medical.
Home Schooling:	Regulated. Parental notification, test scores, and/or professional evaluation of student progress required.
Military Targets:	**Fort Shafter**, Oahu. Command center for Army in Asia-Pacific; primary target. **Schofield Barracks**, Oahu. Army Barracks and target range; not a target. **Kunia Field Station**, Oahu. Navy Security Group, Military intelligence and cryptology; tertiary target. **Wheeler Army Airfield**, Central Oahu. AWACS and airlift; primary target. **Kaneohe Marine Corps Station**, East Oahu. P-3 and SH-60 anti-submarine squadrons, alternate base for Marine Fighters; primary target. **Camp Smith Marine Corps Base**, NE of Pearl Harbor. US Pacific Command and Marine Forces Pacific HQ; secondary target. **Pearl Harbor NAS**, Honolulu. Nuclear weapons storage, naval warship harbor; primary target.

Military Targets continued: | **Laulaulei Naval Weapons Magazine/Radio Station**, between Nanakuli and Schofield Barracks. Naval magazine and very low frequency submarine radio transmitters; primary target.
Wahiawa Naval Reservation, Schofield barracks. Large communication station including satellite management; primary target.
Hickam AFB, Pearl Harbor. Airlift and air refueling; primary target.

Notes

The primary objections to Hawaii as a safe place are 1) it is an island a long way from the US mainland, 2) it is a prime target for foreign military occupation and nuclear attack (Oahu), 3) it is very expensive to live there, 4) it is very crowded on Oahu, 5) there is significant racial tension, with caucasians being the targeted group (especially if part of the military) and 6) it is far from self-sufficient in electricity, food, and fuel as 90% of everything is imported by ship.

During good times, Hawaii is deceptively viewed as a paradise. The Aloha spirit is mostly for tourists. Behind the façade, tourists are despised and there is a lot of vulnerability, corruption and ethnic friction. Racial tension abounds within this state. The native Hawaiians are a minority and are constantly battling with other Pacific Islanders for their rightful place in the islands' government and business. Japanese, Tongans and Samoans are the main rivals. Gangs pertaining to each ethnic group rule the streets in the areas they tend to dominate. In state government, those of Japanese descent rule and even Hawaiians are discriminated against. There is a huge military presence on the Island, representing all four major services, and military personnel are deemed the lowest on the social totem pole.

Corruption on the islands is high and is reflected in racial prejudices. One attorney that worked on several cases involving public servants noted that "We live in a culture of corruption which permeates most of our public institutions." Public records are full of convictions for both elected and appointed public servants. There would have been many more if Hawaii had independent prosecutors. As it is, mayors appoint prosecutors and governors appoint the Attorney General. There is racial prejudice in state hiring which favors mostly those of Japanese ancestry. There are reports of police corruption and lots of tension between police and ethnic groups and gangs based mostly on race or culture.

Hawaii is a very liberal state, and prosperous—at least while serving as a tourist and retirement destination. Even in the recession, Hawaii's unemployment rate was the lowest in the country. But few job hunters dare relocate to Hawaii without being transferred there or hired directly. Businesses and government pay higher than normal salaries, but it doesn't go very far. Hawaii's cost of living is one of the highest in the nation and housing is outrageous in both high prices and low-quality construction. Property values exceed those of California and rent is sky-high. Most people also want to travel back to the mainland to attend family events once or twice a year and this travel to anywhere is expensive.

As for threats, the two worst in Hawaii are military targets and the extreme vulnerability to the supply line of food and fuel oil to run Hawaii's power plants. Pearl Harbor (Honolulu) is a primary nuclear target. There are 2 or 3 others as well, all on Oahu. While we do not expect any nation to occupy the US mainland during war, US pacific islands and territories could very well be occupied by the Chinese—which won't be nice.

Hawaii doesn't have a lot of severe weather in the mid pacific, but extremely heavy rains come on occasion. Hawaii has a significant earthquake hazard. This combined with the many earthen dams on the island that are on the government's warning list does not bode well for preparedness. 37 out of the 53 dams across Hawaii are rated as "high hazard." Built from dirt and stone for irrigation during the glory days of sugar cane and pineapple over a century ago, they are fragile and subject to damage during heavy rain.

Population density is another threat: 1.3 million people and 72% of those live on Oahu, giving it a density of 1,650 ppl/sq mile. On Oahu, 75% live in Honolulu county giving it a population density of 4,336. That's way to much population for such a small island with almost no self-sufficiency. Most of the arable land is used to grow pineapple.

There is plenty of sun for solar energy on certain parts of the islands, but you must be careful to avoid the rainy areas on the windward side of the mountains which collect most of the rain and clouds. You can still get sun on the windward sides, but not right next to the mountain ranges. The islands can be lush and wet on one side and nearly a desert on the other, so pick your micro climate according to your needs.

City-Specific Strategies

Oahu: Many must live here (because that's where the jobs are), but try to live on the windward side (Kaneohe or Kailua) but stay 3 miles away from Kaneohe Marine Air Base. This is within commuting range of Honolulu. If you don't need to commute to the capitol, pick the windward side farther north up around Laie and the North Shore. That keeps you away from all the military targets and as far away from people as possible.

Big Island: Of course, it is much safer on the bigger islands. If you must choose an island, choose the Big Island. It has enough agriculture to sustain its modest population and has enough size to find some privacy. It also has sufficient land at higher altitudes to escape hot, humid temperatures. There are large cattle ranches on the big island as well as extensive valley farms.

Kauai: Our second choice would be the island of Kauai. It has a lot of agriculture and only a small population, and is fairly close to Oahu.

Maui: Maui also has extensive farmlands, but property is more expensive due to the competition with developers on this smaller, sought after tourist destination. There are many small farming plots on all the smaller islands like Molokai that can lend themselves to some self-sufficiency, but Kauai, Maui and the Big Island are the only ones with sufficient commerce and travel links to do well in the good times.

Retreat Areas

There is a lot of jungle and tree cover in parts of the islands to provide retreat privacy. Pick locations near the mountains, outside the heavy wet zones, with a water course nearby (but watch out for flooding during heavy rains). Best locations on Oahu are on the North Shore up in the pine forests. Kauai and the Big Island have the most undeveloped areas for hideaways. On Maui, the windward eastern part of the Island (Hana) is the best because it is isolated from the rest of the island by the longest, most circuitous highway on earth, the "Road to Hana." This road is famously treacherous with many one-way, tiny cement bridges that would be easy to block.

A hint from those who plan to live in Hawaii: Prepare a way off the island. To mitigate the risks of island living, have enough stockpiles so you can pick your time to leave. Having an ocean-capable sailboat is a necessity for those serious about staying, plus the arms and ammunition to defend yourself on land and at sea if necessary. The odds aren't good even then, depending on what you are up against, but it is better than no odds at all.

IDAHO ★★★★★

Summary Facts and Ratings

Climate:	High desert climate in southern Idaho and the central mountains. Pacific maritime climate north of Lewiston. Pacific Northwest moist air flows eastward until hitting the Idaho mountains, where it drops its moisture, yielding forests at altitudes down to 2500 ft.
Population Density:	Low: 19 ppl/sq.mi. (44th ranking in the nation). Hispanic 10% mixed 1.7%, American Indian 1.6%, Asian 1.2%, Black 1%.
Cost of Living Index:	Very low. 88 (average is 100) makes this the third cheapest state in the nation after Mississippi and Indiana.
Private Land Availability:	Poor. 66% is state or federally owned including most of the best forests and mountain land.
Building Permits:	Not required in some northern counties. Flathead and Idaho Counties, for example, do not require permits except for septic or electric. Basements are common.
Land and Urban Planning:	There are local zoning regulations. Land use planning is only at local level.
Food Production:	Only with irrigation. Sandy soil. Most crops are possible below 5500 feet elevation if in full sun. Hay and cattle above this. Highly productive farms are in the Snake River Valley from Payette to Burley. 120-180 day growing season in the north and 180-200 in Snake River Valley. Average rainfall is 18 in/yr because of heavier rain in the mountains of the north, but main population centers in the south get only 12 in/yr.
Health Environment:	Water quality is excellent where fed by mountain springs. Quality is only fair from wells in the valleys. Only 36% of the population's water is fluoridated. Air pollution is only a problem in Boise though steady westerly winds keep the air moving on. Dry climate is very healthy. Good solar potential in the south.
Traffic:	Low. There is some during rush hour on the I-84 metro corridor near Boise. No red light or speed cameras.
Politics:	Conservatives predominate everywhere except northern Idaho which has a liberal bent. Dem 34%, Rep 60, Ind/3rd party 6%.
Taxes:	Below average. Ranked 24th at 9.5% of income (avg. is 9.8%). Up to 7.4% income tax, 6% Sales tax. 35th lowest property taxes.
Corruption:	Low. Some in-state government and metro police, but very little in rural areas. Police and conduct of judges is better than average.
Crime:	Lower. Violent crime 217/100K, property crime 1864/100K. Crime index for Boise is 30 (100 is safest).
Personal Liberty:	Very good. 6th best in the nation.
Gun Liberty:	Excellent. No permit to purchase firearms. "Shall issue" state for carrying a concealed firearm. No prohibited firearms. Open carry without a permit, even in a car.
Alternative Medicine:	Very good availability, full range of natural health practitioners. Direct entry midwives are licensed by the state. School vaccine exemptions: philosophical, religious and medical. A permanent commission has been set up in the ID legislature whose goal is to increase immunization rates there.
Home Schooling:	No regulation. State does not require parents to notify.
Military Targets:	**Mountain Home AFB**. 366th Fighter wing (F-15's); secondary target. **Boise Air Terminal**. ANG A-10s, KC-130 and Apache helicopters; secondary target. **Idaho National Labs**, west of Idaho Falls. Nuclear research laboratory; primary target.

Notes

Idaho is tied with Utah as our top-rated states for overall secure relocation. Utah has some advantages because it is more centrally located in the Intermountain West, such as access to better international air traffic. From anywhere in Idaho, you have to fly first to some other hub like Salt Lake City, Portland or Denver. Conversely, Idaho is further from population centers and is superior in climate, forestation and available retreat and farming sites. Like Utah, Idaho has minimal government intrusion in people's lives. Unlike Utah, many of Idaho's best retreat areas are in counties that have only minimum building code requirements (septic, zoning and state electrical or plumbing only). Car registrations in Idaho are cheap. Idaho is very low in crime and ranks almost at the bottom in car thefts—yielding very low auto insurance rates.

Most people driving through Idaho on I-15 or I-84 don't realize it is primarily a mountain state. It is a hunting and camping paradise in the northern half of the state which is sitting on a massive mountain backbone. Most of this; however, is tied up in US protected wilderness areas which limit the public's vehicular access. Hunting and fishing are allowed in all areas and add to the state's survival rating.

There are three distinct zones in Idaho and each has their own culture. The center and northern half of the state is nearly uninhabited and is covered by the Sawtooth, Challis, Nez Perce and Clearwater National Forests. These are highly forested mountain ranges where you need significant outdoor skills to venture deep into this area. The second is the Snake River farming area in southern and eastern Idaho which has a similar feel to Utah since many of the communities were settled by Mormons; although Evangelical Christians now outnumber the Mormons in most rural areas. The farms have more water for irrigation. The third area is northern Idaho where it is lower in altitude and milder in climate. It is actually an extension of the eastern Oregon and Washington desert basin, but captures more rain as the clouds back up against the Idaho mountains. It is a former mining area and has a non-religious, liberal bent to it common to most mining areas. There are a lot of Christian churches in this region too.

Most importantly, there are few nuclear targets in Idaho. It also boasts little corruption, low population densities, well-prepared communities, fertile land, isolating climate and secure hills and mountains.

Strategies for Populated Living Areas

Boise: This is the only metro area in Idaho that deserves caution relative to normal living areas. Most people who move to Idaho for a job come to the Boise area. The area is developing into a sort of corridor city paralleling I-84 from Boise to Nampa/Caldwell, with Meridian in between. Development has started again at a slower pace after the real estate boom ended in 2008. If you need to work downtown, consider living in Eagle. It is across

the Boise River which acts as a kind of barrier against social unrest if it happens. Eagle is also far enough away from the Boise Air Terminal, which hosts several Air National Guard units. The town is also close to prime retreat areas up Hwy 55 in and around Cascade and McCall.

Meridian is also close to Boise. Choose one of the several subdivisions in North Meridian which border Chinden Blvd, the last road before the Boise River. That road gives you the quickest access back and forth to Boise and yet is at the edge of the populous areas. It also allows you quick access to cross the river at 3 points or allows you to go west to Caldwell, avoiding I-84. Nampa and Caldwell are at the far end of Boise commuting range and have experienced an increase in Mexican gang violence. Gangs do tend to follow wherever Mexicans gather for agricultural work. The gangs have gotten into human trafficking and drugs throughout the US. Idaho is low in crime, but it is still there, thanks to government permissiveness on illegal immigration.

Magic Valley is a rich agricultural area along the Snake River in southern Idaho. This valley is the potato capitol of the USA and perhaps the world, but many other crops do well here too. There are no major population centers nearby and so even though I-84 connects all of the towns in the valley together, people can find rural farms anywhere along the river and have relative safety. Just make sure you are at least 3-5 miles from the freeway. This valley is nicely situated between Salt Lake and Boise for travel to major shopping.

Treasure Valley extends from Boise to Payette along the Snake River, but we only recommend the farmlands in Canyon County where you are far enough away from the Boise population. Our top recommendation goes to Payette, Idaho. It is a great farming community and is just across the river from Ontario, Oregon where one can go shopping without sales tax. Another favorite farm valley nearby is Weiser, Idaho, just up Hwy 95 from Payette. These are not retreat areas but you can find safe farm residences here. Hwy 95 leads north into the prime retreat areas north of New Meadows.

Coeur D'Alene in northern Idaho is packed with gorgeous scenery and lakes. This city puts you in the heart of great camping and boating country. It has a semi-dry climate with enough moisture from the Pacific Northwest to grow beautiful pine forests. It is not nearly as conservative as the rest of Idaho, but retreat sites abound in the areas north of the city including Lake Pend Oreille, Sandpoint and Boundary County. It does have a nuclear target close by in Spokane (Fairchild AFB) so you need to have fallout protection.

Eastern Idaho, from Pocatello to St. Anthony is another fine farming area that has general safety simply by virtue of being so far away from problem population centers. Like the Magic Valley, this valley is a mix of Evangelical Christians and Mormons that has the kind of cultural values that make for peaceful living. The real drawback of this area is the cold winters. Winter temperatures of 60 below are not uncommon for a few weeks in January and it is far enough to the east that cold Canadian air drifts down for deeply chilling temperatures in December through March. The areas east of Rigby give you access to the Grand Teton Mountains without the high prices of Jackson Hole. The country is beautiful and there are lots of game and plenty of good fishing. We do not recommend Idaho Falls because it is downwind of the Idaho National Labs near Arco, with advanced nuclear power engineering. Heavy isotope fallout is possible.

Retreat Areas

Long Valley is the area around McCall, Idaho. It has the Cascade Reservoir at the south end and Payette Lake in the north. It is a secluded ranch valley between two ranges of mountains. There are lots of cabins in the area and a great mix of forests and lakes. The weather is cold in the winter and you can expect snow up to your waist.

Sun Valley is more than just a world famous ski resort. It is also cowboy country and has a lot of ranches in the area. There are lots of wealthy, liberal people here so you'll have to endure the local politics in order to have access to the fine mountain and cabin areas that abound. There is a good homeschooling network in the area for those who choose this private route to education. The winters are cold but there is lots of sun to compensate. Twin Falls is the closest major shopping. For cheaper land you have to be about 30 miles from the resort. On the east side of these mountains, there are 3 fingers of mountains with ranch valleys in between. Hwy 93 runs up the most southern valley and leads to Challis and Ellis—two more potential retreat locations where land is much cheaper than Sun Valley and Ketchum. It's colder there, being on the east side of the mountains.

Swan Valley and Teton Valley in Idaho are on the other side of the Wyoming Teton Mountains and are much safer (and cheaper) than the Jackson Hole area. Both have good agricultural populations and Swan Valley has the added benefit of the lovely Palisades Reservoir. Highly recommended if you can handle cold winters and snow. Nearest medium-sized town is Rexburg, Idaho (college town of BYU Idaho) or St. Anthony.

Northern Idaho: North of Coeur D'Alene, we find some of Idaho's best retreat areas, even though the influx of Californians has driven up land prices, especially in and around Coeur D'Alene. Hayden Lake, in Kootenai County, got a bad reputation early on in the survival movement because of the Aryan Nations organization which is no longer located there. Aryan Nations was a group of radical followers of Reverend Richard Butler (now dead) who developed a strange mix of a Christian Identity religious doctrine ("We are Israel, not the Jews") and National Socialism, NAZI style. Sadly, he claimed to be "conservative" and gave everyone a bad name. How anyone can claim to be a conservative and promote NAZI socialism is beyond me, unless the leader himself turns out to be a government dupe. Butler's group was heavily infiltrated by the FBI with agent provocateurs who worked to give the movement a bad name and succeeded tremendously. This danger has past, but I still believe it wise to avoid joining militia groups as they are all targeted for infiltration by the feds.

Bonner County is further north and has a good mix of rural development and remoteness (limited building permit requirements). This county is home to the spectacular Lake Pend Oreille. Sandpoint is a great location since it is on the north side of the lake. There are also good sites along Hwy 200 leading around the lake toward Clark Fork and beyond (to Montana). There is a natural barrier created by the lake and the Priest River, which leads off into Washington, that makes all the area north to the Canadian border very secure. Hwy 95 leads north from Coeur D'Alene to Bonner's Ferry in Boundary County. Hwy 2 is on the north side of the Priest River. While there is private land on both sides of the highway in most locations, it is better to find retreat property out of sight of these highways.

Boundary County is the best for really getting away from civilization, but you pay for it in driving time when you need to do major shopping. Prices are cheaper and there is less regulation (also minimal building permits). Bonner's Ferry is the only town in the region. Priest Lake is another gem of water in this area, but there is not too much land available around it.

Lewiston and Moscow are western dry farming areas near the WA border and are next to some of the nation's best retreat areas. Take Hwy 8 from Moscow east toward or into the mountains around Bovill. Although cold, this area is beautiful and remote with a mix of rolling prairie and forests. The people are hardy but good natured and the soil is rich.

From Lewiston take Hwy 12 along the Clearwater River past the Nez Perce Indian Reservation. Great retreats sites abound in or near the mountains of the Clearwater and Nez Perce National Forests. While you can buy property on the Indian reservation, we don't recommend it. The native rights movement may demand it back someday. Most of these properties are in Idaho county which doesn't require building permits, although state zoning and septic requirements must be met. Jobs are almost non-existent here, so bring your own income. All of this leads to a subtle depressed atmosphere among many people who live here, despite the beauty. This is also a well-known survivalist haven made popular by Col. Bo Gritz and his followers. There were some serious infighting surrounding this group which is now abandoned, but still the residents are embarrassed by the way the mainstream media labeled them as "extremists." The ones that remain are not associated anymore with the group and are good people. Above the Clearwater River to the north and east of Kamiah, there are some tracts of land on the Camas Prairie that are very nice. This is fairly flat agricultural land northeast of Grangeville. Remember, this area gets Pacific Northwest weather in the winter and spring. There is low-level rain and fog particularly along the Clearwater River where the cold air settles. However, it is sunny and dry in the summer and fall.

ILLINOIS ★★☆☆☆

Summary Facts and Ratings

Climate:	Northern Illinois has a humid continental climate with cold, windy winters. Southern IL from Carbondale southward has a more humid subtropical climate where winter is not quite as severe. IL averages 27 tornados per year.
Population Density:	Moderately high: 179 ppl/sq.mi. (16th highest rank in the nation). Hispanic 15.2%, Black 14.9%, Asian 4.4%, mixed 1.2%.
Cost of Living Index:	Moderate at 96.5 (Average is 100).
Private Land Availability:	Good. Only 2.3% of the land is state or federally owned.
Building Permits:	Required everywhere for most new construction and big renovations. Codes and inspections are enforced by the local jurisdiction. Many have basements in the deep soil here except near rivers where the water table is high.
Land and Urban Development:	A statewide planning body exists, but it has limited involvement in land use and smart growth issues at the local level.
Food Production:	Good with a growing season of 150 in the north to 210 days in the south. Rainfall averages about 48 inches in the south and 35 inches per year in the north. Rich soil in most places.
Health Environment:	Surface water pollution is below average, except for high levels in Lake Michigan. Ground water around commercial farms has traces of farm chemicals. 99% of the state's drinking water is fluoridated—very bad.
Traffic:	Heavy traffic problems in Chicago which is rated #9 of the 75 worst traffic cities. Red light and speed cameras are used.
Politics:	There is a split between the corrupt, leftist political center in Chicago and the conservative agricultural core in the rest of the state. Dem 55%, Rep 40%, Ind/3rd party 5%.
Taxes:	Above average. Ranked 13th highest with an average tax burden of 10.2% of income. Income tax is 3.75%, property taxes are average and sales tax is 6.25%.
Corruption:	Very high, particularly in Chicago where politicians, judges and police are corrupt—often in combination with organized crime.
Crime:	High. Violent Crime 380/100K, property crime 2274/100K Chicago is still high in crime with a crime index of 12 (100 is safest).
Personal Liberty:	Very low. Ranked 45th overall. A vague "eavesdropping law" is being used to punish recording encounters with police as a felony (as of 2016).
Gun Liberty:	Bad (was "terrible" until courts overturned several bad gun laws). Firearm ID (FOID) card is required to purchase and own firearms or ammunition. All sales/transfers require background and FOID check with State Police. Open carry is prohibited. IL is a shall-issue state. Some counties have 10 to 15 round magazine limits. Chicago and Cook County have banned "assault weapons." Chicago requires guns be registered.
Alternative Medicine:	Natural health practitioners are free to practice. Lay midwifery is prohibited. School vaccine exemptions: religious and medical.
Home Schooling:	No regulation. No state requirement for parents to initiate any contact. Considering the regulatory atmosphere in IL, we wouldn't count on this lasting.
Military Targets:	**Scott AFB**, 15 mi. outside East St. Louis on I-64. HQ for Air Mobility Command, and home of refueling tanker aircraft; primary target. **Argonne National Laboratory**, 25 miles SW Chicago. Classified nuclear research; secondary target. **Fermi National Labs**, 25 mi. west of Chicago in Batavia. High energy particle accelerator research; secondary target. **Rock Island Arsenal**, Between Moline and Rock Island, IL. Only active US Army foundry manufactures equipment and ordinance including artillery; secondary target
Nuclear Power Plants:	**Braidwood I and II**, 20 mi. south of Joliet. **Byron I and II**, 17 mi. southwest of Rockford. **Clinton I**, 6 mi. east of Clinton..

Nuclear Power Plants, Cont'd:	**Dresden II and III**, 9 mi. east of Morris.
	LaSalle I and II, 11 mi. southeast of Ottawa.
	Quad Cities I and II, 20 mi. northeast of Moline

Notes

Illinois is a powerful manufacturing state and agricultural processing center like many of the cities on the south shore of Lake Michigan. It is also a major transportation corridor and has the highest number of spills on highways, rails, and waterways than any other state. As in Indiana, union workers are a strong political force in Illinois (especially in Chicago), and the local economies suffer when manufacturing is down. Central Illinois is a broad flat plain with sandy loam soil that makes for great farmland. Given the extreme corruption in this state, no one is safe from the evils of corrupt law in the long term.

The history of corruption in Chicago continues in this state. There were only 16 public corruption convictions last year, but they were all low-level convictions. Higher level corruption tends to be protected even when discovered. Historically, Illinois has had many corrupt governors with links to the mob. Elections are bought and sold in the Chicago area, including even national offices. Rod Blagojevich is the seventh governor of the state to be arrested or indicted since Governor Joel Aldrich Matteson tried to cash in $200,000 of stolen government scrip in the 1850s.

Strategically, this state is not safe, mostly because of the massive potential of crime and social unrest emanating from the Chicago metro area, which will affect not only Illinois but southern Wisconsin and northern Indiana. It is a disaster waiting to happen, and there is hardly any way to avoid it except to not live close to the Chicago metro area. The state has a declining population due to its many problems. IL is surrounded on 3 sides by major rivers and is criss-crossed with numerous freeways, making it a trap zone with limited crossing points. If you live in Illinois, you really do need a retreat further west or north, but it's a tough job to map out a route to safety.

Strategies for Populated Living Areas

Chicago: If you have no choice but to live near this city, here are the key issues: The city is ringed and criss-crossed with beltways and freeways, so it is important to stay outside the outer 355 Beltway for starters. While the best exit routes are to the west, you have potentially dangerous nuclear targets in Batavia, plus two nuclear power plants to the south of I-80. There is also a nuclear power plant SW of Rockville in Byron. To get past these potential problems, pick one or two rural routes either I-88 and I-90 to the northwest or between I-88 and I-80 straight west. In either case, you'll have to find a passage over or under I-39 to the west and also the ring of I-74 and I-88 later on—always do so where there is no on or off ramp to the freeway that is likely to be congested in an emergency. Always plan on crossing the Mississippi at non-freeway bridges in the smaller river either above

or below Davenport/Moline. If your retreat direction is NW to Wisconsin, try to locate in the northern wedge of cities between I-90 and I-94. You should plan your direction of travel in Wisconsin to go to the west of Madison, since refugees fleeing Milwaukee may block roads to the east.

East St. Louis: We would recommend only the sector north of I-70 and outside the 270 Beltway (Edwardsville area) and also not in the Alton corridor sandwiched between the river and Hwy 255. To retreat west, you have to go north to Hwy 16, then west to 96 and then north to 54 which will take you over the Mississippi at Pike.

Rockford and other cities on freeways: Locate outside the Beltways and map out rural road exit strategies (more than one) in the direction to where you decide to retreat.

Retreat Areas

Rural farmland: Illinois has plenty of rural farm land. Farm retreats are not as safe as being in hill country, but if you follow our guidelines about locating for privacy, they can be fairly safe for all but massive social unrest where all of the cities empty out into the countryside looking for food. Because of the mass of population in Chicago, there isn't much hope of not being overrun unless you are at least 100 miles away. The secret is making sure you are not near a major refugee path (usually traveling down secondary roads). Indiana has lots of rural farm land, but little concealing foliage. The only safe strategy is underground concealed rooms where you and your stores can't be found.

Southern tip of Illinois: There are forested areas here from Cape Girardeau to the Shawnee Forest. This land backs up to state forest land giving you some chance of privacy and security. It is not ideal since it is surrounded by rivers on 3 sides, but that may also help keep people out.

INDIANA ★★☆☆☆

Summary Facts and Ratings

Climate:	Indiana has a humid continental climate with cold winters and hot humid summers. The extreme southern portion of the state is within the humid subtropical climate area like Kentucky and gets more rain than the northern parts. Indiana averages 23 tornados per year.
Population Density:	Moderately high: 179 ppl/sq.mi. (16th highest rank in the nation). Black 9.2%, Hispanic 5.5%, Asian 1.5%, mixed 1.3%.
Cost of Living Index:	Low. 88 (average is 100), ranked 22nd least expensive state.
Private Land Availability:	Good. Only 2.2% of the land is state or federally owned.
Building Permits:	Required everywhere for most new construction and renovations. Codes and enforcement vary by local jurisdiction. Basements are common except in a few areas where it is marshy.
Land and Urban Development:	Planning is done almost exclusively at the county and municipal level.
Food Production:	Good productivity with a growing season of 150-210 days. Rainfall averages about 44 in/yr in the south and 40 in the north. Rich soil in most places.
Health Environment:	Indiana surface water pollution is above average. Ground water around commercial farms has traces of chemicals. 95% of the state's drinking water is fluoridated.
Traffic:	moderate traffic problems in Indianapolis which is rated as #56 of the 75 bad traffic cities. No red light or speed cameras.
Politics:	Indiana is conservative in its agricultural core but liberal in the three Lake Michigan counties and in a few industrial counties (Muncie, Terre Haute, Evansville) plus the one university county (Bloomington). Like other states, there was a major conservative shift in 2010 toward more conservative and Republican candidates. Dem 40%, Rep 55%, Ind/3rd party 5%.
Taxes:	Average. Ranked 22nd highest with an average tax burden of 9.5% of income. 3% income tax and average property taxes, plus a 7% sales tax.
Corruption:	High. Local conspiracies and election fraud are examples of corruption in this state.
Crime:	Average. Violent crime 357/100K, property crime 2854/100K. Crime is high in Indianapolis which has a crime index of 3 (100 is safest)
Personal Liberty:	Good. Rated 16th in the nation.
Gun Liberty:	Good. No permit to purchase firearms. "Shall issue" state for concealed or open carry but applicants must submit name, address and gun information to federal government via form 4473.
Alternative Medicine:	Natural health practitioners are not licensed but are allowed to practice. Lay midwifery is unregulated and not sanctioned by law, making it effectively illegal. School vaccine exemptions: religious and medical.
Home Schooling:	No regulation. No state requirement for parents to initiate any contact.
Military Targets:	**Crane Naval Weapons Center**, 10 miles south of Bloomfield. Development and maintenance of electronic warfare systems; secondary target. **Grissom AFB**, 8 miles SW of Peru. KC-135 USAF Reserve refueling base; secondary target. **Fort Wayne Airport**. ANG F-16s; tertiary target, if at all.

Notes

Indiana itself has the nation's highest percentage of manufacturing workers (20%) and is second in products from manufacturing. Refrigerators, engines, cars, truck bodies, engine-electrical equipment, recreational vehicles and mobile homes are built here. There are still a few automated steel mills on the south shore of Lake Michigan and other smaller mills around the state, making it the second largest steel producing state. For this reason, union workers are a strong political force and the local economy suffers during economic downturns.

Strong unions are one source of corruption in the state. There were 40 public corruption convictions last year, but they were all low level convictions. Higher level corruption tends to be protected. Since the 1920s, Indiana has had a history of corruption and bribery at the level of Governor and Attorney General. County prosecutors and higher state judiciaries are complicit in overly aggressive efforts to take children from parents in order to extort federal incentives on child welfare, which is a typical problem in many states. There are also many examples of election fraud, especially in the Democratic counties on the shores of Lake Michigan.

Central Indiana is a broad flat plain with sandy loamy soil that makes for great farmland, but the central plains also have a good mix of forested land. The Whitewater Valley is noted for the best farming in the state. In northwest Indiana, there are sand hills and dunes built by lake and wind action. In the Kankakee River Basin there are a lot of lakes, marshes and prairies. The state is flat except for the tall moraine hills in the northeast.

Indianapolis is the largest city by far and encompasses about a million people. Only four other cities top 100K people: South Bend, Evansville, Gary and Fort Wayne (about 300,000).

Strategies for Populated Living Areas

Indianapolis: An extensive spoke-shaped freeway system and the White River divide the city into various trap zones, none of which are difficult to circumvent. There are no major threats of physical destruction to this city, so one must only prepare for social unrest, especially with its fairly large minority population. We recommend locating well outside the 465 beltway. The best retreat areas are in the forest to the SW, so we prefer the towns of Plainfield, Mooresville and Greenwood.

Fort Wayne: This is one of the few cities where the major beltway was built far into the countryside in anticipation of future growth. The outskirts of the city are within the beltway, so that is where you will most likely reside. It is still important to map out crossing points around the beltway barrier that don't have exits on them. The same goes for the I-69 N-S freeway to the west.

Evansville: This town sits on top of a big bend in the Ohio River just across from Kentucky and is surrounded by I-164 to the east, I-64 to the north and the Wabash River to the west. There are no particularly safe retreat areas close by but there is plenty of rural land within a 10 mile radius that should provide some medium term safety in a crisis.

South Bend: This major industrial town is bounded by I-80/90 to the north and by Hwy 20 on the west and the south. We strongly recommend locating SW of the city, outside Hwy 20. You need to travel about 40-50 miles SW to find rural farm areas with retreat potential.

Gary: This is a suburb of East Chicago. The only safe direction for getting out of the area is to the southeast, so locate on that side of the city in rural country.

Retreat Areas

Rural farmland: Rural farm retreats are not as safe as being in the hill country, but if you follow our guidelines about location and conceal for privacy, they can be fairly safe for all but massive social unrest where all of the cities empty out into the countryside looking for food. The secret is making sure you are not near a major refugee path (usually traveling down secondary roads). Indiana has lots of rural farm land, but little cover from being sighted from a long way off. We recommend underground concealed rooms for storage and safety.

Bloomington Area: The forested areas 5 or more miles outside this city in south-central Indiana provide the most potential for finding retreat property among a low population density and out of the way of refugee flows. The closest metro problem area is Clarksville and Louisville, Kentucky. The Ohio River may keep most of the Louisville people on the other side.

IOWA ★★☆☆☆

Summary Facts and Ratings

Climate:	Iowa lies in the humid continental zone and generally has hot summers, cold winters and wet springs. Iowa averages 35 tornados per year, which is high.
Population Density:	About average. 53 ppl/sq.mi. (35th ranking in the nation). Though the state remains mostly white, there is a steady influx of Latinos to do agricultural work. Hispanic 4.5%, black 2.8%, Asian 1.7%, mixed 1.1%.
Cost of Living Index:	Medium. 92 (average is 100) ranked 13th least expensive.
Private Land Availability:	Excellent. Only 1% of the land is state or federally owned.
Building Permits:	Permit requirements are very reasonable and are hardly required in rural counties like Clinton and Jackson but the biggest cities are onerous (Cedar Rapids requires a permit just to reroof). Basement potential is good in the deep soil except in river flood plains.
Land and Urban Planning:	There is no statewide comprehensive plan for zoning or land use, but there is a statewide Water Allocation and Use Plan.
Food Production:	Very good throughout the state. Long growing season of 180-240 days. Rainfall averages about 33 inches per year and usually eliminates the need to irrigate. Rich soil where it hasn't been depleted by modern agribusinesses. Crops cover 60% of the state, hay and grass cover 30%, and forests take up only 7%.
Health Environment:	Iowa ground water is cleaner than the average farm state but there are still concentrations of agricultural pollution and chemicals. Well water is good in non high-intensity agricultural areas. 92% of people's water is fluoridated (bad).
Traffic:	Low. Even Des Moines and Cedar Rapids are mild. Red light and speed cameras are used.
Politics:	Iowa has been a steady Democratic state for decades, but is getting more conservative over time. Dem 26.8%, Rep. 46.2%, Ind/3rd party 27%.
Taxes:	Average. Ranks as 31st highest taxes, with a state tax burden of 9.3% of income. Income tax is 0.4%-9% ($0 to $63K/year), property taxes are 15th highest in the nation and state and local sales taxes average 6.9%.
Corruption:	Moderate. Election fraud and corruption between judges, law enforcement and politicians.
Crime:	Below average. Violent crime 271/100K, property crime 2194/100K. As in most rural states, meth labs are increasing. Crime index in Des Moines is 7.
Personal Liberty:	Average, ranks 25th.
Gun Liberty:	Fair. Annually renewed permit is required to purchase handguns but rifle purchase is not restricted. "Shall issue" state for concealed weapon permits. CCW permits also allow firearm purchase and open carry (good for 5 years). Private party sales must have background check.
Alternative Medicine:	Natural health practitioners are free to practice in IA except direct entry midwives which are prohibited. School vaccine exemptions: religious and medical.
Home Schooling:	Moderate regulation. State requires parents to send notification, test scores, and/or professional evaluation of student progress. Iowa is proud of being where standardized testing was made famous.
Military Targets:	**Iowa Army Ammunition Plant**, west of Burlington. High explosive conventional munitions plant; secondary target. **Camp Dodge Johnston**, northeast of Des Moines. Iowa NG HQ; not a target. **Sioux City Airport**. ANG KC-135 air refueling; secondary target. **Ames Laboratory**, Iowa State University. Lab for energy resources, material processes. Historically part of Manhattan project; secondary target.
Nuclear Power Plant:	**Duane Arnold Plant**, NW of Cedar Rapids.

Notes

Iowa is typical of a Great Plains state with muggy summers, cold winters and lots of gradual rolling hills. There is good wind and solar potential in many parts of the state. Northwest Iowa is home to some of the largest concentrations of wind turbine farms in the world. Iowa is one of the better plains states for rural farm retreats as long as you are not next door to a large farm with GMO crops.

Politically, Iowa is a conflicted state. It was specifically chosen to hold the first political primary in presidential elections because the people pride themselves on being contrarian or independent-minded, but they seemed to be easily swayed by populist notions presented by politicians and the media. In truth, Iowa can't be pigeon holed in any uniform manner--there is simply a wide divergence of political opinion and one of several divergent factions can come to the forefront depending on how much political activism is directed toward them. Sometimes Democrats will prevail, and then Republicans or independents. For example, Iowa was at the forefront in promoting openness about gays, and then later three activist pro-homosexual State Supreme Court judges were thrown out of office by voters in 2010.

Iowa doesn't seem to lend itself to much corruption except in the dominate area of agriculture. There were 48 public corruption convictions last year. Republican governor-elect Branstad won the 2010 on a campaign to end the corruption under a former Democratic governor. There have been complaints about government lack of transparency and some police brutality has occurred. Former Iowa Governor, Tom Vilsack, actively pushed local legislation that strongly favored the giant agribusiness Monsanto and their genetically engineered seed products. Monsanto is famous for strong-arming and aggressively suing local farmers into only using their genetically modified seeds. Vilsack was known to travel via Monsanto's private jet. Vilsack was later appointed as Secretary of Agriculture by President Obama.

The only direct nuclear target is near Burlington where the Iowa Army Ammunition Plant stores and assembles a full variety of missile and ammunition warheads.

Strategies for Populated Living Areas

Des Moines: Des Moines is the largest city in Iowa, but just barely surpasses the half million mark. We offer no special instructions since there are no major threats near large cities in Iowa and no major metro areas. The only threats within cities come from the city's population density itself. Those near major freeways will have potential refugee problems someday. As always, locate near the outer limits of cities for maximum safety and maintain access to self-sufficient farm land.

Retreat Areas

Rural farmland: Northeast Iowa has many steep hills and deep valleys, checkered with forest and terraced fields, which helps for seclusion of a retreat. Our favorite area is northwestern Iowa where there are many small, friendly towns with family farms in hilly country with some trees. Avoid the area in SW Iowa around Council Bluffs. It is nice country but directly downwind of Offut AFB in Nebraska, a major nuclear target. We would also avoid low lying areas along the Mississippi river that are in the flood plain---and the weather in the Mississippi valley is extremely muggy in the summer.

KANSAS ★★⯪☆☆

Summary Facts and Ratings

Climate:	The eastern two-thirds of the state (especially the northeastern portion) have a humid continental climate with very cold winters and hot, humid summers. Most of the precipitation falls in the summer and spring. The western third of the state is semi-arid like eastern Colorado. Summers are hot and less humid. Winters are cold but can get warmer Chinook winds from the south. The far south-central and southeastern reaches of the state have a similar climate but a bit more rain in winter. Kansas has 48 tornados per year on average, 3rd worst in the nation.
Population Density	Below average: 34 ppl/sq.mi. (40th ranking in the nation). Hispanic 9.3%, Black 6.2%, Asian 2.3%, mixed 1.9%.
Cost of Living Index:	Lower. 90.9 (average is 100) ranked 8th cheapest.
Private Land Availability:	Excellent. Only 1% of the land is state or federally owned.
Building Permits:	Required statewide. Basements are not uncommon.
Land and Urban Planning:	City and county level. Some "Smart Growth" inroads on light rail transportation.
Food Production:	Very good. Growing season is 150 to 220 days. Precipitation is about 35 in/year in the east and 16-20 in/year in the west.
Health Environment:	Water Quality is not good in Kansas due to agricultural pollution and the state's reliance on wells. Elevated concentrations of the popular weed killer, Atrazine, infiltrates public drinking water across Kansas in April, May and June when spraying of farm chemicals is greatest and rainfall the heaviest. Chicken and hog farm operators tend to dump manure on their lands and it runs off into the water supply. 64% of people's water is fluoridated.
Traffic:	Moderate rush hour traffic in Kansas City and Wichita. Lawrence and Overland Park (KC suburb) have the largest number of speed traps in Kansas. Red light or speed cameras are used.
Politics:	Kansas used to be a fertile ground for Democratic Populism in the wake of the great depression, but has now turned into a conservative state. Dem 26%, Rep 47%, Ind/3rd party 27%.
Taxes:	Average: ranked 25th, with a tax burden of 9.4% of income. High income taxes, sales tax is 5.3%, property taxes are 13th highest in the nation.
Corruption:	Good old boy network very prominent in this state. There is a lot of police corruption and judges are often complicit in the cover-ups.
Crime:	High violent crime: 340/100K. Property crime is above average: 2947/100K. Crime index for Kansas City is 4 (100 is safest).
Personal Liberty:	Average, ranked 26th.
Gun Liberty:	Fair. No permit to purchase firearms. "Shall issue" state for concealed permits. Open carry is legal in most areas.
Alternative Medicine:	Good availability, full range of natural health practitioners. Direct-entry midwives allowed by lack of statute or regulation. School vaccine exemptions: religious and medical.
Home Schooling:	Low regulation. State only requires parental notification.
Military Targets:	**Fort Riley**, SE of Manhattan. "Home of the Army." Armor units and aviation; primary target. **Fort Leavenworth**. Training college and high security military prison; not a target. **Kansas Army Ammunition Plant**, near Parson. Mostly inactive ammunition storage site; tertiary target. **McConnell AFB**, SE Wichita. Air Force KC-135 refueling; primary target. **Forbes AFB** (Previously Topeka Army Airfield). ANG KC-135 refueling; secondary target.
Nuclear Power Plant:	**Wolf Creek Plant**, Burlington. Began operation 1985, 1 reactor.

Notes

Kansas is the geographic center of the US, which provides good access to many parts of the country as well as distance from border threats. Kansas is one of the most productive agricultural states, producing mostly wheat, sorghum and sunflowers. Big agricultural businesses are squeezing out the family farms leaving many people to seek better options in the big cities. This trend has made KS one of the slowest growing states in the nation and has created over 6000 ghost towns and many empty barns and farm houses.

What remains is still a prairie state with a combination of discouraged but hard working farm families (still diminishing) and lots of big city corruption. This combination has made for a bad history of exploitation of the poor farmers being manipulated by politicians to vote for populist and democratic subsidy schemes during the Depression. But the religious roots of most farm families have allowed Kansans to finally forge a conservative majority in the state. Kansas has not elected a Democrat to the US Senate since the 1932 election.

Corruption that is endemic to a large metropolis never goes away completely. Kansas City has been the capitol of state corruption ever since the years of Tom Pendergast and his political machine built itself up around the "Good ol' Boy" network that linked police and politicians together in immoral businesses. Even though a major reform took place in the 40s, the machine just went farther underground. Corruption, gambling, vice and kickbacks are all still there, just more hidden. There were 46 public corruption convictions last year. Kansas also has problems with a corrupt and arrogant Department of Human Services. Case workers have long had absolute immunity from negligent and criminal behavior, which has produced no shortage of family custody horror stories.

Oil and water are both important natural resources in Kansas. It ranks 8th in oil and natural gas production, but the oil is declining rapidly. Water irrigation is necessary in western parts of the state (KS was one of the dust bowl states). There is some access to parts of the Ogallala aquifer but nothing compared to Nebraska. Kansas has the Dakota aquifer which is being depleted faster than it can be replenished each year. The salt beds and brine-containing aquifers that are near the surface in much of central Kansas cause wells in those areas to have a salty taste. Consistent farm water can be had along the various rivers and most places with well water.

Several large aircraft corporations have manufacturing facilities in Wichita and Kansas City, in addition to several military contractors like Raytheon and the Kansas City Nuclear Plant (on the Missouri side of the city).

Threats in this state are primarily from tornados and military targets. Nuclear threats are few but significant: McConnell AFB in the SE corner of Wichita and the nuclear manufacturing plant in Kansas City. Additionally, a new security campus of the National Nuclear Security administration is being built east of Olathe just across the MO border. Kansas is in the heart of "Tornado Alley" and has more F5 hurricanes per year than any other state, although Iowa has more per sq. mile. In any case, we consider the tornado shelter a necessity here—and make sure it doubles as a fallout shelter.

Strategies for Populated Living Areas

Kansas City: The city sits astride the Missouri border and has a high crime rate as well as a threat of a direct nuclear strike on the nuclear manufacturing plant in the city. This target is on the Missouri side, so select a western location. Overland Park and Olathe are the best of the suburban areas, although you have to deal with a fair amount of bad traffic if you commute into the city. Be sure and check out the high crime maps for KC at neighborhoodscout.com—they might surprise you.

Wichita: Stay to the north and west of the city to find safety and low crime areas. The southeast area should be avoided because of McConnell AFB.

Topeka: Aside from the fact that it is located on a major freeway, there are a lot of rural suburban areas north and south that are very nice. We also like the river valley towns east and west of the city (Grantville and Silver Lake). Grantville is just west of the Billiard community airport.

Retreat Areas

Rural hill country: You can find good rolling hill farm country north and south of Kansas City. The farther you are from the city the greater the safety, but sometimes a compromise is necessary for access to work and shopping. We like the rolling hill counties west of St. Joseph, MO. They have a low population density and no major roads intrude into this area. The same can be said of the SE corner of Kansas around the towns of Independence, Thayer and Parsons.

Western Kansas: The prairie land here creates more wide open spaces than in east Kansas but it's lower in population density. If you can find good well water, and stay far away from major highways, medium term security and self-sufficiency are possible. Be aware that this area will likely be downwind of Colorado's nuclear targets, so prepare a shelter system for tornados and fallout.

KENTUCKY ★★★☆☆

Summary Facts and Ratings

Climate:	Humid subtropical climate, hot summers and cold winters. KY averages 9 tornados per year.
Population Density:	Moderately high: 109 ppl/sq.mi. (22nd rank in the nation). Black 7.9%, Hispanic 2.7%, mixed 1.1%, Asian 1.1%.
Cost of Living Index:	90 (Average is 100) ranked fifth least expensive state.
Private Land Availability:	Good. Only 3.5% of the land is state or federally owned.
Building Permits:	Required everywhere for most new construction and renovations. However, smaller rural counties have more relaxed requirements. Basement construction is feasible, but rock layers under the soil make it expensive in much of the state.
Land and Urban Planning:	KY has a state planning law, but no sanctions nor incentives for counties to comply. About 1/3 of counties don't have a comprehensive plan.
Food Production:	Good with a growing season of 150-210 days on the plains, 30 days less in the mountains. Rainfall averages about 48 inches per year. Rich soil in most places and good gardening, but rocky in areas like the mountains.
Health Environment:	Surface water pollution is about average, and ground water away from commercial farms is fine. 99.9% of people's water is fluoridated—all cities.
Traffic:	Traffic problems in Louisville, but not one of the 75 worst traffic cities. Lexington also has traffic because it was designed as a quaint southern town, not a busy tourist center. Traffic can be slow near racing tracks and other tourist destinations. No red light or speed cameras in KY.
Politics:	Kentuckians are mostly very conservative and religious, but until 2010 the state was evenly split between Democrats and Republicans. A major conservative shift in 2010 elected a staunch conservative-libertarian for US Senate. Protecting Kentucky's massive coal industry has always been a powerful issue. Dem 57.5%, Rep 36.0%, Ind/3rd party 6.5%.
Taxes:	Average. Ranked 23rd highest with a tax burden of 9.5% of income. It has average income tax and slightly higher property taxes (32nd in nation), plus a 6% sales tax.
Corruption:	High in the cities.
Crime:	Below average. Violent crime 210/100K, property crime 2362/100K. Crime index: Louisville is 6 (nearly double the state average). Crime in Lexington is 9 - low compared to similar sized cities.
Personal Liberty:	Average. Ranked 26.
Gun Liberty:	Very good. No permit to purchase firearms. "Shall issue" state for concealed permits. Open carry state, even in a car.
Alternative Medicine:	Natural health practitioners are free to practice, but Lay midwifery is prohibited, which is a bad sign of medical doctor control in the legislature. School vaccine exemptions: religious and medical.
Home Schooling:	Low regulation. State requires parental notification only.
Military Targets:	**Fort Knox**, 15 miles SW of Louisville. Armor school, 1st infantry, bullion deposit (with no audit no one knows if there's any gold in the depository); secondary target. **Fort Campbell**, SW on the TN border. Army airborne school, reserve aviation fighters; secondary target. **Blue Grass Army Depot**, near Richmond. Conventional and chemical weapons storage; secondary target. **Louisville Airport**. ANG C-130. Not a target.
Nuclear Power Plant:	**Paducah Plant**, on Ohio River. Uranium enrichment plant that was shut down in 2013. Currently undergoing cleanup operations. Not a target.

Notes

Kentucky is known for 3 major products: Horses, coal and bourbon. Lexington is the city that best exemplifies the fine southern country lifestyle of this state. It is the center of horse country and much of the bourbon whiskey industry as well. The farms are beautifully kept and sometimes palatial. There are still lots of family farms in western Kentucky where the flattest ground lies.

Kentucky is a state much like Tennessee with good retreat geography and terrain, but with none of the benefits of low taxes. It also has the disadvantage of being too close to the Eastern population centers. Corruption level is about the same as other southern states (very high), but crime is low.

There were only 8 public corruption convictions last year, which attests to the Good ol' Boy's ability to cover up misdeeds. Six county officials were arrested for changing electronic votes and teaching other election officers to do the same thing. A Circuit Court judge and a Superintendant of Schools were a controlling part of the process. Then there was the Bluegrass Conspiracy in the 70s and 80s about corruption in the Lexington police department—organized crime, drug running, corrupt cops. These kinds of actions are more carefully covered up now, but still there.

Coal production is mostly concentrated in all of the eastern mountain counties. The following western counties surrounding Madisonville also have large coal deposits: Butler, Christian, Crittenden, Daviess, Henderson, Hopkins, McLean, Muhlenberg, Ohio, Union, Webster. You can often get cheap land in these counties because all the mineral rights have been sold off. Sometimes, that can mean significant disruption to your land, so we recommend locating in non coal counties for farms. The best retreats sites, however, are all found in eastern Kentucky. One must still be careful buying land, especially if it has been reclaimed.

Strategies for Populated Living Areas

Louisville is a typical Ohio River town with the full range of high rise office towers and run down old sections. This city has higher-than-average rates of cardiovascular disease, diabetes, asthma and obesity. Blue collar Whites and African Americans are particularly prone to these problems. Poor quality water and air, plus chemical pollution are also endemic here. Louisville is also the center of corruption in the state.

Louisville backs up against the Ohio River on the north and west, which only has 3 bridges crossing to Indiana—a formidable barrier to travel or retreat in a crisis. There are two beltways around the non-river side of the city, 264 and 265. In a situation of social unrest, you don't want to get trapped inside a sea of humanity, so locate outside the 265 beltway.

There are many upscale and lovely communities inside the beltways, but the risk of not being able to get out increases. If you do locate inside either beltway, be sure and scope out underpasses or overpasses that do not have a freeway exit in order to have a better chance of unimpeded crossing in a crisis.

Lexington is a safe town during normal times, but could still become panicky in a crisis of no public services, so it pays to locate on the periphery of development. The other problem is I-75 which blocks easy access to the mountains. If you have a mountain retreat to the east, we would suggest locating on that side of I-75 and south of I-64 heading into West Virginia. The towns of Winchester and Mt. Sterling are ideal for being fairly close to Lexington but are also very close to the mountains.

Bowling Green is a fine city in the midst of the agricultural belt and is a great small city with friendly people and low crime. It is surrounded with country farms and many patches of forest and trees. While getting trapped inside a small town during social unrest is not probable, Bowling Green is surrounded by freeways and small rivers which present lots of trap zones and few roads over the rivers. Map out several routes out of the city that match your retreat direction.

Retreat Areas

Rural farmland: Rural farm retreats are not as safe as being in the hill country, but if you follow our guidelines about locating for privacy, they can be almost as good. The secret is making sure you are not near a major refugee path (usually traveling down secondary roads). Kentucky has the advantage of huge swaths of forested land out in the main farm areas of the state. If you look on the satellite view of any internet map site, you can see a very broad swath of forest land starting just south of Louisville and meandering back and forth, east and west off I-65 on its way south to Bowling Green. When you find farm land backed up to these forested areas, you get both farm self-sufficiency and forested retreat privacy.

Eastern Kentucky Mountains: This is all coal country, but the region is highly depressed financially as coal has been strangled by environmental regulations. The forestation is heavy and the eastern counties have hundreds of small, mostly dying towns. The down side is that newcomers to the area are looked upon with some suspicion. Why would anyone want to come to a place where there are few jobs? There is lots of private land available with many water courses. You have to be careful of pollution from mining as well as the uncertainties of not owning the mineral rights under your property.

LOUISIANA ★☆☆☆☆

Summary Facts and Ratings

Climate:	Louisiana is the most humid of the subtropical areas of the south-central US. It has long, hot summers and short, mild winters. Heat and humidity produce frequent thunderstorms in the summer, on average 60 days of thunderstorms each year. On average 27 tornados occur here each year.
Population Density:	Moderately high: 103 ppl/sq mile (24th ranking in the nation). Black 32%, Hispanic 3.6%, Asian 1.5%, mixed 1.1%.
Cost of Living Index:	Below average. 93.4 (average is 100) and ranked 19th least expensive.
Private Land Availability:	Good. Only 7.6% of the land is state or federally owned.
Building Permits:	Required for any new construction and significant renovations or demolition. Due to high water table only about 50% of the state can have basements.
Land and Urban Planning:	Louisiana does not have a centralized state planning agency. It delegates the authority to plan and zone state growth to a number of state agencies.
Food Production:	Very good with a growing season of 240-270 days. There is a higher incidence of blight, mold and insects typical of warm climates. Rainfall averages about 65 inches per year. Rich soil for good gardening but sometimes too wet.
Health Environment:	Louisiana ground water pollution is one of the worst in the nation, due to heavy shipping and chemical factories along the Mississippi seaway. Only streams up north are clean. 43% of the population's water is fluoridated (major cities).
Traffic:	Heavy traffic problems in New Orleans along I-10 (#27 of 75 bad traffic cities). LA does use red light and speed cameras.
Politics:	Despite chronic corruption locally, Louisiana folk are fairly conservative (60/40 conservative/liberal split even though Democratic registrations outnumber Republicans by 2:1). Republicans swept most offices in 2010. Dem 55.4%, Rep 24%, Ind/3rd party 21%.
Taxes:	Low. 5th lowest in the nation, with an average tax burden of 7.6% of income. Income tax up to 6%, plus a 4% sales tax but property taxes are lowest in US.
Corruption:	Very high. Louisiana has a chronic reputation of being the most corrupt state in the union, from judges on down to police and even congressional politicians.
Crime:	High violent crime 519/100K, property crime rate is 3582/100K. Crime rate in New Orleans is only 3/4 the state average, but that's because New Orleans' police fudge the numbers. Crime index for Baton Rouge is 5, New Orleans 5 (100 safest).
Personal Liberty:	Low: 37th in the nation.
Gun Liberty:	Good. No permit to purchase firearms. "Shall issue" state for concealed handgun permits. Open carry friendly state.
Alternative Medicine:	Natural health practitioners are free to practice. Lay midwifery in the state is legal and regulated. School vaccine exemptions: philosophical, religious and medical.
Home Schooling:	Moderate regulation. State requires parents to send notification, test scores, and/or professional evaluation of student progress.
Military Targets:	**Fort Polk**, 7 mi. south of Leesville. Army training center; not a target. **Louisiana Ordinance Plant**, Minden. Conventional mortars and artillery munitions manufacturing; secondary target. **Camp Beauregard**, NE of Alexandria. NG training facility; not a target. **New Orleans Naval Air Station**, Joint reserve base. Marine Corps F-18 and ANG; secondary target. **Barksdale AFB**, E of Shreveport. B-52 strategic bombers; primary target.
Nuclear Power Plants, Oil Reserve Sites:	**River Bend Nuclear Power Plant**, St. Francisville, 1 reactor. **West Hackberry Strategic Petroleum Reserves,** near Lake Charles, 227 million barrels; secondary target. **Bayou Choctaw Strategic Petroleum Reserves,** near Baton Rouge, 76 million barrels; secondary target.

Notes

New Orleans and southern Louisiana are quite distinct from the central and northwestern areas. Not only is New Orleans the cradle of crime here, it (along with Baton Rouge) is the home of many chemical companies. These two cities are constantly facing the risks of pollution and the further threat of death should a major attack fall on those river and industrial areas. Worse, there are very few escape routes out of New Orleans, as everyone found out during Hurricane Katrina. It is easy to get trapped between Lake Pontchartrain and the city when everyone is trying to get out at the same time. At that time corruption, looting (even by police) and martial law made true the old adage "Nowhere to run, nowhere to hide." There are more than 100 petro-chemical facilities located along the Mississippi River between Baton Rouge and New Orleans. Even part of New Orleans was built on a toxic landfill. Meth labs also abound in the ghettos of this area and have made inroads into the rural areas.

We further downgraded our rating because of major corruption in state and local affairs. It's mostly petty greed and power but there is no greater example in the US of the Good ol' Boy network. Their ability to cover up almost all corruption is seen in the fact that there were only 4 convictions for public corruption last year amid hundreds of potential cases. Congressman William Jefferson was sentenced to 13 years in prison for taking millions in cash bribes. Louisiana police, state and local, are notorious for making traffic stops looking for revenue. A high number of complaints were filed after Hurricane Katrina of police abuse of authority, rough treatment and excessive force. New Orleans cops are very corrupt and often inept.

The prime military targets are the chemical plants (turning the area into an instant death zone) and Barksdale AFB, home of many of the remaining B-52 bombers, nuclear weapons, the 8th Air Force and one fighter wing. It is just east of Shreveport and south of I-20.

Strategies for Populated Living Areas

New Orleans: Our first advice is to not settle in this city, period. This city rivals Manhattan in that it is nearly surrounded by water traps. Worse, there are few routes out of the area except on freeways and causeways, which are certain to be jammed in a major crisis or shut down by authorities. Some try to avoid the crush of New Orleans by living around the north shore of Lake Pontchartrain, but the commute into the city over I-10 or the Lake Pontchartrain Causeway is a risky scheme. The north shore communities of Mandeville and Covington Springs, or Slidell and Pearl River can give you better and quicker escapes to the north, but not if you are trapped in the city when a sudden crisis happens. We would only recommend this if you don't have to commute each day, or if you have no other choice. It's better than living in the trap zone full time. We believe that a slightly less risky alternative is to live in the SW suburbs like Willowdale that put you on the west side

of the Mississippi with close access to HWY 90 leading further west to Lafayette. There are some secondary roads roughly paralleling I-10, but they all lead to the Baton Rouge area which is bound to be another trap zone. The big problem overall in devising exit routes out of the New Orleans area is that virtually all the roads cross bayous and swamps with no possibility of getting off the road and four-wheeling it around traffic jams. Once on these roads, you're stuck.

Baton Rouge: While better than New Orleans, you still have the Mississippi river and various freeway trap zones to deal with. As usual, pick the area of the city that gives you unimpeded access to your retreat direction. If north, locate on the periphery of Baton Rouge between I-12 and I-110. If you want to exit west to Texas, locate on the Port Allen side of the river but close to Hwy 190, your best route out to the Opelousas area. Be sure to map out crossings of I-49 where there are no freeway exits.

Smaller Coastal Cities: We prefer Lafayette to Lake Charles because it has much fewer traps zones. Lake Charles is surrounded by rivers with very few exits. Lafayette is fairly wide open. Pick a spot north of the I-10 freeway.

Shreveport: Because of the military bases on the east side of the city, the safest areas are to the west in Texas. We recommend locations outside the 220 beltway and in the southwest sector between I-49 and I-20. That gives you several routes toward Carthage, Texas. The northwest sector outside 220 is also safe from the military threats, but there are a lot more rivers, lakes and water traps that could limit your retreat. It is, however, the best area if your retreat is in the Ozarks of Arkansas, via Hwy 71.

Retreat Areas

Rural farmland: There are marginal farm retreats located above the E-W Hwy 190 (several miles north and somewhat parallel to Hwy I-10). This gives you some distance from the larger cities along I-10. There are several state and national forests around Alexandria in the center of the state that have small rural towns around them. That's where to start. There is no strategically defensive hill country since the highest hill is only 500 ft. high. Don't forget the hurricane and flooding threat in the south.

The other slightly safer area is in the north near the Arkansas border above I-20. Stay at least 5 miles away from the freeway and also away from N-S secondary roads feeding to and from I-20. This, coupled with a location shielded by trees and small forests, gives you the highest probability of maintaining your privacy from roaming refugees. Keep in mind, however, that this won't ensure long-term safety in an area with this much population density. Eventually, you will have to defend yourself against point threats from specific groups of mobile marauders.

MAINE ★★★☆☆

Summary Facts and Ratings

Climate:	Humid coastal climate. Summers are moderately hot and humid with lots of insects. Winters are cold, down to -30 and -40 degrees with deep snow. Winter on the coast is moderated by the ocean and is comparable to upstate New York.
Population Density:	Below average. 42.7 ppl/sq mile (ranked 40th in the nation). Hispanic 1.4%, Black 1.2%, Asian 1%, mixed 1.1%.
Cost of Living Index:	Moderate. 115 (average is 100) makes this the 13th most expensive state.
Land Ownership:	Very good, only 5.3 % of the land is state or federally owned.
Building Permits:	Required for all new construction. Basements are not uncommon.
Land Use and Urban Planning:	Highly regulatory land use planning. The state plans and zones all unincorporated areas. The Maine Land Use Regulation Commission plans, zones and approves all developments in the unorganized and de-organized areas of the state.
Food Production:	The soil is very rocky, acidic and not particularly fertile except for blueberries. Aroostook County is known for potatoes. Growing season is fairly short, 90-120 days. Rainfall averages about 47 inches per year.
Health Environment:	One of the healthiest states for surface water cleanliness. Very little air pollution. 79.4% of public drinking water is fluoridated.
Traffic:	No major traffic problems. ME does not use red light and speed cameras.
Politics:	Independent voters outnumber both major political parties, but they most consistently vote for left/liberal causes. Dem 31%, Rep 28.7%, Ind/3rd party 40%.
Taxes:	High. One of the highest state and local tax burdens—11.2%. Income tax is 6.5-7.95%, property taxes are among the nation's highest and sales tax is 5.5%.
Corruption:	About average for the US - high. There is a lot of political corruption in Maine.
Crime:	Low - 1/3 the national average. Violent crime 129/100K, property crime 2292/100K. Crime index for Portland is 16, Bangor is 5.
Personal Liberty:	Low. Ranked 39th nationwide.
Gun Liberty:	Good. No permit to purchase firearms, but dealers must retain sales records. "Shall issue" state for concealed weapon permits. Open carry friendly state. Background checks are not (yet) required.
Alternative Medicine:	Natural health practitioners free to practice. Naturopathic Physicians can be licensed. The practice of lay midwifery is legal and unregulated. School vaccine exemptions: philosophical, religious and medical.
Home Schooling:	Must register with the state. State requires parents to send notification, test scores and/or professional evaluation of student progress.
Military targets:	**Bangor Airport**. ANG Air refueling; secondary target. **Portsmouth Naval Shipyard**. Remodel and repair of navy ships; secondary target. **Brunswick Naval Air Station**. Closing in 2011; not a target. **US Naval Radio Station**, Cutler. Very Low Frequency transmitter for submarine communication; primary target.

Notes

The best thing Maine has going for it is its backwoods country seclusion, considering it is the most heavily forested state in the nation. Unfortunately, you pay a price for this quality in mosquitoes and insects during the summer and with the cold in winter. Black Flies are a lot like gnats, but they come in thick swarms and their bites can draw blood. You won't enjoy being outdoors when they are thick no matter what you do. The forests of Maine also took a major hit during the ice storms of 1998 and 2008. Maine also boasts more than 3,000 miles of coast line.

As a state government, Maine has been begging for acceptance from the establishment and doing everything wrong about building a solid free market atmosphere for business. Maine is destined to always have a depressed economy, demanding handouts from the federal government. There are few jobs, and much of the timber is being logged off in the north. Large areas of forest are owned by paper companies. These owners fear the UN will designate this land as a wilderness heritage site and are trying to get their use of the land while they can.

Amity Shlaes writes in www.jewishworldreview.com that "Maine shunned the smaller government model, following an exclusive 'spend to grow' plan. Budgets increased each year; Washington funneled more cash into the state. Taxes stayed high. And Maine has stayed–in the words of its governor–'ambivalent' about courting investors from outside. The result has been an environment hostile to the entrepreneurial Everyman." Since 2009 Maine has improved slightly on fiscal policy, cutting taxes to be comparable to other (high) East Coast states like Vermont. They have brought state debt back to below average but still high for such a small state. As a result there has been a net gain in Maine's population in recent years.

Politically, the population is very liberal, reflecting the influence of Boston to the south. Maine has a reputation of pretending to be Republican, but always votes for the left/liberal agenda. Nothing is more symptomatic of this than Maine's RINO (Republican In Name Only) Senator Susan Collins, and the Independent (but Left voting) Senator Angus King. Maine is, for all the faults of its people and politicians, the safest physical location in the northeast USA with enough distance even for the population time bomb of the Boston area—and that is worth something. Except for taxes, having a retreat in Maine doesn't require that you have many dealings with the politicians or corrupt judges. If, however, a general round-up is decreed for dissidents in the US, you can be sure Maine's police will not object to the violation of your rights. One man brought his two daughters to a very remote cabin in the woods there and was surrounded by FBI (within a month) over a custody dispute in Florida. He never exposed himself to the authorities, stores, local/state government, etc. Some people are just suspicious of all newcomers.

Strategies for Populated Living Areas

Portland is Maine's largest city and is just big enough to be a source of social unrest if services are cut off. Strategic threats will come up the I-95 corridor from Boston, so it is safer to be outside the 295/95 beltway. Falmouth to the north is better yet, because it puts the city of Portland to your south to absorb the refugees.

Bangor is preferred over Portland and is the gateway to the Maine hinterland. You can safely locate anywhere around this city as long as you stay clear of the freeway. As always, the outskirts of town are better than inside in case you have to maneuver.

Retreat Areas

Highway 2 coming out of Gorham, NH represents the northern boundary of development in Maine. Above that highway, extended on toward Bangor, the state is riddled with lakes and rivers with very few roads. This makes for ideal retreat country, though it also creates numerous trap zones that are difficult to get around should you have to maneuver for safety. Know the back roads and rivers better than others and it becomes an advantage. Best recommendations for retreats are above this highway and Bangor.

That said, the most available cabins are in the more populated sections south of Hwy 2, and they are fairly safe if you can find a place away from well travelled roads and behind the cover of trees and forest. The long-term danger is of people fanning out into the country side searching for food and shelter once the cities become unlivable through panic and crime.

MARYLAND ★☆☆☆☆

Summary Facts and Ratings

Climate:	Most of the lowlands fall within the humid subtropical climate zone. Coastal areas of the state have fairly mild winters. Summers are hot and muggy. MD averages 3 tornadoes a year.
Population Density:	High. 592 ppl/sq mile (5th highest in nation). Black 30%, Hispanic 5.5%, Asian 5.3%, mixed 1.1%.
Cost of Living Index:	High. 122 (average is 100) making this the 11th most expensive state.
Land Ownership:	7% of the land is state and federally owned.
Building Permits:	Required for new structure or remodeling. Normally only county permits are needed for construction projects, but some towns and cities may also require a local permit.
Land and Urban Planning:	MD has state-wide planning. The government brags about its Smart Growth program.
Food Production:	Good productivity in the central farm area of the Piedmont. The growing season is 180 to 200 days per year. Precipitation averages 43 inches annually.
Health Environment:	Some of the worst surface water pollution in the country. Aquifer water quality is not very good even in rural areas due to agricultural pollution, but mountain water is fine. Air quality around Baltimore is poor. Most of the EPA superfund sites are located in the most populous corridor and include landfills. 97% of the population's drinking water is fluoridated—very bad.
Traffic:	Baltimore has the 21st worst traffic in the nation. MD uses red light and speed cameras.
Politics:	Maryland is a reliable democratic state whose high percentages of black residents maintain powerful roots in the Democratic Party. Dem 54.6 %, Rep 30%, Ind/3rd party 16%.
Taxes:	Very high. Ranked 7th highest nationally with a tax burden of 10.6% of income which is well above the national average of 9.8%. 2%-5.75% progressive income tax rate, property taxes are average and its sales tax rate is 6%.
Corruption:	High. Corrupt state politicians, links to organized crime, big bank fraud, local nepotism and insider favors.
Crime:	Very high. Violent crime 474/100K, property crime 2664/100K. Crime index for Baltimore is 3 (100 is safest) where violent crime is nearly 4 times the national average.
Personal Liberty:	Bad. Ranked in 44th place nationally.
Gun Liberty:	Bad. No permit to purchase firearms, but handgun buyers must work through licensed dealers and undergo fingerprinting and target training. The state, thus maintains a firearm registry on all new weapons. "Assault weapons" are banned. Permits to carry firearms openly or concealed "may be issued" by the secretary of the Maryland State Police (MP) if applicants can demonstrate a "good and substantial reason."
Alternative Medicine:	Alternative medicine is discouraged by medical practice laws but is largely unprosecuted. Lay midwifery is prohibited by statute. School vaccine exemptions: religious and medical.
Home Schooling:	Moderate regulation. State requires parents to send notification, test scores and/or professional evaluation of student progress.

Military Targets:	**Aberdeen Proving Grounds** and Edgewood Chemical Activity. Chemical research, testing grounds and unknown chemical storage; secondary target.
	Fort Detrick, outside Frederick. Biological weapons and communications link for Raven Rock, PA, the Pentagon's bunkers; primary target.
	Fort Meade, near Odenton. NSA HQ and offices for various Department of Defense and government organizations; primary target.
	NAS Patuxent River, east of Lexington Park. Naval Research Institute, Navy flight testing and test pilot training; secondary target.
	Blossom Point Field Test Facility, 25 mi. south of DC. Satellite control and tracking center on restricted land labeled as testing range; primary or secondary target.
	Andrews Air Force Base, SE of DC. Global communications, Air Force One, support fighters, helicopters, refueling, High frequency global radio transmitter for nuclear forces; primary target.
	Globecom Radio Receiving Station and US Naval Receiving station, 2 locations south of Andrew's AFB. Central communications station for defense network including UHF to satellites; primary targets.
	Camp David, White House, US Naval Observatory. President and vice-president's bunkers (some in DC area); primary and secondary targets.
	NSS Annapolis. Very Low Frequency (VLF) transmitter - all but 3 towers are demolished; secondary target at best.
	Naval Surface Warfare Center Indian Head, south of DC. Research and development of warheads and weapons; secondary target.

Notes

Maryland has a lot of variety in geography and climate. There are sand dunes, lowland marshes in the coastal areas, oak country in the Piedmont middle region and farms and pines in the western mountains. Unfortunately, it is too deeply connected to the Washington DC metro area with its government and military installations to provide much safety. It is not a large state so citizens can't find much safety in the countryside. The state is trapped on the east by the Chesapeake Bay and on the west by the mountains which are home to various US bunkers and thus a nuclear target.

Corruption always follows power and few states are centered around as much power as Maryland. Mark Sapperstein, an accused Maryland/Florida crime syndicate boss, was sued for criminal contempt of court for falsifying an affidavit in a FL RICO suit about a $9 million payment made to Sapperstein by Pinnacle Towers (out of Sarasota Florida), a $325 million IPO underwritten by Goldman Sachs. Former Baltimore mayor Sheila Dixon gave no-bid contracts to companies that employed her sister and her former campaign chairman. She resigned after being convicted of embezzlement. There is also a lot of corruption in Maryland's prison system.

Overall, we rate this state very poorly in security because of many nuclear targets, high crime levels, high population density, corruption and liberal politics. Most of these problems are a result of being near Washington DC (see Virginia for limited information on the capitol).

Strategies for Populated Living Areas

Baltimore: This city has nothing going for it. It has both polluted air and water, and is home to major chemical companies near the bay. It has a high minority population with a high crime rate and some of the worst corruption. The city is trapped on the east by the bay, Washington DC metro area to the south and the Susquehanna River to the north. The only safe place is to be outside the 695 beltway, north of I-70 and to the west of I-83.

Retreat Areas

General advice: Because the state narrows to the north as it goes west, there is very little rural farm land to find safety. The best retreats will be farther to the south and the west into West Virginia or Virginia. The eastern part of Maryland on the Delaware Peninsula is almost completely separated from the mainland. This would only provide a short to medium term benefit as the only entrance or exit by land is very narrow and dominated by fairly high population densities. A retreat here would most likely require a boat option for getting to or from the area if your work took you off the peninsula every day. You would certainly have to prepare concealed underground safe areas in your home for fallout and to avoid confrontation with eventual refugees searching the area.

MASSACHUSETTS ★☆☆☆☆

Summary Facts and Ratings

Climate:	The eastern part of the state has cold winters and moderately warm summers. The Berkshires in the west have both the coldest winters and the coolest summers. The coastal areas have milder winters.
Population Density:	Very high: 841 ppl/sq mile (3rd highest in nation). Hispanic 8.8%, Black 7.1%, Asian 5.1%, mixed 1.5%. Most of the population is concentrated in the Boston area.
Cost of Living Index:	High. 130 (average is 100) ranked 6th most expensive state.
Land Ownership:	Very good. 5.5% of the land is state or federally owned.
Building Permits:	Required for all new construction and are strictly enforced. Basements can be built in most places in the east, with strong waterproofing against damp soil. There are some problems with rock in the Berkshire region.
Land and Urban Planning:	The Commonwealth of Massachusetts delegates primary planning authority to municipalities, but there is a fair amount of pressure from the state to accept "Smart Growth" restrictions.
Food Production:	The soil is Paxton type glaciated soil—rocky, acidic and not particularly fertile. But it holds water well. Growing season is good with 120-150 days. Rainfall occurs about once every three days through the year averaging around 47 inches total.
Health Environment:	Highly polluted air in the Boston metro, but much more healthy in the western hills. Way above average surface water pollution, particularly in the coastal plains and Boston. 70% of public drinking water is fluoridated.
Traffic:	Boston has the 14th worst traffic in the nation. No red light and speed cameras.
Politics:	Independent voters outnumber both major political parties, but they still vote mostly Democratic and for many left-liberal causes. MA is considered a safe Democratic state. For a Republican to win, he must pander to the state's liberal demands. Dem 37%, Rep 13%, Ind/3rd party 50%.
Taxes:	High. State tax burden is 10.3% of income, 11th highest. Income tax is a flat 5.15% and property taxes are about average. State sales tax is 6.25%.
Corruption:	High. Politicians are notorious for receiving luxury accommodations on the tab of private lobbyists. There are many reports of police officers caught drunk driving who are let off easy even if involved in serious collisions (this is a problem in many police dept.'s around the country).
Crime:	Very high for violent crime 413/100K. Property crime is a moderate 2,051/100K. Most crime is centered around the Boston area. Crime index: Boston is 14 (safer than 14% of other cities), Lexington is 85.
Personal Liberty:	Bad: 30th in the nation.
Gun Liberty:	Highly restrictive. Certain firearm purchases require a permit that is valid for 10 days. "May issue" state with two classes of licenses allowing possession and concealment of certain types of weapons for 4 years. Class A: large capacity firearms, rifles, and shotguns. Class B: non-large capacity firearms and large capacity rifles and shotguns. Open carry only with a license.
Alternative Medicine:	Although there are many well-trained naturopathic doctors in this state, naturopathic medicine is not currently licensed in MA. There is an active effort to pass licensing legislation by the Massachusetts Society of Naturopathic Doctors (msnd.org), but their efforts have failed so far, largely due to heavy opposition from the Massachusetts Medical Society. The practice of lay midwifery is legal and unregulated. School vaccine exemptions: religious and medical.
Home Schooling:	High regulation. Parents must register with the state; send notification, achievement test scores and/or professional evaluation and fulfill other requirements.

Military Targets:	**Fort Devens**, SE of Lowell. Army reserve training site; not a significant target.
	Natick Laboratories, W of Boston. Army Soldier Systems Center; not a target.
	US Army Reserve Center, S of Boston. Command center of US army reserve; not a target.
Military Targets continued:	**Hanscom AFB**, Boston area. Air Force electronics systems center; secondary target.
	Otis AGB, Buzzards Bay. ANG base and precision radar warning system; primary target.
	Westover AFB, N of Springfield. Airlift air reserve base; secondary target.
	Barnes Airport. ANG base; not a significant target.
Nuclear Power Plant:	**Pilgrim Nuclear Power Plant**, Plymouth. 1 reactor activated in 1972.

Notes

Massachusetts is dominated by the Boston area, which is extremely liberal and crime ridden. There are no major nuclear threats to the state, but the potential of massive social unrest emanating from the Boston area is very real. The eastern coastal plains will also be a major path northward for refugees fleeing the New York metro area. Massachusetts is a highly regulated state.

Massachusetts had 25 public corruption convictions last year. In 2008 a state senator took a $10,000 bribe and collected over $70,000 in illicit donations during the decade. The FBI sting operation that caught him eventually netted a mayor, city council president and other state senators for their part in the corruption scheme. There are also numerous reports of citizen abuse by law enforcement. This pattern is pervasive in Massachusetts where police are never investigated and the Attorney General never sees any public corruption. In their ranking of *Freedom in the 50 States*, The Mercatus Center reports MA has "the worst possible asset forfeiture laws" and "completely fails to check eminent domain abuse."

Western Massachusetts does offer some respite from the crowding of the east. The Berkshire Mountains have long been a haven of summer homes for the rich. Because of that, there will be a tendency for people to flow out of the Boston area seeking refuge toward the west. We would expect that any retreat in western MA would eventually be overrun by unwanted people seeking safety. It will also receive those refugees fleeing from states to the south when they become overwhelmed.

Strategies for Populated Living Areas

Boston metro area has such a high density population that you really have to locate outside the 495 Beltway in order to have any chance of getting out during a panic. We would recommend the NW sector as the best avenue for retreat. You want to avoid being sandwiched in between Boston and Worcester. If you want to retreat west, stay to that side of Worcester itself. Be aware too that there are many small lakes and rivers throughout the coastal plain route leaving the Boston and Worcester areas, so map out various escape routes carefully to avoid these traps. You must also give Fort Devens a wide berth. To get east to the Berkshires, we suggest going north on route 2 rather than trying to follow I-90 to the west, which will surely be clogged at Springfield.

Cape Cod: Avoid getting trapped in the Cape Cod peninsula (anything east of I-95 between Providence and Boston) as there is no way out once the I-95 corridor becomes a mass of fleeing humanity. If you already live in this area, be prepared to hunker down in concealed safe rooms, because you will have to deal with refugees and pillagers. If you live near the coast, be sure and make secure arrangements for a seaworthy boat as your best way to exit the area. We don't consider either of the two offshore islands (Martha's Vineyard and Nantucket) suitable safe havens. An island may give you distance from trouble on the mainland for a while, but when trouble comes ashore, you have no good escape without a fast boat—and it better be fast to outrun predator boats.

Retreat Areas

The Berkshires: Only the small Berkshire Mountains west of I-91 provide any degree of safety in Massachusetts. We prefer the sector north of I-95—the interstate itself will help serve as a barrier to people fleeing northward through Connecticut. Because this area will eventually receive some refugees, you must take great care to locate where you have extra privacy and can conceal safe rooms and stores to avoid confrontation.

MICHIGAN ★★★☆☆

Summary Facts and Ratings

Climate:	Continental climate with hot, humid summers and cold winters. Temperatures are warmer in the Lower Peninsula. MI averages 18 tornados per year.
Population Density:	Moderately high. 175 ppl/sq mile (17th highest in the nation). Black 14.2%, Hispanic 4.2%, Asian 2.4%, mixed 1.6%.
Cost of Living Index:	Average. 91.2 (average is 100) ranked 9th least expensive state.
Private Land Availability:	Good. 22% of the land is state and federally owned.
Building Permits:	Required everywhere for most new construction and renovations of existing buildings. Deep soil allows for many basements except in a few northern areas where the water table is high.
Land Use and Urban Planning:	Michigan requires a local comprehensive plan, but the statute does not require internal consistency nor consistency between local regulations and developments and the master or county plan.
Food Production:	Fair productivity with a growing season of 90-120 in the north to 150-180 days in the south. Rainfall averages about 35 inches per year (more, depending on lake effect). Rich soil in most places.
Health Environment:	Surface water pollution is some of the worst in the nation. Ground water is only bad around commercial farms that sometimes pollute the aquifers. The Upper Peninsula (UP) has much better water all around. 90% of the public's drinking water is fluoridated—bad.
Traffic:	Heavy traffic problems in Detroit, which is rated as #39 of the 75 worst traffic cities. No red light or speed cameras.
Politics:	Michigan has long been highly democratic due to large numbers of unionized workers in the urban areas. However, as union jobs whither and Detroit is shrinking in population, Michigan is turning more conservative. Dem 51%, Rep 42%, Ind/3rd party 9%.
Taxes:	Average. 21 out of 50 in high taxes with a state tax burden of 9.6% of income. Income tax is a flat 4.25% (good), but local jurisdictions can add to this (bad). The state sales tax is 6.0%. Property taxes are high, #9 in the nation.
Corruption:	High. MI had 34 public corruption convictions last year, mostly at lower levels, so higher level stuff isn't being caught. There is corruption in the judiciary, family courts, state housing contracts and union politics. Only in small rural towns do you have low corruption.
Crime:	High. Violent crime 450/100K, property crime 2,328/100K. Detroit is one of the worst crime cities in the nation with 1220 violent crimes per 100K. Crime index for Detroit is 2, Lansing 10, Ann Arbor 25, Grand Rapids 15.
Personal Liberty:	Poor. Ranked 35th in the nation.
Gun Liberty:	Not good. A license is required to purchase each handgun which is only valid for 10 days. Built-in locking devices shall be sold with each handgun. "Shall issue" state for concealed handgun. Some open carry is permitted.
Alternative Medicine:	Bad. Medical practice law requires that anyone who performs diagnosis or treatment of any kind must be a licensed medical doctor or health care provider—even if their treatment is not potentially harmful, thus leaving all alternative practitioners to prosecution. Lay midwifery status is unclear. Direct entry midwifery is currently "legal" through judicial interpretation or statutory inference, but the state could step in and regulate at any time. School vaccine exemptions: philosophical, religious and medical.
Home Schooling:	No state requirement for parents to initiate any contact.

Military Targets:	**Camp Grayling and Fort Custer**. NG training areas; not significant targets.
	Detroit Arsenal. Tank research; possible tertiary target.
	Selfridge AGB near Mt. Clemens (25 mi. North of Detroit). KC-135 air refueling base and the largest ANG base; primary target.
	Kellog Airport. Reserve A-10 base of the ANG; tertiary target.
Nuclear Power Plants:	**Fermi 2 Plant**, on Lake Erie south of Detroit.
	Donald Cook Nuclear Power Plant, on Lake Michigan S of Benton Harbor.
	Palisades Nuclear Power Plant, on Lake Michigan 5 mi. S of South Haven.

Notes

Michigan is the only state in the union built entirely on two separate peninsulas. The Lower Peninsula is highly populated and industrialized (referred to as "L.P." or the "Mitten" owing to its shape), and the Upper Peninsula (the "U.P.") is lightly populated and mostly rural. The two are separated by the Straits of Mackinac, only 5 miles wide. For all of these geographical reasons, the U.P. is by far the better retreat location. However, for those living on the Lower Peninsula, it is as if the U.P. were in Wisconsin due to the separation by water. While the Mackinaw suspension bridge connects the two peninsulas (I-75) you should not count on that access in a major crisis.

It's worth noting the precipitation difference caused by the "Lake Effect" over Lake Michigan. Moisture from the lake can add significant moisture to storms. Milwaukee on the western shore (upwind) of Lake Michigan received an average of 52.6 inches of snow for the period 1971-2000 compared to Muskegon on the eastern shore (downwind) that received an average of 106.0 inches of snow over the same time period.

The collapse of Detroit as a viable city deserves mention here as it shows what happens to a city which comes under the grip of unionism and benefit-corrupted politics at both the federal and state level. More than one in three homes in Detroit has been foreclosed on in the last 10 years. Roughly half of Detroit's property owners have not paid their taxes, and the city can't afford to continue providing power or water to sparsely populated neighborhoods. In 2013 Detroit became the largest city to declare for bankruptcy with a debt of $18.5 billion in debt. The city is increasingly turning to foreclosure to collect back taxes on properties. 40% of houses at auction go for less than $1,000 and are soon stripped by looters and become part of the "blight" of vacant houses in Detroit, waiting for demolition that the city can't yet afford.

Here is a personal analysis from former resident and author, Frosty Wooldridge of NewsWithViews.com: "From the mid 1970s to 1990, I worked in Detroit, Michigan. I watched it descend into the abyss of crime, debauchery, gun play, drugs, school truancy, car-jacking, gangs and human depravity. I watched entire city blocks burned out. I watched graffiti explode on buildings, cars, trucks, buses and school yards. Trash everywhere! Detroiters walked through it, tossed more into it and ignored it.

"Tens of thousands and then, hundreds of thousands today exist on federal welfare, free housing and food stamps! With Aid to Dependent Children, minority women birthed eight to 10 and in one case, a woman birthed 24 kids as reported by the Detroit Free Press—all on American taxpayer dollars. I saw Lyndon Baines Johnson's 'Great Society' flourish in Detroit. If you give money for doing nothing, you will get more hands out taking money for doing nothing.

"Mayor Coleman Young, perhaps the most corrupt mayor in America, outside of Richard Daley in Chicago, rode Detroit down to its knees. He set the benchmark for cronyism, incompetence and arrogance. As a black man, he said, 'I am the MFIC.' The IC meant 'in charge'. You can figure out the rest. Detroit became a majority black city with 67 percent African-Americans. [82.7% in the 2010 Census.]

"As a United Van Lines truck driver, I loaded hundreds of American families into my van for a new life in another city or state. Detroit plummeted from 1.8 million citizens to 912,000 today [Down to 713,777 in 2010]. At the same time, legal and illegal immigrants converged on the city, so much so, that Muslims number over 300,000. Mexicans number 400,000 throughout Michigan, but most work in Detroit. As the Muslims moved in, the whites moved out. As the crimes became more violent, the whites fled. Finally, unlawful Mexicans moved in at a torrid pace. Detroit may be one of our best examples of multiculturalism: pure dislike and total separation from America."

Obviously, we exclude Detroit as a viable city in Michigan. Grand Rapids, the next biggest is a refreshing relief.

Strategies for Populated Living Areas

Detroit: This high density urban area borders Lake St. Clair on the east and the Detroit Strait (River) on the SW together with the border near Windsor, Ontario, Canada. The worst crime areas are in the city's core, but there are patches of heavy crime even in the suburbs. The metro area is surrounded by other cities with similar problems, but to a lesser degree. Normally, we would suggest one locate on the periphery of the metro area, but in this area of Michigan, the automotive industry has spawned a ring of other industrial towns around Detroit that make exiting the area in a social meltdown crisis very difficult. Within a 50 mile ring you have Toledo (Ohio), Ann Arbor, Lansing, and Flint. To the north of Flint you have Saginaw. All these areas have some degree of the crime and racial tension of Detroit. In this 50 mile area around Detroit (which is a "must-retreat-from" city), you need to map out rural roads that avoid any of the previously mentioned mini-industrial towns.

Grand Rapids: This nice Michigan city has low crime and a good base of decent people. It still has enough population density, combined with the necessity of constant imports to sustain itself, that one should plan a retreat strategy—probably to the north in the general direction of Hwy 131. To retreat north, we recommend locating in the Walker area of Comstock Park because this is beyond the Grand River and north of I-96.

None of the other small and medium cities present trap zones for exiting as long as you stay near the periphery of development. Kalamazoo is problematic because of how far south it is situated. It is still safer to retreat north from here, however, than attempt to get through traffic blockages to the south.

The Lower Peninsula cannot be exited to the south in a crisis, since you will run into the hoards exiting from Chicago. It's like heading into New Orleans during Katrina. We don't recommend trying to thread that gauntlet. Fortunately, the northern half of the Peninsula is very rural with few cities and has good retreat potential. Of course, it only has one exit (the Mackinaw Bridge) so a boat might not be a bad addition to one's contingency plans.

Retreat Areas

Rural farmland: Michigan is fifty percent forested land, which makes it ideal for finding farmland retreats that back up to state forests, such as we find in abundance in the UP and in the northern half of the LP. Only farms that are out in open land, with no tree lines or cover should be excluded. Keep in mind that a farm retreat should have an alternate exit strategy if refugee influx becomes an untenable problem. There will always be small numbers of point threats of individuals or small groups that come to farms searching for food or to steal, but probably not overwhelming numbers 50 miles away from cities. Do implement the safe strategy of putting in underground concealed rooms where you can't be found, so you don't have to confront starving, desperate people. The Lower Peninsula is safe for retreats north of a line between Muskegon and Saginaw, but stay at least 50 miles from those towns.

Upper Peninsula: The entire Upper Peninsula is one medium-term safe haven. It's a very long way from civilization, especially if the Mackinaw Bridge is closed. Besides, all the lands and towns to the south would have already absorbed a lot of pillaging by the time anyone gets that far north. Highly rated for the East.

MINNESOTA ★★★☆☆

Summary Facts and Ratings

Climate:	Minnesota endures temperature extremes characteristic of its continental climate: cold winters, hot humid summers, heavy rain, snow, blizzards, thunderstorms, hail, tornadoes and high-velocity horizontal winds. Major rivers in the south are flood prone. MN averages 19 tornadoes per year, 18th rank in US.
Population Density:	About average. 66.2 ppl/sq mile (31st in the nation). Mostly of German, Scandinavian and Irish descent. Protestants of which Lutheran are dominant. Black 4.7%, Hispanic 4.5%, Asian 3.8%, mixed 1.6%, American Indian 1.3%.
Cost of Living Index:	Average. 101.5 (average is 100) ranked 28th least expensive.
Private Land Availability:	Good. Only 17.5% of the land is state and federally owned.
Building Permits:	Required for all construction, specifics per local jurisdiction. There are other permits at county level for flood plain and shoreline construction. Deep soil everywhere, so good basement potential, except where high water table is a problem (up north).
Land and Urban Planning:	Counties and municipalities may establish comprehensive plans. Once a plan has been adopted, all future decisions and ordinances must be consistent with that plan. There is no state review of the process.
Food Production:	Good productivity in southern 2/3rds of the state with growing season of 90-150 days. Shorter in the North. Rainfall averages about 28 inches per year. Rich soil, good for gardening.
Health Environment:	Surface and well water in the south and eastern corporate farm districts have elevated concentrations of agricultural pollution and chemicals. Good elsewhere. Overall, air and water pollution levels are below national average. 99% of people's water is fluoridated—very bad.
Traffic:	Heavy traffic problems in Minneapolis-St. Paul rated as the 17th worst traffic city. Radar detectors are legal, but not if mounted on front windshield. No red light or speed cameras.
Politics:	Minnesota is generally a liberal state, controlled from Minn.-St. Paul and its liberal newspapers. Dem 51%, Rep 44%, Ind/3rd party 5%.
Taxes:	High. Ranked 6th highest, with a state and local tax burden of 10.7% of income. Income tax is 5.4-9.85%, property taxes are 22nd in the nation and sales tax is high at 6.88% with some exemptions (food, drugs and clothing).
Corruption:	High, including the Attorney General and State Attorney's Office on down to local voter fraud.
Crime:	Average violent crime 234/100K, but above average property crime 2420/100K. Crime index for Minn./St Paul is 4, violent crime there is 2.5 times the state average.
Personal Liberty:	Low. Rated 34th nationally.
Gun Liberty:	Moderate. Transferee permit required (valid for 1 year) to purchase handguns and assault weapons. "Shall issue" state for concealed permits which also constitute as transferee permits. Otherwise buyer must undergo a background check for each purchase. Licensed open carry state.
Alternative Medicine:	Alternative practitioners have been prosecuted on a broad definition of the practice of medicine that includes all diagnosis. However, naturopathic doctors are licensed here. Direct entry midwives practice legally in the state. School vaccine exemptions: philosophical, religious and medical.
Home Schooling:	Low regulation. State requires parental notification only.
Military Targets:	**Arden Hills Army Reserve Command**, Minn./St. Paul. Distribution facility; not a target. **Camp Ripley**, 20 mi. north of Little Falls. NG training facility; not a significant target. **Minneapolis/St Paul Airport**. C-130 Airlift for ANG; not a significant target. **Duluth International Airport**. F-16s of ANG; tertiary targets.
Nuclear Power Plants:	**Monticello Plant**, 30 mi. NE of Minn./St. Paul, 2 reactors. Began operation in 1971. **Prairie Island Plant**, 25 mi. SE of Minn./St. Paul. 2 reactors. Began operation in 1974.

Notes

Minnesota provides good survival retreats in the forests and lakes in the northern part of the state and good farm and ranch living in the rest of the state, at the price of a difficult and bug-ridden climate. The more populated region in the center and south of the state suffers from the general defect of all plains states—flat land without enough cover. Flooding is a problem from the large rivers that drain the lake country. Ice flows can occasionally block river waters and cause flooding.

Politically, this northern state has historically had a leftist or populist background grown out of the Farmer and Labor Party which have now largely merged with the Democratic Party. Conservatives, however, made a huge comeback in 2010 that left Republicans in control of the legislature for the first time since 1972. The elections of independent governor Jesse Ventura and Republican governor Tim Pawlenty were anomalies. Both were thwarted in their efforts to cut government spending by democratic control of the legislatures. After Republicans took control, reforms were thwarted by a democratic governor and the legislature returned to democratic control in the next election. Very liberal voter registration laws have led to higher registrations of poor, indigent and illegal alien voters—and significant election fraud.

There were 47 public corruption convictions last year. MN Attorney General, Lori Swanson, politicized her office by illegally transferring state funds from a credit-card settlement to ACORN and the leftist Legal Aid (quarter million dollars each). Dept. of Human Resources in MN is also scandal ridden and is protected by judges from most civil suits. There is evidence of a conspiracy between state bankruptcy judges and US attorneys to allow cronies to control bankrupt assets. Significant vote fraud took place in the election of left/liberal Senator Al Franken.

Strategies for Populated Living Areas

Minneapolis-St. Paul is split into several sections due to the Mississippi and Minnesota Rivers joining up in this huge city. One must always prepare to leave a large metro area simply because the threat of social unrest or disruption of food and services can send millions into a panic. Where you locate in the city should be coordinated with where you plan to exit the city, either to a rural retreat or some other city where you have family or friends. The key is not to get trapped inside natural or man made barriers like rivers or freeways.

If your exit plan is west, you should locate to the north of the Minnesota River, west of the 495 Beltway and south of I-94. The suburban towns of Maple Grove, Plymouth and Eden Prairie match these criteria generally. If your exit plan is to the south, you should be in the Eagan and Apple Valley areas. In reality, anywhere between the Minnesota and Mississippi Rivers but at least 5 miles away from I-35 will work. If your exit plan is north into the wooded lake country, you have to decide which side of I-35 you want to be on, since there are few roads that cross it without an exit, which may be jammed with traffic.

There are no other large cities in Minnesota that require special exit route planning, except for Rochester, which can be in the path of refugees leaving Minn/St. Paul. Be prepared to go west before the city becomes inundated.

Retreat Areas

Rural farmland: Follow the general rule to stay at least 10 miles away from a major interstate, and find a good place with water and trees for windbreaks, shade and seclusion. The best locations are those that are not visible from any main road. The disadvantage of using isolation for retreat safety is that you are isolated from commerce and friends. Fortunately, in MN there are small towns not too distant from farm/retreat sites. We prefer the towns to the west and north of Minneapolis-St. Paul. We would not have a retreat closer than 50 miles to this major city.

Lakes Country: Minnesota has thousands of lakes and thousands of acres of forest into which one can find good retreat and cabin sites. High water table is a problem in many areas, as is vandalism of cabins left vacant for long periods. Duluth is the only moderate sized city nearby to service your commercial needs.

MISSISSIPPI ★★☆☆☆

Summary Facts and Ratings

Climate:	Humid subtropical climate with long summers and short, mild winters. The coastal area is significantly warmer in wintertime than the central and northern part of the state. Average of 26 tornados per year.
Population Density:	Moderately high: 63 ppl/sq mile (ranked 32nd in the nation). Black 37%, Hispanic 2.5%, Asian 1%, mixed 1%.
Cost of Living Index:	Very low. 83.5 (average is 100) ranked least expensive state in the nation.
Private Land Availability:	Good. Only 5.5% of the land is state and federally owned.
Building Permits:	Required for any new construction, renovations and demolition work. Local jurisdictions can make exceptions where it is not a statewide mandate. Basements are not common but feasible unless high water tables are an issue.
Land and Urban Planning:	Municipalities and counties may adopt comprehensive plans and form planning commissions, but they are not required to do so. If a jurisdiction decides to adopt a comprehensive plan, it must have at a minimum four elements.
Food Production:	Very good with a growing season of 240-270 days. Rainfall averages about 57 inches per year. Rich soil, good gardening, sometimes too wet.
Health Environment:	Surface water pollution is some of the worst in the nation, but ground water away from big commercial farms is acceptable. 58% of the population's water is fluoridated. Mississippi has the third highest combined level of obese plus overweight adults at 70.7 percent.
Traffic:	Moderate traffic problems in Jackson, MS, rated #74 of 75 bad traffic cities. No red light or speed cameras.
Politics:	Mississippians are mostly conservative and religious Democrats. Dem 55%, Rep 40%, Ind/3rd party 5%.
Taxes:	Below average. Ranked 11th lowest taxes, with a state tax burden of 8.4% of income. MS has 3-5% income taxes, very low property taxes (46th in nation) and a 7% sales tax.
Corruption:	High. Major corruption in state and local affairs.
Crime:	Moderate. Violent crime 275/100K, property crime 2725/100K. Crime index for Jackson is 2, (violent crime is more than twice the state average), Gulfport is 6 (100 is safest). Meth labs also abound in the ghettos of this area and have made inroads into the rural areas.
Personal Liberty:	Poor: 41st in the nation.
Gun Liberty:	Good. MS does not require a permit to purchase firearms. A permit is required to carry a concealed handgun. Licensed open carry state.
Alternative Medicine:	Natural health practitioners are free to practice. Lay midwifery is unregulated. School vaccine exemptions—only this state and WV do not allow you to opt out even for religious reasons; medical exemption required.
Home Schooling:	Low regulation. State requires parental notification only.
Military Targets:	**Camp Shelby**, 12 mi. S of Hattiesburg. Battalion sized military training site including tank and artillery; secondary target. **Stennis Space Center** (Nat'l Space Tech Lab), west of Gulfport. Rocket testing, space technology center; primary or secondary target. **Gulfport Naval Construction Battalion Center**. Seabees base; not a target. **Meridian NAS**. Navy/MC jet training base; possible tertiary target. **Columbus AFB**. Air force training base; possible tertiary target. **Jackson Airport**. 8 C-17 Airlift flown by ANG; secondary target. **Key Field**, Meridian. KC-135 Air refueling; secondary target. **Keesler AFB**, Biloxi. C-130 airlift and training field for airlift pilots and electronic operators; possible tertiary target.

Notes

Mississippi lacks mountain retreats, but has good farmland. The population density is moderate but poverty is rampant, much of it is due to personal corruption, obesity and laziness. On the other hand, Mississippians are generally friendly, gentle and gracious. As in all states, there is a significant left-liberal element which plays upon the poor, welfare class, mainly black families. Even though Democrats out-register Republicans, they are conservative Democrats. This state passed a ban on gay marriage by the largest margin in the country: 86% to 14%.

Corruption is too easy to find in the South. 55 of Mississippi's 410 county supervisors, one county road foreman, two state highway commissioners and 13 road vendors were convicted of bribery, extortion and other felony charges. The rural counties have a working Good ol' Boys network that extends to the top. At the state level, Mississippi, like Alabama, has gone after high politicians on corruption charges in order to ruin their political careers. Corruption is easy to find, even among judges and local police. Revenue seeking police stops have occurred.

There are few specific military targets in this state, but in a crisis we see serious problems. With its high welfare population this is one of the highest dependency states upon federal dollars in the nation, so we expect considerable social unrest and scavenging/pillaging to occur. Mississippi is also in the path of refugee flows from other areas such as I-10 from points east, including all of Florida and parts of Alabama, I-20 from Birmingham and I-55 from Memphis. All these cities have a large chance of social meltdown in the future.

Mississippi will have to absorb a lot of those people as it did during hurricane Katrina. Mississippi's major towns are all along freeways so readers will want to position themselves away from those areas. One of the big problems in getting out of MS to the west is the Mississippi River itself. There are very few bridges that aren't freeways—which may be shut down. One is at Natchez, another is at Greenville. The farthest north before Memphis is a bridge on Highway 49. Know where they are and familiarize yourself with the few remaining options like ferry boats.

Hurricanes and flooding are serious threats to this state, particularly along the Mississippi River which has historically always been a problem. Levee systems abound, but the danger is still there, particularly during hurricane season. A lot of rain in the wrong place can often cause more damage than the hurricane-force winds.

Strategies for Populated Living Areas

Biloxi: To avoid Keesler AFB, stay west of the city in Gulfport or better yet north of I-10 near Landon (but not near the freeway). Jackson: Almost any of the suburbs outside the perimeter of this city are as safe as another as long as you are away from the major freeways and secondary roads. If you plan on leaving the state in a crisis, plan routes to the south (Natchez) or to the north (Greenville) where you can cross the mighty Mississippi without getting on a freeway.

Meridian: Stay 5 miles south of NAS Meridian and clear of the freeways, and you should be fine. Again, much depends upon your exit strategy and ease of commute, which will determine the quadrant you choose.

Columbus: Stay south of the city to avoid the air base threat, but west of the river since a safe exit is either to the west or northwest.

Smaller Coastal Cities: You should only choose one of the gulf coast cities if your work depends on it. Avoid Biloxi and you will be free from nuclear targets, but not social unrest. Make sure you scope out ways to get north of I-10 outside of an off or on ramp, which will be clogged.

Retreat Areas

Rural farmland: Rural farm retreats are about the only retreats available. Fortunately, Mississippi has a lot of southern pines and other deciduous trees that give privacy and cover. There are many rivers and creeks that can block your ingress or egress in an area, so learn the terrain and obstacles well—including the Mississippi River itself. Give yourself some distance from the larger cities along I-10. There are several state and national forests around Alexandria in the center of the state that have small rural towns around them. That's where to start. Our favorite places are in the NE corner above I-22, near Tennessee.

MISSOURI ★★★☆☆

Summary Facts and Ratings

Climate:	Missouri generally has a humid, continental climate with cold winters and hot, humid summers. It averages 27 tornados per year.
Population Density:	About average. 86.9 ppl/sq mile (ranked 28th in the nation). Mostly of German, Scandinavian and Irish descent. Protestants are dominant. Black 4.7%, Hispanic 4.3%, Asian 3.8%, mixed 1.6%, American Indian 1.3%.
Cost of Living Index:	Low. 91.5 (average is 100) makes this the 11th least expensive state.
Private Land Availability:	Good. Only 6% of the land is state and federally owned.
Building Permits:	Required for all construction per requirements of local jurisdiction. Deep soil everywhere, so good basement potential.
Land and Urban Planning:	All cities, towns and villages are authorized to plan and adopt zoning regulations in accordance with a comprehensive plan. However, the statute does not require these local agencies to adopt the state comprehensive plan.
Food Production:	Very good. Growing season of 150-210 days. Rainfall averages about 38 inches per year. Rich soil, good gardening. Rocky soil in the Ozarks.
Health Environment:	Ground water has some concentrations of agricultural pollution and chemicals in commercial farming areas. Overall, pollution levels are below national averages. 76% of the population's water is fluoridated.
Traffic:	Heavy traffic problems in Kansas City and St. Louis: #58 and #45, respectively, on the list of 75 worst traffic cities. Red light and speed cameras are used.
Politics:	Missouri is a divided state. Pollsters called it a bellwether state because "as Missouri goes, so goes the nation." But that isn't a compliment, nor is it always true. It voted for McCain over Obama. It indicates that farm-based people with populist tendencies can often be swayed to what the national media propagandizes. Dem 32%, Rep 43%, Ind/3rd party 25%.
Taxes:	Average. Ranks 18th lowest with a tax burden of 9% of income. There are 10 income tax brackets from 1.5%-6%, property taxes are 23rd in the nation and state sales tax is 4.23%.
Corruption:	High.
Crime:	High violent crime 433/100K, property crime is above average 3137/100K. Crime index for St. Louis is 1, Kansas City is 4 (100 is safest). Violent crime rates in St. Louis are 4 times the state average. Kansas City is 3 times.
Personal Liberty:	Good: 7th in the nation.
Gun Liberty:	Moderate. A permit is required for handgun purchase and is only valid for 30 days and one handgun. "Shall issue" state for concealed permits and is open carry friendly.
Alternative Medicine:	Natural health practitioners are free to practice. The practice of midwifery is now legal for anyone who is certified by the ACNM or NARM. School vaccine exemptions: philosophical (daycare, nursery and preschool only), religious and medical.
Home Schooling:	No regulation. No state requirement for parents to initiate any contact.
Military Targets:	**Fort Leonard Wood**, 100 mi SE of St. Louis on I-44. Army basic training base; secondary target. **Lake City Army Ammunition Plant**, Small caliber munitions plant; tertiary target. **Kansas City USMC Mobility Command**, Marine reserves support activity; tertiary target. **Rosecrans Airport**, C-130 airlift and ANG; tertiary target. **Kansas City Nuclear Weapons Plant**. New campus is being built near Richards-Gebaur airport south of KC; primary target. **Whiteman AFB**, South of Knob Noster. B-2 Strategic Bombers (ICBMs have been removed); primary target.
Nuclear Power Plant:	**Calloway Power Plant**, Jefferson City. 1 reactor. Operating since 1984.

Notes

Missouri's self reliant culture is generally pro gun and pro private property and respects people's privacy, but as with most states, Missouri is getting more bureaucratic and intrusive with its regulations every year. There is very low population density in many rural counties, and the cost of living is lower here. The native population is mostly Scotch-Irish and tough, so they have the makings for good, self-sufficient neighbors. The Ozarks area is particularly suited for retreats: there's a natural food supply in wild game, lots of fish and plenty of wood for stoves. The water is excellent from both springs and wells. Property is cheap so you might consider some fertile land in addition to a rocky retreat in the Ozarks.

The northern part of the state lies in plains with gentle rolling hills, and the southern portion is part of the Ozark Mountain Plateau. The Missouri River divides these two parts, generally. There's a lot of good farm and forest land with a good growing season. It would have better long-term security if it were farther west. Some refugees from the East will make it this far west, but primarily to the larger cities.

The land in Missouri is better than its leaders. There were 24 public corruption convictions last year, which is way too low for the amount of corruption in this state—revealing the immunity corrupt leaders give one another. In the last year, four Missourians were barred from casinos for crimes of "moral turpitude." Three were civil servants who authorities say used embezzled tax dollars to feed their gambling habits. But these were small fish. Corruption like this is often facilitated by higher authorities. Consider this: the offices of Governor, Attorney General, State Treasurer and Auditor have all had just three different incumbents since 1920 and no incumbent since 1974 has lost an election for those offices. That's how machine politics work. Moreover, this is the state where the CIA creates a good portion of its front companies. That's telling. Police and judicial corruption is very much a part of protecting the Good ol' Boys network. This network is powerful here, so if you choose to retreat in MO you need to keep a low profile. The connections between all state and local law enforcement (particularly the ones that are corrupt or bullish) allow them to work together with judges and politicians to act with wide latitudes of impunity.

Both the bullish attitude of police and the systemic corruption to protect them was revealed during and after the shooting of Michael Brown in Ferguson, a suburb of St. Louis. Officer Darren Wilson was not indicted by the grand jury and his actions were defended by U.S. Dept. of Justice investigation despite having shot Brown instead of de-escalating the situation. More than anything else the Ferguson riots revealed the level of militarization among the St. Louis and Missouri police. Armored vehicles and full para-military gear on hundreds of officers made it clear that the feds are gearing up police in a major way to handle even stronger future citizen unrest.

Both Kansas City and Whiteman AFB (60 mi SE of KC) are prime nuclear targets, so stay clear of those areas and their near downwind fallout patterns. Winds are mainly N-S. Fortunately for Missouri, all of the missile silos have been removed from the state.

Missouri is one of the states with tornado threats, so you have an excuse to build a safe room and call it a tornado shelter—contractors won't blink an eye over that.

Strategies for Populated Living Areas

St. Louis: This is one of the most difficult cities for planning an exit strategy. It is a metro area cut into numerous trap zones defined by freeways and multiple rivers. Because of the minority problems and crime and corruption endemic to this city, you must plan on a distant rural retreat if you live here. It is wise to select an area of town that gives you clear access to your exit direction without being blocked in by a freeway or a river. All best retreat areas will be north, south or west—not east. St. Louis is surrounded by the Missouri and Mississippi rivers, with only a few bridges allowing you to cross. Most of these are freeways, which will likely be clogged or shut down by authorities.

Here is your best exit strategy: The only outlet between the two-river encirclement is to the southwest, between I-64 and I-55, with I-44 in the middle. You have to pick one or the other halves of this pie shaped area since there is another river meandering along the I-44 corridor blocking your ability to cross from one sector to another. Locate outside the 270 beltway to make sure you don't have that as a barrier. Plan to travel on rural roads and to get out of town before major social unrest or panic clogs the roads.

If your exit route is to the north, we suggest you locate to the north of the Missouri such as in north St. Charles or O'Fallon, above I-70. If you are already located inside the two beltways surrounding parts of St. Louis, you are in a trap zone. You need to take careful note of the instructions we provide in the previous section on how to pick a route including choosing to go under or over a freeway where there is no exit ramp, these will be clogged.

Kansas City: This is a nuclear target city because of the government's nuclear weapons assembly plant. If your exit route is southeast toward the Ozarks, locate outside the 470 beltway in the Lees Summit area. If your retreat direction is north, locate outside the 435 beltway and within the arc between the Missouri river (Liberty area) on the south, and I-29 on the NW. Be aware that I-35 cuts this wedge area in half, so map out where you need to cross it outside of an exit area. As you get farther into the countryside, it may be possible to get onto rural freeways where they are not clogged.

Retreat Areas

Rural farmland: Missouri has abundant hilly farmland intermixed with small forests and lines of trees that give this state more retreat possibilities than the other plains states. Our favorite area in the north is above the line between St. Joseph in the west and Hannibal in the east, excluding those two cities. This is prime rolling hill country far away from any city social unrest and crime. The Lake of the Ozarks forested country in western Missouri is our next favorite rural farm retreat area. Don't go further north than the east-west line between Versailles and Lincoln. The best land is surrounding the Lake state park, extending down to the SW.

The Missouri Ozarks: This and the Arkansas Ozarks are the prime retreat areas for the Midwest. The Missouri portion is encompassed roughly by staying south of I-44 (excluding the Springfield area) and staying west of I-55 which runs N-S along the Kentucky border. The southeast corner of the area is more flat farm land, but the rest is composed of hills and mountains covered mostly by deciduous trees. Much of the most beautiful forest land is contained in the Mark Twain Forest, but there are thousands of private acres elsewhere in this huge area. The resort town of Branson is in the southwest portion. It's a nice place to visit for entertainment, but land prices close by are too high.

MONTANA ★★★★⯪

Summary Facts and Ratings

Climate:	High and dry continental climate east of the Rockies. Pacific Northwest moist air flows bring more precipitation to the northwest corner in the winter and spring. Montana has cold winters everywhere, but it is especially cold in the central and eastern portions.
Population Density:	Very low. 7 ppl/sq mile (ranked 48th in the nation). American Indian 6.4%, Hispanic 3.1%, mixed 1.8%, others below 1%.
Cost of Living Index:	Moderate. 102.7 (slightly below the average of 100).
Private Land Availability:	Fair. 34% of land is state or federally owned, including a good portion of the best forests and mountain land.
Building Permits:	Required for all cities and counties, but many rural jurisdictions have limited requirements for farm and ranch buildings.
Land and Urban Planning:	Montana does have a comprehensive development plan, but it only mandates that each jurisdiction have a zoning commission and does not mandate conformity with any state plan.
Food Production:	Poor. Average rainfall is only 11.4 in/yr. Dry land farms and ranches are common. Some irrigated lands along rivers can grow more. Growing season is 90-150 days on the plains and 30-120 days in the mountains.
Health Environment:	Water quality is excellent where fed by mountain springs. Quality is only fair from wells in the valleys. Only 32% of the population's water is fluoridated. Air pollution is not a problem except downwind of a few factories. There is very good solar potential in the east, fair in the west.
Traffic:	No major traffic problems except, perhaps, in Billings (Heights area).
Politics:	Conservative-liberal split. Montana has been a Democratic leaning state for years, but they have a slight majority now. Conservatives dominate the agricultural areas, and liberals dominate the old mining areas. The influx of Californians brings even more liberal attitudes to the best retreat areas. Dem 40%, Rep 38, Ind/3rd party 22%.
Taxes:	Low. Ranked 13th lowest with a tax burden of 8.6% of income. Up to 6.9% income tax, no sales tax and average property taxes (ranked 26th in the nation).
Corruption:	Moderate. Corruption has always plagued states with strong mining and railroad backgrounds. It still exists at the state level and wherever big corporate influence is felt in mining. Some corruption in judicial system and police.
Crime:	Medium. Violent crime 253/100K, property crime 2557/100K. Crime index for Billings is 7 (same as US average), Helena 10 (100 is safest).
Personal Liberty:	Good: ranked 12th nationally. Raw milk is banned, asset forfeiture laws need to be reformed.
Gun Liberty:	Excellent. No permit to purchase firearms. "Shall issue" state for concealed firearm permits. Open carry state, even in a car.
Alternative Medicine:	Very good availability, full range of natural health practitioners. Direct entry midwives are licensed by the Alternative Health Care Board, which also licenses Naturopathic Physicians. School vaccine exemptions: religious and medical.
Home Schooling:	Low regulation. State requires parental notification.
Military Targets:	**Malmstrom AFB**, Great Falls. Largest Minuteman III missile base; massive primary target for hundreds of warheads. **Fort Harrison**, NW of Helena. Helicopters, some armor; secondary target.

Notes

Montana is considered by some to be the last great frontier in the continental US. With the decrease in mining, the economy is now mostly service-based and is fairly weak. It still has significant remnants of its traditional economic activities: ranching, wheat farming, lumber mills, hard rock mining and some oil and coal in the east. Eastern Montana is more like a Midwestern state, but with little rainfall, very few roads and a declining population. There are no towns over 10K in the east except for Billings which is the largest in the state at 100K+. The best ranches are around Miles City and Forsyth. Eastern Montana has a significant security risk in being downwind from the largest existing Ballistic Missile fields near Great Falls. The Minuteman III missile silos extend many miles around Malmstrom AFB and each must be hit directly by nuclear weapon to stop the missile inside, so this nuclear target area will take an enormous number of nuclear hits someday. Don't be downwind without massive fallout protection.

Western Montana is where the great outdoor living experience begins and where the best retreat sites are located. However, even in this beautifully forested area, Montana has a Dr. Jekyll-Mr. Hyde personality. There is significant tension between the liberal, rough, anti-religious segment of the population (a combination of the old miner mentality and the wealthy and liberal Californian immigrants) and the arch-conservative Christians who are increasingly drawn to Montana for liberty. Democrats and liberals have had their way for so many years they often react with real hostility toward the conservative-Christian resurgence such as what has been happening in the Whitefish area.

There is a decided libertarian mindset to how Montana deals with many issues. It often leaves individuals to do their own thing rather than think of the state as the "protector" and needed "regulator." This also allows people their "right to corrupt themselves" on issues such as semi-unlimited speed limits on the open plains. But the trend toward Laissez-Faire liberty is in fragile tension between the two conflicting political and religious cultures. People should watch Montana as a destination for liberty. The population of Montana is low, and the side that attracts the most immigrants to the state in the future will determine which way the state turns.

Montana would rate 5 stars except for the wide area around Great Falls that houses the largest base of nuclear missiles in the nation. This puts a great portion of the state at risk of massive fallout, depending on which way the wind is blowing. The only safe bet is to be west of this threat.

Strategies for Populated Living Areas

Billings is the largest city in Montana, a town that sprang up around the great Northern Railroad. It has been a financial, energy and service center for Montana ever since. It is also home to the main Montana State University campus (also at Bozeman). These historical and modern influences make this a liberal center of influence in the state. We do not recommend anything east of Bozeman due to the threat of fallout from both the Great Falls missile fields and, to a lesser extent, the Seattle targets.

Bozeman is one of the few cities along I-90 that is situated south of the freeway, and that is where you should find housing. This gives you unimpeded access to the mountains via Hwy 191 and the extensive agricultural areas around Bozeman and Four Corners.

Helena is the closest anyone should locate to the city of Great Falls (which is surrounded by missile silos). Helena does have one minor military training base in the valley which is a secondary target. Avoid the mining towns of Butte, Anaconda and Missoula, which still harbor some hard-drinking, anti-religious elements. Of course, all of these towns have become more moderate since the real mining days, but the influence still lingers.

Great Falls: This is a DO NOT INHABIT city like Colorado Springs. The missile fields spread out like two big butterfly wings to the NW and the SE of the city.

Retreat Areas

The Flathead Lake region: This is one of the two best areas for rural and farm homesteads in Montana that are surrounded with mountains and forests. A growing number of Christian-conservative families are moving into this valley every year and that will probably continue, as will the opposition from those who resent this becoming a haven for preparedness-oriented Christians. We recommend the northern towns of Whitefish and Columbia Falls more than Kalispell. Whitefish is the more beautiful and active of these two, but property values have gone up there and the influx has been more liberal than the locals. Land is cheaper outside of town including fertile land East of Kalispell. Properties up in the hills have more trees for concealment. Make sure you can garden there before buying.

The Bitterroot Valley region is a ranching area at 3,500 ft elevation close to the Idaho border in the secure backdrop of the massive Bitterroot mountain wilderness area. The slightly lower elevation and distance from the Montana plains also makes this a bit warmer in the wintertime, though still cold and with plenty of snow. A lot of wealthy people have built cabins and ranches in the area, so prices are no longer cheap. The town of Hamilton itself is not recommended ever since the government built a Level 4 biohazard laboratory there as part of Rocky Mountain Laboratories. This facility has begun operations using highly-pathogenic organisms, which could be very dangerous if somehow released or leaked. Darby, at the southern-most end of the valley is the safest area.

The Clark Fork Valley Region is an extension of the drainage system feeding Lake Pend Oreille in Idaho. This valley is a mountain range apart from the I-90 freeway that feeds traffic from Idaho to Montana. It is very isolated and safe—perhaps too isolated if you need to travel often. It is situated between the Bitterroot and Cabinet Mountains. There are numerous small towns in the valley that are safe: Plains, Thompson Falls, Belknap, Trout Creek, Noxon, and Heron. The growing season is shortened in the valley by the restrictions to available daylight and being in a mountainous area.

There are hundreds of other retreat sites in these mountain valleys, too numerous to mention. As long as you avoid being close to the I-19 corridor, you should be relatively safe. There are no major population centers here, so there is no threat of mass social unrest, except perhaps those fleeing from the Northwest on I-90. Your biggest threat in Montana will be from what we call "point threats"—small groups of rough locals who have pickup trucks and weapons who think they can take what they want.

NEBRASKA ★★★☆☆

Summary Facts and Ratings

Climate:	Continental climate with cold winters and hot humid summers. The eastern half is the most humid, and the western panhandle is semi-arid and higher in altitude. Blizzards in the winter and droughts in summer are always a threat. Ranked 5th state for tornados, averaging 48 per year.
Population Density:	Low. 23 ppl/sq. mile (ranked 43rd in the nation). 90% of Nebraska's towns have less than 3,000 people. Hispanic 8.4%, Black 4.6%, Asian 1.7%, mixed, 1.3%, American Indian 1.1%.
Cost of Living Index:	Below average. 92.3 (average is 100), ranked 14th cheapest state in the nation.
Private Land Availability:	Excellent. Only 1.6% of the land is state or federally owned.
Building Permits:	Required statewide. Deep soil allows for basements in most places.
Land and Urban Planning:	Local planning prevails; no state mandate.
Food Production:	Very good. 120-180 day growing season. Average yearly rainfall is 30 inches in the eastern part and 17 in the west near Wyoming. The massive Ogallala aquifer underlies almost the entire state. The top soil is deep and rich, though overused and laced with weed killers and chemicals on commercial farms. Consistent farm water can be had along the various rivers and most places with well water.
Health Environment:	Nebraska ground water has elevated concentrations of agricultural pollution and chemicals (both in air and water), but it still rates below average compared to other states because there are fresh sources away from big commercial farms. 71% of the population's water is fluoridated, unfortunately.
Traffic:	Only some rush hour traffic in Omaha, the largest city. Nebraska does not use red light and speed cameras.
Politics:	Nebraska is a conservative farm-belt state that also votes for moderate democrats. Christian conservatives came out in strong opposition to the democratic policies of President Obama and voted out Nebraska's democratic Senator, Ben Nelson, in 2012 in part due to his support for Obamacare. Dem 34%, Rep 50%, Ind/ 3rd party 16%.
Taxes:	Average. Ranked 25th, with a state tax burden of 9.4% of income. Income Tax is 2.6%-6.84%, very high property taxes (3rd highest in the nation) and a state sales tax of 5.5%.
Corruption:	High. State law enforcement and judges are often part of the "Good ol' Boy" network which has led to huge scandals and cover-ups in the past.
Crime:	Average. Violent crime 262/100K, property crime 2623/100K. Crime index for Omaha is 3, Lincoln 14, Bellevue 27 (100 is safest).
Personal Liberty:	Fairly good. Ranked 22nd.
Gun Liberty:	Fair. A transfer certificate is needed to receive a handgun which is valid for up to 3 years and can be used for an unlimited number of purchases. "Shall issue" state for concealed firearm permits. Open carry is allowed in most areas. Omaha maintains a gun registry and prohibits open carry in a vehicle.
Alternative Medicine:	Good availability, full range of natural health practitioners, but state licensing is not available. Lay midwives are not specifically prohibited nor licensed. School vaccine exemptions: religious and medical.
Home Schooling:	Low regulation. State only requires parents to notify.
Military Targets:	**Cornhusker Army Ammunition Plant**, west of Grand Island. Conventional munitions manufacturing plant on standby since 1973; tertiary target. **Lincoln ANG**. KC-135 refueling aircraft; secondary target. **Offutt AFB**, south of Omaha. Secondary bunker complex for Strategic Command (STRATCOM), electronic warfare and reconnaissance; primary target. **Prototype Low Frequency Communications System**, near Silver Creek. Deactivated in 1986, tower removed in 1995; not a target.

| Nuclear Power Plants: | **Cooper Plant**, North Platte, 1 reactor. Began operation in 1974. |
| | **Calhoun Plant**, south of Omaha, 1 reactor. Began operation in 1973. |

Notes

Nebraska is just above the geographic center of the US, which provides good access to many parts of the country as well as distance from border threats. As the nation's top farm and ranch state, NE is famous for its corn and soybeans. However, its agricultural base has attracted thousands of Latinos for labor. Latino gangs and crime are an increasing concern in Omaha and other moderately sized cities. Omaha has double the murder rate of the rest of the state and 40% of the state's murders come from a small northeast area of Omaha, where black gangs are prominent and historic racial tensions run deep.

Like Kansas, the family farm has been mostly replaced by huge corporate farms that can successfully play the finance and subsidy game of big agriculture. Families continue to lose children to the big cities, and most towns in Nebraska are small and shrinking (and will probably remain small). The silver lining here is that this is good for survival and some security in the rural areas.

Sadly corruption is all too prevalent in this big-farm state, which has grown to include corporate, finance and government-centered entities as well. There is a high degree of government control in this state, centered on Omaha and Offut AFB just to the south. This AFB has a huge underground bunker system built by the military and is home to the E-4B, a 747 flying command post. This is the same bunker system President Bush went to during 9/11 together with hundreds of corporate CEOs (many from the World Trade Center itself).

There are powerful forces at work controlling Nebraska regardless of who gets elected. Nothing is more symptomatic of this than the shut-down of an official investigation into Omaha's Franklin Community Federal Credit Union, raided by federal agencies in November 1988. This case involved over $40 million that was missing but the trial unearthed an even bigger scandal that extended all the way to Washington, D.C. and implicated several powerful politicians. The credit union's manager was Larry King, Jr., a powerful figure behind many of the establishment Republican candidates that ruled the state. Former Nebraska State Senator and attorney John De Camp wrote that "What looked like a financial swindle, soon exploded into a hideous tale of drugs, Iran-Contra money-laundering, a nationwide child abuse ring, and ritual murder."

The initial grand jury trial investigated but exonerated most of the perpetrators and let King off with a minimal fine and prison sentence. A key witness was sent to prison for ten years over "perjury" for not retracting her story. The astounding cover-up would only come to light when the Franklin Committee of the Nebraska Legislature launched its own independent investigation—in the face of vigorous opposition from local and state law enforcement, from the FBI, and from the powerful Omaha World-Herald newspaper. An exposé by CBS was dropped from the airways when political pressure was put on the broadcasting station and copies of the material were destroyed. Indeed, there was good reason to want this affair covered up as it would have led to exposure of many dark side government activities in this area, just like what are also occurring in Arkansas, Florida and Colorado (Denver). It is little wonder that even today, drug trafficking in the Madison County area is said to be the highest in the surrounding six states. We recommend reading John DeCamp's book, *The Franklin Cover-Up: Child Abuse, Satanism, and Murder in Nebraska* (see sources).

Major threats in Nebraska are tornados and nuclear weapon attacks. A key nuclear target in the nation is the Offut AFB bunker system, which also serves as the secondary command center for missile forces. More importantly, most of Nebraska is potentially downwind of the huge Minuteman missile fields in NW Nebraska which are part of Warren AFB in SE Wyoming. A tornado shelter that will also protect against fallout is a necessity here.

Strategies for Populated Living Areas

Omaha: Stay to the north of all interstate freeways and beltways and west of the city. Be sure and check out the high crime maps for Omaha at www.neighborhoodscout.com and avoid the NE area of the city. Also avoid all suburbs in the south of the metro area, within 10 miles of Offut AFB.

Ogalla, North Platte, Grand Island: These are the largest of the moderately sized cities along I-80 which in certain crises will be flooded with refugees. There are many other smaller towns along I-80 as well—most of which have freeway exits, a necessary disadvantage. If you locate in any of these towns, stay to the north beyond the town so that the city is between you and the freeway to give you time to maneuver as the city absorbs the first refugees.

Retreat Areas

Rural farmland: This analysis excludes the rural farmland within 100 miles of the missile fields in NW Nebraska since the fallout potential on these rural properties exceeds what you want to prepare against economically. Outside of that area, and at least 10 miles away from a major interstate, you can take your pick of fertile rural farmland to buy. Pick those that have some stands of trees or small patches of forest to provide a wood supply. All of the existing farms have wells, and some have rain water cisterns. The best locations are those that are not visible from any main road. Try to find soil that has not been depleted by commercial farming practices.

Valentine area: This is an example of a rural farm area in northern Nebraska that is pretty far away from everything and offers good medium term security, plus good living. There are more areas like this than we can list here, but look for similar attributes. This is cattle country, with some tourism, including floating along the Niobrara River. There is also a lot of hunting, fishing and recreational opportunities. In the Fort Niobrara Wild Life Refuge and the Samuel McKelvie National Forest, there are many lakes and places to roam where no development will happen. Pure air and water are plentiful. Clear, star-filled skies occasionally offer a sighting of the aurora borealis each year which brings astronomers to Merritt Reservoir.

NEVADA ★★★☆☆

Summary Facts and Ratings

Climate:	Very dry, high desert climate. Hot summers up to 100-120 degrees. Less than 10 inches of rainfall/year.
Population Density:	Very low. 24 ppl/sq mile (8th least dense in the nation). Las Vegas metro area is very high density with 4,154/sq. mile. Hispanic 16.5%, Black 8.3%, Asian 6.6%, American Indian 1.5%, mixed 2.6%.
Cost of Living Index:	Above average at 106.5 (average is 100).
Private Land Availability:	Poor. 80% of land is state and federally owned, including almost all the best forest and mountain land.
Building Permits:	Required throughout the state. Requirements in Las Vegas and surrounding Clark County rival big cities in California. Basements are common, except in Las Vegas where hardpan subsoil makes it extra costly.
Land and Urban Planning:	Land use planning is at the local level. Restrictions are very high in the Lake Tahoe area and elsewhere where water restricts most development.
Food Production:	Only possible with lots of irrigation. Sandy or clay soil. Hay and cattle are more common in northwestern Nevada near the mountains (Carson City area) and a bit more water here provides good farming potential. Very long growing season of 280 days on average.
Health Environment:	Water quality is poor in major metros. Significant chlorine and fluoride are added. 74% of people's water systems are fluoridated. Air Pollution is high in the Las Vegas valley, which traps the air. Clean air almost everywhere else. High desert climate outside of Las Vegas is very healthy.
Traffic:	Moderately heavy during rush hours in Reno and Las Vegas thanks to highways that have been revamped. Traffic is light elsewhere in Nevada. No red light or speed cameras.
Politics:	Liberal-conservative split in Las Vegas and Reno. Conservative dominance elsewhere with a trend toward libertarian opinion. Dem 40%, Rep 40%, Ind/3rd party 20%.
Taxes:	Very low. Ranked 8th lowest with a state tax burden of only 8.1% of income. No income tax, ranked 36th lowest in property taxes but sales tax is high: 7.6% on average.
Corruption:	Very high in the state and near total corruption in Las Vegas and Reno city governments due to gambling and mafia interests. Significant corruption among police and judges, especially in Vegas.
Crime:	High. Violent crime 603/100K, property crime 2837/100K. Crime index: Las Vegas 13, Reno 16, Carson City 41 (100 is safest).
Personal Liberty:	Above average, 20th nationally.
Gun Liberty:	Good except in Las Vegas. No permit to purchase firearms. "Shall issue" state for concealed firearm permits. Some reciprocity with other states. Clark County (Las Vegas) requires handgun registration. Open carry, even in cars (except Las Vegas).
Alternative Medicine:	Very good availability, full range of natural health practitioners. Midwives are relatively unregulated and practice openly in many areas of the state. School vaccine exemptions: religious and medical.
Home Schooling:	Low regulation. State requires parents to send notification only.
Military Targets:	**Hawthorne Army Ammunition Depot**, 80 mi. SE of Carson City. Largest ammunition depot; primary target. **Fallon Naval Air Station**. TOP GUN fighter-attack school; secondary target. **Area 51 or Groom Lake**, 100 mi NW of Las Vegas. Top secret weapons development area; primary target. **Creech AFB**, Indian Springs. Control of UAV Predators and Reapers Drones; primary target. **Nellis AFB**, Las Vegas. Fighter base and storage location of nuclear munitions at foot of Sunrise Mountain; primary target. **Reno-Tahoe Airport**. ANG C-130's, 152d Airlift Wing; tertiary target. **Tonopah AFS**. Active airbase with unknown airplanes. Home to F-117's (now mothballed at this facility); primary or secondary target.

Notes

Nevada is generally dry, arid and austere, but the few good places here are very protected due to the isolation the wide open spaces provide. We particularly like the low taxes, but not the lack of good agricultural land with water. Registering a car is easy and cheap outside of Las Vegas and Reno. Property tax on new cars is high but there is no safety inspection, so if you live outside the two major cities, you don't have that yearly car hassle.

Nevada was hit hard during the 2008 depression with the crash of the real estate boom that was driving a significant part of the economy in Las Vegas and Reno. Las Vegas, in particular, has experienced a massive amount of foreclosures from which it will probably never entirely recover. It is growing again but at a more modest pace. The low taxes keep attracting Californians who are looking for tax relief or are ready to cash out of the high home prices there. Bay area people often like Oregon or Reno, which still gives them access to the Sierra Nevada recreation areas. Many in the LA basin choose Phoenix or Las Vegas.

Nevada has more than its share of threats, however, including some of the largest secret military bases in the US. Groom Lake (Area 51), for instance, has dozens of underground facilities that we estimate will be primary nuclear targets for multiple warhead strikes. Las Vegas has several nuclear targets in the valley itself and others right over the path north via I-15. Social unrest from a major war or economic collapse will impact Nevada's two major cities very hard. Both sit in the path of California's inevitable flood of refugees from LA and SF. Even without this influx, Las Vegas is in trouble as a virtual island completely dependent on air conditioning and trucking supplies.

Nevada's dry barren deserts are a significant threat to anyone trying to flee. It will be hard to survive, especially if you have a breakdown or run out of fuel trying to cross them. There are very few roads in this state. The two major freeway arteries from California, Interstate 15 and 80 can leave you almost no alternate pathway if they become shut down. Las Vegas is a serious roadblock for anyone trying to get further north into Utah. Everything coming north from Phoenix or LA has to pass through Las Vegas or go around to Flagstaff. The impassible Colorado River gorge blocks the path from the Hoover dam on east through the Grand Canyon. The only way to get around the Las Vegas confluence of roads is to take California Hwy 395 north along the eastern edge of the Sierras and then get to Utah through Nevada via Hwy 6. Plan on a lot of water and fuel to make this trip.

Strategies for Populated Living Areas

Las Vegas: If you must live around Las Vegas, we only recommend North Las Vegas. Much of the new growth is slowly pushing out into the desert north and south of Las Vegas. We don't recommend any of the housing areas in South Las Vegas or Henderson because you become sandwiched between the influx from California and the

traffic blockage of Las Vegas itself. The growth rate has been stunted in Sin City, so housing in the northern area along belt route 215 will probably remain on the periphery of the growth area for several years.

The areas near the junction of Hwy 95 and 215 will probably continue to grow if things keep improving, but this area offers the most options for getting north in a crisis (via Hwy 95). This area of Las Vegas is also close to Mount Charleston to the northwest which offers a respite from the heat. My second choice would be in Summerlin farther to the west around 215 where many wealthier homes are built. There are some moderately priced homes too.

There's no avoiding the fact that both Hwy-95 and I-15 north are too close to nuclear targets. If possible, consider the commuting sacrifice to live in one of two rural areas beyond these targets. One is Pahrump which has access north to the Hwy-95 beyond the Creech AFB target. The second, Moapa valley near Overton, is around I-15 and is a fine agricultural valley at the tip of Lake Mead where many good Christians live a quieter life.

Mesquite: A lot of retirees from Utah live just across the border in Mesquite to take advantage of low taxes. It's still a border town and gambling city but has recently grown despite its dry, desert surroundings. Mesquite is not viable as a retreat since it's on the I-15 corridor and bound to be overrun by refugees from Vegas and perhaps California, but it will allow you to head north before they get there. You should still limit your exposure, so live on the high ground area to the south of I-15 where homes are not as visible.

Reno: If you have to live and work here, pick an area north of town (e.g. Sun Valley) which is farthest from the I-80 freeway from Sacramento. Here you have better access to retreat areas in the northern Sierras. It is realistic to assume that the Lake Tahoe area will also get overwhelmed by refugees from California, and perhaps also as far south as Carson City. So the farmland even further south around Garden City would be best for permanent residences.

Retreat Areas

The Carson Valley, especially south of Carson City, offers probably the best farm-type retreat potential in Nevada. This valley also provides ready access to the beautiful Sierra Nevada Mountains and even Lake Tahoe. The area around Gardnerville is ideal. There is mostly cattle ranching and hay growing here, but you have access to irrigation water from the mountains which can improve the gardening possibilities and high quality drinking water. The area is very conservative in politics, but expensive because of California investors that like the area. Even farther south, you can find a few isolated valleys with irrigated farmland—the Smith Valley and Yerington Valley, where prices are dramatically cheaper. While lacking trees, they are fairly safe due to great isolation. Stay away from Hawthorne, a major nuclear target.

Elko, Ely and Wells: In northern Nevada, there are nice high desert retreat areas outside Elko and Spring Creek (the Ruby Mountains) and north of Winnemucca west of Hwy 95 leading to Oregon. Also consider properties around Wild Horse Reservoir north of Elko on Hwy 225. Wells, near I-80 is not good itself, but farther north you find the Humboldt National forest which has ample ranch land around it. In central Nevada, Ely provides some nice mountain properties along Hwy 6 and 93, but it's a long way to anywhere.

NEW HAMPSHIRE ★★★☆☆

Summary Facts and Ratings

Climate:	Humid continental climate with warm, humid summers and cold, wet winters. Temperatures can hit 20 below zero. Three feet of snow can easily pile up in local yards—and sit there until Mother's Day.
Population Density:	Average. 148 ppl/sq mile (21st highest in nation). Hispanic 2.8%, Asian 2%, Black 1.4%, mixed 1.1%.
Cost of Living Index:	Above average. 118 (average is 100) ranks this as the 12th most expensive state.
Land Ownership:	15.8% of the land is state or federally owned.
Building Permits:	Required for new buildings and most renovations involving the structure. Some jurisdictions may require a permit for small projects like a fence or shed. NH has homes with basements outside of mountain areas with granite near the surface.
Land and Urban Planning:	New Hampshire has been very active recently in promoting statewide "Smart Growth." But so far there is no mandate to do so at the local level.
Food Production:	Adequate in lower elevations. Granular and alluvial soils may need some remediation. Growing season of 90 to 180 days. Most of the state is 150 days. Rainfall averages about 43 inches per year.
Health Environment:	Medium water quality. Surface water has average water pollution. Aquifer water quality is good except near the coast where the ground is porous and susceptible to industrial pollutants. 46% of the population's drinking water is fluoridated. Air quality is a problem in the SW part of the state near Boston.
Traffic:	Mild traffic near Lawrence and Portsmouth. No red light or speed cameras.
Politics:	Independents make up a large proportion of this state and although libertarian candidates often win, liberal candidates and policies are usually favored. Dem 26.7%, Rep 31.2%, Ind/3rd party 42.1%.
Taxes:	Low. Ranked 7th lowest with a state tax burden of 8% of income (US average is 9.8%). No income tax, but there is a flat 5% rate on dividend and interest income. There is no sales tax but the property taxes are the third highest in the nation. Property taxes are collected by both state and local governments.
Corruption:	Low at state government level, high in law enforcement and family courts.
Crime:	Average violent crime of 215/100K, but a moderately high property crime rate of 2194/100K. Crime index for Manchester is 10, Salem 24, Hanover 47, Portsmouth 29 (100 is safest). What little crime there is occurs around NH's cities and near the coast.
Personal Liberty:	High, 4th. NH used to rate highest in the freedom-index report by Mercatus.org but after 2010 they hiked taxes and increased gov't spending.
Gun Liberty:	Good. No permit is required to purchase firearms. "Shall-issue" state for concealed carry (required for carrying a firearm in a vehicle). Open carry is permitted. Firearms need not be registered but gun dealers keep records of sales.
Alternative Medicine:	Naturopathy is legal and regulated by a licensing board and allows Naturopaths to prescribe drugs. Direct entry midwifery is legal but regulated. CPM certificates from other states are usually accepted. A Midwifery Council has been established by the state. School vaccine exemptions: religious and medical.
Home Schooling:	Low regulation. Parents must notify the state or non-public school principle every year and keep a portfolio from each student for two years in case of audit.
Military Targets:	**Portsmouth Naval Shipyard**. Remodel and repair of navy ships; secondary target (mostly in ME). **New Boston Air Force Station**, 10 mi. west of Manchester. Satellite tracking station; primary target. **Pease Air National Guard Base**, Portsmouth. Air refueling; secondary target.
Nuclear Power Plant:	**Seabrook Plant**, near Portsmouth.

Notes

New Hampshire was selected as the top state for liberty potential by the Free State Project—a libertarian grass roots movement that encourages like-minded people to relocate to this state. Presumably it has the best potential for being controlled by libertarian minded people. There has been considerable backlash in the local press over the idea of "being taken over," which never sets well with people. The cost of living here is high, especially for gasoline, heating oil and food.

NH has historically valued its independence and low taxes. The historic conservative nature of the state, however, has been watered down by liberal media dominance from Boston broadcasters who seem to manipulate voters toward liberal/left causes. Political bosses continue to demand NH be one of the 3 early primary states because voters can be manipulated.

The state's motto is "Live Free or Die!" but it means little given NH's growing reputation as a police state with corrupt police and judges. There are many horror stories of the police taking property, killing animals and arresting people without warrants. There were 49 public corruption convictions last year, which is in the high range and reflects a strong intolerance for public corruption. There is, however, much to complain about the state's propensity to take children from homes with little justification—a problem in many states.

There are two significant nuclear targets in NH: the tracking station at New Boston and the Pease Air Guard base at Portsmouth near the Naval Shipyards. Upstate New York, Vermont, New Hampshire and Maine are the only potential retreat sites for those in the ultra-high density Boston-New York corridor.

Strategies for Populated Living Areas

Portsmouth: This city by the coast and on the border with Maine is one big trap zone, surrounded by water and freeways. Being so close to Boston, one really needs to be prepared to retreat. If you plan a retreat in Maine, live on that side of the border. If your retreat is further north into NH, live on the west side of I-95, but watch out—there is only one bridge allowing you to get over the river.

Manchester: This will be one of the first cities to receive the waves of future refugees from Boston who are going north. This small city also has a major nuclear target 10 miles to the east (New Boston satellite tracking), and is surrounded by freeways without many clear, non-exit roads over or under it. We'd recommend the South Hooksett area (anywhere east of I-93), but watch out for water courses and plan how to get around them.

Concord: This is almost as close to Boston social unrest as Manchester. Stay east of I-93. There are also lots of water courses in the area, so map out bridges carefully in your retreat direction.

Hanover: The Home of Dartmouth College has its problems. The high cost of housing drives many locals to outlying areas. Some retirees are also settling on the outskirts in somewhat less-expensive places such as Grantham and Quechee, VT.

Retreat Areas

Look for areas in the northern half of NH—from the surroundings of Lake Winnipesauke northward. In this upper half of the state everything with forestation will make for a good retreat (for the East Coast). You will still have to watch out for eventual influxes of refugees, so select locations far from secondary roads.

NEW JERSEY ☆☆☆☆☆

Summary Facts and Ratings

Climate:	Humid coastal climate. Summers are moderately hot and humid. Winters are cold and damp (average high of 34°F). NJ averages 2.5 tornados per year.
Population Density:	Extremely high. 1,174 ppl/sq mile (highest in nation). Hispanic 17%, Black 15%, Asian 7.8%, mixed 1.4%.
Cost of Living Index:	Very high. 126 (average is 100) ranks this as the 8th most expensive state.
Land Ownership:	Poor. 17.7% of the land is state or federally owned.
Building Permits:	Required everywhere for even small new construction or renovations of existing buildings. Some localities even require a permit to replace kitchen appliances. There is good basement potential in most locations.
Land and Urban Planning:	The State Planning Act created the State Planning Commission (SPC) and mandated that the SPC prepare and adopt the State Development and Redevelopment Plan (SDRP). This preempts local planning.
Food Production:	Good productivity with rich soil and a growing season of 120 to 180 days depending on location. Rainfall averages about 47 inches per year.
Health Environment:	One of the 10 worst states for surface water pollution. Ground water aquifers are also easily polluted with the many chemicals and pesticides from industrial and agricultural sources. Only 15% of the population's drinking water is fluoridated.
Traffic:	Heavy traffic problems in the NJ-NY metro area. Rated as 2nd worst traffic area in America, after Los Angeles. NJ does use red light and speed cameras.
Politics:	NJ has the highest percentage of independent voters but these historically vote left/liberal. Dem 23.2%, Rep 17.7%, Ind/3rd party 60%.
Taxes:	Second highest tax burden of any state with an average state tax burden of 12.3% of income. Income tax rates go up to almost 9%. Sales taxes are 7% and property taxes are the highest in the nation.
Corruption:	Very high. NJ had only 11 public corruption convictions last year when there should have been hundreds.
Crime:	Moderately high. Violent crime 289/100K, property crime 1,883/100K. Crime index for Jersey City is 35, Newark 11, Atlantic City 2 (100 is safest). Newark violent crime rates are almost on par with Atlantic City, one of the highest crime cities in the nation.
Personal Liberty:	Very low. Ranked 48th. NJ rates second-worst in the overall freedom rating due to high regulation of both personal and economic freedoms.
Gun Liberty:	Very bad. A permit is required to purchase firearms. "May issue" state for concealed firearm permits and rarely issues them to normal residents. Open carry requires a permit. Transportation of a weapon through the state is restricted. State requires record of all legal weapon transfers.
Alternative Medicine:	Natural health practitioners free to practice but not state licensed. The practice of direct entry midwifery is licensed by a state board. School vaccine exemptions: religious and medical.
Home Schooling:	Low regulation. No notification to the state required.
Military Targets:	**Fort Dix**, McGuire AFB, SE of Trenton. NG training site, airlift and refueling; primary target. **Fort Monmouth**, Oceanport. Scheduled for closure, but currently houses army communications, intelligence, surveillance and FBI and HSA offices; secondary target. **Picatinny Arsenal**, north of Dover. Munitions research and manufacturing; secondary target. **Earle Naval Weapons Station**, SW of Eatontown. Ship loading port for ammunition; secondary target. **Lakehurst Naval Air Station**. Maintenance of naval search and rescue aircraft and equipment; tertiary target.

Nuclear Power Plants:	**Oyster Creek Plant**, on the coast near Ocean City.
	Salem Plant, in Delaware Bay.
	Hope Creek Plant, in Delaware Bay.

Notes

New Jersey is the most densely populated state in the Union and is filled with trap zones, including being surrounded on three sides by water. From Hackensack and Newark on down to Trenton and Philadelphia, it is almost wall to wall city and suburban communities. It only thins out a little bit between New Brunswick and the 295 Beltway around Trenton. The trouble with New Jersey is that this population corridor blocks any potential of exit from the less populated farm and pineland areas on the Jersey Peninsula. If you live on the Jersey shore or anywhere on the peninsula, you had probably better plan to have a boat or stick it out in the relatively unpopulated pinelands rather than try and run the gauntlet of the corridor, which will be crammed with people fleeing New York and the various cities in and around Jersey City.

The large population centers of New Jersey historically vote Democrat, but the split widens in the suburbs and rural areas leaving the Democrats with a lead of only about 10 percentage points at the end of the last few elections. New Jersey almost went bankrupt in 2010 and elected a Republican governor with a mandate to slash spending.

Three mayors, two state assemblymen, three rabbis and a total of 44 people were caught bribing officials, money laundering and trafficking in human organs on an international scale. Ed Kahrer, the FBI agent in charge said, "New Jersey's corruption problem is one of the worst, if not the worst, in the nation." Lots of politicians get elected on anti-corruption platforms, but little ever changes. Gov. Chris Christie's office was caught creating lane closures during peak traffic times on George Washington Bridge forcing 4 lanes of traffic to merge into one toll booth, creating havoc among commuters to punish the mayor of Fort Lee who refused to endorse Christie in the 2013 election. To date, only one official appointed by Christie to the Port Authority has been prosecuted, although two have resigned and one fired.

There are over 200 listed superfund sites in NJ. Chemical manufacturers, landfills and refineries are and were common in this area. One of the greatest threats in the Camden area is still from the numerous chemical plants. One chemical plant that processes chlorine gas is so close to Manhattan that the Empire State Building seems to rise up behind its storage tanks. According to federal EPA records, the plant poses a potentially lethal threat to 12 million people who live within a 14-mile radius. That chemical plant is just one of dozens of chemical manufacturing sites in the area.

Strategies for Populated Living Areas

Newark/Jersey City: If you live on the west of the Newark metro area, you should develop an exit strategy and follow the principles we outlined in Chapter 13. In fact, we even chose a sample exit strategy from the Newark area precisely because it is so difficult. A color version of that map is at the end of this section before the state color maps. The two closest retreat areas are in central Pennsylvania and the three northeast states of Vermont, New Hampshire and Maine. If heading north to Vermont, you will have to go west before trying to go north. In fact we recommend going almost 10 miles west of the 287 Beltway and catching one of the two roads that go under I-80 where there isn't an on-ramp. Keep to the west of I-87 going north until you get above I-84. From there it is advisable to get across the Hudson River and travel toward VT on the east side. You might have to go as far north as Kingston-Ulster to avoid problems crossing at Poughkeepsie (the first crossing you come to).

If you plan on travelling west to central Pennsylvania, you can either stay south of I-80 until you get away from the crowds or cross as before and go west on the secondary roads north of I-80. The other retreat area that is safer for the long term is the Cumberland Plateau in eastern Tennessee. To get there you need to go west to Harrisburg, PA and then parallel (one valley over) I-81 going to Knoxville. All roads point SW due to the lay of the Appalachian Mountains.

Retreat Areas

Southern New Jersey: There are no good retreat areas within New Jersey because the population density is so high that in any long-term food or social crisis, pillaging will eventually reach everywhere in the rural zone of the peninsula. Still, if you live in southern New Jersey, you can survive by picking a very rural forested location and using basement concealment to ride out any threats that may come your way, avoiding confrontation. The forested area in the trough formed by the Garden State Parkway and the Atlantic City Parkway (centered around Harrisville and Speedwell) is very lightly populated if you get five miles away from either expressway. There is rural land at the most southern tip of New Jersey, around Woodbine, but it is entirely too close to Atlantic City to be safe.

NEW MEXICO ★★☆☆☆

Summary Facts and Ratings

Climate:	Mountainous continental climate in the north and continental plains climate in the east. Hot summers with occasional thunderstorms and cold, dry winters are common to both areas. 8 or 9 tornadoes per year, mostly in the east.
Population Density:	Low. 16.5 ppl/sq. mile (ranked 45th in the nation). Hispanic 45%, American Indian 9.7%, Black 3.1, mixed 2%, Asian 1.5%.
Cost of Living Index:	Slightly below average. 98.5 (average is 100).
Private Land Availability:	Below average. 40% of land is state or federally owned, including a good portion of the best forests and mountain land. Basements are not common but are possible except in hard soils.
Building Permits:	Permits are required in the whole state. Water and energy conservation codes add requirements to your permits and affect landscaping.
Food Production:	Moderate to low. The state averages only 14 in/year of rain. Reduced growing seasons 90-150 days in the northern mountains, over 200 days in the south where it is very hot and limited by water. Most farming areas, such as in Farmington, are near rivers.
Health Environment:	Water quality is excellent where fed by mountain springs. Water from wells is only fair in the valleys. 77% of water supplies are fluoridated. Air pollution is not a problem except in Albuquerque. There is excellent solar potential everywhere.
Traffic:	No major traffic problems except in Albuquerque which is heavy during rush hour. Albuquerque employs red light cameras.
Politics:	New Mexico is a conflicted state with heavy Democratic majorities in Albuquerque that won many state wide races. But that trend reversed in 2010 with significant Republican wins, including the governorship. Dem 50% Rep 33%, Ind/3rd party 18%.
Taxes:	Below average. Ranked 14th lowest, with a state tax burden of 8.6% of income. 4.9% income tax, property taxes ranked 8th lowest in the nation and sales tax is 5.13%.
Corruption:	Very high. New Mexico has a long list of corrupt politicians and the list could be growing. Corruption also occurs in the judicial system and police force.
Crime:	High. Violent crime (very high) 613/100K, property crime 3,705/100K. Crime index for Albuquerque is 3, Farmington 11 (100 is safest). Crime is especially bad in Albuquerque due to the high incidence of Latino gangs.
Personal Liberty:	Moderate. ranked 21st.
Gun Liberty:	Very good. No permit to purchase firearms. "Shall issue" state for concealed firearms. No weapons banned. Open carry permitted in the state, including cars.
Alternative Medicine:	Very good. Full range of natural health practitioners. The practice of midwifery is legal and licensed in the state. School vaccine exemptions: religious and medical.
Home Schooling:	Regulated. State requires parents to send notification, but no test scores. Parents must have a high school education to teach. School vaccine exemptions: religious and medical.
Military Targets:	**Holloman AFB** and White Sands Test Facility, Alamogordo. Satellite communications, NASA, rocket engine testing, F-22 fighters; primary target. **Cannon AFB**, Clovis. F-16 and air refueling; primary target. **Kirtland AFB**, SE Albuquerque. Nuclear Weapons Center, F-16, KC-130, Osprey. research laboratories; primary target. **Sandia National Laboratory**. Nuclear weapon storage, research and development; primary target. **National Enrichment Facility**, near Eunice, NM. Power plant fuel rod enrichment plant under construction. Tertiary target.

Notes

New Mexico has a lot of crime and poverty associated with illegal immigration and low productivity of the land. Eastern New Mexico is a dry farming belt extension of the Great Plains, but at higher altitudes ranging from 3500 to 5500. NM is not nearly as productive as the central plains states—due to limited irrigation water from wells and streams. No state has a higher percentage of Hispanics—a whopping 45%. Democratic dominance is now shifting toward the Republicans, but it is doubtful that much will change overall in New Mexico.

High historic levels of corruption in state government also count against this state as a safe haven. Thomas McClenaghan, a retired FBI agent in the state, said New Mexico may be the most corrupt state in the nation. High-profile political figures and associates have been convicted, and ongoing investigations are making frequent headlines. State Treasurers seem to be particularly prone to corruption. Whenever there is state and city corruption, there is the potential of complicity with the dark side of government which uses the threat of prosecution to gain cooperation of corrupt elements in the state.

New Mexico has numerous nuclear threats during a future war: Los Alamos NW of Santa Fe, Sandia Labs around Albuquerque and Carlsbad, White Sands Missile facility in Las Cruces, Cannon AFB in Clovis (Special Ops) and Holoman AFB in Alamogordo. To find safe places in New Mexico, one has to carefully locate away from the major population centers, the nuclear targets and the hostile zone with Mexico. Generally, that leaves the far northern area and the mountains bordering Arizona. Avoid buying and building on indian lands, due to lease restrictions and law changes specific to their councils.

Strategies for Populated Living Areas

Albuquerque: There are numerous threats in and around Albuquerque which make it hard to find places of safety. The weather in the area presents alternating wind and dust storms with flash floods and torrential rains 2 or 3 times a year. This is the crime capitol of New Mexico, complete with dozens of Latino gangs. Winter is relatively mild with a few dustings of snow and some strong winds. You must have a retreat somewhere else if you live here, so you have to be worried about exit paths as well. You don't want to go north on I-25 to Santa Fe in a crisis because it is downwind of a major nuclear target (Los Alamos).

The Sandia Labs at Kirtland AFB are just south of I-40 near the airport, so one must stay in north Albuquerque to be out of this potential blast zone. There are two north-south barriers cutting through Albuquerque: the Rio Grande River and I-25. Unfortunately, there is only one non-interstate highway leading to Farmington's haven of safety in NW New Mexico and that is Hwy 550. To get to it you have to take the 528 Beltway to Hwy

313 or 448 and 528 going north and you have to cross I-25 and the Rio Grande to reach 448 and 528. For this reason, it is better to live on the west side of both obstacles, along the 448 or 528 corridors, but not in Rio Rancho. Rio Rancho is a boom town with too many problems like corrupt mayors, bad city infrastructure (water mains keep breaking), flash floods and the huge Intel semiconductor plant that puts out some damaging pollutants.

Santa Fe: This is a lovely town north of Albuquerque and much closer to the safety of the mountains. However, it is a Mecca for the wealthy and is also a New Age haven with occult overtones, directly downwind from Los Alamos, depending on which way the wind is blowing. It has plenty of distance from potential blasts but you'll need a fallout shelter with good protection if you choose Santa Fe.

Retreat Areas

Kirtland/Farmington/Bloomfield/Aztec area: This used to be a poor irrigated farm area, but since the discovery of oil, gas and coal, it has become an energy hub. While not a mountain retreat area, this line of towns is close to the Four Corners area that is so far distant from most threats that one can find rural farm retreats here that promise a great deal of safety, without having to live in the mountains. The Animas, La Plata, and San Juan Rivers flow through Farmington, accounting for two-thirds of the surface water in New Mexico. In a state as dry as New Mexico, that accounts for a lot. Durango, Colorado is the closest commercial city. Farmington itself is a nice town with a regional airport, but the smaller farm towns along the rivers are really nice too. The Kirtland/Fruitland area is an old Mormon colony. Bloomfield, La Plata and Aztec further east on each of the incoming rivers are also nice towns. Navajo Lake to the NE is the major recreation area. If the dam ever fails, it will flood all the San Juan River basin, so make sure you don't locate in the flood plain along these small towns.

Espanola/Santa Cruz: This farm community along the upper Rio Grande valley is a fine farm retreat site with reasonable prices, unlike Santa Fe to the south. There are numerous other small towns along the tributary streams that feed the Rio Grande, like Chimayo, to consider.

Taos: This town is the symbol of alternate energy and adobe solar homes in New Mexico. It is located in the high desert at the foot of the gorgeous Sangre de Cristo Mountains. Taos has a rich culture and history, fine restaurants, art galleries and world renowned recreation. It is very isolated from any major city—which is good for retreats, but usually hard for full time living. The smaller towns like Arroyo Seco/Valdez and Questa provide more mountain retreat areas.

NEW YORK ★★⯪☆☆

Summary Facts and Ratings

Climate:	Humid continental climate. Upstate NY is subject to long cold winters with averages below −13 °F. Summers are moderately hot and humid in the 80s °F. New York City is hotter and more humid.
Population Density:	Very high: 414 ppl/sq mile (7th highest in nation). Black 18%, Hispanic 17%, Asian, 7%, mixed 1.6%.
Cost of Living Index:	High. 136 (average is 100) ranks as the 3rd most expensive state.
Land Ownership:	Moderate. 36.9% of the land is state or federally owned.
Building Permits:	Required everywhere in large cities for most new construction or renovations of existing buildings. Small projects like decks, sidewalks, etc. often require a permit. There are rural counties with fewer requirements. Basements are common, except in the lake districts where the water table is high.
Land and Urban Planning:	There is no central planning agency; however, there are a number of state agencies that mandate aspects of plans for the entire state.
Food Production:	Adequate. Good soil and a growing season of 90-210 days, average is 150 days. Rainfall is about 42 inches per year.
Health Environment:	Average water quality. Better surface and aquifer water quality in the northern and eastern part of state. Long Island water quality is very poor. 72% of the population's drinking water is fluoridated.
Traffic:	Heavy. New York City is rated as the fourth worst traffic city in the nation. Most serious bottlenecks are around bridges and tunnels. NY does use red light cameras.
Politics:	Democrats are favored by voters in NYC (almost half the state population) and in larger cities like Buffalo but rural areas of the state vote largely republican. Dem 46.8%, Rep 27.1%, Ind/3rd party 26.1%.
Taxes:	Highest in the nation with a state tax burden of 12.6% of income. Incremented income tax rates are 4%-8.82% (around 6.9% for most). Local and state sales taxes average at 8.3% and property taxes are the fifth highest in the nation (collected locally).
Corruption:	Extremely high in New York City and high in the state capitol.
Crime:	High. Violent crime 394/100K, property crime 1825/100K. Crime index for NYC is 25, Brooklyn 37, Queens 49, Albany 7 (100 is safest)
Personal Liberty:	Terrible. Ranked as by far the lowest state in the freedom study by Mercatus.org.
Gun Liberty:	Considered the worst state in the US. A permit is required to purchase firearms. Firearms must be registered. "May issue" state for concealed firearm permits but it's almost impossible to obtain in NYC. Open carry or in a vehicle requires a permit. Transportation of a weapon through the state is restricted. NYC requires a license just to have a gun in the home—big fees and lots of paperwork. New law in 2013 further restricts guns including a 7 round limit on magazines.
Alternative Medicine:	Alternative medicine is practiced in the state but is often harassed and sued. The practice of lay midwifery in NY is legal but regulated. Certified midwives must meet state specific requirements. School vaccine exemptions: religious and medical.
Home Schooling:	High regulation. Parents must notify the state and provide quarterly reports of curriculum, annual test reports and keep attendance records.
Military Targets:	**Fort Drum**, 10 mi. west of Watertown. Training site and home of 10th Mountain Division; tertiary target. **Fort Hamilton**, west end of Long Island. Army NG and reserve base; not a target. **Watervliet Arsenal**, north of Albany. Artillery manufacturing; tertiary target. **West Point** on the Hudson River. US Army Military academy; not a target. **Hancock Field ANG**, Syracuse. F-16 jets and Reaper UAVs; secondary target.

Military Targets continued:	**Stewart ANG**, west of Newburgh. C-5's for airlift; secondary target. **Brookhaven National Laboratory**, Upton, Long Island. Nuclear and high-energy physics research; primary target. **West Milton Area Knolls Atomic Lab**, on 2 sites near Schenectady. Naval nuclear propulsion laboratory; secondary target.
Nuclear Power Plants:	**Fitzpatrick Plant and Nine Mile Point Plant**, southeast shore of Lake Ontario. **Ginna Plant and Indian Point Plant**, near Buchanan on the Hudson River.

Notes

New York State has some beautiful rural, forested land in the upstate area, particularly above Albany and Syracuse that would be great for retreats except it is tied to the politics of NYC in the south. High taxes, high regulations, high cost of living and restricted liberties are too expensive a price for the scenery and rural living benefits.

New York had 20 public corruption convictions last year, where it should have had a thousand. New York City has a huge democratic political machine that is every bit as crooked as Tammany Hall in the 1800s. The New York vote has often been manipulated by as much as 10%. Corruption is chronic with high leaders. State Senate President and Majority Leader, Pedro Espada, of the Bronx stole $14 million from his nonprofit charity. Congressman Charlie Rangel was guilty of 11 ethics violations, not including the really bad stuff that got covered up. He got away with a censure instead of expulsion. Former Governor Eliot Spitzer was caught using a call-girl service.

Police corruption is rampant, and judges are complicit by almost always ruling in their favor. NY was the home of Bernie Kerick the city's most corrupt police commissioner and also of America's Most Corrupt Mayor—Rudolph Giuliani. Historically high crime areas on Long Island are rated lower in crime than many populated upstate areas leading us to think that some of this is due to differences in reporting methods (or hiding statistics).

Natural medicine has been under attack for many years. In 1994 New York alternative healthcare advocates managed to pass the Alternative Medical Practice Act designed to help guarantee that people would have access to alternative medical doctors by barring the State of New York from taking away the licenses of alternative medical doctors just because they practiced alternative or non-conventional medicine. Despite the passing of this legislation, the medical board bureaucrats found a way to avoid the intent of the law and alternative medical doctors were once again targeted and eliminated from medicine. NY medical boards vigorously prosecute any medical doctor who uses alternative therapies.

Despite all the military facilities in this state, there aren't many serious targets in a nuclear war. New York City itself is a tempting target for an enemy as it is the financial center of the nation. There are several nuclear power plants north of NYC which are a concern if they are destroyed. But the biggest threat, by far is the huge and highly dense NYC metro area itself with its millions of people. New York is highly dependent on truck and train supplies for food and necessities each day. Even though most people are honest and hardworking, even small percentages of criminals and contentious minorities amount to hundreds of thousands of problem people who will look for a way out of the urban areas in a major crisis. Everyone who lives or works around this huge metropolitan area needs multiple escape plans.

Strategies for Populated Living Areas

New York Metro Area: You couldn't ask for a worse geography to create multiple trap zones. Every inch of Manhattan is high density city. Long Island can almost only be accessed through the dense urban areas to the west. The rest of the metro cities (e.g. Yonkers and Mt. Vernon to White Plains, etc.) are on a peninsula bounded by the Hudson River on the west and Long Island Sound on the east. There is simply no way to exit this area in a crisis of panic except north, along with countless millions unless you get a couple of hours advanced warning or have a boat. An airplane on Long Island wouldn't be a bad idea either. It won't do any good to get on the Jersey side of the Hudson either, it's just as crowded.

You should live no closer than White Plains in the north (outside of the 287 Beltway) or Brentwood on Long Island. Living outside the densest areas at least gives you some time to react, and if prepared in advance, a head start in leaving. Naturally, there is no option of leaving Long Island by car once a major panic crisis happens. You can either hunker down to survive in place (if you have prepared concealed safe rooms somewhere—hopefully below ground) or you can leave via boat. We strongly recommend the boat option in this area since everything on the New York side of the Hudson is surrounded by water. There are numerous marinas in both Manhattan and Long Island, and there are no geographic restrictions on your ability to sail off to safety. Naturally, you need to have a retreat either north or south with an old car stationed at a remote boat house on the coast or up a river. It doesn't have to be a fancy yacht, as long as it is large enough to handle open seas or the current of the Hudson if going up north. When the freeways are packed, you can go a lot farther north via the Hudson, even if at 3-6 knots.

As for using a light aircraft to exit the area, hangar your plane at an untowered airport ("uncontrolled airport") so you can get into the air even if the government is shutting down commercial air traffic.

Albany-Schenectady: There are three different retreat directions from Albany (in order of safety): North toward the Canadian border, east into Vermont or west into rural New York or even north-central Pennsylvania. If retreating east to Vermont, locate on the east side of I-90 and the Hudson River. If going west, locate on that side of I-87 and I-90 further north. If going north, we recommend locating in or around East Grenville in order to beat the traffic out of both Albany and Schenectady.

Syracuse: Stay south and either east or west of I-81 depending on whether you are heading for the Finger Lakes region on the west or the farm/forest retreat areas centered around Sherburne.

Rochester: Locate south of I-90 and either east or west of I-390 to be able to gain quick access to rural farm land retreats in either the Carlton Hill State Forest area or the Finger Lake district to the East. The Finger Lakes have more people, so we would recommend the west.

Buffalo: Stay southwest of the city. The best retreats are in that direction or into north-central Pennsylvania.

Retreat Areas

Upstate New York: Despite the population density of the NYC area, Upstate New York in the forest and lake district bounded by I-87 on the east and I-81 on the west and north of I-90 is pretty good for the East coast. The rural lands south of Albany will absorb most of the refugee and pillaging potential of the crowds fleeing NY and Newark. There aren't that many main roads in the north, so it's fairly easy to find property off in the backwoods for privacy.

Western New York: If you look at a map of New York State, you will see four trapezoidal or triangular shaped areas south of I-90, each bounded by two other interstate freeways. Each of these has some retreat potential depending on how well concealed your property is from major roads and view.

Area SW of Albany between I-87 and I-88: This is the area that is least safe overall because it will be most impacted by the flood of refugees fleeing NYC someday. Most refugees stay fairly close to the roads and only get into the countryside out of desperation for food. Even then they follow signs to small towns hoping to find organized relief. If you choose something in this area, which fortunately is quite large, make sure it is very rural and distant from main or secondary roads.

Area west of Schenectady between I-90 and I-88: This is much safer than the previous area because it is more distant from the source of urban flight and the area just mentioned will absorb a good deal of the refugee problems. There are no major resorts in this area.

The Finger Lakes District southwest of Syracuse: This area has some remote retreat possibilities south of the Finger Lakes, but around the Finger Lakes themselves we find too much commercial activity. For those that want something that doubles as a vacation home and a retreat, this has possibilities.

The area southwest of Rochester: This will receive refugees from Buffalo to the west so it is not quite as good as area #2 above. However, in the eastern sector there are numerous small state forests and rural farms that can provide relative safety.

The area south of I-86 and west of Hwy 15 is better than the areas described above since it is an extension of the northern Pennsylvania retreat areas that we rate fairly highly for the East. There are no major highways in this area, and few refugees will go that direction.

Catskill Mountains: Forget about these. They are the domain of the wealthy from NYC and are much too close to the NYC metro area for comfort.

NORTH CAROLINA ★★☆☆☆

Summary Facts and Ratings

Climate:	Most of the lowlands fall within the humid subtropical climate zone. The mountains in the west are more than 300 miles from the coast and have a subtropical highland climate. NC averages 13 tornadoes a year.
Population Density:	Above average. 192 ppl/sq. mile (ranked 15th highest in nation). Black 21.6%, Hispanic 8%, Asian 2%, mixed 1.3%.
Cost of Living Index:	Below average. 96 (average is 100) making this the 21st least expensive state.
Land Ownership:	Good. 7% of the land is state and federally owned.
Building Permits:	Required for new buildings and major renovations. Some rural counties give wide exceptions to farm buildings or buildings below a certain cost. Basements are easily built except in the mountains where rock would require blasting or jack-hammering.
Land and Urban Planning:	The Land Policy Act mandates that the Land Policy Council enact and update a state comprehensive policy plan. However, the Council has no enforcement powers. Political forces in NC have attempted to mandate Smart Growth but so far it hasn't succeeded.
Food Production:	Excellent in the central and eastern plains. The hill country is more difficult to farm due to rocky, acidic soil mixed with clay. The growing season is 180 to 220 days in the east and 150-180 in the west. Average annual precipitation is 50 inches per year and 70-90 inches in the Smokey Mountains above Georgia.
Health Environment:	One of the worst 20 states for industrial pollution per the EPA. Surface and aquifer quality are better in rural and farm areas. Many EPA superfund sites are between Charlotte and Greenville corresponding to the worst air pollution. 88% of the population's drinking water is fluoridated.
Traffic:	Charlotte has the 35th worst traffic in the nation and Raleigh is 50th (out of 75 cities). NC uses red light cameras.
Politics:	Politics are very polarized as the progressive liberals try and overcome NC's traditional conservative values. Dem 46%, Rep 35%, Ind/3rd party 19%.
Taxes:	Average. NC ranks 17th highest with a state tax burden of 9.8% of income. Income tax is a flat 5.75%, property taxes are average and state and local sales tax averages at 8.1%.
Corruption:	High, particularly within the state government.
Crime:	High. Violent crime 342/100K, property crime 3128/100K. Crime index for Charlotte is 11, Greensboro 11, Raleigh 15 (100 is safest). These cities are where most of the crime occurs (largely due to racial and cultural gang components). In the mountains meth labs seem to be increasing.
Personal Liberty:	Average. 24th in the nation.
Gun Liberty:	Fair. Permit is required to purchase a handgun including stating the purpose for it; valid for 5 years. "Shall issue" state for concealed firearm permits. A person who may possess a machine gun is required to obtain a permit from the county sheriff as well as the BATRE. Open carry state, even in a car.
Alternative Medicine:	Alternative medicine is discouraged by medical practice laws, but largely unprosecuted. Naturopaths still practice in NC but are being increasingly regulated and restricted. Lay midwifery is effectively prohibited because statutes are unclear. School vaccine exemptions: religious and medical.
Home Schooling:	Moderate regulation. State requires parents to send notification and test scores or professional evaluation of student progress.
Military Targets:	**Fort Bragg**, Camp Mackall, Pope AFB, NW of Fayetteville. Special Forces, Airborne, USAF airlift; primary target. **Sunny Point Military Ocean Terminal**, Wilmington. Key ammunition shipping point and storage; primary target. **Camp Lejeune**, New River MCAS, Jacksonville. Large USMC Base with C-22 Osprey and helicopters; primary target. **Cherry Point Marine Corps Air Station**, north of Havelock. F-18, Harrier, F-35 (planned), A-6, helicopters; primary target. **Charlotte Douglas Airport**, C-130 ANG; not a target.

| Military Targets continued: | **Seymour Johnson AFB**, **Goldsboro**. F-15 fighters and air refueling; primary target.
Harvey Point Defense Testing Activity, 35 mi east of Kitty Hawk on the bay. CIA training base with secret operations; secondary target. |
| Nuclear Power Plants: | **Brunswick Plant**, south of Wilmington. 2 reactors. Operating since 1977.
McGuire Plant, 20 mi north of Charlotte. 2 reactors. Operating since 1984.
Shearon Harris Plant, 20 mi. southwest of Raleigh. 1 reactor. Operating since 1987. |

Notes

North Carolina used to be a rural agricultural state. Its major products were tobacco, hogs and furniture. Most of the textile jobs have gone to China now and tobacco jobs are down, but new industry has made NC one of America's leading growth states. The high growth area of Research Triangle Park between Raleigh, Durham and Chapel Hill, has become one of the world's leading pharmaceutical and high-tech research centers; including semiconductors, nanotechnology, and security technology. There are also many corporate headquarters in the area. The population grew by 45% from 1980 to 2005 bringing wealth, pollution, corruption and liberal people which do not share the state's traditional family values. The state's Hispanic population was the fastest growing in the country in the past decade and a half, which has contributed to the crime rate.

North Carolina's religious, tradition-minded citizens had been overwhelmed politically by the leftist-progressive citizens in the big growth areas and around the two major liberal universities until 2011 when Republicans also won a majority among state legislators and in 2013 the governor's seat. Voters still often split along cultural lines. In the 2004 exit poll, 85% of blacks voted Democrat while conservative, white Protestants voted 95% Republican.

There were 36 public corruption convictions last year. In the past six years, corruption convictions included North Carolina's House Speaker, its Agriculture Commissioner and a State Representative. In early 2010, a federal grand jury was investigating former democratic Governor Mike Easley, but only indicted his top adviser—typical of corruption investigations.

North Carolina rates fair for the East, thanks to the Smokey Mountains in the western parts. There are a lot of military targets here, particularly in the coastal plains. We would only recommend retreats west of Hickory in the mountains. Asheville is the center of the hill country but has grown so much it has its own problems now. The mountains south of Asheville get almost 80 inches of annual rainfall from Franklin down through Clayton, GA. North of Asheville the mountains are drier. Depending on the winds, these areas are downwind of potential fallout from Oak Ridge Labs west of Knoxville.

Strategies for Populated Living Areas

Raleigh Durham area: This is the new high tech center of NC, so your chances of having to locate in this area are high if you are employed by one of the major corporations. Since the safest areas of retreat are west, we would recommend locating around Chapel Hill. It is surrounded by low density rural land and yet is to the west of significant cities and suburbs but not too far away to commute.

Greensboro, Winston-Salem, High Point area: We recommend you locate west of Hwy 70 from Lexington to Winston-Salem. If you work in High Point, Lexington isn't a bad commute and puts you to the west for a quick exit during social unrest. Depending on where you choose your retreat in the mountains, pick the sector leading away from Winston-Salem that gives you unimpeded access without having to cross a major freeway, which can be a formidable barrier. If you can't, and need to cross a freeway in your exit route, pick a crossing that is not an access ramp. Each sector west of Winston Salem will have to cross I-77 on their way west. Hunting Creek Church Rd, Union Grove, and Jennings are secondary roads that cross with the potential conflict of an off ramp, but there are several smaller roads you can find on maps.

Charlotte: Stay west of both the 85/485 Beltway and also the river that leads to Lake Wylie. Mt. Holly would be an ideal location to commute from and gives you multiple barriers between the metro area and your residence. It also gives you the best way out of town to the west without having to go through Gastonia.

Retreat Areas

General advice: There are lots of potential rural farm retreats all over, especially in the coastal plains, but they aren't safe in the long term due to potential confrontation with refugees someday. There are a lot of nuclear military targets in eastern NC that will drive thousands toward the cities in the center of the state. That, in turn, will create a great deal of social unrest there. If you have to get out on the roads and retreat west, it would be a major problem getting past those population centers in turmoil. That is why we recommend strongly that you locate to the west of the Charlotte-Greenville line to start with. If you are already settled in the east and aren't close to a nuclear target, be sure and follow the recommendations about making your place safer and more concealed behind plenty of tree cover and away from major roads.

Smokey Mountains: The NC mountains are the first area that people from the east will flock to for safety if there is a meltdown in the cities. That is why we don't rate them as safe as the Cumberland Plateau in Tennessee. However, there is a lot of cover and concealment available in these mountains and the old timers there have a "don't tread on me" attitude. That's good for survival but doesn't equate to an open arms attitude toward flatlanders coming into the mountains to build recreation cabins. Take your time to get to know the neighbors before you buy. Real hostility can ruin all of your retreat plans no matter how safe the hills and forests can be. There is less private land south of Ashville but we prefer the land north as it is less rainy. Andrews is probably the best moderately sized town near good retreat property.

NORTH DAKOTA ★★⯪☆☆

Summary Facts and Ratings

Climate:	Northern continental climate. Summers are hot (and humid in the east), winters are very cold with snowfall above 40 inches annually. Rainfall is sparse and droughts are common. ND averages 20 tornados per year.
Population Density:	Very low. 9.3 ppl/sq.mi. (47th ranking in the nation). 90% of ND's towns have less than 2,000 people. 65% of the population is from European descent. American Indian 5.6%, Hispanic 2.3%, Black 1.2%, mixed 1.2%.
Cost of Living Index:	Near average. 101.2 (average is 100) ranks this as the 27th least expensive state.
Private Land Availability:	Good. Only 5% of the land is state or federally owned.
Building Permits:	Required for all construction but local jurisdiction requirements vary. Consistent deep soil is good for basements.
Land and Urban Planning:	No state plan. Townships, cities, and counties have planning and zoning power. However, cities with populations greater than 25,000 people have exclusive control over land located within two miles, for planning purposes.
Food Production:	Good. Especially in the east which gets more rain. Severe conditions such as drought, early frost and storms are common but are manageable if they don't persist. Water is scarce in the western part, but soil is all sandy loam and good for growing gardens—particularly if irrigation is available. Growing season is 90–150 days. Average yearly rainfall is only about 16in.
Health Environment:	Ground water in the eastern farm district has elevated concentrations of agricultural pollution and chemicals, but the drier ranching country in the west does not. 96.5% of the state's water is fluoridated—very bad. Almost no air pollution.
Traffic:	No heavy traffic problems.
Politics:	ND has populist tendencies like all the plains states. Many once supported a socialist party, the Non-Partisan League—now merged with the Democrats. But the state is now mostly conservative. Dem 25%, Rep 50%, Ind/3rd party 25%.
Taxes:	Lower than average. Ranked 15th for low taxes with a state tax burden of 8.8% of income. The income tax increments from 1.8%-3.22%, property taxes are 10th in the nation and the local and state sales tax average is 5%.
Corruption:	Average. North Dakota had only 3 public corruption convictions recently, but on a per capita basis, that is fairly high. ND lacks any campaign financial disclosure laws which aids corruption of politicians.
Crime:	Low. Violent crime 270/100K, property crime 2094/100K. Even Fargo, the largest city, has low crime (crime index of 20).
Personal Liberty:	Very Good. Rated first out of 50 states by Mercatur.org.
Gun Liberty:	Fair. No permit to purchase a firearm. "Shall issue" state for concealed weapon permits. Open carry requires the same permit.
Alternative Medicine:	Natural medicine is less restricted but there are few Naturopathic Doctors in the state. Direct-entry midwifery is legal and unregulated. School vaccine exemptions: philosophical, religious and medical.
Home Schooling:	High Regulation: State requires parents to send notification, achievement test scores or professional evaluation and other requirements such as curriculum approval by the state, teacher qualification of parents, or home visits by state officials.
Military Targets:	**Camp Grafton Training Areas**, Devil's Lake. Army NG training areas; not a target. **Cavalier AFS**, 10 mi. E. of Cavalier near Canada border. Phased array radar and space warning; primary target. **Grand Forks AFB**. KC-135 air refueling; primary target. **Minot AFB**, 10 mi. north of Minot. Minuteman III missile maintenance and B-52s capable of carrying nuclear weapons; multiple primary targets.

Notes

This state was part of the ancient tribal grasslands of the Lakota Sioux Indians. These grasslands provide rich soil and good growing conditions when there is sufficient water. There is abundant grassland game, such as pheasant and antelope. The population is light throughout the state and there are no large cities. Fargo is the only city over 100,000 people. The other significant towns are Bismarck (the capitol), Grand Forks and Minot.

The low population and isolating climate are good here, but the climate is a bit too harsh, cold and dry. Moreover ND is too regulated in freedoms essential to conservatives. Flooding is a major threat in most river courses of North Dakota due to the flat lay of the land, especially the Red River which backs up when major ice flows clog the river banks.

There are significant strategic nuclear targets in the state, two of which are close to larger cities. Minot is surrounded on the north, west and southeast with missile silos which are each likely to be hit with nuclear weapon in war. Avoid the areas north and south, corresponding to the prevailing wind directions. The missile sites around Grand Forks AFB have been deactivated and destroyed, but long range refueling aircraft are still a target.

Strategies for Populated Living Areas

Fargo is in the fallout shadow of Grand Forks AFB, so residents should have tornado shelters with concrete roofs that also protect against fallout. Watch out for the many areas in potential flood zones from the Red River, which is constantly threatening, especially north of the city. Unlike most US rivers, the Red flows northward, which means that thawed water often builds up against snow and river ice dams downstream flooding easily. The Red River flows right through the middle of Fargo.

Grand Forks: Surprisingly, we think this city is relatively safe from the nuclear blast threat on Grand Forks AFB even though it is only 24 miles east. It is sufficiently far away that the prevailing north-south winds will likely push the fallout elsewhere. Just keep your distance from the freeway which will always be the main channel for refugees.

Bismarck: North Dakota's capitol is downwind of Minot AFB, when north winds blow. Pick the SE part of the area, away from the river.

Retreat Areas

Rural farmland: Excluding the rural farmland within 50 miles of the missile fields surrounding Minot, and the areas north or south subject to fallout, we consider these areas fairly safe for farm retreats. The wind rarely blows east, so the least susceptible areas are east of the line between Minot and Bismarck. Like South Dakota, this state's harsh and arid reputation will discourage refugees fleeing war, economic or social unrest from settling here, nor will they dare venture very far from the freeway towns. Follow the general rule to stay at least 10 miles away from a major interstate, and find a good place with water and hopefully some trees for windbreaks and shade. The best locations are those that are not visible from any main road. In this state, that means distance more than tree cover. The disadvantage of using isolation for retreat safety is that you are isolated from commerce and friends.

OHIO ★★☆☆☆

Summary Facts and Ratings

Climate:	Humid continental climate with hot muggy summers and cold winters. OH averages 16 tornados per year.
Population Density:	Moderately high. 284 ppl/sq. mile (9th highest in the nation). Black 12%, Hispanic 2.8%, Asian 1.6%, mixed 1.1%.
Cost of Living Index:	Below average. 92.5 (average is 100) makes this the 16th least-expensive state.
Private Land Availability:	Good. Only 2.6 % of the land is state or federally owned.
Building Permits:	Required everywhere for new construction or big renovation of buildings. Deep soil is good for basements. Possible bedrock in Appalachian area.
Land and Urban Planning:	No statewide plan exists. Everything is determined at the local level.
Food Production:	Good. Rich soil and a growing season of 150-180 days. Rainfall averages about 39 inches per year.
Health Environment:	Surface water pollution is higher than average. Aquifers are susceptible to chemicals and pesticides around commercial farms. 92% of Ohioan's drinking water is fluoridated.
Traffic:	Heavy traffic problems are common in Cincinnati, Cleveland and Columbus, rated as #36, #42, and #52, respectively of the 75 worst traffic cities. Red light and speed cameras are used.
Politics:	Ohio is nearly evenly split. Democrats dominate the northeast urban areas with their industrial unions and republicans have the rest of the rural areas. Democrat's actions under Obama led to more republican votes in 2010. Dem 41%, Rep 42%, Ind/3rd party 17%.
Taxes:	High. Ranked 18th highest, with a state tax burden of 9.7% of income. Income tax is 0.6%-5.33%, state and local sales tax average to 6.8% and property taxes are 12th highest in the nation (collected by state and local governments).
Corruption:	High. Corruption at all levels from State Representatives to election officers.
Crime:	Moderately high. Violent Crime 286/100K, property crime 2928/100K. Crime index for Columbus is 7, Cincinnati 3, Cleveland 2 (100 is safest). In Cleveland, violent crime was almost four times the national average.
Personal Liberty:	Low, ranked 33rd in the nation.
Gun Liberty:	Good. No permit to purchase firearms. "Shall issue" state for concealed firearm permits. No gun registry. Open carry or in a vehicle only with a permit.
Alternative Medicine:	Natural health practitioners are free to practice. The status of lay midwifery is not legally defined, but not prohibited. School vaccine exemptions: philosophical, religious and medical.
Home Schooling:	Moderate regulation. State requires parents to send notification, test scores, and/or professional evaluation of student progress.
Military Targets:	**Defense Construction Supply**, Columbus. Supply facility for military materiel; not a target. **Lima Army Tank Plant**. Manufactures M1 tanks; secondary target. **Ravenna Arsenal**, between Ravenna and Newton Falls. NG training site; not a target. **Mansfield-Lamm Airport**, Mansfield. C-130 airlift for NG; not a target. **Rickenbacker Airport**, 10 mi south of Columbus. KC-135 air refueling NG; secondary target. **Springfield-Beckley Airport**, Springfield. F-16 Air National Guard; tertiary target. **Toledo Express Airport**, Toledo. F-16 Air National Guard; tertiary target. **Wright-Patterson AFB**, Dayton. C-5 Heavy airlift, air force research; primary target.

| Military Targets continued: | **Piketon Uranium Enrichment Facility** or **Portsmouth Facility**, 60 miles south of Columbus in Piketon. Gaseous diffusion plant for weapons and a centrifuge plant, operated through Oak Ridge Laboratories; primary target. |
| Nuclear Power Plants: | **Perry Plant** on Lake Erie, NE of Cleveland.
Davis Besse Plant, southwest shore of Lake Erie. 10 miles north of Oak Harbor. |

Notes

Ohio is a large and powerful state in terms of manufacturing, agriculture and political power—not as much as New York, Illinois and California, but close. The cost of living isn't bad here, and a new survey shows that it's cheaper to insure a home in Ohio than in most other states. Ohio's population has held steady at about 11 million for decades, but with the declining economy its people are on the move and crime has increased. Said one observer, "They are heading to what they perceive as the country, resulting in a clash of cultures in rural areas." Mostly property crimes keep officers busy in rural areas. In cities surrounding Columbus, overworked departments have too much territory to cover, too little cash and too few deputies. Between 1993 and 2002 the number of thefts alone nearly doubled to 1,353 and burglaries skyrocketed 83 percent between 2000 and 2001 in Delaware County. Car thefts in western Licking County increased 50%, residential burglaries rose 34% in 2002 while business burglaries increased 150%.

Cincinnati and Cleveland are major problem urban centers—beset by crime and other big city problems. Dayton, Toledo, Canton and Youngstown all have the same faults. Part of the crime problem is owing to the high percentage of Hispanic immigrants (36-37%) moving into the state. The cold winters haven't seemed to deter them. Columbus is considered more clean and safe, but it is also where the most political corruption is centered. The northern Ohio industrial cities have a reputation for not being too friendly. Said one resident after moving to a rural town, "I live in Zanesville, Ohio. I was taken aback by how friendly people were. In Cleveland, you wouldn't look a stranger in the eye, let alone say hello."

Ohio is a major transportation corridor, the gateway to the Midwest. It has the fifth highest volume of truck traffic in the US and sadly, has the second-highest number of hazardous materials spills nationwide (highways, railways and waterways) in each of the past 10 years, according to the U.S. Department of Transportation reports.

One of the reasons why Ohio residents are susceptible to government power is because so many work for the local, state and federal government. Only Virginia and Maryland have higher percentages of government related workers and that's due to the close connection with the nation's capitol.

Ohio had 13 public corruption convictions last year—all at lower levels, but corruption is extensive at the top too. Rep. James Traficant, an Ohio Democrat, was expelled from Congress after being found guilty of bribery and racketeering. Ohio was caught corrupting ballots in the 2008 election. There have been numerous scandals over favoritism and

kickbacks in public contracting. Democratic state Sen. Marc Dann got elected Attorney General on a campaign against corruption but was found to harass female employees in his office. After years of a federal investigation, FBI agents this year arrested the head of Cleveland's Cuyahoga County Board of County Commissioners and two judges on multiple corruption charges. The county's auditor was arrested the week before. Naturally, there is police corruption too.

There are some health issues to watch for in Ohio. Some of the ground water smells and tastes like sulfur which is more unpleasant than dangerous. Radon is also a problem in many central Ohio homes. Radon is a colorless, odorless gas generated by decaying uranium. It's like low-level exposure to radioactivity. Radon is heavier than air so special care has to be taken in building basements to make them impervious to it. Licking and Franklin Counties are the worst. You can get home test kits from several locations and often from local government agencies.

Ohio has relatively few nuclear military targets and is considered a "safe" destination for the wealthy and well-connected within government. Retail billionaire Les Wexner is typical of that crowd, hobnobbing with globalists George W. Bush and Arnold Schwarzenegger, and building palatial mansions in east Columbus with large bunker systems. He is one of the privileged few that have been warned by government insiders that a nuclear war will someday descend upon America. This area may have some safety from nuclear devastation but it still may not be safe for the rest of us that don't have connections with government for preferential protection during social unrest and martial law.

The big government orientation of some leaders here has had an effect on how the local National Guard units are used. During the Y2K concerns, Ohio's National Guard was practicing maneuvers to shut down the 270 Beltway around Columbus to prepare for possible martial law control. That's another reason not to plan on using the freeways for an exit strategy.

Strategies for Populated Living Areas

Cleveland is surrounded by other suburban cities that have merged into one high density urban zone, so we do not recommend the core of this city. Even locating at the periphery of any of the outlying suburbs, there is only one sector that is safe for a better exit, and that is in the Strongsville area. The closest retreat area is around New Philadelphia so don't locate on the eastern or southern sectors because you have to travel between the two industrial towns of Akron and Youngstown, and there are only 5 or 6 rural roads to choose from. It can be done, but it is much safer and less populated to go west around Akron on rural roads, making sure you know how to cross I-71 at a point where there are no access ramps.

Columbus: Our recommendation for Columbus is to stay outside the 270 Beltway. If you have a retreat site in the nearby "Little Appalachia" area, locate on the SE sector toward Lancaster or Circleville. If you are retreating southward, avoid picking a retreat location downwind of the nuclear processing plant at Portsmouth, on the Ohio River.

Cincinnati: There are several trap zones in this city, including the Ohio River which snakes its way around in a loop. If your retreat is in southern OH, you should stay outside the 275 Beltway, north of the river and toward the eastern sector. If your intended direction is to retreat west, we recommend you be north of I-75 and the 275 Beltway in or west of the Pleasant Run area. That will give you first access to the secondary roads leading into Indiana.

Toledo: Stay south of and east or west of I-75 to the south, depending on which way you intend to go. If going west, you must plan a route south to the middle of Indiana first to avoid the crush of refugees leaving the industrial centers along the Lakes, like Chicago. You may be the first out of Toledo, but you won't be free of traffic blocks by the time you get south of Chicago unless you are quite far south.

Dayton: There is only one beltway to work around (Hwy 675) on the eastside of town. Wright-Patterson AFB is also nearby, so stay south of 675 on the SE side if retreating to central or southern Ohio, and stay west of I-75 at the periphery of development if retreating west. The most natural route is Hwy 44 to Shelbyville, but from there, we recommend going further south before continuing west to avoid crowds leaving Indianapolis.

Freeway towns and others: They may be small and in a generally rural part of the state, but there will be problems from travelers, eventually. For example, in Zanesville on I-70, citizens see a lot of crime similar to larger cities (crack, gangs and property crime). None of the other small and medium cities away from freeways have these problems, and none present trap zones for exiting the area as long as you stay near the periphery of development.

Retreat Areas

The population density is too high in Ohio generally for any of these areas to compare favorably to areas further west, but the following are the best you can find in Ohio if you need something close. Sometimes it's better to pick something close than to risk being out on the roads for days at a time after a nuclear strike or in the midst of general social unrest.

Northeastern Ohio: This area is the only semi-safe rural area within the Cleveland-Columbus-Pittsburgh triangle. It is hilly and forested with lots of small family farms mixed in. Specifically, it is bounded by the following towns (connect the dots): Start at New Philadelphia on I-77, west to Millersburg, Mt Vernon, south to Newark and I-70, east to Wheeling, north to Steubenville and East Liverpool, then west to Carrollton and New Philadelphia. Of course, it doesn't include the cities within 5-10 miles of the Interstates.

Southeastern Ohio. This area is Ohio's "little Appalachia." That's not only true in terms of forestation and geography but in poverty as well. Some 21 counties in Ohio take part in various federal welfare schemes developed by the Appalachian Regional Commission, created by Congress. This region has thousands of good retreat sites, but most of the poor people in the area, especially coal miners, have become welfare dependent. There have even been food lines formed for the needy in recent years. There are plenty of trees and the people are generally more friendly than in the cities. Crime has increased in all rural areas as drug traffickers and amateur meth labs are built away from law enforcement. There are plenty of rednecks too, but they aren't all bad. Often it's more a label applied by snobbish city dwellers to the "down home" country person.

One astute observer told us about some occult problems: "While there are many honest, decent, hard-working, struggling folks with good character in southeastern Ohio, there's also a 'dark' side to this area, and for decades it seems to center around Athens, Ohio–home of Ohio University. A pretty, wooded, hilly town…Athens, which might have been one of Ohio's shining jewels, has been clouded with bizarre, evil shadows that seem to never fade away. Athens is one of the 'occult capitals' of the nation according to people in the occult community."

Rural farmland: "America's–best kept secrets," said one contributor. "This would be the village of Granville, Ohio (an example of small town America, east of Columbus). I know many people who are world travelers and they tend to agree that Granville is one of the safest, prettiest places they ever visited. A radon problem exists here, but Granville is far enough away from any large cities, yet still close enough to commute easily. People are very friendly here if you ignore the minority of snobs who frequent the Denison University campus area or the gorgeous country inns and restaurants along Broadway, the town's main thoroughfare. Travelers from all over come to sparkling little Granville and usually say the same thing – 'We came here just to get away for awhile.' Granville is, indeed, a great 'get away' spot and is ideal for retirees or anyone who appreciates natural beauty, country elegance, and a quiet, simple lifestyle among the trees, flowers and emerald hills."

Southern Ohio: Most towns in this area are like Granville, but not as grand. The country is not as hilly as Little Appalachia, but there are lots of forested plots next to state forests that can be had fairly reasonably. Avoid Cincinnati by 100 miles on the west and don't get downwind of Portsmouth Nuclear facility in the central portion.

OKLAHOMA ★★★☆☆

Summary Facts and Ratings

Climate:	Continental plains climate with extremes of hot humid summers and dry, cold, windy winters. Second highest tornado state with an average of 53 per year.
Population Density:	Below average. 54 ppl/sq. mile (36th ranking in the nation). Hispanic 8.2%, Black 8.1%, American Indian 8%, mixed 4%, Asian 1.7%.
Cost of Living Index:	Low. 89.7 (average is 100) makes this the 4th cheapest state.
Private Land Availability:	Excellent. Only 2% of the land is state or federally owned.
Building Permits:	Required statewide, but requirements are moderate in rural areas. Basements can be built everywhere.
Land and Urban Planning:	No state planning mandate. Control is by local jurisdictions.
Food Production:	Good. Long growing season of 180-240 days. Average rainfall is over 40 inches in the east but less than 17 inches in the western panhandle.
Health Environment:	Water quality is not good due to agricultural pollution and the state's reliance on wells. Chicken and hog farm runoff also leaches into the water supply. Nitrate levels are high in well water. 70% of the state's water is fluoridated.
Traffic:	Moderate. Rush hour traffic is only heavy in Oklahoma City, Tulsa and Norman, which also use red-light traffic cameras.
Politics:	OK is a safe Republican state in national politics but Democrats are often elected to local offices. Dem 43.7%, Rep 43.6%, Ind/3rd party 13%.
Taxes:	Ranked 12th lowest, with a state tax burden of 9.8% of income. Income tax is 5.25% for most, property taxes are ranked 30th in the nation and state and local sales taxes average 8.4%.
Corruption:	Good ol' Boy network is very prominent in this state. There is also a lot of police corruption and judges are often complicit in the cover-ups.
Crime:	High. Violent crime 441/100K, property crime 3274/100K. Crime index for Oklahoma City is 6, Tulsa 4, and Norman 19 (100 is safest).
Personal Liberty:	Good, rated 5th best in the nation.
Gun Liberty:	Good. No permit to purchase firearms. "Shall issue" state for concealed firearm permits. No open carry permitted even though OK legislature recently affirmed Oklahoman's right to keep and bear arms and transport them in vehicles.
Alternative Medicine:	Good availability, full range of natural health practitioners. Lay midwives prohibited, unfortunately. School vaccine exemptions: philosophical, religious and medical.
Home Schooling:	No regulation. Parents do not have to notify the state.
Military Targets:	**Fort Sill**, north of Lawton. Artillery training school and battery of Marines are stationed here; secondary target. **McAlester Army Ammo Plant**. Conventional ammunition manufacturing plant; secondary target. **Altus AFB**, 40 mi. east of Lawton. C-17 and KC-135 training; secondary target. **Tinker AFB**, southeast of Oklahoma City. Strategic Communications with E-3 AWACS planes; primary target. **Vance AFB**, south of Enid. USAF Training wing, T-38's; not a target. **Will Rogers Airport**, OKC. Air National Guard C-130; not a target.

Notes

Oklahoma has a good central location in the heartland of the US and is the home of more man-made lakes than any other state in the union—a reflection of Oklahoma's continual battle to secure water after the dust bowl years. Its land ranges from grassy plains to the forested regions of the Ouachita Mountains and its own portion of the Ozark Mountains near the Arkansas border. Fortunately, Oklahoma has mostly deep, sandy loam soil and is suitable for basements and underground safe rooms.

Oklahoma is a productive agricultural state (ranked 26th) with access to the giant Ogallala aquifer in the panhandle area. However, only about half of the rest of the state has access to big wells for large food production. Lack of water is a problem in half of the state (OK was one of the dust bowl states). Consistent farm water can be had along the various rivers, but the western half of the state lacks rainfall despite its better climate.

This state is flatland country except for the Ozarks. The plains area can't match the more highly mountainous areas for strategic relocation, which have more forests and hills or mountains that provide better cover and concealment for maneuvering, if necessary. If you choose to retreat in the flat plains of America, make sure it is safe enough to stay put. You do not want to have to flee in that vast open area in a crisis.

Oklahoma is also an oil and gas energy hub whose players have contributed to the decades of corruption in state government. This state holds the record for the most governors impeached for corruption. Three Supreme Court justices received $200,000 to reverse a tax claim against an investment company, and were impeached. During the 1980's, over 200 of Oklahoma's County Commissioners and suppliers were indicted for kickbacks. The FBI described the kickback scandal as "the largest local corruption investigations in American history." The State Highway Patrol Officers seem to be more professional and courteous, while the local town police and county sheriff types are becoming more arrogant and abusive with their authority. Oklahoma's Dept. of Human Services (DHS) has a bad reputation for running over the rights of parents, even at times fabricating drug test evidence to justify taking children from indigent or unwed mothers. The state actively seeks federal subsidies for number of children "rescued" which rewards this behavior.

Oklahoma is home to more Indian tribes (55) than any other state. We don't recommend locating on Indian lands due to tribal infighting and the extra layer of government imposed. There is a huge Latino population in the state, which has been an increasing source of crime. Because of this increasing crime, Oklahoma passed a law that incarcerates all illegal aliens and deports them unless they have a green card and are on a path to becoming an American citizen. State law now requires English as the official language. Still, crime in and around Oklahoma City, makes this city a dangerous place in certain sections. Petty crime is becoming more of a problem, as is the manufacture of methamphetamines in small mountain labs by welfare recipients and redneck types who have corrupted the local police to a degree.

Oklahoma's largest employer is the government (Federal, State and Local, including schools). States with high rates of government employment typically grow more liberal each year. Politically, Oklahoma is a conservative state, but from the New Deal until 1964 it was run by Democratic majorities which have only recently lost control of the state government. Until 1964, support of Democrats and Republicans kept swinging back and forth, but thereafter they have reliably voted for Republicans in national elections.

One of Oklahoma's major threats is tornados. The state sits astride a boundary area between dry continental air in the north and warm tropical air coming up from the south. When this transition of air masses collides, it produces perfect conditions for huge thunderstorms with lightning and tornados. Oklahoma has an average of 54 tornadoes a year, the highest concentration (per sq. mile) in the country. One F-5 tornado in 1999 (a very bad year for OK) reached wind speeds of 318 mph. However, the eastern part of Oklahoma gets most of the southerly winds bringing moisture from the Gulf, so the western part of the state from Lawton towards Colorado gets less thunderstorm activity.

Strategies for Populated Living Areas

Oklahoma City is a sprawling metropolitan area which has merged with neighboring towns Norman and Edmund in the north and south. The crime maps at neighborhood-scout.com clearly show that the outer living areas are the safest. The older, central locations of Oklahoma City are where most of the crime is. Do not locate closer than 5 miles to Tinker AFB (in the SE part of the city) and avoid the downwind fallout patterns that will probably spread east. Select locations to the far west of the city or to the north around Edmund and, as usual, stay on the periphery of residential development.

Tulsa's high crime areas are not clearly concentrated in the center, as in most cities, so although it is always safer on the outskirts of town, it's not that simple. Crime areas are more widely distributed, but most low crime areas generally correspond to wealthy housing areas, even in central Tulsa.

Retreat Areas

Garfield County: This is merely an example of the hundreds of small town farm/ranch areas in Oklahoma that may provide self-sufficient retreats as long as refugees don't come down your road en masse. The town of Garfield is a few miles north of Enid, a moderate commercial hub in the county, and home to Vance AFB. The area is typical of the good living possible on a farm or ranch, though it is hard to hide if a point threat targets your farm—the bane of rural plains living.

This is largely an agricultural region, growing wheat and cattle. South of Enid is Vance AFB, a potential nuclear target, so locate away from such targets, and prepare against fallout in a basement security shelter. There are other similar rural ranch and farm areas—too many to be mentioned individually. They all have the liability of "no place to hide" except underground, due to lack of forestation. The small towns surrounding Lawton are of the same quality, but select only those west of Altus AFB.

The Ouachita Mountains: These are the Oklahoma Ozarks in the SE part of the state. This area is good for retreat property with privacy and forestation. The big problem you have to deal with here, however, is an increasing threat of petty vandalism and crime. One resident wrote us: "There is a big problem with thieves and redneck types breaking into any property left unattended in the countryside and the mountains. I have friends who have had their 'secure' cabin and mountain retreat walls chain sawed to gain entry. A secure retreat will have to be hardened and have good security to survive." That's proper advice for any retreat you don't live in full time.

OREGON ★★★☆☆

Summary Facts and Ratings

Climate:	West coast marine climate west of the Cascades with 9 months of cloudy wet weather, mild temperatures, steady breezes and few major storms. Semi-arid climate in the east with dry, sunny weather.
Population Density:	Low. 39 ppl/sq. mile (ranked 39th highest). 3500 ppl/sq. mile in Portland metro area, but less than 20 ppl/sq. mile east of the Cascades. Hispanic 11.2%, Asian 3.7%, Black 2%, American Indian 1.6%, mixed 2.6%.
Cost of Living Index:	Above average. 129.5 (average is 100) makes this the 7th most expensive state.
Private Land Availability:	Good. 32% of land is state or federally owned, including most of the best forests.
Building Permits:	Required everywhere. Basements are common and possible almost everywhere.
Land and Urban Planning:	Oregon was the original perpetrator of Smart Growth and has state-wide restrictive land use planning imposed on local communities— the worst in the nation. Small building parcels can only be had in the restrictive Urban Growth Boundaries.
Food Production:	Very good. Plenty of rain in the west (80 inches per year), but irrigation required in the east (less than 10 inches of rain). Long growing season of 120-210 days. Fishing and hunting are excellent. Organic farming is popular.
Health Environment:	Water quality is good, except where 23% of communities have fluoridation (mostly Portland area). Air Pollution is very low because of constant wind.
Traffic:	Heavy in Portland, Salem and along the I-5 and I-84 corridors near these cities; low in rural areas. Oregon has red light and speed cameras.
Politics:	Very liberal in Portland, Eugene, and Salem. Conservative in rural parts of the state. Dem 38%, Rep 30%, Ind/3rd party 32%.
Taxes:	Average. Ranked 16th highest with a tax burden of 10.1% of income. Income tax is 5%-9.9%, property taxes rank 26th but there is no sales tax.
Corruption:	Average. Higher in Portland and Eugene, low in eastern OR. Police conduct has some amount of corruption in Portland, but state police are generally professional and fair. Corruption is common among judges in the Portland area.
Crime:	Average violent crime 254/100K, higher property crime 3174/100K. Crime index for Portland is 4, Salem 8, Eugene 9, Bend 25 (100 is safest)
Personal Liberty:	Below average, rated 28th. According to Mercatus.org Oregon "earned the dubious distinction of having the greatest loss of freedom in the country [from 2009 to 2011]."
Gun Liberty:	Fair. No permit to purchase firearms. "Shall issue" state for concealed weapon permits, but no reciprocity for other state's permits. Open carry permitted except where restricted by city ordinance (most large cities). Portland city ordinance restricting concealed weapon permit holders was struck down in court.
Alternative Medicine:	Good. Lots of natural health practitioners. Direct entry midwifery is legal as a completely unregulated practice. There is voluntary licensure to recieve Medicaid reimbursement for midwife work. School vaccine exemptions: religious and medical.
Home Schooling:	Moderate regulation. State requires parents to send notification, test scores, and/or professional evaluation of student progress.
Military Targets:	**Umatilla Chemical Weapons Depot**. Weapons depot being decommissioned; until then, secondary target. **Boardman Naval Bombing Range**. Active training site with drone base and live fire exercises. Unknown quantity, probably tertiary target. **Kingsley Field ANG Base**, Klamath Falls. F-15C training base; secondary target. **Portland Airport**. F-15s for Oregon ANG; tertiary target. **Over the Horizon Radar**, Christmas Valley, southeast of Bend. Mothballed; not a target. Idaho Nat'l Labs at Oregon State Univ., Corvallis, small energy research facility; not a target.

Notes

Oregon is a breathtakingly beautiful state with somewhat better weather than Washington. It has the same moderate marine climate, but the farther south you get from the Canadian border, the greater the percentage of sun you find amidst the many storm systems that pass through this area. Oregon state parks are numerous, well kept, and beautifully situated in both the Cascade Mountains and the Oregon coast. The Oregon coastline is cold and foggy but with a dramatic mix of jagged rocks, cliffs, trees, and periodic fine sandy beaches with driftwood and abundant sea life. The forestation is a wonderful mix of firs, pines and deciduous trees. Water is abundant and pure, except in the major metros where chlorine and fluoride is often added.

Oregon would be perhaps the best state in the country for preparedness and safety if it hadn't been taken over by liberal/left environmentalists with a passion for controlling private property. A lot of these liberals came up from California. Ever since Oregon adopted uniform land use planning for the entire state, individual cities and counties lost the liberty to make reasonable development decisions at the local level. When the citizens finally had enough and passed an initiative to allow aggrieved property owners to gain compensation for loss of property rights, the liberal/left courts overturned it—just like in California.

Oregon has been at the forefront of every draconian and excessive land control law in the country—from demands to destroy all hydroelectric dams to save the fish, to almost total strangulation of the logging industry to save the owls. The propaganda machine emanating from the single leftist newspaper in Portland broadcasts its tainted opinions throughout the state, followed in lock-step by the major television stations. All of the universities are extremely liberal and continue to churn out advocates for state power.

This agenda to control private property led to a desperate protest with the (unadvised) takeover of the Malheur Wildlife Refuge in 2015 to bring attention to ranchers who were being intimidated and targeted by state and federal agencies to give up their land and long-standing grazing rights on public land. Democrat Gov. Kate Brown was completely unsympathetic and called the standoff "intolerable" and ordered the feds to "end the occupation." Editorials in the Oregonion newspaper lambasted the police for being easy on the Bundy's and called for them to be arrested or shot. Local and state police allowed the FBI to dress up like militia and stalk local county officials to foment antagonism among the locals. Oregon police also worked closely with the FBI to stage the final highway traps that led to their arrest and it was state police that ultimately shot Lavoy Finicum. Lesson: don't expect OR police to hesitate over an order that may conflict with your fundamental rights.

Oregon is a state of many contradictions. One would never know by listening to the media that almost half of Oregonians are very conservative, because they are a big, largely disenfranchised minority that rarely has any say. Oregon still requires no safety inspections of vehicles, and it has no greater accident rate because of it. Then again, Oregon doesn't consider it safe to let individuals pump their own gas at service stations. Once the safety excuse was debunked by the experience of the rest of the nation, the cry became one of "preserving jobs" no matter how unnecessary. Oregon has become a socialist state almost to the degree of California, with correspondingly severe budget problems caused by overly generous state worker pensions and numerous welfare programs. All land use is tightly controlled. Oregon has no state sales tax, but state officials keep trying to convince voters to change that every few years.

The Portland Metro traffic situation is better than Seattle. There is a traditional rush hour in the morning and afternoon on the main highways leading into Portland, but traffic is normally moderate during the day and evening. Housing costs are higher in the Portland area than the rest of the state, but not as high as in Seattle. Overall, restrictive zoning keeps Oregon property more expensive than it would be without it. With no sales tax, the cost of living seems cheaper.

There are almost no major nuclear threats in Oregon, and none are in or around the urban areas—only a few secondary or tertiary targets in the east. The Christmas Valley backscatter radar site in central Oregon is in "cold storage" and unlikely to be hit with anything nuclear, so we have removed it from our strategic target maps. It's so remote in location that it isn't a threat in any case. What this means is that Oregon has one of the few coastal areas with no nuclear threats, so it is a place where a person might not have to prepare for fallout. There are, however, major volcanoes embedded within the Cascade Mountains which will someday erupt. Prime candidates are Mt. St. Helens, Mt. Hood and Mt. Bachelor.

Strategies for Populated Living Areas

Portland: If you must live here to make a living, you must consider where you work relative to the Willamette River which divides Portland in two. You don't want to get stranded on one side of the river in a crisis during working hours, when you live on the other side. For example, if you work on the east side of Portland, then locate in an eastern suburb such as Gresham on the fringe of the suburbs. If you work downtown, on the west side of the river, then find a location further west, beyond the West Hills, but not in the Beaverton sprawl area which is too crowded. Joel likes the area north of Hillsboro (North Plains, Banks, or Skyline Drive) as it has fairly low population density and gives you an alternate route into town via Hwy 30 which runs along the scenic Columbia River. There is a lot of rural land south of Hillsboro as well, in the Newberg area.

The best places are likely along the fringe of the Urban Growth Boundary which separates subdivisions from farm land. If you can afford a farm home on farm acreage, so much the better. Both of these east and west locations give you unimpeded access to retreat sites in the Coast range farther to the west or in the beautiful Cascade Mountains to the east.

The best agricultural areas are in the Willamette Valley, but these are only safe from major social unrest if you locate near the eastern margins of the valley or west near the mountains. The major population centers are clustered around the I-5 corridor north and south in the middle of the valley.

Retreat Areas

The Hood River Valley is a wonderful area on the Columbia Gorge about an hour east of Portland. It is just to the east of the transition line between the wet and dry areas of Oregon and the air mass differences push a lot of wind through here. In fact, the town of Hood River is often called the "Wind Surfing Capitol of the World," a reputation that turned this sleepy orchard valley into a sort of trendy and upscale place. While the lower valley is now suitable only for good times, the upper valley around Parkdale is still prime agricultural retreat property. Hwy 35 gives you a back door over Mt Hood and into eastern Oregon should the Gorge route become closed, as it sometimes is in winter. A few hundred people even commute to Portland from here.

The Oregon Coast has abundant retreat areas, though rarely right on the beach itself, where prices are high and houses are sandwiched between Hwy 101 and the ocean. But on the other side of the highway are the Coast Mountains with rising views, lots of forest and cheaper land (though not much is available due to development restrictions). The big down side is the near constant flow of cloudy, wet weather. As long as you avoid locating within the major seaside resort towns (Astoria, Seaside, Newport, Florence) everything else has a good rating.

The Umpqua River Valley is an excellent location in southwestern Oregon. This is the valley that extends east from Roseburg towards Glide, and there is also a more remote tributary further south at Canyonville that goes up toward the Cascades through Day's Creek. Alternatively, for more farm country in the valley, check out Umpqua and Elkton areas east of Roseburg which have great growing seasons. Housing is much cheaper than in northern Oregon locations.

Southern Oregon: Further SW in Oregon is the traditional retreat area made famous by Mel Tappan: the land surrounding Grants Pass and Medford. It is no longer so highly rated due to charges of corruption among the Douglas County Sheriffs and the influx of thousands of California transplants bringing with them many of their liberal ideas and biases. This is the home of the beautiful Rogue River Valley which, away from the freeway cities, offers great retreat sites on the river. Go east at least until White City or Eagle Point.

We recommend the areas around towns further from the freeway corridor such as Cave Junction to the west, and Klamath Falls to the east, particularly the mountain country between Medford and Klamath Falls. The Klamath area has good water supplies and soil with a decent growing season, but it is more remote.

Eastern Oregon: The better retreat areas for long term security from social unrest are all in eastern Oregon, where long distances over the mountains and dry desert areas provide a suitable buffer. While the areas just mentioned that are west of the Cascade Range are suitable for full time living with some hope of employment, very little of the better sites in eastern Oregon have job opportunities.

The most prosperous of the cities in central and eastern Oregon are Bend and Sun River, but that prosperity is ephemeral since it relies mostly on spending from the many Californian transplants and retirees from the Northwest, tired of the rain on the western side of the state. The Bend area is beautiful but it is in the shadow of several volcanoes.

Ontario on the Idaho border, in contrast, is a legitimate agricultural center and, while not rich, has consistent rural business and farm markets. The area around the town of Vale to the east is better than Ontario itself and far enough away from I-84.

Northeast Oregon: The best retreat areas for those who really want seclusion are found in the northeast corner of Oregon: Grande Ronde Valley Union, Wallowa, and Baker Counties. Elgin has wonderful pine tree ranch country that is surrounded by national forests. The Wallowa Valley centered around Joseph is another favorite. Many of these towns have mountain-fed water supplies which gives them better self-sufficiency than valley cities that rely on wells. LaGrande and Baker, while too close to the freeway themselves, are the gateway to good retreat sites in and on the east side of the Blue Mountains. This area is higher in elevation and thus is more suited to ranching and cold-resistant fruit orchards.

Southeast Oregon: Further remote still is the Steens Mountain Region in southeastern Oregon. This is strictly a remote, dry cattle ranching area with fairly large spreads of at least a thousand acres. It does have some water in small streams, which provides the life blood of ranchers in the area. No one is going to bother you here. It's an area that few Oregonians even visit, and it's a long way to town for commercial dealings. Burns is the major city in the region.

PENNSYLVANIA ★★⯪☆☆

Summary Facts and Ratings

Climate:	Humid continental climate with hot, muggy summers and cold winters. Philadelphia has a more humid subtropical climate like Washington DC. PA averages 10 tornados per year.
Population Density:	Moderately high. 281 ppl/sq. mile (ranked 10th highest in the nation). Black 11%, Hispanic 5%, Asian 2.5%, mixed 1.1%.
Cost of Living Index:	Average. 103 (average is 100) makes this the 33rd least expensive state.
Private Land Availability:	Good. 15% of the land is state or federally owned.
Building Permits:	Required for major new construction or renovations, but there is a lot of variation in the requirements at the local level. Many homes have basements in the deep alluvial soil in valleys, but the Allegheny Mts. can present difficulties.
Land and Urban Planning:	No statewide plan exists nor does the state mandate comprehensive plans for local governments.
Food Production:	Good productivity except in mountainous areas where sunlight is reduced. Growing season is approx 150-180 days. Rainfall averages about 42 inches per year.
Health Environment:	Surface water pollution is worse than the national average. Ground water has some pollution in farm and mining areas. 55% of the state's drinking water is fluoridated—mostly major cities.
Traffic:	Heavy traffic problems in Philadelphia and Pittsburgh, rated #20 and #30 of the 75 worst traffic cities in America. PA uses red light cameras.
Politics:	Registered Democrats are in the majority. However, after 2010, some Democrats have broken ranks and elected conservatives. Philadelphia and Pittsburgh are highly unionized and minority-oriented cities that are democratic strongholds. Dem 49.5%, Rep 36.7%, Ind/3rd party 14.8%.
Taxes:	High. Ranked 10th highest with an effective rate of 10.3% of income. Income tax is a flat 3.1%, property taxes are 11th highest in the nation and sales tax is average at 6%.
Corruption:	High. Collusion between big industries and politics has corrupted people for years, particularly in Philadelphia.
Crime:	High. Violent crime 335/100K, property crime 2,061/100K. Crime index for Philadelphia is 10, Pittsburgh 11 (100 is safest).
Personal Liberty:	Poor, 31st in the nation. Somewhat better than its neighbors NY, NJ and MD which isn't saying much.
Gun Liberty:	Good. No permit to buy a firearm. "Shall issue" state for concealed firearm permits. Open carry permitted except in Philly. Weapon transfers or sales must be through gun dealer and these transactions are recorded by the state.
Alternative Medicine:	Natural health practitioners are free to practice. Lay midwifery is effectively prohibited. School vaccine exemptions: religious and medical.
Home Schooling:	High regulation. State requires achievement test scores and sometimes curriculum approval, teacher qualification of parents or home visits by state officials.
Military Targets:	**Letterkenny Army Depot**, 35 miles SW of Harrisburg. Repair and maintenance facility for Patriot Missiles and other high tech equipment; secondary target. **Raven Rock and Fort Ritchie**, SW of Gettysburg. National security bunker; primary target. **New Cumberland Defense Depot**, Susquehanna. Distribution supply depot; tertiary target. **Willow Grove NAS**, near Philadelphia. Reserve heavy helos, A-10 aircraft and C-120 transport; secondary target. **Harrisburg and Pittsburgh airports**. ANG stations; not a target.

Nuclear Power Plants:	Peach Bottom Plant, York County, Susquehanna River. 2 reactors.
	Beaver Valley Plant, 34 miles NW of Pittsburgh. 2 reactors.
	Limerick Plant, Montgomery County, NW of Philadelphia. 2 reactors.
	Susquehanna Steam Electric Station, 15 miles SW of Wilkes-Barre. 2 reactors.
	Three Mile Island, 15 miles SE of Harrisburg. 1 reactor.

Notes

Pennsylvania is a large state with stark contrasts between its ugly urban centers and pleasant rural land. It has been a steel and manufacturing powerhouse until these industries declined or moved out of the US. Its rural acreage is mostly family farms and horse country. Its rugged, low elevation mountains and valleys in the Allegheny region provide a partial barrier to the populations in Philadelphia and Pittsburgh to the east.

Pennsylvania has a long history and culture of corruption. Big oil and railroad corporate influences corrupted the Legislature early in PA's development. PA had only 15 public corruption convictions last year, which doesn't come close to reflecting the amount of corruption in the state. There was bribery in an infamous scandal involving the furnishing of the ornate state capitol building. Philadelphia is the center for corruption. Recently, former Philadelphia Mayor John Street was the target of a secret FBI corruption investigation that only ended up prosecuting his underling, city treasurer Corey Kemp, on charges of conspiracy, fraud and tax evasion. That is typical of how the big fish normally escape prosecution. Malfeasance and collusion with criminal elements are part of all PA's big city political machines. Elections are always tweaked if not rigged. Even now, more than 25 individuals associated with the general assembly are under investigation, have been indicted, have pled guilty or await trial due to scandals such as "Bonusgate." The list goes on and on.

Philadelphia has grown rapidly along with the high density population corridor between DC and New York City. It is this link to the high density East that makes Philadelphia vulnerable and part of the problem of social unrest. The southern route across the state (I-70) is a massive transportation corridor feeding rail, truck and automobile traffic not only from the New York-New Jersey region to Ohio, but also from the Washington DC-Baltimore area as well. The Virginia Mountains to the west of Washington DC force most traffic NW into Pennsylvania. The high traffic portion of Pennsylvania (I-80 and below) can expect overwhelming numbers of people fleeing the east coast someday.

Pennsylvania has numerous river and mountainous obstacles which will tend to funnel refugees into the main corridors. When refugee travel is halted (either through blockages or shortages of fuel and food) the communities nearest to these corridors will suffer the most. That is why the lightly populated areas of northern PA will survive better, at least in the medium-term.

Strategies for Populated Living Areas

Philadelphia is such a dangerous city that it isn't enough to simply stay outside the 276/476 Beltway. We recommend being 5 to 10 miles outside this boundary. To survive a major social crisis in this area, one must be able to get on the roads first and leave before the crush of traffic jams shut everything down. Whatever you do, don't choose the Jersey side of the city where you have the Delaware River to cross before heading west. Most people are going to have to head west to get out so keep your travel on rural and secondary roads away from the numerous fingers of freeway extending outward from Philly. Make sure you map out in advance where you can cross the freeways north and south of your direction of travel where there are no exits. You can probably travel close to Lancaster or Reading, but you should give Allentown a wide birth.

Harrisburg is divided by a river with only a few crossings. This fact coupled with social unrest and massive traffic jams can help you understand the need to find a more rural crossing. If you live in this city, locate on the NW or SW so as not to be surrounded by multiple freeways; stay west of the Beltway.

Pittsburgh: This city has 3 river barriers to contend with. We recommend staying northeast of I-76, on either side of Hwy 8, or to the west beyond I-79 on either side of Hwy 22. Take note that if you plan to retreat into Ohio, you still have the Ohio River to deal with. Select possible secondary crossings in advance.

Scranton/Wilkes-Barre: Scranton is encircled by a beltway with not much development on the west side, which is the preferred route of retreat. Also pick the west side of Wilkes-Barre and the Susquehanna River to keep all your barriers to the east, if possible.

Retreat Areas

The population density is too high in the southern part of Pennsylvania, but very light above I-80, so that is where the best PA retreats are found.

North Central PA: This is the area to the north of I-80 that spans from Hwy 220 in the east (near Wilkes-Barre) to the western towns of Oil City and Titusville. The private land backing up to the numerous state forests in the middle are ideal. The Allegheny National Forest area is further west, but has the liability of some future buffer zone being designated around federal property. Stay at least 5 miles north of I-80 in non-exit areas and 10 miles from any exit.

Central Allegheny Mountains: These are the rural lands and valleys in the Alleghenies south of I-80. While not as secure as the North-Central area, they can be acceptable. There are two areas split by I-99. The eastern area is centered around Lewiston. Keep a distance of at least 30 miles from Harrisburg which is at the southern boundary of this area. In the western sector, stay above Hwy 422 to give you distance from the Pittsburgh area.

Southwest PA: There are good potential retreats in the sector south of I-70/76 and on into northern West Virginia. The population density is not heavy, and there are several state forests in the area. Again, keep a normal distance from the freeways.

Lancaster: This is the famous Amish country of PA. In past years, we have recommended this area for those in the Philadelphia area, but no longer. It is simply too well known and will attract too many refugees under social chaos conditions.

RHODE ISLAND ☆☆☆☆☆

Summary Facts and Ratings

Climate:	This small state has a northeastern continental or coastal climate. The winters are cold and humid but relatively mild compared to inland states due to the moderating affects of the sea.
Population Density:	Very high. 1008 ppl/sq. mile (2nd highest in the nation). Hispanic 12.1%. Black 6.4%, Asian 2.8%, mixed 1.7%. Most of the population is concentrated in the Providence metro area.
Cost of Living Index:	High. 123 (average is 100) ranking this as the 10th most expensive state.
Land Ownership:	Fair. 9.4% of the land is state or federally owned.
Building Permits:	Required for all new construction and are strictly enforced. Basements can be built in most places but damp soil means you must have good waterproofing.
Land and Urban Planning:	Rhode Island is a highly centralized planning state. There is a state comprehensive plan and mandatory comprehensive planning at the local level.
Food Production:	Fair. Good growing season of 120-150 days. It rains on average every 4 days for an annual average of about 48 inches. The soil is Paxton type glaciated soil, rocky, acidic and not particularly fertile, but it holds water well.
Health Environment:	Only moderate air pollution thanks to sea breezes. Dangerous surface water pollution as reflected in the coastal bays. There is very little pollution inland. 84% of public drinking water is fluoridated.
Traffic:	Providence has the 41st worst traffic in the nation. Red light cameras are used in Providence.
Politics:	Heavily Democratic state. Republicans must pander to the Rhode Islander's liberal demands. Independents most often vote left. Dem 41.5%, Rep 11%, Ind/3rd party 47.5%.
Taxes:	Ranked 8th highest with an average state tax burden of 10.5% of income. Income tax varies 3.8%-6%. Property taxes are the 16th highest. Sales tax is 7%.
Corruption:	High. Politicians have been blatantly corrupt including taking bribes in office, working with the mob and serving jail time.
Crime:	Moderate. Violent crime 257/100K, property crime 2442/100K. Most crime is in the Providence area whose crime index is 10 (100 is safest).
Personal Liberty:	Bad, ranked 46th and getting worse.
Gun Liberty:	Poor. No permit to purchase firearms but 7 day waiting period. "Shall issue" but local authorities and the attorney general often impede the process making this an effective "may issue" state for concealed permits. Open carry only with a license.
Alternative Medicine:	Normal medical hostility towards alternative medicine. Midwifery is legal and regulated. Rhode Island has one of the oldest midwifery laws on the books. However, as the health care system has changed, the rules and regulations for this statute have been amended to effectively deny women access to attended out-of-hospital birth. School vaccine exemptions: religious and medical.
Home Schooling:	High regulation. Parents must register with the state and send notification, test scores and/or professional evaluation, plus other requirements.
Military Targets:	**Newport Naval Education and Training Center**. Naval War College, pier facilities for inactive ships; not a target. **Naval Underwater Systems Center**, Aquidneck Island. Fleet support center for submarines. Part of Newport Training Center; secondary target. **Quonset State Airport**. ANG; not a significant target.

Notes

Rhode Island is a very small state measuring barely 20 miles across, so it is very difficult to gain distance from the capitol city of Providence. The state is mostly flat with no real mountains. Narragansett Bay cuts deep into the state and separates the eastern portion of RI from the mainland. Outside the bay there is Block Island, approximately 12 miles away toward Long Island. Within the bay, there are over 30 islands, 3 that are quite large. The eastern-most land in RI can only be accessed by traveling around the bay through Massachusetts.

Strategies for Populated Living Areas

Providence is a tangle of streets and water barriers that make numerous trap zones. We recommend you locate outside the I-294 Beltway in order to be clear of any potential social unrest emanating from within the city. Avoid East Providence as it is on the far side of the bay and puts you into the Massachusetts region of the state. That side is a trap zone with no escape except via water. That said, there might be a certain amount of safety in the far reaches of the southern coast of RI and MA, if you care to gamble that people won't go that direction when turmoil arises. As in other such areas with no exit, it is absolutely essential to locate in a forested area with maximum privacy and have concealed safe rooms that cannot be found. For most people, the best strategy will be to retreat further west and then north, getting around the major population centers. It is vital that you plan a route that allows you to cross all freeways at places where there is no on or off ramp, as described in Chapter 14.

Retreat Areas

Northwest: There are many smaller lakes and creeks to cross if traveling to the northwest. If you can find good privacy in this area, you still run the risk that refugees or criminals will reach you if people start to empty out of Providence. It is just too close. But it is better than being south of I-95 where you are trapped between the freeway and the ocean (unless you have a boat for an emergency exit). If you have a retreat in NW Rhode Island, plan an exit route or two farther to the NW into CT and MA. The most difficult part of planning that route is getting past I-395 that travels north-south in eastern CT. Most of the roads from RI cross 395 only at towns which may be impassable. Only if you head toward Thompson in CT can you get across 395 outside of a major city. Take US 44 into CT and just after the border, go north to Thompson.

SOUTH CAROLINA ★★☆☆☆

Summary Facts and Ratings

Climate:	Most of the lowlands fall within a humid subtropical climate zone. Winter temperatures vary between the upland cold winters and the mild temperatures in coastal areas. Summers are hot and muggy. The mountainous section to the west approaches the Blue Mountains of Georgia and has a subtropical highland climate with colder winters and rare snowfall. SC averages 10 tornadoes a year.
Population Density:	Above average. 148 ppl/sq. mile (20th highest in nation). Black 28.2%, Hispanic 4.5%, Asian 1.3%, mixed 1.1%.
Cost of Living Index:	Below average. 97.5 (average is 100) making this the 23rd least expensive state.
Land Ownership:	Good. 5% of the land is state or federally owned.
Building Permits:	More strict here than in NC or Georgia. Counties with major cities require permits for any construction project that creates a new structure or alters, adds to, renovates or demolishes an existing building. This can include new fences, decks, sheds, detached garages, and roofing and siding work. Basements are common except in rocky hill areas.
Land and Urban Planning:	No statewide plan for Smart Growth exists, but the state does mandate local comprehensive planning.
Food Production:	Good productivity in the central and eastern plains. The Upstate, or western region is hilly with thin, stony, clay soils and contains few areas suitable for farming. Some of the coastal areas are swampy. The growing season is 180 to 240 days. SC has an average annual precipitation of 50 inches.
Health Environment:	SC contains some of the worst surface water pollution. The air quality throughout the state is not bad—particularly around Columbia, Spartanburg and Darlington. Several EPA superfund sites are located in the most populous corridor including landfills. Aquifer water quality is not very good even in rural areas due to agricultural pollution. 94% of the population's drinking water is fluoridated.
Traffic:	Columbia has the 73rd worst traffic in the nation. SC uses speed cameras.
Politics:	Before the boom years of the 80s and 90s SC Black citizens were nearly a majority and established powerful roots with the Democratic Party. Since then most of the newcomers have been white or businessmen with conservative attitudes. The black percentage has now fallen below 30% and Republicans dominate. Dem 39%, Rep 44%, Ind/3rd party 17%.
Taxes:	Low. Ranked 9th lowest with an average tax burden of 8.3% of income. Graduated income tax tops out at 7% for income over $13.7K. Property taxes are low and state and local sales taxes average 7.0%.
Corruption:	Extremely high. State officers down through judges, police and attorneys.
Crime:	Very high. Violent crime is 509/100K, property crime 3624/100k. SC's crime rate is always above the national average. Crime index for Myrtle Beach is 0 (absolute worst rating), Greenwood 2, and Spartanburg 2. Even many small towns have high crime like Dillon and Walterboro (both 0).
Personal Liberty:	Above average. 15th overall.
Gun Liberty:	Fair. No permit to purchase firearms. "Shall issue" state. Open carry is not permitted. Most restrictive of southern states.
Alternative Medicine:	Naturopathy is prohibited by law. Alternative medicine in general is discouraged by medical practice laws, but is largely un-prosecuted. Lay midwifery is legal and licensed within the state. School vaccine exemptions: religious and medical.
Home Schooling:	Moderate regulation. State requires parents to send notification, test scores, and/or professional evaluation of student progress.
Military Targets:	**Fort Jackson**, east of Columbia. Largest army basic training camp; secondary target. **McEntire Joint National Guard Base**, SE of Columbia. F-16 and C-130s of SC NG; tertiary target. **Naval Weapons Station**, Charleston. Key port for transfer of weapons, nuclear power propulsion and training; primary target.

Military Targets continued:	**Beaufort MC Air Station/Naval Hospital**. Six F-18 squadron base; primary target. **Parris Island MC Recruit Depot**, Beaufort. USMC recruit training; tertiary target. **Shaw AFB**, northwest of Sumter. Largest F-16 fighter base; primary target. **Charleston AFB**. 21 squadrons of C-17s for airlift. Part of Charleston Naval Weapons Station; primary target. **Savannah River Plant**, 25 miles SE of Augusta. Previous nuclear weapon material plant, now nuclear material processing site; secondary target or primary target depending on secret use.
Nuclear Power Plants:	**Catawba Plant**, SW of Charlotte, NC, 2 reactors. Operating since 1986. **Oconee Plant**, Lake Keowee in Seneca, 3 reactors. Operating since 1974. **Robinson Plant**, near Hartsville, 1 reactor. Operating since 1971. **Summer Plant**, Jenkinsville, 1 reactor. Operating since 1984.

Notes

South Carolina has a kind of underdeveloped feel to it in the rural areas reminiscent of second world countries. While there is a top layer of wealthy people, this has traditionally been among the nation's poorest states with income levels less than half the national average and with high levels of illiteracy and disease. Then in the 1980s, SC began to aggressively sell itself as business friendly, attracting European car and aviation companies to set up factories here. The fastest growth in the 1990s happened in coastal resort areas around Hilton Head and Myrtle Beach and in suburban counties outside Columbia and just south of Charlotte, North Carolina.

The effects have been good for the economy but bad for state debt as it increased new infrastructure. Now there exists a near constant tension between those that hold to southern, if not confederate, values of states' rights versus the new wealthy elite who are embarrassed about southern conservatism and want to be all things modern and politically correct. Nowhere was this more obvious than in the debates over official displays of the Confederate Flag—including at a Civil War memorial at SC's state capitol. In 2015 republican governor Nikki Haley removed the Confederate symbol from flying at the capitol and the legislature approved it in a final win for political correctness.

Corruption has also grown with the state. There were 42 public corruption convictions last year. A former Union County Tax Assessor pled guilty to a range of corruption charges including money laundering, extortion and bribery. He also ran drugs out of the office and stored them on site. A former Republican State Treasurer, Thomas Ravenel, was arrested on drug charges. SC has an outrageous reputation for police and prosecutorial corruption that includes the governor's office and most of the state's high judges. If they decide to take you down, there is no attorney in the state that will stand up for you against the pressure they can bring to bear on lawyers who challenge them.

As for terrain, SC is about half coastal plain, which makes for good farmland, except next to the coast. This land, however, is relatively unsafe from the effects of social unrest. The hillier piedmont region is to the northwest of I-20 from Augusta to Columbia and beyond.

In this area, you find a good mix of forest and fields with good privacy for permanent residences. You don't get into the mountains in this state until about 10 miles from the Georgia and NC borders. Most of that is national forest, but the land abutting the forest in the foothills is the most secure property in the state. Earthquakes do occur in South Carolina. The greatest frequency is along the central coastline of the state, in the Charleston area.

Strategies for Populated Living Areas

Charleston and North Charleston: There are military nuclear targets nearby in the bay and estuary so the only safe place to locate in this area is to the west of Charleston. As long as you stay in the smaller towns to the southwest of I-26 you should be able to commute into Charleston and live outside the target areas. This entire coast is subject to hurricanes, which is another reason to locate inland.

Columbia: The best and safest areas are to the northwest of I-20 and Augusta Hwy 1. In that northern sector, we would also recommend staying west of I-77 where the population is not heavy.

Augusta-Richmond County: Stay on the SC side of the border to keep the major population on the other side of a river. It's even better if you locate to the north of I-20 such as in Murphy's Estates.

Retreat Areas

General advice: There are lots of potential rural farm retreats all over, especially in the coastal plains and sand hills region, but they aren't safe in the long term due to potential confrontation with refugees seeking food in the countryside. There are a lot of nuclear military targets on the coast that will drive thousands toward the cities and towns in the center of the state. That, in turn, will create a great deal of social unrest in the major cities. If you have to get out on the roads and retreat west, it would be a major problem getting past those population centers in turmoil. If you are already settled in the SC flat farm lands and aren't close to a nuclear target, be sure your residence is behind plenty of tree cover and away from major roads. The 5 mile wide strip of mountains along the border with Georgia and NC are the last areas that refugees will reach when looking for food. They always tend to head for cities first. That's what makes the mountains better. Still, over time, starving people or criminal minds will eventually arrive. That is why these mountain areas are not as safe as the Cumberland Plateau in TN, for example. However, there is a lot of cover and concealment available in these mountains.

Greenville and Spartanburg: These are the largest cities closest to the mountain country and are within 5-10 miles of good retreat sites. You could possibly even live in a retreat full time and commute into town. Rock Hill is another nice town close to NC. It isn't attached to the mountains but does have a lot of forested hill country to the west.

SOUTH DAKOTA ★★★☆☆

Summary Facts and Ratings

Climate:	Continental climate, with hot summers (humid in the east) and very cold winters. Blizzards in the winter and droughts in summer are always a threat. SD is on the edge of Tornado Alley and averages 28 tornados per year.
Population Density:	Very low. 10 ppl/sq. mile (ranked 46th in the nation). 80% of South Dakota's towns have less than 2,000 people. 65% of the population is from German, Norwegian and Irish stock. American Indian 8.5%, Hispanic 2.9%, mixed 1.8%, Black 1.2%.
Cost of Living Index:	Average. 102.5 (average is 100) makes this the 30th least expensive state.
Private Land Availability:	Good. Only 7.6% of the land is state or federally owned.
Building Permits:	Required for all construction statewide. Basic requirements in most areas. Deep soil everywhere allows for good basement potential.
Land and Urban Planning:	There is a state comprehensive development plan. Counties and local governments are authorized, but not required, to adopt comprehensive plans.
Food Production:	Good, especially in the east where it rains more. This was a dust bowl state and water can be scarce in the western half. Soil is sandy loam and good for growing gardens. 150-180 growing days throughout the state. Average yearly rainfall is 25 inches in the east and only 15 in the west.
Health Environment:	Ground water in the eastern corporate farm district has elevated concentrations of agricultural pollution and chemicals, but the drier ranching country in the west does not. 94% of people's water is fluoridated. Very little air pollution.
Traffic:	No heavy traffic problems. In fact, Sioux Falls, the largest city, has the second highest insurance rating in the country for safe driving.
Politics:	Like all the plains states, SD used to have a populist tendency supporting Democratic leaders who promised relief. Former Senate leader Tom Daschle hailed from SD. But conservatism now rules most of the time as the lure of salvation by government programs has been shown to have major problems. Dem 34%, Rep 46%, Ind/3rd party 20%.
Taxes:	Low. Ranked 3rd lowest with an average state tax burden of 7.1% of income. No income tax, high property taxes and low state and local sales taxes of about 5.5%.
Corruption:	High. The fact that there have only been 7 public corruption convictions indicates that most corruption is deep and protected. There are some ongoing cover-ups involving state law enforcement who refuse to keep local deputies at bay in several counties from breaking and entering private homes.
Crime:	Medium high violent crime 316/100K, average property crime 1914/100K. Crime index for Sioux Falls is 17, Rapid City 10 (100 is safest).
Personal Liberty:	Very good. Rated 2nd in the nation, right behind North Dakota.
Gun Liberty:	Good. Permit required to purchase guns. "Shall issue" state for concealed permits which double as purchasing permits. Open carry permitted including in vehicles.
Alternative Medicine:	Good availability for the full range of natural health practitioners, except lay midwives which are prohibited and prosecuted. School vaccine exemptions: religious and medical.
Home Schooling:	Regulated. State requires parents to send notification, test scores, and/or professional evaluation of student progress.
Military Targets:	**Camp Rapid**, west of Rapid City. Active Army NG base; tertiary target. **Joe Foss Field**, Sioux Falls Airport. ANG F-16s; tertiary target, if at all. **Ellsworth AFB**, 10 mi. NE of Rapid City. B-1s, nuclear weapons; primary target—possibly multiple hits.

Notes

This state includes the ancient tribal grasslands of the Lakota Sioux Indians and has some of the largest Indian reservations. Eastern South Dakota is home to most of the state's population and has the most fertile soil, with access to part of the Ogallala aquifer for irrigation. In western South Dakota, ranching predominates and water is scarce. The economy is somewhat dependent upon the draw of Mt. Rushmore and the Black Hills to compensate for lack of industry. The Black Hills is the most spectacular mountain country in the state and would be rated highly for retreats except Ellsworth AFB is situated nearby just NE of Rapid City and north of I-90. Ellsworth is home to strategic B-1 bombers so it is a first strike target.

South Dakota has some good geographic qualities, but rates poorly in safety because of corrupt officials and law enforcement. Although it is a flatland state without any major geographic protection, it does have a lot of rural isolation, at least where the land is dry. There is a major nuclear threat in the SW corner where the missile fields from Warren AFB in Wyoming extend around and over the state line.

In an example of deep corruption in South Dakota consider State Prosecuting Attorney Mick Strain who, according to reports, allowed local police and sheriffs (though not all were involved) to ride roughshod over individual and family rights. The Good ol' Boy network was very much afraid to buck Strain. This is the worst kind of corruption pertaining to family security and survival. Deputies can break into your home without a warrant and the state's chief law enforcement officer won't help or prosecute and neither will any other enforcement agent, state or federal, for fear of getting on the wrong side of this corrupt legal officer.

Indian reservations can be a problem too where alcoholism and now drugs are constant issues. Methamphetamine is the drug of choice among the young problem people of SD. Pine Ridge Indian Reservation in southwestern South Dakota has a big problem with this drug as well as cocaine.

Like Kansas, the family farm here has been mostly replaced by huge corporate agribusinesses that can successfully play the finance and subsidy game of big agriculture. But this is mainly in the eastern part of the state where big farm operations proliferate. Families continue to lose children to the big cities, and most towns in S. Dakota are small and shrinking. They will probably remain so, but that is actually good for survival and increased security in the rural areas.

Strategies for Populated Living Areas

Sioux Falls: Stay to the north and west of the city and at least 5 miles from I-90 (which goes E-W) and I-29 (N-S). On the east side of the city it's easy to get boxed in between the city and the Missouri river. Safety is to the west, so locate on that side or north of town.

Rapid City: Except for being right on Interstate 90, Rapid City is a very nice town. Fortunately, Ellsworth AFB with its B-1 bombers is far enough to the east that people here are out of the blast zone. Locate anywhere west or south of the city for best security.

Retreat Areas

Rural farmland: Avoid the rural farmland within 50 miles of the missile fields in the SW corner. The prevailing wind is from the NW so fallout will likely drift toward Nebraska, especially in winter. However, during a few periods the winds can switch and come from the SW. The unique thing about SD rural farm and ranch land, even though flat as a pancake in most parts out west, is that SD's arid reputation in the west will act as a strong deterrent for refugees fleeing war and economic or social unrest from venturing out very far from the freeway towns. Follow the general rule to stay at least 10 miles away from a major interstate, and find a good place with water and hopefully some trees for windbreaks and shade. The best locations are those that are not visible from any main road. In this state, that means distance more than tree cover. The disadvantage of using isolation for retreat safety is that you are isolated from commerce and friends.

Black Hills: The retreat areas here are among the small towns that ring the Black Hills, but avoid Sturgis which has an annual Harley Davidson convention each year. This ring of small towns each has its own farm and ranch communities close to the mountains around the Black Hills in both SD and Wyoming. Take your pick. It's the best area in South Dakota.

TENNESSEE ★★★☆☆

Summary Facts and Ratings

Climate:	Humid subtropical climate, except for the higher elevations in the Appalachians, which have a cooler mountain climate with considerable rain. TN alternates between warm humid flows from the Gulf of Mexico and cool dry air from the north. TN averages 12 tornados per year.
Population Density:	Moderately high. 153 ppl/sq. mile (ranked 18th in the nation). Black 16.8%, Hispanic 4.2%, Asian 1.4%, mixed 1.2%.
Cost of Living Index:	Very low. 90.3 (average is 100) ranks as the 7th least expensive state in the nation.
Private Land Availability:	Good. Only 10.6% of the land is state or federally owned.
Building Permits:	Required everywhere for new construction, renovations and demolition work. Basement construction is feasible, but rock layers under the soil make it expensive in much of TN.
Land and Urban Planning:	Tennessee is a hybrid planning state. There is no state plan. Its growth management program is largely voluntary—the state's role is to encourage, rather than require, local jurisdictions to adopt comprehensive plans. However, following some heated annexation disputes, Tennessee began mandating urban growth boundaries and service area planning.
Food Production:	Good with a growing season of 150-210 days. Rainfall averages about 50 inches per year. Rich soil in most places but some places are rocky.
Health Environment:	Surface water pollution is higher than average, but ground water away from big commercial farms is OK. 90% of people's water is fluoridated—all cities and towns.
Traffic:	Heavy traffic problems in Nashville, rated #44 of 75 bad traffic cities. Knoxville is #70. TN does use red light and speed cameras.
Politics:	Tennesseans are mostly very conservative and religious. Dem 35%, Rep. 47%, Ind/3rd party 18%.
Taxes:	Low. Ranked 6th lowest with an average state tax burden of 7.6% of income. No income tax except on dividends and interest. Property taxes are 34th highest in the nation but state and local sales taxes average at 9.2%.
Corruption:	High. State lawmakers down to local police are corrupt, although many instances remain under wraps thanks to the Good ol' Boys network.
Crime:	Very high. Violent crime 591/100K, property crime 3181/100K. Crime index for Nashville is 7, Knoxville 2, Memphis 1 (100 is safest). Violent crime in Memphis is over twice the state average and four times the national average. Meth labs also abound in the ghetto areas of the big cities and have become a problem in rural TN, especially in the "safe" Amish areas which were so highly rated in our last edition.
Personal Liberty:	Good. 3rd in the nation behind the Dakotas.
Gun Liberty:	Good. No permit to purchase firearms. "Shall issue" state for concealed weapon permits. Open carry with a license.
Alternative Medicine:	Naturopathy doctors are prohibited from practice in TN. Direct entry midwives are licensed if they pass the CPM exam and apply to the state for certification. School vaccine exemptions: religious and medical.
Home Schooling:	Regulated. State requires parents to send notification, test scores, and/or professional evaluation of student progress.
Military Targets:	**Fort Campbell**, north of Clarksville. Joint reserve base. Marine Corps F-18 and ANG; secondary target. **Holston Army Ammo Plant**, Kingsport. Explosives research and manufacturing. Makes Trident missile motors; secondary target. **Milan Arsenal**. Loading and packing of conventional munitions; tertiary target. **Volunteer Army Ammo Plant**, NE of Chattanooga. Standby status; not a target unless status changes. **Arnold Engineering Development Center**, south of Manchester. Testing and simulation of aircraft, missile and space systems; primary target. **Nashville Airport**. Airlift and training for ANG; tertiary target.

Military Targets continued:	**Memphis Airport**. Airlift for ANG, tertiary target. **Oak Ridge National Laboratory**, Oak Ridge. Uranium processing, neutron research and supercomputer laboratory; primary target. **Nuclear Fuel Services Facility**, Irwin. Processing plant for Navy's fuel rods and reprocessing uranium for power plants; primary target.
Nuclear Power Plants:	**Sequoyah Plant**, 30 mi. NE of Chattanooga. 2 reactors. Active since 1982. **Watts Bar Plant**, TN River valley 80 mi NE of Chattanooga. 1 reactor active since 1996, 1 reactor under construction. This facility has produced Tritium rods for Nuclear weapons material—primary target.

Notes

Tennessee is a famous battleground state with deep sentiments and great music including blues, country and bluegrass. TN gets our best rating for retreat areas in the East. Land is cheap, there is no income tax, garden potential is good, there is lots of forest and you can be within a tank of gas from many large eastern cities. Of course, the last benefit is also why it is not a perfect recommendation—it is too close to population centers. The best safe haven is the Cumberland Plateau, which has less rain and is safer from refugee influx than the highly rated Blue Ridge Mountains.

Tennessee's overall rating would be higher if not for the high amount of corruption and collusion with government in the state. There were only 8 public corruption convictions, which attest to the Good ol' Boys network's ability to cover up misdeeds. In operation Tennessee Waltz, seven state lawmakers and two men identified as bagmen were indicted on bribery charges. The FBI also arrested two county commissioners from Hamilton county and one member of the prominent Hooks family of Memphis. The stories of local police and judicial corruption are too numerous to retell.

Tennessee has also been recently downgraded because of Republican Governor Bill Haslam's willingness to sell resident's rights for favor with the federal government. As of 2014 TN will join only 9 other states that currently require retailers like Amazon to charge state sales tax on online purchases. Additionally the TSA said it was "invited" by TN to conduct five random checkpoints during three days along the state's highways. The federal government is working to expand TSA's presence beyond airports to all forms of transportation—bus, train and cars—and they are looking for states to facilitate this agenda. Similarly TN has formally acknowledged that DHS agents can act as officers of the peace. TN is a willing party to these unwarranted searches despite the infringement on her citizen's fourth amendment rights.

Fifty percent of the US population is within 600 miles of Nashville, which is both an advantage and a disadvantage. The advantage is that people who have to make a living in the big eastern cities can find refuge at a reasonable distance. The disadvantage is that you can't expect to evade refugees that flee the social unrest that will hit the population centers of the East coast. Most of those waves will move inland along the major highways and branch off into the rural countryside only after scavenging what they can from the towns closest to the big highways.

That is why the Cumberland Plateau is such a haven. The elevation of the plateau ranges from 1,500 to 1,800 feet and is very lightly populated. This height is readily visible from the roads below which should discourage most people when compared to the valleys with more food and commerce. There is plenty of water available up on top and relatively cheap forested land. The people are also not as reclusive as those in the mountain country of the Carolinas.

The Blue Ridge Mountains are also highly rated—perhaps too much. They have attracted moonshiners for hundreds of years as well as law enforcement surveillance. The western Blue Ridge Mountains have several sub categories such as the Great Smoky Mountains, the Bald Mountains, the Unaka Mountains, the Unicoi Mountains, Roan Highlands and the Iron Mountains. The peaks are higher than the Cumberland Plateau by about 3500 feet. While that helps deter people it also makes for tougher homesteading. The original Cumberland Gap is way up on the Tennessee/Kentucky border at the town of Harrogate. Hwy 25E goes through the gap. There are many other gaps now accessible by roads. The primary one is I-40 which crosses the plateau to Crossville.

Between the Blues and the Cumberland Plateau is a series of ridges and valleys traveling at an angle parallel to the Blue Ridge Mountains. These ridges and plateaus are important barriers to travel and one of the reasons why this area provides good retreats. Make sure you know the lay of the land in the area you choose because you often have to go NE or SW a fair distance before being able to cut through a ridge to go west. The valleys between the ridges and plateaus are all fertile, with a river, but not as safe as the mountains or plateaus themselves. The Tennessee River flows down the "Great Valley" next to the Cumberland Plateau and is dammed up at intervals by TVA dams. Knoxville is found in the north of this ridge/valley system and Chattanooga in the south.

In western TN, the prominent land mass is called the Gulf Coastal Plain and is where the most commercial farms are situated. These old plantation lands are what brought most of the black slaves to western TN. Blacks now predominate in and around Memphis. South central Tennessee is home to a lot of Amish people. The farms are smaller but very productive. Tennessee is also home to the most caves in the United States, with over 8,350 in the mountains and hills.

Strategies for Populated Living Areas

Memphis is not a recommended city due to its location along the mighty Mississippi and this city's high crime rate. There are only two bridges across the Mississippi at Memphis: I-40 and Hwy 61. That's too few for comfort, considering the experience of people trying to flee Hurricane Katrina. The next nearest bridge to the north is close to the Missouri border, and to the south, you take Hwy 61 as it joins Hwy 49 which takes you into Arkansas. There is considerable pent up anger and crime in sections of this town. The mostly black ghettos in Memphis are some of the most dangerous in the metro area and need to be given a wide berth. If you need to live near Memphis, live on the Arkansas side or locate to the east outside the 240 beltway. You will not be able to retreat west from this side of Memphis except by going north or south and finding those few routes across the Ol' Mississippi. It is best to have a rural retreat in north or south central TN.

Nashville has some fine cultural features, and some ghetto areas with high crime, so it pays to commute into this town rather than live inside the 440 beltway. There are actually several beltways around the southern portion of Nashville where most of the urban growth is heading. We would recommend staying out past Brentwood but preferably as far as Franklin on I-65 or Murfreesboro out along I-24. If you have retreat property in the Lawrenceburg area (Amish country, but with increasing local drug crime) then pick the Franklin area. If you select a higher rated retreat area such as the Cumberland Plateau, pick the outskirts of Murfreesboro, which gives you unimpeded access to Hwy 1 to McMinnville, the gateway to the plateau.

Chattanooga is one of the higher rated cities in eastern TN. It is culturally more laid-back than Nashville, but pleasant. It gives you good access to either Atlanta or Nashville, but is far safer than both—although Chattanooga will certainly receive the brunt of the refugees coming out of Atlanta. This is the biggest major city within an hour of the high security Cumberland Plateau. The Tennessee River runs through town and is an occasional flooding threat. There are also two nuclear plants up river to worry about, although the prevailing winds will take the fallout north towards Knoxville. We recommend living on the north side of the river (Hill City or North Chattanooga) so that you have unimpeded quick access out of the city in a panic. The quickest route up to the Plateau is via Hwy 27 and then Hwy 111. But that goes close to the Nuclear Power plant. If that plant is damaged, take Hwy 8 instead.

Knoxville itself is sufficiently far away from the Oak Ridge nuclear complex that residents will not need blast protection, but any suburbs to the south, east or north of Oakridge is at risk of fallout, depending on which way the wind is blowing. If your retreat route is west to the northern portion of the Cumberland Plateau, you must be cognizant of the winds and plan to go north on Hwy 25W or south on Hwy 1 from Knoxville in order to penetrate the mountain ridges away from Oakridge. The ridges run perpendicular to your direction of travel, so you can't get west in a straight line of travel.

If your direction of retreat is to the SE toward the Blue Ridge Mountains, then make sure you locate on the east side of the river that blocks the way for most of the city. Only if you choose to live toward the NE part of the city (outside of the 640 beltway and between I-75 and I-40) does your exit route run parallel to the ridges. It doesn't really help that much because there are lots of rivers and watercourses in those same valleys and few roads.

Retreat Areas

Rural farmland: Rural farm retreats are not as safe as being in the hill country, but if you follow our guidelines about locating for privacy, they can be almost as good. The secret is making sure you are not near a major refugee path (usually traveling down secondary roads). Also make sure you are not downwind of major nuclear targets or one of the nuclear power plants.

Cumberland Plateau: The plateau actually extends from into Alabama on the south up part way into Kentucky in the north. However, we prefer the southern portion where there are no major traffic flows over the mountains. I-40 cuts through the Middle and I-24 between Nashville and Chattanooga cuts through the plateau to the south. The town of Spencer is approximately in the middle of the tabletop. The best locations are along routes 8 and 111 that cross over the plateau south of Spencer. McMinnville is the largest medium sized city closest to this area of the plateau. There is good forestation throughout the plateau. On the bluffs, grand views of the lower countryside are magnificent, but too far away for anyone to notice from the valleys below. The only downside of the plateau is that rock layers under the soil can sometimes inhibit basements. In many cases there is enough to permit partial basements and with landscaping you can obtain full basement protection.

TEXAS ★★★☆☆

Summary Facts and Ratings

Climate:	Multiple climate zones, from continental (hot and dry) in the west to humid subtropical near the Gulf coast. The panhandle has colder winters than north Texas, while the Gulf Coast has very little winter. TX averages 139 tornadoes a year and commonly gets hit by hurricanes on the coast.
Population Density:	Average. 95 ppl/sq. mile (ranked 26th in the nation). Hispanic 37%, Black 12%, Asian 3.6%, mixed 1.4%, American Indian 8%.
Cost of Living Index:	Low. 92.6 (average is 100) ranks this state as the 17th lowest in the nation.
Private Land Availability:	High. Only 2% of land is state or federally owned.
Building Permits:	Required statewide, but many local towns have easier requirements. Most cities have jurisdiction for property close to but outside of the official city limits.
Land and Urban Planning:	No state-wide planning mandate.
Food Production:	Good growing season from 180 days in the north to 330 days in the south. The top five crops are: cotton, greenhouse & nursery, corn, wheat and hay. Rainfall varies from 55 inches per year in the east to less than 10 inches in the west. Dallas gets a moderate 37 inches. Only the coastal plain gets enough rain to raise crops without irrigation or well pumping.
Health Environment:	Many natural springs abound and have good water except in urban areas or near extensively fertilized crops. 80% of water supplies are fluoridated. Air pollution is not a problem except in the major cities. There is excellent solar potential almost everywhere.
Traffic:	Houston and Dallas/Ft. Worth have heavy traffic problems. Some red light cameras in use, but no state law per se.
Politics:	Texas is a conservative state except in the large cities. Dem 37%, Rep 41%, Ind/3rd party 12%.
Taxes:	Below average. Ranked 4th lowest with an average state tax burden of 7,5% of income. No income tax, property taxes rank 8th lowest in the nation but state and local sales tax average 7.4%. Car registration fees are reasonable.
Corruption:	Very high at the state level. Police and judges in large cities are also subject to corruption.
Crime:	High. Violent crime 408/100K, property crime 3258/100K. Crime index for Houston is 4, Dallas 10, San Antonio 4, Corpus Christi 6 (100 is safest)
Personal Liberty:	Fair. 14th best nationally.
Gun Liberty:	Very good. No permit is required to purchase firearms. "Shall issue" state for concealed weapon permits. Banned weapons include machine guns and sawed-off rifles and shotguns. Open carry is not permitted in the state except in special cases such as when hunting or transporting a gun.
Alternative Medicine:	Very good. There is a full range of natural health practitioners. Direct entry midwifery is legal through apprenticeship and approved courses if they pass the NARM exam. School vaccine exemptions: philosophical, religious and medical.
Home Schooling:	Unregulated. State requires no notification and no test scores.
Military Targets:	**Brooks AFB**, San Antonio. Aerospace medicine training. Not a target. **Camp Bullis**, San Antonio. Maneuvering and training area. Not a target. **Fort Bliss**, north of El Paso. Patriot Missile training, 1st armored Division, large maneuver area and range; primary target. **Red River Army Depot**, west of Texarkana. Ammunition storage and repair of Bradley army vehicles; secondary target. **Fort Hood**, north of Kileen. Large army base with armor, artillery and air corps; primary target. **Fort Sam Houston**. US Army command center and home of 5th and 6th armies; secondary target. **Corpus Christi Naval Air Station**. Includes Naval Hospital, Naval Station and Ingleside Army Depot; secondary target.

Military Targets continued:	**Kingsville Naval Air Station**. Navy's premier jet aviation training; secondary target.
	Fort Worth NAS/Air Force Plant 4 (formerly Carswell AFB). Joint reserve base with F-16, F-18 and production of F-16 and F-22 parts; secondary target.
	Randolph AFB, east San Antonio. Training base for jets and large aircraft; tertiary target.
	Lackland AFB, San Antonio. ANG F-16s and C-5s; NSA intercept and data storage; secondary target.
	Sheppard AFB, Wichita Falls. Training wing; tertiary target.
	Dyess AFB, west Abilene. B-1s and C-130; primary target.
	Goodfellow AFB, San Angelo, Cryptology training; not a target.
	Laughlin AFB, Ciudad Acuna. Largest pilot training base in USAF; secondary target.
	Hensley Field, east Arlington. Texas Air National Guard—no target.
	Chesapeake ROTH Radar, Corpus Christi. Relocatable Over-the-Horizon Radar (ROTHR). Enlisted for counter narcotics; tertiary target.
	Pantex Nuclear Weapons Plant, Amarillo. America's only plant for assembly/disassembly/storage of nuclear weapons; primary target.
	NSA Cryptological Center, San Antonio. Built into the old Sony building; tertiary target.
Nuclear Power Plants, Oil Reserve Sites:	**South Texas Plant**, Gulf Coast between Galveston and Corpus Christi. 2 reactors.
	Commanche Peak Plant, 40 mi. southwest of Fort Worth. 2 reactors.
	Bryan Mound Strategic Petroleum Reserve, near Freeport, 254 million barrels underground storage; secondary target.
	Big Hill Strategic Petroleum Reserve, near Winnie, 160 million barrels underground storage; secondary target.

Notes

Texas is great because of what remains of the spirit underlying its unofficial motto "Don't Mess with Texas." Texas has a long history of independence and resistance to tyranny and being controlled by the eastern establishment. That still lives on today in the good humble people of rural Texas but not so much in its big cities. Along with the Texas oil boom came tremendous wealth and fat cat living which corrupted much of the fighting spirit of the state. What's left of Texas bigness is of the bawdy and showy variety rather than a strength of resistance.

Texas politicians are especially adept at playing the role of the tough Texan but most sell out to financial interests. Texas used to be solidly democratic, but started to change after the state's disgust of Lyndon Johnson. Rural Texans still demand protection of their rights, but are often betrayed by politicians claiming to be conservative but who are controlled by the establishment. Even the big mega-churches have become soft and worldly with money and fame.

Corruption is widespread in the Lone Star State, especially when mixed with political power. The legislature passed a state lottery on the grounds that the profits would all go to fund education in the state and prevent escalation of property taxes, but the taxes just keep rising despite the money from the lottery. There have been several cases of corrupt lottery officials absconding with funds. There were 27 public corruption prosecutions last year, which is way too low for the level of corruption here. Cronyism, payoffs and kickbacks for state contracts are common. The NAFTA highway scandal, complete with toll road sales to foreign companies, continues to be pushed by the governor despite local rejection. Corruption in the judicial system and among police is chronic.

Texas has several major advantages over other states as a relocation destination, including the low cost of living, no income tax, wide open spaces, available land and a fairly strong "don't mess with Texas" attitude (largely outside of big cities like Dallas). On the other hand, we see several negatives about Texas such as the deep roots of corruption, the lack of principled toughness in politics and the steady encroachment of illegal immigrants. Like all southern border states, the illegal alien threat will eventually overwhelm the area. Latino gangs are driving up crime and wielding increasing voter support of democratic socialism and benefits.

There are also some major threats to Texas in a nuclear war. Texas senators have used their insider connections with Washington for many years to bring military installations to Texas. This has been good for jobs, but these bases put civilians at risk during war. Naturally, the largest metro areas in Texas are also subject to mass social unrest following a major attack or any crisis accompanied by the cutoff of supplies and public services. Dallas/FortWorth and Houston are the worst. But also at risk are San Antonio, Austin and Amarillo.

In short, because of the sheer size of this state, you can find medium-term safety in rural areas and enjoy a low cost lifestyle. However, in like manner, conservative Texans are easily fooled by politicians who talk and walk like traditional Texans and who say what conservatives want to hear, but are in league with powerful and corrupt national forces which intend to subvert traditional values in this once great state.

Texas has very diverse weather because of its huge size where it encounters two huge air masses that meet, the Rocky Mountain and Canadian cold air masses and the Gulf of Mexico's warm, moist air. Thunderstorms and tornados are persistent threats. We recommend below-ground shelters from all these threats but watch out for rock-like soils like Caliche, or the infamous Vertisols types. Vertisols are expansive clay soils that cause buildings to heave upwards in the rainy season or sink during dry spells. Both types make building secure basements an expensive and costly project. Before you buy land in Texas, you must check local soil maps at the county extension office to make sure you aren't buying land that is useless for growing or where basements are not feasible.

Strategies for Populated Living Areas

All of the major metros in Texas are too big to survive social unrest in a major crisis, so you should plan on a rural retreat; and your retreat should not be toward the south. In general, you should locate in the suburban towns on the outer ring of any metro area, and near to the non-freeway exit routes you plan out of the city. We want to emphasize living on the periphery of the metro area because if you're in the middle of Plano or Garland, for example, you will have a hard time escaping the local traffic, not to mention the traffic from all the people inside the metro area. Remember, if you can't get out quickly, you might as well stay put. Don't get stranded on the freeways or roads.

Dallas area/Fort Worth: Your best retreat sites are east in the pine forest country around Athens, Palestine, etc. Also consider retreats in the north around Sherman and Denison or northwest toward the small towns near Wichita Falls. You can't go west without first going north because of the targets and populations in your way. If you move to Dallas for a job, we recommend the small suburban towns near the periphery of Dallas in an arc from east to northwest. Your selection must coincide with where you plan to exit the area.

In the Fort Worth area, locate on the periphery of the housing developments in an arc beginning above the I-30/I-820 junction and ending with I-35W. There are several subdivisions outside this freeway arc (Crest Ridge and Saginaw) that eliminate your need to evade the encirclement of roads.

Houston area: Locate on the periphery in a northerly arc, centered around Spring, Texas. Your best retreat sites are NW into the pine country of east Texas. If you prefer the retreat sites in the Hill Country west of Austin and San Antonio (Kerrville area), you can pick a suburban city on Houston's west side. Choose a route west and around San Antonio on rural roads. You must also find a way to cross under I-35 where there isn't an exit to bar your way.

Austin: Select a location in a west suburb of the city near Hwy 290 leading to Fredericksburg or Hwy 71 leading to Llano. There are retreat sites between Llano and Austin. In San Antonio, we recommend you locate outside the Charles Anderson Loop Highway to the north. Best exit routes are Hwy 281 to Fredericksburg, or 16 to Kerrville.

Amarillo: Avoid the nuclear assembly plant (Pantex) 17 miles northeast of the city, above Hwy 60. Amarillo is not in the blast zone, nor is it in the normal fallout wind pattern if the plant is struck. It is very likely to be hit since nuclear weapons are being stored there. It would be better to locate on the west side of town and have a secure home or retreat.

Retreat Areas

East Texas: This is the beautiful pine country near the Louisiana border and the Gulf Coast. This area encompasses the outer ring of suburban cities around Houston, along the Gulf Coast to Port Arthur and includes all the small towns going north to Tyler, Texas. Lastly, there are several small towns even farther north between I-20 and I-30, but one must stay at least 5 miles from the freeways themselves to ensure against having to deal with those stranded on the major highways. Naturally, the Gulf Coast portion of this area within 25 miles of the water is not recommended due to the threat of Hurricanes. This is a huge area where one can find mild weather, good water, rural farm land clearings and down-to-earth people. However, keep in mind that the towns closest to Dallas and Houston will eventually receive a lot of refugees, so keep to the central zone around the Angelina National Forest. We should also mention the area above I-30 which approaches the Oklahoma Ozarks. Farm retreats outside of Clarksville and Paris are very rural and provide good safety.

Texas Hill Country: This is the only suitable retreat area in southwest Texas, and it is especially suitable for people who live in the south of Texas. It encompasses the counties to the NW of I-35 between Austin and San Antonio. The central cities in the hill country are Kerrville and Fredericksburg, though it extends farther north toward Llano as well. It has a mix of Pines, Live Oaks and Juniper forestation together with good well water. Its major liabilities are rock outcroppings and hardpan Caliche soils (making basements expensive). It is also close to Mexico and the problems of eventual "reconquista" of southern states.

Texas Panhandle: There are some fine agricultural areas in the panhandle from Lubbock north to Amarillo, particularly in the Plainview areas. Flat land doesn't make for good retreats per se, but this area is so vast and rural that it can be considered relatively safe. Remember that a key part of survival is being able to grow food in areas that don't have a lot of starving people. There are ranges of hills and rough country where rural retreat cabins can be located. While rougher and less forested, the rugged country north of Amarillo and its small towns provide good long-term safety if you have water.

UTAH ★★★★★

Summary Facts and Ratings

Climate:	High altitude desert and arid climate. Summers are hot at 90-105 °F. Winters are cold but sunny at 30 °F. Low humidity. UT averages 2 tornadoes per year.
Population Density:	Low. 32 ppl/sq. mile (41st ranking in the nation). Salt Lake metro area density is 1218 ppl/sq. mile). Hispanic 12.3%, Asian 2.1%, Native American 1.4%, Black 1.4%, mixed 1.7%.
Cost of Living Index:	Below average. 92.4 (average is 100) ranks this as the 16th lowest cost state.
Private Land Availability:	Poor. 70% of land is state or federally owned, including most of the best forests and mountain land.
Building Permits:	Required statewide for new construction and remodel. Basements are built everywhere.
Land and Urban Planning:	Smart Growth is being pushed, but not yet taken hold so land use planning stays at the local level.
Food Production:	Good but requires irrigation. Adequate growing season of 90-150 days. Sandy soil in most places, but clay is common at valley bottoms and around lakes. Rain averages 15 in/year in the north and only 12 inches in the south.
Health Environment:	Mountain spring water is excellent but the quality from wells in the valleys is only fair. 51.7% of the population's water is fluoridated. Air pollution is bad in Salt Lake and Utah Valleys during the winter inversions. Good solar potential all year.
Traffic:	Moderate except during rush hour on I-15 metro corridor, Ogden to Springville. Traffic is light in rural areas. No red light or speed cameras.
Politics:	Conservatives predominate everywhere except Salt Lake City, partly because of the conservative Mormon religious culture. Dem 26%, Rep 59%, Ind/3rd party 15%.
Taxes:	Average. Ranked 23rd lowest with an average state tax burden of 9.4% of income. Income tax is a 5% flat rate, sales taxes average 6.6% and property taxes are low, ranked 40th in the nation.
Corruption:	Moderate. Some corruption in state government and metro police, but almost non-existent in rural areas.
Crime:	Moderate. Violent crime 224/100K, property crime 2950/100K. Crime index for SLC is 1, Ogden 7, Provo 27, St. George 37 (100 is safest). Gangs only a problem in the Salt Lake metro area.
Personal Liberty:	Good, 10th best nationally.
Gun Liberty:	Very good. No permit to purchase firearms. Background check required for purchase from gun dealers. "Shall issue" state for concealed firearm permits. Recognizes most other states' permits. Open carry permitted if no round in chamber.
Alternative Medicine:	Very good availability for full range of natural health practitioners. Direct entry midwives can choose to be licensed or operate free of licensing. School vaccine exemptions: philosophical, religious and medical.
Home Schooling:	Low regulation. State requires parents to send notification only.
Military Targets:	**Tooele Army Depot** and Deseret Chemical Depot, west of SLC. Storage of chemical and conventional munitions; primary target, 2 locations. **Dugway Proving Ground**, east of SLC. Air Force range containing Michael Army Airfield, the "new Area 51" secret underground base. Decommissioned MX missiles stored here; primary target. **Camp Williams NG**, south of SLC. This includes the **NSA datacenter** near Bluffdale, UT; secondary target. **Hill AFB**, Ogden Defense Depot. F-16 Fighters, MX missile parts, major repair depot; primary target. **Air Force Plant No. 78**, west of Logan. Now Thiokol plant manufacturing rocket motors; secondary target.

Notes

Utah is the center of the Intermountain West and has become known for its mountains, skiing and arid desert scenery (including its unique red rock formations). Utah has some of the greatest distances in any direction from potential sources of social unrest, thus making it one of the safest long-term places in the nation. It is the only top rated state with access to an international airport (SLC is a major hub for Delta Airlines). This is important for businessmen seeking safety in combination with ease of travel.

Mountain snowmelt and reservoirs provide good, clean water for most of Utah's needs, including irrigation. Parts of some old pioneer towns still have pure public water supplies coming out of the mountains, although most have to add some chlorine due to federal requirements. It is still a desert, so find a community with good water sources. The mountains provide gravity feed, so water could continue flowing even in an extended power outage.

After years of farming, the native sandy soil has now become fertile, sandy-loam soil which is easy to work with. Ample sunshine helps almost all crops grow if below an elevation of 6,000 feet. Hay and cattle are more common in the higher mountain valleys. The growing season is longer at lower elevations in southern Utah along rivers (Utah's Dixie). As in all other high desert climates in the West, Fir and Pine forests don't grow on the hot western face of the mountains, nor below 6,000 ft. Shaded snowpack provides the steady melt of water needed to grow conifer trees, found only on the northern and eastern sides of the mountains. The populated cities along the Wasatch front and I-15 corridor back up to the west face of the mountains which don't show the beauty of the forests behind.

Many people are intimidated by the Mormon religion in Utah. But we consider the Mormon population base to be a strategic advantage in a crisis. The Church of Jesus Christ of Latter-day Saints (LDS) as a culture contributes to making this the most conservative state in the Union, and Mormons generally have a much higher level of personal preparedness that is encouraged by their religious beliefs and state cultural history. The Latter-day Saints are, for the most part, friendly and tolerant of other faiths in their midst, despite the distortions and rumors that come from the prolific anti-Mormon opposition. Other Christian churches are found in every Utah community.

The only place the Mormons are the minority is in Salt Lake City (SLC), where non-Mormons tend to congregate, and sometimes create friction with anti-Mormon hostility. Much of it is driven by Democrats, liberals and homosexuals chaffing under the overwhelming majority of Mormon Republican voters and their religious doctrine which espouses liberty but does not consider homosexuality an acceptable moral lifestyle. Others dislike the "follow the leader" mentality of many Mormons, which is certainly a valid criticism. However, a sizable minority of Mormons are even further to the right of mainstream Mormon Republicans and considers themselves constitutional conservatives.

The bottom line is that the vast majority of Mormons are good Christian people, and don't deserve the bad rap that critics promote. Our experience with clients moving into the state is that they find the people open and tolerant of other Christians and even non-religious people as long as newcomers don't harbor a lot of anti-Mormon feelings.

LDS high moral standards helps to keep corruption at low levels among Mormon public office holders, with occasional glaring exceptions. All states have corruption, including Utah, but it is significantly lower here. In theory, if any church member has knowledge of significant dishonesty among a leader in the Church (and many LDS government officials also hold lay leadership positions in local congregations), they can raise an objection and the local leaders are required to hold a hearing on the matter. While few members ever exercise that right, some have and it has resulted in a leadership change. This potential for public embarrassment acts as a deterrent to corruption. Naturally, that doesn't stop some from hiding their corruption, but it does form a second avenue for discipline—especially when political parties join ranks to protect one of their own from dismissal. There has been corruption among local police, but particularly in the Salt Lake Valley when over a dozen officers were suspended or dismissed for alcohol, moral, or policy offenses. Corruption among local judges is lower than the national average, but it does exist.

Utah is not free from the nuclear threat. Hill Air Force Base is a primary target since it is a major logistics and repair depot for complex aircraft and missiles. Parts of the MX missile system are stored there as well as in the Dugway Proving Grounds in the West Desert and the Tooele Army depot. There are also well documented rumors of a secret underground military base out in the West Desert. It's logical that there are several of these scattered around the US since Cheyenne Mountain is such an obvious target for a Russian nuclear attack. The new NSA spy data computer center in the desert NW of Camp Williams is also a possible future target.

Most mountain areas in the West are subject to some earthquakes, and Utah is no exception. Take steps to prepare a home here for earthquakes by securing heavy bookcases and water heaters to the walls, etc. If you are building a new home consider the soil conditions and implement appropriate reinforcing such as shear walls and foundation anchor bolts.

Strategies for Populated Living Areas

Salt Lake City area: The main metropolitan areas in Utah are about 4500 feet in elevation and sit right next to the towering Wasatch Range of the Rocky Mountains. These valleys offer the best growing areas in northern Utah. Everything else is higher in altitude. We don't recommend the Salt Lake Valley itself because of its congestion, liberal/left tendencies and winter air pollution. Most people have to locate near SLC for work, but they should note that most traffic out of the city travels via the I-15 freeway around the "Point of the Mountain." One of the few alternates is Redwood Road which leads to Utah Valley from the south Salt Lake Valley areas of Herriman and Bluffdale. If you are a pilot and want to use an airplane to leave the city in a crisis, locate in West Jordan near the South Valley Regional Airport. Here are other areas in the SL Valley with alternate paths out:

Cottonwood Heights is close to the 215 beltway and Big Cottonwood Canyon for business access and there are jeep roads over the mountains into the secure Heber Valley. This area is also a secondary business district with professional offices.

East Sandy is around Little Cottonwood Canyon Road, which leads up to the famed ski resorts of Snowbird and Alta. That canyon also has unpaved roads leading over the mountains to greater safety. Further south in the valley is the new housing areas above Draper (Suncrest) which has a road leading to Alpine in Utah Valley.

Northern I-15 Corridor: It is more difficult to find anything safe north of Salt Lake City because of the proximity to Hill AFB, but a few small cities qualify for some safety if properly located away from the freeway. These are North Salt Lake, Bountiful and perhaps Farmington. We recommend areas on the high foothills (called the "benches") because you will have to go further into the mountains on jeep trails to get around the traffic blockages north and south. Jeep trails lead off above Bountiful Blvd.

There is nothing safe north between Kaysville and Ogden because of the presence of Hill AFB. You really have to go north past Willard Bay and on to Brigham City to find another valley city outside the danger zone. Willard Bay is a huge freshwater bay on the Great Salt Lake and a favorite for large sailboats. Brigham City is a little too far for commuting, though some do it. This nice little town is the gateway to the excellent high valley retreat sites in Cache Valley.

Utah County: Because most of the threats are in the north and west parts of the State, we recommend clients pick normal living areas in the valleys south of Salt Lake City for the best safety. Utah Valley has good commuting access to SLC and yet better retreat access to the safe areas further south. There is no major metro area to the south of Utah Valley. In addition, Utah valley has closer access to the mountains and some excellent retreats via Heber Valley than does Salt Lake (via Hwy 189). Utah Valley is the home to two universities (BYU in Provo and UVU in Orem) and thus offers a wide variety of education and culture. Our favorite locations are the ring of cities along the mountains south of the Provo-Orem area: Springville, Mapleton, and Salem. The first two have mountain fed spring water. Spanish Fork (near Springville) is out in the middle of the valley and is perhaps the best run city in the county in terms of low cost and efficiency (with fiber-optic internet). It has a non-towered airport as well. Avoid buying in the wind flows of Spanish Fork Canyon unless you want to put up your own wind generator. The best area in the southern part of Utah valley is the part of Spanish fork that joins the mountains on the east, but just south of Hwy 6, going up Spanish Fork Canyon. Most of Spanish Fork

is in the center of the valley where the water table is high and where you cannot build basements. However, in this area near the mountains, you can build basements and the price of land is lower than north of Hwy 6 in Mapleton.

Retreat Areas

The closest retreat areas to the Salt Lake Valley are Parley's Summit at the top of the canyon near the Park City ski resorts on I-80. This is where many of the original settlers had their summer cabins. The real estate is expensive, but beautiful and convenient. The mountain-fed water is excellent as are the high mountain forests. Further on around the mountains is a very secure upper valley retreat area, the Heber Valley. While a thousand feet higher than Salt Lake Valley, you still have a full growing season for normal crops. Prices are not cheap here either as the higher prices of Park City and Deer Valley have made this the destination for overflow demand. Even so, it is a beautiful agricultural valley with its own airport and one of the best lakes in Utah, Deer Creek Reservoir under the spectacular Mt. Timpanogos. We like the town of Midway best. The town of Midway, on the west side of Heber valley up against the mountains is particularly sought after, and has beautiful views of the back side of Mt. Timpanogas and the reservoir. However, do not locate in the lower parts of Heber valley along the river. A new reservoir has been built to the north (Jordanelle) which puts the low parts of the valley at risk in case the dam breaks in an earthquake.

Northern Utah: North of Salt Lake City and east of Ogden in a higher mountain valley is a jewel of a farm-retreat area surrounding the Pineview Reservoir. The names of the towns of Liberty, Eden and Huntsville tell their own story. Even farther north is the larger Cache Valley, home of the city of Logan and Utah State University. This is one of the cold high mountain valleys in Utah, but it still has a full growing season once the frost has passed. The best retreat areas are in the southern part of Cache valley around the towns of Hyrum, Paradise and Avon. Even more remote (over the mountains on Hwy 89), is the Bear Lake area around Garden City—a small resort town which is famous for its raspberry crops and berry shakes. Bear Lake is one of the most beautiful blue lakes in the West, and there are many cabin sites in the mountains to the West of the Lake.

Near Utah Valley: The mountains near here are mostly undeveloped and rugged but there are three possible retreat areas with power and water amenities: Sundance has numerous private cabins in the mountains around Robert Redford's iconic Sundance ski resort. It is not as crowded or popular as Park City, (home of the Sundance Film Festival) being lower in altitude, but the scenery is spectacular on the wooded backside of Mt. Timpanogos. It is too high and shaded to grow food at Sundance, but it is only a few miles from farmland and 20 minutes from Provo-Orem. Hobble Creek Canyon runs east up from Springville and is known for its canyon golf course. It is lower in elevation and can grow some crops, though the mountains on either side limit the hours of sunshine. Spanish Fork Canyon also has one or two cabin subdivisions and is at about the same elevation as Hobble Creek canyon.

Central Utah: The best overall retreat area in the entire state is in Sanpete County. The 5500' to 6000' altitude valley extends from Mt. Pleasant and Fairview in the north (highest elevation in the valley) down to Sterling and Manti (with the lower elevations). All the towns have excellent water, good soil and no major threats. The primary agriculture in the valley is turkey farms and hay. It is too far away from Salt Lake City to experience much social unrest overflow, and it has a good base of farm people and hunters that will survive well in hard times. The valley has forested mountains on both sides offering dozens of cabin sites, ample hunting (deer and Elk) and lakes and trails. Our favorite places are Mt. Pleasant and Spring City.

Central Utah and Highway 89 corridor: Going south from Sanpete County, you come into Sevier County, which has a lot of rich irrigated farmland, at a moderate altitude and centered around the town of Richfield. I-70 passes through this area on its way to join I-15 further West, but has little traffic this far West. Hwy 89 follows the Sevier River south. There are pioneer homesteads and farmland on both sides of the highway. All of this area is relatively safe since the construction of I-15 on the other side of the mountains took most of the traffic. All of the farms in this area have easy access to higher mountain valleys and retreat sites, as well as clear mountain lakes like Fish Lake.

Highway 12 corridor: Some of the real gems of southern Utah are isolated farm and ranch areas along scenic Hwy 12, which takes you from Panguitch up to the gorgeous Bryce Canyon Plateau through Red Rock Canyon. The real retreat sites don't show up until you go down the other side of the mountain into Tropic. There you enter the spectacular world of the Grand Staircase National monument and the towns of Tropic, Escalante and Boulder, including the Aquarius Plateau Mountains. This is an isolated world known to very few in Utah, and it is a wonderful area to retreat to if you don't mind the isolation and are content to soak in the beautiful landscape. Tropic is the closest to civilization and Boulder is the farthest—a real sanctuary.

Southern I-15 corridor: Even though the interstate is not safe due to high traffic, it is still possible to find retreat sites in the mountains to the east of the freeway and not visible from it. Each of the communities of Beaver, Parawan and Cedar City has such limited sites. The tough thing is finding one for sale.

Southern Utah past Cedar City has a different climate due to the fifteen hundred feet lower elevation. It is called Utah's Dixie due to the warmer climate. St. George became a destination boom town after Las Vegas started to fill up with Californians, but all that leveled off after 2008. It's now a first rate shopping and commerce area, but not quite a good place to retreat to itself. The smaller and older pioneer communities of Hurricane, LaVerkin and Toquerville are better. You can still find properties close to the Virgin River which flows out of Zion's National Park, but there is so much traffic along Hwy 9 going to and from the park, that it might be hard to gain any privacy. Consider the irrigated lands around Toquerville which is off the freeway and has clear water pressurized for irrigation. The farm belt in Hurricane also has its own non-towered airport as well as a high end gated airport community (Sky Ranch) providing some excellent possibilities for pilots who need an aviation retreat to escape the LA basin.

On the west side of St. George, you find the old pioneer communities of Santa Clara and Ivins in Green Valley, which offer good isolation. Beyond these you can find even better remote retreat sites when you climb back up into the mountains on the Hwy to Veyo, Central and Pine Valley. The road keeps going over the mountains to Enterprise, which is another good retreat site, though very isolated by distance to the markets.

Eastern Utah: We must mention the areas around Vernal in the northeast part of the state. They make good retreat sites because few people want to live there. It's very cold in the winter, being on the east side of the Wasatch Range, and it's a long drive to major commercial centers. But there are good ranching sites near the mountains close to the small towns in the area. It's also part of the oil boom going on in the US, so there is considerable growth in the apartment and rental markets---so don't go to rent. There are a couple of stunning reservoirs in the area so recreation is a real draw as well.

In the southeastern part of the state, Monticello and Blanding have the same safety factor due to isolation with the added advantage of a warmer climate. Monticello really belongs more to the economic district of southwestern Colorado, due to proximity and type of agriculture. To get there, you pass through the spectacular red rock country of Moab and Arches National Monument, the mountain biking paradise of the US. The climate is drier and warmer than northern Utah.

VERMONT ★★⯪☆☆

Summary Facts and Ratings

Climate:	Humid continental climate with wet springs, mild summers, brightly colored fall leaves and long, cold winters. Snowfall varies between 60 to 100 inches depending on elevation.
Population Density:	Medium low. 67 ppl/sq. mile (20th lowest in nation). Hispanic 1.5%, Black 1%, Asian 1.2%, mixed 1.2%.
Cost of Living Index:	High. 124 (average is 100) ranked as the 9th most expensive state.
Land Ownership:	Good. Only 8.2% of the land is state or federally owned.
Building Permits:	Required for new buildings. Localities may require permit for small projects like replacing the heating system, but most do not. Some areas have onerous zoning restrictions on new construction (Wal-Mart found it easier to use preexisting buildings). Basements are common outside of some mountain areas with granite near the surface.
Land and Urban Planning:	Vermont has "Smart Growth" implementation by stealth. Despite the lack of mandatory local planning, the state Land Use and Development Law (Act 250) requires permits for certain types of development activity which must comply with Growth Management Act (1988) which is a form of Smart Growth.
Food Production:	Moderate. Rocky, glaciated soil and a growing season of 90 to 180 days. Most of the state gets 150 days. Rainfall averages about 42 inches per year.
Health Environment:	Good water quality. Surface and aquifer water is among the top 20 states. 56.1% of the population's drinking water is fluoridated.
Traffic:	No significant traffic observed. VT does not use red light or speed cameras.
Politics:	VT is considered a heavily Democratic state and attracts independents and environmentalists who (together with the state news media) carry things even further left. VT has liberal laws on marijuana and gay unions. Dem 47%, Rep 31%, Ind/3rd party 23%.
Taxes:	High. Ranked 9th highest with an average state tax burden of 10.5% of income. Income tax rate is 7% up to $34K and 8.95% after $82.4K. Sales tax is 6% and property taxes are the sixth highest in the nation (collected by both state and local governments).
Corruption:	Moderate. Vermont has always prided itself on being a low corruption state. But there are political and judicial improprieties.
Crime:	Low violent crime rate of 121/100K and average property crime rate of 2214/100K. Crime index for Burlington is 15, (100 is safest).
Personal Liberty:	Poor. VT rates 7th lowest in overall freedom rating.
Gun Liberty:	Excellent. Considered one of the most open states in the nation. No permit is required to purchase firearms. "Shall issue" state for concealed weapon permits, but open carry is unrestricted (even in a car) outside of convicted criminals. Firearms need not be registered but gun dealers keep records of sales.
Alternative Medicine:	Naturopathy is legal and regulated by a licensing board and allows naturopaths to prescribe drugs and perform mild surgeries. The practice of midwifery is legal but regulated. Certified midwives must meet state specific requirements. School vaccine exemptions: religious and medical.
Home Schooling:	High regulation. Parents must notify the state and submit an annual record and portfolio of each child's work or the child must take an annual test.
Military Targets:	**Burlington Airport**. F-16s and C-130s of Air National Guard; tertiary target.
Nuclear Power Plant:	**Vermont Plant**, in Vernon (SE tip of state), 1 reactor.
Overall Rating:	Good for the East Coast, because of rural retreat potential. Basically, same situation as New Hampshire except it is downgraded for proximity to big cities, left/liberal politics and restrictions to liberty.

Notes

Vermont's big advantage is that it has very few people. The largest city, Burlington, barely surpasses the 50,000 population mark. All the other towns are well below the 20,000 mark. Unlike other low population states, Vermont is very liberal and considered to be the least religious in the union. It ranks with Upstate NY as a retreat site, which is good, considering how close these areas are to the high density urban zones of the East. It is safer than New Hampshire, which is closer to people exiting from Boston. VT will remain a refuge longer because the major transportation corridors do not pass through the state. Nevertheless, with that kind of population center fairly close, we expect only medium-term safety here.

Economically all is not well in the state. VT had the highest decline in household income in 2010 and high rates of people are leaving this state, largely because of high taxes. Air quality is good except in the I-89 corridor where pollution from Boston drifts northwest. Vermont's culture is oriented toward frugality and healthy living. It rates highest in the nation in a survey on healthful behaviors such as healthy eating, exercising and not smoking. Other good things are low crime and a fairly high life expectancy.

In 1987 three of Vermont's five Supreme Court justices were accused of judicial improprieties with a former assistant woman judge. VT had 30 public corruption convictions last year, but no prosecutions of politicians. William H. Sorrell, Attorney General of Vermont, told the U.S. Supreme Court in 2010 that political corruption in Vermont is a serious problem, but admitted under questioning that he hadn't prosecuted anyone for it. Sorrell is rated the 6th worst AG in the country for corruption of law. VT has in recent years begun to charge exorbitant fees to access public records—not a good trend. Several counties have reported police misconduct toward victims, including improper tasering.

Vermont is anxious to be known as a pro-gay state. It has legalized homosexual marriage and as you enter the state, you can't miss a sign that says, "Welcome to Vermont – home of one of the 13 original gay bars." Vermont is a hotbed of homosexual activism, some of which is even supported by tax funds.

Strategies for Populated Living Areas

Burlington: While Burlington is not a large city (less than 50,000), there are enough people to present some social unrest in a shortage crisis. It has several trap zones, being bordered by Lake Champlain on the west and freeways on the east. Essex Junction to the east is outside the trap zones and closest to retreat sites further north. South Burlington is the place to locate if you have a retreat in that direction.

Retreat Areas

Almost any area in Vermont qualifies as retreat property if it is at least 10 miles away from the freeways and secondary roads with some forestation for privacy. We prefer the area to the north of I-89, although the area south of this interstate is almost as good.

VIRGINIA ★★☆☆☆
(Including Washington DC)

Summary Facts and Ratings

Climate:	There are at least 3 different climate types: coastal sub-tropical in the east, humid subtropical, and humid continental in the west. The air mass becomes increasingly warmer and humid the farther south and east you go. During the fall and winter, cold air from Canada gives a respite to the humidity and insects, but can bring significant snowfall, such as the huge blizzards in 1996 and 2009. Chesapeake Bay vulnerable to hurricanes. Thunderstorms are a regular occurrence in the west. VA averages 7 tornadoes a year.
Population Density:	Above average. 200 ppl/sq. mile (14th highest in nation). Black 20%, Hispanic 8%, Asian 5%, mixed 2%.
Cost of Living Index:	Below average. 94.5 (average is 100) ranks this as the 20th least expensive state.
Land Ownership:	Good. 9.5% of the land is state and federally owned.
Building Permits:	Required for new buildings and most renovations involving the structure. This includes small structures such as decks and sheds as well as interior remodeling. In 2007 Virginia put into law the draconian Oregon model of Urban Development boundaries, into which all residential development must fit—which often prohibits anything but expensive 40 acre and larger parcels outside those urban growth boundaries, which is where you want to be. Basements are built in VA except in mountain areas where the underlying rock requires blasting.
Land and Urban Planning:	In 2007 Virginia implemented a draconian urban development plan similar to Oregon. Mandated boundaries restrict all residential development to specific areas. This is bad for rural property rights where one has to have one, two or even five acre lots to build.
Food Production:	Excellent productivity in the central and eastern valleys. The hill country is more difficult to farm due to rocky, acidic soil mixed with clay. The growing season is 150 to 220 days, west to east. Average annual precipitation is 43 in.
Health Environment:	Rural VA is very healthy except when winds bring pollution from urban areas. 96% of the population's drinking water is fluoridated.
Traffic:	Washington DC Beltway is the 9th worst traffic in the nation. Richmond also has traffic problems, but rural VA does not. VA uses red light cameras and radar detectors are prohibited, even when driving in from out of state.
Politics:	Virginia is a Republican state, although the Republicans they elect always tend to do the bidding of the federal government which heavily influences the state with its many agencies. Dem 40%, Rep 42%, Ind/3rd party 18%.
Taxes:	Average. Ranked 21st lowest with an average state tax burden of 9.2% of income. The income tax tops out at 5.75% (DC is 8.5%), sales tax is 5.3% (none in DC) and property taxes are average except in the DC area where they are high.
Corruption:	Lower than average (which is still high). There were 14 public corruption convictions last year, which is relatively low. DC corruption is very high.
Crime:	Average. Violent crime 196/100K, property crime 2066/100K. Crime index for Arlington is 41, Richmond 8, DC 3 (100 is safest).
Personal Liberty:	Good, 8th best nationally.
Gun Liberty:	Good. No permit to purchase firearms. "Shall issue" state for concealed weapon permits. Open carry is permitted, even in a car. A permit issued by a circuit court is needed to carry a concealed handgun. Firearms in DC must be registered with police—no permits for concealed or open carry. DC ban on guns was struck down by Supreme Court.
Alternative Medicine:	Alternative medicine is discouraged by medical practice laws, but largely unprosecuted in VA. Licensure is available for Certified Professional Midwives (CPMs) in VA but they are prohibited in DC. School vaccine exemptions: religious and medical (same for DC).
Home Schooling:	Moderate regulation. State requires parents to send notification, test scores, and/or professional evaluation of student progress. Same requirements in DC.

Military Targets:	**Radford Army Ammunition Plant,** SW of Blacksburg. Active explosives and propellant manufacturing plant; secondary target. **Mount Pony**, near Culpeper. Dated bunker for Federal Reserve, to be changed to archive for Library of Congress; tertiary target.
Richmond Area:	**Fort Lee**. Ordinance research and development and testing; not a target. **Fort Pickett**. Army NG training; not a target.
Norfolk/Newport News Area:	**Fort Eustis**. Army transportation facility; primary target. **Camp Peary. C**overt CIA training facility known as "The Farm"; secondary target. **Yorktown Naval Weapons Station**. Fleet ordinance supply dock; secondary target. **Langley AFB**. F-22s, presidential aircraft; primary target. **Naval Base Norfolk**. Carriers, US 2nd Fleet; primary target. **Oceana Naval Air Station**. 17 squadrons of F-18's. Navy jet base; primary target. **Craney Island Disposal Area**. Naval fuel depot and stockpile; primary target. **Naval Facility Engineering Command**. Also listed as Naval Security Group Activity. Possible intelligence gathering; primary target.
Washington DC Zone:	**Fort Belvoir**. Army office and housing; primary target. **Marine Corps Base Quantico**. Command General HQ, officer school and training base. Also major FBI training facility; secondary target. **Naval Surface Weapons Center Dahlgren Lab**, W of Fredericksburg. High tech naval research lab; secondary target. **Mount Weather Bunker**, 3 mi. SW of Bluemont; primary target.

Notes

We found it easier to include Washington DC in with Virginia because of its close ties with Arlington. Nevertheless, we limit our information about DC because it is a DO NOT INHABIT area because of the multiple primary targets it contains.

Virginia is divided into five regions from east to west: Tidewater, Piedmont, Blue Ridge Mountains, Ridge and Valley, and Cumberland Plateau. The Chesapeake Bay separates the contiguous portion of the Commonwealth from the two-county peninsula of Virginia's eastern Shore—which are separate from the rest of Virginia except by going around the bay via Maryland.

The Tidewater area is the coastal plain closest to the Atlantic coast and includes the eastern shore and the major peninsulas and estuaries that lead to Chesapeake Bay. The Piedmont area is further inland and includes the rock-based foothills east of the mountains. This region is known for its heavy clay soil and includes the Southwest Mountains.

The Blue Ridge Mountains are part of the Appalachian chain and filled with state parks and public scenic areas. The Ridge and Valley region is just west of these mountains and includes the Great Appalachian Valley. The Cumberland Plateau and the Cumberland Mountains are in the southwest corner. There are also more than 4,000 caves in the hills and mountains of Virginia with ten open for tourism. These last three regions form the best areas for retreats in Virginia, excluding the northern mountainous area west of Washington DC where the government has several bunkers which are all primary targets.

The southern suburbs of Washington DC and northern Virginia have become overcrowded due to continued expansion of the federal government. Fifteen of these northern counties received failing grades in air quality from the EPA, with Fairfax County being the worst, primarily due to automobile pollution from the Washington DC beltway system. Average surface water quality in the state is better than average. Aquifer water quality is good in rural farm areas. Mountain areas suffer from mining pollution in aquifers. There are various EPA superfund sites relative to mining and landfills that are pollution concerns.

Basically, there are two Virginias: Northern Virginia, which is now dominated by government agencies and corporate headquarters that want to be near the center of power, and southern Virginia which maintains some of its southern manners. Northern VA now hosts software, communication technology, and consulting companies, particularly in the Dulles Technology Corridor. Tyson's Corner and nearby Reston are now the hub of all the secret companies connected to the dark side of government. Northern Virginia's data centers now carry more than 50% of the nation's internet traffic. All of these make tempting targets for an enemy intent on shutting down this nation someday.

Virginia has its share of corruption but it mostly occurs in northern VA as influenced by the heady power around the capitol. Southern VA has corruption too, but it has a reputation of doing it in a genteel manner, as befitting Virginians. For example, John W. Forbes II, former State Secretary of Finance won a $5 million grant from the commission to set up the Literary Foundation of Virginia. The foundation was designed to promote adult literacy, but it was used to provide $1 million in salaries for Forbes and his spouse and help buy a million-dollar house. He's now doing time. Police in Virginia have a good reputation for fairness, except in and around Arlington where judicial corruption also takes place.

Strategies for Populated Living Areas

Washington Metro area: This includes all of the DC bedroom cities such as Alexandria, Arlington, Annandale and McLean. The traffic in the entire region is horrendous during normal times, let alone during a panic when people will all be trying to leave the area at once. We would recommend living outside the 495 Beltway and to the west; avoid the south corridor. Going south to Woodbridge and Dale City is a popular commute direction because the homes being built there were initially cheaper. Now it's a crowded corridor. It still allows you fairly clear access to the west, so it isn't out of the question—just not as good as locating yourself in the west sector. The nearest we would recommend in the west sector would be the Vienna or Fairfax area. There is a metro stop in Vienna on the Orange Line which will allow you to get into the city without driving. Eventually the Orange line will go farther west, so the towns of Lees Corner, and Centerville are even better. I-66 is the north-south divider for safety for exiting the area and it takes you out to western VA. Plan non-interstate routes west, as is standard in case the freeways are closed or jammed. Many commute from as far as Harrisonburg, Virginia along I-81 in the Shenandoah Valley (which is much further than Manassas) to avoid the high density areas.

Richmond: The James River cuts through the city from the west and then flows south, separating the city in two parts. I-95 separates it north and south, and there is a continuous beltway surrounding the city. Safest locations are outside the 288 beltway to the west. Stay north or south of the James River depending on which direction you plan on retreating to.

Retreat Areas

General advice: We don't recommend any of the rural or mountainous areas north of a line from Fredericksburg to Front Royal in the western foothills. All of these areas will quickly be flooded with refugees fleeing the Washington DC metro area someday. Even south of that line, one must stay at least 20 miles south and west of the Richmond-Norfolk corridor which are major sources of social unrest from military target destruction. The best retreat areas are west of a line from Culpeper, Charlottesville and Lynchburg heading south along the Blue Ridge Mountains. Security increases with each successive ridge you put between your position and the Virginia flatland. You can even get into the Cumberland Plateau while still in Virginia. Unfortunately, the best and safest areas of the state taper down to nothing at the western end, but it is not heavily populated, so there is safety there. Because all of Virginia is susceptible to having to cope with refugees from the major popu-

lation centers, be sure and follow the recommendations about building your retreat behind plenty of tree cover, and away from major roads.

WASHINGTON ★★★⯪☆

Summary Facts and Ratings

Climate:	West coast marine climate with mild temperatures and steady breezes west of the Cascades; semi-arid climates to the east. Few major storms, but cloudy 9 months of the year in the west, more sun in the east. Winters are moderate in the west but wet and overcast; colder and drier in the east.
Population Density:	Average. 101 ppl/sq. mile (3000 ppl/sq. mile in Seattle area) but only 35 ppl/sq. mile east of the Cascades. Hispanic 11%, Asian 7%, mixed 4.7%, Black 4%,
Cost of Living Index:	Above average. 106 (average is 100).
Private Land Availability:	Fair. 37% of land is state or federally owned, including most of the best forests.
Building Permits:	Required statewide. Stricter regulations around Seattle area. Basements can be built in most places in the state.
Land and Urban Planning:	"Smart Growth" land use planning is in vogue here, with statewide planning boards controlling local boards.
Food Production:	Very good in the west, irrigation required in the east. Growing season in west 150-210 days. Shorter in the east, but has more sun. Rainfall is about 40 in/yr west of the Cascades and 17 in/yr to the east. Fishing and hunting are excellent.
Health Environment:	Water quality is good, except in 64% of communities that have fluoridated water. Air Pollution is moderate because of constant sea breezes into the Seattle Metro area which blows it northeastward. There is nuclear pollution around the Hanford site in eastern WA (tri-cities area).
Traffic:	Terrible in Seattle-Everett (rated 2nd worst in nation behind LA). Tacoma and Spokane also have their share but it is low in rural areas. WA cities use red light and speed cameras.
Politics:	Very liberal population in Seattle overpowers conservatives in rural WA. Dem 45%, Rep 37%, Ind/3rd party 18%.
Taxes:	Average. Ranked 24th lowest with an average state tax burden of 9.4% of income. No income tax. Gross receipts tax of 2-3% for all businesses. State and local sales tax is a high 8.8%. Property taxes are high in Seattle, but statewide average ranks 25th in the nation.
Corruption:	Medium high in Seattle, low in eastern WA. Fair amount of corruption in Seattle police and judges. Overall, WA ranks below average in corruption compared to other states.
Crime:	Average. Violent crime 289/100K, property crime 3710/100K. Most crime is in the Seattle area. Crime index for Seattle is 2, Tacoma 2, Spokane 1.
Personal Liberty:	Low, rated 29th. High debt, bad asset forfeiture laws, too many residential regulation laws.
Gun Liberty:	Good. No permit to purchase firearms. "Shall issue" state for a concealed weapon permit. Open carry friendly state. We expect more gun restrictions however given the liberal legislators and prevailing anti-gun atmosphere accelerating after 2012.
Alternative Medicine:	Excellent access to natural health practitioners. Several alternative medical schools. Lay midwives are legal and have many free-standing birth centers or perform home birth. School vaccine exemptions: philosophical, religious and medical.
Home Schooling:	Moderate. State requires parents to qualify and then send notification annually with test scores, and/or professional evaluation of student progress.
Military Targets:	**Fort Lewis (Joint Base Lewis-McChord)**, Tacoma. Only Army power projection base west of Rockies for infantry, Special Forces and Stryker Brigade via C-17 airlift or ship transport; secondary target. **Bangor Submarine Base and Bremerton Naval Base**, Puget Sound. Trident missile submarines, naval ship storage; primary target. **Indian Island Naval Ammo Depot**, north of Bremerton. Air refueling; primary target. **Whidbey Island Naval Air Station**, Puget Sound. Naval aviation; primary target. **FEMA Regional Bunker** at 130 228th St. SW, Bothell. Cold war bunker; not currently a target.

Military Targets continued:	**Naval Reservation or Jim Creek Naval Station**, west of Lakewood. Very low frequency submarine communication station; primary target. **Fairchild AFB**, Spokane. Airlift and refueling; primary target. **McChord AFB**, Tacoma. Airlift Command; secondary target. **NSA Listening Post**, at Yakima Firing Center; primary target
Nuclear Power Plants:	**Columbia Station**, north of Richland on Hanford Site. 1 reactor.

Notes

Washington is a state of tremendous variety, from rain forests in the Olympic Peninsula to the deserts in the east. The geography here is very similar to Oregon, except that it is even more wet and cloudy west of the Cascades. It is gorgeous in Seattle when the sun shines, but that isn't very often. Worse than this, the traffic situation in Seattle and Everett are terrible if you have to commute in it every day. Traffic here during rush hour took 81% longer to travel freeways and major arterial roads than it would without traffic, according to a traffic study performed by Texas A&M.

The volcano danger is significant in western WA. Mt. Saint Helens is rebuilding after blowing its top and Mt. Rainier is threatening. When the latter blows and its glaciers melt, the mud flows will be devastating to most of the valleys around the mountain where there are many people. Both WA and OR have become home to dedicated environmentalists and liberals that have tied up development for years, but this mostly affects the rural areas of the east, which need more local freedom. It's way too late for the overcrowded Seattle corridor.

While we love the lush forests and waterways of the Cascade Mountains and Puget Sound, the oppressiveness of Seattle's left/liberal establishment dominates the state and its major newspapers. This influence continues to grow and has led us in 2013 to reduce WA's rating because of recent sweeping gun bills in the state legislature that were only narrowly defeated because they tried to restrict so much at once. This is likely only a temporary setback, however, and we expect state laws to become increasingly restrictive of many freedoms.

The picturesque coastal side of the state is also infamous for its rain and cloud cover making it dreary much of the year, so we prefer the drier climate east of the Cascades. We especially like the northeastern parts of the state where you can find coniferous forestation at low altitudes. It is still cloudy there most months of the year, but at least it has a longer and drier summer.

Washington has no income tax, which is a big plus, particularly if you live close to Oregon where you can shop without a sales tax. The cost of living is quite high in the Seattle area but lower in the east, particularly for housing.

Major threats to your long-term safety include multiple first-strike military targets very close to Seattle, and its three dormant volcanoes in the Cascade Mountains. Northwestern WA is also in an elevated earthquake risk zone, which creates potential tidal wave threats to the sound. The Bangor Trident Submarine base is a key nuclear target and will most certainly be hit in the next world war. There are also various auxiliary service and nuclear weapons storage facilities north and south that will be hit. All of this means you should not locate in the Seattle Metro area. Massive social unrest will be the guaranteed result of any major crisis. If traffic is heavily congested in good times, it will be impossible to travel in a severe panic. There are only three main exits out of the area: north and south on I-5 and east on I-90. That means the towns in those areas will be inundated with refugees. Avoid even the small cities of Ellensburg and Yakima to the east as they will be overwhelmed.

Strategies for Populated Living Areas

Seattle: If you must live in or near the Seattle area for work, stay far away from the main freeway corridors, north and south. These freeways cross many bridges and will trap many thousands of cars in a crisis. Pick a commute from east or west that avoids most freeways. On the west, across the sound, the valleys around Skokomish on the Olympic Peninsula are one compromise. This area is outside the range of destruction and fallout from military targets, and we believe large groups of refugees will not go in that direction during a crisis. You can always go deeper into the peninsula to a retreat for further safety. To the east, a good compromise is to locate toward the foothills of the cascades, staying at least 4-5 miles away from I-90. Fallout is easy to contend with compared to the potential social unrest fanning out from the traffic corridors. If social unrest creeps toward the hills, you must be prepared to have a retreat or exit through the Cascades, but not along I-90.

North of Seattle: You have to go as far as Mount Vernon and Bellingham to give you a sufficient buffer zone from the high density population areas of Seattle. If you choose a southern Washington location, go as far as Centralia, and then stay east or west of the freeway by 4 or 5 miles.

Vancouver: This city is across the Columbia River from Portland. Locate east of I-5 to have access to retreat areas east in the Columbia Gorge. Don't go north where Mt. St. Helens is still a threat.

Spokane: This is a delightful city with a much better climate than Seattle. Stay on the east or northeast side of the city to avoid Fairchild AFB which is a military target in the west.

Retreat Areas

Eastern Washington: The best areas in WA are east of the Cascades. We recommend the vast valleys and pine forests north of a line between Chelan in central WA and Newport on the eastern border with Idaho, excluding the large Indian reservation marked in red. These are where you also find the best long term retreat areas. Spokane is the largest city in the area where jobs are available, but it too has a nuclear target in Fairchild AFB.

Farther south is the community of **Walla Walla** which is great farm country and far away from the danger zones. The Tri-cities area (Richland, etc.) is a bigger economic center—still relatively safe, but you have to be careful of the proximity to the Hanford nuclear reservation with all its nuclear clean-up problems.

Besides the northern zone previously mentioned, another good retreat area is east of **Clarkston**, sister city of Lewiston, Idaho. Although these two cities are in the dry plains, they are the gateway to the Orofino/Kamiah area of Idaho.

In the south, there are nice areas in and around Yakima, but Yakima itself is not included, being downwind of Mt. Saint Helens, a dormant volcano. Yakima also has a NSA listening station and is in line to receive huge inflows of people fleeing Seattle someday. That doesn't mean you can't find an out-of-the-way place for safety, but you must prepare for the increased threats.

WA/OR Border—the Columbia Gorge: For people wanting to take advantage of the two-state tax preference policy, there are nice cities on the Washington side of the Columbia Gorge. You want to be about an hour's drive east of the Portland and Vancouver area to avoid refugee flows coming from that direction. Most of that will flow down the Oregon side, unless the freeway is closed, and then all the refugee flow will switch to the non-freeway Washington side. If you locate in White Salmon, WA, across from Hood River, make sure you find property outside the Colombia Gorge Scenic Area and its draconian building restrictions.

WEST VIRGINIA ★★⯪☆☆

Summary Facts and Ratings

Climate:	The mountainous terrain creates a humid continental climate, with hot humid summers and cold winters similar to northern New England. This is one of the cloudiest states in the union with fog problems in the valleys. WV has an average of 2 tornadoes per year.
Population Density:	Below average. 74 ppl/sq. mile (21st lowest in nation). Black 3.7%, Hispanic 1.2%, Asian 0.7%, mixed 1%.
Cost of Living Index:	Above average. 104 (average is 100) ranked as the 34th least expensive state.
Land Ownership:	Good. 10% of the land is state or federally owned.
Building Permits:	Required for new buildings and most renovations involving the structure. Requirements are set on the local level and can vary throughout the state. Basements are difficult to build in WV due to the underlying rock strata of sandstone, shale, bituminous coal, and limestone.
Land and Urban Planning:	Regional level planning state. The governor creates Regional Planning Councils and these bodies have most of the planning and zoning power.
Food Production:	Adequate in the valleys and sloping hills. Growing season of 120 to 180 days. Rainfall averages about 45 inches per year. Soil is shallow and acidic with a lot of clay (or rocky in the mountains). River flood plains have more fertile black soil. Limestone areas neutralize the acidity.
Health Environment:	Surface water quality and air pollution are better than most states. Aquifer water quality is good in rural farm areas. Mountain areas suffer from mining pollution in aquifers. There are various EPA superfund sites related to mining and landfills that are pollution concerns. 91% of the population's drinking water is fluoridated.
Traffic:	No major traffic snarls. No red light or speed cameras.
Politics:	WV has been solidly Democratic for half a century, but the lure of Democratic promises is wearing down. Dem 49%, Rep 29%, Ind/3rd party 22%.
Taxes:	Average. Ranks 19th highest with an average state tax burden of 9.7% of income. Income tax tops out at 6.5% after $60K, property taxes are below average and sales tax is a flat 6.0%.
Corruption:	Very high.
Crime:	Below average. Violent crime 300/100K, property crime 2103/100K. Most of the crime is in and around Charleston, the industrial center. Crime index for Charleston is 1 (100 is safest).
Personal Liberty:	Low. 8th lowest in the nation.
Gun Liberty:	Fair. No permit to purchase firearms. "Shall issue" state for concealed weapon permits. Open carry friendly state.
Alternative Medicine:	Very restricted. Alternative medicine is discouraged by medical practice laws, but largely unprosecuted. Direct entry midwives are effectively prohibited. Practicing midwifery without a medical license (which doesn't even exist for midwives) is a misdemeanor. Vaccines are required to enroll in elementary, middle and high schools unless a waiver is signed by a doctor (only for contraindications) and approved by State Health Officer.
Home Schooling:	Moderate. State requires parents to be "qualified" and send notification, test scores, and/or professional evaluation of student progress annually.
Military Targets:	**Sugar Grove Radio Station**. NSA ECHELON listening post for all communications; primary target. **Shepperd Field**, S of Martinsburg. C-5 airlift for ANG; secondary target. **Yeager Airport**, Charleston. C-130 airlift ANG; not a significant target. **Greenbrier Resort**. Decommissioned bunker; might still be a tertiary target if enemy suspects it will be reactivated.

Notes

West Virginia is a mountin state completely within the Appalachian Mountain range. Valleys alternate with prominent ridges in an oblique NE-SW angle that is typical from PA down through Tennessee. West Virginia is laced with coal both in deep seams and near the surface. There is minable coal in 53 of its 55 counties, and mines are still in production in 26 counties. The abundance of coal and rock salt mines made this a favorable area for heavy industry and chemical companies which settled in the Kanawha Valley around Charleston. There were steel mills and glass factories as well near the Monongahela River Valley.

The United Mine Workers organized most of the West Virginia mines, and the state went union in a big way, which meant shifting political allegiance to Democrats. There were 17 public corruption convictions in 2010. In the past decade, 2 governors, 2 senate presidents, a high-ranking delegate, a state school superintendent and several county officials resigned or went to prison for corruption. The Charleston Gazette told of payoffs involving paper bags filled with cash transferred in parking lots. According to the trial transcript from his first bribery trial, Gov. Arch Moore was found with $200,000 in cash in his desk.

This is one of the densest Karst regions in the world, which allows the formation of many natural limestone caves. The forestation of the state is mixed hardwood and softwood trees like Chestnut, Maple, Oak and Beech. There are also some White Pine and Spruce.

Overall, West Virginia is rated better than other states in the East because of the extensive mountainous terrain available for retreats. WV loses points because the state is poverty stricken, full of welfare recipients and has a majority of liberal Democrats.

Strategies for Populated Living Areas

Charleston: This metro area houses about 300,000 people, although the city proper only has 50,000. Interstates 79, 77 and 64 intersect in Charleston. Combined with the intersection of the Kanawha and Elk Rivers, you have some significant barriers to travel in a retreat situation. However, since the city is not large and there is little threat outside the populated area, simply pick a rural country retreat and commute or locate on the outskirts of the city nearest your retreat.

Retreat Areas

The state abounds in forested retreat areas with access to well water, streams and sloping land that can support a garden. However, these are not all equally safe. We would recommend staying clear of the old mining towns where many people are still on the federal Appalachian welfare dole. This rules out most of the old towns that are losing people every year. There are several new mountain subdivisions not associated with any town that are your best bet, buy a lot (or two for privacy) and build a nice retreat. You'll get new land and new territory without the bias of old timers who may not look kindly on newcomers. You will have to build your retreat with substantial secure construction to avoid vandalism when you are not present.

WISCONSIN ★★★☆☆

Summary Facts and Estimates

Climate:	Humid continental climate with hot, humid summers and cold winters. WI averages 21 tornados per year.
Population Density:	Moderately high. 104 ppl/sq. mile (ranked 23rd highest in the nation). Black 6.2%, Hispanic 5.3%, Asian 2.2%, mixed 1.2%, American Indian 1%.
Cost of Living Index:	Below average. 98.1 (average is 100) ranks this as the 24th least expensive state.
Private Land Availability:	Good. 16% of the land is state or federally owned.
Building Permits:	Required everywhere for new construction and renovations. Basements are easy to install in the deep soil here except in a few areas in the north where the water table is high.
Land and Urban Planning:	The state does not mandate comprehensive plans for local governments.
Food Production:	Good with a growing season of 90-120 days in the north to 150-180 in the south. It is warmer near Milwaukee. Rainfall averages about 32 inches per year in the north. Rich soil in most places.
Health Environment:	Surface water pollution is good, except for Lake Michigan which is bad. Ground water around commercial farms has traces of farm chemicals, but it is much cleaner up north. 89% of the state's drinking water is fluoridated.
Traffic:	Heavy traffic problems in Milwaukee which is rated as #34 of the 75 worst traffic cities. WI does not use red light and speed cameras.
Politics:	Milwaukee and Madison are the most liberal cities in the state and tend to vote strongly Democratic, but elections have swung to the Republicans since 2010 due to conservative suburbs. Dem 43%, Rep 41%, Ind/3rd party 16%.
Taxes:	High. Ranked 5th highest with an average state tax burden of 11% of income. Income tax ranges from 4.6% to 7.65%. The state and local sales tax averages 5.4%. Property taxes are high.
Corruption:	Average. Wisconsin politics remained mostly corrupt until the turn of the century.
Crime:	Moderate. Violent crime 278/100K, property crime 2189/100K. Crime index for Milwaukee is 3, Madison 17 (100 is safest). Madison violent crime is lower than the US average.
Personal Liberty:	Low, 38th in the nation but rising in part due to Gov. Walker's Act 10 that restricted union bargaining rights.
Gun Liberty:	Not good. State law does not yet provide for concealed firearm permits, but is considered an open carry friendly state.
Alternative Medicine:	Natural health practitioners free to practice. Certified Professional Midwives are legal and licensed to practice in Wisconsin. School vaccine exemptions: philosophical, religious and medical.
Home Schooling:	Low regulation. State requires parental notification only.
Military Targets:	**Fort McCoy**, Monroe County, near Sparta. Military training center; not a target. **Camp Williams**, East of Tomah on I-90, part of Volk Field. National Guard training; also not considered a target. **General Mitchell Field**, Milwaukee. ANG refueling aircraft; tertiary target at best.
Nuclear Power Plants:	**Kewaunee Plant**, east of Green Bay. 1 reactor. **Point Beach Plant**, north of Manitowoc. 2 reactors.

Notes

Wisconsin used to pride itself on being a left-progressive state, but after many years of liberal spending and overspent budgets, there was a strong backlash that gave Republicans a big majority in the state legislature and the governor's seat in 2010, although Wisconsin remains a strong state for the Democrats in the past six presidential elections. Counties in western WI are more liberal—a holdover from their Scandinavian background; The other rural farm areas are solidly republican or independent. That said, the people of WI in general are good, friendly, and helpful in a crisis and it is this character of the people that counts.

In 2011 Gov. Scott Walker proposed the Wisconsin Budget Repair Bill (or "Act 10") to ease the union grip on bargaining power and the fiscal burden from years of insurance benefits, high wages and generous pensions for state employees. Once people get hooked on benefits they have a hard time giving them up. The entrenched liberals in WI were up in arms and fought the Act tooth and nail. When union-driven teacher strikes and protests all over the state failed to slow down the bill, all 14 Democratic state senators fled to Illinois so the 19 Republicans could not form a quorum (required for any fiscal bill). Republicans finally amended the fiscal provisions out of the bill to pass it without a quorum. After many more debates and compromises by Walker (including allowing collective bargaining on big items like salaries, and overtime pay), it passed. Lawsuits set the bill back several times by state and federal judges but so far these have been overturned.

Despite the dire predictions from Democrats, five years later teachers are not much worse off. Teacher's unions memberships are down by half after teachers were freed from the mandatory union dues collection (a real evil). Union employees were used to fat salaries of over $95K/year thanks to enforced dues. The City of Milwaukee expects to save $25 million per year just from not having to negotiate with the unions for healthcare benefits. Although this was a big win for conservatives, the fiscal benefits are limited by the big compromises in the bill.

Corruption in WI is moderate because the people here pride themselves on clean, progressive state government, but it is mostly an illusion. In 2002, State Senate Majority Leader, Chuck Chvala (D-Madison), and Assembly Speaker, Scott Jensen (R-Waukesha), were both charged with felony misconduct in office, including allegations of extortion. There were 35 public corruption convictions last year, which reflects the fact that Wisconsin citizens don't like political corruption. It still happens, however. Former DA, Joe Paulus, is now doing federal time for bribery.

Wisconsin has a lot of rural farm land and forested areas that are suitable for retreats for those coming from the East. Retreat areas are best in the north; prospects are marginal south of Madison. Southern Wisconsin will suffer a significant inrush of refugees from Chicago someday, but it takes hardy people to live in the far north.

Strategies for Populated Living Areas

Milwaukee: The only proper exit strategy for those living in the Milwaukee area is to head north and then west. Locate outside the 894/I-43 beltway. Unfortunately, Waukesha creates a possible obstacle of urban density to the west, so if you locate in New Berlin, for example, you need to travel parallel to I-43 going west staying on rural roads. Franklin, to the south of I-43 is also a good location, but to travel west one must cross over to the north of I-43 once past Waukesha. Those in the northern wedge of the suburbs between I-94 and Hwy 41 have clear exit paths to the NW. If you choose retreats in central or northern WI, you should pick routes to the NW, bypassing Madison. The rural farm country at least 25 miles north of Madison will give some safety.

Madison: While Madison is large enough to experience some social unrest from within if public services and food supplies are lost, it is mostly a problem because it will attract refugees fleeing from the turmoil of Milwaukee. Thus, locals should definitely plan for retreats further north or west. Two lakes sit astride Madison, Lake Mendota and Lake Monona. In combination with I-90 to the east and the Hwy 12 beltway, there are some tight trap zones to avoid. We would suggest that the only way to avoid this squeeze play of exit traffic is to be in Middleton. Don't pick communities along Hwy 113 on the east side of the lake because only Hwy 113 crosses the marshes to the north—too risky.

Retreat Areas

Rural farmland: Wisconsin has plenty of rural farm areas north or west of Madison. That's where the semi-safe areas begin. There will be eventual point threats of small groups of refugees that come to farms, but you probably won't see overwhelming numbers 50 miles away from Madison. Rural farm retreats are not as safe as being in the hill country, but if you follow our guidelines about locating for privacy, they can be fairly safe. Implement extra safety by putting in underground concealed rooms where you can't be found and so you don't have to confront starving, desperate people.

Northern lake and forest country: The best retreat sites are north of a line along Eau Claire, Wausau and Green Bay, but stay at least 25 miles from these cities. There are numerous small towns spread out in this area which can provide a semblance of commerce. They represent most of the private land relative to the state-owned forests. Get land backing up to these state forests. Well water is easy to get. Pick the highest ground for better basement potential.

WYOMING ★★★★☆

Summary Facts and Ratings

Climate:	High desert, continental climate with low humidity but windy through the I-80 corridor on the continental divide. Moderate summers but cold winters.
Population Density:	Very low. 5.6 ppl/sq. mile (ranked 49th in the nation). Hispanic 8%, American Indian 2.6%, mixed 1.5%, Black 1.4%.
Cost of Living Index:	Below average. 92.8 (average is 100).
Private Land Availability:	Poor. 55% of land is state or federally owned, including a good portion of the best forests and mountain land.
Building Permits:	Reasonable permits and regulations in most areas. Basements are possible in most parts of the state.
Land and Urban Planning:	No statewide planning mandate, other than to have a general plan, but no oversight for enforcement.
Food Production:	Moderate. Mostly ranching and dry land farms. Some irrigated farmland along rivers. Reduced growing season 90-180 days depending on altitude. Average annual rainfall is 13 inches.
Health Environment:	Water quality is excellent where fed by mountain springs and fair from wells in the valleys. 43.6% of people's water supplies are fluoridated. Air pollution is not a problem due to steady westerly winds. There is good solar potential everywhere.
Traffic:	No major traffic problems except during rush hour in Cheyenne. No Red light or speed cameras.
Politics:	Wyoming is a conservative state with libertarian tendencies. Conservatives dominate the agricultural areas and Democrats the larger cities like Cheyenne. Dem 20%, Rep 67%, Ind/3rd party 13%.
Taxes:	Ranked lowest state in the nation with an average state tax burden of 6.9% of income. No income tax, state and local sales tax averages 5.4% and low property taxes are ranked 41st in the nation.
Corruption:	Generally below average. Some in state government and judicial system. There is also some evidence of police brutality.
Crime:	Low. Violent crime 205/100K, property crime 2198/100K. Crime Index for Cheyenne is 21, Evanston 21 (100 is safest).
Personal Liberty:	Above average. 36th in the nation down from 31st in 2011. State spends too much being used to income from oil and gas industry.
Gun Liberty:	Good. No permit to purchase firearms. "Shall issue" state for concealed firearms. Open carry permitted everywhere (even a car) except schools, courts and federal buildings.
Alternative Medicine:	Very good availability for the full range of natural health practitioners. Lay midwives are technically not regulated, but since 2007 they have been prosecuted for practicing medicine without a license, which is a bad precedent. School vaccine exemptions: religious and medical.
Home Schooling:	Low regulation. State requires parental notification only.
Military Targets:	**Francis E. Warren AFB**, east of Cheyenne. 150 nuclear Minuteman III missiles in the SE corner of state and extending into SD and Nebraska; primary target (direct hit expected at each silo). **Naval Strategic Oil Reserves** No. 3, NW of Casper near Natrona. "Teapot Dome" oil reserve; tertiary target.

Notes

Wyoming came in second for the Free State Movement—an effort by libertarians to build up enough like-minded people in a state to gain a majority and turn it into a haven of liberty. New Hampshire won out but the movement failed there because it caused too much resentment among existing residents. We would have picked Wyoming.

This state has some of the finest mountains and forests in the nation, including the Grand Tetons and Yellowstone areas. Also of note are the Big Horn Mountains. Much of the rest of the state is a flat, nearly barren desert with some windblown prairies which are not particularly hospitable. Wyoming is lightly populated for good reasons—but that is a big part of its attraction to us as a great survival state. It has lots of wide open spaces and is rich in gas and oil deposits to pay the bills, allowing this sparsely populated state to have no income tax and low taxes in other areas.

Most of the property around the Tetons and Yellowstone is expensive cabin country bought up long ago by the rich and elite. But you can still find beautiful mountain meadow ranch country in places like Star Valley, south of Jackson Hole.

There are two major threats to one's physical wellbeing at opposite ends of the state: the volcanic danger of the huge Yellowstone caldera—a seething, boiling pot of unstable geothermic action, and the nuclear targets of Warren AFB around and southeast of Cheyenne.

Strategies for Populated Living Areas

Cheyenne: The largest city in Wyoming sits astride I-80 and hosts Warren AFB on its western border. The actual missile fields are farther away to the north, east and southeast, but the base is still a target since it houses the headquarters of the missile wing. The base is too close to Cheyenne for the city to avoid destruction if the base is hit. The only housing development outside the 5 mile circle of damage from the base is in South Greeley, south of I-80. The missile fields themselves are fairly close if you locate to the north or to the east of the city.

Casper: This is the preferred city of the two largest in the state. It has no major threats in the area, other than its own population if social unrest develops.

Retreat Areas

Star Valley: This is one of the premiere retreat valleys in the nation for beauty and safety from threats. The closest fair-sized town is Jackson to the north but Star Valley doesn't have the high prices of Jackson Hole where the global elite have chosen to vacation and build second homes. This is a high mountain valley inhabited mostly by farm and ranch families, and a growing group of retirees. It was originally a Mormon colony, established by pioneers who knew how to find good ranch land with mountain-fed irrigation water. The valley is actually composed of two valleys separated by a small rise where Hwy 89 and 238 meet. The southern valley centers around the town of Afton which has a nice airport, and the northern valley centers around the towns of Thayne, Freedom, and Etna. Freedom sits astride the Wyoming-Idaho border. In this valley you choose which state you live in by picking the east or west side. Most pick east to be in Wyoming's no income tax jurisdiction. This is a high altitude valley that gets about 3 feet of snow in the winter. It is surrounded by rugged mountains with abundant game and fish. There isn't much private land in the mountains, but you can find forested retreat sites along the foothills of the valley. Star Valley Ranch is a nice mountain cabin subdivision built around a golf course with views of the valley. The entire valley is sufficiently distant from any threats to provide a safe haven without separate mountain retreats.

Evanston Area: Evanston itself is out in the windy plain, but there are numerous forested hills with private land and cabins to the south along the border with Utah. It backs up to the rugged Uintah Mountains of Utah.

Casper Area: Look for forested cabin sites south of the city up on Casper Mountain, a lovely pine country with rustic cabins.

Sheridan: The towns of Buffalo and Sheridan are the gateways to the Big Horn National Forest. This is the traditional land of the Sioux Indian with plenty of grass for Buffalo and timber in the forests for cabins and retreats. You can find similar farmland and retreat sites on the other side of the forest near Lovell.

Black Hills: Wyoming runs up against the fabled Black Hills on the east border near the towns of Sundance, Four Corners, and Newcastle. Water is not plentiful, but improves closer to the hill country where excellent retreat sites can be found. The area will never be heavily populated.

South and east of Yellowstone: There are a couple of fingers of valley land that approach the park in these directions. We do not, however recommend anything East of the Yellowstone caldera---a potential super volcano eruption. While there is a lot of hype about a future eruption destroying the entire West, this is not true. It will only affect areas downwind in an arc from the northeast to the southwest and going out about 100 miles for significant ash fall. However, as in Mt. St. Helens, the ashfall is benificial in the long-term to soil, and the earth will recover.

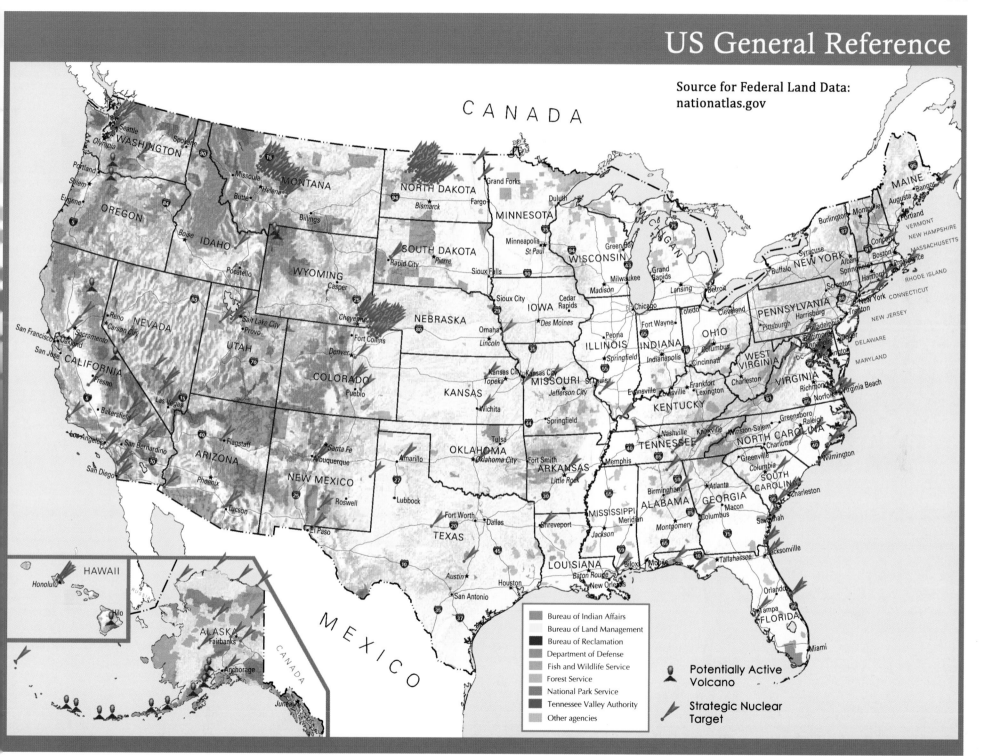

US General Reference

Source for Federal Land Data:
nationalatlas.gov

CANADA

MEXICO

WASHINGTON
Seattle • Spokane
Olympia •
Portland
Salem •
Eugene •
OREGON
MONTANA
Missoula • • Helena
Butte •
Billings •
Bismarck ★
Helena ★
NORTH DAKOTA
Grand Forks
Fargo •
Duluth •
MINNESOTA
Minneapolis •
St Paul
WISCONSIN
Green Bay •
Milwaukee •
Madison •

IDAHO
Boise ★
Pocatello •
WYOMING
Casper •
Cheyenne ★
SOUTH DAKOTA
Rapid City • Pierre ★
Sioux Falls •
IOWA
Sioux City •
Cedar Rapids •
Des Moines •

NEVADA
Reno • • Carson City
UTAH
Salt Lake City ★
Provo •
COLORADO
Denver ★
Pueblo •
NEBRASKA
Fort Collins •
Lincoln •
Omaha •

San Francisco • Oakland
San Jose •
Sacramento •
CALIFORNIA
Fresno •
Los Angeles •
San Bernardino •
San Diego •
Bakersfield •
Las Vegas •

ARIZONA
Flagstaff •
Phoenix ★
Tucson •

NEW MEXICO
Santa Fe ★
Albuquerque •
Roswell •
El Paso •

KANSAS
Wichita •
MISSOURI
Kansas City Kansas City
Topeka ★
Jefferson City ★ St Louis •
Springfield •

OKLAHOMA
Amarillo •
Lubbock •
Oklahoma City ★
Tulsa •
Fort Smith •
ARKANSAS
Little Rock ★

TEXAS
Fort Worth • • Dallas
Austin ★
San Antonio •
Houston •

MINNESOTA / WISCONSIN / MICHIGAN
Grand Rapids •
Lansing •
Detroit •
Chicago •
Fort Wayne •
Peoria •
ILLINOIS
Springfield ★
INDIANA
Indianapolis ★
OHIO
Toledo •
Cleveland •
Columbus ★
Cincinnati •

KENTUCKY
Evansville • Louisville •
Lexington •
Frankfort ★
TENNESSEE
Nashville ★ Knoxville •
Memphis •

MISSISSIPPI
Jackson ★
Meridian •
ALABAMA
Birmingham •
Montgomery ★
LOUISIANA
Shreveport •
Baton Rouge ★
New Orleans •
Biloxi • Mobile •

GEORGIA
Atlanta ★
Columbus •
Macon •
Savannah •

FLORIDA
Tallahassee ★
Jacksonville •
Orlando •
Tampa •
Miami •

WEST VIRGINIA
Charleston ★
VIRGINIA
Richmond ★
Norfolk • Virginia Beach

NORTH CAROLINA
Winston-Salem • Greensboro • Raleigh ★
Charlotte •
Greenville •
Columbia ★
SOUTH CAROLINA
Charleston •
Wilmington •

PENNSYLVANIA
Pittsburgh •
Harrisburg ★
Philadelphia •
NEW YORK
Buffalo •
Syracuse •
Albany ★
MAINE
Augusta ★ Bangor •
Portland •
Burlington • Montpelier ★
VERMONT
NEW HAMPSHIRE
Concord ★
Boston ★
MASSACHUSETTS
Springfield •
Hartford ★ Providence ★
RHODE ISLAND
CONNECTICUT
New York •
Trenton ★
NEW JERSEY
Dover ★
DELAWARE
MARYLAND
Baltimore •
Annapolis ★
DC ★
Scranton •

HAWAII
Honolulu •
Hilo •

ALASKA
Fairbanks •
Anchorage •
Juneau ★

RUSSIA
CANADA

Legend

- Bureau of Indian Affairs
- Bureau of Land Management
- Bureau of Reclamation
- Department of Defense
- Fish and Wildlife Service
- Forest Service
- National Park Service
- Tennessee Valley Authority
- Other agencies

Potentially Active Volcano

Strategic Nuclear Target

Earthquake Hazard

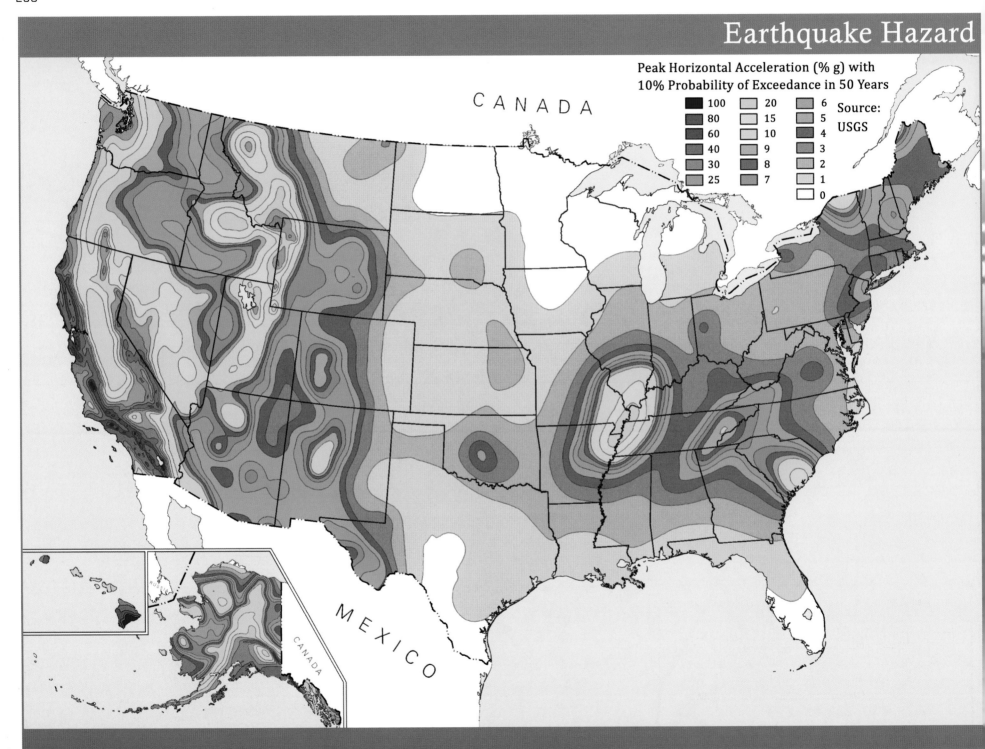

Peak Horizontal Acceleration (% g) with
10% Probability of Exceedance in 50 Years

100	20	6
80	15	5
60	10	4
40	9	3
30	8	2
25	7	1
		0

Source: USGS

US Nitrate in Groundwater

Source: USGS

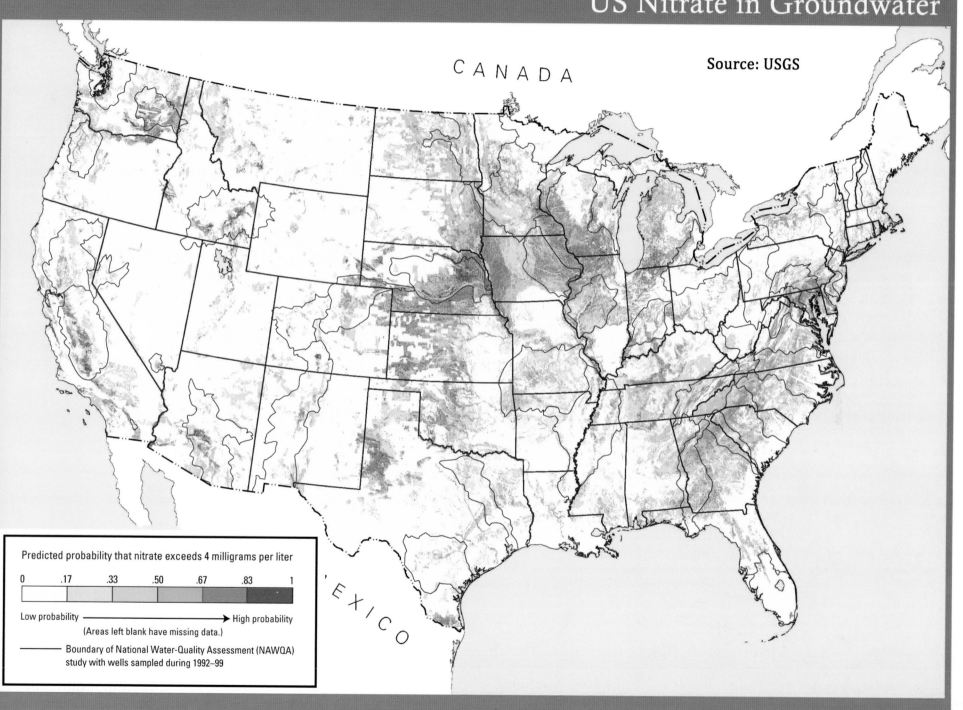

CANADA

MEXICO

Predicted probability that nitrate exceeds 4 milligrams per liter

| 0 | .17 | .33 | .50 | .67 | .83 | 1 |

Low probability ——————————→ High probability

(Areas left blank have missing data.)

—— Boundary of National Water-Quality Assessment (NAWQA)
study with wells sampled during 1992–99

Retreat Route Example: Livingston, NJ to Newton, NJ

Note: This is just an example. Newton, NJ is too close to NYC to be a good ultimate retreat location. We would recommend rural PA instead.

Don't plan on using freeways or principle thoroughfares

Rivers are important obstacles to plan around

Livingston

Plan "B" route over Columbia Bridge (more traveled)

Home
45 min. from Manhattan (2hrs w/traffic)

Pass under/over freeways where there are no on or off-ramps

Plan "A" route: over Lower Chatham Bridge (looks less traveled)

Newton

Stay away from target areas

Consider alternate routes and mark in lighter color on your map

Picatinny Arsenal

Find a balance between options. In this case: crossing many rivers/streams or risking congestion on residential roads through town.

Succasunna

Randolph

Livingston

Once on rural roads, avoid going through moderate or dense populations.

Manhattan

Newark

New York City

Elizabeth

ALABAMA

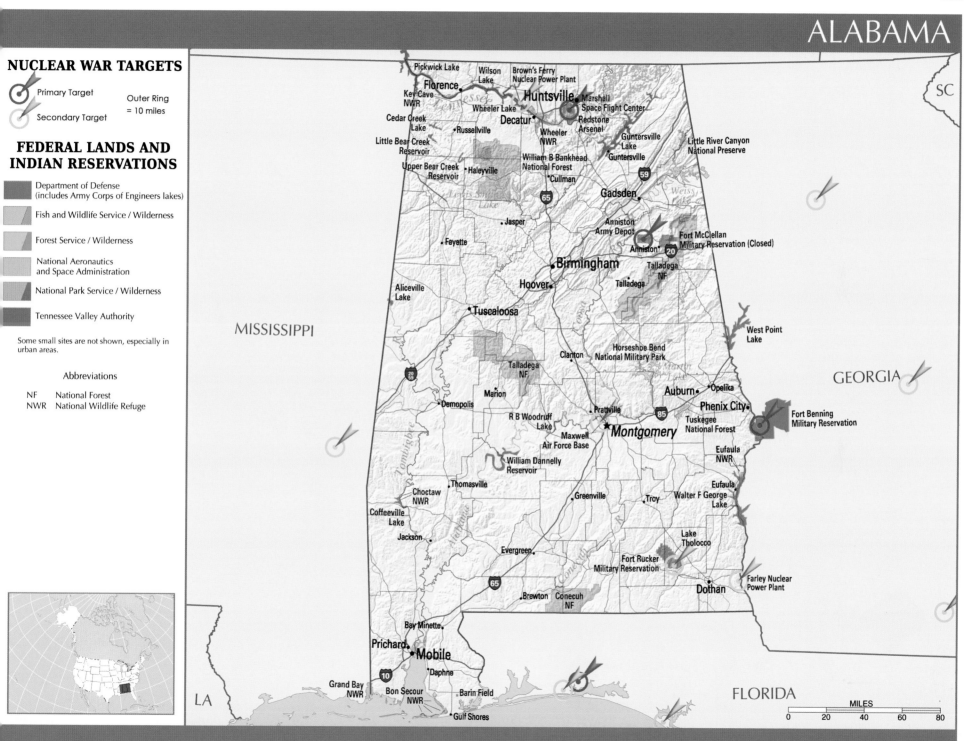

NUCLEAR WAR TARGETS

⊚ Primary Target

⊘ Secondary Target

Outer Ring = 10 miles

FEDERAL LANDS AND INDIAN RESERVATIONS

▰ Department of Defense (includes Army Corps of Engineers lakes)

▱ Fish and Wildlife Service / Wilderness

▱ Forest Service / Wilderness

▱ National Aeronautics and Space Administration

▱ National Park Service / Wilderness

▰ Tennessee Valley Authority

Some small sites are not shown, especially in urban areas.

Abbreviations

NF   National Forest
NWR   National Wildlife Refuge

MISSISSIPPI

GEORGIA

FLORIDA

LA

SC

Pickwick Lake
Wilson Lake
Brown's Ferry Nuclear Power Plant
Florence
Key Cave NWR
Huntsville
Marshall Space Flight Center
Wheeler Lake
Decatur
Redstone Arsenal
Cedar Creek Lake
Russellville
Wheeler NWR
Guntersville Lake
Little Bear Creek Reservoir
Little River Canyon National Preserve
Upper Bear Creek Reservoir
Haleyville
William B Bankhead National Forest
Guntersville
Cullman
Gadsden
Jasper
Anniston Army Depot
Fort McClellan Military Reservation (Closed)
Fayette
Anniston
Birmingham
Talladega NF
Hoover
Talladega
Aliceville Lake
Tuscaloosa
West Point Lake
Horseshoe Bend National Military Park
Talladega NF
Clanton
Marion
Auburn
Opelika
Demopolis
Prattville
Phenix City
Fort Benning Military Reservation
R B Woodruff Lake
Montgomery
Tuskegee National Forest
Maxwell Air Force Base
Eufaula NWR
William Dannelly Reservoir
Eufaula
Choctaw NWR
Thomasville
Greenville
Troy
Walter F George Lake
Coffeeville Lake
Jackson
Lake Tholocco
Evergreen
Fort Rucker Military Reservation
Brewton
Conecuh NF
Dothan
Farley Nuclear Power Plant
Bay Minette
Prichard
Mobile
Grand Bay NWR
Daphne
Barin Field
Bon Secour NWR
Gulf Shores

MILES
0   20   40   60   80

ALASKA

VOLCANO

 1 Eruption in last 100 years

1 Eruption in last 1000 years

NUCLEAR WAR TARGETS

Primary Target

Secondary Target

Outer Ring = 10 miles

FEDERAL LANDS AND INDIAN RESERVATIONS

Bureau of Indian Affairs

Bureau of Land Management / Wilderness

Department of Defense (includes Army Corps of Engineers lakes)

Fish and Wildlife Service / Wilderness

Forest Service / Wilderness

National Park Service / Wilderness

Some small sites are not shown, especially in urban areas.

Abbreviations

NCA   National Conservation Area
NF   National Forest
NHP   National Historic Park
NM   National Monument
NP   National Park
NPres National Preserve
NRA   National Recreation Area
NWR   National Wildlife Refuge

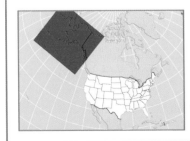

MILES
0   100   200   300   400   500

ARCTIC OCEAN

RUSSIA

BEAUFORT SEA

NORTHWEST TERRITORIES

NUNAVUT

Pt Barrow

Alaska Maritime NWR

National Petroleum Reserve In Alaska

Noatak NPres

Gates of the Arctic National Park

Arctic NWR

Cape Krusenstern NM

Gates of the Arctic NPres

Kobuk Valley NP

Bering Land Bridge National Preserve

Selawik NWR

Kanuti NWR

Yukon Flats NWR

Yukon-Charley Rivers National Preserve

Koyukuk NWR

White Mountains NRA

Steese NCA

Nowitna NWR

Fairbanks

St Lawrence Island

Innoko NWR

Tatalina Long Range Radar Site

Fort Wainwright

Clear Air Force Station

Fort Greely

CANADA

Denali NP and NPres

Wrangell-Saint Elias National Park and Preserve

YUKON TERRITORY

St Matthew I

Yukon Delta NWR

Yukon Delta NWR

Spurr

Redoubt

Fort Richardson

Wrangell

Tetlin NWR

Klondike Gold Rush NHP

BRITISH COLUMBIA

Nunivak I

Lake Clark NP and NPres

Anchorage

Chugach NF

Kenai NWR

Cape St Elias

Tongass NF

Juneau

Togiak NWR

Katmai NPres

Kenai Fjords NP

Glacier Bay NPres

Glacier Bay NP

BERING SEA

Becharof NWR

Katmai NP

Augustine

Tongass NF

Misty Fiord NM

Attu I

Alaska Maritime NWR

Alaska Peninsula NWR

Kodiak NWR

KODIAK I

GULF OF ALASKA

Aniakchak NM

Pavlov

Aniakchak NPres

Alaska Maritime NWR

Annette Islands Indian Reservation

Alaska Maritime National Wildlife Refuge

Kasatochi

Cleveland

Okmok

Izembek NWR

Unimak I

Alaska Peninsula NWR

Veniaminof

Korovin

Alaska Maritime National Wildlife Refuge

PACIFIC OCEAN

ARIZONA

VOLCANO

- 1 Eruption in last 100 years
- 1 Eruption in last 1000 years

NUCLEAR WAR TARGETS

- Primary Target
- Secondary Target

Outer Ring = 10 miles

FEDERAL LANDS AND INDIAN RESERVATIONS

- Bureau of Indian Affairs
- Bureau of Land Management / Wilderness
- Bureau of Reclamation
- Department of Defense (includes Army Corps of Engineers lakes)
- Fish and Wildlife Service / Wilderness
- Forest Service / Wilderness
- National Park Service / Wilderness

Abbreviations

AFB	Air Force Base
IR	Indian Reservation
NCA	National Conservation Area
NF	National Forest
NHP	National Historic Park
NHS	National Historical Site
NM	National Monument
NP	National Park
NRA	National Recreation Area
NWR	National Wildlife Refuge
Res	Reservoir

MILES
0 25 50 75 100

NEVADA

CALIFORNIA

NEW MEXICO

MEXICO

BAJA CALIFORNIA

SONORA

Gulf of California

Glen Canyon NRA
Lake Powell
Pipe Spring NM
Kaibab IR
Vermilion Cliffs NM
Page
Navajo NM
Kayenta
Grand Canyon National Game Preserve
Kaibab NF
Navajo Indian Reservation
Kaibab NF
Grand Canyon-Parashant NM
Grand Canyon NP
Havasupai IR
Grand Canyon National Park
Grand Canyon
Chinle
Canyon de Chelly NM
Lake Mead NRA
Lake Mead
Lake Mead NRA
Kaibab NF
Hopi Indian Reservation
Polacca
Hualapai Indian Reservation
Lake Mohave
Lake Mead NRA
Window Rock
Navajo Indian Reservation
Wupatki NM
Coconino NF
Navajo Army Depot
Kaibab NF
Sunset Crater Volcano NM
Flagstaff
Lake Mead NRA
Kingman
Bullhead City
Fort Mojave IR
Naval Obervation Station
Walnut Canyon NM
Winslow
Holbrook
Petrified Forest National Park
Havasu NWR
Prescott NF
Tuzigoot NM
Coconino NF
Lake Havasu City
Bill Williams River NWR
Camp Verde IR
Prescott NF
St Johns
Yavapai IR
Prescott
Montezuma Castle NM
Sitgreaves NF
Alamo Lake
Agua Fria NM
Payson
Show Low
Parker
Horseshoe Res
Tonto National Forest
Colorado River Indian Reservation
Wickenburg
Bartlett Res
Fort Apache Indian Reservation
Apache National Forest
Saguaro Lake
Theodore Roosevelt Lake
Fort McDowell IR
Canyon Lake
Luke AFB
Salt River IR
Tonto NM
San Carlos Indian Reservation
Phoenix
Scottsdale
Apache Lake
Cibola NWR
Kofa NWR
Palo Verde Nuclear Power
Tempe
Mesa
Chandler
Globe
Superior
Clifton
Hohokam Pima NM
Gila River IR
Imperial Reservoir
Gila Bend IR
Sonoran Desert National Monument
Florence Military Reservation
Imperial NWR
Gila Bend
Maricopa IR
Casa Grande Ruins National Monument
Safford
Gila Box Riparian National Conservation Area
Yuma
Yuma Proving Ground
Eloy
Cocopah IR
Yuma Marine Corps Air Station
Barry M. Goldwater Air Force Range
Ironwood Forest NM
Oro Valley
Coronado National Forest
Willcox Dry Lake Bombing Range
Willcox
Fort Bowie NHS
Cabeza Prieta National Wildlife Refuge
Ajo
Saguaro NP
Tucson
Chiricahua NM
Air Force Plant No. 44
Davis-Monthan AFB
Benson
Tohono O'odham Indian Reservation
San Xavier IR
Coronado National Forest
Tumacacori NHP
Buenos Aires NWR
San Pedro Riparian NCA
Coronado National Forest
Organ Pipe Cactus NM
Lukeville
Sierra Vista
Fort Huachuca
Leslie Canyon NWR
Coronado National Forest
Nogales
Coronado NF
Coronado NF
Douglas
Coronado National Memorial
San Bernardino NWR

Colorado
Lake Havasu

ARKANSAS

NUCLEAR WAR TARGETS

⊕ Primary Target

⟋ Secondary Target

Outer Ring = 10 miles

FEDERAL LANDS AND INDIAN RESERVATIONS

Department of Defense (includes Army Corps of Engineers lakes)

Fish and Wildlife Service / Wilderness

Forest Service / Wilderness

National Park Service / Wilderness

State Park

Some small sites are not shown, especially in urban areas.

Abbreviations

NF   National Forest
NWR   National Wildlife Refuge

OK

TEXAS

Table Rock Lake

Pea Ridge National Military Park

Rogers•

Springdale•

Beaver Lake

Ozark NF

•Fayetteville

540

Buffalo National River

Bull Shoals Lake

Harrison•

Ozark NF

Norfork Lake

Mountain Home•

Buffalo National River

Ozark NF

Walnut Ridge•

Paragould•

Big Lake NWR

Eaker Air Force Base (Closed)

MO

Ozark NF

Batesville•

•Jonesboro

55

Ozark National Forest

Newport•

Cache River NWR

TN

Ozark Lake

40 •Clarksville

Dardanelle Lake

Arkansas Nuclear Power Plant

•Fort Smith

•Russellville

Greers Ferry Lake

Cache River NWR

Bald Knob•

Bald Knob NWR

Cache River NWR

West Memphis•

Fort Chaffee (Closed)

Blue Mountain Lake

Ozark NF

Arkansas

Holla Bend NWR

•Conway

Cache River NWR

Forrest City•

Cache River Mitigation Project

St Francis River

OK

Nimrod Lake

Little Rock Air Force Base

Ouachita National Forest

Lake Ouachita

Camp Joseph T Robinson

40 Cache River NWR

Cache River Mitigation Project

Saint Francis National Forest

•Mena

Little Rock ★

Hot Springs National Park

Benton•

Stuttgart•

Helena•

•Hot Springs

530

Pine Bluff Arsenal

DeGray Lake

Malvern•

•Pine Bluff

White River NWR

Gillham Lake

Lake Greeson

Arkansas Post National Memorial

Dierks Reservoir

DeQueen Reservoir

Arkadelphia•

White River NWR

Pond Creek NWR

30

Millwood Lake

Fordyce•

Ashdown•

•Hope

Monticello•

•Texarkana

Camden•

Warren•

Lake Village•

TEXAS

Magnolia•

•El Dorado

Felsenthal NWR

Overflow NWR

MISSISSIPPI

MILES

0 10 20 30 40 50 60

CALIFORNIA

VOLCANO

1 Eruption in last 100 years

1 Eruption in last 1000 years

NUCLEAR WAR TARGETS

Primary Target

Secondary Target

Outer Ring = 10 miles

FEDERAL LANDS AND INDIAN RESERVATIONS

Bureau of Indian Affairs

Bureau of Land Management / Wilderness

Department of Defense (includes Army Corps of Engineers lakes)

Fish and Wildlife Service / Wilderness

Forest Service / Wilderness

National Park Service / Wilderness

Abbreviations

AFB	Air Force Base
IR	Indian Reservation
MCAS	Marine Corps Air Station
MCB	Marine Corps Base
NAF	Naval Air Facility
NAS	Naval Air Station
NF	National Forest
NHS	National Historic Site
NM	National Monument
NP	National Park
NRA	National Recreation Area
NS	Naval Station
NTC	Naval Training Center
NWR	National Wildlife Refuge
WMA	Wildlife Management Area

MILES
0 25 50 75 100 125 150

COLORADO

NUCLEAR WAR TARGETS

- ◎ Primary Target
- ○ Secondary Target

Outer Ring = 10 miles

FEDERAL LANDS AND INDIAN RESERVATIONS

- Bureau of Indian Affairs
- Bureau of Land Management / Wilderness
- Bureau of Reclamation
- Department of Defense (includes Army Corps of Engineers lakes)
- Fish and Wildlife Service / Wilderness
- Forest Service / Wilderness
- National Park Service / Wilderness
- Other agencies

Some small sites are not shown, especially in urban areas.

Abbreviations

AFB	Air Force Base
NCA	National Conservation Area
NF	National Forest
NG	National Grassland
NHS	National Historic Site
NM	National Monument
NP	National Park
NRA	National Recreation Area
NWR	National Wildlife Refuge
Res	Reservoir

MILES
0 20 40 60 80

WYOMING
NEBRASKA
UT
KANSAS
NEW MEXICO
OKLAHOMA

Medicine Bow NF
Browns Park NWR
Dinosaur NM
Roosevelt National Forest
Horsetooth Reservoir
Pawnee NG
Pawnee NG
Juleburg
Steamboat Springs
Routt NF
Arapaho NWR
Sterling
Holyoke
Craig
Fort Collins
Loveland
Greeley
Routt NF
Rocky Mountain NP
Carter Lake Res
Fort Morgan
Akron
Wray
Meeker
Routt NF
Arapaho NF
Shadow Mountain Lake
Longmont
Arapaho NRA
Boulder
White River National Forest
Green Mountain Reservoir
Two Ponds NWR
Broomfield
Rocky Mountain Arsenal NWR
Naval Oil Shale Reserve
Rifle Gap Res
Vail
Arapaho NF
Arvada
Lakewood
Denver
Buckley AFB
Glenwood Springs
Ruedi Reservoir
White River National Forest
Federal Correctional Complex
Cherry Creek Reservoir
Arikaree River
Colorado Canyons NCA
Colorado NM
Vega Res
White River NF
Aspen
Leadville National Fish Hatchery
Turquoise Lake
Twin Lakes Reservoir
Pike National Forest
US Air Force Academy Farish Memorial Recreation Area
Limon
Burlington
Grand Junction
Grand Mesa NF
Black Canyon of the Gunnison NP
Paonia Res
Taylor Park Reservoir
San Isabel NF
Florissant Fossil Beds National Monument
United States Air Force Academy
Grand Mesa NF
Delta
Gunnison Gorge NCA
Crawford Res
Curecanti NRA
Gunnison National Forest
Colorado Springs
Peterson AFB and Schriever AFB
Cheyenne Wells
Manti-La Sal NF
Uncompahgre NF
Montrose
Gunnison
Salida
NORAD COC Center (Cheyenne Mt)
Fort Carson
High Speed Ground Test Center
Ridgway Res
Silver Jack Res
Federal Correctional Complex
Pueblo Chemical Depot
Uncompahgre NF
Uncompahgre National Forest
Rio Grande National Forest
San Isabel National Forest
Pueblo Res
Pueblo
John Martin Reservoir
Lamar
Canyons of the Ancients NM
Gunnison NF
Baca National Wildlife Refuge
Great Sand Dunes NP
Bent's Old Fort NHS
La Junta
San Juan National Forest
McPhee Res
Mesa Verde National Park
Lemon Reservoir
Vallecito Res
Del Norte
Monte Vista
Monte Vista NWR
Alamosa
Walsenburg
Comanche NG
Fort Carson (Planned Pinyon Canyon Maneuver site)
Springfield
Hovenweep NM
San Juan NF
Platoro Reservoir
Alamosa NWR
San Isabel NF
Trinidad
Comanche National Grassland
Durango
Pagosa Springs
Antonito
Ute Mountain Indian Reservation
Southern Ute Indian Reservation
Navajo Reservoir
South Platte River

CONNECTICUT

NUCLEAR WAR TARGETS

⊕ Primary Target

⬙ Secondary Target

Outer Ring = 10 miles

FEDERAL LANDS AND INDIAN RESERVATIONS

Bureau of Indian Affairs

Department of Defense (includes Army Corps of Engineers lakes)

Fish and Wildlife Service / Wilderness

Bureau of Prisons

State Park

Some small sites are not shown, especially in urban areas.

MASSACHUSETTS

Colebrook River Lake

NEW YORK

Torrington

Hartford ★

New Britain

Mansfield Hollow Lake

Waterbury

Norwich

Mashantucket Pequot Indian Reservation

Danbury Federal Correctional Institution

Danbury

New London Submarine Base

New London

New Haven

Millstone Nuclear Power Plant

RI

Bridgeport

Stewart B. McKinney National Wildlife Refuge

Norwalk

Long Island Sound

Stamford

MILES

0   5   10   15   20

NEW YORK

DELAWARE

NUCLEAR WAR TARGETS

⊘ Primary Target

⊘ Secondary Target

Outer Ring
= 10 miles

FEDERAL LANDS AND INDIAN RESERVATIONS

Department of Defense
(includes Army Corps of Engineers lakes)

Fish and Wildlife Service / Wilderness

State Park

Some small sites are not shown, especially in urban areas.

PENNSYLVANIA

Wilmington

Newark
95

NEW JERSEY

Middletown

Smyrna

Bombay Hook
National Wildlife Refuge

Dover
★
Dover Air Force Base

Delaware Bay

MARYLAND

Chesapeake Bay

Milford

Prime Hook
National Wildlife Refuge

Rehoboth Beach

ATLANTIC OCEAN

Seaford

MILES

0   5   10   15   20   25

FLORIDA

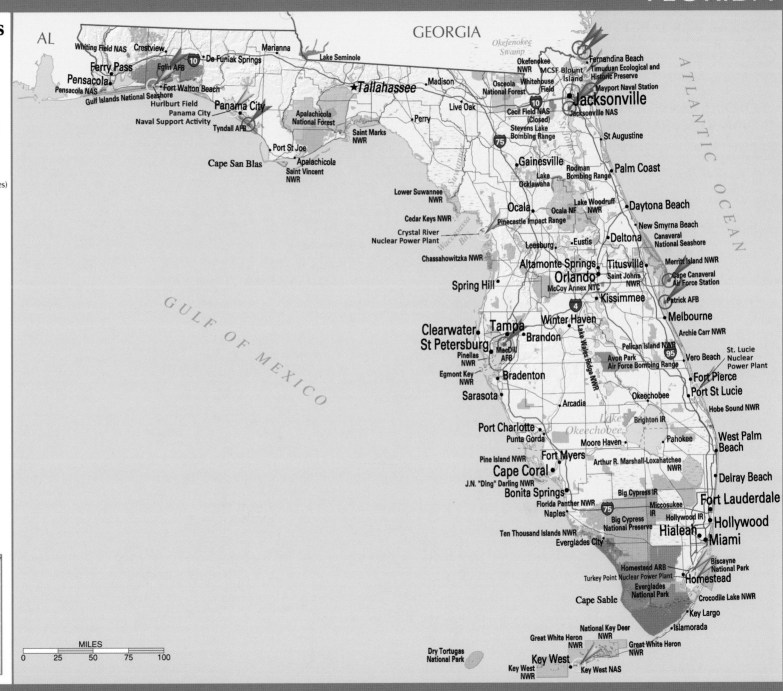

NUCLEAR WAR TARGETS

◎ Primary Target

◎ Secondary Target

Outer Ring = 10 miles

FEDERAL LANDS AND INDIAN RESERVATIONS

Bureau of Indian Affairs

Department of Defense (includes Army Corps of Engineers lakes)

Fish and Wildlife Service / Wilderness

Forest Service / Wilderness

National Park Service / Wilderness

State Park

Some small sites are not shown, especially in urban areas.

Abbreviations

AFB — Air Force Base
IR — Indian Reservation
NF — National Forest
NAS — Naval Air Station
NTC — Naval Training Center
NWR — National Wildlife Refuge

MILES
0   25   50   75   100

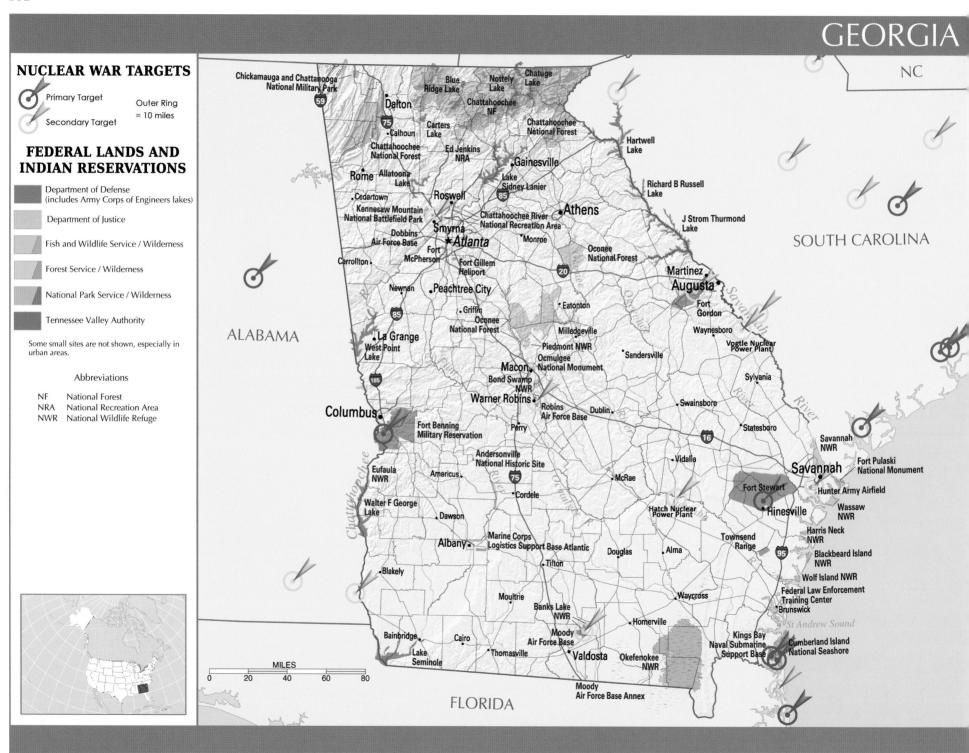

GEORGIA

NC

SOUTH CAROLINA

ALABAMA

FLORIDA

NUCLEAR WAR TARGETS

Primary Target

Secondary Target

Outer Ring = 10 miles

FEDERAL LANDS AND INDIAN RESERVATIONS

Department of Defense (includes Army Corps of Engineers lakes)

Department of Justice

Fish and Wildlife Service / Wilderness

Forest Service / Wilderness

National Park Service / Wilderness

Tennessee Valley Authority

Some small sites are not shown, especially in urban areas.

Abbreviations

NF   National Forest
NRA   National Recreation Area
NWR   National Wildlife Refuge

MILES

0   20   40   60   80

Chickamauga and Chattanooga National Military Park

Dalton

Blue Ridge Lake

Nottely Lake

Chatuge Lake

Chattahoochee NF

Calhoun

Carters Lake

Chattahoochee National Forest

Hartwell Lake

Chattahoochee National Forest

Ed Jenkins NRA

Gainesville

Richard B Russell Lake

Rome

Allatoona Lake

Lake Sidney Lanier

Cedartown

Roswell

Athens

J Strom Thurmond Lake

Kennesaw Mountain National Battlefield Park

Chattahoochee River National Recreation Area

Dobbins Air Force Base

Smyrna

Atlanta

Monroe

Oconee National Forest

Martinez

Augusta

Carrollton

Fort McPherson

Fort Gillem Heliport

Fort Gordon

Newnan

Peachtree City

Eatonton

Waynesboro

Griffin

Milledgeville

Vogtle Nuclear Power Plant

La Grange

Oconee National Forest

Piedmont NWR

Sandersville

Sylvania

West Point Lake

Macon

Ocmulgee National Monument

Bond Swamp NWR

Warner Robins

Swainsboro

Columbus

Robins Air Force Base

Dublin

Statesboro

Fort Benning Military Reservation

Perry

Savannah NWR

Eufaula NWR

Andersonville National Historic Site

Savannah

Fort Pulaski National Monument

Americus

McRae

Vidalia

Fort Stewart

Hunter Army Airfield

Walter F George Lake

Cordele

Hinesville

Wassaw NWR

Dawson

Harris Neck NWR

Albany

Marine Corps Logistics Support Base Atlantic

Douglas

Alma

Townsend Range

Blackbeard Island NWR

Blakely

Hatch Nuclear Power Plant

Waycross

Wolf Island NWR

Federal Law Enforcement Training Center

Brunswick

Moultrie

Banks Lake NWR

St Andrew Sound

Bainbridge

Cairo

Moody Air Force Base

Homerville

Kings Bay Naval Submarine Support Base

Cumberland Island National Seashore

Lake Seminole

Thomasville

Valdosta

Okefenokee NWR

Moody Air Force Base Annex

HAWAII

VOLCANO

- 1 Eruption in last 100 years
- 1 Eruption in last 1000 years

NUCLEAR WAR TARGETS

- Primary Target
- Secondary Target

Outer Ring = 10 miles

FEDERAL LANDS AND INDIAN RESERVATIONS

- Department of Defense (includes Army Corps of Engineers lakes)
- Fish and Wildlife Service / Wilderness
- National Park Service / Wilderness

Some small sites are not shown, especially in urban areas.

Abbreviations

AFB	Air Force Base
MCAS	Marine Corps Air Station
NAS	Naval Air Station
NHP	National Historical Park
NP	National Park
NS	Naval Station
NWR	National Wildlife Refuge

Map labels

NIIHAU
Puuwai

KAUAI
Barking Sands
Pacific Missile Range Facility
Hanalei NWR
Kekaha
Huleia NWR
Kapaa

Wahiawa Naval Reservation
Oahu Forest NWR
Camp H M Smith Marine Corps Base
Schofield Barracks
Wheeler AFB
Schofield Barracks
Dillinghan AFB
Makua Military Reservation
Lualualei Naval Radio Station
Lualualei Naval Reservation
Pearl Harbor NS
Barbers Point NAS (Closed)
Hickam Air Force Base
Fort Shafter
Red Hill Naval Supply Center
Haiku Naval Reservation
Kaneohe MCAS
Tripler Military Hospital
Bellows Air Force Station
Honolulu
OAHU

MOLOKAI
Maunaloa
Kalaupapa NHP

LANAI
Lanai City
Kealia Pond NWR
Haleakala NP
Hana
MAUI

KAHOOLAWE

Upolu Pt
Hawi
Honokaa
Waimea
Hakalau Forest NWR
Pohakuloa Training Area
Kaloko-Honokohau NHP
Hilo
Captain Cook
Pahoa
Cape Kumukahi
HAWAII
Pahala
Hawaii Volcanoes National Park
Ka Lae

PACIFIC OCEAN

MILES
0 20 40 60 80

IDAHO

VOLCANO

 1 Eruption in last 100 years

 1 Eruption in last 1000 years

NUCLEAR WAR TARGETS

 Primary Target

 Secondary Target

Outer Ring = 10 miles

FEDERAL LANDS AND INDIAN RESERVATIONS

 Bureau of Indian Affairs

 Bureau of Land Management / Wilderness

 Bureau of Reclamation

 Department of Defense (includes Army Corps of Engineers lakes)

 Fish and Wildlife Service / Wilderness

 Forest Service / Wilderness

National Park Service / Wilderness

Other agencies

Some small sites are not shown, especially in urban areas.

Abbreviations

IR	Indian Reservation
NF	National Forest
NG	National Grassland
NHP	National Historic Park
NRA	National Recreation Area
NWR	National Wildlife Refuge

WASHINGTON

Kaniksu NF
Kaniksu NF
Kootenai IR
Kootenai National Forest
Kootenai NWR
Kaniksu NWR
Sandpoint
Kaniksu NF
Lake Pend Oreille
Coeur d'Alene National Forest
Kaniksu NF
Coeur d'Alene
Kellogg
Wallace
Coeur d'Alene Indian Reservation
St Maries
Saint Joe National Forest

Nez Perce NHP
Moscow
Clearwater National Forest
Dworshak Reservoir
Lewiston
Nez Perce IR
Nez Perce NHP

Nez Perce NHP
Nezperce National Forest
Bitterroot NF

Hells Canyon NRA

Payette National Forest
Salmon NF
Salmon

Payette NF
New Meadows
McCall
Salmon National Forest

Cascade Reservoir
Cascade
Deadwood Reservoir
Challis
Challis NF
Challis NF
Dubois
Sheep Experiment Station
Targhee NF
Targhee NF

Weiser
Boise NF
Boise National Forest
Sawtooth NRA
Challis NF
Targhee National Forest
Dubois
Island Park Reservoir
St Anthony

Black Canyon Reservoir
Idaho City
Arrowrock Reservoir
Caldwell
Boise
Deer Flat NWR
Air NG
Lucky Peak Lake
Ketchum
Sun Valley
Sawtooth National Forest
Hailey
Arco
Idaho National Engineering Laboratory
Camas NWR
Rexburg

Anderson Ranch Reservoir
Little Wood Reservoir
Idaho Falls

OREGON

Mountain Home Small Arms Range Annex
Mountain Home Air Force Base
Craters of the Moon National Monument
Blackfoot
Grays Lake NWR
Palisades Reservoir

Snake River Birds of Prey National Conservation Area
Hagerman Fossil Beds National Monument
American Falls Reservoir
Fort Hall IR
Caribou National Forest

Saylor Creek Air Force Range
Pocatello
Blackfoot Reservoir

Twin Falls
Burley
Minidoka NWR
Rupert
Sawtooth NF
Caribou NF
Soda Springs

Duck Valley Indian Reservation
Sawtooth NF
City of Rocks National Reserve
Curlew NG
Caribou NF
Downey
Preston
Cache NF
Bear Lake NWR

MONTANA

Yellowstone National Park

WYOMING

MILES
0 25 50 75 100

ILLINOIS

NUCLEAR WAR TARGETS

⌖ Primary Target

Outer Ring = 10 miles

⌖ Secondary Target

FEDERAL LANDS AND INDIAN RESERVATIONS

Department of Defense (includes Army Corps of Engineers lakes)

Fish and Wildlife Service / Wilderness

Forest Service / Wilderness

Other agencies

State Park

Some small sites are not shown, especially in urban areas.

Abbreviations

NWR   National Wildlife Refuge

MILES

0   25   50   75   100

IOWA

MICHIGAN

INDIANA

MISSOURI

KENTUCKY

Savanna Army Depot (Closed)

Waukegan

Rockford

Great Lakes Naval Training Center Fort Sheridan (Closed)

Upper Mississippi River Wildlife and Fish Refuge

Byron Nuclear Power Plant

Glenview Naval Air Station (Closed)

Evanston

De Kalb

Elgin

Skokie

Dixon

Chicago

Quad Cities Nuclear Power Plant

Sterling

Fermi National Accelerator Laboratory

Argonne National Laboratory

Rock Island   Moline

Joliet

Joliet Army Ammunition Plant

Rock Island Arsenal

Dresden and Braidwood Nuclear Power Plants

Midewin National Tallgrass Prairie

Kewanee

La Salle Nuclear Power Plant

Port Louisa NWR

Streator

Kankakee

Galesburg

Chautauqua NWR

Monmouth

Peoria

Normal

Canton

Bloomington

Macomb

Pekin

Rantoul

Emiquon NWR

Chautauqua NWR

Lincoln

Champaign

Danville

Great River NWR

Beardstown

Urbana

Quincy

Clinton Nuclear Power Plant

Meredosia NWR

Decatur

Springfield

Pittsfield

Great River NWR

Pana

Lake Shelbyville

Effingham

Two Rivers NWR

Alton

Vandalia

Charles Melvin Price Support Center

Olney

East St Louis

Carlyle Lake

Belleville

Centralia

Scott Air Force Base

Mount Vernon

Carmi

Rend Lake

Crab Orchard NWR

Carbondale

Marion Federal Penitentiary

Shawnee National Forest

Cypress Creek NWR

Cairo

Mississippi

Illinois River

Kaskaskia River

Wabash River

Ohio River

River

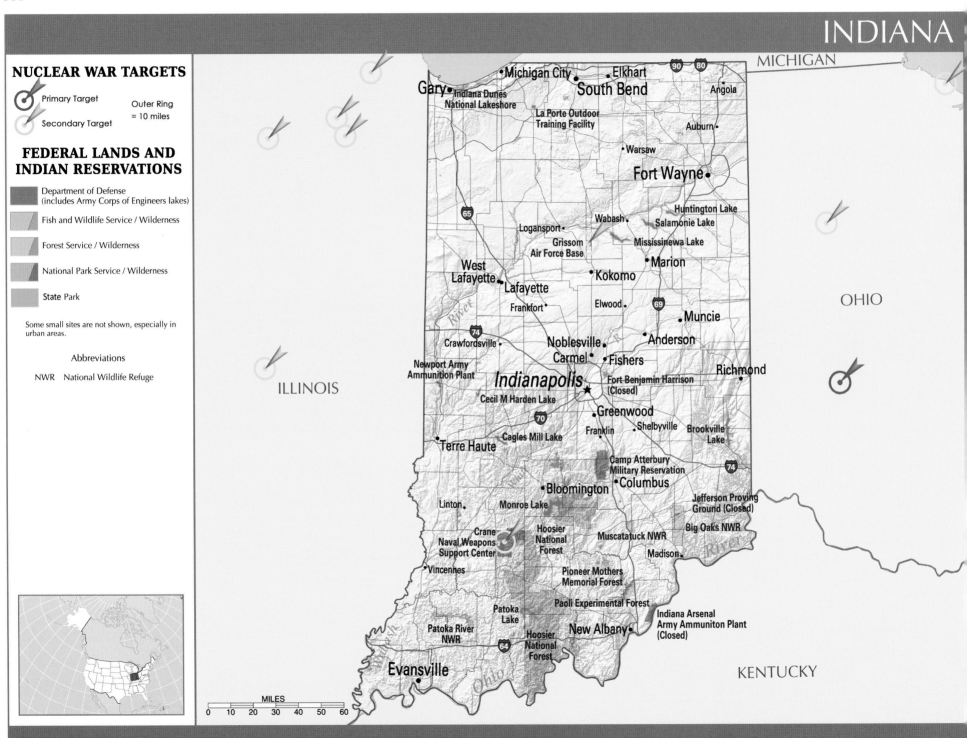

INDIANA

MICHIGAN

OHIO

ILLINOIS

KENTUCKY

NUCLEAR WAR TARGETS

Primary Target

Secondary Target

Outer Ring = 10 miles

FEDERAL LANDS AND INDIAN RESERVATIONS

Department of Defense (includes Army Corps of Engineers lakes)

Fish and Wildlife Service / Wilderness

Forest Service / Wilderness

National Park Service / Wilderness

State Park

Some small sites are not shown, especially in urban areas.

Abbreviations

NWR   National Wildlife Refuge

MILES
0   10   20   30   40   50   60

Gary
Michigan City
Indiana Dunes National Lakeshore
Elkhart
South Bend
Angola
La Porte Outdoor Training Facility
Auburn
Warsaw
Fort Wayne
Huntington Lake
Wabash
Salamonie Lake
Logansport
Mississinewa Lake
Grissom Air Force Base
Marion
West Lafayette
Kokomo
Lafayette
Elwood
Frankfort
Muncie
Crawfordsville
Noblesville
Anderson
Carmel
Fishers
Richmond
Newport Army Ammunition Plant
Indianapolis
Fort Benjamin Harrison (Closed)
Cecil M Harden Lake
Greenwood
Terre Haute
Shelbyville
Franklin
Brookville Lake
Cagles Mill Lake
Camp Atterbury Military Reservation
Bloomington
Columbus
Linton
Jefferson Proving Ground (Closed)
Monroe Lake
Big Oaks NWR
Crane Naval Weapons Support Center
Hoosier National Forest
Muscatatuck NWR
Madison
Vincennes
Pioneer Mothers Memorial Forest
Paoli Experimental Forest
Indiana Arsenal Army Ammuniton Plant (Closed)
Patoka Lake
New Albany
Patoka River NWR
Hoosier National Forest
Evansville

IOWA

NUCLEAR WAR TARGETS

⊙ Primary Target

Outer Ring = 10 miles

◎ Secondary Target

FEDERAL LANDS AND INDIAN RESERVATIONS

Bureau of Indian Affairs

Department of Defense (includes Army Corps of Engineers lakes)

Fish and Wildlife Service / Wilderness

National Park Service / Wilderness

Some small sites are not shown, especially in urban areas.

MINNESOTA

WISCONSIN

Upper Mississippi River Wildlife and Fish Refuge

SD

Spirit Lake

Estherville

Union Slough National Wildlife Refuge

Decorah

Sheldon

Spencer

Mason City

Charles City

Effigy Mounds National Monument

Emmetsburg

Le Mars

Cherokee

Waverly

Upper Mississippi River Wildlife and Fish Refuge

Storm Lake

Iowa Falls

Cedar Falls

Waterloo

Dubuque

Sioux City

Fort Dodge

Webster City

Iowa Air National Guard

Duane Arnold Nuclear Power Plant

Winnebago Indian Reservation

Ames Nat'l Labs

Boone

Marshalltown

Marion

Maquoketa

Denison

Carroll

Ames

Sac and Fox Indian Reservation

Cedar Rapids

Clinton

NE

Saylorville Lake

Coralville Reservoir

Camp Dodge

Ankeny

Grinnell

DeSoto National Wildlife Refuge

Urbandale

West Des Moines

Des Moines

Newton

Iowa City

Davenport

Bettendorf

Atlantic

Neal Smith (Walnut Creek) National Wildlife Refuge

Muscatine

Council Bluffs

Indianola

Lake Red Rock

Washington

Port Louisa National Wildlife Refuge

Red Oak

Creston

Osceola

Chariton

Knoxville

Ottumwa

Fairfield

Shenandoah

Clarinda

Rathbun Lake

Burlington

Iowa Army Ammunition Plant

Centerville

Fort Madison

Keokuk

ILLINOIS

MISSOURI

MILES

0 10 20 30 40 50 60

KANSAS

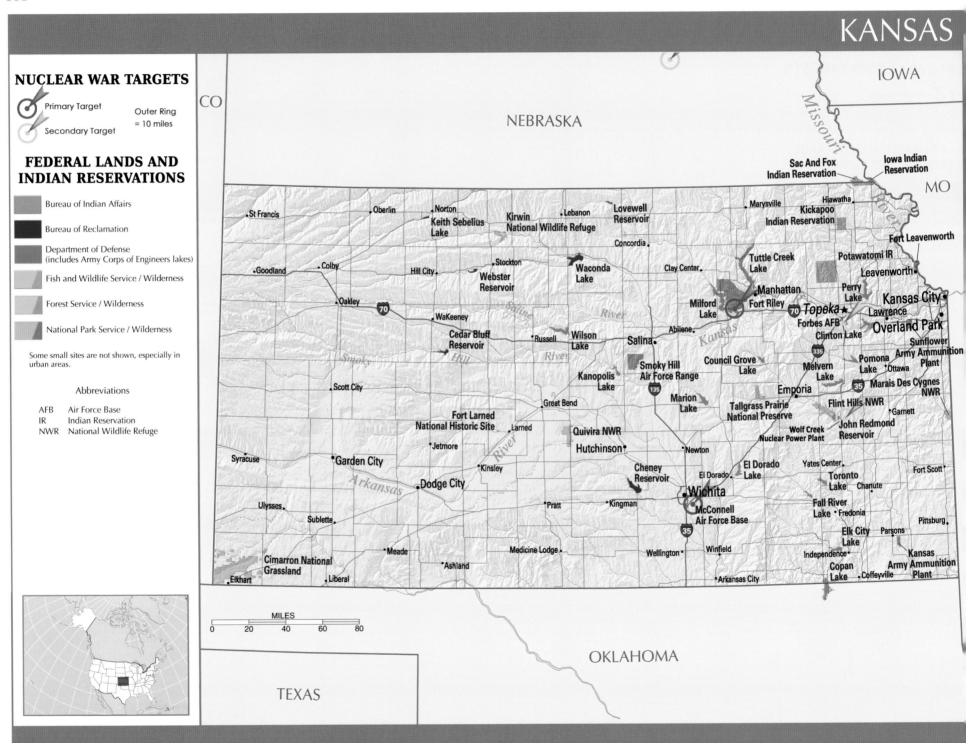

NUCLEAR WAR TARGETS

- Primary Target
- Secondary Target

Outer Ring = 10 miles

FEDERAL LANDS AND INDIAN RESERVATIONS

- Bureau of Indian Affairs
- Bureau of Reclamation
- Department of Defense (includes Army Corps of Engineers lakes)
- Fish and Wildlife Service / Wilderness
- Forest Service / Wilderness
- National Park Service / Wilderness

Some small sites are not shown, especially in urban areas.

Abbreviations

AFB	Air Force Base
IR	Indian Reservation
NWR	National Wildlife Refuge

MILES
0 20 40 60 80

IOWA

NEBRASKA

MO

CO

OKLAHOMA

TEXAS

Sac And Fox Indian Reservation
Iowa Indian Reservation
Fort Leavenworth
Marysville
Hiawatha
Kickapoo Indian Reservation
Potawatomi IR
Leavenworth
St Francis
Oberlin
Norton
Lebanon
Lovewell Reservoir
Kirwin National Wildlife Refuge
Keith Sebelius Lake
Concordia
Tuttle Creek Lake
Perry Lake
Kansas City
Stockton
Waconda Lake
Clay Center
Goodland
Colby
Hill City
Webster Reservoir
Milford Lake
Manhattan
Fort Riley
Topeka ★
Lawrence
Overland Park
Oakley
WaKeeney
Cedar Bluff Reservoir
Salina
River
Russell
Wilson Lake
Salina
Abilene
Kansas
Forbes AFB
Clinton Lake
Sunflower Army Ammunition Plant
Smoky Hill Air Force Range
Council Grove Lake
Pomona Lake
Melvern Lake
Ottawa
Scott City
Kanopolis Lake
Marion Lake
Emporia
Marais Des Cygnes NWR
Flint Hills NWR
Garnett
Great Bend
Tallgrass Prairie National Preserve
John Redmond Reservoir
Fort Larned National Historic Site
Larned
Wolf Creek Nuclear Power Plant
Syracuse
Jetmore
Quivira NWR
Hutchinson
Newton
El Dorado
Yates Center
Fort Scott
Garden City
Kinsley
Cheney Reservoir
El Dorado Lake
Toronto Lake
Chanute
Dodge City
Ulysses
Pratt
Kingman
Wichita
Fall River Lake
Fredonia
Pittsburg
Sublette
McConnell Air Force Base
Elk City Lake
Parsons
Meade
Medicine Lodge
Wellington
Winfield
Independence
Kansas Army Ammunition Plant
Cimarron National Grassland
Ashland
Arkansas City
Copan Lake
Coffeyville
Elkhart
Liberal

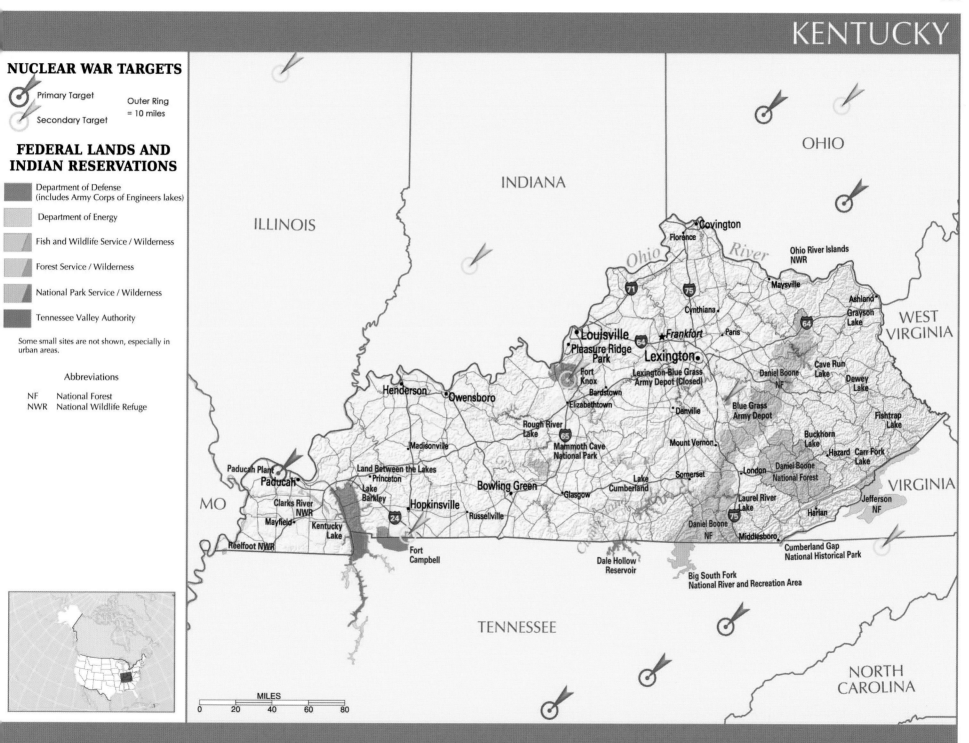

NUCLEAR WAR TARGETS

Primary Target

Secondary Target

Outer Ring
= 10 miles

FEDERAL LANDS AND INDIAN RESERVATIONS

Department of Defense
(includes Army Corps of Engineers lakes)

Department of Energy

Fish and Wildlife Service / Wilderness

Forest Service / Wilderness

National Park Service / Wilderness

Tennessee Valley Authority

Some small sites are not shown, especially in urban areas.

Abbreviations

NF   National Forest
NWR   National Wildlife Refuge

310

LOUISIANA

NUCLEAR WAR TARGETS

⊕ Primary Target

Outer Ring
= 10 miles

◎ Secondary Target

FEDERAL LANDS AND INDIAN RESERVATIONS s)

- Bureau of Indian Affairs
- Department of Defense (includes Army Corps of Engineers lakes)
- Fish and Wildlife Service / Wilderness
- Forest Service / Wilderness
- National Park Service / Wilderness
- State Park

Some small sites are not shown, especially in urban areas.

Abbreviations

NF   National Forest
NWR   National Wildlife Refuge
SPR   Strategic Petroleum Reserve

ARKANSAS

Upper Ouachita NWR
Handy Brake NWR
Kisatchie National Forest
Minden
D'Arbonne NWR
Bastrop
Poverty Point National Monument
Shreveport
Ruston
Black Bayou Lake NWR
Barksdale Air Force Base
Louisiana Ordnance Plant
Monroe
Tallulah
Tensas River NWR
MISSISSIPPI
Mansfield
Kisatchie NF
Winnfield
Natchitoches
Tullos
Catahoula NWR
Bayou Cocodrie NWR
Kisatchie NF
Kisatchie NF
Alexandria
Lake Ophelia NWR
Fort Polk Military Reservation
Leesville
Kisatchie NF
Grand Cote NWR
Fort Polk Military Reservation
TEXAS
Cat Island NWR
Bogalusa
De Ridder
Kisatchie NF
Oakdale
River Bend Nuclear Power Plant
Bogue Chitto NWR
Ville Platte
Kinder
Atchafalaya NWR
Hammond
Big Branch Marsh NWR
Slidell
Eunice
Opelousas
Baton Rouge
Sulphur
Jennings
Lake Charles
Lafayette
Bayou Choctow SPR
Bonnett Carre Spillway
Bayou Sauvage NWR
Crowley
Cameron Prarie NWR
West Hackberry SPR
Waterford Nuclear Power Plant
Kenner
Metairie
New Orleans
Sabine Lake
New Iberia
Abbeville
Lacassine NWR
Chitamacha Indian Reservation
New Orleans Naval Air Station
Breton NWR
White Lake
Jean Lafitte National Historical Park and Preserve
Sabine National Wildlife Refuge
Morgan City
Thibodaux
Houma
Marsh I
Mandalay NWR
Breton NWR
GULF OF MEXICO
Atchafalaya Bay
Delta NWR

MILES
0 10 20 30 40 50 60

MAINE

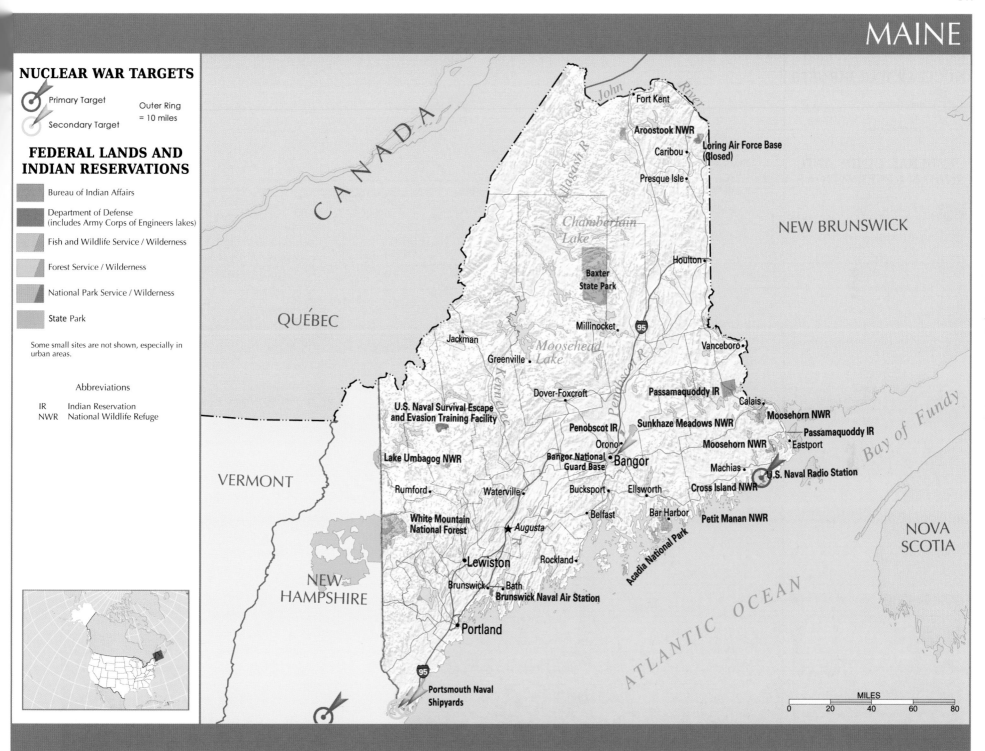

NUCLEAR WAR TARGETS

Primary Target

Secondary Target

Outer Ring
= 10 miles

FEDERAL LANDS AND INDIAN RESERVATIONS

Bureau of Indian Affairs

Department of Defense
(includes Army Corps of Engineers lakes)

Fish and Wildlife Service / Wilderness

Forest Service / Wilderness

National Park Service / Wilderness

State Park

Some small sites are not shown, especially in urban areas.

Abbreviations

IR   Indian Reservation
NWR   National Wildlife Refuge

CANADA

QUÉBEC

NEW BRUNSWICK

NEW HAMPSHIRE

VERMONT

NOVA SCOTIA

St. John River

Fort Kent

Aroostook NWR

Loring Air Force Base (Closed)

Caribou

Presque Isle

Allagash R.

Chamberlain Lake

Baxter State Park

Houlton

Millinocket

95

Jackman

Moosehead Lake

Greenville

Vanceboro

Penobscot R.

Dover-Foxcroft

Passamaquoddy IR

Calais

Moosehorn NWR

U.S. Naval Survival Escape and Evasion Training Facility

Kennebec R.

Penobscot IR

Sunkhaze Meadows NWR

Passamaquoddy IR

Orono

Moosehorn NWR

Eastport

Lake Umbagog NWR

Bangor National Guard Base

Bangor

Machias

U.S. Naval Radio Station

Rumford

Waterville

Bucksport

Ellsworth

Cross Island NWR

Bay of Fundy

White Mountain National Forest

Augusta

Belfast

Bar Harbor

Petit Manan NWR

Lewiston

Rockland

Acadia National Park

Brunswick

Bath

Brunswick Naval Air Station

Portland

95

Portsmouth Naval Shipyards

ATLANTIC OCEAN

MILES
0   20   40   60   80

MARYLAND

NUCLEAR WAR TARGETS

⊚ Primary Target

⊚ Secondary Target

Outer Ring = 10 miles

FEDERAL LANDS AND INDIAN RESERVATIONS

■ Department of Defense (includes Army Corps of Engineers lakes)

■ Fish and Wildlife Service / Wilderness

■ National Park Service / Wilderness

■ Other agencies

■ State Park

Some small sites are not shown, especially in urban areas.

Abbreviations

NAS — Naval Air Station
NB — National Battlefield
NHP — National Historical Park
NWR — National Wildlife Refuge

PENNSYLVANIA

NEW JERSEY

Youghiogheny River Lake

68 Frostburg • Cumberland

Hagerstown

Catoctin Mountain Park
Camp David
Fort Ritchie (Closed)

70 Antietam NB

Fort Detrick
Frederick

Harpers Ferry NHP

Army Chemical Center
Edgewood Arsenal
83 95
Towson
Baltimore
Dundalk

Aberdeen Proving Ground Military Reservation

Columbia

Jennings Randolph Lake

WEST VIRGINIA

Chesapeake and Ohio

Canal

Rockville

US Naval Surface Weapons Center

National Bureau of Standards
Fort George G Meade
Patuxent NWR

NSS Annapolis

Eastern Neck NWR

Annapolis ★
US Naval Academy
USAF Transmitter Station

NASA Goddard

DC

Andrews Air Force Base
US Naval Radio Receiving Station

Easton

DELAWARE

Piscataway Park

St Charles
Globecom Radio Receiving Station

Cambridge

Naval Surface Warfare Center, Indian Head Division

Blossom Point Test Facility

Calvert Cliffs Nuclear Power Plant

Blackwater NWR

Salisbury

Ocean City

VIRGINIA

Solomons Complex

NAS Patuxent River

Bloodsworth Island US Naval Reservation

Chincoteague NWR
Pocomoke City

NAS Patuxent River Webster Field Annex

Martin NWR

Chesapeake Bay

ATLANTIC OCEAN

Susquehanna

Delaware Bay

Potomac R

MASSACHUSETTS

NUCLEAR WAR TARGETS

- Primary Target
- Secondary Target

Outer Ring = 10 miles

FEDERAL LANDS AND INDIAN RESERVATIONS

- Department of Defense (includes Army Corps of Engineers lakes)
- Fish and Wildlife Service / Wilderness
- National Park Service / Wilderness
- State Park

Some small sites are not shown, especially in urban areas.

Abbreviations

NWR   National Wildlife Refuge

VERMONT

NEW HAMPSHIRE

ME

NEW YORK

• North Adams

• Greenfield

Pittsfield

Fitchburg
Fort Devens (Closed)

Haverhill

Lawrence

Parker River NWR

Lowell

Gloucester

Oxbow NWR

Great Meadows NWR

Assabet NWR

Hanscom Air Force Base

Minute Man National Historical Park

Natick Laboratories
Military Reservation

Great Meadows NWR

★ Boston

Holyoke

Westover Air Force Base

Worcester

Framingham

Quincy

U.S. Army Reserve Center

Westfield

Springfield

South Weymouth Naval Air Station (Closed)

Colebrook River Lake

Brockton

Provincetown

Cape Cod National Seashore

Cape Cod Bay

Taunton

Pilgrim Nuclear Power Plant

RHODE ISLAND

CONNECTICUT

Otis Air Force Base

Fall River

Hyannis

New Bedford

Mashpee NWR

Monomoy NWR

Nantucket Sound

Martha's Vineyard

Nantucket I

Nomans Land Island NWR

ATLANTIC OCEAN

Long Island Sound

MILES
0   10   20   30   40

NEW YORK

MICHIGAN

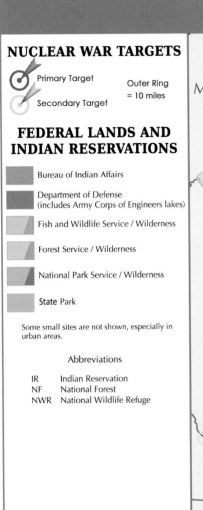

NUCLEAR WAR TARGETS

Primary Target

Secondary Target

Outer Ring = 10 miles

FEDERAL LANDS AND INDIAN RESERVATIONS

Bureau of Indian Affairs

Department of Defense (includes Army Corps of Engineers lakes)

Fish and Wildlife Service / Wilderness

Forest Service / Wilderness

National Park Service / Wilderness

State Park

Some small sites are not shown, especially in urban areas.

Abbreviations

IR   Indian Reservation
NF   National Forest
NWR   National Wildlife Refuge

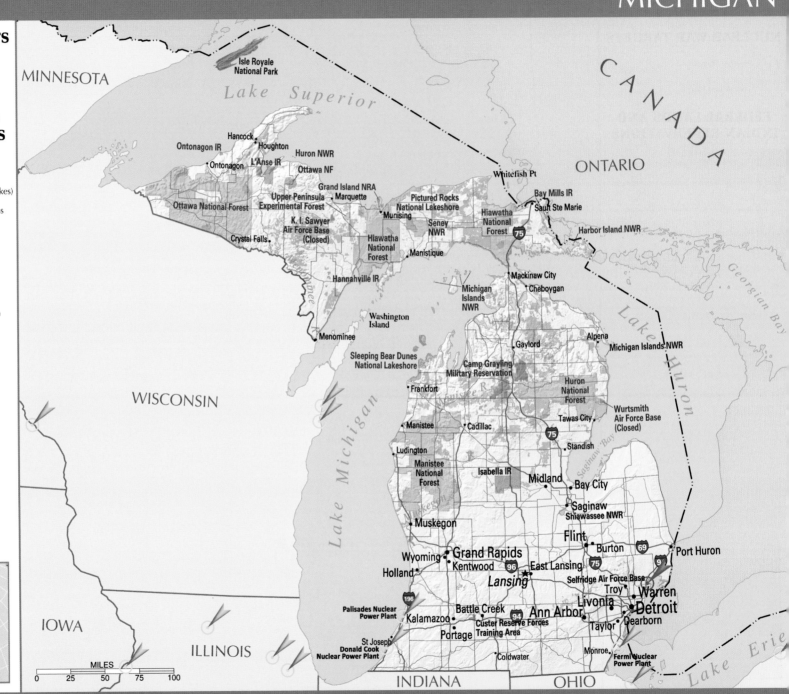

MINNESOTA

CANADA

Lake Superior

ONTARIO

Isle Royale National Park

Hancock
Houghton
Ontonagon IR
Ontonagon
L'Anse IR
Huron NWR
Ottawa NF
Whitefish Pt
Grand Island NRA
Upper Peninsula Experimental Forest
Marquette
Bay Mills IR
Sault Ste Marie
Ottawa National Forest
Pictured Rocks National Lakeshore
Munising
Seney NWR
Hiawatha National Forest
Harbor Island NWR
K. I. Sawyer Air Force Base (Closed)
Crystal Falls
Hiawatha National Forest
Manistique
Mackinaw City
Cheboygan
Hannahville IR
Michigan Islands NWR
Washington Island
Gaylord
Alpena
Michigan Islands NWR
Menominee
Sleeping Bear Dunes National Lakeshore
Camp Grayling Military Reservation
Huron National Forest
Wurtsmith Air Force Base (Closed)
Frankfort
Tawas City
Manistee
Cadillac
Standish
Ludington
Manistee National Forest
Isabella IR
Midland
Bay City
Saginaw
Shiawassee NWR
Muskegon
Flint
Burton
Port Huron
Wyoming
Grand Rapids
Kentwood
East Lansing
Holland
Lansing
Selfridge Air Force Base
Troy
Warren
Livonia
Detroit
Palisades Nuclear Power Plant
Battle Creek
Ann Arbor
Kalamazoo
Custer Reserve Forces Training Area
Taylor
Dearborn
Portage
St Joseph
Donald Cook Nuclear Power Plant
Coldwater
Monroe
Fermi Nuclear Power Plant

Lake Michigan
Lake Huron
Georgian Bay
Saginaw Bay
Lake Erie

WISCONSIN

IOWA

ILLINOIS

INDIANA

OHIO

MILES
0   25   50   75   100

MINNESOTA

NUCLEAR WAR TARGETS

- ⊚ Primary Target
- ⊿ Secondary Target

Outer Ring = 10 miles

FEDERAL LANDS AND INDIAN RESERVATIONS

- Bureau of Indian Affairs
- Department of Defense (includes Army Corps of Engineers lakes)
- Fish and Wildlife Service / Wilderness
- Forest Service / Wilderness
- National Park Service / Wilderness
- State Park

Some small sites are not shown, especially in urban areas.

Abbreviations

IR	Indian Reservation
NF	National Forest
NP	National Park
NWR	National Wildlife Refuge

MANITOBA

CANADA

ONTARIO

Lake of the Woods

Red Lake IR

Rainy

Agassiz NWR

Red Lake IR

Voyageurs NP

Bois Forte IR

Superior NF

East Grand Forks

Red Lake IR

Chippewa NF

Vermilion Lake IR

Superior NF

Grand Portage IR

NORTH DAKOTA

Rydell NWR

Bemidji

Lake Winnibigoshish

Superior NF

Lake Superior

White Earth IR

Leech Lake IR

Hibbing

Leech Lake

Pokegama Lake

MICHIGAN

Chippewa NF

Hamden Slough NWR

Tamarac NWR

Fond du Lac IR

Moorhead

Big Sandy Lake

Duluth

Cross Lake

Gull Lake

Rice Lake NWR

Fergus Falls

Brainerd

Mille Lacs IR

Crane Meadows NWR

St Croix National Scenic Riverway

Lake Traverse

St Cloud

Sherburne NWR

Big Stone Lake NWR

Monticello Nuclear Power Plant

Marsh Lake

Anoka

WISCONSIN

Lac qui Parle

Minneapolis

St Paul

SOUTH DAKOTA

Upper Sioux IR

Minnesota Valley NWR

Mississippi National River and Recreation Area

Prairie Island IR

Shakopee IR

Lower Sioux IR

Northfield

Prairie Island Nuclear Power Plant

New Ulm

Mankato

Upper Mississippi River Wildlife and Fish Refuge

Pipestone National Monument

Rochester

Worthington

Austin

MILES

0   25   50   75   100

MISSISSIPPI

NUCLEAR WAR TARGETS

◎ Primary Target

◎ Secondary Target

Outer Ring = 10 miles

FEDERAL LANDS AND INDIAN RESERVATIONS

Bureau of Indian Affairs

Department of Defense (includes Army Corps of Engineers lakes)

Fish and Wildlife Service / Wilderness

Forest Service / Wilderness

National Aeronautics and Space Administration

National Park Service / Wilderness

Tennessee Valley Authority

Some small sites are not shown, especially in urban areas.

Abbreviations

NF   National Forest
NMP   National Military Park
NWR   National Wildlife Refuge

ARKANSAS

LOUISIANA

ALABAMA

FLORIDA

Southaven
Corinth
Pickwick Lake
Holly Springs
Arkabutla Lake
Holly Springs NF
Bay Springs Lake
Sardis Lake
55
New Albany
Oxford
Enid Lake
Tupelo
Coldwater River NWR
Water Valley
Holly Springs National Forest
Aberdeen Lake
Tallahatchie NWR
Tombigbee NF
Aberdeen
Columbus AFB
Cleveland
Grenada Lake
Columbus Lake
Dahomey NWR
Columbus
Indianola
Greenwood
Starkville
Noxubee NWR
Aliceville Lake
Greenville
Mathews Brake NWR
Morgan Brake NWR
Tombigbee NF
Louisville
Multipurpose Target Range
Yazoo NWR
Belzoni
Hillside NWR
Mississippi Choctaw Indian Reservation
Alpha Naval Auxiliary Air Station
Delta NF
Panther Swamp NWR
Bravo Naval Auxiliary Air Station
Canton
Ross Barnett Reservoir
Okatibbee Lake
Meridian Naval Air Station
Vicksburg NMP
Meridian
Vicksburg
★ Jackson
20
Mississippi Choctaw Indian Reservation
Bienville NF
Jackson-Evers Airport Air Nat'l Guard
55
Key Field Air National Guard
Grand Gulf Nuclear Power Plant
Hazlehurst
Magee
Mississippi Choctaw Indian Reservation
Collins
Laurel
Waynesboro
Saint Catherine Creek National Wildlife Refuge
Natchez
Brookhaven
Monticello
DeSoto NF
Columbia
Hattiesburg
Homochitto NF
McComb
Camp Shelby
DeSoto NF
59
Bogue Chitto NWR
Picayune
Mississippi Sandhill Crane NWR
Grand Bay NWR
10
Gulfport
Biloxi
Pascagoula
National Space Technology Laboratories
Gulf Islands National Seashore
Keesler AFB

MILES
0   20   40   60   80

MISSOURI

NUCLEAR WAR TARGETS

⊕ Primary Target

⊘ Secondary Target

Outer Ring = 10 miles

FEDERAL LANDS AND INDIAN RESERVATIONS

Bureau of Prisons

Department of Defense (includes Army Corps of Engineers lakes)

Fish and Wildlife Service / Wilderness

Forest Service / Wilderness

National Park Service / Wilderness

Some small sites are not shown, especially in urban areas.

Abbreviations

NF   National Forest
NWR   National Wildlife Refuge

NE

IOWA

ILLINOIS

Maryville

Squaw Creek National Wildlife Refuge

Princeton

Bethany

Kirksville

Great River National Wildlife Refuge

Trenton

Chillicothe

Brookfield

Macon

Hannibal

St Joseph

Cameron

Swan Lake National Wildlife Refuge

Mark Twain Lake

Clarence Cannon National Wildlife Refuge

Moberly

Bowling Green

Big Muddy NWR

Fort Leavenworth Federal Penitentiary Farm

Liberty

Big Muddy NWR

Kansas City

Big Muddy National Wildlife Refuge

Mexico

Independence

Lake City Army Ammunition Plant

Columbia

Mark Twain National Forest

Florissant

St Charles

Lees Summit

Whiteman Air Force Base

Calloway Nuclear Power Plant

St Louis

Richards-Gebaur Air Force Base (Closed)

Sedalia

Big Muddy National Wildlife Refuge

Jefferson City

KANSAS

Harry S Truman Reservoir

Sullivan

Festus

River

Lake of the Ozarks

Rolla

Nevada

Pomme de Terre Lake

Fort Leonard Wood Military Reservation

Farmington

Perryville

Stockton Lake

Mark Twain NF

Mark Twain National Forest

Salem

Mark Twain National Forest

Bolivar

Clearwater Lake

Cape Girardeau

Carthage

Wilson's Creek National Battlefield

Springfield

Ozark National Scenic Riverways

Mingo NWR

Joplin

Mountain Grove

Mark Twain NF

Neosho

Monett

Willow Springs

Mark Twain NF

Wappapello Lake

Sikeston

Mark Twain National Forest

Table Rock Lake

Mark Twain National Forest

Ozark National Scenic Riverways

Dexter

Branson

Malden

OKLAHOMA

Bull Shoals Lake

Norfork Lake

Kennett

KY

ARKANSAS

TN

MILES
0   20   40   60   80

MONTANA

VOLCANO

- 1 Eruption in last 100 years
- 1 Eruption in last 1000 years

NUCLEAR WAR TARGETS

- Primary Target
- Secondary Target

Outer Ring = 10 miles

FEDERAL LANDS AND INDIAN RESERVATIONS

- Bureau of Indian Affairs
- Bureau of Land Management / Wilderness
- Bureau of Reclamation
- Department of Agriculture
- Department of Defense (includes Army Corps of Engineers lakes)
- Fish and Wildlife Service / Wilderness
- Forest Service / Wilderness
- National Park Service / Wilderness

Some small sites are not shown, especially in urban areas.

Abbreviations

IR	Indian Reservation
NB	National Battlefield
NF	National Forest
NHS	National Historic Site
NM	National Monument
NRA	National Recreation Area
NWR	National Wildlife Refuge

CANADA

BRITISH COLUMBIA

ALBERTA

SASKATCHEWAN

IDAHO

WYOMING

Kaniksu National Forest
Lake Koocanusa
Eureka
Lake Sherburne
Glacier National Park
Cut Bank
Creedman Coulee NWR
Lake Thibadeau NWR
Scobey
Plentywood
Kootenai National Forest
Libby
Flathead NF
Blackfeet Indian Reservation
East Glacier Park
Lake Elwell
Fresno Reservoir
Havre
Black Coulee NWR
Hewitt Lake NWR
Nelson Reservoir
Medicine Lake NWR
Kalispell
Hungry Horse Reservoir
Conrad
Rocky Boys Indian Reservation
Fort Belknap IR
Bowdoin NWR
Glasgow
Fort Peck Indian Reservation
N
Kootenai NF
Lost Trail NWR
Flathead NF
Swan River NWR
Lewis and Clark National Forest
Upper Missouri River Breaks National Monument
Fort Peck Lake
Charles M Russell NWR
Sidney
Kaniksu NF
Flathead NF
Pablo NWR
Benton Lake NWR
Fort Benton
UL Bend NWR
Lolo NF
Lolo NF
Flathead IR
Gibson Reservoir
Pishkun Reservoir
Great Falls
Circle
National Bison Range
Nine-Pipe NWR
Flathead NF
Willow Creek Reservoir
Malmstrom Air Force Base
Lewis and Clark National Forest
Malmstrom AFB MM Missiles (Old)
Jordan
Glendive
Lolo NF
Lolo NF
Helena NF
Lewistown
War Horse NWR
Lolo NF
Missoula
Fort William H Harrison
Helena NF
Lewis and Clark National Forest
Lamesteer National Wildlife Refuge
Rattlesnake NRA
Helena NF
Lake Mason NWR
Lee Metcalf NWR
Bearmouth National Guard Training Area
Helena
White Sulphur Springs
Baker
Lolo NF
Grant-Kohrs Ranch NHS
Canyon Ferry Lake
Lewis and Clark National Forest
Miles City
Hamilton
Townsend
Roundup
Forsyth
Lake Como
Deerlodge National Forest
Hailstone NWR
Fort Keogh Livestock and Range Research Lab
Butte
Helena NF
Gallatin National Forest
Halfbreed Lake NWR
Pompeys Pillar NM
Northern Cheyenne Indian Reservation
Ekalaka
Bitterroot NF
Deer Lodge NF
Big Timber
Hardin
Bozeman
Billings
NG Base
Big Hole NB
Beaverhead National Forest
Livingston
Little Bighorn Battlefield National Monument
Custer NF
Broadus
Beaverhead National Forest
Virginia City
Gallatin National Forest
Bighorn Canyon NRA
Crow Indian Reservation
Custer National Forest
Dillon
Red Lodge
Custer NF
Clark Canyon Reservoir
Gallatin NF
Custer NF
Bighorn Lake
Beaverhead NF
Beaverhead National Forest
Red Rock Lakes NWR
Gallatin NF
Custer NF
Centennial Mountains Sheep Experimental Station
Yellowstone National Park
Milk River
Missouri River
Yellowstone River

MILES
0 25 50 75 100

NEBRASKA

NUCLEAR WAR TARGETS

⊙ Primary Target

◎ Secondary Target

Outer Ring = 10 miles

FEDERAL LANDS AND INDIAN RESERVATIONS

▪ Bureau of Indian Affairs

▪ Bureau of Reclamation

▪ Department of Agriculture

▪ Department of Defense (includes Army Corps of Engineers lakes)

▪ Fish and Wildlife Service / Wilderness

▪ Forest Service / Wilderness

▪ National Park Service / Wilderness

Some small sites are not shown, especially in urban areas.

Abbreviations

AFB — Air Force Base
IR — Indian Reservation
NF — National Forest
NG — National Grassland
NM — National Monument
NRA — National Recreation Area
NWR — National Wildlife Refuge

WY

SOUTH DAKOTA

MINNESOTA

MISSOURI

IOWA

COLORADO

KANSAS

Missouri National Recreational River

Lewis And Clark Lake

Santee Sioux Indian Reservation

Winnebago Indian Reservation

Omaha Indian Reservation

Fort Calhoun Nuclear Power Plant

DeSoto NWR

Oglala NG

Pine Ridge NRA

Samuel R McKelvie National Forest

Valentine

Fort Niobrara NWR

Gordon

Nebraska NF

Box Butte Reservoir

Valentine NWR

Merritt Reservoir

O'Neill

Neligh

Norfolk

Nebraska NF

Agate Fossil Beds National Monument

Alliance

North Platte NWR

Scottsbluff

Lake Minatare

Scotts Bluff NM

Bridgeport

Hyannis

Crescent Lake National Wildlife Refuge

Thedford

Nebraska National Forest

Calamus Reservoir

Burwell

Prototype Low Frequency Communications System

Davis Creek Reservoir

Boyer Chute NWR

Fremont

Omaha

Offutt AFB

Bellevue

Kimball

Sidney

Lake McConaughy

Broken Bow

Sherman Reservoir

Army Training Area

Columbus

Mead

Army National Guard Facility

Army Reserve Outdoor Training Area

Ogallala

North Platte

80

Cornhusker Army Ammunition Plant

Lexington

Kearney

Kearney Rifle Range

York

Lincoln Air NG Base

Lincoln

Nebraska City

Imperial

Enders Reservoir

Harry Strunk Lake

Holdrege

Hastings

Roman L Hruska US Animal Meat Research Center

Cooper Nuclear Power Plant

Beatrice

Iowa IR

Swanson Lake

Benkelman

Hugh Butler Lake

Alma

Harlan County Lake

Superior

Fairbury

Falls City

Sac And Fox Indian Reservation

Niobrara River

Middle Loup

North Loup

Elkhorn River

Loup River

Platte River

Republican River

MILES

0   25   50   75   100

NEVADA

VOLCANO

🌋 1 Eruption in last 100 years

🌋 1 Eruption in last 1000 years

NUCLEAR WAR TARGETS

◎ Primary Target

◎ Secondary Target

Outer Ring = 10 miles

FEDERAL LANDS AND INDIAN RESERVATIONS

Bureau of Indian Affairs

Bureau of Land Management / Wilderness

Bureau of Reclamation

Department of Defense (includes Army Corps of Engineers lakes)

Department of Energy

Fish and Wildlife Service / Wilderness

Forest Service / Wilderness

National Park Service / Wilderness

Abbreviations

AFB — Air Force Base
IR — Indian Reservation
NAS — Naval Air Station
NCA — National Conservation Area
NF — National Forest
NP — National Park
NWR — National Wildlife Refuge
WMA — Wildlife Management Area

MILES
0   25   50   75   100

NEW HAMPSHIRE

NUCLEAR WAR TARGETS

⊙ Primary Target

⊙ Secondary Target

Outer Ring = 10 miles

FEDERAL LANDS AND INDIAN RESERVATIONS

▨ Department of Defense (includes Army Corps of Engineers lakes)

▨ Fish and Wildlife Service / Wilderness

▨ Forest Service / Wilderness

▨ State Park

Some small sites are not shown, especially in urban areas.

CANADA
QUÉBEC

MAINE

VERMONT

NEW YORK

Lake Umbagog National Wildlife Refuge

White Mountain National Forest

Lancaster
Berlin
Littleton

White Mountain National Forest
Conway

Hanover
Lebanon

Lake Winnipesaukee

Laconia
Franklin

Claremont

Concord

Pease Air National Guard

Hopkinton Lake

Great Bay National Wildlife Refuge
Portsmouth

New Boston Air Force Station

Keene

Manchester
Exeter

SeaBrook Nuclear Power Plant

Wapack National Wildlife Refuge

Nashua
MA

ATLANTIC OCEAN

Connecticut

MILES
0 10 20 30 40

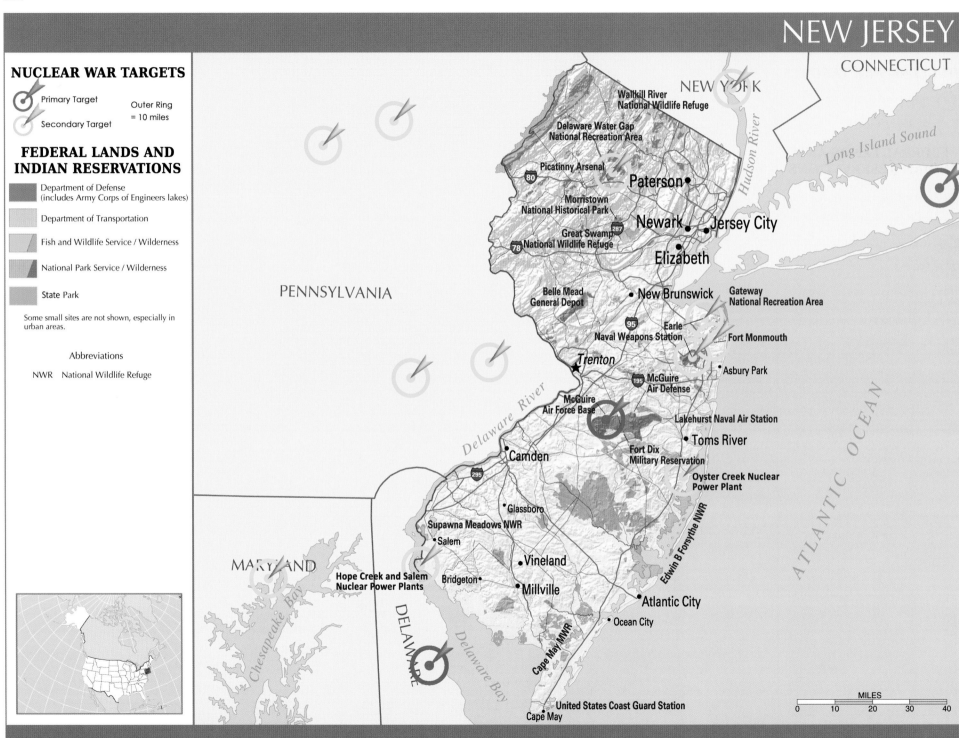

NEW JERSEY

NUCLEAR WAR TARGETS

- Primary Target
- Secondary Target

Outer Ring = 10 miles

FEDERAL LANDS AND INDIAN RESERVATIONS

- Department of Defense (includes Army Corps of Engineers lakes)
- Department of Transportation
- Fish and Wildlife Service / Wilderness
- National Park Service / Wilderness
- State Park

Some small sites are not shown, especially in urban areas.

Abbreviations

NWR   National Wildlife Refuge

CONNECTICUT

NEW YORK

Long Island Sound

Hudson River

Wallkill River National Wildlife Refuge

Delaware Water Gap National Recreation Area

Picatinny Arsenal

80

Paterson

Morristown National Historical Park

Newark

Jersey City

Great Swamp National Wildlife Refuge

78

287

Elizabeth

Belle Mead General Depot

New Brunswick

Gateway National Recreation Area

95

Earle Naval Weapons Station

Fort Monmouth

Trenton

195

McGuire Air Defense

Asbury Park

McGuire Air Force Base

Lakehurst Naval Air Station

Toms River

Fort Dix Military Reservation

Oyster Creek Nuclear Power Plant

PENNSYLVANIA

Delaware River

Camden

295

Glassboro

Supawna Meadows NWR

Salem

MARYLAND

Vineland

Bridgeton

Edwin B Forsythe NWR

Hope Creek and Salem Nuclear Power Plants

Millville

Atlantic City

Ocean City

Chesapeake Bay

DELAWARE

Delaware Bay

Cape May NWR

United States Coast Guard Station

Cape May

ATLANTIC OCEAN

MILES

0   10   20   30   40

NEW MEXICO

NUCLEAR WAR TARGETS

⊕ Primary Target

Outer Ring
= 10 miles

⊘ Secondary Target

FEDERAL LANDS AND INDIAN RESERVATIONS

Bureau of Indian Affairs

Bureau of Land Management / Wilderness

Bureau of Reclamation

Department of Defense (includes Army Corps of Engineers lakes)

Fish and Wildlife Service / Wilderness

Forest Service / Wilderness

National Park Service / Wilderness

Other agencies

Some small sites are not shown, especially in urban areas.

Abbreviations

AFB	Air Force Base
IR	Indian Reservation
NCA	National Conservation Area
NF	National Forest
NHP	National Historical Park
NL	National Laboratory
NM	National Monument
NRA	National Recreation Area
NWR	National Wildlife Refuge
Res	Reservoir

OKLAHOMA

TEXAS

ARIZONA

CO

CHIHUAHUA

MEXICO

SONORA

MILES
0   25   50   75   100

NEW YORK

NUCLEAR WAR TARGETS

⊕ Primary Target

⊕ Secondary Target

Outer Ring = 10 miles

FEDERAL LANDS AND INDIAN RESERVATIONS

▮ Bureau of Indian Affairs

▮ Department of Energy

▮ Department of Defense (includes Army Corps of Engineers lakes)

▮ Fish and Wildlife Service / Wilderness

▮ Forest Service / Wilderness

▮ National Park Service / Wilderness

▮ State Park

Some small sites are not shown, especially in urban areas.

Abbreviations

IR   Indian Reservation
NHS   National Historic Site
NWR   National Wildlife Refuge

QUÉBEC

CANADA

ONTARIO

Lake Champlain

VERMONT

NEW HAMPSHIRE

MASSACHUSETTS

CONNECTICUT

PENNSYLVANIA

NEW JERSEY

ATLANTIC OCEAN

St Lawrence R

Lake Ontario

Lake Erie

Delaware R

Allegheny Reservoir

LONG ISLAND

Saint Regis Indian Reservation

Ogdensburg

Potsdam

Plattsburgh

Plattsburgh Air Force Base (Closed)

Saranac Lake

Lake Placid

Tupper Lake

Fort Drum

Long Lake

Watertown

Fitzpatrick and Nine Mile Point Nuclear Power Plants

Oswego

Ginna Nuclear Power Plant

Camden Test Annex

Hancock Field U S Air Force

Griffiss Air Force Base (Closed)

Glens Falls

Rochester

Syracuse

Utica

West Milton Area Knolls Atomic Power Laboratory

Saratoga Springs

Saratoga National Historical Park

Air Force Plant No. 38

Tuscarora IR

Iroquois NWR

Tonawanda IR

Montezuma NWR

Onondaga IR

Schenectady

Troy

Niagara Falls

Albany

Buffalo

Mount Morris Lake

Seneca Army Depot (Closed)

Cortland

Finger Lakes National Forest

Oneonta

Cattaraugus IR

Ithaca

Whitney Point Lake

Oil Springs IR

Allegany IR

Wellsville

Corning

Binghamton

Jamestown

Olean

Elmira

Vanderbilt Mansion NHS

Home of F D Roosevelt NHS

Eleanor Roosevelt NHS

Poughkeepsie

Stewart Air National Guard Base

Newburgh

Middletown

West Point U S Military Academy

Indian Point Nuclear Power Plant

Montauk

Wallkill River NWR

White Plains

Brookhaven National Laboratory

Naval Weapons Industrial Reserve Plant

New York

Oyster Bay NWR

Wertheim NWR

Levittown

Fire Island National Seashore

Gateway National Recreation Area

MILES

0   20   40   60   80

NORTH CAROLINA

NUCLEAR WAR TARGETS

- ◎ Primary Target
- ◎ Secondary Target

Outer Ring = 10 miles

FEDERAL LANDS AND INDIAN RESERVATIONS

- Bureau of Indian Affairs
- Department of Defense (includes Army Corps of Engineers lakes)
- Fish and Wildlife Service / Wilderness
- Forest Service / Wilderness
- National Park Service / Wilderness
- Tennessee Valley Authority
- Department of Transportation
- State Park

Some small sites are not shown, especially in urban areas.

Abbreviations

AFB	Air Force Base
IR	Indian Reservation
MCAS	Marine Corps Air Station
NF	National Forest
NHS	National Historic Site
NMem	National Memorial
NP	National Park
NS	National Seashore
NWR	National Wildlife Refuge

MILES
0 25 50 75 100

KENTUCKY

WEST VIRGINIA

VIRGINIA

MD

Chesapeake Bay

TENNESSEE

John H Kerr Reservoir

Great Dismal Swamp National Wildlife Refuge

Naval Facility Engineering Command

Mount Airy

Reidsville

Henderson

Harvey Point Defense Testing Activity

Mackay Island NWR

Boone

Winston-Salem

W Kerr Scott Reservoir

Greensboro

Falls Lake Reservoir

Roanoke River NWR

Wright Brothers NMem
Fort Raleigh NHS

High Point

Chapel Hill

Durham

Pisgah National Forest

★ Raleigh

Wilson

Pocosin Lakes NWR

Alligator River NWR

Great Smoky Mountains NP

Asheville

Hickory

Salisbury

B Everett Jordan Lake

Shearon Harris Nuclear Power Plant

Greenville

Dare County Range

Fontana Lake

Nantahala NF

Kannapolis

Uwharrie NF

Sanford

Seymour Johnson AFB

Mattamuskeet NWR

Pea Island NWR

Appalachia Lake

Eastern Cherokee IR

Gastonia

Charlotte

Pope Air Force Base

Swanquarter NWR

Cedar Island NWR

Hiwassee Lake

McGuire Nuclear Power Plant

Pee Dee NWR

Fort Bragg

Fayetteville

Cherry Point MCAS

Chatuge Lake

Camp Mackall

Oak Grove Holt Navy Airfield

Croatan NF

Atlantic Field

Cape Lookout NS

Jacksonville

Lumberton

Camp Lejeune Marine Corps Base

Bogue Field

Cape Hatteras NS

Wilmington

SOUTH CAROLINA

Military Ocean Terminal Sunny Point and Brunswick Nuclear Power Plant

GEORGIA

ATLANTIC OCEAN

326

NORTH DAKOTA

NUCLEAR WAR TARGETS

Primary Target

Secondary Target

Outer Ring
= 10 miles

FEDERAL LANDS AND INDIAN RESERVATIONS

Bureau of Indian Affairs

Bureau of Land Management / Wilderness

Bureau of Reclamation

Department of Defense (includes Army Corps of Engineers lakes)

Fish and Wildlife Service / Wilderness

Forest Service / Wilderness

National Park Service / Wilderness

Some small sites are not shown, especially in urban areas.

Abbreviations

IR   Indian Reservation
NG   National Grassland
NHS   National Historic Site
NWR   National Wildlife Refuge

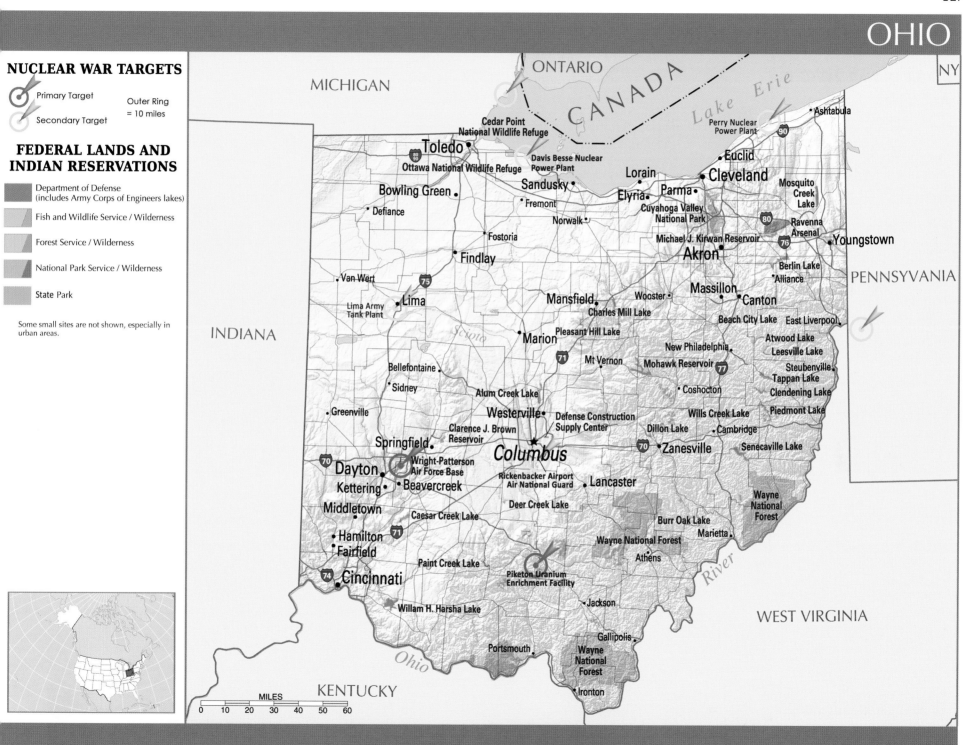

OHIO

NUCLEAR WAR TARGETS

◎ Primary Target

◎ Secondary Target

Outer Ring = 10 miles

FEDERAL LANDS AND INDIAN RESERVATIONS

Department of Defense (includes Army Corps of Engineers lakes)

Fish and Wildlife Service / Wilderness

Forest Service / Wilderness

National Park Service / Wilderness

State Park

Some small sites are not shown, especially in urban areas.

MICHIGAN

ONTARIO

CANADA

Lake Erie

NY

Ashtabula

Cedar Point National Wildlife Refuge

Perry Nuclear Power Plant

Toledo

Davis Besse Nuclear Power Plant

Euclid

Cleveland

Ottawa National Wildlife Refuge

Lorain

Mosquito Creek Lake

Bowling Green

Sandusky

Elyria

Parma

Defiance

Fremont

Cuyahoga Valley National Park

Ravenna Arsenal

Youngstown

Norwalk

Michael J. Kirwan Reservoir

Fostoria

Akron

Berlin Lake

Alliance

PENNSYVANIA

Findlay

Van Wert

Mansfield

Wooster

Massillon

Canton

Lima Army Tank Plant

Lima

Charles Mill Lake

Beach City Lake

East Liverpool

Pleasant Hill Lake

Atwood Lake

Leesville Lake

INDIANA

Marion

New Philadelphia

Steubenville

Bellefontaine

Mt Vernon

Mohawk Reservoir

Tappan Lake

Sidney

Scioto

Clendening Lake

Alum Creek Lake

Coshocton

Piedmont Lake

Greenville

Westerville

Wills Creek Lake

Clarence J. Brown Reservoir

Defense Construction Supply Center

Dillon Lake

Cambridge

Springfield

Columbus

Zanesville

Senecaville Lake

Dayton

Wright-Patterson Air Force Base

Rickenbacker Airport Air National Guard

Lancaster

Kettering

Beavercreek

Wayne National Forest

Middletown

Deer Creek Lake

Caesar Creek Lake

Burr Oak Lake

Hamilton

Paint Creek Lake

Wayne National Forest

Marietta

Fairfield

Athens

Cincinnati

Piketon Uranium Enrichment Facility

River

WEST VIRGINIA

Willam H. Harsha Lake

Jackson

Gallipolis

Portsmouth

Wayne National Forest

Ohio

KENTUCKY

Ironton

MILES

0 10 20 30 40 50 60

OKLAHOMA

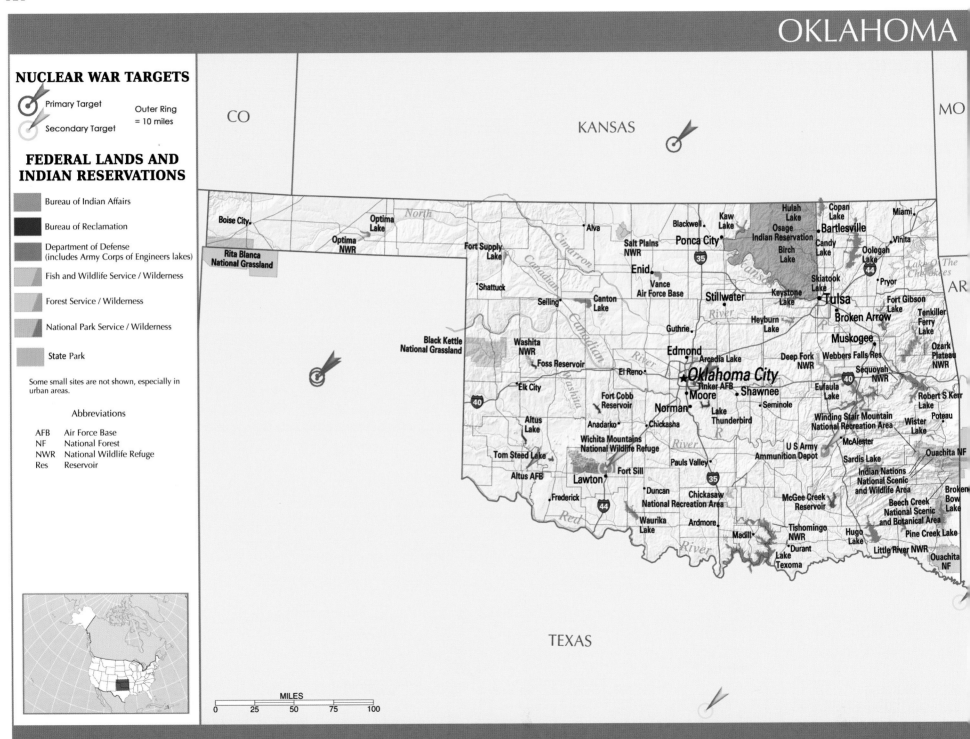

NUCLEAR WAR TARGETS

- Primary Target
- Secondary Target

Outer Ring = 10 miles

FEDERAL LANDS AND INDIAN RESERVATIONS

- Bureau of Indian Affairs
- Bureau of Reclamation
- Department of Defense (includes Army Corps of Engineers lakes)
- Fish and Wildlife Service / Wilderness
- Forest Service / Wilderness
- National Park Service / Wilderness
- State Park

Some small sites are not shown, especially in urban areas.

Abbreviations

AFB — Air Force Base
NF — National Forest
NWR — National Wildlife Refuge
Res — Reservoir

CO
KANSAS
MO
AR
TEXAS

Boise City
Optima Lake
Optima NWR
North
Rita Blanca National Grassland
Shattuck
Seiling
Black Kettle National Grassland
Elk City
Altus Lake
Tom Steed Lake
Altus AFB
Frederick
Waurika Lake

Alva
Fort Supply Lake
Canton Lake
Washita NWR
Foss Reservoir
Fort Cobb Reservoir
Anadarko
Wichita Mountains National Wildlife Refuge
Fort Sill
Lawton
Duncan

Blackwell
Salt Plains NWR
Enid
Vance Air Force Base
Guthrie
El Reno
Norman
Chickasha
Chickasaw National Recreation Area
Ardmore
Madill
Lake Texoma

Ponca City
Stillwater
Edmond
Oklahoma City
Tinker AFB
Moore
Lake Thunderbird
Pauls Valley

Kaw Lake
Hulah Lake
Osage Indian Reservation
Birch Lake
Keystone Lake
Heyburn Lake
Shawnee
Seminole
U S Army Ammunition Depot
McGee Creek Reservoir
Tishomingo NWR
Durant

Copan Lake
Bartlesville
Candy Lake
Skiatook Lake
Tulsa
Broken Arrow
Muskogee
Deep Fork NWR
Webbers Falls Res
Eufaula Lake
Winding Stair Mountain National Recreation Area
McAlester
Sardis Lake
Hugo Lake

Miami
Vinita
Oologah Lake
Pryor
Lake O' The Cherokees
Fort Gibson Lake
Tenkiller Ferry Lake
Ozark Plateau NWR
Sequoyah NWR
Robert S Kerr Lake
Poteau
Wister Lake
Ouachita NF
Indian Nations National Scenic and Wildlife Area
Beech Creek National Scenic and Botanical Area
Broken Bow Lake
Pine Creek Lake
Little River NWR
Ouachita NF

Cimarron
Canadian River
Washita
Red River

MILES
0 25 50 75 100

OREGON

VOLCANO

- 1 Eruption in last 100 years
- 1 Eruption in last 1000 years

NUCLEAR WAR TARGETS

- Primary Target
- Secondary Target

Outer Ring
= 10 miles

FEDERAL LANDS AND INDIAN RESERVATIONS

- Bureau of Indian Affairs
- Bureau of Land Management / Wilderness
- Bureau of Reclamation
- Department of Defense (includes Army Corps of Engineers lakes)
- Fish and Wildlife Service / Wilderness
- Forest Service / Wilderness
- National Park Service / Wilderness
- State Park

Some small sites are not shown, especially in urban areas.

Abbreviations

IR	Indian Reservation
NF	National Forest
NG	National Grassland
NM	National Monument
NP	National Park
NRA	National Recreation Area
NWR	National Wildlife Refuge
Res	Reservoir

PENNSYLVANIA

NUCLEAR WAR TARGETS

Primary Target

Secondary Target

Outer Ring = 10 miles

FEDERAL LANDS AND INDIAN RESERVATIONS

Department of Defense (includes Army Corps of Engineers lakes)

Fish and Wildlife Service / Wilderness

Forest Service / Wilderness

National Park Service / Wilderness

State Park

Some small sites are not shown, especially in urban areas.

Abbreviations

NHP   National Historical Park
NHS   National Historic Site
NRA   National Recreation Area
NWR   National Wildlife Refuge

CANADA

Lake Erie

NEW YORK

OHIO

WEST VIRGINIA

MILES

0 10 20 30 40 50 60

VA

MARYLAND

DE

NEW JERSEY

Delaware R

Erie

Corry

Allegheny National Recreation Area

Bradford

Sayre

Erie NWR

Woodcock Creek Lake

Titusville

Erie NWR

Allegheny Reservoir

Allegheny National Forest

Kane

Coudersport

Mansfield

Wellsboro

Prompton Lake

Greenville

Tionesta Lake

Franklin

East Branch Clarion River Lake

St Marys

Susquehannock State Forest

Carbondale

Honesdale

Scranton

Shenango Lake

Williamsport

Susquehanna Nuclear Power Plant

Wilkes-Barre

Delaware Water Gap NRA

Sharon

Du Bois

Tobyhanna Army Depot

New Castle

Punxsutawney

Clearfield

Blanchard Lake

Bloomsburg

Butler

Mahoning Creek Lake

Curwensville Lake

Bellefonte

Sunbury

Hazleton

Beaver Falls

Crooked Creek Lake

State College

Beltzville Lake

Aliquippa

Indiana

Lewistown

Pottsville

Easton

Beaver Valley Nuclear Power Plant

Pittsburgh

Altoona

Huntingdon

Allentown

Bethlehem

Loyalhanna Lake

Conemaugh River Lake

Fort Indiantown Gap Military Reservation (Closed)

Blue Marsh Lake

Limerick Nuclear Power Plant

U.S. Naval Air Development Center

Bethel Park

McKeesport

Allegheny Portage Railroad NHS

Raystown Lake

Harrisburg

New Cumberland General Depot (US Military Reservation)

Reading

Willow Grove Naval Air Station

Johnstown

Washington

Mechanicsburg Naval Ship Parts Control Center

Hopewell Furnace NHS

Norristown

Valley Forge NHP

Three-Mile Island Nuclear Power Plant

Columbia

Lancaster

Philadelphia

Somerset

Waynesburg

Uniontown

Friendship Hill NHS

Fort Necessity National Battlefield

Letterkenny Army Depot

Chambersburg

Eisenhower NHS

Gettysburg National Military Park

Hanover

York

John Heinz NWR

Philadelphia Naval Base (Closed)

Youghiogheny River Lake

Greencastle Military Reservation

Fort Ritchie Raven Rock Site

Peach Bottom Nuclear Power Plant

RHODE ISLAND

NUCLEAR WAR TARGETS

Primary Target

Secondary Target

Outer Ring
= 10 miles

FEDERAL LANDS AND INDIAN RESERVATIONS

Department of Defense
(includes Army Corps of Engineers lakes)

Fish and Wildlife Service / Wilderness

State Park

Some small sites are not shown, especially in urban areas.

CONNECTICUT

MASSACHUSETTS

Woonsocket

Pawtucket

Providence ★

Scituate Reservoir

Warwick

Bristol

Narragansett Bay

Davisville Naval Construction Battalion Center (Closed)

Newport Naval Educational and Training Center

Newport

Sachuest Point National Wildlife Refuge

John H Chafee National Wildlife Refuge

Trustom Pond National Wildlife Refuge

Westerly

Ninigret National Wildlife Refuge

NY

NY

Block Island Sound

Block I

ATLANTIC OCEAN

MILES

0   5   10   15

SOUTH CAROLINA

NUCLEAR WAR TARGETS

⌖ Primary Target

Outer Ring
= 10 miles

⌖ Secondary Target

FEDERAL LANDS AND INDIAN RESERVATIONS

Department of Defense
(includes Army Corps of Engineers lakes)

Department of Energy

Fish and Wildlife Service / Wilderness

Forest Service / Wilderness

National Park Service / Wilderness

State Park

Some small sites are not shown, especially in urban areas.

Abbreviations

NWR   National Wildlife Refuge

MILES
0   10   20   30   40   50   60

NORTH CAROLINA

GEORGIA

ATLANTIC OCEAN

Kings Mountain National Military Park
Cowpens National Battlefield
Catawba Nuclear Power Plant
Oconee Nuclear Power Plant
Greer
Spartanburg
Rock Hill
Sumter National Forest
Easley
Greenville
Union
Chester
Lancaster
Cheraw
Carolina Sandhills NWR
Clemson
Hartwell Lake
Anderson
Laurens
Sumter National Forest
Robinson Nuclear Power Plant
Hartsville
Darlington
Newberry
Summer Nuclear Power Plant
Camden
Marion
Mullins
Abbeville
Ninety Six National Historic Site
Fort Jackson
Florence
Richard B Russell Lake
Columbia
Shaw Air Force Base
Sumter
Lake City
Conway
Sumter National Forest
Congaree Swamp National Monument
J Strom Thurmond Lake
Kingstree
Waccamaw NWR
Myrtle Beach
Aiken
Lake Marion
Santee NWR
Orangeburg
Bamberg
Lake Moultrie
Francis Marion National Forest
Cape Romain
Savannah River Plant
Charleston Naval Weapons Station
Cape Romain NWR
Allendale
Charleston Naval Weapons Station South Annex
Walterboro
Charleston Air Force Base
Charleston Naval Shipyard (Closed)
Charleston
Charleston Naval Shipyard East Cooper Spoil Area (Closed)
ACE Basin NWR
Ace Basin NWR
Beaufort Marine Corps Air Station
St Helena Sound
Laurel Bay Naval Area
Parris Island US Marine Corps
Savannah NWR
Pinckney Island NWR

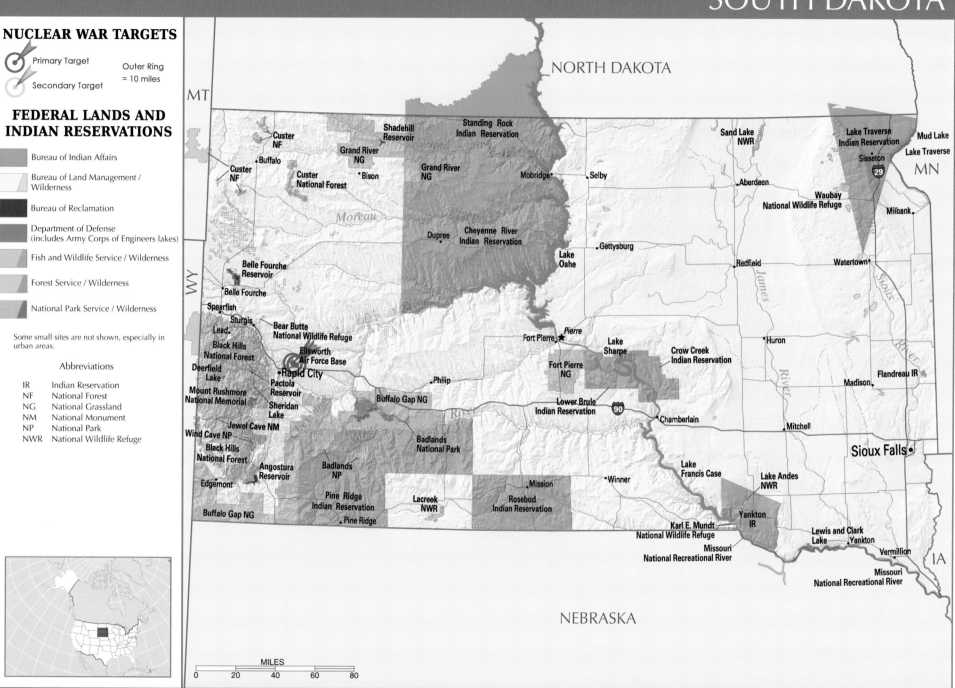

TENNESSEE

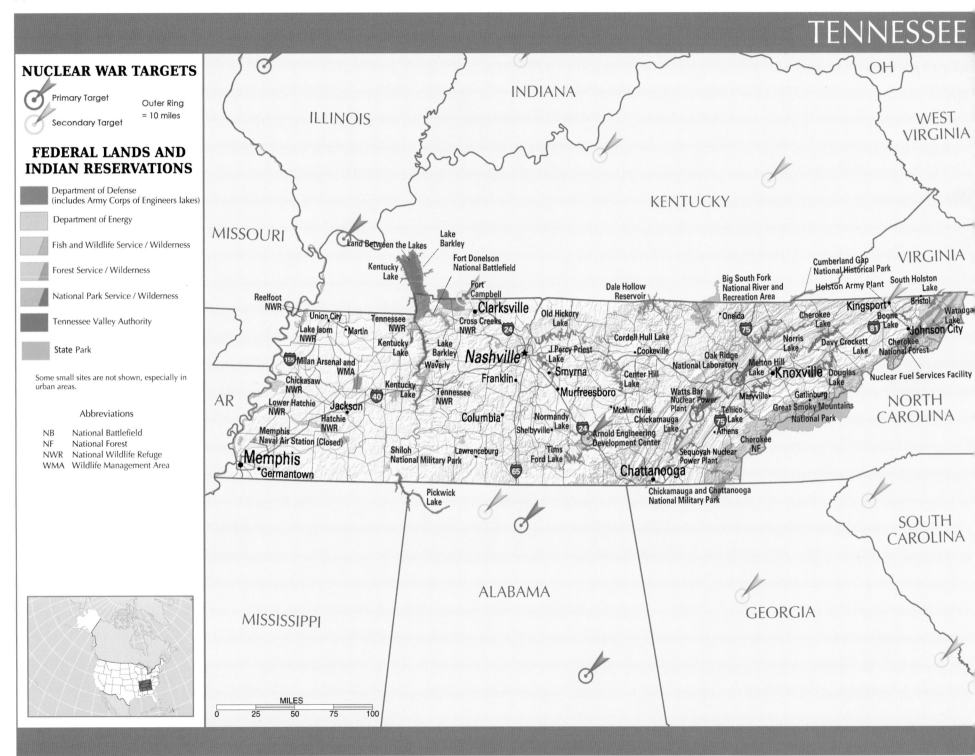

NUCLEAR WAR TARGETS

Primary Target

Secondary Target

Outer Ring = 10 miles

FEDERAL LANDS AND INDIAN RESERVATIONS

Department of Defense (includes Army Corps of Engineers lakes)

Department of Energy

Fish and Wildlife Service / Wilderness

Forest Service / Wilderness

National Park Service / Wilderness

Tennessee Valley Authority

State Park

Some small sites are not shown, especially in urban areas.

Abbreviations

NB   National Battlefield
NF   National Forest
NWR National Wildlife Refuge
WMA Wildlife Management Area

MILES
0   25   50   75   100

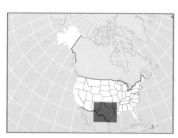

UTAH

VOLCANO

1 Eruption in last 100 years

1 Eruption in last 1000 years

NUCLEAR WAR TARGETS

Primary Target

Secondary Target

Outer Ring
= 10 miles

FEDERAL LANDS AND INDIAN RESERVATIONS

Bureau of Indian Affairs

Bureau of Land Management / Wilderness

Bureau of Reclamation

Department of Defense (includes Army Corps of Engineers lakes)

Fish and Wildlife Service / Wilderness

Forest Service / Wilderness

National Park Service / Wilderness

Some small sites are not shown, especially in urban areas.

Abbreviations

AFB   Air Force Base
IR   Indian Reservation
NF   National Forest
NM   National Monument
NP   National Park
NRA   National Recreation Area
NWR   National Wildlife Refuge

MILES
0   20   40   60   80

WYOMING

NEVADA

COLORADO

Caribou NF
Sawtooth National Forest
Air Force Plant No. 78
Newton Reservoir
Hyrum Reservoir
Logan
Randolph
Golden Spike National Historic Site
Brigham City
Cache NF
Woodruff
Woodruff
Bear River Migratory Bird Refuge
Causey Reservoir
Flaming Gorge Reservoir
Ogden
Roy
Pineview Reservoir
Lost Creek Reservoir
Flaming Gorge National Recreation Area
Great Salt Lake
Hill AFB
Morgan
East Canyon Reservoir
Bountiful
Echo Reservoir
Hill Air Force Range
Utah Air NG
Wasatch NF
Wendover
Salt Lake City
West Valley City
Wasatch NF
Rockport Lake
Wasatch NF
Ashley National Forest
Moon Lake
Steinaker Reservoir
Dinosaur NM
Timpanogos Cave National Monument
Tooele
Sandy
Wendover Range
Wasatch NF
Deer Creek Lake
Vernal
Camp Williams
Uintah and Ouray Indian Reservation
Ouray NWR
Skull Valley IR
Orem
Uinta NF
Strawberry Reservoir
Deseret Test Center
Dugway Proving Grounds
Tooele Army Depot
Provo
Duchesne
Lake Boreham
Ashley NF
Michael Army Airfield
Wasatch NF
Army NG Base
Uintah and Ouray IR
Uinta NF
Goshute IR
Fish Springs NWR
Uinta NF
Nephi
Scofield Reservoir
Price
Uintah and Ouray IR
Delta
Uinta NF
Mt Pleasant
Fishlake NF
Joes Valley Reservoir
Ephraim
Manti-La Sal National Forest
Castle Dale
Gunnison
Green River
Fillmore
Utah Launch Complex White Sands Missle Range
Richfield
Fishlake National Forest
Arches National Park
Paiute IR
Canyonlands NP
Moab
Desert Range Experimental Station
Paiute IR
Loa
Manti-La Sal NF
Milford
Canyonlands National Park
Beaver
Junction
Capitol Reef National Park
Dixie National Forest
Monticello
Panguitch
Manti-La Sal National Forest
Cedar Breaks NM
Dixie National Forest
Bryce Canyon National Park
Blanding
Cedar City
Paiute Indian Reservation
Grand Staircase-Escalante National Monument
Glen Canyon NRA
Natural Bridges NM
Dixie NF
Zion NP
Paiute IR
Lake Powell
Hovenweep National Monument
St George
Kanab
Rainbow Bridge National Monument
Navajo Indian Reservation

VERMONT

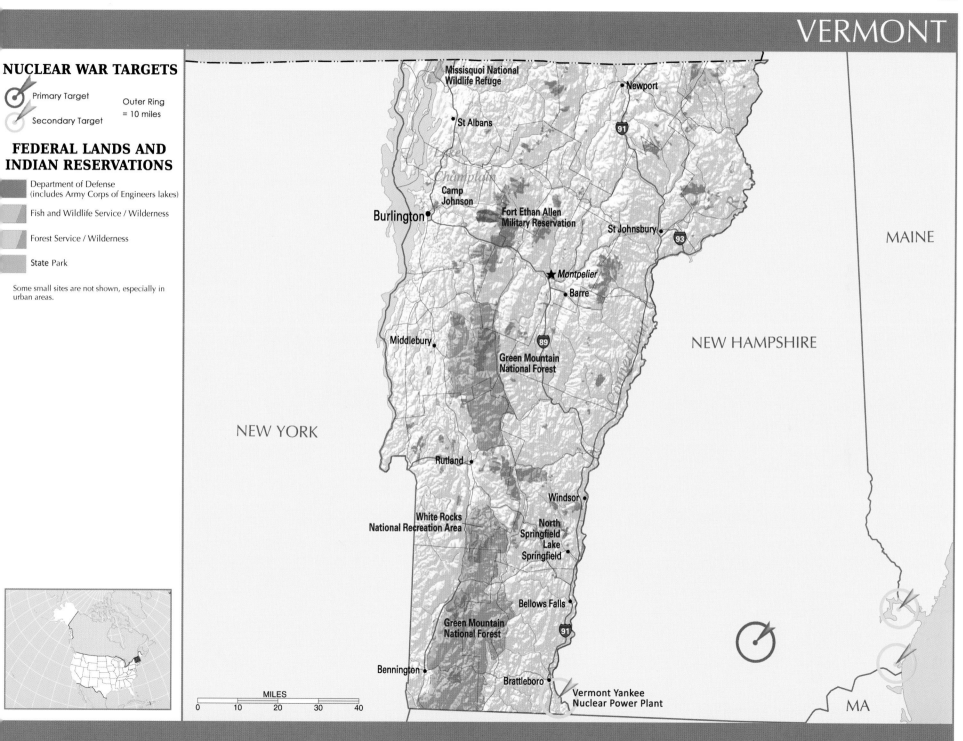

NUCLEAR WAR TARGETS

Primary Target

Outer Ring = 10 miles

Secondary Target

FEDERAL LANDS AND INDIAN RESERVATIONS

Department of Defense (includes Army Corps of Engineers lakes)

Fish and Wildlife Service / Wilderness

Forest Service / Wilderness

State Park

Some small sites are not shown, especially in urban areas.

MILES

0   10   20   30   40

Missisquoi National Wildlife Refuge

Newport

St Albans

91

Lake Champlain

Camp Johnson

Burlington

Fort Ethan Allen Military Reservation

St Johnsbury

93

★ Montpelier

Barre

Middlebury

89

Green Mountain National Forest

Rutland

Windsor

White Rocks National Recreation Area

North Springfield Lake Springfield

Bellows Falls

91

Green Mountain National Forest

Bennington

Brattleboro

Vermont Yankee Nuclear Power Plant

MAINE

NEW HAMPSHIRE

NEW YORK

MA

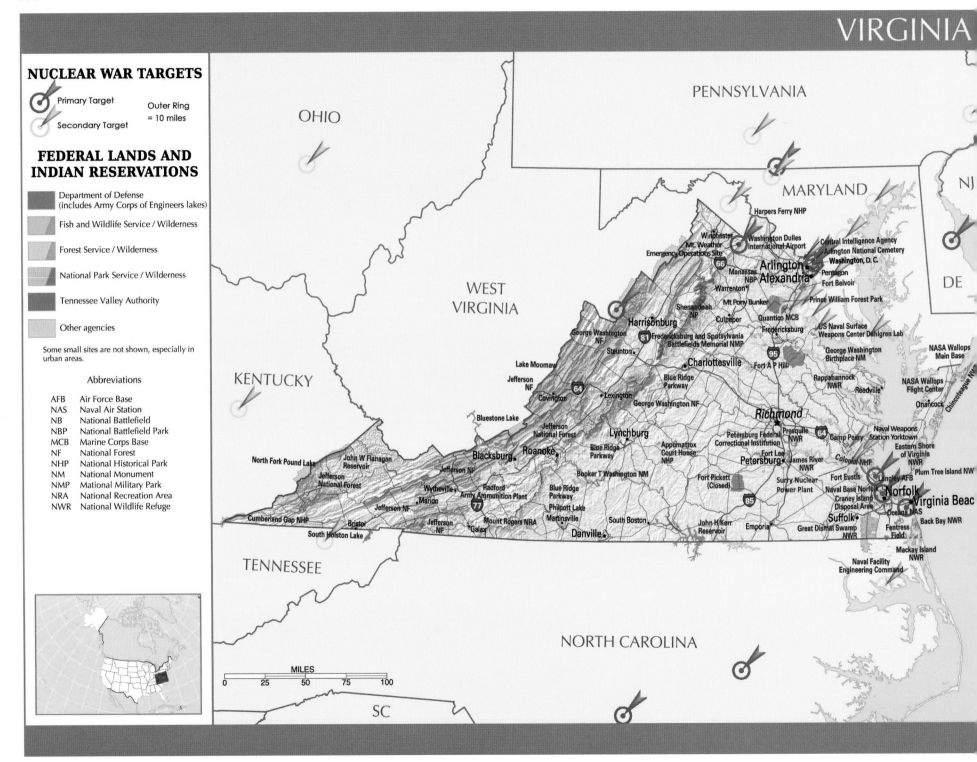

338

VIRGINIA

NUCLEAR WAR TARGETS

Primary Target

Secondary Target

Outer Ring
= 10 miles

FEDERAL LANDS AND INDIAN RESERVATIONS

Department of Defense
(includes Army Corps of Engineers lakes)

Fish and Wildlife Service / Wilderness

Forest Service / Wilderness

National Park Service / Wilderness

Tennessee Valley Authority

Other agencies

Some small sites are not shown, especially in urban areas.

Abbreviations

AFB   Air Force Base
NAS   Naval Air Station
NB   National Battlefield
NBP   National Battlefield Park
MCB   Marine Corps Base
NF   National Forest
NHP   National Historical Park
NM   National Monument
NMP   Mational Military Park
NRA   National Recreation Area
NWR   National Wildlife Refuge

OHIO

PENNSYLVANIA

MARYLAND

WEST VIRGINIA

KENTUCKY

TENNESSEE

NORTH CAROLINA

SC

NJ

DE

Harpers Ferry NHP

Winchester
Mt. Weather
Emergency Operations Site

Washington Dulles
International Airport

Central Intelligence Agency
Arlington National Cemetery
Washington, D. C.
Pentagon
Fort Belvoir

Manassas
NBP

Arlington
Alexandria

Warrenton

Mt Pony Bunker

Prince William Forest Park

Shenandoah
NP

Culpeper

Quantico MCB

Fredericksburg

US Naval Surface
Weapons Center Dahlgren Lab

Harrisonburg

George Washington
NF

Fredericksburg and Spotsylvania
Battlefields Memorial NMP

George Washington
Birthplace NM

Staunton

Charlottesville

Fort A P Hill

Rappahannock
NWR

Reedville

NASA Wallops
Main Base

Lake Moomaw

Blue Ridge
Parkway

NASA Wallops
Flight Center

Jefferson
NF

Lexington

George Washington NF

Onancock

Covington

Richmond

Bluestone Lake

Jefferson
National Forest

Lynchburg

Presquile
NWR

Camp Peary

Naval Weapons
Station Yorktown

North Fork Pound Lake

John W Flanagan
Reservoir

Blacksburg

Roanoke

Appomattox
Court House
NHP

Petersburg Federal
Correctional Institution

Petersburg

Fort Lee

James River
NWR

Colonial NHP

Eastern Shore
of Virginia
NWR

Plum Tree Island NW

Booker T Washington NM

Fort Pickett
(Closed)

Surry Nuclear
Power Plant

Fort Eustis

Naval Base Norfolk

Langley AFB

Jefferson
National Forest

Wytheville

Radford
Army Ammunition Plant

Blue Ridge
Parkway

Philpott Lake

Martinsville

South Boston

John H/Kerr
Reservoir

Emporia

Great Dismal Swamp
NWR

Craney Island
Disposal Area

Oceana NAS

Norfolk

Virginia Beac

Cumberland Gap NHP

Marion

Jefferson NF

Jefferson
NF

Mount Rogers NRA

Suffolk

Fentress
Field

Back Bay NWR

Bristol

Galax

Danville

Mackay Island
NWR

South Holston Lake

Naval Facility
Engineering Command

MILES

0   25   50   75   100

WASHINGTON

VOLCANO

- 1 Eruption in last 100 years
- 1 Eruption in last 1000 years

NUCLEAR WAR TARGETS

- Primary Target
- Secondary Target

Outer Ring
= 10 miles

FEDERAL LANDS AND INDIAN RESERVATIONS

- Bureau of Indian Affairs
- Bureau of Land Management / Wilderness
- Department of Defense (includes Army Corps of Engineers lakes)
- Department of Energy
- Fish and Wildlife Service / Wilderness
- Forest Service / Wilderness
- National Park Service / Wilderness
- State Park

Abbreviations

AFB	Air Force Base
IR	Indian Reservation
NAS	Naval Air Station
NF	National Forest
NHP	National Historic Park
NHR	National Historical Reserve
NM	National Monument
NP	National Park
NRA	National Recreation Area
NWR	National Wildlife Refuge

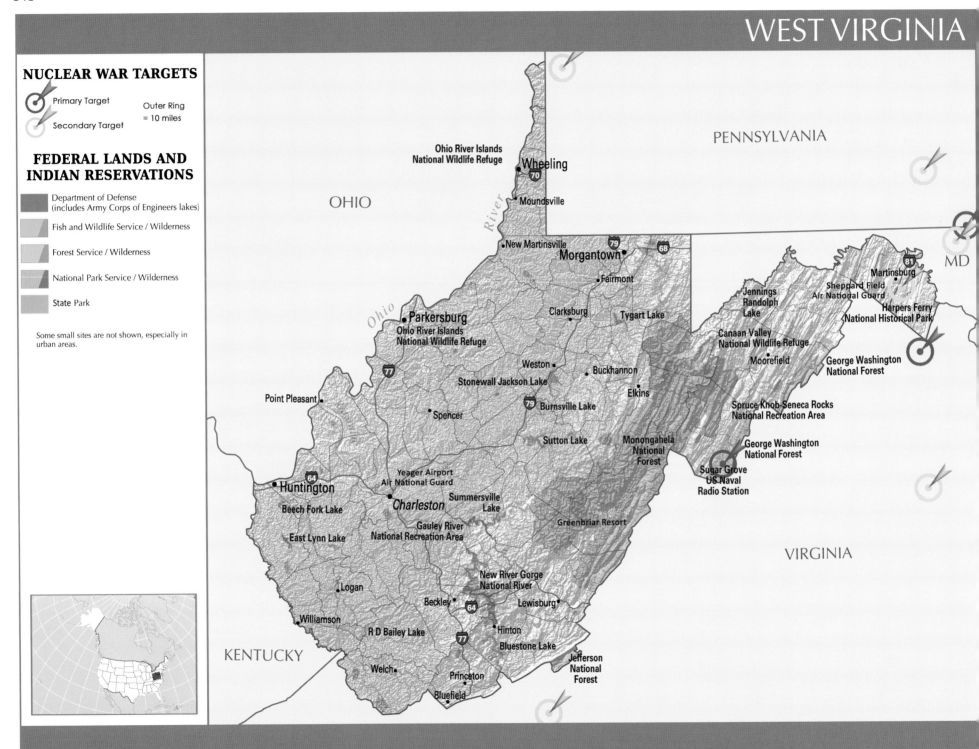

WEST VIRGINIA

NUCLEAR WAR TARGETS

Primary Target

Secondary Target

Outer Ring
= 10 miles

**FEDERAL LANDS AND
INDIAN RESERVATIONS**

Department of Defense
(includes Army Corps of Engineers lakes)

Fish and Wildlife Service / Wilderness

Forest Service / Wilderness

National Park Service / Wilderness

State Park

Some small sites are not shown, especially in
urban areas.

PENNSYLVANIA

OHIO

Ohio River Islands
National Wildlife Refuge

Wheeling

Moundsville

New Martinsville

Morgantown

Fairmont

Clarksburg

Tygart Lake

Parkersburg

Ohio River Islands
National Wildlife Refuge

Weston

Buckhannon

Stonewall Jackson Lake

Elkins

Point Pleasant

Spencer

Burnsville Lake

Sutton Lake

Monongahela
National
Forest

Yeager Airport
Air National Guard

Huntington

Charleston

Summersville
Lake

Beech Fork Lake

Gauley River
National Recreation Area

East Lynn Lake

Greenbriar Resort

Sugar Grove
US Naval
Radio Station

Jennings
Randolph
Lake

Canaan Valley
National Wildlife Refuge

Moorefield

Spruce Knob-Seneca Rocks
National Recreation Area

George Washington
National Forest

Martinsburg

Sheppard Field
Air National Guard

Harpers Ferry
National Historical Park

George Washington
National Forest

MD

VIRGINIA

Logan

New River Gorge
National River

Beckley

Lewisburg

Williamson

R D Bailey Lake

Hinton

Bluestone Lake

KENTUCKY

Welch

Princeton

Jefferson
National
Forest

Bluefield

WISCONSIN

NUCLEAR WAR TARGETS

Primary Target

Secondary Target

Outer Ring
= 10 miles

FEDERAL LANDS AND INDIAN RESERVATIONS

Bureau of Indian Affairs

Department of Defense
(includes Army Corps of Engineers lakes)

Fish and Wildlife Service / Wilderness

Forest Service / Wilderness

National Park Service / Wilderness

State Park

Some small sites are not shown, especially in urban areas.

Abbreviations

IR   Indian Reservation
NWR   National Wildlife Refuge

Lake Superior

Apostle Islands
National Lakeshore

Red Cliff IR
Bayfield

Bad River
Indian Reservation

Superior

Ashland

Hurley

MICHIGAN

Chequamegon
National
Forest

Clam Lake ELF
Transmitter

Lac du Flambeau IR

Saint Croix National Scenic Riverway

Hayward

Park Falls

Eagle River

Nicolet
National
Forest

Menominee R

Pembine

Saint
Croix
Indian
Reservation

Spooner

Lac Courte
Oreilles IR

Chequamegon
National
Forest

Rhinelander

Sokaogon Chippewa IR

Rice Lake

St Croix Falls

Tomahawk

Potawatomi
Indian Reservation

Washington
Island

Chequamegon
National
Forest

Merrill

Antigo

Marinette

Menomonie

Chippewa Falls

Wausau

Menominee IR

Shawano

Sturgeon
Bay

Eau Claire

Stockbridge IR

MINNESOTA

Marshfield

Oneida IR

Green Bay

Lake
Michigan

Black River Falls

Winnebago IR

Stevens Point

Wisconsin Rapids

De Pere

Kewaunee

Appleton

Kaukauna

Kewaunee and Point Beach
Nuclear Power Plants

Trempealeau NWR

Necedah National Wildlife Refuge

Two Rivers

Fort McCoy

Oshkosh

Lake
Winnebago

Manitowoc

MI

Camp Williams

Fond du Lac

Sheboygan

La Crosse

Wisconsin Dells

Fox River NWR

IOWA

Viroqua

Portage

Horicon NWR

Beaver Dam

West Bend

Lake
Michigan

Badger Army
Ammunition Plant

Watertown

Menomonee Falls

Wauwatosa

Prairie du Chien

Madison

Waukesha

West Allis

Milwaukee

Upper Mississippi River Wildlife And Fish Refuge

Platteville

Janesville

Racine

Monroe

Beloit

Kenosha

MILES
0   20   40   60   80

WYOMING

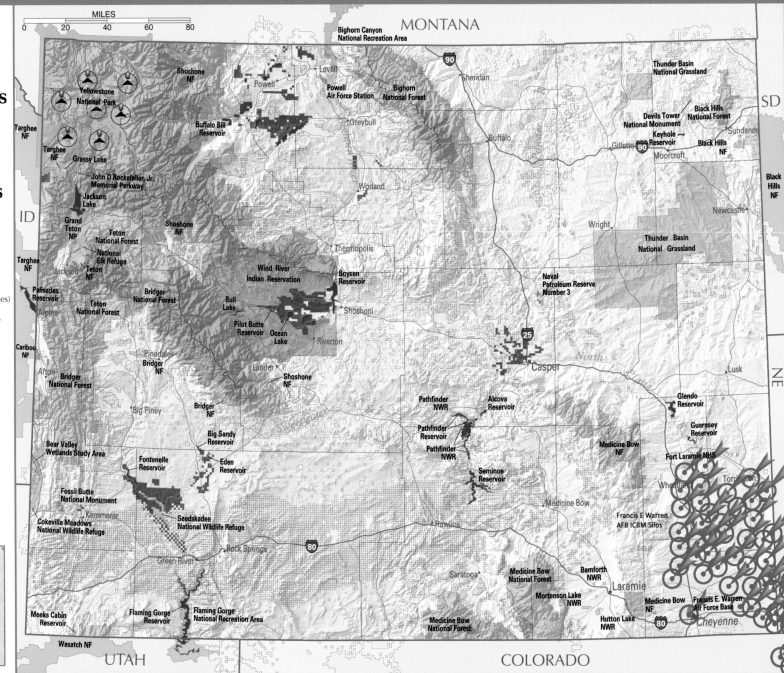

VOLCANO

🌋 1 Eruption in last 100 years

🌋 1 Eruption in last 1000 years

NUCLEAR WAR TARGETS

◎ Primary Target

◎ Secondary Target

Outer Ring = 10 miles

FEDERAL LANDS AND INDIAN RESERVATIONS

Bureau of Indian Affairs

Bureau of Land Management / Wilderness

Bureau of Reclamation

Department of Defense (includes Army Corps of Engineers lakes)

Fish and Wildlife Service / Wilderness

Forest Service / Wilderness

National Park Service / Wilderness

Some small sites are not shown, especially in urban areas.

Abbreviations

NF   National Forest
NHS   National Historic Site
NP   National Park
NWR   National Wildlife Refuge

MILES
0   20   40   60   80

Bighorn Canyon National Recreation Area

Shoshone NF

Powell

Sheridan

Powell Air Force Station

Bighorn National Forest

Buffalo Bill Reservoir

Greybull

Thunder Basin National Grassland

Targhee NF

Yellowstone National Park

Targhee NF

Grassy Lake

John D Rockefeller, Jr. Memorial Parkway

Jackson Lake

Devils Tower National Monument

Black Hills National Forest

Keyhole Reservoir

Gillette

Moorcroft

Sundance

Black Hills NF

ID

Grand Teton NP

Teton National Forest

National Elk Refuge

Teton NF

Shoshone NF

Worland

Wright

Newcastle

Black Hills NF

SD

Targhee NF

Jackson

Thermopolis

Palisades Reservoir

Bridger National Forest

Wind River Indian Reservation

Boysen Reservoir

Thunder Basin National Grassland

Teton National Forest

Alpine

Bull Lake

Pilot Butte Reservoir

Ocean Lake

Shoshoni

Naval Petroleum Reserve Number 3

Caribou NF

Pinedale

Bridger NF

Lander

Riverton

North

Afton

Bridger National Forest

Shoshone NF

25

Casper

Lusk

Big Piney

Bridger NF

Sweetwater

Pathfinder NWR

Alcova Reservoir

Glendo Reservoir

Bear Valley Wetlands Study Area

Big Sandy Reservoir

Pathfinder Reservoir

Pathfinder NWR

Medicine Bow NF

Guernsey Reservoir

Fontenelle Reservoir

Eden Reservoir

Seminoe Reservoir

Fort Laramie NHS

Fossil Butte National Monument

Kemmerer

Medicine Bow

Francis E Warren AFB ICBM Silos

Cokeville Meadows National Wildlife Refuge

Seedskadee National Wildlife Refuge

Rawlins

80

Saratoga

Medicine Bow National Forest

Bamforth NWR

Wheatland

Torrington

Rock Springs

Green River

Laramie

Medicine Bow NF

Francis E. Warren Air Force Base

Meeks Cabin Reservoir

Flaming Gorge Reservoir

Flaming Gorge National Recreation Area

Mortenson Lake NWR

Medicine Bow National Forest

Hutton Lake NWR

80

Cheyenne

Wasatch NF

UTAH

COLORADO

NE

RESOURCES

Books by Joel Skousen

- *The Secure Home* (683 pages, $45)
- *The High Security Shelter - How to Implement a Multi-Purpose Safe Room in the Home* (109 pages, $25)
- *10 Packs For Survival, a list for storage and barter* (booklet, $5)

Go to *www.joelskousen.com* and click on the appropriate links on the front page. Prices listed here are subject to change.

World Affairs Brief

Mr. Skousen puts out a weekly news analysis service via email. He concentrates on revealing key facts and analysis that the establishment media leave out concerning the hot topics of each week. These weekly briefs also serve subscribers as an early warning system for global crisis and war. Go to *www.worldaffairsbrief.com* and click on "subscribe" or contact *editor@worldaffairsbrief.com* for a sample brief.

Consultation and Custom Design Services

Joel Skousen pioneered the concept of the "Secure Home" by developing cost-effective solutions for self-sufficient home designs. To help people prepare over the years he has done everything from designing and overseeing the entire project to just consulting on key issues. Several years ago Joel retired from design work to concentrate on consulting and book writing; however, he has recently teamed up with Andrew to create *The Secure Home Design Group*, a flexible network of professionals that can provide many services to help accomplish your self-sufficient project. Andrew is a licensed PE (professional engineer) with a background in structural work and has worked with Joel on many projects.

As consultants, we specialize in helping people with site selection, contingency planning, self-sufficient living and overall coordination of the preparedness aspects of a project. We can work with your architect, local designer or builder or we can put together a team of professionals and self-sufficiency experts from our group. We maintain connections with professionals all over the country who subscribe to our criteria for security and produce good results while being discreet about your private security.

Our goal is to help you implement your own best option whether that is high-tech or farm-basic but we emphasize economy wherever possible. Simple things like concealing instead of hardening or relocating instead of fortifying can save significant costs. We also recommend, for example, using stock plans of your choice which can be modified to implement a few key survival aspects. In general, self-sufficiency and security can be designed into a full range of styles, from classical to modern. We emphasize the need, however, to keep a low profile so the finished product does not draw undue attention to itself. We design with the goal of complete integration of the applicable technical equipment you need to become more self-sufficient and secure.

Feel free to call us to discuss your needs at (801) 224-4746 or email Joel at *joel@joelskousen.com*. We can help you make a quick determination of your needs or set up for a more in-depth consultation. If you could be one of the professionals described above, we'd also like to hear from you and consider adding you to our group.

Fee Schedule

Hourly consultation: $60 per hour for telephone consultation. Design work is at $60 per hour or 6% of the construction cost.

Travel and on-site consultation: $500 per day plus travel expenses.

We quote these numbers to help you plan for your needs, but we have the flexibility to work within every budget. These numbers are subject to change.

BIBLIOGRAPHY

The following sources have been mentioned in the book or are listed to provide additional information to some of the controversial things discussed in the text. Some of these books may not be in print, but in these cases they represent some of the only information on the subject, so we recommend looking for them from used booksellers via the Internet.

Conspiracy

Cuddy, Dennis and Robert Goldsborough. *The Network of Power and Part II The New World Order: Chronology and Commentary*. American Research Foundation Inc, 1993.

DeCamp, John. *The Franklin Cover-Up: Child Abuse, Satanism, and Murder in Nebraska*. AWT publishers, 1992.

Jenson-Stevenson, Monika and William Stevenson. *Kiss the Boys Goodbye; How the United States Betrayed Its Own POW's in Vietnam*, McClelland & Stewart, 1999.

Kellett, Michael. *The Murder of Vince Foster, One More Link*. CLS Publishers, 1997.

Lee, Robert W. *The United Nations Conspiracy*. Western Islands, 1981.

Lifton, David. *Best Evidence*. Signet, 1992.

Livingstone, Harrison and Robert Groden. *High Treason: The Assasination of Pres. John F. Kennedy and the Case for Conspiracy*. Carroll & Graf Publishers, 1998.

Monteith, Stanley, MD. *Brotherhood of Darkness*. Hearthstone Publishing, Ltd., 2000.

Pearloff, James. *The Shadows of Power*. Western Islands, 1988.

Roberts, Craig. *The Medusa File: Secret Crimes and Coverups of the U. S. Government*. Consolidated Press International, 1997.

Ruddy, Christopher. *The Strange Death of Vincent Foster: An Investigation*. Free Press, 1997.

Sanders, James, et al. *Soldiers of Misfortune*. National Press Books, 1992.

Sanders, James. *The Downing of TWA Flight 800*. B & B Audio, Inc., 1997.

Stinnett, Robert. *Day of Deceit*. Free Press, 2001.

Skousen, W. Cleon. *The Naked Capitalist*. Ensign Publishing Company, 1972.

Skousen, W. Cleon. *The Naked Communist*. Ensign Publishing Company, 1960.

Stich, Rodney. *Defrauding America* (4th Edition). Silverpeak Enterprises, Inc., 2005.

Sutton, Antony C. *Wall Street and the Rise of Hitler*. Clairview Books, 2010.

Sutton, Antony C. *How the Order Creates War and Revolution*. Research Publications, 1984.

Sutton, Antony C. *Wall Street and the Bolshevik Revolution*. Veritas Publications, 1981.

International Betrayal

Fanning, Louis A. *Betrayal In Vietnam*. Arlington House, 1976.

Lazo, Mario. *Dagger in the heart: American Policy Failures in Cuba*. Twin Circle Publishing, 1968.

Rowe, David N. *Ally Betrayed . . . The Republic of Korea*. Western Goals, 1982.

Somoza, Anastasio and Jack Cox. *Nicaragua Betrayed*. Western Islands, 1980.

Wittmer, Felix. *The Yalta Betrayal*. Caxton Printers, 1954.

Medicine and Homebirth

Harper, Barbara, RN. *Gentle Birth Choices* (3rd Edition). Healing Arts Press, 2005.

Mendelsohn, Robert S., MD. *Confessions of a Medical Heretic*. Contemporary Books, 1979.

O'Brien, Lawrence J., MD. *Bad Medicine: How the American Medical Establishment Is Ruining Our Healthcare System*. Prometheus Books, 2004.

Pryor, Karen and Gale Pryor. *Nursing Your Baby* (4th Edition). Harper Paperbacks, 2005.

Romm, Aviva Jill, MD. *Vaccinations: A Thoughtful Parent's Guide*. Healing Arts Press, 2001.

Simkin, Penny. *The Birth Partner, A Complete Guide to Childbirth for Dads, Doulas, and All Other Labor Companions* (3rd Edition). Harvard Common Press, 2007.

Stewart, David. *The Five Standards for Safe Childbearing* (4th Edition). Napsac Intl, 1997.

Wootan, George, MD and Sarah Verney. *Take Charge of Your Child's Health: A Parents' Guide to Recognizing Symptoms and Treating Minor Illnesses at Home*. Marlowe & Company, 2000.

Nutrition

Balch, Phyllis A., CNC. *Prescription for Nutritional Healing: A Practical A-to-Z Reference to Drug- Free Remedies Using Vitamins, Minerals, Herbs & Food Supplements* (5th Edition). Avery Trade, 2010.

Fallon, Sally. *Nourishing Traditions: The Cookbook that Challenges Politically Correct Nutrition and the Diet Dictocrats*. New Trends Publishing, 1999.

Hickey, Steve. *Vitamin C: The Real Story*. Basic Health Publications, 2008.

Madigan, Carleen. *The Backyard Homestead: Produce all the food you need on just a quarter acre!* Storey Publishing, 2009.

Planck, Nina. *Real Food: What to Eat and Why*. Bloomsbury USA, 2007.

Shanahan, Catherine, MD and Luke Shanahan. *Deep Nutrition: Why Your Genes Need Traditional Food*. Big Box Books, 2008.

Printed Periodicals

Access to Energy. Art Robinson, PhD. *http://www.accesstoenergy.com*; PO Box 1250, Cave Junction, OR 97523. Monthly newsletter for $40 (as of 2010).

The Freeman. Foundation of Economic Education (FEE). *http://www.fee.org*; 30 S. Broadway, Irvington-on-Hudson, NY 10533; Tel. (914) 591-7230. Monthly magazine for $50 donation per year (as of 2010).

The New American. John Birch Society (JBS). *http://www.thenewamerican.com*; 770 Westhill Boulevard, Appleton, WI 54914; (920) 749-3784. Twice-monthly magazine for $39 per year (as of 2010).

INDEX